LIBRARY OF AMERICAN LABOR HISTORY

THE

LABOR MOVEMENT

THE
LABOR MOVEMENT

THE PROBLEM OF TODAY

EDITED BY

GEORGE E. McNEILL

[1887]

REPRINTS OF ECONOMIC CLASSICS

AUGUSTUS M. KELLEY · PUBLISHERS

NEW YORK 1971

First Edition 1887

(Boston: A. M. Bridgeman & Company;
New York: The M. W. Hazen Co., 1887)

REPRINTED 1971 BY
AUGUSTUS M. KELLEY · PUBLISHERS
REPRINTS OF ECONOMIC CLASSICS
New York New York 10001

. . . .

I S B N 0-678-00713-6
L C N 66-21683

. . . .

PRINTED IN THE UNITED STATES OF AMERICA
by SENTRY PRESS, NEW YORK, N. Y. 10019

Yours Truly
U. S. Stephens

THE LABOR MOVEMENT:

THE PROBLEM OF TO-DAY.

THE HISTORY, PURPOSE AND POSSIBILITIES OF LABOR ORGANIZATIONS IN EUROPE AND AMERICA; GUILDS, TRADES-UNIONS, AND KNIGHTS OF LABOR; WAGES AND PROFITS; HOURS OF LABOR; FUNCTIONS OF CAPITAL; CHINESE LABOR; COMPETITION; ARBITRATION; PROFIT-SHARING AND CO-OPERATION; PRINCIPLES OF THE KNIGHTS OF LABOR; MORAL AND EDUCATIONAL ASPECTS OF THE LABOR QUESTION.

EDITED BY

GEORGE E. McNEILL,

First Deputy of Mass. Bureau of Statistics of Labor; Sec.-Treas. of D. A. 30, Knights of Labor.

ASSOCIATE AUTHORS:

TERENCE V. POWDERLY, G. M. W., K. of L.; DR. EDMUND J. JAMES, University of Pennsylvania; HON. JOHN J. O'NEILL, of Missouri; HON. J. M. FARQUHAR, of New York; HON. ROBERT HOWARD, of Massachusetts; HENRY GEORGE, of New York; ADOLPH STRASSER, Pres. Cigar Makers' Union; JOHN JARRETT, of Pennsylvania; REV. R. HEBER NEWTON, of New York; F. K. FOSTER, of Massachusetts; P. M. ARTHUR, Chief Engineer Locomotive Brotherhood; W. W. STONE and W. W. MORROW, of California; FRANKLIN H. GIDDINGS, "Springfield Union"; JOHN McBRIDE, Secretary Coal Miners' Union; D. J. O'DONOGHUE, of Toronto, Canada; P. J. McGUIRE, Secretary Carpenters' Brotherhood, Ohio.

BOSTON:
A. M. BRIDGMAN & CO.

NEW YORK:
THE M. W. HAZEN CO.

C. V. LECRAW & CO., *New York;* O. H. P. APPLEGATE, *St. Louis, Mo.;* A. ROMAN, *San Francisco, Cal.;* J. DEWING & CO., *San Francisco, Cal.;* GATELY & CO., *Cincinnati, O.;* JOHN W. ILIFF & CO., *Chicago, Ill.;* M. M. ELLSWORTH & CO., *Detroit, Mich.;* N. G. HAMILTON & CO., *Cleveland, O.;* N. D. McDONALD & CO., *New Orleans, La.;* A. T. HUBBARD, *Philadelphia, Penn.;* GATELY & HASKELL, *Baltimore, Md.;* WESTERN INSTALLMENT BOOK CO., *Kansas City, Mo.;* BRYAN, TAYLOR & CO., *New York.*

1887.

PREFACE.

THE worker, the thinker, the student, the statesman and the capitalist are all forced, by the pressure of events, to consider the Labor Movement and the Labor Problem. All are witnesses of the power of combination for good or evil. All may know that systems of industry change by slow, evolving processes, and that these processes of growth culminate in crises of mighty import. The capitalist, seeking profit or gain, and the worker, seeking better and easier condition, may work as partners, with common interests, or wage unrelenting war for the mastery. That the victory will come to the side of justice and equity, is the certain prophecy of history.

This book is an attempt to contribute something to the peaceful solution of the Labor problem. The history of the Labor Movement is the history of civilization. It has manifested itself in all times and under all conditions of life. The eternal query of life is, How to obtain comfort? The prayer, "Give us this day our daily bread," is uttered by Pagan and Christian alike; and this demand for sustenance is supplemented by the hope for equity. So long as outward evidences of aggregate prosperity are present, we are apt to forget or neglect to know the conditions of some of those who contribute to the results. In Europe, the frequent and almost continuous periods of distress have compelled attention; and philanthropist, statesman and student have done much, especially in England and France, to provide a literature covering almost every phase of the movement. Dr. Edmund J. James, of the University of Pennsylvania, has so admirably condensed that history in his three chapters of this book, as to need no editorial comment. In this country, the extent of our territory, the variety of our pursuits, and the form of government have tended to lead us to overlook and underestimate the importance of the Labor movement. It is only when some great strike has checked the wheels of material progress that our business-crazed community has stopped to think. We claim for our work an earnestness of purpose to find the causes, to trace the movement, and to point out some of the measures that will culminate in a Republic of Labor. The history that we present is the compilation of such facts as could be gathered from records of labor organizations, newspapers and pamphlets, and from the varied experiences of a large number of thinking men in all parts of the country.

The growth of the national and international labor-unions, trades-assemblies, central-trades and labor-unions and trades-congresses, have furnished much of the more recent history. These efforts to unite the men of all trades under one central body have been supplemented by the most wonderful organization of modern times,—the Knights of Labor. Its history is largely secret, and we are permitted to present only that part of its work which is open to public view. Its declaration of principles is a bill of grievances and a platform of measures, as broad as human hopes and desires, and it is built in symmetry of proportion, like the pyramid, to remain an enduring monument of human intelligence and human effort.

In this volume, we have stated the laborers' side of the question; and, while making no claim for a scientific presentation of the whole question, we have presented what will be provocative, we trust, of a deeper investigation, and a more thorough appreciation of the relation of man to man, regardless of conditions, or opportunities of immediate gain,—believing that the security of all that is good is achieved when all are participators in the full enjoyment of the opportunities of civilization.

The chapters devoted to the history of the various organizations of labor were compiled from information received from their accredited officers. The history of the Knights of Labor was mainly furnished by the six surviving founders of the Order. To all who have in any way assisted us in this work, we tender our grateful acknowledgments, and especially to the *North American Review*, for granting us the privilege of republishing Mr. Powderly's article, "The Army of the Unemployed."

In addition to those who contributed, and whose names appear on the title-page, it is the pleasurable duty of the Editor to here express his thanks for valuable contributions, to Thomas B. Barry, member of General Executive Board K. of L.; Josiah B. Dyer, Secretary Granite Cutters' National Union; George C. Block, Secretary Journeymen Bakers' National Union; Joseph Wilkinson, Secretary Journeymen Tailors' Association; Thomas O'Dea, Secretary Bricklayers' and Masons' International Union; H. Emrich, Secretary International Furniture Workers' Union; J. T. Elliott, Secretary Brotherhood of Painters; W. S. Higbie, Secretary National Silk and Fur Hat Finishers' Association; T. J. Curran, President Boiler Makers' and Helpers' Protective and Benevolent Union; H. H. Lane, Secretary National Wood Carvers' Union; Archibald M. Taylor, National Secretary of United States Wool Hat Finishers' Association; Joseph Dean, Corresponding Secretary of New York Stereotypers' Union; Louis Arrington, Manager of Improved Druggists' Ware Glass Blowers' League; E. F. O'Shea, Secretary and Treasurer of Brotherhood of Railroad Brakemen; E. V. Debs, Secretary and Treasurer of Brotherhood of Locomotive Firemen; James B. Graham, of New York; Joseph R. Buchanan, Denver, Col.; Henry J. Skeffington, Philadelphia, Pa.; Dr. S. S. Robie and E. H. Rogers, of Boston.

THE EDITOR.

LIST OF PORTRAITS.

GENERAL ILLUSTRATIONS.

TRADES-UNION LEADERS.

NATIONAL LEGISLATORS.

TRADES-UNION LEADERS.

CALIFORNIA LEADERS.

GENERAL ILLUSTRATIONS.

CONTENTS.

APPENDIX.

THE LABOR MOVEMENT.

CHAPTER I.

THE RISE OF THE MODERN LABORER.

THE STUDY OF ECONOMIC HISTORY NECESSARY TO AN UNDERSTANDING OF THE LABOR MOVEMENT — THE LABORER IN GREECE — IN ROME — AMONG THE ANCIENT GERMANS — AMONG THE ANGLO-SAXONS — IN THE MIDDLE AGES — IN ENGLAND AFTER THE NORMAN CONQUEST — SOCIAL CLASSES ON MEDIÆVAL ESTATE — THE LORDS, SERFS, COTTAGERS, FREE TENANT — THE GROWING FREEDOM OF THE SERF — THE BLACK DEATH — THE RISE IN WAGES AND EMANCIPATION OF THE SERF — THE COMBINATION OF LORDS TO REDUCE WAGES AND COUNTER-COMBINATIONS OF THE LABORERS — THE ATTEMPT TO REDUCE THE LABORERS TO SERFDOM — THEIR INSURRECTION — GROWING DEBASEMENT OF THE LABORER DURING THE SIXTEENTH CENTURY — STATUTE OF APPRENTICESHIP — FIXING OF WAGES BY PUBLIC AUTHORITY IN THE INTEREST OF EMPLOYERS — THE POOR LAW OF ELIZABETH — ADDITIONAL STEPS IN THE DEGRADATION OF THE LABORER — THE LAW OF PAROCHIAL SETTLEMENT AND ALLOWANCE AND SYSTEM OF SUPPLEMENTARY ALLOWANCES — PRESENT CONDITION AND FUTURE PROSPECTS OF THE AGRICULTURAL LABORER.

IF we would comprehend our present labor problems we must study carefully the conditions out of which they have grown. The modern laborer is a historical product. He has been evolved out of a former condition by a set of influences and forces of which he himself has been a prominent part. If we would understand fully either his present condition or his future prospects we must investigate carefully the course of development by which he has become what he is, and the means which are open to him to become what he should be. How great the difference between the condition of manual labor to-day and two or ten centuries ago can be fully comprehended only by a careful study of the vastly different social and economic conditions now and then.

The materials for such a study are being gathered slowly and with much difficulty by a large number of enthusiastic and patient economists of the new school in Germany, England, France and America. Until very recently, indeed, historians have given almost no attention to the social and economic conditions of respective periods. The things which have attracted their attention have been chiefly the striking phenomena of national life, the course of wars, the outcome of battles, political changes, the rise and fall of dynasties, and other similar movements. The quiet and often vastly more important changes in the economic spirit and system of the age and country have escaped even the merest notice. We are dependent for our knowledge of such things almost entirely on the accidental mention of facts which may justify us in inferring what conditions must have existed with such facts, or on the accidental preservation of accounts, rent-rolls, bills of sale and similar items. It is scanty, at best, and for some periods is lacking almost altogether.

There is a special difficulty in the way of getting at all the facts in regard to the history of the laborer in past times, owing to the circumstance that history has nearly always been written by authors representative of, and in the interest of, the ruling classes. We may consequently be tolerably sure that everything will be presented from the standpoint of the aristocrat and gentleman, or master and despot. We owe, therefore, a special debt of gratitude to such men as Brentano, Schoenberg, Rogers, and many others who have worked in their spirit, all of whom have made an earnest effort to find out the exact facts about labor conditions and labor movements in the past and have presented them without fear or favor, though the simple presentation of the facts constitute in many cases a terrible indictment of the policy and honesty of the ruling classes in one country as well as in another.

The materials for a history of agricultural labor are more ample in the case of England than in that of any other country, while the rise of mechanical labor can be traced more satisfactorily in the history of Germany than elsewhere. In the following sketch, accordingly, we shall pursue the history of agricultural labor chiefly in England, and that of mechanical labor on the Continent, and particularly in Germany. This plan will not interfere seriously with the continuity of the account since much the same conditions prevailed in all the countries of Western Europe down to recent date. The authorities for the statements of fact are chiefly the students of economic history, mentioned above, upon whose writings liberal drafts have been made wherever they would serve our purpose.

Until very recent times the great majority of men were in a condition of personal dependence, which, although varying much in different countries and at different times, may be fairly termed personal slavery. The many have been compelled to labor for the few, who, in the light of law and custom, were alone entitled to the fruits of the labor, and could give little or much to the persons who actually did the work. This condition is so different from those which prevail nowadays, that it would at first seem as if it called for little attention. But a careful study of the history of legislation and economic progress shows that it is simply impossible to understand many of our existing laws unless we go back to a time when the great mass of laborers were practically the slaves of the few.

In Greece and Rome slavery was recognized as a fundamental institution of the state — the absolute condition of any progress in the arts and sciences. The slaves consisted of captives in war, or of those who had been purchased from those who had captured them, or those who had fallen into debt and had no other way of payment than that of selling themselves and children into slavery to the creditor, and of those who in times of disturbance had no way of protecting themselves except by giving themselves up body and soul into the protection, *i. e.*, the slavery of a superior. It was the hands of slaves "that tilled the soil, dug the mine, wove the cloth, and built the walls of ancient Greece and Rome." Labor with the hands, except that on a farm, was considered beneath the dignity of a free Greek or Roman. It had to be performed by the slaves or by free hired labor from the lower class of citizens who aspired to no position of honor in the state. It is estimated that in the early ages of Rome there were more slaves than free servants, and it is certain that in the times of the latter republic the large landowners found it more profitable to cultivate their fields by slaves than by free labor. It has been claimed that the free citizens in the provinces of the Roman Empire supported themselves in agriculture by their own labor without the assistance of slaves, but this is not likely to be true. The great mass of the craftsmen, smiths, carpenters, metal workers, shoemakers, tailors, dyers and others were all slaves, either of those who wore or used the products of their labor or of those who sold the results of their exertions. The condition of these slaves was hopeless in the extreme. They were regarded as mere animals with no rights which their masters were bound to respect. They could be tortured to death, struck dead, or flogged at the mere order of the master, and no one, not even the magistrate, had any right to interfere.

The Germans who conquered the Roman Empire and established their dominion over every part of modern Europe were also familiar with the institution of slavery. Tacitus, the great Roman historian, describes the condition of the slaves among the Germans in a few short but telling sentences. The slave, he says, may be sold, punished or killed by his master. He is not recognized as being a member of society and is not allowed to dress himself as a citizen. It is true that the actual treatment of the slave was not as cruel and severe as one might suppose from the utter lack of rights. It was much milder than among the Romans. The children of slaves grew up side by side in the same house with the children of the masters. This, of itself, would of course tend to do away with some of the most common forms of cruelty. Marriage between a free person and a slave, however, was forbidden under severe penalty. In some tribes the free person so marrying was subjected to slavery and in other cases was punished by death. The greater independence of the German slave from his master is also partly explained by the fact that he often lived on a small piece of land which his master assigned him and from which he made his living undisturbed by the latter, except when called upon for service or for a yearly contribution consisting in a part of the crops which he had raised. The development of this condition of things from this state of absolute slavery up through the intermediate stages, until slavery gave way to personal freedom in the present century, was a very slow one and one which progressed very unequally in different countries. All the modern European countries commenced with this condition of affairs and have finally ended with the legal independence of the present century.

The Anglo-Saxons who conquered England in the fifth and sixth centuries after Christ, took with them the institution of slavery. Two-thirds of the people were either absolute slaves or in an intermediate state of bondage to the remaining third. They might be put in bonds and whipped, they might be branded, and on one occasion are spoken of as if actually yoked: "Let every man know his team of men, of horses and oxen." Cattle and slaves formed, in truth, the live money of the Anglo-Saxons and were the medium of exchange by which the value of commodities was measured.

For centuries the Anglo-Saxon subdivisions of society were maintained and the inhabitants of England were divided into two great classes of freemen and slaves. Except the baronial proprietors of land and their vassals, the free tenants and seamen, the rest of the nation was depressed in servitude, which, though qualified as to its effects, was uniform in its principle that none who had been born in or had fallen into bondage could acquire an absolute right to any species of property.

The condition, however, of the people who were thus debarred from the first of social rights was not in other respects equally abject and miserable. One class of villains or villagers, though bound to the most servile offices of rural industry, were permitted to occupy small portions of land to sustain themselves and families. Other ranks of men equally servile are noticed in the ancient records, particularly the bordars and cottars, the former in consideration of being allowed a small cottage were required to provide poultry, eggs and other articles of diet for the lord's table; and the latter were employed in the trades of smith, carpenter and other handicraft arts in which they had been instructed at the charge of their masters. Inferior to these were the thralls or servi, principally employed in menial services about the mansion. Their lives were professedly protected by law and with the consent of their owners they were allowed in some cases to purchase their manumission. In other respects they were in the lowest degradation, so much so as to be considered mere chattels and regular articles of commerce. Giraldus relates that the number of them exported to Ireland for sale, in the reign of Henry the II., was so great that the market was absolutely overstocked, and from William I. to the reign of John scarcely a cottage in Scotland but possessed an English slave. In the details of the border wars mention is frequently made of the number of slaves taken prisoners as forming a principal part of the booty.

It is not easy to ascertain from writers the precise immunities of the several classes of bondmen mentioned; the chief differences in their condition arose probably from the relative utility of their occupations, the servi or serfs as least valuable being a more ordinary article of traffic and transfer than the bordars and cottars who had been trained to useful arts or obtained a fixed habitation.

All, however, alike appear to have been denuded of the substantial attributes of freedom; the law recognized in none the uncontrolled right to property or change of place without the consent of their superiors; the lord had the absolute disposal of their persons; they might be attached to the soil or transferred by deed, sale, or conveyance from one owner to another; in short they were slaves in the strictest sense of the word, men under an obligation of perpetual servitude, which the consent of the master could alone dissolve, and in all probability enjoyed less legal protection from the ill-usage of their oppressors than the humanity of modern legislation has extended to the brute creation.

Attempts have been made to class the population existing at the close of the Anglo-Saxon period into its several proportions of nobles, freemen, and those of servile condition, but with no great pretence to accuracy. In thirty-four counties the burgesses and citizens are made to amount to 17,105, the villains to 102,704, the bordars to 74,823, the cottars to 5,947, the serfs or thralls to 26,552. The remaining population consisted of freemen, ecclesiastics, knights, thanes, and landowners. In the opinion of Sir James McIntosh, the persons strictly slaves were not above one out of every seven of the higher laborious classes of villains, bordars and cottars.

In 1060 Anglo-Saxon England was conquered by the Normans, under the leadership of William the Conqueror. This conquest appears to have completely supplanted the Anglo-Saxon aristocracy, and to have put the soldiers who accompanied William into the places of those nobles who had ruled the peasantry. There is no proof, however, that the great mass of the people were any worse off after the conquest than before, nor is it at all likely that they were any better off. The thane, as the Saxon lord was called, had his villains and slaves, and there is no reason to believe that the Norman baron was a worse master than the Saxon thane, whom he superseded.

In order to get a fairly satisfactory picture of the economic and social condition of the English people in the period following the conquest, we must glance at the life of the people in town and country. Under the feudal system of society, which had been developing under the late Anglo-Saxons, and which was fully developed under the Normans, society was sharply divided into different classes, with a peculiar and complicated system of mutual rights and duties which has never been satisfactorily explained in all its details. It seems that in rural districts, *i. e.*, outside of the chartered cities, the whole country was divided into a series of landed estates, some in the hands of powerful barons, and some in the hands of the church. The great mass of the people lived on these estates in various degrees of dependence on the lord of the manor, as the superior was called, whether a baron or the church or other corporation.

On each of these great estates there was one or more villages where the freer part of the dependents lived. The settlement contained several orders of social life. First there was the lord who usually had a manor-house or mansion in which he lived. He had about this his special farm, which he cultivated by means of his slaves and the labor which the other dependents owed him as rent for their farms. The next class was that of free tenants, *i. e.*, tenants who were freemen. They were independent of the personal power of the lord, and had the right to take part in the village court, etc. The other tenants were cottagers and bordars, who did not have the same liberty as the free tenants, and finally the serfs who at one period were regarded as the slaves of the lord, but who were gradually acquiring certain rights. The lord of the manor was recognized as the owner of the serfs and the superior of the villagers and cottars. But there were many customs which limited very materially the power of the lord over the land and his estate. It became usual for the lord to assign to his serfs lots of land which they might cultivate for themselves in return for giving a certain portion of their products, and rendering labor at certain periods. It soon became a custom, with all the force of law, that as long as the serf or cottager performed his services, the lord might not disturb him in possession. The lord could do what he pleased with the lot which belonged to himself, but he was entitled only to certain services from the holders of the rest of the manor. There was also always a large portion of the estate which was held in common by the lord of the manor and his tenants, viz., the woodlands and pasture land. It was recognized to be a right of the tenant to take as much wood from the forest, and pasture as many cattle on the pastures as he chose. It is evident that this was a most valuable right, and one intimately connected with the welfare of every tenant. As the serfs became tenants, these same rights passed over to them. The villagers and cottars, after they had performed the services due the lord of the manor, had their time for their own work. They had ample time after they had tilled their own fields, to go out as day-laborers either for their lord for such wages as he might pay, or for other lords or fellow-tenants. The serfs acquired the same rights in course of time.

As civilization progressed, it became usual for the tenants to offer their lord money instead of labor for the services due him. It was for the interest of both parties that this commutation of payments in kind for money payments should be made. In the first place it was very burdensome to the tenant to have to leave his own work and go and help his lord harvest just at the time when his own field needed his attention most. On the other hand it was very difficult for the lord's overseer to get any amount of work out of the unwilling tenant. The interest of both parties thus combined to favor the new custom of commutation. As the services of the tenants were not very valuable, since labor was cheap, the lords were willing to let them off with easy payments. The serf shared in all these advantages, and was rapidly becoming almost as independent, so far as his earnings were concerned, as the cottager or free tenant, the lord becoming, in the meantime, more and more dependent on hired labor. Everything was thus rapidly progressing toward a time when the serf should be free and independent, and the free tenant his own man in every respect except the payment of a small cash rent, when a sudden event happened which proved to be a disturbing cause of the most powerful and far-reaching kind. The Black Death appeared in England on the 1st of August, 1348, and within a short time one-third of the population of England had perished. The economic and social effects of this terrible plague were far-reaching and long-working. One of the immediate consequences was, of course, a great dearth of labor, a very great enhancement of wages, and a serious difficulty in collecting the harvests of those landlords who depended on a supply of hired labor for the purpose of getting in their crops. We are told that crops rotted in the fields for want of hands; that cattle and sheep roamed at large over the country for want of herdsmen; and that great estates went out of cultivation.

Two important results showed themselves immediately. The process of commutation for money payments became more rapid, each landlord being willing to give his tenants the best terms he could to prevent them from leaving, and being willing to favor the serf to prevent him from running away to some other lord who would defend him against his old master, in order to utilize his labor. The second result was the final emancipation of the serfs over a great part of England.

It soon became evident to the lords that, what with rising wages and falling prices of farm products, they would soon be in a bad way. The remedy to which they resorted was characteristic. They secured the passage of the celebrated statute of laborers, in 1350, which remained on the statute books of England for more than two hundred years, until, in the reign of Elizabeth, 1562, it was replaced by another. The statute contained eight clauses: 1. No person under sixty years of age, whether serf or free, shall decline to undertake farm labor at the wages which had been customary in 1327, except they lived by merchandize, were regularly engaged in some mechanical craft, were possessed of private means or were occupiers of land. The lord was to have the first claim on the labor of his serf, and those who declined to work for him or for others were to be sent to the common jail. 2. Imprisonment is decreed for all persons who may quit service before the time which is fixed in their agreements. 3. No other than the old wages are to be given, and the remedy against those who seek more is to be sought in the lord's court. 4. Lords of manors paying more than the customary rates are liable to treble damages. 5. Artificers are to be liable to the same conditions, the artificers enumerated being: saddlers, tanners, farriers, shoemakers, tailors, smiths, carpenters, masons, tillers, plasterers, carters and others. 6. Food must be sold at reasonable prices. 7. Alms are strictly forbidden to able-bodied laborers. 8. Any excess of wages taken or given can be seized for the king's use. The statute provides for the difference between summer and winter wages, and guards against the emigration of the town population to country places in summer. In answer to complaints from employers this statute was re-enacted again and again from year to year with accumulated penalties and precautions —penalties sometimes laid on the employers, sometimes on the laborers, and sometimes on both. An attempt was made in the beginning of the fourteenth century to enforce apprenticeship in the handicrafts with the view of making it difficult to get into them and thus make the number of those who had to take their recourse to agriculture larger, and thus secure cheap labor for the landlord and tenant-farmer. It was in other words a gigantic attempt on the part of employers to keep down the wages of labor.

The rise in agricultural wages in all kinds of men's work taken together, some years after the plague, when the rates had become pretty steady, was fifty per cent., and of women's work fully one hundred per cent. When taken together the rise in the wages of artisans' labor was almost exactly the same as that effected in the case of the husbandmen. The result is marked, universal, permanent and conclusive, even if we did not have on record the complaints of the landowners in Parliament that the statute of laborers was entirely inoperative.

The combination of employers to depress wages to the old rates shown by this statute, might, however, have been successful if it had not been met by counter-organizations on the part of the laborers. They formed societies; subscribed, as we are expressly told, considerable sums of money for the defense and protection particularly of the serfs and for the payment of fines. In plain English, the serfs entered into what are now called trades-unions and supported each other in resistance to the law and demands for higher wages. This is especially noticeable among the peasantry, the upland folk as they were called, to distinguish them from artisans and townspeople generally. These facts are proved by the averages of agricultural wages, which at first were only occasionally very high in comparison with what they had been before the plague. At last, twenty years after the first incidence of the plague, the combination seemed to have been completely successful, and the prices of harvest-labor were more than double those before the plague. Thus the results of this great economic revolution in favor of the laborer were only saved by the combinations of the laborers themselves to protect and guard their own interests.

But the lords were by no means ready to let the case go by default. They had not yet tried all experiments. They next attempted to do away with the bargains which they had made with their serfs to accept money payments in place of labor rents, and tried to compel the serfs to render again the old labor rents which had been usual before the beginning of the century, *i. e.*, to reduce them again to villainage in the old sense. But the time for this had gone by. The serfs had learned their own power and how to use it. They organized anew and waited for their opportunity The secret was well kept. The storm which no politician of the time anticipated burst on June 10, 1381. The uprising of peasant and serf was simultaneous. For a time it looked as if the government of England was destined to pass into other hands. Finally, by the use of treachery, the ruling party killed the leader of the insurrection, Wat Tyler; and, persuaded by the promises of the king, the peasants and the serfs returned home. No sooner had the king seated himself securely again than he proceeded to take summary vengeance on the rioters. A commission was sent into the disturbed districts and some 1,500 persons were taken and hanged.

The peasants were dispersed and defeated; their leaders were tried, sentenced and hanged; but the solid fruits of victory remained with the insurgents of 1381. The peril had been so great and the success of the insurrection so near, that wise men saw it was better silently to concede that which the Parliament had so stoutly refused to grant. It is absolutely certain the claims of the serfs were conceded and that the claims of the landlords were dropped. The custom of commuting old labor rents for money became universal; the serfs became free tenants and the insurrection of Tyler became characteristically enough in the accounts of the historians of the time a mere outbreak of a mob which had been stirred to indignation by a brutal tax-gatherer. It is improbable that the serfs would have held all the advantages which they had at one time gained even if Tyler had not been assassinated. But they caused such terror by what they did do that they gained all they claimed, and that right speedily. The English laborer for a century or more became virtually free and constantly prosperous; and this again by his own efforts in combination with his fellow laborers.

According to the investigations of Professor Rogers, and most other investigators agree with him, the fifteenth century and the first quarter of the sixteenth were the golden age of the English laborer, if we are to interpret the wages he earned by the cost of the necessaries of life. At no time were wages so high or the cost of food so low, and seldom were the hours of labor so few. Within a century he sunk, from perfectly intelligible causes, to so low a level as to become practically hopeless. He then improved again, until in the first half of the eighteenth century he reached a condition of comparative plenty though not so prosperous a condition as in the fifteenth. He then began to sink again, and the workman experienced the direst misery during the great Napoleonic wars. Latterly, almost within our own memory, the state of the laborer has experienced a slow and partial improvement, the causes of which are to be found in the liberation of industry, in the adoption of certain principles which restrained employment in certain directions, and most of all in the concession to laborers of the right so long denied of forming labor unions.

Several causes conspired during the sixteenth century to make the condition of the laborer worse than it had been before. There was, in the first place, a great debasement of the currency followed by an enormous rise in prices which was not followed by a proportional rise in wages. It is possible that in the course of time wages might have risen to the full extent of the rise in prices if the laborers had combined to defend their own interests effectually. But not only did they not combine, but the ruling classes combined to keep wages from rising, and they succeeded in this attempt. To make the matter worse the king of England, Henry VIII., destroyed the guilds, which were the mediæval trades-unions, as will be fully described in the next chapter, and confiscated their property. This prevented them from extending their aid to poverty-stricken members and threw the latter on the community for support. The artisan was thus attacked simultaneously from two sides. His cost of living was increased while wages remained the same, and the assistance which his benefit society gave him in times of trouble, which allowed him loans without interest, apprenticed his sons and pensioned his widow, was confiscated. The agricultural laborer was driven to the wall by the increasing habit of enclosures of the common lands by the landlords, thus depriving him of the rights of pasturage for his cattle and hogs, and making the keeping of these impossible. They deprived him also of the right to take wood and timber from the common wood-lot. All these things contributed to increase the number of the hopelessly poor who had no prospect of rising above the lowest level of society. So rapidly did this class increase that a law was passed in 1547 to restrain pauperism and vagabondage by reducing the landless poor, who were made poor by this policy of enclosures on the part of the lord, to slavery by branding them and making them work in chains. This act endured, however, only two years. It was followed by a law providing for the support of the poor. A few years after, in 1562, the statute of apprenticeship was passed, prescribing a period of seven years before practising any handicraft and empowering the justices of the peace to fix the rate of wages in husbandry and handicrafts. In 1601 the famous poor law was enacted which, with the supplementary acts, completed a system of legislation which did as much to degrade the laboring man and prevent him from rising out of a condition of hopeless dependence and poverty as the most bitter enemies of labor or most warm-hearted partisans of privilege could desire.

The law provided for the regular appointment of assessors, for the levy of rates, for supplying work to the ablebodied, for giving relief to the infirm and old, and for binding apprentices. It is evident that had the act of Elizabeth been carried out in all its details the whole revenue of land might have ultimately been swallowed up in the relief of the poor. Now, it was plain that if the magistrates were to fix the rates at which labor should be paid, as they regularly did in the sixteenth and seventeenth centuries, they would have every inducement to put the rate at the lowest sum which could maintain life, knowing well that if the laborer should become destitute all occupiers would have to assist in his maintenance while the benefit of cheap labor would remain to those who employed labor, to which class the magistrates themselves always belonged.

Only one more step remained to be taken to consummate the degradation of the laborer, and that was taken in 1662, in the law of parochial settlement, by which the laborer was prevented from going from one parish to another in search of labor. It made him, and has left him up to the present time, a serf without land. It applied equally to the artisan, but he was able to extricate himself from the toils of this hateful law at a much earlier period. The law prescribed that any person on removing into a parish and occupying a tenement of less than ten pounds' annual value might be immediately removed to the parish from which he came. An act passed thirty-five years later recognized that the law of settlement practically imprisoned the laborer in his place of settlement where he could not get work, though workmen were badly wanted elsewhere. It therefore empowered churchwardens to allow laborers to migrate from their parishes if the parish authorities would give security that they should not be allowed to come for their support on the parish whither they went. It is superfluous to say that such certificates would be looked on with suspicion as expedients to relieve a parish of its quota of poor. Hence it became customary for those who employed labor from without the parish to give certificates of indemnity to the parish that they would bear the risk of the newcomer's charge. The effect of this law was to annex the laborer to the parish of his residence, and to make him the serf of the community. Those persons, however, who owned the whole of a parish took care, whenever they could, to tear down cottages on their estate and rely on labor from a distance. By this system, they hired labor at the justice's rate, *i. e.*, a factitiously low rate, while the parish of the man's residence had to supplement his wages and to bear all those contingencies which were enhanced by the laborer's being constrained to travel a considerable distance to his work in all weathers. The law of settlement, therefore, not only fixed the tenant to the soil but enabled opulent landowners to rob their neighbors and to wear out prematurely the laborer's health and strength. All this was done, too, when the patriots and placemen chattered about liberty and arbitrary administration, and fine ladies and gentlemen talked about the rights of man and Rousseau and the French Revolution; and Burke and Sheridan were denouncing the despotism of Warren Hastings! Why, at his own doors at Beaconsfield, Burke must have daily seen serfs who had less liberty than those Indians whose wrongs he described so dramatically and pathetically.

No trifling percentage of the funds collected for the maintenance of the poor was expended in litigation on the cases which sprang out of this law, since each parish tried to shift the burden of the support of the poor, if possible, on the neighboring parish. It was an evil inheritance of the English people, perhaps the worst act of the worst Parliament which ever sat, but it was an El Dorado to the lawyers. Many a barrister owed his place in Parliament and on the bench to his skill in arguing settlement cases, to the ingenuity with which he was able to tighten the bonds on the peasant. The wealthy landowners clung to it with desperate tenacity; for it increased their rents at the expense of the tenants and the laborers. What mattered it to them that the English peasant's life was aged soon after his prime, if they could get cheap labor and increasing rents? The whole force of law was directed for nearly two centuries toward the solution of this problem; How much oppression can the English people endure, how much privation, misery and starvation without absolutely destroying the labor on which the growing rents depend? The present generation, though a portion of the evil has been prevented for the future, inherit the outcome of these two centuries and with it problems of the gravest kind daily pressing for solution, and to which it is idle to offer the nostrums of over-population, emigration, competition, and other formularies of an ideal society.

Towards the close of the last century the Berkshire magistrates, struck with the appalling discrepancy between wages and the price of food — for the labor of the peasant could procure him, for several years, only one-eighth of the amount of wheat which the same person could have earned before 1540 — met and proposed, not that the mischievous law of Elizabeth, which established legal wages, should be repealed or that the infamous law of parochial settlement should be done away with, but that able-bodied laborers should have their wages supplemented by allowances from the overseer of the poor, proportionate to the number of their children or the general charges of the family. By this means they were enabled to prevent a general increase of wages, to fix the wages of the single and childless at a low amount, and compel all tenants to contribute to the expense of agricultural operations.

It is no wonder that the condition of the agricultural laborer is to-day a very unhappy one. Men do not come out of such a state of debasement as that into which such a policy as this, pursued for two centuries, has thrown them, in a few days or years, or even decades. The very name Hodge, which is applied to the British agricultural laborer, has come to be used as a synonym of stupidity. In 1865 Prof. Fawcett wrote in his work on the economic condition of the British laborers, that theirs is a life of incessant toil for wages too scanty to give them a supply even of the first necessaries of life. No hope cheers their monotonous careers: a life of constant labor brings them no other prospect than that when their strength is exhausted they must crave as suppliant mendicants a pittance from parish relief.

The most hopeless feature in the case is the almost insurmountable obstacles in the way of any improvement on the part of the laborers themselves. The condition of the agricultural laborer is very different from that of the artisan in this respect. Scattered and incapable of combined action with his fellows, bowed down by centuries of oppression, hard usage and hard words, with, as he believes, every social force against him, the landlord in league with the farmer, the clergyman in league with both; the latter preaching resignation, and the former enforcing it, he has lived through evil times. Several attempts have been made of late years to bring about an organization of agricultural laborers, but they have been only very partially successful. It is difficult to organize laborers who live so widely scattered. The present laborer can give absolutely nothing from his scanty wages toward defraying the costs of organization, and it costs something to conduct a successful organization. Those who attempt to form such unions have to contend with the apathy of despair, with the sluggishness of ignorance, with the habitual mendacity of distrust, and with the low cunning with which the oppressed shirk duty. In other words, the long policy of oppression has ended in sinking the laborer so low that he has neither intelligence enough nor virtue enough to combine with his fellow-laborers in order to raise their condition.

We have thus traced the process by which the condition of the English laborer has been continuously deteriorated by the acts of government. It was first impoverished by the issue of base money. Next it was robbed of its guild money by the land thieves of Edward's regency. It was next brought into contact with a new and more needy set of employers, the sheep-masters who succeeded the monks. It was then by a pretence subjected to the justices' assessment of wages, mercilessly used in the first half of the seventeenth century, the agricultural laborer being still further impoverished by being made the residuum of all labor. The agricultural laborer was then further mulcted by enclosures of common lands and the extinction of those immemorial rights of fuel and pasture which he had enjoyed so long. The poor law professed to find him work, but was so administered that the reduction of his wages to a bare subsistence became an easy process and an economical expedient. When the monarchy was restored, his employers, who fixed his wages by their own authority, relieved their own estates of their ancient dues at the expense of his poor luxuries, by the excise; tied him to the soil by the law of settlement, and starved him by a prohibitive corn law. The freedom of the few was bought by the servitude of the many. Fletcher, of Saltoun, an ardent republican for a narrow class, suggested hopeless slavery as the proper doom of the laborers, argued that the people existed only to work, and that philosophical politicians have the power to limit their existence by labor. Throughout the eighteenth century the most enlightened men gave the poor their pity, occasionally their patronage, and would sometimes assist them at the cost of other workers; but beyond a bare existence never imagined that they had rights or remembered that they had suffered wrongs. The weight of taxation fell on them in every direction and with searching severity. It was necessary to find funds at all risks and from every source; and it is obvious that the most fruitful source of taxation is that of necessary consumption and cheap luxuries. It was, of course, impossible to tax the absolute necessaries of the individual workman, else he would starve and perish. But the process left him nothing but a bare subsistence. To crown the whole, the penalties of felony and conspiracy were denounced against all laborers who associated together to better their lot by endeavoring to sell their labor in concert, while the desperation which poverty and misery induce, and the crime they suggest, were met by a code more sanguinary and brutal than any which a civilized nation had ever heretofore devised or a high-spirited one submitted to.

Such was the education which the English workmen received from those days when the government employed and developed those means for oppressing and degrading him. It is no marvel that he identifies the policy of landowner, farmer and capitalist employer with the machinery by which his lot has been shaped and his fortunes in the distribution of national wealth have been controlled. He may have no knowledge, or a very vague knowledge, as to the process by which so strange, so woeful an alteration has been made in his condition. But there exists, and always has existed, a tradition, obscure and uncertain, but deep seated, that there was a time when his lot was happier, his means more ample, his prospects more cheerful than they have been in more modern experience. From one point of view the annalist of the good old times may be able to show that life was shorter, disease more rife, the market of food more unsteady, the conveniences of life fewer and more precarious than they are now. From another point of view, and that by far the most accurate and exact, the relative position of the workman was one of far more hope and far more plenty in the days of the Plantagenets than it has been in those of Hanover. Wages were, relative to their purchasing power, far higher, and the margin of enjoyable income over necessary expenditure was, in consequence, far wider.

T. V. Powderly

CHAPTER II.

HISTORY OF MECHANICAL LABOR.

The Mechanic in Greece — In Rome — Among the Ancient Germans — On the Mediæval Estates — Differentiation of Employments and Rise of Cities — Official Organization of the Mechanics — Rise of the Guilds — Characteristics of the Guild System — Division into Masters, Apprentices and Journeymen — Privileges of the Guilds — Duties of the Guilds (a) to their Own Members; (b) to the General Public — Police and Judicial Functions of the Guilds — Gradual Rise of Distinct Social Classes within the Guild — The Differentiation of a Laboring Class and the Consequent Appearance of the "Labor Question" — Degeneration of the Guilds — Selfish Policy of the Masters (a) toward their Workmen; (b) toward the Public — Demand for the Abolition of the Guilds in the Interest (a) of General Liberty; (b) of the Laborer Himself; (c) of the Large Capitalist — Fall of the Guilds and Rise of the Modern System of Industry.

THE preceding chapter was chiefly devoted to a history of agricultural labor in England. It may serve also as a general description of the course of development of agricultural labor in modern times in all the countries of Western Europe. The same general forces have been at work in these nations for more than one thousand years, bringing about the same general result in all, each case being, however, somewhat varied owing to local circumstances and influences.

Many of the laws mentioned in the preceding chapter applied equally to laborers in the mechanical callings and, of course, the forces and influences which determined the condition of the agricultural laborer could not but affect in the most intimate way the condition and welfare of the mechanic. It is impossible to discuss one of these topics without touching upon the other at various points. But there are certain features in the history of mechanical labor which make it desirable to discuss the subject somewhat more in detail. Indeed, in order to understand at all the labor legislation and labor movements of the last and present century, it is necessary to comprehend the condition of things which preceded them; and we cannot do this without a glance, at least, at the previous development of mechanical labor up to that time.

As the history of agricultural labor can be traced most satisfactorily in the case of England, owing to the greater wealth of annals, accounts and other materials; so that of the rise and development of mechanical labor can be followed most completely in the history of the Continent, and particularly of Germany, where the followers of these trades became at one time the freest and most powerful classes of society. The free cities of the German Empire, which played such an important part in the history of mediæval Europe, owed in many cases their freedom and their prosperity to the handicraftsmen who constituted the bulk of their population.

We know but little of the condition of mechanical labor among the Greeks and Romans. That it was highly developed in many ways we may be sure from the most incontestable of all evidence, viz., the products of their industry and art, which have remained in many respects the models for all subsequent time. We know from the writings of their philosophers that mechanical labor was regarded as degrading and was performed chiefly by slaves and the lower classes of free citizens. We have very good evidence that the artisans at Rome, *i. e.*, the free artisans, were organized into unions called "collegia," but we do not know the purposes of these associations or what particular rights or duties they had. The condition of mechanical labor in the ancient world, however, has only a historical interest for us, since our modern system is built up on an entirely different basis which has been but slightly modified by the system or habits of the ancients. Even if the mediæval trade guilds sprung from the old Roman "collegia" and the modern trades-unions from the guild, as many claim, yet the connection between the first two is so slight and the influence of the former so untraceable that the question has for us only an antiquarian interest.

The history of mechanical trades among the Germans may be traced back to a time before the rise of modern nations.

In the earliest period of German history of which we know anything, viz., that which preceded the attack by the Germans on the Roman Empire, mechanical labor, with the single exception, perhaps, of casting and forging, had not become a separate calling which men followed for the sake of a livelihood. Social conditions were very primitive. The houses were mere rude hovels which it did not require much skill to construct, and the furniture was, if possible, still ruder. The head of the family with the aid of his slaves and the members of the family built his own house, made his own furniture and wove his own cloth. The household work, such as spinning and weaving, fell to the lot of the women. In only one department does it seem probable that separate classes of artisans existed, and that was in the department of metal working. We know from Roman accounts that the Germans used weapons of iron in battle, and iron utensils in the worship of the gods. To prodúce these required skilled workmen, and it can hardly be supposed that every German possessed this skill.

This state of things continued to exist for the great mass of the people for a thousand years, at least, after we first learn something of the Germans from the accounts of Cæsar and Tacitus. When the Germans issued from their ancient home beyond the Rhine, and in one campaign after another conquered the Romans and broke the power of the ancient empire in pieces and settled themselves down in the fair fields of what is now France, Spain, Italy and Greece as masters, they made large numbers of the Romans their slaves, and from them learned the customs and habits of civilized life. When the disintegrating influences of this period of conquest had done their perfect work and the old territory of the Empire was divided into almost as many different countries as there were estates, we find that, although the great mass of the people still remained in the same low state of civilization as before, the lords themselves had acquired a taste for the comforts and conveniences of life which attend a developed system of handicrafts. The great feudal lords collected on their own estates artisans acquainted with all the known arts. It was on these estates that mechanical labor among the Germans was first divided into separate callings. But in this early period there were few, if any, free laborers who followed these callings as a means of earning a living. The mechanics were dependent persons, bondmen of the feudal lords; and they worked for their masters, just as other serfs and bondmen, according to the service and law of the manor. The rise of this new class of laborers among the Germans was a natural consequence of the growth of the feudal system and the gradual spread of civilization among the conquerors. A large number of families were collected on these great estates for whose wants (food, clothing, housing, etc.) the lords were naturally expected to provide. The latter needed, moreover, for the proper defence and cultivation of such an estate, a large quantity of utensils, instruments and arms. The wants of the lord and his family kept increasing in number, and they kept desiring finer quality as they came more and more in contact with Roman civilization or with those whom Roman civilization had affected. These wants could only be satisfied by increasing skill on the part of the mechanics. Many of the lords took great trouble to purchase skilled mechanics from distant centers and import them for work on their own estates. The Emperor Charlemagne, who at one time ruled over the most of what is now modern Europe, made a special effort to spread abroad through his realms a knowledge of the mechanic arts and passed a law that on all royal estates there should be collected a sufficient number of skilled artisans.

These mechanics usually lived about the household of their master, and received from them what they needed for their living and performed their services in return. One portion of the mechanical labor about the court of the lord, viz., the making of cloth, was done by female laborers who were brought together for this purpose into special houses. It was at the courts of the lords that the first official organization of the mechanics took place. In order to supervise them and their labor more easily they were organized into small societies and placed under control of a court officer whose business it was to supervise their work and look out for the proper training of the children for their future calling as mechanics. There was no trace of independence in these bodies. The individuals had no right to choose their calling. The lord could take them from one business and set them at another at his own pleasure. Discipline and jurisdiction, as well as the regulation of the labor and service, pertained to the officer appointed by the lord. There is no evidence that they had any special court of self-government of any kind. Occasionally some unusually able mechanic would acquire a position of influence about the estate and would acquire a certain degree of practical freedom, but the class as a whole was strictly dependent, subordinate and without legal rights of any kind, *i. e.*, slaves.

Some of the mechanics, probably those who performed service for the various villages on the estate, lived in a somewhat freer position. In many cases they were allowed to cultivate a lot of land on their own account and were bound only to perform certain services to the lord at stated times. That which was at first a mere grant of the lord came in course of time to be considered a right of the servant, and the holding of the lot of land and the following of the trade became a hereditary right, and thus certain trades became the privilege of certain families. In the course of time, owing to a multitude of causes, the absolute right of the lord over his tenants became very much modified, and those who had been slaves became assimilated more and more to the class of free tenants which was described in the preceding chapter.

It seems likely that there were also free mechanics in the few free communities which still existed, who combined the following of a trade with the pursuit of farming. Out of these three classes of mechanics, viz., the free mechanics in the free communities, the serf mechanics in the household of the lord and the tenant mechanics on the estates of the lords, sprang the modern class of mechanics.

The process by which this took place is too long and intricate to be adequately described in this connection, but two or three of the more important causes may be mentioned. The chief circumstance in this new development, which began about the eleventh century, was the rise of cities. The origin of the leading cities which played the most important part in this period was very various. Owing to the circumstances of the time it was easy for any band of men who would combine and entrench themselves in some stronghold to develop an independent city, if they could hold their own against the strong barons and knights who were always quarreling among themselves. In some cases the lords encouraged the growth of the villages on their estates by offering special encouragements to foreign laborers to immigrate and to the artisans on other estates to run away from their masters, offering them in many cases a large degree of liberty. In course of time these villages, enlarged and fortified, felt themselves strong to demand a greater share of liberty from their masters, and in case these refused they often declared their independence and maintained it through long and stubborn contests. It was in these cities that the artisans organized themselves into the famous unions of the middle ages which are known by the name, "guilds." The origin of these guilds is not known. It would be idle to seek any one source for them perhaps. The circumstances of the time were favorable to the development of such bodies; and as with one accord we find them springing up in nearly every European country, though their career in Germany was the most successful and brilliant.

We cannot follow the rise and development of the system of guilds in detail. Their rise dates from the twelfth century, in a few cities and a few callings. In the thirteenth and fourteenth centuries they became more numerous, and in the fifteenth century the system becomes almost universal in all Continental and English cities and embraces all callings. The history of the guilds was very different in different cities and in different branches of trade, conditioned largely by the political development of the city. But in spite of all the differences in detail the guilds in the German cities toward the close of the middle ages formed an organization of industrial labor with a homogeneous nature, with similar ultimate aims and purposes and with a similar social and economic significance.

There were many different classes of guilds, but those

which chiefly interest us in this connection are the craft-guilds. These craft-guilds were, according to Professor Schoenberg, who has made special investigations into their history, fraternal unions of the mechanical laborers (in the rule, belonging to one branch of industry), for the promotion of their common interests. The most prominent was their social and economic interest, though they did not by any means neglect their political or other interests. They were, however, not merely unions of laborers for their private purposes, but they were recognized organs of the city government. With the approval and under the supervision of the city authorities they could issue regulations for the conduct of their particular branches of trade which were binding on all mechanics of that branch in the city. They were entrusted by the city with the execution of city ordinances in regard to trade, and were held responsible for their enforcement.

The following features were characteristic of the guild system when it was in its flourishing period. It was based, in the first place, on a legal division of its members into three classes of masters, journeymen and apprentices. The masters were the members in full standing, the journeymen and apprentices were the minor members who were under the protection of the guild-masters as a corporation. They were subject to the jurisdiction of the guilds not only in matters pertaining to the trade, but also in their disputes with one another or with the masters and in all violations of the custom or honor of the guild. The journeymen and apprentices were usually members of the master's household. They were personally free. The access to each class was regulated by a detailed body of rules and was dependent on certain conditions. The apprenticeship and journeymanship formed a preparatory stage, a school for the mastership. The journeymen did not, in the earlier period, at least, form a separate class by themselves whose members could only follow their calling as dependent laborers; but were merely those who had not yet finished their preparatory training or did not desire to become masters, or who had not been able to fulfill the conditions of the mastership.

The right to follow a trade as a master was, as a rule, dependent on membership in the guild to which the trade belonged. This was called the guild-right, and was nothing more than the right granted to the guild of forcing every one who wished to practice the trade to join the guild. In later times, when the guild decided upon the admission of new members, this privilege was extended in some places so as to include the right to refuse membership to any one whom they did not wish and thus prevent him from pursuing the trade in the city. In most places, however, the city authorities reserved the right to grant license to non-members of the guilds to follow their handicraft in the city.

Mastership in the guild was dependent on the proof of certain qualifications on the part of the applicant, both as respecting his moral character and his technical skill. They demanded a spotless reputation and a thorough knowledge of the business. The method of acquiring the skill was not at first regulated by guild rule, but in course of time it was prescribed that every one who wished to become master must serve a period as apprentice and afterwards as journeyman. The qualifications were gradually raised so that it was difficult, if not impossible, for the average man to comply with them. Legally, however, every one who could become an apprentice could also become master by fulfilling the conditions.

The right to employment, the protection of guild-labor, and an assured market were secured by certain privileges conferred on the guild. Every guild had the monopoly of certain kinds of mechanical labor as its specified field of production, and only its members had, as such, the right to make or sell those products within the jurisdiction of the city. This was a privilege which the individual guild had not only against foreign laborers but also against the merchants and dealers and other craft-guilds. But it was not intended that the welfare of the city should suffer by this monopoly. The right carried with it the corresponding duty to see that the consumer received good wares or services at a reasonable price. If the guild did not do this the city authorities might at any time introduce foreign laborers or give to its merchants the right to sell foreign goods in the city. In order that consumers might not suffer, market days and times were established when outside mechanics might offer their wares for sale, provided that they complied with the same conditions as those imposed on local mechanics.

With the design of securing for the individual laborer an independent existence and a sufficient income and creating an honorable and worthy class of mechanics, and on the other hand of guarding the interests of consumers by a proper organization of labor a whole system of regulations governing the action of the guild members was adopted, which was characteristic of the guilds. They may be divided into two classes, those in the interest of producers and those in the interest of consumers. The measures in the interest of consumers aim at securing a good quality and a fair price for commodities and services. The care for this was entrusted to the guild. The first condition of good service is good training; and this was required, as we have seen, before entering the guild. In addition to this, regulations were adopted in regard to the method and manner of production, prescribing the material to be employed, and the method of its use, form, size and quality of the product. Fines and bodily punishments were threatened for violation of these provisions. Very severe punishments were inflicted for the manufacture or sale of bad wares or for cheating. Poor commodities were confiscated and destroyed. Regular visitation of the shops, inspection of the individual masters while at work, examination of the manufactured commodity by the guild inspectors, compulsory marking of manufactured commodities with the name of the manufacturer, and many similar regulations made the way of the slovenly or dishonest workmen a hard one. Undue delay with the work was also punishable and the guild police watched over the conduct of its members toward the public. A fair price was secured by fixing the price of the manufactured or partially manufactured article or service.

This regulation of industry aimed also at securing to the guild members an income suitable to their social position and an independent business. The idea of fraternity, moreover, was to be realized among the members and the difference between the rich and the poor was to be kept as slight as possible, and the poor were to be properly cared for. The necessary consequence of all this was the exclusion of competition among the members and a far reaching restriction of the individual in production and of the market in the interests of the guild as a whole, They took care to hinder the growth of large capital as far as possible by a complicated series of regulations which aimed at making large business comparatively unprofitable. They aimed at restricting capital as a factor of production and a source of income within very narrow limits, and tried to make the income of mechanics chiefly the income of labor.

In order to carry out these rules and regulations the guilds were entrusted with very extensive police and judicial functions, though they were much greater in some places than in others. All disputes between guild members, no matter on what subject, had to be taken before the guild court before they could be taken before the ordinary courts.

There is but little doubt that the guild system was of great advantage, not only to the laborers but also to the whole system of mediæval industry. It quickened the best elements of the time and was a most judicious and happy form of the organization of industry, with the great merit of being fully in harmony with the other institutions of the time. But it was by no means a system which did away with all conflict of interest between the various classes within the system itself, to say nothing of the large masses of labor outside of the organization. It can be easily seen that the tendency of the system was toward monopoly; not only monopoly of trade and business by the guild, as distinguished from outsiders, but also monopoly of the masterships within the guilds by a few individuals and families, to the exclusion of the great mass of members.

From the rise of mechanical industry in the cities until the time when the guilds succeeded in obtaining independence in the management of industrial affairs, *i. e.* in general, until the middle of the fourteenth century, there was, according to Professor Brentano, no special class of laborers as distinguished from the masters. The journeymanship, so far as it existed at that time, was only one stage in the life of an artisan, not a special calling followed by particular persons. It was a transition period on the way to a mastership. But it did not exist at all in most places before the middle of the fourteenth century. This was owing to the character of the mechanical industry of the time. The trades were chiefly local industries and were carried on for the most part, if not entirely, by native born inhabitants of the cities. An inflow of laborers and an overcrowding of the trades was thus made impossible. The guilds of that time were not "close," *i. e.*, neither the number of masters was limited nor was it difficult to become a master by reason of any undue restrictions. The masters themselves were, moreover, chiefly laborers themselves, for, although it was necessary to have some capital in order to start in as a master, yet the amount demanded was very small and was within the reach of almost everyone. In consequence of this, the apprentices, as soon as they had learned their business, commenced immediately as masters and very few of them served as journeymen. What few journeymen there were soon became masters themselves, so that in spite of the authority vested by the law in the master over the journeyman where he existed, there was no social difference between the two classes, no conflict of interests and consequently no distinct social class.

The only exception to this state of things was in such branches of industry, few in number, as were prosecuted from an early period on a large scale or those in which from other causes as, for instance, cost of material, a large capital was necessary. Among such branches was the manufacture of cloth; and we learn that at an early period, in certain cities of Flanders and Brabant, there were enormous numbers of weavers crowded together in an incredible condititition. It was in this branch, too, that there first came into existence a large class who had no hopes of ever becoming independent workmen, *i. e.*, that a class of laborers arose. But this class does not seem to have been completely within the power of the masters. They had large labor unions as far back as the thirteenth century. Two of the four directors of the guild were always journeymen. Journeymen were members of the body which issued regulations in regard to guild matters. The wages of the journeymen were regulated in proportion to the reward of the masters, and in some instances in such a way as must have given the journeymen a regular participation in profits. Even in those cases where the inspecting body consisted entirely of nobles, no regulation was issued without first hearing the ideas of the journeymen unions on the subject.

The harmony of these relations became disturbed more and more as the guilds became richer and more independent, as they got the power more and more completely of determining the rules of their respective trades and as larger and larger quantities of capital became necessary to prosecute the trade. The rapid growth of the industries, particularly that of cloth manufacture, and the great amount of capital expended, attracted great masses of serfs from the rural districts to the cities. In this way the increased number of laborers, which the continued growth of industry made necessary, was obtained, and, on the other hand, every new laborer became a possible competitor. The profit of the capital already expended was thus made uncertain. The anxiety of the masters was thus excited, and as the regulation of industrial affairs gradually passed into the hands of the guilds, the masters of the latter kept introducing new restrictions in order to keep down the rising families who threatened their position. High apprentice fees, a long period of apprenticeship, a long period as journeyman, wandering of the journeymen from place to place; during this time costly masterpieces and expensive master banquets were demanded. In consequence of these regulations it soon became impossible for any one to become master and carry on the trade independently who was not already in the possession of property, or was the son of a master, or did not marry the daughter or widow of a master. Instead of the original requirement for a mastership, viz., personal worth and skill of the individual, they now demanded capital or family connection. The various trades became more and more the vested property of a number of families, and this tendency, once started, grew in the next century with ever increasing rapidity.

This degeneration of the guild could not fail to have a very decided effect on the condition of the laborer. As already stated the number of these laborers increased very rapidly, just about the time that the guilds began their policy of restriction, by a large and growing immigration from the country. This flight to the cities was about the only means open to a serf upon a great estate to get rid of the bondage in which he lived, without the consent of his master, as it was a law that a serf who remained in a city for a year and a day without being claimed by the lord was a freeman. The restrictions adopted prevented, of course, the most of these laborers from becoming masters; and the course which the masters took of following out exclusively their own interests, could not fail to call into existence a similar spirit on the part of the journeymen. Toward the end of the fourteenth century we find plain signs that such a separation of interests had, at least, begun in the formation by the journeymen of special journeymen's unions.

The earliest references which we can find in regard to these unions do not say that they occupied themselves from the first with the regulation of the industrial interests of the members. If we may conclude from this that they did not do this, we may also conclude that it was because the organization of the guilds was, at first, sufficient to protect these interests without any special action of the journeymen within their own organizations. At any rate it is evident that the guild had ceased to satisfy the demands of the journeymen in other respects. Whereas the guilds had originally united all members, masters and journeymen, together for common religious and social services, banquets, etc., and had taken care equally of all poor and sick, whether masters or journeymen, it may be taken as a pretty good proof of the aristocratic separation of the classes that now these journeymen unions are formed for these purposes. And where, as it often happened, the masters, now grown fat and ease-loving, shifted the military burdens upon the shoulders of the journeymen, the organization of the latter for military purposes must have encouraged the growth of these unions. But after the custom became universal, in the fifteenth century, that the journeymen should wander from city to city for a term of years, it became necessary that there should be some organization to take care of poor journeymen and afford the wanderers food, shelter and protection. Thus the journeymen unions seem to have been at first, as a rule, a sort of supplement of the guild; and while the industrial interests of this class seem to have been sufficiently cared for by the guild, the religious, social and eleemosynary wants of the journeymen were provided for by their own unions.

But this separation of master and journeyman could not long remain without some influence on the labor relations of the latter. The authority of the master over the journeyman, even where it was abused, would seem bearable as long as every journeyman had prospect of soon becoming master himself. But so soon as the journeymanship became a life-calling it became intolerable that the master should strive to keep wages down; should cheat him out of the wages he had agreed to give, by paying in truck instead of in money; should keep him in dependence, by encouraging him to run in debt to him, and thus prevent him from ever rising to the level of a worthy workman. As early as the second half of the fourteenth century we find traces of attempts on the part of the masters to debase the condition of the journeymen by the occupation of excessive numbers of apprentices. As time passed on the guilds became more and more associations of masters which used their journeymen as mere instruments by which to increase their own wealth and power.

In opposition to this the brotherhoods for religious, social and eleemosynary purposes became the cloak under which the journeymen concealed a union for the protection of their own economic and other class interests. Toward the close of the fourteenth century we find repeated complaints on the part of the masters that journeymen under pretense of religious and social organizations united themselves together to force up the rate of wages, and that attempts by the masters to repress these unions, even though made by several guilds of different cities together, had not been at all successful. The efforts of these journeymen's unions did not aim at the equality of master and journeyman and the acknowledgment of equal honor for both classes; such an effort was not suited to that time. Corresponding to the general line of development of the middle ages, what they aimed at was a special journeyman law and a particular journeyman honor and spirit as a security against contempt and arbitrary acts of power. The particular things which they demanded varied with different conditions; but in general they attempted to gain an influence in determining the relation of labor and service, particularly to keep up wages and control the matter of apprentices and to regulate the movement of labor. In order to get these ends they tried to secure a representation of the journeymen in the directorate of the guilds. In order to obtain this they resorted to strikes; and even where they were represented in the guilds they often resorted to the same means to carry through their measures. In those branches in which the conditions of the time favored the application of large capital and numerous laborers who had no prospect of ever becoming masters, like the woolen industry in England, France and Germany, there were great strikes in the second half of the fourteenth century which differ from those of the nineteenth century only in the time of their occurence, and in the following centuries we find such strikes in all branches of industry.

It thus appears that, contrary to a widely received opinion, the guilds not only did not solve the labor question, but that the labor question arose in just the same proportion as the guilds flourished. In all places and in all industries in the same proportion as the industries improved in technics and wealth and the guilds became more independent in the regulation of industrial relations, a separation took place among the members of the guild. The masters used the autonomy which they had acquired in the regulation of the industry to limit with one hand competition, by making it difficult to become master, and to regulate the conditions of the laborers with the other exclusively in the interests of the masters. This policy aroused in the laborers, who had now no chance of becoming masters and of carrying on the business independently, the consciousness of peculiar class interests and wants. There arose the class of masters and the class of laborers, and with them the labor question. The question then arose how shall the wants of this laboring class be best satisfied. The journeymen formed their unions for the protection of their interests within and by the side of the guilds; and the demands which they made for the furtherance of their interests led, at an early period, to quarrels which bear a close resemblance to the labor difficulties of to-day. This was so generally true that wherever in the fourteenth century we find no traces of such troubles or such special unions, we may take it for granted that in that place and in that industry the relations were so little developed that as yet the separation between the masters and journeymen had not taken place, and that there was consequently no great difference of interests.

The system of regulating the relations of labor for the solution of the labor question, and particularly the system of measures in favor of unemployed and indigent journeymen, did not rest upon the legal equality of master and journeyman and the responsibility of the latter for his own welfare. The relation of master to journeyman was one of authority. The masters in a guild, as a whole, were the rulers of the journeymen. The journeyman was a member of the guild, it is true, but he was a subject member. The guild regulated the wages of the journeyman and the other conditions of labor. But this positive authority was limited by the power of these journeymen unions, and, out of the struggles of the latter for their objects there was developed in the course of time a peculiar body of laws and privileges which secured the laborer against despotism and contempt. And just as the individual laborer was not dependent on the individual master for the amount of his wages, so the union secured for him employment by regulating the number of apprentices in proportion to journeymen, by acknowledging the right of the unemployed to employment, by securing labor for the stranger or granting assistance to the journeyman who wished to go further and by assisting the laborer who could not find employment. The journeymen were required to pay a part of their wages into the treasury of their unions for the purpose of defraying their expenses. The guild was required to assist the unions where they could not pay all these expenses themselves. This was recognized to be the proper thing, since the masters had limited to their own advantage the opportunity of the laborer to rise to the position of master. If all these means of assistance failed, and an individual could not get help from them, there still remained the church, which possessed, at this time, a large part of the property of the community, and which was bound to help the poor.

This system of industrial organization existed in Germany from the end of the fourteenth century to the beginning of the seventeenth, and, indeed, in the free cities, where the authority in industrial matters remained in the hands of the guilds much longer than elsewhere, to a much later date. A similar system existed in France for the same period, but in England the journeymen's unions never got the strong hold which they obtained on the continent. The system took a somewhat different form wherever the government became strong enough to take the regulation of industrial matters into its own hands. This took place in several European countries toward the close of the sixteenth century.

As a rule the government approved the general system developed by the guild and extended it to all forms of new industry as well. But there was a great difference between the management of the two systems. The regulation of the labor relations was no longer entrusted to the guilds, which kept following more and more closely the exclusive interests of the masters, whose number had now been limited, but to inspecting authorities who belonged to neither party, or were entrusted to the guilds under the supervision of the authorities. Thus the rate of wages was fixed by the government officers. The length of the working day was fixed by the same authority. In the same way the length of the period of apprenticeship of journeymen, the conditions of the labor contract, etc., were fixed by law or by officers representing the government. Only apprentices who had finished their apprenticeship could be employed as laborers. Journeymen had a right to employment if there was any, and the right to support, for a certain time, if there was no work, and assistance to go elsewhere. On the other hand, as correlatives of these rights, the government insisted that the laborers should not strike, that they should take work under the legal conditions, wherever there was work, and should pay contributions for the support of their poor brethren.

When the church became too poor to support the indigent, owing to the secularization of its estates, and the Christian and Germanic idea of property as a trust connected with duties gave place to the Roman idea of it as a subjective right, the state undertook to look after the poor who had no claims on the assistance of any union or society. By means of the poor tax it collected from those who were benefited by the guild restrictions (such as the difficulties in the way of settlement, the regulation of wages and prohibitions of labor coalitions) the means of supporting those who, although unable to work, had no opportunity of looking out for themselves owing to the restrictions on labor.

If we disregard those who by these restrictions on entering the trade were prevented from earning their living as laborers in these callings, it is pretty evident that those who once got into the trade had an assured existence so long as the above provisions were carried out. The provisions in regard to the number of apprentices, the limitation of labor to those who had actually served the apprenticeship period, the right of the journeymen to work if it was to be had, made it pretty certain that those journeymen who had passed through the period of training would secure employment. The long period of the engagements secured to them regular employment, no matter what the condition of the trade. The officials were directed to fix the rate of wages so that the laborer should have sufficient, as well in times of scarcity as in times of plenty. All this secured to the laborer a regularity in his income which enabled him to pay his contributions for the support of the unemployed or sick laborer. With all this the working hours were not excessively long, especially as the work itself was not so exacting as that of to-day. If we consider, finally, that the paternal treatment which the laborer received at the hands of the government was in accordance with the ideas of the time and was extended to the employer as well, and that this similar treatment of the two classes corresponded to the growing demand for equality, we may well believe that this system of the organization of labor answered the demands of the laborers of that time very fairly. It is true that in spite of all prohibitions to the contrary there were numerous strikes during the eighteenth century, so that it has been called the century of journeymen rebellions. Yet it is highly probable that, although some may have grown out of the fact that the laborers did not secure new concessions which they were working for, the most of them grew out of the fact that the customary or legal organization of industry was being broken through in all directions by those who were powerful enough to do so with impunity.

In this way the wants and interests of those who were admitted to the ranks of the mechanical laborers were fairly provided for. But the exclusion of so many from any opportunity to enter the trades, which was effected by this system, and the difficulty in the way of starting an independent business, became in more and more striking contrast to the wants and feelings of the time. The constant persecutions of the outsiders by the guilds in Germany; occurrences such as that in France, where, in consequence of a denunciation on the part of the guild, a married journeyman who had made a pair of shoes while hidden in a barn was sent to the galleys; the hinderance which the English guilds placed in the way of the growth of large industries; and the cheating of the public, which finally became characteristic of the guilds, made it impossible for the old organization of labor to continue. On the other hand, the system of caring for the poor had also become unbearable. For the obligation to work for alms received was not insisted upon, and in this way one of the most efficient motives to work was taken away altogether from the poorer class of laborers, and the poor rates were increasing from year to year at an enormous rate.

The complaints about the heartless policy of the guilds began as early as the fifteenth century and did not die out until the guilds themselves died. During the fifteenth century the abolition of the guilds was demanded on this ground. When Henry III. of France, in 1581, extended the provisions of the guilds to all branches of mechanical industry in France, the Parliament refused at first to register the edict. In 1614, the third estate in France moved the abolition of the guilds; in 1624, a party in the city council of Bremen; in 1669, the Elector of Brandenburg, in the German Parliament, made the same motion. In Prussia, beginning with 1688, a series of laws was adopted looking toward the reformation of the guilds in the direction of greater freedom and in the interest of a growing industry. But the chief attack upon the old guild system came on its theoretical side from Adam Smith and the French Physiocrats.

God, said the physiocratic school of economists, made the right to labor the property of every person by giving to every one wants and referring him to labor as a means of satisfying them. This property is the first in order of time, the most holy and the most inalienable. Owing to the restrictions on labor maintained by the guilds, the poor are condemned to protract a precarious existence under the control of the masters, to linger in poverty or to betake themselves and their industry to foreign lands. Just as the whole existing system of law had proceeded from the selfish efforts of privileged classes, who resisted every reform, so in making the regulations in regard to organization of the system of apprentices and journeymen the councilors of the government had always been the employers. They served merely to secure to the masters the labor of the apprentice for a long time at a very low rate of wages or for no wages at all; to keep down the wages of the journeyman and to diminish competition by limiting the number of masters. It is one of the first duties of justice to free those whose only property consists in the skill and strength of their hands from the limitations placed upon them by the guilds.

The pretended care of the state for the welfare of the laborers was, according to this view, not merely a piece of hypocrisy but a shameless presumption. Self-interest will show everyone what is best for his own welfare. And as all men are by nature equal and actuated by the same self-interest, the greatest happiness of each one and, therefore, of all will be secured as soon as the state will leave each one undisturbed to the guidance of his own self-interest and thus let him utilize all his powers and capacities in the best way.

Thus natural justice and economic expediency united in demanding the freedom of labor and the freedom of the laborer. Above everything, therefore, no legal limitation on the freedom of the trades; then, the conversion of the laborer into a free merchant of the commodity, labor. In the place of the previous relation of laborer and master should be put a purely contractual relation, and in place of the subordination of the laborer, he should be placed on a perfect equality with the master as the seller of a commodity which the latter wishes. With equal rights of both parties to make such contracts as they please, there should be no interference by any government officer between them.

The same demand for freedom of industry and freedom of contract was made by those interested in the large industry which was now beginning to rise in England. The guild system was in the interest of the small employer, and, so far as he did not desire to become master, in the interest of journeyman also; but it was opposed to the interest of the large employer. The mere requirement that a man should have passed through an apprenticeship, and, on the continent, a journeymanship also, if one wished to take up a branch of manufacturing, stood greatly in the way of those who wished to utilize their capital rather than their personal powers in the business. But, moreover, those who had passed through the apprenticeship and journeymanship were greatly limited in the expansion of their business by the prohibition of the employment of others than laborers who had learned the business.

The long period of engagement might be of advantage to the employer as long as he worked for a local market which was subject to few disturbances, but with the system of production for a distant market came the danger of gluts in the market which made it necessary for the employer to be able to dismiss his laborers at short notice. Equally inconsistent with the interest of the great manufacturer was the provision fixing the wages for a whole industry, since he wished to be able to attract quickly to him a large number of laborers by the offer of high wages in order to increase his production; and again, by a reduction of wages, to make it possible to compete with a rival for the possession of a given market. When, finally, the progress in machinery began in earnest, and every new discovery made the old machines worthless, the effort of the manufacturers to make the most of the capital invested in a machine by increasing the length of the working day, and so to make the out-put as large as possible to the machine, came into conflict with the laws about the working day. By all the provisions of the old organization of labor this new interest found itself hindered in its development. Its desire was freedom of industry and absence of every governmental interference with the contract between laborer and employer, and it showed itself very skillful in exploiting for its own uses the arguments of Adam Smith for the same thing in the interest of the laborer, while it prevented, for a long time to come, any regard being paid to other demands which Smith made at the same time to secure the interests of the laborer in the new state of things.

Thus theory and pecuniary and class interest united in demanding the abolition of the old system. In the different countries different considerations and occasions gave the decisive impulse, and the course of events was somewhat peculiar in each country. In France the old system was abolished in that memorable night of August 4th, 1789, which saw the old *regime*, in so many departments, swept into oblivion. In Germany, where the various governments had made many changes in the old system in the interest of political and industrial progress, Prussia was the first to adopt the principle of freedom of industry in this sense and to do away with the old system completely. This was done in 1810. England, under the control of the large capitalists, abolished the apprentice law of 1562 in 1814 and thus acknowledged the same principle.

By these laws, in France, England and Prussia, not only was the freedom of the independent workman established, but the relation of contract pure and simple was substituted for the one prevailing under the guilds. The prohibitions of coalitions of laborers were, however, left on the statute books. The impression which the policy of the guilds in their decadence had made on the public mind was so strong that people had come to see the only guarantee of liberty in the complete isolation of each individual, and saw in every agreement of any kind an infringement of this freedom. The French Parliament, in 1791, forbade anew all agreements among laborers or employers or merchants and every union of the members of the same trade. The first state in which the ideas of Adam Smith about labor unions were carried through was England. The prohibitions were abolished by the law of 1824. In France they were not abolished until 1864. In Germany the liberal policy mentioned above was afterwards given up for a generation, and the laws forbidding laborers' coalitions were not passed for all of Germany until after 1871, while Austria had abolished them in the previous year.

If we look back at the course of the development of the class of mechanical laborers, from their origin until the present time, we see that there has been through the centuries a steadily progressing emancipation. At the time when we first hear of mechanics' trades among the Germanic races they are carried on almost exclusively by serfs on the estates of feudal lords. Then there appears a class of free mechanics in which, however, there is no distinction between master and journeyman. But the trade itself is at this time in a very primitive state and all who ply it are in one uniform condition of poverty; and, although the period of serving a mechanic as assistant is a mere transition period toward the mastership, and there is, therefore, no permanent difference in class between the master and the servant, yet the power of the former over the latter during this period of serving is absolute, the one being practically the slave of the other. With the progress in the trade itself and the general advance in prosperity differentiation gradually takes place into a master class and a journeyman class. At the same time a counter-movement begins, having for its object the improvement and the protection of the journeymen class. And if with the progress of time it becomes more and more impossible for the great mass of journeymen to have any prospect of becoming masters, the old relation of master over slave gives place to the different power of master over journeyman, limited as it was by custom and the success of the journeymen unions to a mere fraction of the former power. The power of the master over the journeyman is then still further limited by general laws passed by the chief legislative authority of the state, and, finally, in the nineteenth century, the old relation is abolished entirely and the status is converted into a contract. This mode of treatment converts the laborer into an independent human being on the same footing exactly as the master, and secures to him, nominally at least, perfect freedom in the disposition of his time and labor, which form the commodities which he has for sale. It was reserved for the nineteenth century, therefore, to emancipate the working man fully from the bondage of the guild masters.

CHAPTER III.

RECENT LABOR LEGISLATION.

The Hopes of the Friends of Liberty not Realized under the New System — The Great Advantage of Capital Over Labor — The Growing Debasement of the Factory Laborer — Attempts of the Laborers to Protect Themselves — Rise of Labor Unions — Factory Legislation in England — In France — In Germany — In Switzerland — In other European Countries — Other Legislation in the Interest of Labor — Employers' Liabilities Acts — Insurance against Sickness and Accidents in Germany — Development of the Trades-Unions in England — In France — In Germany — In Italy — Federation of Labor — Progress of Working Classes — The Use Made by Them of their Growing Power.

As we have seen in the preceding chapter, the industrial system which had come down to modern times from the Middle Ages finally succumbed to the combined attacks of the friends of free labor and the owners of large capital. The former saw in the guild system the chief barrier in the way of the laborer's making the most of the only commodity which he had to sell, viz., labor. The latter were prevented by the same system from utilizing the immense advantages for gain which the recent enormous development of machinery had put within their grasp. The barriers, however, were first thrown down which stood in the way of the capitalists, and in the race for supremacy under the new conditions, capital was thus enabled to get a long start of labor. Some of the barriers in the way of the latter, it is true, were also thrown down; but now the greatest obstacles, among others, that prevented labor from resorting to the only effective means of holding its own in the race, viz., combinations, were left in full force.

The immediate result of the new freedom of industry, therefore, was, as might have been expected, a decided deterioration in the condition of the laborer. His old safeguards were all gone, and he was prevented by law and circumstances from erecting any others in their place. The evils of the new system made themselves felt first and most deeply in England, which was the first country to use on any great scale the new means of an increased production in the shape of machinery, which the progress of invention was increasing every day. The capitalist had no obligations toward the laborer; all these had been swept away, and he proceeded to use his newly acquired power in a most heartless way. The mill and factory lords who arose to take the place of the old master mechanic, exploited in the most merciless manner the great mass of laborers who were now delivered bound hand and foot into their hands. The condition of factory operatives in the factory districts and mining regions of England in the latter part of the last century, and away on into the second quarter of the present, was horrible beyond belief. The mere description of the lives they led is enough to make one's blood boil with indignation that such things should be allowed to exist in a so-called Christian land. It seemed, indeed, as if the great mass of the laborers were destined to sink into a condition far worse than that in which even the most miserable of their ancestors had lived, and one little short of slavery in its worst form, viz., that in which the master has no duties, only rights and privileges.

There is no telling how far this process of degradation might have proceeded if the laborers themselves, who were thus being gradually forced down into a state little short of barbarism, had not begun to resist with such means as were in their power. They could not organize openly, as any attempt to defend their rights was met by the strong arm of repression. They had absolutely no representation in any legislative body. The political economists of the time, fully under the capitalistic influences of society, proved that nothing could be done by the government which would not injure the laborer more than it would benefit him, showed how necessary to national prosperity was the accumulation of capital, how surely men would not save unless they could get good returns on their money, and how any interference with the power of the capitalist would so diminish his profits that he would no longer save, and then the country would be completely ruined. The progress of invention made it possible for the employers to get along with women if men would not consent to a lowering of their wages, and soon to resort to the labor of children when they could get neither men nor women. And thus the condition of all classes, men, women and children, was becoming worse and worse.

The natural outcome of this state of affairs was a long series of outrages on persons and property committed by these starving and half-crazed people, which no severity of police power seemed able to prevent, and which increased with every passing year. These people, with no legal way of making their grievances known, resorted in many instances to the foulest and most dastardly crimes; and wise men soon saw that such a condition of things was becoming absolutely untenable, and that something must be done to remedy it. No appeal to his justice or duty could move the unjust judge; nothing but the fear of revolution and loss of life and property could stir the attention of the Parliament of England to a consideration of this question; and when it did begin to do something it was with slow and halting steps, which did not at all keep pace with the growing debasement and enslavement of the laboring class.

The crying evils of the factory system, and the growing demoralization of the laboring class, as a whole, finally forced the English government to inaugurate a system of legislation which has been growing down to the present time, and which has for its object the protection and improvement of the laborers in the various departments of industrial life. Some of the laws have had for their object the protection of the helpless classes of laborers, such as women and children, and the securing of healthful and safe conditions of labor. These are known collectively as factory acts, and have been imitated in the leading countries of Europe. Others have aimed at protecting the laborer against the greed and avarice of the employer, such as those forbidding the payment of wages in anything but money, and insisting on the regular periodical payment and making it unlawful for the employer to insist on any conditions in regard to the mode or place of spending wages when hiring laborers. Still others have given to the laborers the means of protecting themselves by allowing them to form trade-unions for the furtherance of their common interests. Efforts have been made by the government to afford to laborers a safe place to invest their surplus earnings by the establishment of the postal savings banks, and giving them opportunities to buy into the funds at the same rate as the wealthier. Opportunities have been furnished them further to establish investment companies of their own by granting articles of incorporation to various forms of friendly societies and the equally varied forms of the building societies. Some of the Continental governments, notably that of Germany and Switzerland, have even gone further than England in the direction of protecting the laborer against the great calamities of his life, by inaugurating under government auspices companies to insure the laborer against sickness and accident happening in the prosecution of his work.

This century has also seen, for the first time, such an extension of the suffrage as now insures to the laboring man, if he will use his opportunities, adequate representation of his interests in the great legislative bodies of Western Europe. The English laborer has now, under the recent extension of the suffrage, the same relative vote for members of Parliament as any other class in the community; and if he is not represented it can only be his own fault. The new German Empire, established in 1871, was built up on the broad basis of universal manhood suffrage; and Austria, Italy and France extend practically the same privileges. The large mass of legislation, moreover, which has been placed on the statute books of this century in the interest of health and comfort has redounded in a large measure to the benefit of the laboring man, though much was placed there from no particular intention of helping him. We have not space to notice all these various laws; indeed, that would require a pretty complete *resume* of the legislation of Europe for the last eighty-five years; but some of them are important enough to deserve a fuller notice.

Among the most important acts having for their object the protection of the laborer, in his freedom of expending his wages, against the greed of the employer, is the series of acts relating to the truck system of paying wages. The first English act of this kind was passed in 1831, and has been followed up by a series of acts which forbid employers from paying their laborers in other than money of the realm or to give them credit for wares purchased of them or persons dependent on, or connected with, them, or to sell them wares at prices exceeding the current prices, or to compel them to purchase at stores controlled by or worked in the interests of the employers. These laws aim not at limiting the freedom of the laborer in the expenditure of his wages, but at making it impossible for the employer to limit it by imposing injurious conditions. They are intended to prevent that destruction of the family life of the laborer, and to free him from the economic and moral slavery which is sure to be brought about by payment in kind or in wares, by giving credit and by making it a condition of receiving employment that he shall make his purchases in stores conducted by the employers, or, as was once widely the custom, in a grog-shop run by the masters, where he could be persuaded to leave the bulk of his wages before he left the place. As these conditions existed at a time when organization among the laborers was unlawful and they could not act in common to do away with such abuses, it was the duty of the state to interfere and forbid such requirements in the contracts. Such laws do not by any means do away with the necessity of action on the part of the laborers themselves, as experience shows that it is almost impossible to carry out such laws except where the trades-unions are strong enough to enforce it by their action. The custom still prevails where there are no labor unions to insist that it shall disappear. The laws on this subject in Germany are very unsatisfactory, and there are none at all in France.

The first factory law was passed in 1802. It had for its object the preservation of the health and morals of apprentices and others employed in cotton and other mills and in cotton and other factories. This bill owed its passage to the ravages of epidemic diseases in the factory districts of Manchester. The ill-fed and overworked children in the factories formed the very best field for the development and spread of epidemic and contagious diseases. Pauper children were sent in crowds from the agricultural districts of the southern counties to the manufacturing districts of the northern counties. They were apprenticed to the mill owners and mercilessly overworked and under-fed. The act mentioned subjected all mills employing three or more apprentices or twenty other persons to its provisions. The walls were to be whitewashed, windows enough were to be provided, and the apprentices were always to have two suits of clothing, one of which was to be new each year. Twelve hours were declared to be a day's work, and work was altogether prohibited from 9 P. M. until 6 A. M. These provisions applied only to apprentices and not to the labor of children residing in the neighborhood of the factories. In 1819 children under nine years of age were excluded from the cotton mills altogether, and those from nine to sixteen were not to be employed more than twelve hours per day. In 1825 a bill was passed providing for a partial holiday on Saturday. In 1831 night work in the cotton factories was prohibited for persons between nine and twenty-one years of age. The working day for persons under eighteen was to be twelve hours, and on Saturday nine. In 1833 another act was passed which seemed in some respects to be a retrogression, since it restricted night work in factories to persons under eighteen instead of under twenty-one, yet extended the provisions of its protection to a much larger number of callings. It now includes every cotton, woolen, worsted, hemp, flax, tow, linen, or silk mill, or factory wherein steam or water or any other mechanical power is used to propel or work the machinery. The labor of young persons under eighteen remains fixed at twelve hours per day and sixty-nine per week, with one hour and a half for meal-times, and the age for first admission at nine years. The employment of children under eleven, twelve and thirteen years of age, is to be gradually restricted from twelve to nine hours per day and forty-eight a week. Regular holidays for children and young people are secured; medical certificates are required before children may be employed; factory inspectors are to be appointed by the crown; school attendance is made compulsory for all children whose labor is limited to forty-eight hours per week. This measure stood its ground for eleven years, when another act was passed, including more careful provisions for enforcing inspection; for protecting children or young persons engaged in the wet spinning of flax, hemp, jute or tow; for the avoidance of accidents to children; the guarding of machinery; the inquiring into and securing compensation for accidents. The age of first employment of children is lowered to eight years; the hours of their employment are reduced to six and a half or seven hours per day or ten hours on alternate days. The employment of women is brought under the same rules as that of young persons; the cessation of labor is made absolute for the protected classes on Saturday at 4.30 P. M.; the hours for meal-time are to be taken from 7.30 A. M. and 7.30 P. M., with additional regulations as to meal-times and half-holidays and for school attendance for children. In the next year the workers in print works were brought under the same provisions. In 1847 was passed the famous ten-hour law which restricted the hours of labor for young persons under eighteen and for women of all ages after May 1, 1848, to ten hours per day and fifty-eight hours per week. It is well known that this act has practically operated (until quite recently when means seemed to have been devised by some employers for employing adult males only) as a general reduction of the hours of labor in consequence of the interdependence of the labor of men and that of women and young persons, thus showing how powerful the effect of law may be in fixing the length of the working day. In 1850 work was prohibited for the protected classes between the hours of 6 P. M. and 6 A. M., except on Saturdays, when work was to cease at 2 P. M.; thus finally establishing the half-holiday. By a series of subsequent acts these same provisions were extended to bleaching and dyeing works, lace factories and match factories. In 1874 the minimum age of children in the factories was fixed at ten years, and the provisions of the act extended to nearly every branch of manufacturing industry. In 1878 a consolidating act was passed which included in one bill the substance of all previous acts. It is worthy of special notice as containing the present provisions on the subject. Part 1 contains the general law relating to workshops and factories under the following heads: 1, sanitary provisions; 2, safety; 3, employment and meal-hours; 4, holidays; 5, education; 6, certificates of fitness for employment; 7, accidents.

1. Under the first head, the buildings must be kept in a clean state and free from any effluvia arising from any drain, privy or other nuisance. 2. The second contains provisions for the fencing of dangerous machinery and restrictions on the employment of children and young persons in cleaning machinery while in motion. 3. No child, young person, or woman shall be employed except during the period of employment fixed as follows: 1st. In textile factories. For young persons and women the period shall be from 6 A.M. to 6 P.M., or 7 A.M., to 7 P.M.; on Saturdays from 6 A.M. to 1 P.M. for all manufacturing processes, and 1.30 for all other employment, if one hour is allowed for meals, otherwise at 12.30 and 1 P.M. respectively. Or if the work begins at 7 A.M. it shall end on Saturdays at 1.30 and 2 P.M. respectively. For meal-times two hours at least on week days, and on Saturdays half an hour must be allowed. Continuous employment without a meal-time of at least half an hour must not exceed four and one-half hours. For children, employment must be for half time (only in morning or afternoon sets, or on alternate days, the time to be the same as above). A child must not be employed for two successive periods of seven days each in the same set whether morning or afternoon, nor on two successive Saturdays nor on Saturday in any week if he has already on one day been employed more than five and one-half hours. Nor shall a child be employed the whole time on two successive days nor on the same day in two successive weeks. 2d. In non-textile factories. For young per-

sons and women: period of employment same as in textile factories, ending at 2 P.M. on Saturdays; meal-times not less than an hour and one-half and on Saturdays half an hour; continuous employment without a meal not to exceed five hours. These provisions also apply to young persons in workshops. For children half time arrangements as before. Women in workshops are subject to the same regulations as young persons, if young persons and children are employed; if not, the period of employment may extend from 6 A. M. to 9 P. M., and on Saturdays to 4 P.M. Absent time for meals, etc., must be allowed to the extent of four and one-half hours (on Saturdays for two and one-half hours). The employment of young children at home when the work is the same as in a factory or workshop but no machine power is used is also regulated, the day being from 6 to 9 for young persons; from 6 to 1 or from 1 to 8 for children. Meal-times in factories or workshops must be simultaneous, and employment during such meal-time is forbidden. The occupier of a factory or workshop must issue a notice of the hours of employment, etc. No children under ten may be employed. 4. The following holidays shall be allowed to all persons: Christmas day, Good Friday and eight half-holidays, two of which may be commuted for one entire holiday. 5. Occupiers must obtain a weekly certificate of the school attendance for every child in their employment. 6. Medical certificates of fitness for employment must be secured in the case of children and young persons under sixteen. When a child becomes a young person a fresh certificate is necessary. 7. Notice of accidents causing loss of life or bodily injury must be sent to the inspector and certifying surgeon of the district. The word child as used in the act means a person under ten years of age, young person means one between fourteen and eighteen; and woman means a female person over eighteen. It will be seen that the government now undertakes to protect the whole class of women, children and youth employed in manufacturing industries. The protection of laborers over eighteen comprises only the general provisions in regard to sanitation, safety, remedies for wages, etc.

In 1842 the first of a series of mining acts was passed which forbade the working of women and girls absolutely and that of boys under ten years of age, in all mines and collieries. In 1850 and 1855 other acts were passed providing for the more thorough inspection of mines. In 1860 an important act was passed forbidding the employment of boys under twelve, except such boys between ten and twelve as can produce a schoolmaster's certificate that they can read or write, or who attend school for not less than three hours a day two days in the week each lunar month. Eighteen is fixed as the age at which youths may be placed in charge of steam-engines or machinery for hoisting persons. Provisions are made for the removal of dangers by the inspectors which are not provided for by the rules. Wages are to be paid in money and in an office not contiguous to a spirit, or wine or beershop; and where the payment is made by weight, measure or guage they may at their own cost station one of their own number at the place of weighing to take an account of the weight.

Several other important acts have been passed relating to different callings with the intention of securing a more satisfactory degree of protection to laborers employed in their daily labor, such as that relating to chimney-sweepers, bake-houses, Merchant Shipping Act, etc., etc., which cannot be further discussed in this connection. It is worthy of notice that nothing appears in this long list looking toward bettering the condition of the agricultural laborers. The Agricultural Gangs Act of 1867 did aim to put a stop to an abuse which was quite equal to anything which ever existed in the cotton or woolen mills, but that afforded little protection to children or laborers except against this one evil.

The most important act for the protection of laborers which has been passed of late years is that known as the Employers' Liability Act of 1880. This gives to the employees a right to a suit against their employers in case they are injured while performing their duties, unless it can be shown that the accident was caused by the fault of the employee himself.

The first law in regard to child-labor in France was passed

in 1841, and contained provisions which would have been very satisfactory for that period if they had been enforced thoroughly. One of the immediate consequences of the Revolution of 1848 was the passage of the so-called twelve hour law which introduced a normal working day of twelve hours for adult male laborers, but which has always remained a dead letter. A law was passed in 1874 in regard to the labor of children and young girls, the provisions of which will be noticed in another connection.

Prussia began in 1839, at a time when the evils of the factory system were not very great and had attracted but little attention. The government issued a decree in regard to the working of children in factories, which was superseded by a more general one in 1853. A general factory law passed in 1849 provided for the establishment of industrial councils in each factory district, composed partly of employers and partly of laborers and partly of government officials, which was to fix the number of hours in a working day for the various branches of industry. This provision did not meet with much success, and has always remained a dead letter. The same law forbade the truck system of paying wages. The law of 1853 was of considerable importance, as it was the basis of subsequent legislation, not only for Prussia but also for the new German Empire. The law of 1869 of the North German Confederation contained important provisions in regard to this subject and became general imperial law of the German Empire.

Switzerland has the honor of going further in this direction than any other country. Previous to 1874 the only power which could pass factory acts were the various states of the Swiss Union, but since that year the Federal Government has power to make such legislation. The consequence of this new extension of power of the Federal Government, was the passage of a law in 1877, subsequently approved by a popular vote on the subject, which may serve as a model so far as its formal provisions are concerned, which goes much farther than any other law on the subject now in existence.

Factory laws have been passed in Austria, Hungary,

Netherlands, Denmark and Sweden. The other European countries appear to have nothing on the subject on their statute books, though Russia has been contemplating one for some time, and strong efforts have been made for years in Belgium. All such attempts have failed hitherto, through the opposition of the powerful capitalists and factory lords, who show themselves as lacking in all regard for humanity in their dealings with their laborers as the English lords of fifty years ago.

The law in the German Empire, at present, forbids absolutely the employment of children in factories under twelve years of age. Those between twelve and fourteen may be employed only six hours per day, and those between fourteen and sixteen, ten hours per day. The labor must be performed between 5.30 in the morning and 8.30 in the evening, with certain pauses, and not at all on Sundays or holidays. In the complete prohibition of labor of children under thirteen Germany goes much further than most countries. The French law forbids labor under thirteen, but allows a great number of exceptions which go far toward making the law of little use. Switzerland goes further than Germany by making the age for admission to the factories fifteen. Comparatively few children, however, are employed in Germany who are under the age of fifteen. The compulsory school-law makes it necessary for the children to attend school so many months in the year, until they reach the age of fifteen, that it is hardly worth the while of employers to engage them. The number of children under thirteen employed in the cotton factories alone in England amounted in 1878 to over sixty-seven thousand, and was increasing all the time. The French law affords but little protection to the youths, since those between twelve and sixteen may work twelve hours per day, which shows also how far the law limiting the day of the full-grown laborer is carried out, since twelve hours is his day also. The German law provides that young persons between fourteen and sixteen, who, according to the local law, must still attend school, may not work more than six hours. The Swiss law protects all classes of laborers. Those especially mentioned are children under fifteen, who may not be employed at all; young persons between fifteen and sixteen, and those between sixteen and eighteen, and women over eighteen. The legal working day is eleven hours, shortened to ten on the days before Sundays and holidays, with a noon pause of one hour. Work is absolutely forbidden on Sundays and holidays. Night work for all laborers is forbidden, except in those branches of industry where continuous working is necessary to the business. The working day may be shortened by decree in the unhealthy branches of industry. In the case of youths who have to attend school after the age of admission to the factories, they shall not be employed more than six hours. Pregnant women are not to be employed in those branches which are unhealthy, and they are to be excluded in all factories for at least two weeks before, and six weeks after, delivery. Women must not be employed to clean machinery in motion.

It will be seen from the foregoing that a normal working day has been established in no Continental country except France, where the law is a dead letter, and in Switzerland. A normal working day of ten hours was, as we have seen, practically established in England by the law limiting the working hours of women and youth to ten, which had the effect of making the day for all ten, owing to the intimate connection of the work of the protected classes with that of adult men.

The legislation in regard to the shops and factories as regards lighting, ventilation, etc., is very different in different countries. That of England has been mentioned. Germany goes further in its laws on such subjects than even Switzerland, since it requires every master, no matter how small the number of his laborers, to comply with certain police regulations of the most far-reaching kind in regard to all the details of building and operating his machinary so far as they affect the health and morals of the operatives.

According to the German law the employer must pay the wages in cash. Payment in any other form is invalid, and the employer so paying may be fined or imprisoned. The employer is not permitted to give the laborer credit for goods or to loan him money. Nor are any members of his family, assistants or agents permitted to do what is forbidden to the employer. Employers are not permitted to make any contracts with their laborers, by which the latter bind themselves to purchase wares in his or any other stores.

The German Federal law on the liability of employers was passed in 1871. It provides for the payment of damages in case of the death of any employee by accident in railroads, mining, quarrying and factories. It presumes that the accident occurs through the fault of the employer, and thus puts the burden of proof on him to show that it occurred through the fault of the injured party, in which case he is not liable for damages. The law makes some differences in case of the railroads and other classes of undertakings. The damages include, in the case of bodily injury, the payment of costs of treatment and making good the loss of earnings which is incident to the accident. In the case of death, they include the cost of treatment up to the time of death, the cost of burial, and the loss of property incident to the sickness and death of the person injured, and a sum to be decided by the court to those persons who were dependent on the person so killed. If the employer and the persons whom the deceased was bound to support can not agree as to the gross sum to be paid in damages, the court is to grant an annuity, which it is to fix after examining all the circumstances of the case.

This law was very materially modified by the passage of the Compulsory Insurance bill, in 1884. Under this act employers are bound to insure their employees against all accidents happening to them while engaged at their work, whether owing to their own fault or not, unless it can be shown that the employee himself intentionally caused the injury. It is claimed that this law will afford much more efficient protection than the liability act, which it largely supersedes, owing to the fact that no question is raised as to whose fault the accident was, but payment must be made anyhow.

A series of friendly societies to insure the laborer against sickness has also been organized under the supervision of the public authorities, to some one of which every laborer must belong.

We must pass with the mere mention the laws intended to facilitate the banking operations of the workmen, which ended in the establishment of loan and savings banks; those which concern the applications of his savings and energies, resulting in the vast net-work of friendly and building societies; those relating to his physical and intellectual advancement, which have led to the multiplication of libraries, mechanics' institutes, gymnasiums and schools of all kinds; those aiming at securing a better housing of the laborer, which conferred upon the public authorities of boroughs and cities the power to take land by the right of eminent domain and erect tenement houses upon them for the use of laborers, and which thus incorporated the principle in the English law that the same power that is so continually exercised in order to secure opportunities for the investment of capital may also be used in the interests of labor. Those which facilitated the establishment of co-operative societies of various kinds, such as co-operative stores, co-operative factories and co-operative banks, and many similar acts which testify powerfully to the great advancement of the laborers themselves and the newly awakened interest of every class of society in everything which concerns the condition of the wage-receiving class.

The efforts to solve the labor question by substituting for the present system of wage-payer and wage-receiver a plan of co-operation cannot be said to have assumed importance enough as yet to enable us to judge as to its ultimate success. Curiously enough the different forms of co-operation succeed very differently in different countries. Consumptive co-operation has succeded best in England; productive co-operation, in France; and banking or credit co-operation, in Germany. The stores of England, the factories of France and the credit unions of Germany prove the possibility of substituting co-operation under very favorable conditions for the wage system in some departments of their respective spheres. But as yet only a mere fraction of the laboring class has been brought within the range of the working of these various establishments.

A very different means of meeting many of the difficulties of the present situation is to be seen in the trades-union. This institution, organized in the dark days which followed the destruction of the old industrial system and for a long time unlawful and still discriminated against in the legislation of nearly every European nation, has been steadily growing in influence and power for the last fifty years, until to-day it is recognized as the most powerful instrument in the hands of the working class. Trades-unions have grown up within the limits of each trade; but during the last few years an effort is making to organize them all into a sort of federation of labor unions, which shall stand as a unit in the defense of the rights of the laborer and work as a unit for his improvement.

The trades-union took its rise in England and has there reached its highest development. It is now recognized by employers themselves that the most stable and satisfactory conditions prevail in those branches where the trades-unions are the strongest and best developed, *i. e.*, these associations are now recognized as among the most conservative elements in the industrial system, and as offering to the honest and well meaning employer the best guarantee that he will not be outbid in the market by unscrupulous competitors who rely for their profits on the possibility of lowering wages whenever they think they see a chance to cut under the prevailing rate.

The trades-union sprang up also in France about the same time as in England. Some of these unions can be proved to have developed out of the old journeymen's associations, and others grew up under the mask of friendly societies; but the most of them sprang up spontaneously out of strikes, as in England. Not only in their origin, but also in their nature, as well as in the conception and limitation of their functions, in their tendencies and in the particular measures in regard to wages and industry, as well as in the importance which they have finally obtained in the life of the laborer; these labor syndicates (as the French call them) resemble in the most striking way their English counterparts, a circumstance which, owing to the spontaneity of their rise in both countries, speaks loudly for their timeliness and their fitness to satisfy a great demand. The organization, however, in France is not so complete as in England, and they do not yet embrace all branches of skilled labor.

In Germany the trades-unions have not run such a career as in England or France. According to Brentano, those which have been organized since 1860 may be divided into two classes, — those founded by the laborers themselves from a feeling of their own needs, and those which were started by people interested in the welfare of the laborers, though not belonging to their numbers. The German Printers' Union belongs to the first class, which grew out of a strike in Leipsic, in 1865; also the hat-makers' association, established in 1871; and the union of tobacco-workers, started in 1865. Some other classes of workers also have unions stretching over the German-speaking countries. To the second class belong the unions started by the Social Democrat party, and by Hirsch and Duncker.

The Social Democrat unions were all dissolved by the Government under the provisions of the Socialist law, and have disappeared, from the surface, at least. The Hirsch and Duncker unions are modelled after the best English trade-unions, but they have never succeeded in getting a firm hold except among the engineers of Berlin.

The trade-unions in Italy did not take their rise until after 1870, but since that time, in spite of prohibitions and severe police regulations, they have continued to grow. The old friendly societies are being rapidly converted into real trade-unions with similar organizations and ends to those of England. They seem destined to grow and multiply, as they fill a great demand wherever there is a class of laborers somewhat raised above the lowest level of existence.

We can take but the merest glance at the development of the trade-unions, and must limit ourselves to a few of those in England. The largest individual trade society in England is reckoned to be that of the Amalgamated Society of Engineers, Machinists, Mill-wrights and Pattern-Makers, founded by the amalgamation of a large number of different societies in 1851. This society had, the year before the great lock-out in 1852, 11,829 members, and a balance of cash of £21,705. That fierce fight with employers brought down the numbers to 9,737, and the reserve fund to £17,812, in 1853. At that time it was thought that trade-unionism had received its death-blow. This calculation was premature. In 1865 this society numbered 30,984 members, with an income of £75,672, and a clear balance in hand of £115,357. It had 229 branches in England and Wales, 32 in Scotland, 11 in Ireland, 6 in Australia, 2 in New Zealand, 5 in Canada, 1 in Malta, 8 in the United States, and 1 in France; a total of 295. The total expended by it had been, during fifteen years, £484,717.

The Amalgamated Society of Carpenters and Joiners affords another instance of these vast trade organizations. Although it was not established until 1860, it grew rapidly, having in 1865 more than 8,000 members, in 187 organizations. It expended in the last mentioned year £11,808.

Eighteen of these societies, which were examined by the Trades-Unions Commission of 1869, had more than two hundred thousand members; and, besides these, many societies existed which did not come forward by delegates before the Commission. The number of members in all these various trades-unions in 1865 was estimated by the unionists themselves to be not far from seven hundred thousand. In the face of these figures, and of the evidence given before the Trades-Unions Commission, the accusation of secrecy against these bodies — so commonly launched against them — must disappear. Such accusations simply show that those who make them know nothing of the facts, and wish to prevaricate the facts for bad purposes. It is difficult for four or five hundred men to conspire secretly at any time; especially so when they meet in conference at public rooms and halls, under the eye of newspaper reporters, and publish their proceedings afterward to the whole world. Nor can anything be franker than the testimony of the officers of these societies before the Commission. The Secretary of the Amalgamated Engineers brought forward the unprinted by-laws, which are read to candidates for admission, and whether these may be considered bad or good political economy they have certainly nothing criminal about them. The details given by him and others relating to the constitution of the societies are both most copious and most interesting. It is true that all this power of organization, instead of being accepted as an evidence of social development, was treated by some as only a cause of alarm to other classes. "I shall not refer to the subject of strikes," said Mr. Lowe, in his speech of May 3, 1865, on Mr. Baine's motion of reform, "but it is, I contend, impossible to believe that the same machinery which is at present brought into play in connection with strikes would not be applied by the working classes to political purposes. Once give the men votes, and this machinery is ready to launch those votes in one compact mass upon the institutions and property of the country." As if the Amalgamated Society of Engineers, with its thirty thousand members which, in 1865, spent over £14,000 in donations, sending members to situations and beds for non-free members, £13,785 for sick benefits, stewards and medical certificates, £5,184 for superannuation benefit, £4,887 for funerals, £1,860 for accidents, etc., etc., were not an institution! As if the workman's labor were not as truly property as that capital which it enables to accumulate. As if it were likely that the great trade societies have accumulated their capital of thousands of pounds, — tens of thousands, — invested them, as many of them have, in post-office savings banks, at two and a half per cent., rendered tens of thousands of widows and of sick men and of the disabled and aged dependent on those funds in order to "launch" votes in a compact mass at institutions or property! The calumny is so preposterous that it surely needed an unreformed House of Commons to listen to it, and it went far to justify the trade societies in claiming such a measure of political reform as has rendered the like impossible henceforth to be uttered. No man of sound mind would make any such statement nowadays.

There remains but one more point. The progress of democracy in Europe is continuous and irrresistible. Surely, though in some places slowly, the power is slipping from the hands of the privileged few into the hands of the burdened many. What use will the latter make of it? Will they be as shorted-sighted and selfish as the few have been? If so, the latter can not complain and some good at least will be done since more will be benefited by such selfishness than at present. But we have good reason to believe that their rule will be characterized by more good sense, probity and wisdom than that of their predecessors. Surely it is cause for pride on the part of the friends of the workingman to hear such testimony as that of J. M. Ludlow, who says, at the end of an extended history of labor legislation in England since 1832, that in looking back over the intervening time and calling to mind the great contests, social, moral and political, which have occurred, it will be found that the workingmen of England, in all the great centers of industry, gave what strength and influence they possessed to that side, which experience has since demonstrated to have been in the right. Their course, wherever they have been fairly treated, has been marked by as much thought and unselfishness as that of any other large class in the community. They have wisely used every advantage which has come to them. They have disappointed the Cassandrian prophecies of their enemies, who claimed that it was unsafe to shorten their hours of labor, because they would but use their leisure for the purpose of dissipation. They have fulfilled the most hopeful anticipations of their friends. They have given ample evidence that they will use their rapidly increasing preponderance in politics in the interest of freedom and justice. No better illustration of this can be found than in their course in regard to Catholic emancipation and the abolition of wage-slavery.

It is certain that at a time when the workingmen of England had, as God knows, grievances enough to complain of, they never turned a deaf ear to pleadings for the rights of the

African slave; that anti-slavery meetings were always largely attended by workingmen. But there is one crowning instance which Americans above all people in the world should never forget, in which the working classes may be said to have decided the policy of England, when the voice of the people proved truly to be the voice of God. At a time when every evil influence under heaven seemed combined to force England into abetting the slaveholders' secession, when the cotton famines and blackade-runners' profits, the French despot and the *Times*, the country-party and the ship-owners, Mr. Carlyle and half the piety of England, were urging the country on to a course which all now feel would have been one of headlong and ruinous folly, the workingmen of Lancashire stood firm and fast to the holy principle of human freedom. Sublimely patient, far-seeing beyond speculators and statesmen, they could meet in the midst of their own deep distress caused by the continuance of the war, to congratulate Abraham Lincoln on his proclamation of emancipation; and at the time when any expression of sympathy with the cause of the "Union" was sure to meet with fierce scorn and self-complacent derision in the House of Commons as well as on every 'change throughout the country, they never wavered in their firm faith of its ultimate triumph. Abraham Lincoln recognized the meaning of this expression of sympathy, and replied in a letter of the 19th of January, 1863: "Under the circumstance I can not but regard your decisive utterances upon the question as an instance of sublime Christian heroism which has not been surpassed in any age or country." May this prove to be a forecast of the way in which the laboring man will use his growing power in every country for all time to come.

The history of the laborer and his condition in every European country, whether in agriculture or the mechanic arts, whether in the fifteenth or the nineteenth century, proves indisputably the result of two facts: first, that the laboring class owe nearly the whole improvement of their condition to their own efforts; second, that they have ordinarily been able to protect their own interest only by combination. Whenever the laborers have been too poor, too indolent, too selfish, too short-sighted to combine, there they have fallen an easy prey to their enemies; wherever they have had the requisite public spirit and wisdom, they have never failed to better their own condition and with that the condition of the great majority of their fellow-countrymen.

CHAPTER IV.

THE LABOR MOVEMENT IN AMERICA TO 1861.

Plymouth the Starting-point of the Free Labor Movement — Free and Slave Labor — Early Associations of Labor — Class Distinctions — Wages Regulated by Law — An Early Boycott — Early Strikes and Organizations — First Epoch of the Present Movement — First Experiment in Community Life — Time Money, 1829 — Labor Men Pioneers in the Anti-slavery Movement — Yankee Girls — Agitation for the Ten-hour Work-day — Workingmen's Party — Protest against Land Traffic — New England Convention of Farmers and Mechanics — Ship-carpenters and Calkers and Merchants of Boston — Connecticut Carpet-workers' Conspiracy Case — Fourth of July Celebration, Boston, 1834 — Strikes of Carpenters, Stone Cutters, Horseshoers, Longshoremen and Riggers — Military under Arms in New York City — Factory-girls' Strike of 1838 — Ten-hour Proclamation of President Van Buren — Journeymen Bootmakers' Conspiracy Case — Judge Shaw's Decision — Labor Literature, 1838 to 1851 — New England Protective Union — New England Workingmen's Association — Ten-hour Movement in Pittsburgh — First Industrial Congress, 1845 — Convention of Carpet Weavers — Public Meeting of Machinists — Sympathy with the Chartists and Repealers of England and Ireland — Protest against Cheap Labor — Wendell Phillips on the Labor Question, 1847 — Attempt to Boycott a Labor Man in Maine — Typographical Society to the Printers of Paris — Industrial Conventions and Congresses — Co-operative Iron Moulders — Horace Greeley before the Printers — Factory Operatives' Strike of 1851 — Ship-workers on Old Work gain the Eight-hour Day — First Epoch of the Social Revolution ends in the War against Chattel Slavery.

PLYMOUTH and Jamestown are the two starting points of the labor movement in this country; Plymouth representing free, and Jamestown chattel labor. For nearly two hundred and fifty years these systems contended with each other for the mastery. Out of the first grew the free school, the public library, the forum of free debate, the wonderful control and mastery over an unyielding soil and untold natural difficulties, the wonderful inventions of the human brain to produce things with rapidity and cheapness, giving to labor the highest prosperity and highest attainments ever reached. Under this free labor system the laborer became the sovereign citizen, holding an equal right under the law to make laws and enforce them, each increasing responsibility leading to greater development, opening avenues of advancement in the political, social and industrial world. The labor movement of to-day came over in the "Mayflower," the founders of the colony, building more wisely than they knew, engrafting into their contract the spirit of co-operation. The first industry established by them, the fisheries, partook of this spirit, and each man who handled a line handled also his share of the profit of the venture. In addition to the profit-sharing system thus introduced, the colony still further protected the fisherman by setting aside a certain part of their corn for the use of the fishers in case the cruise should be unprofitable.

The planting of the chattel system of labor at Jamestown constituted the establishment of an oligarchy. The virgin soil of the South was outraged by mammon. To labor in the field was degradation. Education was for the master; ignorance, for the laborer. The employer was mounted in the saddle, the laborer was on foot; the one holding the whip, the other the hoe. From the leisure of the master, in the days of the Revolution, great men were grown. The white laborer became the "trash" of the South. Civilization was stagnant. The Plymouth colony built up the free West, ringed the continent with homes, newspapers and churches. The Jamestown colony became dangerous, and was restricted within a self-destroying area.

The history of the struggle of free labor on this continent is not complete without an analysis of the spirit of commerce, as manifested in the settlement of New York. The compromise between these three factors — sentiment in affairs, commerce, and slavery — has resulted in the destruction of the latter, the subversion of the former, and the enthronement of the spirit of commerce. The struggle now pending is for the restoration of sentiment, or the restoration of the moral relation of man to man.

Ship-building, being the most important of the early industries, and the skilled craftsmen being emigrants from England, where trades organizations then existed, it is very evident that some form of organization existed among them. Their acts show an agreement or mutual understanding in reference to rules governing their craft, — rules that finally had the strength of custom, and were maintained after many struggles.

The first historical mention we have of a craftsman is found in the History of Plymouth, in which it is stated that in 1621 a carpenter and saltmaker were sent to the colony by the adventurers. "The carpenter," says Governor Bradford, "is an honest and very industrious man, who very quickly built us two very good and strong shallops, with a great and strong lighter;" but it seems that this carpenter died during the summer, as Governor Bradford says, "to our great grief, loss, and sorrow." This industry grew to such large proportions as to necessitate the bringing over of a comparatively large number of ship-workers. They came mostly from the county of Kent, where organizations of labor existed. The extent of the industry at that time is but very little known or appreciated at the present day. The workmen were necessarily strong, vigorous men, physically and mentally. Their hours of labor were from sun to sun. That they were the pioneers of the labor movement in this country will be clearly seen by a perusal of the chapter on the "Building Trades," to an investigation of which Mr. Edward H. Rogers, himself a ship-builder, has given much time.

It is probable that in the early days no attempt was made to form special labor organizations, the condition of the colonies being such that what was the interest of one was the interest of all; but it was not long before class distinction became clearly marked, and an aristocracy as strict as that existing in England had become established. A man of wealth and position was termed "gentleman," and a man of humble means, a craftsman, etc., "goodman." The social nature of man necessitated association, and this desire for association necessarily led to organization, and the mingling together of men at their several crafts naturally led to organizations of fellow-craftsmen; but these associations were at first wholly of a social character, with benevolent features.

That shortly after the close of the first century and a half of the history of the colonies, they commenced to discuss the question of wages, is evident from the legislation enacted in the several towns establishing the maximum wages to be paid.

In the town of Newburyport (1777) the following vote was passed:

Pursuant to "an Act of the General Court to Prevent Monopoly and Oppression," it was voted by the Selectmen to establish the following as the Maximum Wages to be paid:

Carpenters	5 shillings	4 pence	per	day.
Calkers	6 "		"	"
Day Laborers, not found	4 "		"	"
Day Laborers, found	3 "		"	"
Joiners	4 "	8 pence	"	"
Masons	6 "		"	"

It will be noticed that by this vote the employers were prohibited from paying more than a certain sum per day, but they were not prohibited from paying the lowest possible price for labor.

Of strikes we have no record up to the present century, unless the refusal to work on Christmas, as referred to by a recent historian, can be considered as such.

The question of the relation of the colonies to Great Britain commanded the special attention of the workingmen. Their places of meeting were the centers of the discussions that precipitated the Revolutionary War, and the ship-carpenters and calkers, and others of the building trades were among the most earnest followers of Samuel Adams. They doubtless belonged to the several secret organizations like the Sons of Liberty, who, like the order of Tammany, wore the paraphernalia of the native Indian. Events proved that Tories were not found among the workingmen, but in the ranks of

Geo. E. McNeill.

the aristocratic. The class distinctions, if not also the oppression of the poor, which existed at this time, are evidenced by the following quotation from a paper published in 1775:

> Do not the threats of the rich to distress the poor in any shape, if the last should not in an approaching election give their votes to such men as the former direct, show an enslaving disposition? Can we expect representatives chosen in this manner will be faithful to preserve our liberties? Have not the tradesmen and laborers a glorious opportunity now offered them of asserting their freedom by voting, one and all, according to their own minds and consciences, without paying the least regard to the lordly dictates of their employers?

It is a matter of tradition that the idea of overturning the tea in Boston Harbor was first promulgated at a meeting of the ship carpenters and calkers, and that these men before that sometimes acted together in political matters.

The Revolutionary War naturally tended to the elimination of the class distinctions which had prevailed, and a spirit of individual independence permeated the laboring masses—a spirit that has not yet been wholly obliterated.

It is said that the first strike in the country occurred in New York City, in 1803, when a number of sailors struck for an advance of wages. It seems to have been settled by the arrest of the leader and his lodgment in jail. That strikes of craftsmen had occurred prior to this time it is but natural to suppose, but as they were matters of minor importance it is difficult to find any record of them.

Beginning with this century, the tailors appear to be the first to establish the present form of trades-unions, their organization claiming to date back to 1806. Prior to that date members of that craft coming from England continued their membership in the Journeyman Tailors' Unions of the old country. The same is true of the hatters, who organized a union of their craft as early as 1819. The Columbia Charitable Association, of Shipwrights and Calkers, was organized between 1825 and 1830. Local unions of the printers are traced back to 1831.

The especial point of interest as the formative period of the labor movement is from 1825 to 1851. This development was in the direction of a demand for less hours of labor and higher wages, and in co-operative experiments. The labor men of that day were reformers in every sense of the word. They were among the first to denounce chattel slavery and capital punishment, and the first to call attention to the displacement of laborers by the introduction of labor-saving machinery. The building trades were in the advance line, as will be seen by reference to the chapter on that subject. They were sustained, doubtess, by the factory operatives, the bootmakers, tailors, printers, and other craftsmen.

New Harmony, Ind., was the scene of the first experiment at community life under the idea of common property. This experiment (1825) had the advantage of Mr. Owen's ability and money. With $1,000,000 at command, 28,000 acres of very good land, two libraries, which cost $30,000 each, sets of scientific instruments, and 800 persons to try the experiment, it failed after about two years' trial. Mr. Josiah Warren, who was a member of this community, and whose writings upon questions of labor, money, commerce, etc., commanded the attention of the labor reformers of early days, was on the point of abandoning all such enterprises, when, as he says, "a new train of thought seemed to throw a sudden flash of light on past errors, and to show plainly the path to be pursued. This led directly in the opposite direction to that which had just been travelled." Mr. Warren gave as the problem to be solved: first, the proper, legitimate and just reward of labor; second, security of person and property; third, the greatest practical amount of freedom to each individual; fourth, economy in the production and uses of wealth; fifth, to open a way to each individual to the possession of land and all other natural wealth; sixth, to make it the interest of all to co-operate with and assist each other, instead of clashing with and counteracting each other; seventh, to withdraw the elements of discord, of war, of distrust and repulsion, and to establish a prevailing spirit of peace, order and social sympathy. The means of solution he stated as being, first, individuality; second, sovereignty of every individual; third, cost the limit of price;

You never will find any satisfactory solution of the great problem now up between LABOR and CAPITAL, or SLAVERY and LIBERTY, until you understand what Justice *is*, and what a circulating medium, or money, ought to be.

The above is one specimen of what money ought to be. It should be issued by those men, women, and children who perform some useful service, but by *nobody else.* It should command LABOR FOR LABOR in equal quantities, and the most disagreeable should be highest paid.

Perhaps no class or person is to blame, but the most fatal element of confusion, oppression, and violence ever introduced among mankind is the passing off of metals or any other natural product of the earth, or the earth itself as *pay for labor!* It defrauds, starves, and degrades, and then insults labor, and makes it a thing to be shunned and avoided, and forced upon whoever can be made to bear it. This is the origin of all forms of slavery, in all civilized countries, and of all poverty and crime, the *insecurity of condition*, the worship of money, the antagonisms of classes, and the crisis of these times. Whereas, if Labor were equitably rewarded (with an equal amount of labor), the hardest worker would be the richest man, and all would choose a portion of labor as a means of health and pleasure. For further explanations, see the works mentioned on the opposite page.

This is addressed in a friendly spirit to all parties and nations. *YOU HAVE NO TIME TO LOSE!*

fourth, a circulating medium founded on the cost of labor; fifth, adaptation of the supply to the demand. George Jacob Holyoake speaks of Mr. Warren's system as the developing of the principle of disintegration which has always been well provided for both in savage and civilized societies. In 1842 Mr. Warren again returned to New Harmony and opened a labor exchange on the principle of cost being the limit of price. Of this method Mr. Holyoake writes: —

Mr. Warren's mode of paying commission was by charging the exchanger for the amount of time expended in effecting his business. The manager had a clock before him; he noted the time of the customer's arrival, and, when the transaction was completed, charged him for the time consumed in conducting it. It was not the value of the business done, but the time taken in doing it, upon which the charge was made. It might cost more on this plan to buy a bunch of needles than a sack of flour.

Mr. Warren, speaking of his system, says that cost being made the limit of price would give to a washerwoman a greater income than the importer of foreign goods; that this would entirely upset the present system of national trade, stop all wars arising out of the scramble for the profits of trade, and demolish all tariffs, duties, and all systems of policy that give rise to them; would abolish all distinctions of rich and poor; would enable everyone to consume as much as he produced, and consequently prevent anyone from living at the cost of another without his or her consent. The circulating medium to be used in equitable commerce consisted of a certain number of hours of labor of a definite kind. We give a copy of this form of note with the verbal explanation, as printed by him in "Periodical Letters on Principles of Progress." Mr. Warren afterwards moved to Thompson Station, L. I., where with others he made an attempt to carry out his principles. His attempts may be considered failures, although there is no doubt that his theories left a lasting impression upon many minds. Of the other experiments, notably of that of the Brook Farm Community, at communal life no mention need be made in this volume, as they are already covered by historians of their own.

As early as 1825 the agitation of social and economic questions was commanding the attention of thinkers and philanthropists, representatives of labor organizations bringing to public notice the dangers of overwork, low wages, and poverty. A paper published in Boston in 1826-9 reports that in 1826 five hundred and thirty-one persons were dependent upon charity for support in Portsmouth, N.H., and the Hon. Thomas Hertell, in an article on intemperance, speaks of the poverty of the working classes as one of the causes of intemperance. In the same paper the attention of manufacturers is called to the dangers of factory operatives, and demands are made that suitable rooms, lodgings, etc., be provided for them; means for "preventing the rich from swallowing up the inheritance of the poor of the land" are commended; and "the injurious consequences to the community of individuals amassing large landed property," are commented upon. Social unions of different crafts were springing up in the principal cities and manufacturing centres. The cotton mill operatives, being amongst the most oppressed, were agitating among themselves methods of relief and remedy, the women weavers—Yankee girls—leading in the agitation and perfecting organization.

In New York City the ship carpenters and calkers were commencing the agitation for the ten-hour work day, and all along the Atlantic coast, where ships were being built, and on the rivers, these sturdy men were preparing for the first great movement in the emancipation of labor. In spite of their long hours of toil they found time to discuss their grievances. Strikes of small magnitude occurred, sometimes resulting in success, and sometimes in failure. They were not considered of sufficient importance to command the attention of the public press of that day. It seemed to be the opinion of some of the cultured people, that the workingmen had no legal right to strike, and when the imported laborers on the Chesapeake & Ohio Canal struck, in 1829, they were arrested; but upon being brought before a judge, on a writ of *habeas corpus*, were discharged, the judge deciding that the case did not come under the statute of 1815. We are unable to learn whether these laborers had been imported to take the places of other workmen, or whether they had been imported originally because they could be obtained at lower rates of wages.

The agitation of the preceding years had culminated in demands for legislation, a mechanics' lien law being one of the first measures demanded. In New York a favorable report was presented in 1828, but was not acted upon by the House. In the following year meetings of workingmen were held and protest made against the action of the legislature, and candidates pledged to support that measure. Prominent members of the several local labor organizations finding the importance of public agitation, and the need of legislation, organized a workingmen's party, the operations of that party, being in each instance local, and having at one time its largest membership in Boston, and at others in New York and Philadelphia. At the time of the State election in New York in 1829, a workingmen's ticket was put into the field. Several other tickets were nominated, of which the regular Republican ticket was supposed to be the most popular; but at the close of the first day of the election the workingmen's ticket was found to be ahead of all others, and the New York papers expressed great alarm, and urged the people—"bank gentlemen, and all who opposed regular nominations"—to arouse themselves and oppose the ticket, which they did with such success that only one of the candidates of the workingmen's party was elected—one Ebenezer Ford, who was a candidate for the State Assembly. The possibility of unseating Mr. Ford was suggested, which it was claimed could be done by the Assembly. This movement was unsuccessful. One of the opposition papers said of the successful candidate: "Mr. Ford, who has succeeded on the workingmen's ticket, is said to be an honest and sensible man, and by no means attached to the doctrines of the Free Enquirers or the visionary project of the Agrarians."

At the first meeting of those who got up the workingmen's ticket the following resolutions were passed:

Resolved. In the opinion of this meeting, that the first appropriation of the soil of the state to private and exclusive possession was eminently and barbarously unjust.

2. That it was substantially feudal in its character, inasmuch as those who received enormous and unequal possessions were lords, and those who received little or nothing were vassals.

3. That hereditary transmission of wealth, on the one hand, and poverty on the other, has brought down to the present generation all the evils of the feudal system — and that this, in our opinion, is the prime source of all our calamities.

4. In this view of the matter, that the greatest knaves, impostors and paupers of the age are our bankers — who swear they have promised to pay to their debtors thirty or thirty-five millions of dollars on demand, at the same time that they have, as they also swear, only three or four millions to do it with.

5. That more than one hundred broken banks within a few years past admonish the community to destroy banks altogether.

6. That more than a thousand kinds of counterfeit banknotes, from five hundred dollars down to a single dollar, give double force to the admonition.

7. That exemption is privilege; and as such, the exemption from taxation of churches and church property, and the property of priests, to an amount not exceeding fifteen hundred dollars, is a direct and positive robbery of the people.

No statement of the measures by which the evils complained of were to be remedied can be found in this instance; but the discussions were not only upon the land question, but also upon the question of lien laws, hours of labor, and, in some places, an oppressive militia system. The resolution regarding the taxation of church property is incident to the fact that the free religious movement which was then in the warmth of its inception permeated these reform organizations. The fact that the eloquent and impressive men and women who are termed here "free enquirers" sympathized heartily with all the efforts of the poor and oppressed, made them welcome to the meetings of the workingmen, at the same time frightening away many of the church-going conservative wage-laborers. The papers opposed to the movement made the most of this fact, and stigmatized every effort in the direction of relief of labor as an infidel movement. The appearance of woman upon the platform was also enlarged upon as evidence that the whole movement was visionary and fraught with danger to society. Frances Wright and Robert Dale Owen were especially condemned, in terms not always polite, by the press.

The system of long payments that then prevailed proved

disastrous to the workingmen in many instances, not only because of the truck system, which obtained, but by reason of the failure of some of the manufacturers and the consequent loss of wages to the employees. This led the reformatory papers to demand legislative interference for the protection of the operatives. The Workingmen's Party still continued, and newspapers were established in Rhode Island, Connecticut, Massachusetts and New York. We have been unable to procure copies of these papers, but from extracts in the leading papers of the day, we have reason to believe that they were not supported by the workingmen, although exhibiting considerable editorial ability.

The question had attracted sufficient public attention to warrant the delivery of a lecture by Hon. Edward Everett before the Charlestown Lyceum, in which he commended the organization of the Workingmen's Party.

A meeting of farmers, mechanics, and other workingmen was held at Boston on the 16th of February, 1831. This meeting took steps to organize a delegate convention, which was assembled on the 6th of September, 1832, in the Representative chamber of the State House in Boston. The convention was a dignified and able body, and its proceedings foreshadowed the present stage of the social problem. Charles Douglass, of New London, Conn., presided; and G. W. Light, of Boston, and Thomas Dodd, of Providence, acted as secretaries. All of the New England states excepting Vermont were represented, and delegates from New York were also present. The city of Boston was represented by thirty delegates, among whom were Billings Briggs, Timothy Claxton, George W. Light, W. R. Stacy, afterwards well known as a temperance advocate and the proprietor of Stacy Hall which was for a long time the headquarters of the trades assembly, Ruggles Slack, the father of Charles W. Slack, the well-known editor and proprietor of the *Boston Commonwealth* and Collector of Internal Revenue, Samuel Bassett, of Chelsea, William D. Swan, Colonel J. P. Clapp, of Dorchester, and Ebenezer Seavey, of Roxbury. The meeting was opened by prayer by Rev. Mr. Taylor, who was afterwards invited to take a seat in the convention. The ten points submitted to the convention for consideration were the organization of a central committee for each state, the institution of lyceums or institutes, reform in the militia system, the expediency of calling a national convention of workingmen, the ten-hour system, the effect of banking institutions and other monopolies upon the condition of the laboring classes, the improvement of the system of education, (including the recommendation of such legislative enactments in relation to the internal economies of factories as should insure to the operatives therein a competent degree of instruction), the abolition of imprisonment for debt, the adoption of a national bankrupt law, the extension of the right of suffrage in states where the people were then denied its privileges, and the lien law in favor of journeymen and mechanics. Among the other matters discussed were the landed interests, taxation, and co-operative trading.

The committee on official organ recognized a paper called the *New England Artisan*, and asked for its removal to Boston. The committee on address to the workingmen adopted the addresses of the president and of Mr. Eldredge, as expressing the views of the convention. The remedies which these addresses call for were the organization of the whole laboring population of the republic, the removal of political questions, morality, and economy from the mere personal and party contests of that day, the presentation of facts to the consideration of all citizens, the selection from among the politicians of the respective parties whose moral character, personal habits, relations and employments, as well as professions afforded the best guarantee of their disposition to revise our social and political system and introduce the reforms demanded, to which was added the fixed determination to persevere until all wrongs were redressed, and to imbue the minds of their offspring with a detestation of the habits of the aristocracy. The president of the convention read a letter from the workingmen of the City of New York.

It is a singular coincidence of history that at the time the New England mechanics and farmers were in convention discussing these questions of great social and economic importance, another convention was being held in South Carolina, under the lead of John C. Calhoun, for the purpose of nullifying an act of Congress, and laying the foundation for the Rebellion of 1861. The convention of workingmen had been preceded by the formation of an association auxiliary to the New England Association of Farmers, Mechanics, and Workingmen. The first meeting of this association was held at the old Common Council Room, Court Square, on Wednesday evening, March 14, 1832. The resolutions adopted at the meeting speak of various institutions in the country organized for the same object. On March 21st an adjourned meeting was held for the adoption of the constitution, and the officers and directors of the association were chosen, from which it appears that, in addition to the names already given, S. Loud, W. M. Kendall, W. B. Lowner, Henry Seaver, William Sparrell, S. Batchelder, R. Smith, A. Richardson, S. M. Russell, E. H. Chamberlain, and D. Hinckley appeared. This meeting voted to recommend that the mechanics of all branches have meetings by themselves, for the purpose of consulting together, and if possible come to a mutual agreement upon the system of working hours.

On March 30th the Shipwrights' and Calkers' Association called a meeting for April 4th, inviting master workmen to attend. On May 3d the auxiliary association discussed the question, "Is the ten-hour system a benefit?" On May 23d a meeting of master-carpenters was held, at which it was voted to call a meeting of the master-carpenters, masons, painters and slaters, to take into consideration the expediency of altering the number of hours which then constituted a day's work.

On May 29th an advertisement was published, calling the shipwrights and calkers of Boston and Charlestown to meet at four o'clock of the same day on business of importance. On the same day an advertisement appeared in the papers that one hundred and twenty shipwrights and calkers, first-rate workmen, wanted employment in Boston or elsewhere, to which is appended an additional notice, to the effect that a calker had been employed by one of the committee of the master-builders under misrepresentations, and that he had gone home to his family; ending with the warning that those persons who should come to the city thereafter must govern themselves accordingly. From this advertisement it would appear that the shipwrights and calkers had entered upon a strike, in which the master-workmen were interested in favor of the men.

The ten-hour movement had spread to other cities; strikes had been inaugurated in many places. A strike occurred in New Bedford, in which some five or six hundred mechanics and laborers were engaged, to regulate wages and hours of labor. They held daily meetings and engaged the town crier to announce them.

While this movement of the men for shorter hours was being agitated, the merchants and shipowners of Boston were not idle They held a meeting at the Exchange Coffee Rooms on the 15th of May, at which there was but one sentiment as to the course which ought to be pursued, as the report says, "to discountenance and check the unlawful combination formed to control the freedom of individuals as to the hours of labor, and to thwart and embarass those by whom they are employed and liberally paid." The report continues, "setting forth the pernicious and demoralizing tendency of these combinations, and the unreasonableness of the attempt, in particular where mechanics are held in so high estimation, and their skill in labor so liberally rewarded." A long preamble and resolution was adopted, in which it was claimed that labor ought always to be left free to regulate itself, and that neither the employed nor the employer should have the power to control the other; that all combinations to regulate the price and hours of labor, or to restrain individual freedom and enterprise were at all times attended with pernicious consequences; that they looked with deep regret upon the course pursued by their fellow citizens, the journeymen, in the adoption and maintenance of a system of measures designed to coerce individuals of their craft, and to prescribe the time and manner of that labor for which they were liberally paid. They claimed that such organization and action would drive the trade from the city, and concluded that they would discountenance all associations and combinations, saying: "We will neither employ any journeyman who at the time belongs to such combinations, nor will we give work to any master mechanic who shall employ them while they continue thus pledged to each other and refuse to work the hours which it has been and is now customary for mechanics to work." These resolutions were signed by the representatives of one hundred and six firms.

The merchants at this time were the employers of the master mechanics, and evinced by their action the same spirit that has been manifested in later years; namely, the denial of the right of the workingmen to organize for protection, while claiming that right for themselves. They say that neither the employed nor the employer should have the power to control the other, and then add that they will not employ any journeyman who belongs to an organization, or give work to any master mechanic who employs such a journeyman, thus effectively introducing the boycott in its most pernicious form. On May 19th a general meeting of house and ship-joiners was held, in which Mr. John Hunt acted as chairman, and Mr. Thomas Gould, Jr., as secretary. It was voted that so far as laid in their power they would use every exertion to persuade their employers to allow their hands three hours instead of two for their meals during the hot months of summer, and also allow them to quit work on Saturdays at six o'clock, P.M., commencing June 1st. The history of the movement for ten hours at this time is a part of the history of the building trades, and will be found in the chapter under that head.

It is evident that the movement was a failure, as far as immediate success was concerned. But it resulted in the increase of organization, and in an increased membership.

In July, 1833, the workingmen in the Thompsonville (Ct.) Carpet Factory struck for an advance of wages, and the Carpet Company sued some of the strikers for conspiracy; the question at issue being whether the workmen had a right to refuse to work, or to conspire, or agree together not to work for less than a certain sum. The court charged the jury in the negative, but the verdict was given for the defendants.

The workingmen of Baltimore celebrated the 12th of September, 1833, as a holiday, and nominated two candidates for the State Legislature.

In 1833 the journeymen shoemakers of Geneva, New York, succeeded in forcing their employer to dismiss one of the employees, the reason not being given, but the employer retaliated upon his men by having some of them indicted and punished for conspiracy.

A mechanics' convention met at Utica, N. Y., August 20, 1834, to protest against convict labor.

The leaders of the movement saw the necessity of a more complete organization of the trades. Efforts to bring them together culminated in a meeting January 8, 1834, when a general trades-union of the mechanics of Boston and vicinity was formed. A circular was issued proposing a plan of organization, which was responded to by sixteen local unions, who held a meeting on the first Tuesday in March and adopted a constitution which was subsequently ratified by the different trades. This was the first organization of this kind, and may be considered the parent trade assembly or central trade and labor union. Under the auspices of this organization arrangements were made for the celebration of the 4th of July, consisting of a procession, oration, and dinner. This first effort proved successful. About two thousand men participated. They marched through the principal streets, preceded by bands of music and carrying banners. The oration was delivered by Frederick Robinson of Marblehead in the open air on Fort Hill; and the dinner, at which a thousand plates were laid, was served in Faneuil Hall. A special feature of the procession was the new ship "Mechanic," fully rigged, and manned with four pieces of cannon, drawn by twenty-four white horses. The ship was twenty-four and a half feet long, and thirty-seven and a half feet high to the top of the mast, and was built expressly for the occasion.

On July 8th the committee published a card in the papers, thanking the military company for their escort, the proprietors of the Federal Street Theatre for the use of furniture, the commandant of the Navy Yard for the use of decorations, the North End Artillery for the grand salute, those citizens who decorated their houses, the reader of the Declaration of Independence, the toast-master, and the editors who gave favorable notices. From the oration we quote a few paragraphs: —

We are yet but a half-educated and a half-civilized people. But few are educated in one-half of their faculties, and the people in the other half. The many have been obliged to devote their whole time to bodily labor, while the powers of the mind have been almost wholly neglected. The millions have been lulled into a fatal security, while the thousands have been active in promoting their own interests. The speaker alluded forcibly to the usurpations of the judiciary, and called for legislative interference with the hours of labor in the factories.

The following statement, which is self-explanatory, was made by the committee at the dinner:

The committee of arrangements have an apology to make to their fellow citizens. We regret to say that no one of our respected clergy are present. Application having been made to twenty-two different societies for the use of a meeting-house on this day for trades-unions, the doors of all were shut against us, and under the circumstances your committee felt a delicacy to apply to any clergyman to officiate at the table, lest he might consider it an affront.

One of the toasts was "Our brethren at New York. They have struck the first blow at oppression; may success attend and prosperity crown all their lawful undertakings." From this toast it appears that the movement for ten hours in New York City had culminated in a strike. Very little is known of the connected history of the movement in the building or other trades. In the chapter devoted to that subject, interesting matter will be found from the pen of Captain Richard Trevellick, an apprentice in the shipyards in New York during the early days of the movement, and now general lecturer of the Order of Knights of Labor. It is known that the movement took the same form as in the New England States, public meetings being held, newspapers published, pamphlets issued, trades organized, a central union formed, and the workingmen's party organized as before described.

One peculiar feature of the movement of the shipbuilders — the pioneers in the movement — was the inauguration of a "Mechanics' Bell," the story of which is told in the chapter on the building trades. The first strike of the ship carpenters of New York proved unsuccessful, as also did strikes of other craftsmen in New York and Pennsylvania.

In Bath, Me., the ten-hour question was discussed in every shipyard. It is probable that a strike occurred there which proved unsuccessful.

The failure of the Boston mechanics in 1832, together with the threats of prosecution for conspiracy which were made by the merchants, impeded the movement, and it was not until 1836–7 that the ten-hour day was gained on ship repairs in that city, while on new ship work it was not granted until 1840.

In 1835 the stone-cutters and horse-shoers of New York city went on strike for an increase of wages. A strike occurred in Paterson, N. J., for a shorter work-day. In many places the employers organized and refused to give work to any person belonging to a trades-union, openly declaring that the workmen should not obtain the means of supporting one another.

In the year 1836 some French Canadians were engaged to work on a dam in Maine and struck because they were not permitted to smoke their pipes while at work.

In the same year twenty-one journeymen tailors in New York were punished for striking for higher wages and preventing others by threats and promises and various means from working except for the prices fixed by the Tailors' Union. Judge Edwards in his charge said "This is not a mere struggle between master and workman; it is one on which the whole harmony of the Union depended," and continuing, he said that there was no necessity for such systems in this country, and that they were of foreign origin. The defendants were fined sums ranging from $100 to $150.

The ship carpenters of Boston having failed to gain the

ten hour day, attempted to secure two hours for dinner, the dinner hour then being one o'clock. In November, 1835, the master mechanics of Boston held meetings at the Exchange Coffee House to consider the question of altering the hours of labor. At the last one fifty-two trades were represented, and they resolved to fix the dinner hour at twelve o'clock instead of one, and to petition the city government to have the bells rung at the former hour.

The journeymen house carpenters held a meeting December 29 at which the following resolutions were adopted: —

Resolved, That as the mechanic arts constitute one of the principal constituents on which a social and civilized community is based, we as mechanics claim the sole right, so far as our trade is concerned, of regulating our intercourse with its other important constituents, and that the violation of this right destroys the just relations of society, and further a community actuated by judicious motives will preserve at all times its inviolate rights, the infringement of which will injure the prosperity and happiness of any portion of her citizens.

Resolved, That, believing that ten hours a day is amply sufficient in any well-regulated community to produce all the requisite necessaries and comforts of life, and as it is all that the well-being of society requires, we hereby notify all employers of labor that we shall do all in our power to reduce the hours of labor to that number the ensuing season, and we caution employers to govern themselves accordingly.

Resolved, That we recognize in the example set by the government and citizens of Philadelphia one well-worthy the attention and imitation of our own citizens, inasmuch as they have made a practical application of the principle that man cannot with impunity resist nature's demands.

Resolved, That it affords cause of congratulation to witness the spirited response given to the calls for this meeting, as it evinces no want of zeal to effect the object of our desire the coming season.

The strike of the carpenters in 1836 to secure ten hours was a failure, as were evidently most of the attempts of the workingmen in that year. In an address delivered before the Boston Charitable Mechanics Association in the fall of 1836, Mr. T. L. Holmer congratulates the people on the failure of the trades-unions, in these words: "It must be a source of high gratification to us all to know that a sense of returning reason has induced many of those who took the lead in the late strikes to see the error of their ways. Most cordially do I rejoice at this result that the trades unions have been very generally abandoned by their members." The same spirit is shown by a hat and cap manufacturer of New Brunswick, N. J., in a card which he issued to the public in April of the same year. In it he states that he "has now at work four-and-twenty good, permanent workmen, and several more engaged to commence the first of May, all of whom are alike unaffected with the brutal leprosy of blue-Monday habits and the moral gangrene of trades-union principles. Hence my binders may rely upon steady employment, and the public upon good work punctually performed; and they and myself find just cause to felicitate ourselves upon the prompt and effectual disposal, at once and forever, of the inconvenience, injustice, and nuisance of perpetual vexations, regular combinations and periodical strikes from marauding gangs of transient and tramping trades-unionists, who have proved themselves as destitute of every moral principle as they have become notorious for their wickedness and folly, their presumption, violence and audacity."

In spite of the defections from their ranks, the organizations continued their existence with varied success and failure, extending into other cities and towns, and notably to Philadelphia. A general strike for ten hours was inaugurated in Philadelphia in the latter part of May, 1835, and public meetings were held. The result of the strike seems to have been some modification of the working hours and a more complete organization of the several trades. In August of that year, the mechanics employed in the Navy Yard, at Washington, left their work and waited on the Secretary of the Navy for a redress of grievances. Very little satisfaction was received, and the mechanics returned to their work.

The trades-unions of Boston had at this time leased a hall for a place of meeting, giving it the name of "Trades-Union Hall." A trades-union course of lectures had also been inaugurated, the subjects being phrenology, history, witchcraft, corporations, political economy, political education, Republican education, and the effect of machinery on labor. The Journeymen Cordwainers' Society had become so strong in many places that none but members of the Association could readily find work, as the members of the union refused to work with non-union men. The meetings of the workingmen at this time had become of enough importance to command considerable space in some of the daily papers, the Democratic press more generally favoring the workingmen as far as reports were concerned, and in editorials of a conciliatory nature. Meetings seem to have been held nearly every week in the large cities and manufacturing towns of New York, Pennsylvania, Massachusetts, New Jersey, and Maine, and in Baltimore, Maryland; and strikes were of constant occurrence, that of the journeymen stone-cutters being of considerable importance, the master mechanics offering to compromise on the basis of two hours at noon. This offer was refused, and the strike continued and was successful; in New York first, and afterwards in other places. The carpenters, also, after quite a number of strikes, succeeded in some of the larger towns and cities in securing the ten-hour system. A petition was presented to the mayor and aldermen of Boston to call a public citizens' meeting in Faneuil Hall in the interest of ten-hours. This they refused to do, when a newspaper correspondence ensued, the reply of the mayor being considered very weak. The action which the mechanics desired was to instruct the city authorities to contract with the mechanics or laborers employed by the city government on the public works on the ten-hour system, from the 20th of March to the 20th of September, inclusive. The trades-union of Baltimore had been actively engaged in perfecting their organization, and were the first to memorialize Congress to enact a law to limit the hours of labor by those employed on the public works to ten hours a day. This memorial was brought up in Congress, March 21, 1836, and after a short debate was laid on the table.

In 1836 the longshoremen, riggers and other employees connected with shipping in New York struck for an increase of wages and less hours, and upon finding that their places were being taken by others not members of their organizations, they went from wharf to wharf, first requesting the workmen to leave their work, and then, it is claimed, threatened them.

The mayor ordered the military under arms, and, as the papers of that day say, threatened them with ball cartridges. The same scenes were enacted in Philadelphia, and a riot was feared. The men were finally obliged to return to work under much the same conditions as when they struck.

In the early summer of 1837 an attempt was made by some of the employers to induce the organizations of the ship-workers on repairs to consent to a reduction of wages. The form of the appeal shows that the trades-union organizations had gained great strength, for heretofore they had been ignored or condemned, and now they were recognized. The organizations declined to accept such a reduction, and the journeymen calkers and carpenters presented a method by which the ship-building of the merchants could be economically performed without a reduction of wages. They say: "We are now prepared and ready to contract for the repairs of vessels of any tonnage, either by the day or job, in a workman-like manner, at prices much less than they have been accustomed to pay, giving the merchant the opportunity of furnishing his own stock if he prefers to do it, and save paying a man (the master mechanic) one day's work in every five for doing nothing or worse than nothing." At this time these craftsmen were receiving three dollars per day, but they could not average much more than three days in the week.

The factory girls of this time were school-taught Americans, some working at one season in the mill and teaching school during short school terms. It had been the custom in manufacturing establishments to appoint the superintendent from the ranks of those who had advanced from the lower rounds of the ladder, but, as the manufacturing industries grew, some of the wealthy families found positions for themselves or their sons, as agents of mills. A gentleman of distinguished family had accepted the superintendency of a cotton mill in Dover, N. H., and, having some of the aristocratic habits of the city, was made the subject of ridicule by the townspeople. It is related that one day he stopped at the hotel, and after he had partaken of his dinner in his private room, he ordered a toothpick. As this was a luxury but little known in that locality, the porter brought up an armful of wood, requesting the gentleman to whittle out his own tooth-picks. It is also authentically stated that after moving his family to Dover he was annoyed by the croaking of frogs in the mill-pond, and accordingly had the pond drained off, and employed some of the mill hands to destroy the frogs. They were gathered, and, having been first subjected to a bath of boiling water, they were buried. A proposed reduction of wages caused a strike of the employees. The authority from whom we receive this story, now himself a manufacturer, was then a boy of about nine years, at work in the mill. The girls, by a preconcerted arrangement, gathered in the mill-yard and sent word to the agent, who appeared before them, taking his stand at the pump in the centre of the yard, and addressed the girls. After he had made his speech to the girls, which was received with laughter, the girls proceeded with handfuls of cotton waste to cover his broadcloth garments with a feathery coating of the material. The strike lasted but a few days, but it is believed that the agent never forgave the indignity perpetrated upon him on that occasion. During the strike the girls placarded the fence of the mill-yard and the door of the office with rhymes composed for the occasion. One of them bore an illuminated heading, consisting of a large frog painted green, the only stanza of the rhyme underneath which our informant could remember being: —

The agent to the frog-pond went,
To kill the frogs he was intent;
He gave them a dose of red-hot water,
For he thought to croak they hadn't oughter.

This is but an instance of a peculiar method which some of the early strikers had of revenging themseves by making verses.

The panic of 1837 naturally drove some of these organizations out of existence, to revive when more prosperous times returned, the general economic movement being continually in the direction of less hours and higher wages. The trades that organized prior to 1840 were the ship carpenters, and joiners, calkers, house carpenters, painters, roofers, bricklayers, printers, tailors, hatters, saddlers, cordwainers or shoemakers, factory operatives, marble and freestone-cutters, coopers, and masons, while other craftsmen were enrolled in the Labor Reform Associations or Workingmen's Party of that day. Literary institutes were formed by the workingmen, and some of them were of a conservative nature, notably that of Bath, Me., 1839, in which the "members were pledged to avoid exciting topics," but the people were not long satisfied with the discussion of remote questions, and even the Bath Literary Institute was soon succeeded by a workingmen's union.

Organization and agitation on this subject finally attained such magnitude as to warrant the President of the United States, Martin Van Buren, in issuing a proclamation establishing the ten-hour system for all employees of the United States government in the Navy Yards.

The following is the text of the proclamation, it being an extract from General Orders for the regulation of the Navy Yard, Washington, D. C.: —

NAVY YARD, WASHINGTON, April 10, 1840.

By direction of the President of the United States, "all public establishments will hereafter be regulated, as to working hours, by the ten-hour system." The hours for labor in this yard will therefore be as follows, viz.: From the first day of April to the 30th day of September, inclusive, from 6 o'clock A.M., to 6 o'clock, P.M. During this period, the workmen will breakfast before going to work, for which purpose the bell will be rung, and the first muster held at 7 o'clock, A. M. At 12 o'clock, noon, the bell will be rung, and the hour from 12 to 1 o'clock allowed for dinner, from which hour to 6 o'clock, P. M., will constitute the last half of the day.

From the last day of October, to the 31st day of March, the working hours will be from the rising to the setting of the sun. The bell will then be rung at one hour after sunrise, that hour being allowed for breakfast. At 12 o'clock, noon, the bell will again be rung, and one hour allowed for dinner, from which hour, say 1 o'clock, till sundown, will constitute the last half of the day. No quarters of days will be allowed.

Although this proclamation affected only the employees of the government, it was received with gladness by all branches of organized labor, and stimulated them to renewed efforts in the same direction. By the force of public sentiment created by the public meetings, and the establishment of numerous labor and other reformatory papers, the hours of labor upon Saturday were somewhat reduced without resort to strikes, but in many instances the workingmen were forced to resort to this method to secure their ends. The movement, which had been confined to the larger cities, had now found footing in many of the manufacturing towns, New York and New England leading. The number of organized trades had increased, and the movement had spread as far West as Ohio, while the discussion of the question on the platform and in the press was still more widely diffused.

Governor Fort, of New Jersey, seems to have been the first State executive to recommend legislation. In 1841 he said : "Constant and unremitting toil prevents intellectual improvement, and leads to physical and moral debasement."

It was a period when the intelligence of the country was challenged by men of remarkable ability and power, as well as high social position. The communities that had been formed by Robert Owen, Josiah Warren and others, were the centres to which gathered the radical reformatory spirits of the age. The Brook Farm Community furnished many of the most eloquent speakers for the platform of the workingmen, and, though often disagreeing in methods, these men of culture were united with the men and women of toil in a serious and earnest effort to overturn existing systems by a peaceful revolution, and the establishment of equity and justice among men. In fact, the movement was so broad in its character and universality of demand as to deprive it of the advantage of a definite and distinct aim.

This, indeed, was the period of the birth or awakening of American socialism. If the audiences that gathered to listen to Owen, Brisbane, Ryckman, Charles A. Dana, Horace Greeley, Frederick Robertson, John A. Collins and William H. Channing were not large in numbers, they were remarkable in intelligence. These workingmen and women who met in convention were American by birth as well as by instinct. They were the Americans of Americans, believing not only in the American idea of the largest individual independence, but also in the methods of educational and political revolution.

In some of the crafts, unions practically controlled the industry, many of the employers willingly complying with their conditions, one of which was that none but union men should be employed. Other employers sought to break up the organizations, and a suit was brought against the journeymen bootmakers of Boston for a combination to compel, by force of numbers and discipline, and by imposition of fines and penalties, other journeymen to join their societies and masters to employ none but members. This was called an unlawful conspiracy at common law. The trial took place in the October term, 1840, Robert Rantoul having charge of the journeymen's case. The court ruled against the defendants, and the jury found them guilty. The case was carried up to the Supreme Court on exceptions, and was tried in the March term of 1842. The exceptions were sustained and judgment arrested. Recent events make this case of special interest, and a full account can be found in "Metcalf's Supreme Court Reports," vol. IV., page 111.; Commonwealth *vs*. Hunt and others.

This was an indictment against the defendants (seven in number) for a conspiracy. The first count alleged that the defendants, together with divers other persons unknown to the grand-jurors, being workmen and journeymen in the art and manual occupation of bootmakers, unlawfully, perniciously and deceitfully designing and intending to keep up, form and unite themselves into an unlawful club, society and combination, and make unlawful by-laws, rules and orders among themselves, and thereby govern themselves and other workmen in said art, and unlawfully and unjustly to extort great sums of money, did unlawfully assemble and meet together and agree that none of them should thereafter work for any master or person whatsoever, in the said art, mystery or occupation, who should employ any workman or journeyman or other person, who was not a member of said club, society or combination, after notice given him to discharge such workman.

The second count charged that the defendants did unlawfully assemble, conspire, etc., and agree not to work for any master or person who should employ a workman not being a member of the Boston Journeymen Bootmaker's Society, or who should break any of their by-laws; and that this society did compel a master cordwainer in Boston to turn out of his employ one Jeremiah Horne, a journeyman bootmaker, because Horne would not pay the penalty fixed in the by-laws.

The third count averred that the defendants wickedly and unjustly, intending unlawfully, and by indirect means, to impoverish one Jeremiah Horne, and hinder him from following his trade, and from getting his livelihood and support thereby, in pursuance of such conspiracy did wrongfully, unlawfully, and indirectly prevent him from following his art and occupation.

In the fourth count it was alleged that the defendants, unjustly intending to injure and impoverish one Jeremiah Horne, and to prevent his earning his livelihood, did unlawfully conspire to prejudice the said Horne, and prevent him from exercising his trade.

The fifth count set forth that the defendants unlawfully conspired to impoverish one Isaac B. Wait, one Elias Blanchard, and one David Howard, all being master cordwainers and bootmakers, and prevent and hinder them from employing any journeymen bootmakers who would not become members of the society, or who should refuse or neglect to pay any sums of money demanded from them by such society, as a penalty for the breach of by-laws.

A printed copy of the constitution of the society was put in evidence against the defendants at the trial, and it was agreed that it might be referred to by the counsel in the argument, and by the court in considering the exceptions.

Robert Rantoul for the defendants, claimed: —

As we have no statute concerning conspiracy, the facts alleged in the indictment state an offence, if any, at common law, but the English common law of conspiracy is not in force in this State. We have not adopted the whole mass of the common law of England indiscriminately, nor of the English statute law which passed either before or after the settlement of our country. So much only of the common law has been adopted as is applicable to our situation.

Mr. Rantoul cited numerous authorities, among others, the case of The King *vs.* Journeymen Tailors (8 Mod., 10.) "In that case," said Mr. Rantoul, "it was held that a conspiracy among workmen to refuse to work under certain wages was an indictable offence. The doctrine of that law was not the common law when our ancestors came hither, and is not suited to our condition." He also claimed that the report of that case is not to be depended upon, being of no authority and entitled to no respect. Mr. Rantoul claimed that the English statutes of laborers were the blind struggles of the feudal nobles to avert from themselves the effects of great national calamities. He said, "a conspiracy to raise wages would not be indictable in England, if it were not unlawful for an individual to attempt to raise his wages. And the indictment, in the case at bar is bad, because each of the defendants had a right to do that which is charged against them jointly."

Attorney-General Austen appeared for the Commonwealth, and said that the charge, in effect, was an attempt to monopolize by them certain labor on their own terms, and to prevent others from obtaining or giving employment.

Chief Justice Shaw, in his decision, said:—

The general rule of the common law is, that it is a criminal and indictable offence, for two or more to confederate and to combine together, by concerted means, to do that which is unlawful or criminal, to the injury of the public, or portions or classes of the community, or even to the rights of an individual. This rule of law may be equally in force as a rule of the common law, in England and in this Commonwealth; and yet it must depend upon the local law of each country to determine, whether the purpose to be accomplished by the combination, or the concerted means of accomplishing it, be unlawful or criminal in the respective countries.

And again, he says:—

Without attempting to review and reconcile all the cases, we are of opinion, that as a general description, though perhaps not a precise and accurate definition, a conspiracy must be a combination of two or more persons, by some concerted action, to accomplish some criminal or unlawful purpose, or to accomplish some purpose not in itself criminal or unlawful, by criminal or unlawful means.

After reviewing the indictment, the court stated the case as follows:—

The manifest intention of the association is, to induce all those engaged in the same occupation to become members of it. Such a purpose is not unlawful. It would give them a power which might be exerted for useful and honorable purposes, or for dangerous and pernicious ones. If the latter were the real and actual object, and susceptible of proof, it should have been specially charged. Such an association might be used to afford each other assistance in times of poverty, sickness and distress; or to raise their intellectual, moral and social condition; or to make improvement in their art; or for other proper purposes. Or the association might be designed for purposes of oppression and injustice. But in order to charge all those who become members of an association with the guilt of a criminal conspiracy, it must be averred and proved that the actual, if not the avowed object of the association, was criminal. Supposing the object of the association to be laudable and lawful, or at least not unlawful, are these means criminal? The case supposes that these persons are not bound by contract, but free to work for whom they please, or not to work, if they so prefer. In this state of things, we cannot perceive that it is criminal for men to agree together to exercise their own acknowledged rights in such a manner as best to subserve their own interests, Suppose a class of workmen, impressed with the manifold evils of intemperance, should agree with each other not to work in a shop in which ardent spirits was furnished, or not to work in a shop with anyone who used it, or not to work for an employer who should, after notice, employ a journeyman who habitually used it. The consequences might be the same. A workman who should still persist in the use of ardent spirit would find it more difficult to get employment; a master employing such a one might, at times, experience inconvenience in his work, in losing the service of a skilful but intemperate workman. Still it seems to us, that as the object would be lawful, and the means not unlawful, such an agreement could not be pronounced a criminal conspiracy.

On the charge of depriving Jeremiah Horne of the profits of his business, the court gave, as an illustration, the case of a baker, in a small village, who had the exclusive custom of his neighborhood, and who was making large profits, and the neighbors, believing the price of his bread too high, after proposing to him to reduce the price, and, failing, introduce another baker, who set up a rival establishment and sold his bread at lower prices. "It might be said and proved," said the court,

That the purpose of the associates was to diminish his profits, and thus impoverish him, though the ultimate and laudable object of the combination was to reduce the cost of bread to themselves and their neighbors, We think, therefore, that associations may be entered into, the object of which is to adopt measures that may have a tendency to impoverish another, that is, to diminish his gains, and profits, and yet, so far from being criminal or unlawful, the object may be highly meritorious and public spirited.

The case referred to, in 8 Mod., 10, was the case of the King against the Journeymen Tailors, of Cambridge, Eng., in 1721, and was based on the statute, 7 Geo. 1, c. 13 (1720). As this case shows the operation of the conspiracy law under the acts which held the workingmen practically in a state of bondage, we have given space in the appendix for a brief summary of the case and of the statute under which the defendants were prosecuted.

In 1841 a firm of boat builders, in Bath, Me., consisting of four partners, mutually agreed to adopt the ten-hour system, and in 1844, one of the firm, then having charge of a marine railway, adopted the system on the repair of vessels. The feeling was so strong in favor of a reduction of the hours of labor that a combination was formed of many trades, some of them not directly connected with either house or ship-building. Public meetings were held, and public sentiment was aroused. The failure of the strikes in the preceding years had made the men extremely cautious. So strong was the feeling that the employers organized to offset the management, but public sentiment was too strongly in favor of the men. In a speech made by a judge of one of the courts, the attention of the Masonic fraternity was called to the proper division of time into three equal parts, "eight hours for work, eight hours for sleep, and eight hours for God and the brethren." All but two of the ship-yards in Bath finally yielded, and ten hours became the rule in that city.

The labor literature of 1838 to 1851 was marked by earnestness of purpose, fidelity to principle, and more than ordinary ability. A paper was published in New London, Ct., by Charles Douglass, a prominent member of the workingmen's party, the paper having but a short existence. The *Awl*, another paper advocating the claims of the workingmen, was much copied from. It is believed to have been published in Lynn. No copies of these papers can now be found, and the oldest labor paper before us is entitled the *Voice of Industry*, with the motto, "Hearken to me; I also will show mine opinion." As the oldest labor paper accessible, it deserves extended notice. It was published in Fitchburg,

Mass., by an association of workingmen, W. F. Young, now of Wakefield, Mass., being the editor. The first number was issued Thursday, May 29, 1845, and contained poetry, stories, lectures, editorials, news, and a very few advertisements. Some of the poems were original, and one of those appearing in the first number was "Moral Warfare," by John G. Whittier. The same paper contains an address by the editor before the workingmen's association, at Fitchburg, upon the existing evils of society, in which he says: "In the present state of society, labor becomes disreputable, friendship becomes insincere, and religion becomes hypocritical." Speaking of the Association before which he lectured, he said:

> It has no fellowship with the custom which makes one portion of our fellows workingmen and women, and obliges them to do all the labor, thereby making it irksome, tedious and undesirable, while the other is revelling in affluence and luxury. We believe all should labor, either physically, mentally or morally, and that all should enjoy perfect freedom in selecting those kinds of labor by which it would become a pleasure rather than a task, and lastly, that all should receive such a share of the fruits of their labor, as will conduce in the highest possible degree to their happiness. Thus it will be seen that none are excluded, that our area extends wherever man is known, from the civilized European down to the cannibals of the South Sea Islands.

In the editorial columns is found the statement of the imprisonment of Mike Walsh, incarcerated in a New York prison for an "alleged libel against a mercenary villain who had long glutted his coffers by plundering the poor of that city." On visiting Walsh in his cell, it is said some verses were found penciled on the walls as an apostrophe to a poor, dejected looking creature, which he had skilfully sketched beside them, representing a laborer in search of employment. We quote one verse of the three:

> The wealth which ingrate tyrants wield
>   To crush and starve us — WE create;
> The blood we shed on flood and field,
>   Give greatness to the MISNAMED great:
> But short would reign this favored few,
>   Were we but to each other true.

A touching incident regarding the factory system existing at that time is quoted in an early number of this paper, the gist of which is contained in the statement of a young and delicate girl of not more than eight or nine years, who said: "I go to work before daylight in the morning and never leave it until it is dark, and don't make enough to support mother and baby." In the same paper statistics of several factories in Lowell are given which show the following facts: that in those factories the capital was increased $500,000 in 1844; that the number of spindles was increased 11,624; that the number of females employed was decreased 430; that the wages in 1844 were two dollars per week, and in 1845 were one dollar and seventy-five cents per week; that the number of yards produced per week was increased 64,550; and that the dividends were increased from four and a half to twelve and a quarter per cent. The decrease in the number of operatives was said to have been effected by improvements in machinery. Referring to the increase of two hundred per cent. in the dividends and the decrease of twelve and a half per cent. in the wages of the females, it is stated that "this is the natural result of the state of things in New England — the more wealth becomes concentrated in a few hands, the poorer the great mass becomes." It also says: —

In this state of things the bounty offered to manufacturers by the tariff induced many of the wealthy men of New England to invest their capital in manufactures, which, when the tariff has been high, proved exceedingly profitable, concentrating immense wealth in the hands of a few, whilst the laboring part of the community has increased rapidly, until the demand for employment exceeds the want of the employers, which has enabled them to reduce the wages of the operatives whilst their own profits were very largely increased, and this reduction of wages must continue to go on with the increase of that class of society who depend upon employment for subsistence, until they arrive at a point which will barely afford such necessities as will enable the human system to undergo its daily toil.

Among the papers of this time in sympathy with the labor movement were the *New York Tribune*, *Daily Commercial*, *Weekly Bee*, *Harbinger*, *Ohio Eagle*, *Spirit of the Age*, *Workingmen's Advocate*, *Factory Girl's Friend*, *Young*

American, *Spirit of Liberty*, *People's Press*, *Cabotsville Chronicle*, *Mechanics' Mirror*, *Chronotype*, *People's Journal* (monthly), and *Equal Rights Advocate*.

The effort at co-operation most closely connected with the labor movement originated in Boston in 1844–5, and was organized and conducted by members of trades-unions and labor reform societies, although its first practical experiment was said to be an outcome of a temperance organization known as the Sons of Temperance. It may be noted that this co-operative enterprise of American workingmen originated at about the same time with that of the Rochdale Pioneers in England. In the same year these men, without knowledge of each other's effort, were attempting to solve the labor question by the formation of a combination, first to eliminate profit in traffic, and finally in production. The New England Workingmen's Association, in September of 1845, had resolved that concert of action in the purchase of the necessaries of life was the only means of securing the amelioration of the condition of the working people. The preamble to the constitution of the New England Protective Union shows that the leaders realized the necessity of something more than the mere saving of the profit upon goods, as will be seen by the following extract.

> We most firmly believe it is the imperative duty we owe one another and ourselves to give all the information in our power to the procurance of sure, steady and profitable employment, that we may have deeds of genuine sympathy which not only manifest themselves in relieving the destitute and administering to the sick, but those which strike at the root of poverty, such as will secure good pay and fewer hours of labor, and thereby in no ordinary degree remove the cause of poverty and sickness.

They commenced business with a box of soap and a half chest of tea. The organization grew slowly, the leaders still maintaining the grand idea of the elevation of the working classes. In the report of the committee on the organization of industry we find these words: "The dollar was to us of minor importance; humanitary and not mercenary were our motives." They believed that by the organization of co-operative industry, labor-saving machinery would labor for instead of against the interest of the poor. They say: "Man's muscles are now made to compete with iron machines that need no rest, that have no affections, eat no bread. Why is he who produces everything not only destitute of the luxuries but of the common comforts of life, to say nothing of a shelter he can call his own?" They saw the need of improving the condition of the working women, for they say: "Lamentable as is the condition of the laboring men, that of women is worse and increasingly so." Speaking of the newly-invented sewing machine, they say: "Let us take this and kindred machines and christen them for the good of the race by shortening the hours of labor, while at the same time we increase the product of labor."

These men had felt the tyranny of the employing class. They had witnessed the discharge of their fellows because of prominence in labor matters or because they dared to vote according to the dictates of their own consciences, and they desired to place men in such independent positions "that tyranny cannot say, 'Vote my ticket or leave my employ,' which, with wife and starving little ones before him, obliges him to succumb." Their bright dreams of the future pictured the displacement of the disease-breeding work-shops and the erection of grand palaces devoted to Labor and Love. They were also thoroughly imbued with the free soil sentiment of their time. They say: "We must proceed from combined stores to combined shops, from combined shops to combined houses, to joint ownership in God's earth, the foundation that our edifice must stand upon." They condemned the fugitive slave law as an infamous act, fitted to be trampled under the foot of every lover of justice and liberty, and pledged their lives and fortunes to its overthrow and final repeal. At this time (1850) they had formed 106 divisions, 83 of which returned a membership of over 5,000, with a capital of $71,890.36. In October, 1852, the purchases through the general agency amounted to over $1,000,000, and 167 of the subdivisions reported a capital of $241,712.66. A branch of the organization was formed in New York, under the name of the American Protective Union. These organizations practically ended in 1853 as efforts for the amelioration of the condition of the working classes, but trade was continued through their stores up to about the time of the war. Co-operative efforts were attempted in many parts of the country by members of trades-unions and other labor associations. As a general rule they failed as much from an ability to co-operate among the co-operators as from limited patronage.

The New England Workingmen's Association was organized in March, 1845, and held its first annual convention in Boston, May 28th of that year. Among those who participated we find the names of Charles A. Dana and George Ripley, of Brook Farm; A. Brisbane, of New York; Sarah G. Bagley, of Lowell; and Albert J. Wright, of Boston. A Lowell delegate reported 500 members of the Female Labor Reform Association. Robert Owen of Scotland, was also present and addressed the meeting; Mr. Dana and Mr. Brisbane addressing the convention in the evening. The following delegates were elected to attend the convention of the New York National Reform Association, having special reference to a call for a convention for forming a reformatory Constitution of the United States: From Boston, Albert J. Wright, Wendell Phillips, William Lloyd Garrison, Marcus Morton; Charlestown, Frederick Robertson; Brook Farm, L.W. Ryckman, Charles A. Dana; Lowell, Abijah Watson, A. Smith, Sarah G. Bagley, H. J. Stone, S. Hathaway; Lynn, N. W. Brown, Henry Clapp, William Phillips; Woburn, William Totman, Henry Wendell; Fall River, Thomas D. Chalmer, John Hull; West Roxbury, Theodore Parker; Stonington, A. T. Cowles, Thomas M. Brown; Fitchburg, P. C. Pettibone, John Scism.

A resolution was adopted recommending associations in various election districts to question all candidates for office in respect to their willingness to support and advocate measures of labor reform, general or specific, in which said association may from time to time be interested. Resolutions of regret at the discontinuance of the *New England Mechanic* shows that another labor paper had failed. On the Fourth of July of the same year a convention of the workingmen and women of New England was held at Woburn, at which about two thousand persons were present. Charles A. Dana, in his speech on that occasion, opposed the prevailing system of hard labor, which, as he said, generated hostility, and recommended unity of interest in an organized form as the panacea to cure the affection of oppressed labor and capital. Mr. Albert J. Wright said: "If we can judge future effects by present causes, the signs of the times are indicative of the long-looked-for millennium, and to those who charge us with being disorganizers we put the lie. Our object is to build up, — to promote human happiness, without regard to party, sect, creed or color."

The constitution of the New England Workingmen's Association, as published at that time, contained the following preamble: —

> WHEREAS, we, the mechanics and workingmen of New England, are convinced by the sad experience of years that under the present arrangements of society labor is and must be the slave of wealth; and, whereas, the producers of all wealth are deprived, not merely of its enjoyment, but also of the social and civil rights which belong to humanity and the race; and, whereas, we are convinced that reform of these abuses must depend upon ourselves, and ourselves only; and, whereas, we believe that in intelligent union alone is strength, we hereby declare our object to be union for power, power to bless humanity, and to further this object resolve ourselves into an association.

The terrible increase of want and pauperism in New York led to the issuing of a call for a workingmen's meeting at Croton Hall, on July 16th, 1845. This call states that there were 65,000 paupers in New York City alone; that one-sixth of the entire population of the state was in a condition of pauperism; that the compensation for labor was steadily sinking, until thousands were reduced to starvation; that the white labor of the North was in a worse state than the slave of the South. The call was issued for a general meeting of the trades and useful classes. It was signed with the names and occupations of twenty-four persons, all save one being mechanics, that exception being Dr. Newbury, a physician of Brooklyn.

The specially marked features of the movement during

1845, were the organization of women, and the appointment of women delegates to state and national conventions, and the organization of unskilled laborers, under the name of the "Laborers' Union Association." The organizations of women were very effective, and decidedly more radical in expressions than the organizations of unskilled laborers. Strikes occurred in the latter part of the summer and fall of this year. Welsh puddlers in the works at Pittsburgh and Alleghany City struck for higher wages, and evidently succeeded, as they are said to have had a perfect combination. The second convention of the New England Workingmen's Association was held in Fall River, September 11, 1845, Judge Lapham of Fall River being present and addressing the convention, together with other well-known reformers of that period. It continued in session two days, and adjourned to the 29th of October, at Lowell.

On the 16th of June a mass meeting of the working people of Pittsburgh and Alleghany City was held at Pittsburgh in favor of a ten-hour system, Pittsburgh papers reporting an attendance of at least five thousand persons, a large number of whom were females. During the convention a communication was received from five of the cotton manufacturing firms, in which the manfacturers say: —

> The undersigned manufacturers having received your communication on the subject of adopting the ten-hour system in our city, beg leave to say that although they do not admit the right of persons interfering between them and their operatives, and as they recognize the names of none of their operatives, either on this committee or in the proceedings of your meeting, yet they have no hesitation in saying that they believe it entirely impracticable to adopt that system here whilst in places the twelve-hour system is continued. They would inform you further that at present our mills run about sixty-eight hours per week, whilst the eastern factories of our own country make seventy-two hours per week. Believing, therefore, that the enforcement of such a system here would drive all cotton machinery from our borders, we cannot favor it.

This public meeting in favor of ten hours was followed by a strike in which it is said 4,000 persons were engaged. After remaining out five weeks the operatives returned under the old conditions. The Pittsburgh *Spirit of the Times* in reviewing the strike, said, "The manufacturers will not risk another five weeks' suspension for a slight consideration. They have lost 340 hours (by each person engaged) by the strike — more than half a year's loss at two hours per day."

The first Industrial Congress of the United States convened in New York, October 12, 1845, and was the result of the action of the New England Workingmen's League and the National Reform Association of New York. The Congress was organized by the election of W. S. Wait, of Illinois, as president; Charles Douglass, of Connecticut, E. N. Kellog, of New Jersey, and John Ferral, of Pennsylvania, as vice-presidents; and George H. Evans, Charles Sears and Moses Johnson as secretaries. Sarah G. Bagley represented the Female Labor Reform Association of Lowell and presented a written address. The Congress adopted a constitution. They also proposed a plan for the formation of a secret Industrial Brotherhood. The preamble, after giving its source of authority, states: —

> It is a well-known fact that rich men, capitalists and non-producers associate to devise means for securing to themselves the fruits of other men's labor, and that schemes for this purpose are invented and accomplished by combinations. Believing that no effectual resistance to these combinations can ever take place without united action of the same character on the part of those who labor and produce all, it is deemed expedient to recommend a plan of organization for the adoption of farmers, mechanics and workingmen throughout the United States.

The main feature of the preamble seems to be to secure the right of the soil to all, by limiting the possessions of farmers and corporations or communities; to prevent all further traffic in land by the government, and to make the public lands free to actual settlers, that every man, woman, and child in the nation may have a home. They denounced the then existing system of factory labor which was withering life's energies, even in childhood, producing by excessive toil physical deformity, and through lack of opportunity and means to acquire cultivation, deterioration of both mind and body.

Under Article 3, Section 1, it appears that no employer, overseer or superintendent could be admitted to the Brotherhood.

On the 29th of October the New England Workingmen's

Association convened in the City Hall at Lowell, pursuant to adjournment. Resolutions were introduced to the effect that resort to the polls was the only practical and effectual method that the workingmen could then adopt for the protection of their rights. The apathy of the workingmen and women themselves called for a resolution urging organization and agitation. Resolutions of sympathy and encouragement were passed in favor of the operatives on strike for ten hours in Pittsburgh.

In the latter part of 1845 and the spring of 1846, immense mass meetings were held in Massachusetts, New York, and Pennsylvania. In Lowell, Mass., and Manchester, N. H., the town halls were crowded to their utmost capacity. The people seemed to be aroused from their apathy, and public speakers were in great demand. The labor papers made an active canvass of the towns for subscribers, publishing letters, in which the condition of labor was described.

The ten-hour question was still in the ascendant, and Cassius M. Clay had entered the field as an advocate of that measure, and had taken an advanced position on the land question. In the City of Philadelphia a hundred dollars was raised by the workingmen in one factory, to aid in the universal establishment of the ten-hour system throughout the country. Petitions for ten hours, containing thousands of names, were presented to the Legislature of Massachusetts in 1846. Petitions of previous years had been ignored, and members of the Legislature were charged with attempting to intimidate and brow-beat the representatives of labor who appeared before the committees in advocacy of the measure. The manufacturers, in many places, discharged and victimized persons in their employ who took a prominent part in the movement. Efforts were made to break down the character of leading labor advocates. Especially was this true in the case of John C. Cluer, an eloquent Scotchman, who for a quarter of a century past has been known to the citizens of Boston, as he was then well known throughout all the cotton factory districts of the United States.

The persistent agitation of the Yankee factory girls for

better conditions in the manufacturing centres led at first to a system of obtaining help peculiar to that time. In Cabotville now known as Chicopee, a long, low, black wagon was employed in making regular trips to the northern part of Massachusetts, and around in Vermont and New Hampshire. The man having this team in charge was paid a dollar a head for all the girls he could secure, a larger amount being given, according as the distance travelled was greater. It is charged that he misrepresented facts to the girls thus engaged, telling them that the work was very neat, wages high, and that they could dress in silks, and spend half the time in reading.

The workingmen's associations of that time established libraries and reading rooms. In the Laborers' Union men were obliged to subscribe two dollars a year, and women one dollar for the library. They also established a fund for the relief of destitute members. A memorial was forwarded to Congress protesting against the system of land traffic, as wrong in principle. The memorialists say, "This system is imported to this country from Europe, and is fast debasing us to the condition of dependent tenants, of which condition a rapid increase of inequality, misery, pauperism, vice and crime are the necessary consequences, and therefore now, in the infancy of the republic, we should take effectual measures to eradicate the evil, and to establish a principle more in accordance with our republican theory as laid down in the Declaration of Independence." They proposed as a remedy that the general government should no longer traffic or permit traffic in the public lands, but that they should be laid out in farms and lots for the free use of such citizens, not possessed of other land, as would occupy them, allowing the settler to dispose of his possession to any one not possessed of other land; and that the jurisdiction of public lands be transferred to States only on condition that such a disposition should be made of them.

On January 16, 1846, the New England Workingmen's Convention met at Lynn, Mass., continuing in session two days. The following resolutions adopted by that convention will show the position taken by organized labor on the question of slavery : —

WHEREAS, there are at the present time three millions of our brethren and sisters groaning in chains on the Southern plantation; and, whereas, we wish not only to be consistent, but to secure to all others those rights and privileges for which we are contending ourselves; therefore,

Resolved, That while we honor and respect our forefathers for the noble manner in which they resisted British oppression, we, their descendants, will never be guilty of the glaring inconsistency of taking up arms to shoot and to stab those who use the same means to accomplish the same objects.

Resolved, That while we are willing to pledge ourselves to use all the means in our power, consistent with our principles, to put down wars, insurrections and mobs, and to protect all men from the evils of the same, we will not take up arms to sustain the Southern slave holder in robbing one-fifth of our countrymen of their labor.

Resolved, That we recommend our brethren to speak out in thunder tones, both as associations and as individuals, and to let it no longer be said that Northern laborers, while they are contending for their rights, are a standing army to keep three millions of their brethren and sisters in bondage at the point of the bayonet.

The custom of lighting up the factories in the morning and working an hour or more before daylight was thus treated by a resolution adopted at Peterboro, N. H. : —

Resolved, That although the evening and the morning is spoken of in the Scripture, yet in that book no mention is made of an evening in the morning. We therefore conclude that the practice of lighting up our factories in the morning, and thereby making two evenings in every twenty-four hours, is not only oppressive but unscriptural.

The joint standing committee on manufactures of the Massachusetts Legislature of 1846, to which were referred the petitions for ten hours, unanimously recommended that the petitioners have leave to withdraw. The objections of the committee to a ten-hour law were that it was unnecessary to legislate; that the evils complained of did not exist to an extent sufficient to require legislative interference. The committee thought if a man had the strength and constitution to labor fourteen hours per day, that the Legislature should not interfere. They expressed themselves as being jealous of the right of freedom of contract. They agreed that the Legislature had a right to interfere in the direction of the reduction of hours of labor for all persons employed by corporations, but thought that the less interference with business relations the better. During the fall of this year the labor associations issued circulars to the nominees for Congress and the State Legislatures, asking them to give their views on the land question, homestead exemption, the ten-hour system on all public works and in all establishments chartered by law, and the adjusting of salaries to an equal average compensation for useful and productive labor.

Agreeable to previous arrangements, delegates from several carpet factories throughout the United States met at Tammany Hall in the fall of 1846. Thirty-four delegates, representing thirty-one factories, and 1099 operatives, were present. The principal action of the convention was a protest against a reduction of wages. The statement was made that the manufacturers could make a profit of thirty to forty per cent. under the new tariff which was soon to go into effect, the reduction being on the plea that the new tariff operated against the manufacturers, while it was shown that when the tariff was increased in 1842 the manufacturers declined to raise the wages, saying it was home and not foreign competition they had to contend with, although they had previously cried out that it was foreign competition. A conference with the employers was called for Thursday of that week. Only two of the employers appeared.

About this time Horace Greeley gave his famous definition of slavery, in a private letter — a definition which applied to the white labor of the North with nearly as much force as to the black labor of the South. Corporations in Lowell and other cities were charged with stealing time by altering the clocks, and considerable evidence was submitted showing that it was true.

In January, 1847, resolutions were introduced into the Assembly, of New York, by Representative Walsh, declaring that the hours of labor which may be expected from apprentices and other minors ought to be limited and declared by law; that the number of hours of labor per day, which shall legally satisfy and fulfil a contract to work for any specified term, in the absence of any further agreement between the parties, ought also to be determined and declared by law; and that a select committee be appointed to consider generally the subject of the rights of the State, with regard to the hours of labor, to take testimony if they may deem it expedient, and to report thereon by bill or otherwise. This appears to be the first movement in the direction of state investigation of the relations of labor and capital.

The machinists of Boston held a meeting at Faneuil Hall, in May, 1847, at which it was resolved to hold a meeting on the Common, on May 24th, and that if the employers did not agree to reduce the hours of labor, they would start a co-operative establishment. The New York machinists were working ten hours at this time. The Boston machinists had no union, and one of the speakers said that if a union had been started three years before, the ten-hour system would then be in operation in Massachusetts.

The Second Industrial Congress convened at New York, June 10, 1847. Among the States represented were New York, New Jersey, Massachusetts, Pennsylvania, Delaware, Illinois and Kentucky. At this Congress it was resolved that a committee of seven be appointed to inquire into the extent, objects and means of trades-unions in the United States, and to report to the next Congress or to the executive committee. Several members spoke of the utility of the trades-unions that existed in the United States, and one inquired of Mr. Evans, of Boston, whether he belonged to the general trades-union, and could give any information in regard to it. Mr. Evans replied that his position as an employer at the time prevented his being a member, but that he had published the *Workingmen's Advocate*, which was the organ of the union; that at the largest convention of the union ever held in the City Hall, in 1834, resolutions had been passed in favor of the freedom of the public lands. The congress received a communication from the Fraternal Democrats in London to the Reformers of the United States, which led to considerable discussion as to the object of the Fraternal Democrats. The address was signed by George Julian Harney, a gentleman for a long time a contributor to the *Northern Star*, a Chartist paper, and other papers in England, and for twenty years afterwards connected with the office of the Secretary of State of Massachusetts. At this convention John C. Noble, from the Louisville, Ky., Typographical Union, was admitted as a delegate, and a communication was received from a farmer of Carter County, that state. The Mexican War was condemned in a resolution which stated "That this Congress do hereby recommend to national and all other labor reformers throughout the nation to nominate no candidate for congressional or legislative office who is not pledged to use the influence of his station, if elected, to withhold supplies from the United States Army now in Mexico, and to cause said army to be withdrawn as soon as possible." Miss Fannie Townsend, of Providence, R. I., was admitted as an honorary member of the congress.

The apathy and animosity of the clergymen on the labor question called forth the following resolution:

Resolved, That while we fully appreciate the labors of all in behalf of suffering humanity, we are constrained to declare, more in sorrow than in anger, that the great body of the so-called Christian Church and Clergy of the present day are fearfully recreant to the high and responsible duties upon them. That they sustain the blood-stained banner of capital and fraud in their crusade against labor, and have themselves become the fiercest of the vampire brood that gorge upon the veins of honest industry and justice; therefore we would warn them that if they would have those principles which they preach, and by which they profess to be governed, influence the people of this country, they must infuse into their teachings and practice more of truth, justice, and regard for the rights of humanity.

A long discussion ensued, the resolution being finally rejected.

That there were ministers at that time who joined their protest in favor of the workingmen is well known; and the protest of Rev. E. M. P. Wells in an appeal he made in behalf of the poor contained this strong language: "Why must I, the official servant of Him who went about doing good, only go about talking good?"

The congress voted to cause candidates to pledge themselves to limit the quantity of lands any individual might acquire, to exempt the homestead from alienation on account of any future debt, mortgage or other liability, to prevent all further traffic in the public lands, and to cause them to be laid out in farms and lots for the free and exclusive use of actual settlers, and to limit the hours of labor to ten on all public works and establishments chartered by law. To carry out the work of the congress, members were requested to pay five cents per month, two cents of which was to be at the disposal of the national executive committee, and the rest to be retained for defraying the expenses of their representatives, etc. The Industrial Congress took an advanced and decided ground on the question of temperance.

The three prominent features of the movement at this time were: first, a reduction of the hours of labor; second, a radical reform of the land traffic; third, co-operative or associate effort. Meanwhile the labor reformers of that time were among the most earnest of the anti-slavery men, favoring the abolition of capital punishment and the enfranchisement of woman. They were in full accord with the struggles of the men in England and Ireland, the name of Fergus O'Connor appearing frequently in the columns of the labor press at that time. The labor and reformatory press of that day spoke in no uncertain terms of the dangers that threatened our institutions through the power of accumulated wealth. In a paper published in 1847, the editor says:

> The few whose labor supports the mass will revolt. They will demand all the fruits of their labor. They will revolt against the principle that inanimate matter and ideal creatures are better entitled to legal care and legislative protection than the contracted muscles and mental and physical energies. Social revolutions of this character are inevitable. They will come. Every political organization has witnessed them, and until human nature is perfect and every man becomes so thoroughly civilized and christianized as to make laws and restraints unnecessary, until all men shall seek to do good and to do unto others as we wish them to do unto us, we shall have these discords and troubles.

During the year 1847 many strikes prevailed, some for shorter hours and some for higher wages; some of which were successful. There were strikes among cordwainers, bootmakers, tobacconists, tailors, journeymen-cabinetmakers, painters, and pump and block makers. Wages were low, and provisions and rents were high. A large foreign emigration had already set in, competing with American labor, thus antagonizing race against race, and finally resulting in the establishing of a strong native American sentiment, and in the organization of a native American party. This movement received a severe protest from the workingmen's organizations. But finally the foreigner was looked upon as an enemy, because his presence gave the manufacturer power to reduce wages more and more to the European level.

On receipt of the news of the passage of the ten-hour law by the British Parliament, in the early summer of 1847, mass meetings were held in the principal cities congratulating the people of England on their triumph. At a meeting of the mechanics and laborers at Albany, N. Y., July 2, 1847, it called forth a resolution hailing it as a step in progress not only invaluable in itself considered, but as the harbinger of a great industrial reform which was to sweep over the Old World and the New. They voted to continue the agitation for ten hours, the restoration of the rights of all to the soil, motive power and machinery, the freedom of the public lands to actual settlers, the exemption of the homestead from liability for debts or mortgages, the limitation of the amount of land which might be acquired by individuals, and the organization of industries. The *New York Tribune* of that date in speaking of the passage of the ten-hour bill, says: "The friends of humanity may rejoice at even this one step toward relieving the misery of the poverty-stricken and oppressed operatives. If no other measures had occupied the attention of Parliament during the session, this one would alone redeem all its sins of omission and commission."

On the third day of July, 1847, a law was passed in New Hampshire making ten hours a legal day's work, and although the working people knew this law to be a cheat and a sham, still they hailed it as an event worthy of notice. Newspapers reported tremendous excitement in Manchester and Nashua, N. H., and other factory towns. The largest halls were crowded with enthusiastic working people.

Some of the abolitionists were impatient at the labor

reformers because they used the term "white slaves" when speaking of factory operatives and other classes of low-paid labor. Wendell Phillips in a speech before the Anti-slavery Society during anniversary week, 1847, said, while asking the anti-slavery people to abstain from the use of the products of slave labor, in other words calling for a boycott, "in my opinion the great question of labor, when it shall come up, will be found paramount to all others, and the operatives of New England, peasants of Ireland, and laborers of South America, will not be lost sight of in the sympathy for the Southern slave." A labor paper, in calling attention to these remarks, says: "Mr. Phillips is on the high road to the principles of social reform. May he and like philanthropists be brought to see that slavery, war, poverty, and oppression are inseparable from the system of civilization, the system of antagonism of interests; that the only effectual remedy is the introduction of a higher system of union of interest and union of industry."

An effort was made in 1847 to break down the ten-hour system. The ship-builders of Bath, Me., bound themselves together under heavy penalties to insist on the old hours. When the short days of the winter season had passed, the employers demanded the old system of working from sun to sun, and for some weeks not a stroke of work was done in any of the yards. Public opinion continued on the side of the men, and finally the employers were forced to yield. The success of the movement was hastened by the action of one of the employers, a man who was in sympathy with the men and their cause. As soon as he saw the employers were weakening he visited the men at their houses, and engaged the best skilled labor in the town, setting them to work on the ten-hour system. The prominent position taken by Mr. H. T. Delano in the movement led one of the richest ship-builders to attempt a boycott. Efforts were made to deprive Mr. Delano of his position as superintendent of a marine railway. A man was engaged to take his place, but upon learning the circumstances he refused to be made the tool of injustice, and Mr. Delano retained his place. The panic of

1847 tended to demoralize the trades-union movement, although the agitation by the labor and land reformers, etc., was continued.

In contrast to the employers who were opposing the labor organizations, it is worthy of note that in 1848 the employees of the firm of Knapp & Totten, of Pittsburgh, Penn., three hundred in number, gave a complimentary supper to the members of that firm. Mr. Totten, in his speech on that occasion said that he believed that he was the first employer to adopt the ten-hour system, but that this was not enough, he would like to see the time of labor shortened to eight hours; that the tendency of things was that way, and that society would be vastly the gainer, and no one the loser, if all would agree to it.

The uprising in Europe in 1848 renewed the agitation of American socialism and labor reform generally. Meetings were called by various craftsmen, and resolutions were passed congratulating the French people. The Franklin Typographical Society of Boston met April 1, 1848, and voted to transmit an address to the printers of Paris "in response to the glorious events of the recent revolution in France, in which they bore so noble, patriotic, and conspicuous a part." In their address the printers say:—

We rejoice to learn that the tendency of events in France is to social reform, and that the French people are demanding that reorganization of society which shall secure to the laboring man the fruits of his skill and industry. To us this is the noblest feature of your revolution, for we are convinced that mere political reforms do not effect much for the mass of mankind. The people have done enough for the self-styled higher classes; it is time now to work for themselves. They should proceed as if they knew and recognized the truth contained in the noble words of one who, at different periods of his life, was a citizen of France and of the United States, namely, "That gold in its last analysis is the sweat of the poor and the blood of the brave." As Americans engaged in a vocation which you have honored and illustrated by heroic deeds, as citizens of that community which France was first to welcome to the list of nations, and to sustain whose nationality and freedom she poured out her blood and treasure, as bearing in our united capacity the name of that man who formed the first treaty between France and the United States, and was at once a philosopher, a statesman, a friend of the human race, and a printer, we venture to address the printers of Paris as men.

At a mass meeting of workingmen in Faneuil Hall, May

9th, who met to congratulate each other on the auspicious events in Europe, and to express their views in relation to reform, at which Albert J. Wright presided, the first three resolutions passed were congratulatory to the working people of France and the provisional government, and expressed their grateful sympathy for the Chartists in England and the Repealers in Ireland. The fourth and fifth resolutions were as follows:

While we rejoice in the organization of free institutions in the old world, we are not indifferent to their support at home, and we regret the despotic attitude of the Slave Power at the South, and the domineering ascendancy of the Monied Oligarchy in the North as equally hostile to the interests of labor, and incompatible with the preservation of popular rights. *Resolved*, that if we would procure the passage of just and efficient laws to protect labor, and raise it from its present degrading dependence on wealth, we must purge the halls of legislation of the hirelings who basely pander to the interests of capital, and to accomplish this result we recommend for the laboring classes to try for once the experiment of trusting the management of their political affairs to men of their own class, who know their interests and have a fellow-feeling in supporting them.

They also formulated the following measures: first, reduction of the hours of labor; second, an efficient lien law; third, the freedom of the public lands; fourth, the inalienability of the homestead; fifth, the abolition of the poll-tax as a condition of the elective franchise; sixth, an industrial department in the government; seventh, destruction of all white and black slavery; eighth, reduction of officers and salaries, especially those of eight dollars a day and upwards, to the standard of all useful and necessary labor. The meeting was addressed by Horace Seaver, John Turner, Elizur Wright and John C. Cluer.

On May 11th the ten-hour order was introduced into the Massachusetts House of Representatives, but was rejected in the Senate.

In Philadelphia, in the same month, the male and female loom-weavers adopted resolutions, and were anxious to see some form devised to completely revolutionize the present iniquitous system by which those who toil most receive least, and those who toil least receive most, and see labor organized on the basis preached by St. Paul, so that "if anyone would not work, neither should he eat." An industrial convention was held at Philadelphia, nominating Gerritt Smith, a national land reformer, as a candidate for the presidency.

The discovery of gold in California again stimulated labor, increasing the cost of living, and thus necessarily forcing the demand for increased wages.

Up to this time the agitation and public discussion of the land and labor questions had been conducted largely by open general organizations. The social, economic, and religious ostracism or boycotting of the leaders forced the organization of secret societies. The trades-unions, who were extremely conservative, were rather impatient of socialism, and the several community movements. They wanted less hours of labor and higher wages, and saw the necessity of combining themselves in their several trades to accomplish these objects.

In this year (1848) petitions were sent to Washington, praying for a ten-hour law, and a law restraining persons from employing children in factories over eight hours a day, and obliging those employing them to give them an opportunity to obtain a common-school education.

The trades began to organize as never before. Organization extended so far westward as to warrant the calling of the Industrial Congress, at Chicago, Ill., on the second Wednesday of June, 1850. The platform adopted at that convention was modeled after that of the New England Association. In the same year a city congress of labor was formed in New York, consisting of delegates from the several organizations, and through its instrumentality and the public agitation, the organization of other crafts received a new impetus. The saddlers, silversmiths, iron and metal workers, steam-boiler makers, lady milliners, bookbinders, tanners, lady shoemakers, riggers, sailmakers, watch-case makers, coach painters, sash and blind makers, window-shade painters, carvers, gilders, upholsterers, bakers, laborers, and dry-goods clerks joined their forces with the trades already organized. There were many strikes at about this time among the carpenters, the most notable one being that of the carpenters of New York.

who struck for one dollar and seventy-five cents per day, and marched through the streets in a procession a quarter of a mile long and four deep. A co-operative association of iron moulders was formed in Cincinnati, O., and strikes of iron workers occurred in Pittsburgh, St. Louis and other places.

In Philadelphia the movement had become equally important with a strong tendency towards co-operative effort. Workingmen's conventions were held to discuss the labor question, a demand for homestead exemption and free public lands being included in nearly all of their platforms. The Printers' Union organized a trades bureau of statistics for gathering statistics of labor. Horace Greeley delivered a lecture at a mass meeting of printers in New York, in which he strongly urged the necessity of more thorough organization, and the special necessity of the trades-unions regulating wages and hours of labor, and in which he complained of the indifference and inattention of the laboring classes, especially the printers, to the discussion of truths so great and so important as the rights of labor. He said: "The laboring class, as a class, is just where it was when I came here eighteen years ago, or, if anything, in a worse condition."

The workingmen in Baltimore, Md., succeeded in carrying a bill through the House of Delegates making ten hours a day's work, but they were unwise enough to have an exemption made in the case of a special contract. The sewing women of Philadelphia made a strong effort to form a co-operative establishment. Efforts were made in the principal cities to obtain short hours for persons employed in mercantile establishments, one of the meetings in New York being presided over by the mayor, and addressed by John Van Buren and others.

The ten-hour system had been adopted in some places in some of the mechanical trades, and the movement in its favor had become so strong as to gradually ameliorate the condition of the factory operatives. Strikes occurred in many of the industries, each success giving renewed hope, and each failure awakening renewed efforts for organization. The increased immigration of the cheaper labor of Europe to this country rendered many of the attempts at improvement abortive. When a strike occurred, especially in the factories, foreigners were imported to take the places of the operatives on strike. As an illustration of this, we give an account of a strike occurring in Massachusetts in 1851.

The factory operatives of Amesbury and Salisbury were at the time of this strike very largely American citizens, a great portion of them being the owners of their homes. For years this corporation had been under the management of a Mr. Horton and had declared dividends as high as thirty per cent. The hours of labor were extremely long, being from five in the morning until seven at night, with half an hour for breakfast and three-quarters of an hour for dinner. A custom prevailed for the men to go out at ten o'clock in the forenoon, under what was called the "luncheon privilege," remaining fifteen or twenty minutes, and then returning to their work. With many it was the habit to purchase supplies in the open market, or "Market Square," as it was called. Upon the retirement of Mr. Horton from the position of agent, the employees presented him with a silver service, and great regret was felt by them at losing so good an agent, he having helped many of them to the ownership of their homes.

After assuming control, the new agent had a notice posted in the mills practically abolishing the "luncheon privilege." No attention being paid to it, another notice was posted, stating that any person leaving his work between the hours of starting the wheel and shutting down would be discharged On the day when the notice was to go into effect, the spinners of the large mill left their work in a body, and marched down the yard to the square, the block printers, mechanics, and other employees following. Upon the return of the men they were discharged by the overseers, and, taking their aprons and tools, retired from the yard. A meeting was called and addresses made; great enthusiasm prevailed. On the following day a temperance banner, containing the words "Come with us and we will do you good," was procured, and the men taking this banner at luncheon time, marched to the gate of the mill-yard, when the weavers (women) left their looms, and joined the men, thus practically closing the mill.

A band of music was procured, and the procession marched to the house of the former agent, and giving him three cheers, passed down to the residence of the new agent, and saluted him with hisses. No threats of violence were offered, and the utmost good nature existed until one of the prominent members, A. G. Carey, afterwards elected to the Governor's Council, was arrested, tried and acquitted at Newburyport. Many men and boys walked from Amesbury to Newburyport a distance of six miles, to witness the trial.

Two Boston policemen were engaged to assist in guarding the property, and parties were sent out to procure new help. These agents of the company secured some fifty or more persons, mostly recent immigrants from Ireland, but no private boarding place could be found for them. The proprietor of the hotel fitted up his dance-hall with mattresses and blankets for their accommodation. Boys gathered in the vicinity, and stones were thrown at the building, breaking some glass.

During the strike the overseers, some twenty in number, met at the house of an overseer, who was a deacon of the Orthodox Church, on Saturday night, remaining in session until past the midnight hour, thus infringing upon the Sabbath, to the great scandal of the members of the Church. The result of this meeting was the publication of a manifesto supporting the corporation, as against the employees.

On Sunday morning those ignorant of the fact were surprised to find posted upon the pillars of the Orthodox Congregational Church, written notices to the effect that at the close of divine service the overseers of the Salisbury Manufacturing Company would hold a meeting for the transaction of important business. At the church meeting one of the overseers, a deacon, acknowledged his error in transacting secular business on the holy day. The Amesbury *Villager* contained not only articles in prose but also verse dedicated to the factory bell. It was the custom of the men to gather about the gates in the morning, forming a double line, and every man who entered the gate to go to work was soundly hissed. The strike lasted nearly six months, and during the strike, on the morning of July 5th (the 4th of July coming on Sunday), one of the corporation buildings, a mile from the village, was discovered to be on fire, and was burned to the ground. A reward was offered for the apprehension of the incendiary, but the origin of the fire was never learned. It is said that the hose of the fire engine was cut and the fire buckets rendered useless. The strike resulted in a failure, though many of the men engaged in it never returned to work for the corporation, and the foreign population of the town was considerably increased by the operatives who took their places. The only organization existing there at that time was a branch of the Block-Printers' Union. The block-printers were English, and worked but ten hours a day. They were not discharged upon returning from their luncheon. We remember reading in the village paper the story of "The Old White Horse on a Strike." The corporation was the owner of a powerful white horse which was very vicious. His driver, a tall, raw-boned Yankee, finding that his fellows were discharged for taking the luncheon privilege, refused to return to work, although permitted to do so by the superintendent, and he left the horse in the market square. No one else could induce him to go to the stable, and he remained there, the pet of the men, until his old driver returned him to his stall, where he was obliged to care for him day after day.

It was on the occasion of this strike that the editor of this book, then a boy at work in the mill, received his baptism into the labor cause.

The demand for legislation on the hours of labor was renewed, and many of the men who afterwards became prominent in the history of the country were elected upon that issue, especially in Massachusetts. Among the men elected in that State favorable to ten-hour legislation, as early as 1851 and 1852, were Benjamin F. Butler, Nathaniel P. Banks, Henry Wilson, William Claflin, William S. Robinson, and James M. Stone. Some of the strong Whig towns of the state for the first time sent Democratic representatives, the town of Amesbury, Mass., having the honor to elect the gentleman who introduced the ten-hour bill of that year, which passed the House and was defeated in the Senate.

In 1853 eleven hours was adopted in many parts of the country as the work-day, apparently for the purpose of heading off the ten-hour movement. In some places the factories continued to be run on the old hours until about 1865, when the eleven-hour system was adopted, as the result of strikes; one manufacturer, who owned a small mill, saying, that as they were making a thousand dollars a week, the cheapest way was to grant the request of the strikers and set them to work.

From 1851 to 1857 the isolated trades-unions and labor organizations saw more and more the necessity of national and international organizations. In many of the cities and large towns delegates of the several trades held irregular meetings to discuss any special case then pending, and conventions of different craftsmen were called for the purpose of better organization. National and international trades-unions were organized, granting charters to the local bodies and organizing new branches from Maine to California. Strikes continued to occur, both in organized and unorganized trades, the demands at this time being principally for increased wages. The ship carpenters and joiners and calkers were still the pioneers in the movement for the reduction of hours, and having been the first to gain ten hours, they were the first to gain eight hours. In fact, within a period of sixteen years, they changed their system of working from sun to sun to eight hours per day. The success in supplying the great demand for shipping during the early California days showed the practicability of the ten-hour system under a most severe strain. Local organizations continued to increase, often, as heretofore, the result of strikes.

The organized men began to discover the importance of funds to carry on their work, and adopted a system of allowances from the funds of the associations to such members as needed assistance during strikes. The men who had been compelled to live near their work during the long hour system commenced to move farther and farther back from their places of work, many of them living three and five miles from the shipyards. The panic of 1857, like the preceding panics of 1837 and 1847, tended to break up the organizations, reducing their membership, but leaving a remnant to carry the standard. In 1859 the Machinists' and Blacksmiths' Union held a convention in Philadelphia, at which they strongly advocated the eight-hour movement.

The increased agitation of the question of slavery absorbed the attention of the public, many of the wisest of the labor men being of the opinion that no great progress could be made until after the destruction of the chattel slave system.

The introduction of means for rapid production brought with it extraordinary dangers to life and limb. Under the stimulating influence of profit-gaining, individual employers and corporations took but little heed of the necessity of securing the employees from the dangers incident to belts and machinery and crowded mills and work-shops. In this brief synopsis of the labor movement we could give no space to the accidents in mines, mills, and work-shops and on railroads, but we cannot end this chapter without mentioning the Pemberton Mill catastrophe, which occurred in Lawrence, Mass., January 10, 1860.

While the machinery of the mill was in motion, the main building fell without warning, and a conflagration broke out. Out of the 700 persons in the building at the time, 77 were killed and 134 injured, of whom 14 afterwards died. Cause of the disaster, faulty construction of the pillars and the lack of adhesive power in the mortar. The following is a description by Miss Elizabeth Stuart Phelps: —

> Who shall say what it was to the 750 souls who were buried in the ruins? What to the eighty-eight who died that death of exquisite agony? What to the wrecks of men and women who endure even to this day a life that is worse than death? What to the architect and engineer who, when the fatal pillars were first delivered to them for inspection, had found one broken under their eyes, yet accepted the contract, and built with them a mill, whose thin walls and wide, unsupported stretches never could keep their place unaided?
>
> One that we love may go the battle ground, and we are ready for the worst; we have said our good-bye; our hearts wait and pray; it is his life, not his death, which is the surprise; but that he should go out to his safe, daily commonplace occupation, unnoticed and uncaressed, scolded a little, perhaps,

because he leaves the door open and tells us how cross we are this morning, and they bring him up the steps, by-and-by, a mangled mass of death and horror, — that is hard.

The little band of men who commenced the agitation of the labor movement in 1825 to 1832 had witnessed the growth of that movement until it had commanded the attention of the student and the philanthropist as well as many of the most intelligent wage-workers. Their isolated unions had grown into great national and international organizations of craftsmen, numbering their members by tens of thousands. Members of legislative bodies had been forced to discuss the labor question. The arrogant assumption of power by the controlling classes had been met fearlessly and often overcome, in argument and otherwise, by the organizations of which they were founders. They had witnessed the demand for ten hours, at first ridiculed, now acknowledged by all to be a benefit. The semi-annual and quarterly payments had in many places given way to the weekly and monthly systems. The militia laws had been revolutionized, and in some places lien laws had been enacted. But above all as the very pioneers of the anti-slavery question, they had seen the public sentiment of the community turn from apathy or approval into earnest condemnation. They had clasped hands across the ocean with their brothers of England and Ireland, and France and Germany, and with all peoples who were attempting to secure a better condition in life. No body of men could claim as much as they for statesmanship. They had begun a social revolution which was soon to reach a climax by the abolition of the chattel system through blood, and bright hopes were entertained that with its fall the wage-system would peacefully be evolved out of existence, and the co-operative system come to bless mankind.

CHAPTER V.

PROGRESS OF THE MOVEMENT FROM 1861 to 1886.

Agitation and Organization During the War — First Organization of Horse-Car Drivers — Supreme Mechanical Order of the Sun — Grand Eight-Hour League — Early Closing Movement — Mass Meetings of Working Women — Conspiracy Laws — Return of the Army to Industrial Pursuits — Labor Newspapers — Public Meetings — Processions and Strikes — The Grand Revival of 1866 — Revival of the Eight-Hour Movement — Discussion in Congress — Passage of the Law in 1868 — Non-enforcement of the Law — National Labor Congress in Baltimore — Trades Represented — Knights of Labor Organize, 1869 — Patrons of Husbandry — First Bureau of Statistics of Labor — Great Strike of the Coal Miners — Boston Eight-Hour League — International Workingmen's Association — Great Eight-Hour Strike, 1872 — National Industrial Congress, Rochester, N. Y., 1874 — Railroad Strikes of 1877; Military Called Out; Lives Lost; Property Destroyed; International Labor Union of America — Great Libel Case, Paterson, N. J. — Colored Exodus — Federation of Organized Trades and Labor Unions — The Great Uprising of Labor in 1886.

THE war of the chattel labor masters upon the Republic concentrated the whole force of the patriotic labor masses of the North, East, and West. They left their tools of industry and took up the implements of war. Never was there such a patriotic uprising of the common people. They proved themselves worthy of their inheritance. Their hearts made the breast-work of defence, not only of the Union, but of the possessors of wealth. At first the industries trembled, but the demand for arms and equipments, and the distribution of money by bounties, soon compelled more rapid production. Strikes occurred in some places to compel the advance of wages, and the demand for less hours of labor was voiced by factory operatives and trades-unions.

It may be said that the eight-hour movement obtained its great impetus during the war. An intelligent agitation was commenced, and demands were made for labor legislation. Many old unions were re-organized, national and international trades-unions created, and local unions and labor associations sprung up everywhere. In 1861 the horse-car drivers of New York formed a benevolent association, John Walker, who has been a driver on the Third-avenue line for twenty years, being the founder. This organization discountenanced strikes, but as reduction after reduction took place they were compelled to unite upon the question of wages. The coal miners organized a National Association in 1861. The Boston United Laborers' Society was organized in 1862, the hack-drivers in 1863, and the locomotive engineers in the latter year. The Garment Cutters' Association, from whose members sprung the Order of the Knights of Labor, was organized at this eventful period. In California the scattered trades-unions of the cities, and especially of San Francisco, formed an amalgamation.

This nearly completed the circle of organization of the wage-laborers. Secret associations, with signs and passwords, were established, the largest in point of numbers being the Supreme Mechanical Order of the Sun, an organization with an extensive ritual, having numerous degrees. The Grand Eight-hour League, and other associations whose names were never given to the public, were organized. Through the power of these orders workingmen were elected to legislative bodies in several of the States. At the councils, conventions and congresses of the labor organizations during the war resolutions of a patriotic nature were passed. The cost of living had more than kept pace with the wages of the workers, and discontent was general. The building trades were especially active in the movement.

In the early part of 1863 strikes were prevalent in many of the industries. Ship carpenters demanded three dollars per day, and mechanics and laborers in the Navy Yard were also moving for an increase of wages. It was during this trying time of the Republic that the organized workingmen of England manifested in unmistakable terms their love for our institutions, as referred to by Professor James in Chapter III., and as acknowledged by President Lincoln in the early part of February of that year. The clerks in different departments pressed their claim for the early-closing movement, and mass-meetings of women were held, at which the terrible condition of the working women of the large cities was exposed and a strong public sentiment created in their favor. The shipwrights of New York City formed an association for intellectual and social improvement, established a reading room and library and listened to a course of lectures.

The draft of 1863, which practically exempted the wealthy by the payment of the small sum of three hundred dollars, was felt to be unjust to the laboring men, and advantage was taken of this feeling to create disloyalty to the Union and bitterness against the negro. A meeting of mechanics was held in Tammany Hall, and Horace Greeley was present. Mr. Greeley was called upon and very unwillingly addressed the assembly. After he had retired, he was shamefully abused by some of the speakers. This was followed by monster meetings in which all disloyal sentiments uttered in the name of labor were strongly condemned. Strikes continued to multiply, generally for an advance of wages.

Among the longshoremen and railroad employees assaults were made upon the non-unionists who took the places of the men on strike. In New York negroes were engaged to take the places of longshoremen. The negroes were assaulted, but the police succeeded in restoring order. It was not many years after this that the white and colored men joined in a trades-union procession for eight hours, some of the colored leaders riding in carriages, and the colored organizations being received into the procession with a salute.

In the spring of 1864 efforts were made in some of the State Legislatures for the enactment of laws, termed laws against intimidation, but really so drawn as to practically destroy all trades-union organizations. Section 1 of the bill presented in the New York Assembly read as follows: "Be it enacted, that if any person shall, by violence to the person or property of, or by threats or intimidation, or by molesting, or in any way obstructing another, force or endeavor to force any workman or other person hired in any manufacture, trade or business, to depart from his work before the same shall be finished," etc., giving then the penalty.

Mr. Greeley, in commenting upon this in the *Tribune*, said: "There is force in the objection that the acts it reprobates are already misdemeanors punishable under existing laws. We are inclined to the opinion that Mr. Folger's bill, if enacted, would do more harm than good."

The organizations continued to increase in membership. In 1864 the Cigar-Makers' International Union was formed. The stone-cutters, blacksmiths, carpenters and laborers in the forts in New York struck for twenty-five per cent. advance, the longshoremen asked for $2.50 per day of nine hours, the mechanics in the Brooklyn Navy Yard asked for an advance of wages, pianoforte-makers organized to secure higher wages, the sewing women of New York and Philadelphia held mass-meetings, and the mates of merchant ships held a meeting for an increase of pay. The journeymen tailors formed a national trades-union in Philadelphia in September, 1865.

It was not until the breaking up of the rebellion and the return of the Grand Army of the Republic to the grand army of labor, from the processes of destruction to the processes of production, that the full force of this movement was developed. Labor newspapers began to multiply, perhaps the most important move in this direction being the establishment of the *Daily Evening Voice* by the Boston Typographical Union, which had a continued existence of two or three years. Great public meetings were held, strikes occurred, and labor processions marched through the streets. State conventions of workingmen were held in Indiana, Illinois and New York; at those in Indiana and New York nearly all the trades being represented.

In Massachusetts an order was introduced into the Legislature by a Union soldier, instructing the Judiciary Committee to consider the expediency of regulating and limiting the hours of labor to constitute a day's work. As a result an unpaid commission was appointed by Governor Andrew to investigate the subject of the hours of labor. The report of this committee was unsatisfactory to the labor men, and the next year Governor Bullock appointed three commissioners: the Honorable Amasa Walker, William Hyde and Edward H. Rogers.

The workingmen of some of the large cities celebrated the Fourth of July by processions and orations. The position given the returned soldiers by the labor men contrasted with that given them by the city of Boston, where the Aldermen rode in barouches and the veterans in express wagons. The *Daily Evening Voice*, then published in Boston, in a pungent editorial, commented on this, and said: "When labor is paid as it deserves, and not overworked, it will be impossible to keep the honors of the world from the workingmen, and such an exhibition as that of the Boston procession cannot occur."

The year 1866 witnessed a grand revival of the labor movement. Isolated unions and associations came more and more to see the necessity of amalgamation. An active propoganda was aroused, and new organizations were continually multiplying. From thirty to forty national and international trades-unions and amalgamated societies were in existence, some of them numbering tens of thousands of men. The people of to-day have little conception of the extent of the labor movement of twenty years ago.

In the professional and personal occupations we find among those organized barbers and hairdressers, hostlers, clerks; in trade and transportation, commercial travellers, railroad employees, telegraphers, packers, sailors on the lakes; in manufacturing, mechanical and mining industries, packers, blacksmiths, blind, door, and sash makers, bookbinders, boot and shoemakers, brass founders, brush-makers, cabinetmakers, carpenters and joiners, carpet workers, cigarmakers, clock and watchmakers, coopers, cotton-mill operatives, flax-dressers, gilders, glass-work operatives, gold and silversmiths and jewellers, harness and saddle makers, hat and cap makers, hosiery and kitting-mill operatives, iron and steel workers, leather curriers, dressers, finishers and tanners, machinists, marble and stone-cutters, masons (brick and stone), miners, nail-makers, organ-makers, painters, paper-hangers, pianoforte-makers, plasterers, plumbers, printers, pump and block makers, quarrymen, roofers and slaters, sail-makers, ship-carpenters, calkers and riggers, silk-mill operatives, steam-boiler makers, tailors, trunk-makers, upholsterers, and woolen-mill operatives. These associations had, in many cases, organizations for different parts of their industries.

In the principal cities, and in some of the larger towns, the trades assemblies or central trades and labor councils were continued in various forms, and where none had existed, the meetings of the officers of the different associations convened, and sometimes by correspondence, sometimes through the experience of members of the several unions, they formed their central bodies, many of them at that time being termed trades assemblies. Some of the men who were then prominent in the movement have become employers, some are prominent in public positions, and some finished their work before the present great uprising of labor. To the credit of the cause, it can be said of almost all, living and dead, that they maintained their principles, and if retiring from active participation in the work, still gave their sympathy to it. The few demagogues, failing to make money or fame, have since found both in the service of wealth.

Labor legislation was enacted in many of the States of the Union, especially in the direction of education and of limiting the hours of labor for children. Massachusetts' greatest orator, Wendell Phillips, had taken a prominent position upon the question, and General H. K. Oliver, of Salem, one of the first educators of the State, had spoken in no uncertain words, through his report on factory children.

The eight-hour system had been introduced in the colony of Victoria, Australia by operative stone masons. The stone masons commenced the movement and were joined by the bricklayers, carpenters, joiners, plasterers and slaters, who formed themselves into an association for the purpose of securing it and called the other trades to their assistance. The first meeting was called together by the stone masons on March 27,

1856, the builders and contractors thinking the movement ought to be accepted by the whole of the building trades before it should go into operation. The meeting was the result of this suggestion offered by the contractors. Some of the contractors were present. It was voted to enforce the rule on the 21st of April. The second meeting was held on the 21st of April, at which the mayor, John Thomas Smith, presided, the masons paying all the expenses of the meeting. The mayor offered a cup, valued at £10, as a prize for the best essay showing the advantages to be derived from the eight-hour system to the workingmen in particular and to society in general, the essays to be judged and the prizes awarded by the professors of the university. The first prize was awarded to Mr. Best, a chemist. This movement awakened the ship-carpenters of California to make an attempt in the same direction.

In the early part of the year 1866, eight-hour bills were introduced in the United States Congress by Mr. Rogers, of New Jersey; Mr. Niblack, of Indiana; Mr. Brown, of Missouri, and Mr. Julian, of Indiana; and Mr. Ingersol, of Illinois, introduced a resolution to adopt the eight-hour system for the District of Columbia. After some discussion on Mr. Ingersol's resolution, a vote was taken, no quorum being present. There were but 111 members present at this time. Mr. Ingersol demanded the yeas and nays, but they were not ordered. On the motion to lay on the table the yeas and nays were ordered, the result being—yeas, 156; nays, 92; not voting, 76. As the morning hour had arrived, the resolution went over till the next Monday. March 28, 1867, Mr. Banks, of Massachusetts, introduced an eight-hour bill. The question was taken upon suspending the rules so it could be introduced—yeas, 78; nays, 23; not voting, 63. As two-thirds voted in favor of the motion, the bill was introduced. Mr. Banks moved the previous question, which was ordered, and the bill passed. Senator Conness, of California, and Senator Wilson, of Massachusetts, advocated the bill. It was referred to the Committee on Finance.

On November 29, 1867, Mr. Niblack again introduced

an eight-hour bill. It was referred to the Committee on Education and Labor, and in the Senate, Mr. Sherman of Ohio, reported for the Finance Committee that it asked to be discharged from the further consideration of the Banks bill, which was agreed to. An eight-hour bill was finally passed in 1868, and was signed by President Johnson.

After its passage by Congress, the officers having it in charge failed to report it, and President Grant issued a proclamation on the 19th of May, 1869, directing that no reduction should be made in the wages of laborers, workmen, and mechanics in the employ of the United States, by reason of the reduction of the hours of labor. Still the provisions of this law continued to be evaded, or utterly disregarded on the part of many officers and agents, when the President, on the 11th of May, 1872, issued another proclamation calling attention to the provisions of the act and directing all officers of the executive department having charge of the employment or payment of laborers, workmen and mechanics to make no reduction in the wages on account of the reduction in the hours of labor. The government officials still failed to enforce the law, when pressure was brought to bear upon Congress to pass an additional resolution. On the 18th of May, 1872, Congress passed an act securing to all laborers, workmen and mechanics employed by the government between June 25, 1868, and May 19, 1869, pay or compensation on the basis of a full, regular day's pay for eight hours'labor. Two months afterwards the Navy Yard authorities reduced the wages one-fifth, and a committee appointed by the Columbia Typographical Society of Washington, presented a bill to the President of the United States, who referred the whole matter to Attorney-General Evarts, who made the following decision:—

The act of June 25, 1868, constituting eight hours a day's work for all government laborers, workmen and mechanics does not absolutely require that the employees of the government must receive as high wages for their eight hours' labor as similar industry in private employment receives for a day's labor of ten hours; but it simply requires that the same worth of labor shall be compensated in the public employment at the same rate of wages that it receives in private employment.

This decision led Senator Dawes of Massachusetts to offer a resolution to enquire whether any legislation was necessary to secure uniformity of compensation under the eight-hour law, according to its true intent.

On April 5, 1869, Mr. Stevens of New Hampshire by unanimous consent, introduced a declaratory resolution which provided that the act of June 25, 1868, should not be considered as authorizing a corresponding reduction of wages. This resolution was passed. On April 21st Attorney-General E. R. Hoar gave an opinion that the act of 1868 had nothing to do with the compensation to be paid, and said the rate of compensation was still left by law to be determined under the rule to be prescribed by the statute of July 16, 1862, so as to conform, as nearly as was consistent with the public interests, with those of private establishments in the immediate vicinity. He says: —

I find nothing in the statute which requires you [Secretary of the Navy, Borie] to pay the same price for eight hours' labor which private establishments pay for ten or twelve hours, unless the kind of service rendered or the quality of the work made the fewer hours in the Navy Yard equivalent in value to the longer time required in private establishments, or for some other reasons, make it consistent with the public interest.

The Secretary then issued the following to the commandants of the Navy Yards and stations: —

NAVY DEPARTMENT, WASHINGTON, April 22, 1869.

DEAR SIR: The act of Congress approved June 25, 1868, constituting eight hours a day's work for all workmen, laborers and mechanics employed on behalf of the United States, while establishing the length of a day's work, Congress omitted to repeal the act of July 16, 1862, requiring the wages of the employees in the Navy Yards to conform, as nearly as is consistent with the public interest, to those of private establishments in the immediate vicinity of the Navy Yards. Until these laws are repealed, the Department abides by them. The Department has no authority to extend the hours of labor by making more than eight hours a day's work, but it has the right to employ mechanics, workmen and laborers and pay them *pro rata* for such extra labor. When, therefore, necessity exists for extra labor, you are at liberty to exercise your discretion in the matter so as to assist the working classes and at the same time assist the Government.

Very respectfully,

A. E. BORIE, *Secretary Navy.*

This called forth a letter from Hon. Henry Wilson addressed

to Major-General John A. Rollins, in which he says that the construction put by the officers of the Government upon the eight-hour law is a palpable violation of the spirit and letter of the act, of the intention of Congress and of the desires of the men who petitioned for its passage, and continued: —

During the past third of a century the hours of labor for manual labor have been largely diminished. Thirty years ago the hours of labor in manufacturing establishments, in machine and in various mechanical industries were from twelve to thirteen hours a day. Laboring men and persons who realized the fact that capital has its duties as well as rights sought to reduce the hours of labor to ten hours a day, and they have been generally successful. I think there cannot be a doubt that the hours of labor for persons employed in mechanical and manufacturing industries have been diminished within a third of a century two hours per day. That this reduction of the hours of labor has been conducive to the physical, mental, moral, and social improvement of the workingmen there can be no question whatever.

The trades assemblies of New York City and Baltimore, in the Spring of 1866, issued a call for a national congress. In answer to their appeal over a hundred delegates met at Baltimore, August 20th. The following named organizations being represented: —

Ship-carpenters and Calkers, of St. Louis, Mo.; Grand Eight-hour League, of Detroit, Mich. (this was one of the branches of the Order), Railroad Men's Protective Union; Painters' Union and Moulders' Union, of St. Louis; Miners' Lodge, Illinois; Workingmen's Union, St. Louis; Window-glass Blowers' Union, Birmingham, Penn.; Mechanics' Association, Norfolk, Va.; House Painters' Union, Washington, D. C.; Masons' Union, Newburg, N.Y.; Trades' Union and Eight-hour Association, New Haven, Ct.; Coach Makers' International Unions, of Brooklyn and Philadelphia; Marble Cutters' Association, Boston, Mass.; Trades' Assembly, New Albany, Ind.; Iron Moulders' Union, of Augusta and Savannah, Ga.; Trades' Assembly and Grand Eight-hour League, of Chicago, Ill.; Trades' Assembly, Wilmington, Del.; Workingmen's Convention, Washington, D. C.; Bricklayers' Union, Brooklyn, N. Y.; House-carpenters' Union and Granite Cutters' Association, of Washington, D. C.; Workingmen's Union, New York City; Stone-cutters' Association, Washington, D. C.; Bookbinders' Union, New York; Ship-joiners' Union, New York; Carpenters', Joiners' and Machinists' Union, Lowell, Mass.; Workingmen's Assembly, Boston, Mass.; Ship-joiners' Union, Baltimore, Md.; Bookbinders' Union, Boston, Mass.; Blacksmiths' Union, Baltimore, Md.; Ship-carpenters' Union, Boston, Mass.; Iron Moulders' Union, Boston, Mass.; Journeymen Coopers' Union, Baltimore, Md.; Journeymen Shipwrights' Unions, Baltimore, Md.; Journeymen House Painters' Baltimore, Md.; Wood Turners' Union, Baltimore, Md.; Trades' Assembly, Baltimore, Md.; Harness-makers' Union, Baltimore, Md.; Pattern-makers' Union, Baltimore, Md.; House-carpenters' Union, Baltimore, Md.; Can-makers' Union, Baltimore,

Md.; Bricklayers' Union, Baltimore, Md.; Iron Moulders' Union, Baltimore, Md.; Operative Masons' Union, Baltimore, Md.; Journeymen Curriers' Union and International Union of Curriers, of Baltimore, Md.; Eight-hour League, No. 1, of Iowa; Trades' Assembly, Philadelphia, Penn.; Trades Assembly, Pittsburgh, Penn.; Steam-boilers' Union, Baltimore, Md.; Iron Moulders' Union, Scranton, Penn.; Workingmen's Associations, Rochester, N. Y.; The Trades-Unions of Buffalo, N. Y., and the Grand Eight-hour League, of Buffalo, N. Y.

Committees were appointed on the following subjects: —

On Eight-hours and Political Action; on Permanent National Organization; to wait on President Johnson; on Public Domain and National Debt; on Trades-Unions and Strikes; on Co-operative Associate and Convict Labor; on National Organs (newspapers); to prepare an Address to the Mechanics and Working People of the United States.

The place of meeting of the next Congress was fixed upon as Chicago, Ill. Resolutions were adopted on the following subjects: —

In favor of the Eight-hour System; of Supporting Labor Journals; Favoring the Organization of Co-operative Stores and Work-shops; Opposing Prison Labor unless Paid for at the same Rate as to outside Mechanics; Pledging Support to Sewing Women; Favoring Speedy Restoration of Agriculture in the South; Asking Capitalists to Erect Improved Dwellings; Asserting that the Public Domain should go to Actual Settlers; Deprecating Strikes; Urging the Promotion of Mechanics' Institutes; Advising Unemployed Workingmen to go on Public Land.

The New York *Tribune* warmly commended the convention, concluding with these words: "Altogether the convention has thoroughly represented the intelligence, education and enterprise of the workingmen of the Union, and its influence should be general and permanent."

The following resolution, adopted by the convention, expresses the dissatisfaction which was felt against existing political parties and the determination of the working people to secure eight-hour legislation: —

WHEREAS, the history and legislation of the past has demonstrated that no dependence whatever can be placed upon the pledges and professions of representatives of existing political parties, so far as the interests of the industrial classes are concerned; therefore, be it

Resolved, That the time has come when the workingmen of the United States should cut themselves loose from all party ties and organize themselves into the National Labor Party, the object of which shall be to secure the enactment of a law making eight hours a day's work.

THE MECHANICS' BELL.

This same convention exposed the condition of the dwellings of the poor, and called upon capitalists to take steps for the building of improved dwellings.

The shoemakers' union, known as the Knights of St. Crispin, was organized in 1866 in the city of Milwaukee, Wis., by Newell Daniels. The name was given by F. W. Wallace. The first lodge of the order was formed the 1st of March, 1867. The International Grand Lodge held its first meeting on the the 23d day of April, 1869, at Worcester, Mass., and adopted a constitution. One of its articles forbade the members to teach, or aid in teaching, any part of the trade to any one without permission of three-fourths of the members of the lodge present and voting thereon, provision being made that a father could teach his son. Their methods of settling grievances, etc., together with their further history, will be found in the chapter on Shoemakers.

From this time forward much of the history of the movement is contained in the history of the several organizations. Depression in business resulted in the lessening of membership and depletion of the treasuries of existing organizations, many of the isolated trades-unions passing out of existence or held together by small bands of the faithful members and reviving again with the revival of prosperity, the tendency being always to a better form of organization. Much the same method of agitation was pursued and the same measures of reform were continually demanded.

The movement began again to assume a political character, although the trades-unions, as such, took no part in it. Numerously signed petitions were forwarded to the state legislatures and to Congress.

August 19, 1867, the National Labor Congress convened at Chicago, upwards of two hundred delegates being present, representing labor associations in all the Northern States, and Kentucky, Maryland and Missouri. The president, Z. C. Whalley, in his report, urged the eight-hour movement, and recommended that each State have a vice-president, for the purpose of a more hearty co-operation in the objects of the organization. He suggested the establishment of a national organ, the editorial columns of which should be devoted to the rights of labor. He said: —

> The emancipation of the slaves has placed us in a new position, and the question now arises, what labor position shall they now occupy? They will begin to learn and to think for themselves, and they will soon resort to mechanical pursuits, and thus come in contact with white labor. It is necessary that they should not undermine it, therefore the best thing that they can do is to form trades-unions, and thus work in harmony with the whites.

He strongly urged co-operative effort as well as changes in the methods of the organization, so that a central head should be established, all subordinate unions to be auxiliary to it, paying quarterly dues, and thus establishing a fund to secure the end they sought.

The preamble contains this clause:—

> Heretofore the highest form labor associations have taken, is the national union of some of the trades. Between these organizations, however, there was no sympathy or systematic connection, no co-operative effort, no working for the attainment of a common end, the want of which has been experienced for years by every craft and calling.

The name adopted by the congress was the National Labor Union. This convention appointed Richard F. Trevellick as a delegate to Europe, but on account of a lack of funds, he was unable to attend. It adjourned to meet at Pittsburgh, Penn., on the first Monday in May, 1868.

The Chicago *Tribune* of that date, in an editorial, called attention to the fact that the farmers, who were both capitalists and laborers, were not represented at the convention, and that "this mighty mass of producers" had no sympathy with the labor congress, or with strikes, or eight hours, or movements. This was measurably true of that day, but after the organization of the Patrons of Husbandry a different spirit pervaded the farming community, as was shown by the action of the National Grange at their nineteenth session, assembled in Boston in November, 1885, at which convention the following preamble and resolution was adopted and forwarded to the Secretary-Treasurer of District 30, Knights of Labor, Massachusetts.

WHEREAS, the morning papers inform us that at Brockton a number of workingmen, amounting to five thousand, have been turned out of employment because they belong to an organization called the "Knights of Labor" — this being their offence, and nothing more — by an organization called the Manufacturers' Association, therefore be it

Resolved, That we, the Patrons of Husbandry, in the National Grange assembled, do hereby send greeting and sympathy to our laboring brethren, and assure them that we will ever maintain the right and privilege of any person or class of our fellow citizens to organize themselves for protection.

Resolved, That the Secretary, under seal of the National Grange, send a copy of the above to the Secretary of the Knights of Labor.

JOHN TRIMBLE,
Secretary National Grange P. of H.

November 18, 1885.

The eight-hour men, who had been the unpaid representatives of labor before committees of the Massachusetts Legislature, succeeded in securing the passage of a resolve establishing the Massachusetts Bureau of Statistics of Labor in 1869, the first of the kind ever established. General H. K. Oliver, of Salem, a man with varied experiences as an educator and as the agent of a large cotton mill for ten years, afterwards being specially deputized to enforce the laws in reference to the employment and schooling of children, was appointed chief, and the editor of this work, on August 4th of the same year, was appointed deputy. The chief and deputy constituted the Bureau. In the fall of that year the Labor Reform Party of Massachusetts was formed, and nominated candidates for the State offices, who received about fifteen thousand votes.

Massachusetts was at this time again the centre of the political and public movement, while the trades-unions movement was centering in New York and Chicago, and spreading into California, where the telegraphers organized a benévolent association which spread into the larger cities of the east, and was immediately followed by a strike, which, for a time, paralyzed business, the newspapers suffering severely; but in twenty-four hours after the strike the offices in the cities were manned by operatives from the country, and the strike was a failure.

September 21, 1868, the National Labor Congress convened in New York City. The address of the president was largely occupied with the question of women's labor. He warned the members not to lose their identity in political organizations. Mrs. E. C. Stanton was admitted as a member after a long discussion. The convention seemed to be divided on the question of political action and on the question of currency. W. H. Sylvis, of the Iron Moulders' Union, was chosen chairman. It was voted that the next National Congress should be held at Pittsburgh, Penn.

In 1868 the Workingmen's Benevolent Association, a miners' organization of St. Clair county, asked for a charter from the State of Pennsylvania, which was granted, and an extensive eight-hour strike began on the first of July of that year, during which considerable violence occurred. A grand mass-meeting of all the miners and laborers in Schuylkill county was called in Mahoning city. It is estimated that from twelve thousand to twenty thousand persons were present. They were addressed by many of their fellow-workmen, and all counseled moderation and good order. The miners in Schulykill county had not at that time organized a union, and a charter was granted on the application of John Siney and others, for the Workingmen's Benevolent Association of Schuylkill county, giving them authority to organize sub-districts in that county, and giving the trustees of such sub-districts power to sue in the corporate name. The movement for the eight-hour system was abandoned, and work was resumed in September.

A very strong effort was then made by operators to break up the unions, and a long strike ensued. Men who had used every means in their power to prevent violence and preserve the public peace were stigmatized by the coal operators as demagogues. The difficulties resulted in great suffering among the men, and the failure of some of the wealthy coal operators, which finally gave President Gowen control of Schuylkill county.

In November, 1870, the Delaware & Hudson Canal Co., located in New York City, gave notice to their employees that on and after the first of December miners should be paid eighty-six cents per diamond car, instead of one dollar and thirty-one cents. This proposed reduction of thirty-three per cent., coming as it did so soon after the abandonment of the eight-hour movement, and the attempt to break up the unions, created great excitement. Orders of like character were issued by the Delaware & Lackawanna, and Western Railroad Companies and the Pennsylvania Coal Company. The men struck, and the utmost demoralization prevailed.

In the spring of 1869 the Boston Eight-hour League was formed, the Grand Eight-hour League having gone out of existence in that State some time before. The preamble to the constitution of this organization was a terse statement of the argument for, and the results of, the reduction of the hours of labor to eight. It argued that a reduction of hours is an increase of wages; that this increase is without a corresponding increase in the cost of production; that the increase of wages without increased cost is a better distribution of wealth; that a better distribution of wealth in the process of production lessens profits upon labor, and thus makes co-operative labor practicable; that leisure is the greatest motive power to create wants and desires; that the wage system must gradually become extinct through natural causes.

This society discussed the question as one of political economy solely. It treated the theory that demand and supply governed wages as the false theory as long as capitalists were the masters, and the laborers the slaves of that law. They claimed that wages were governed by the cost at which any class of laborers were compelled to live; that with increased wages, that is, increased purchasing power of a day's labor, the condition of the laborers must be improved, all effort being toward making them better consumers; they claimed that it was Sabbaths, free schools, the elective franchise, frequent elections, etc., that made the New Englander higher priced than the Chinaman, and that leisure must be given as an incentive in the same direction. The society had weekly meetings for the discussion of purely labor questions and held annual conventions. The proceedings of these conventions were given great publicity, and the resolutions adopted by them were widely quoted and translated into many languages.

They were pronounced in their opposition to the discussion of finance reform and other subjects, in the name of labor reform, as will be seen by the following resolutions adopted at one of the annual conventions: —

Resolved, That the Boston Eight-hour League records its most emphatic protest against the discussion or the consideration of financial theories, in the name of Labor Reform.

That financial reform, so called, is interesting and important, chiefly to that small per cent. of our fellow citizens who belong to the capitalist classes; who regard themselves as a permanent class in society, and believe that upon their financial successes must depend all who work with their hands. Who read Labor's advantages in the light of their own, but none of their own interests with the eyes of Labor: who make no distinction between capitalists and capital, between the curse of a class, known only for its wealth and the blessings of wealth itself; and are able through their wealth to fix public attention upon questions of taxation, railroad and banking management, currency and interest, protection and free-trade, franking, mileage, salary, civil service, and economical humbugs, the settlement of which the best way, still leaves the laborer a laborer, and the capitalist a capitalist, between whom there is an irrepressible conflict which must continue until all are laborers and all are capitalists.

Resolved, That it always was, and always will be, too late to secure to the wage-worker any appreciable amount, or any considerable advantage in the management of wealth *that has once been distributed!*

That his attention must be turned to the earnings or productions of the future, and not to those of the past; to wealth in the process of its creation:

That as long as the wage system prevails, the production and the distribution of wealth must proceed together; and any re-distribution of wealth, through a supplementary financial system, can never occur.

That a better labor system, or the present one improved, must precede a better distribution of wealth.

That labor produces everything, and must learn to keep everything, if it would have everything. That all that labor ever had since the world began to divide its work, and all it can ever have until it reaches the higher level of co-operation, is through the wage system: and through higher wages only can the masses ever secure a more equal distribution of wealth, by which the claim of the League is reached, that it assembles in the name of labor, to consider questions of labor, and not financial theories under the banner of labor reform.

And the so-called "Labor Reform" conventions that assemble and discuss almost everything else but labor, and confuse and disgust those who stop to listen, by the impracticable nature of their claim; that furnish a theatre or a platform for a crowd of adventurers who are without a purpose, and without a constituency among those who labor or those who think; that minister to the most superficial and sensational thought or feeling of the movement; that flippantly denounce as narrow and unimportant, or worse, the uprising of labor everywhere for less hours; that present no theory even of the labor and poverty problem, and no measures that could be enacted or repealed with profit to labor, may be regarded as not important to the laborers' movement; and our interest in them begins and ends with the wish, that as often as they call the public to discuss financial theories, they will call in the name of capital and not in the precious name of labor.

Resolved, That with unfaltering confidence we shall be triumphantly sustained in our great claim that less hours for labor is the first step in labor reform.

That less hours mean higher wages, less poverty, a more equal distribution of wealth, more wealth-producing machinery, and wealth far more rapidly produced.

That the vices and crimes and follies of mankind are largely the result of their poverty and of their ignorance, which their poverty increases.

That a monopoly of education, a monopoly of political rights, and a monopoly of wealth in the hands of a few, are the great dangers that now most threaten our Republic.

We therefore call once again, as we have and shall continue to call, for the concentration of the whole power and forces of the labor movement upon the single and simple issue of the legislation necessary to secure the eight-hour system first, for all labor employed at the public expense, whether by contract or by the day.

Resolved, That the congratulations of labor men everywhere may be exchanged upon the fact that the Commonwealth of Massachusetts has at last decided to legislate on the hours of labor.

In the winter of 1869 the Knights of Labor was organized in Philadelphia as described in the chapter devoted to that order.

In 1870 and 1871 the International Workingmen's Association, which was formed in 1863, and which had held international congresses at Geneva, Bruxelles, Basle and London, commenced to form branches in the United States. This was an attempt to combine the disconnected movements of the several countries for the emancipation of the working classes. It declared that all previous efforts had failed from the want of solidarity between the manifold divisions of labor in each country, and from the absence of a fraternal bond of union between the working classes of each country; that the emancipation of labor was a social problem embracing all countries and depending for its solution on the concurrence, practical and theoretical, of the most advanced countries. It declared that all societies and individuals adhering to it would acknowledge truth, justice and morality as the basis of our conduct toward each other and towards all men, without regard to creed, color or nationality; that it acknowledged no rights without duties, no duties without rights. It provided for annual congresses and for a general council. In addition to the general council there were federal councils or committees, local societies, branches and groups. No branch or group was allowed to designate themselves by sectarian names,—such as Positivists, Mutualists, Collectivists, Communists, etc. They established a system of general statistics of labor. This organization had but a short existence in this country. Some of its members were among the ablest and most earnest of the labor advocates.

The year 1872 was one in which the agitation of labor question was most active. The "Report of the Massachusetts Labor Bureau of Statistics of 1873," in speaking of that period, says:—

> Hardly a week has passed in which some trade has not either struck or been struck against, and yet definite knowledge of details cannot be obtained. No strike on a large scale occurred in Massachusetts, though in the spring and summer the building trades reorganized their unions, held meetings, and seemed on the verge of striking for the eight-hour system. The agitation of this subject gave new life to the unions, and woke the enthusiasm of the men; the common expression of the meetings being to persevere until they gained the boon of added leisure and better opportunity. The speeches are singularly free from extravagant statements, many of the speakers defending their claims by able arguments. A spirit of universal brotherhood was evinced and men of all nationalities participated in the discussions. Every night in the week societies of workingmen held meetings and discussed their grievances, some with open, and some with closed, doors. Organizations for mutual benefit and for the building and ownership of houses and homesteads had been formed. Unions exist where least expected, some of them having well-furnished and alluring halls under their own control, never seeking publicity, and some even concealing their membership. In many trades there are union men who keep up a form of organization, meeting monthly or at the call of the officers, often without a quorum, the remaining members seldom paying dues or fines. They are simply rallying points around which the workmen gather in times of danger, such as the contemplated reduction of wages, or in periods of prosperity, to create a scarcity in the labor market and thereby increase wages.

It was in the summer of 1872 that the great strike occurred in the city of New York, in which nearly one hundred thousand men were engaged, as the result of which the following trades secured the eight-hour day: bricklayers, carpenters, plasterers, painters, plumbers, brown and bluestone-cutters, stone masons, masons' laborers, paper-hangers (when working by the day), and plate printers.

In March, 1872, a vast body of workingmen of New York City, mostly of the building trades, struck for the eight-hour system. The strike was conducted with the utmost order, and on June 10th a procession paraded the streets, with bands of music, flags and banners of many descriptions.

On June 19th the employers, four hundred in number, held a conference to secure concerted action for the maintenance of the ten-hour system. Mr. Andrew J. Campbell was elected president, and in his address, said:—

> The present convulsion in the industrial interests of the city demands decisive action. About seven thousand men are walking the streets of New York in behalf of a principle, destructive to the business interests of the entire community. The country is not in such a state of business prosperity as will warrant a concession to the demand for eight hours. It may be in the course of a few years that it will be expedient to grant those terms, but at present it would be ruinous.

The New York *Tribune* of June 24th thus refers to the strike editorially:—

> The great strike still pending in New York City has been, in its various aspects, the most remarkable we have ever had in America. The length of time over which it has extended (nearly three months), the numbers of men and varieties of trades engaged in it, and its disastrous effects on the welfare of the workingmen and the trades, have been unparalleled. Not one trade, but scores, have engaged in it. All the trades have been convulsed, and altogether three-fourths of all the journeymen in the city have been on strike for more time. Of the three-fourths who have struck, more than one-half have gained their point; but over eleven thousand are still unsuccessful and without present clear prospect of success.

On the 22d of May, 1872, Horace Greeley wrote as follows: "The dissatisfaction has extended into all the leading mechanical trades, and in almost every instance the employers have acceded to the demands of their men."

At the Convention of the Boston Eight-hour League, in 1872, Mr. Ira Steward, Chairman of the Committee on Resolutions, presented the following resolutions, which we give space to here, because they form one of the most condensed statements of the question ever presented to the public: —

Resolved, That poverty is the great fact with which the labor movement deals;

That co-operation in labor is the final result to be obtained;

That a reduction in the hours of labor is the first step in labor reform; and that the emancipation of labor from the slavery and ignorance of poverty solves all of the problems that now most disturb and perplex mankind.

Resolved, That we demand legislation on the hours of labor as follows: —

1. An amendment to the Patent Laws of the United States, by which an exclusive right to make or sell shall be forfeited when persons are employed in manufacturing an article patented, more than eight hours a day.

2. An amendment to the Acts of Incorporation of cities and towns, requiring them to adopt the eight-hour rule in the employment of all mechanics and day laborers, and the same hours to apply to the same class at work for the State, whether directly or indirectly, through persons, firms or corporations contracting with the State.

3. Manufacturing corporations to adopt the eight-hour system or surrender their charters.

4. All persons under twenty-one years of age to be employed not more than eight hours a day.

5. Eight hours to be made a legal day's work in the absence of a written agreement.

Resolved, That this legislation, though affecting directly but a small per cent. of the people, will establish the facts most important for the working classes to learn:

That eight hours do not mean less wages;

That men are never paid as a rule according to what they earn, but according to the average cost of living;

That in the long run — within certain limits — *less* hours means *more* pay, whether they work by the day or work by the piece;

That reducing the hours increases the purchasing power of wages as well as the amount of wealth produced;

That dear men mean cheap productions, and cheap men mean dear productions;

That six cents a day in China is dearest, and three dollars a day in America is cheapest;

That the moral causes that have made three dollars a day cheaper than six cents a day, will make higher wages still cheaper;

That less hours mean reducing the profits and fortunes that are made on labor or its results;

More knowledge and more capital for the laborer: The wage system gradually disappearing through *higher* wages;

Less *poor* people to borrow money, and less wealthy ones to lend it, and a natural decline in the rates of interest on money;

More idlers working, and more workers thinking; the motives to fraud reduced, and fewer calls for special legislation;

Woman's wages increased, her household labor reduced, better opportunities for thought and action, and the creation of motives strong enough to demand and secure the ballot;

Reaching the great causes of intemperance — extreme wealth and extreme poverty;

And the salvation of republican institutions.

Resolved, That whether National Banks are abolished or bonds are taxed, or whether taxes or tariffs are high or low, or whether greenbacks or gold, or any system of finance proposed is adopted, or civil service, or one term for President shall prevail, are not *laborers'* questions, because they have no appreciable relation to the *wage system* through which the wage classes secure all that they can ever obtain of the world's wealth, until they become sufficiently wealthy and intelligent to co-operate in its production; and whether the masses have anything to choose between President Grant and Horace Greeley, turns entirely on the question which one of the two will be most likely to secure the legislation we demand, as well as the enforcement, upon all government works, of the law already enacted.

Resolved, That the factory system of Massachusetts that employs tens of thousands of women and children eleven and twelve hours a day; that owns or controls in its own selfish interest the pulpit and the press; that prevents the operative classes from making themselves felt in behalf of less hours, through a remorseless exercise of the power of discharge; that is rearing a population of children and youth whose sickly appearance and scanty or utterly neglected schooling, means a class dangerous to the peace and good order of the State, is proving, year by year, that "the lords of the loom and the lords of the lash" were natural allies in the conflict between Freedom and Slavery; and that those who voted against ten hours legislation in the Massachusetts Legislature would have voted for slavery at the behest of their masters, the cotton lords, as they have voted that this barbarism shall continue to the scandal and shame of the Commonwealth.

Resolved, That the recent onslaught made in the Massachusetts Legislature upon the Bureau of Statistics of Labor, at the command of the banking capital of the State, under the generalship of the Boston *Advertiser*, means stifling investigation concerning the poverty of the working-classes, and argues the efficiency and fidelity with which the Bureau has conducted its investigations.

Resolved, That our greetings and plaudits go out to the Nine-hour Engineers of England, as well as to the workingmen on the Continent, whose strikes for less hours have helped on to victory this simultaneous uprising of labor everywhere; and to the Trades-Unionists of New York, who represent the manhood and conscience, the brains and hope of their class, whose representatives we have summoned, and now welcome to our platform, we return our most profound and hearty congratulations for their triumphant success, and if they faithfully preserve the precious hours they have wrung from toil, by remorsely branding as traitors to the cause all who accept "overwork" for any consideration whatever, they will find themselves sustained in the coming years, and will prove how much this movement has contributed to the grander civilization of the future, while the whole world of workers will be filled with the sound of their praises and the inspiration of their example.

At this time the great strike for the eight-hour system was going on in New York, some recent strikes in that city having been successful, and delegates from the New York Workingmen's Unions were present at this convention, addressing the audience in the evening. One of the speakers said that at that time there were fifty trades-unions in New York City holding weekly meetings.

During this year, in some places, the manufacturers combined, binding themselves in one place in the sum of one thousand dollars each to break up the organizations of the workmen.

Strikes of the coopers occurred in 1872 and 1873 against the sugar refineries using barrels made in other localities. The men admitted that the sugar refiners had a right to purchase barrels where and of whom they chose, but claimed that they had a right to work for whom they chose, and would not work for the refineries that purchased barrels elsewhere.

It was also during the agitation of 1872 that a new form of labor organization came into existence, called the Christian Labor Union of Boston. The best known members of this organization were Hon. T. Wharton Collens, of New Orleans, La., a lawyer and ex-judge, and a member of the Catholic Church; Rev. Jesse H. Jones, of North Abington, Mass., a Congregational clergyman; Henry T. Delano, senior deacon of the First Congregational Church, of Charlestown, Mass., and Edward H. Rogers, of the Warner Street M. E. Church, of Chelsea, Mass. This union was active for several years, and commanded the respect of the labor organizations. It held two conventions and conducted two periodicals, one succeeding the other. It raised and expended about two thousand dollars during its existence in the promulgation of its principles. It was brought to a close by the death of its principal patron, Judge Collens, in 1878. Its preamble set forth its object to be to obey Christ's command, "follow me," and to secure obedience to it in the conduct of every form of human labor. It adopted the Bible principle of the Hebrew Church, in its relation to land, labor and capital. Its objects were to lift men out of their poverty by moral and religious influences, and reform measures. It presented the following questions for prayerful consideration:—

1st. Do not the teachings, example and spirit of Jesus require of his churches to day, that there should be mutual care in sickness, and such systematic provision for the help of those who have need, that the degrading sense of pauperism which now too often embitters their hard lot may be removed?

2d. Do they not now require the church to establish labor partnerships and other industrial co-operative organizations, as a part of its Christian duty to its members?

3d. Do they not also now require that the principle of labor service of each other as exemplified by the Master, in washing the feet of his disciples, should constitute the Law of Industry and Exchange, and inasmuch as this requires concert of action, is it not the duty of the church to sustain those who abandon the present maxims of trade, and endeavor to act upon the principle which is inspired by Philosophy and Religion, that Cost is the just limit of Price?

The winter of 1873-4 was one of extreme suffering, especially in the large cities. Midwinter found tens of thousands of people on the verge of starvation, suffering for food, for the need of proper clothing, and for medical attendance. Meetings of the unemployed were held in many places, and public attention called to the needs of the poor. Many of the charitable societies, as well as private individuals, did all it was possible for them to do to relieve the distress. The men asked for work and found it not, and children cried for bread.

On the announcement of public meetings of the unemployed, the conscience-pricked communities took alarm and feared that the bringing together of so many heretofore patient sufferers might imperil their lives and property. From the earliest days of the agitation of the question of the relations of labor and capital, free speech had been often restrained, and sometimes forbidden. This had been especially true in those smaller towns and manufacturing centres where the owner of the principal industry was practically the owner of the community — of the halls, churches, school-rooms and the press, but up to this time no great outrage upon the freedom of speech had attracted public attention.

The unemployed and suffering poor of New York City determined to hold a meeting and appeal to the public by bringing to their attention the spectacle of their poverty. They gained permission from the Board of Police to parade the streets and hold a meeting in Tompkins Square, on the 13th of January, 1874, but on the 12th of January the Board of Police and Board of Parks revoked the order and prohibited the meeting. It was impossible to notify the scattered army of this order, and at the time of the meeting the people marched through the gates of Tompkins Square. No officer of the government and no method excepting the public press had been utilized to inform the people of the determination of the city authorities. When the square was completely filled with men, women and children, without a moment's warning, the police closed in upon them on all sides.

One of the daily papers of the city confessed that the scene could not be described. People rushed from the gates and through the streets, followed by the mounted officers at full speed, charging upon them without provocation. Screams of women and children rent the air, and the blood of many stained the streets, and to the further shame of this outrage it is to be added that when the General Assembly of New York State was called to this matter, they took testimony, but made no sign.

John Swinton, a man whose unswerving fealty to the cause of the poor has challenged the admiration of even his enemies, in his appeal to the Legislature, addressed to the Committee on Grievances, well said: —

> Never has the Committee on Grievances been asked to investigate any grievance more cruel, flagrant or lamentable, — more repugnant to human nature, more insulting to human misery, more deeply taken to heart by those who suffered from it or who sympathise with the sufferers, more subversive of the living principles of our political system, more pervasive and portentous in its influence, or bearing upon a larger number of your fellow-citizens, than the grievance about which you have consented to give us a hearing. We have come to ask you to investigate the facts — to make inquiry, take evidence and receive affidavits — to adjudge whether the municipal authorities of New York, who exist through your legislation and permission, perpetrated an appalling wrong, grossly violated popular rights, shamefully outraged helpless suffering, disregarded the ordinary amenities of civilized society, disturbed

public order and assassinated constitutional liberty. These are formidable words, yet they but feebly represent the things for which they stand, and which have now brought us here.

He then described the suffering of the terrible winter which led to the convening of the meeting, and described in detail the scenes there, and ended as follows: —

We ask, in brief, then, gentlemen of the Committee on Grievances, that you make such report to the Legislature as will immediately secure a thorough investigation of this whole matter, to be made in the city of New York, where the witnesses are at hand.

We further ask that the Police Board which perpetrated these cruel, flagrant and horrible outrages against the unemployed and suffering workingmen of New York, be *abolished*, and that instead thereof a new Board be created, to be elected by popular suffrage, according to the orthodox political system of our Government.

These are my two propositions, dealing not with party politics, but with popular rights, which cannot be subverted without the subversion of the fundamental basis of American liberty. I pray you so to deal with the matter — and I stand here, not as a hired agent or attorney of anybody or any cause, but merely as one whose heart has been touched by the wrongs of those who have had but few to speak for them, and who, on that account, has been asked to become one of their spokesmen — I pray you so to deal with it that you may vindicate for all time those great constitutional principles which lie at the foundation of our Republic, and by which alone the public welfare can be maintained.

I close with the prophetic warning of Longfellow, which, let us hope, may never hereafter be applicable to any wronged or victimized class in our country: —

"There is a poor blind Samson in our land,
Shorn of his strength and bound with bonds of steel,
Who may in some grim revel raise his hand,
And shake the pillars of the commonweal."

Gentlemen, we have done.

One of the most important of the many industrial congresses was held at Rochester, N. Y., commencing April 14, 1874, Robert Schilling, of the Coopers' Union, acting as president. Among the trades' organizations represented were machinists and blacksmiths, binders, coopers, shoemakers, tailors, cigarmakers, miners, quarrymen, iron moulders, printers, tobacco laborers, iron and steel roll makers; and of other organizations there were present the Industrial Council, Labor Council, the Workingmen's Central Council of New York, Trades Assemblies, Industrial Brotherhood, the Grand

Division of the Conductors' Brotherhood, Sovereigns of Industry, and Daughters of St. Crispin.

President Schilling, in his address, called upon the Congress to devise means by which the public could be informed as to the real objects and purposes of its assembling. He said: "It is a well-known fact that many oppose us in our efforts, merely because they do not understand or comprehend the principles which we advocate." The public press at that time practically ignored the movement. Mr. Schilling sent circulars to over three hundred daily and weekly papers in every State and Territory, and only one newspaper outside of the labor press took any notice of it, while at the same time great publicity was given to a letter written by a deposed officer of one of the most powerful labor organizations, with a view of disrupting that order. He especially commended the *Workingmen's Advocate*, of Chicago; the *Independent Workingman*, of Nashville; the *Iron Workers' Journal*, the *Machinists' and Blacksmiths' Journal*, and the *Coopers' New Monthly*. He strongly favored political action; he said: "To this end it is not necessary that we should form ourselves into a new party or attach ourselves to any party now existing, or that may hereafter be formed, but merely that we vote for men of honesty and ability, and against corruptionists and monopolists." He desired to see some form of organization similar in its objects and purposes to the Patrons of Husbandry, so that they would be able to co-operate with farmers and all other classes of producers. Letters were received from the president of the Mechanics' State Council of California, and from the Executive Board of the Connecticut Labor Union.

Among the resolutions adopted was one which says: "We are opposed to strikes on principle, and advocate the settlement of all grievances by arbitration. This would be the means of creating a better feeling beween employers and employees, and would be a guarantee against advantage being taken on either side during business prosperity or adversity." A very large part of the time of the convention was taken up in considering the question of organization and constitution, some of the delegates desiring to create an order similar to the Industrial Brotherhood, while others favored the Sovereigns of Industry plan. The leaders of these two great organizations were present, and the Committee on Constitution was made up of the author of this history as chairman; John Ferrenbatch, of Ohio, then president of the Machinists' and Blacksmiths' Union; George Blair, of New York; M. H. Smith, of Vermont; T. Dwyer, of Michigan; W. H. Earle, of Massachusetts, the representative of the Sovereigns of Industry; and E. Warner, of Missouri, who represented the Industrial Brotherhood.

The *Workingmen's Advocate* in reviewing the work of this Congress, said: —

For nine successive years we have had the honor and pleasure of attending the deliberations of these national assemblages, and it has never been our privilege during that time to meet a more intelligent, truth-seeking, persistent and enthusiastic body of men than were present at the Rochester Congress. The all-pervading, all-engrossing idea manifested was the necessity of devising, perfecting and adopting a plan of organization, which will secure the co-operation of the industrial classes under one banner, irrespective of trades and callings, and this idea happily overshadowed all other considerations. Although no definite line of policy has as yet been adopted, the committee to whom the duty of drafting a constitution has been entrusted are gentlemen who bring to the discharge of their duties a ripe experience and comprehensive judgment. The platform adopted is certainly an admirable document, setting forth in clear and terse terms the principles upon which the organization is founded.

Executive officers were appointed for Massachusetts, New York, Indiana, West Virginia, Ohio, Minnesota, Virginia, New Jersey, Michigan, Pennsylvania, Maryland, Wisconsin, Connecticut, Tennessee and Vermont.

The platform containing their declaration of principles, adopted in 1874, read as follows: —

WHEREAS, The recent alarming development and aggression of aggregated wealth, which, unless checked, will inevitably lead to the pauperization and hopeless degradation of the toiling masses, renders it imperative, if we desire to enjoy the blessings of the government bequeathed us by the founders of the Republic, that a check should be placed upon its power and unjust accumulation, and a system adopted which will secure to the laborer the fruits of his toil; and

WHEREAS, This much desired object can only be accomplished by the thorough unification of labor, and the united efforts of those who obey the Divine injunction that "In the sweat of thy face thou shalt eat thy bread;" and

WHEREAS, The great desideratum of the hour is the organization and direction, by co-operative efforts, of the power of the producing masses for their substantial elevation, yet we recognize in the ballot-box the great agency through which our wrongs can be redressed; and

WHEREAS, While we fully recognize the power and efficacy of trade and labor unions, as now organized, in regulating purely trade matters, yet upon all questions appertaining to the welfare of the masses as a whole, the influence of these organizations, without closer union, must prove comparatively futile; therefore

Resolved, That we submit to the people of the United States the objects sought to be accomplished by the Industrial Congress: —

1st. To bring within the folds of the organization every department of productive industry, making knowledge a standpoint for action, and industrial, moral, and social worth — not wealth — the true standard of individual and national greatness.

2d. To secure to the toilers a just share of the wealth they create; more of the leisure that rightfully belongs to them; more society advantages; more of the benefits, privileges, and emoluments of the world; — in a word, all those rights and privileges necessary to make them capable of enjoying, appreciating, defending, and perpetuating the blessings of our Republican government.

3d. To arrive at the true condition of the producing masses in their educational, moral and financial condition, we demand from the several States and from the National Government the establishment of Bureaus of Labor Statistics.

4th. The establishment of co-operative institutions, productive and distributive.

5th. The reserving of the public lands, the heritage of the people, for the actual settler; not another acre for railroads or speculators.

6th. The abrogation of all laws that do not bear equally upon capital and labor, the removal of unjust technicalities, delays and discriminations in the administration of justice, and the adoption of measures providing for the health and safety of those engaged in mining, manufacturing and building pursuits.

7th. The enactment of a law to compel chartered corporations to pay their employees at least once in every month, in full, for labor performed during the preceding month, in the lawful money of the country.

8th. The enactment of a law giving mechanics and laborers first lien on their work; and also preventing stays of execution in case of labor lien judgments.

9th. The abolishment of the contract system on national, State, and municipal work.

10th. To inaugurate a system of public markets to facilitate the exchange of products of farmers and mechanics, tending to do away with middle-men and speculators.

11th. To inaugurate a system of cheap transportation, to facilitate the exchange of commodities.

12th. The substitution of arbitration for strikes, whenever and wherever employers and employees are willing to meet on equitable grounds.

13th. The prohibition of the importation of all servile races, and the discontinuance of all subsidies granted to national vessels bringing them to our shores.

14th. To advance the standard of American mechanics, by the enactment and enforcement of equitable apprentice-laws.

15th. To abolish the system of letting by contract the labor of convicts in our prisons and reformatory institutions.

16th. To secure for both sexes equal pay for equal work.

17th. The reduction of the hours of labor to eight per day, so that the laborers may have more time for social enjoyment and intellectual improvement, and be enabled to reap the advantages conferred by labor-saving machinery, which their brains have created.

18th. The establishing by Government of a just standard of distribution to labor and capital, by providing a purely national circulating medium, based on the faith and resources of the nation, issued directly to the people, without the intervention of any system of banking corporations, which money shall be a legal tender in the payment of all debts, public and private, and interchangeable at the option of the holder for registered Government bonds, bearing a rate of interest not to exceed three and sixty-five one-hundredths per cent., subject to future legislation by Congress.

From 1873 to 1876 many strikes occurred in the cotton and woollen factories of Massachusetts, Rhode Island and Connecticut. In many of these places the men had no organizations, but after striking they proceeded to form themselves into unions, which at the end of the strikes were generally dissolved until reorganized into Assemblies of the Knights of Labor.

The industries were becoming somewhat relieved from the industrial depression of 1873. The working people had suffered four years of low wages and all its consequent evils; millions of men had been unable to obtain employment, and tens of thousands of families were suffering for the necessities of life. Great strikes occurred in all parts of the Union, especially in the States of Pennsylvania, Illinois, Indiana, Missouri, Maryland, Ohio, and New York. In one of the strikes of the coal miners at this time thirty thousand persons were involved, — men, women, and children. The miners were reduced almost to starvation, and dwelt in communities in camps, subsisting on coarse food provided from the common fund. In Susquehanna, Penn., twelve hundred machinists employed on the Erie Railroad paraded, carrying the

American flag. The militia guarded the railroad property. The men claimed that the superintendent created the strike. They also claimed that they had not been paid for months. Ten thousand cigarmakers were on strike in New York City.

In the strikes that occurred at this period a great deal of bitterness was evinced against trades-union organizations, and men were blacklisted to an extent hardly ever equaled. In many instances when men struck against a reduction or for an increase, or were locked out, employers in the same trade were notified of difficulties and requested not to employ any workmen from their vicinity. The difficulty in the settlement of the disputes was not so much the objection of the employers to pay the prices asked, as a false sense of dignity and a refusal to recognize labor organizations. Labor troubles occured in Washington,—and the departments were visited by unemployed men seeking work.

The movement in 1874 had reached colossal proportions. At this time the nations of the earth were at peace with each other, while the Labor question threatened to develop into open war. A Boston paper published in May of that year, said: "Great hostile combinations of capitalists and laborers stand facing each other. In the agricultural sections of England the farmers are determined to starve more than four thousand of their fellows, not into working for a certain amount of pay, but into withdrawing from a union into which they entered for the maintenance of their common interests."

A Labor Reform Convention was held at Worcester in 1875, at which resolutions were adopted with reference to the hours of labor, and many other matters concerning the Labor question.

In 1877 the Workingmen's Party of the United States held a State Convention in Boston, October 1st. It proposed, among other things, to adopt measures to protect the people from the extortions of monopolists and speculators, and nominated Wendell Phillips for Governor.

The great railroad strikes of 1877 began on the Baltimore & Ohio Railroad in consequence of a reduction of ten per cent. in the wages of the employees. The reduction was to go into effect on Monday, July 16th. A circular containing this announcement created almost a panic among the workmen. Meetings of employees were held at different points along the road, and a plan of action was agreed upon. A committee was appointed to confer with the officers of the company. The vice-president was appealed to, but declined to hear their complaints. Efforts were then made to have the order rescinded. Many men expressed themselves in favor of striking, but it does not appear that up to the morning of the 16th any movement had been agreed upon. That day found the men all at work as usual. The officers had partly anticipated a strike, but as the day wore and dispatches were received from the different stations on their fourteen hundred miles of railway, they began to be satisfied that the hard times would deter the men from entering upon a strike. At four o'clock on the afternoon of that day about forty-five of the firemen at Camden Junction quit their engines and persuaded twenty or thirty brakemen to join them in deserting the trains. Another force of firemen and brakemen were engaged to take out the waiting trains. The announcement was then received that the railroad men at Cumberland, Martinsburg and other places were discontented and insubordinate, and that the canal boatmen had quit work and abandoned their boats. At six o'clock of the same day the box-makers, sawyers and can-makers engaged in the shops at Baltimore struck for an advance of ten per cent. in their wages. The strike of these workmen naturally affected the railroad men. Late in the evening the general strike was set on foot in Martinsburg, and all trains were side-tracked while brakemen and firemen who manifested an intention to continue at their posts were forced to leave their engines and trains. At Cumberland the situation was the same. At Geyser and Grafton the train men had obtained complete possession and no freight trains were moved. Vice-president King telegraphed to Governor Matthews of West Virginia to furnish troops to protect the interests of the company, and the Governor telegraphed to Captain Faulkner to afford the officers of the road all the aid and protection necessary.

At two o'clock on the 17th a freight train was thrown from the track at South Baltimore, and the engineer and firemen were both injured. At an early hour on the morning of the 17th Captain Faulkner arrived at Martinsburg in command of seventy-five men and deployed them to guard a western-bound freight train, but before the train had reached the switch one of the strikers seized the switch-ball for the purpose of side-tracking the train. One of the guards attempted to replace the switch, in order to allow the train to proceed, when the striker drew a pistol and fired two shots at the guard. Upon this a number of shots were fired at the striker, who was shot in the head and arms. The report of firearms attracted a multitude of railroad men and citizens to the spot. The engineer and fireman engaged to run the train fled when the firing commenced. Captain Faulkner then led his men back to the armory. The strikers in possession of the road, the cars were uncoupled and link-pins were either hidden or broken. The strikers were greatly assisted by the citizens of the town and the rural population. Railroad men from the Chesapeake & Ohio Railroad arrived in considerable numbers. Governor Matthews, with the Matthews Guard, left Wheeling for Martinsburg, and had proceeded as far as Cumberland when he received intelligence that the strike had reached the capital, when he hastily returned. Two military companies at Martinsburg affiliated with the strikers. Governor Matthews, upon his return to Wheeling, appealed to President Hayes for assistance. The President issued a proclamation and ordered a body of regulars to Martinsburg.

On the third day the workmen at Baltimore issued a circular containing a statement of the causes which led to the strike. They declared that they had submitted to three reductions of wages in three years; that they would have acquiesced in a moderate reduction; that they were frequently sent out on a trip to Martinsburg and there detained at the discretion of the company, for which detention they were allowed pay for but two days; that they were compelled to pay their board during the time that they were detained, which was more than the wages they received, so that they had nothing left with which to support their families; that many times out on the road they could not get more than fifteen days' work in a month; that many sober, steady, economical men became involved in debt; that honest men had their wages attached because they could not meet their expenses, and that by the rules of the company any man whose wages were attached should be discharged; that this was a tyranny to which no rational being should submit; and that it was utterly impossible for a man with a family to support himself and family.

At about ten o'clock on the third day an attempt was made to start a freight train from Martinsburg towards Baltimore. The locomotive was fired up while guarded by United States troops. A large number of strikers had assembled. The Sheriff was present with a posse and an engineer named Bradford was found willing to take out the train. He got upon the engine, and just as the train was about to move away, his wife mounted the engine and with agonizing cries besought him to leave the position. The engineer heeded the entreaty and departed from the engine, followed by the fireman. Another engineer was found, but he was prevailed upon to abandon the undertaking.

At Baltimore the excitement had become intense. While the troops were marching through the streets, which were practically blockaded with a crowd of people, the men, without orders from their commander, fired into the crowd. Many men were seen to drop; women screamed and fainted in the streets, and children mingled their piercing cries with the general uproar. The crowd shrank back and the militia marched down, but before they had proceeded two squares the crowd was as large as before. When opposite the office of the *American* newspaper a halt was called and another volley was received by the people with mingled cries of agony, threats, and jeers. Paving stones were gathered and hurled into the ranks of the soldiers. The military again took up their march and another fusillade left more dead and dying in the streets.

On the morning of July 19th the men of the Pennsylvania

Central Railroad, apparently without previous agreement, refused to take out any freight trains from Pittsburgh. Not a freight train left the station that day. The men explained that their action was in consequence of the determination of the company to introduce what was known as "double-headers," a system by which the company could dispense with a number of employees and increase the work of the remaining men. The men on this road had already had their wages reduced ten per cent., commencing June 1st. A conference between the representatives of the road at Pittsburgh and the workmen was held, but the road would make no concessions.

Colonel Thomas A. Scott, the President of the road, was absent from the city during the trouble, but was in constant communication with his representatives and dictated the policy to be pursued by the officers. There is no doubt but that he could have averted the strike and could have ended the conflict after it was begun.

On the morning of the 21st the infantry forces of Alleghany County, Pennsylvania, which had been called out for duty, were re-enforced by two batteries and two bodies of calvary. To these were added the First Division of the National Guards of Pennsylvania which had been called out at Philadelphia the preceding night. This force was under command of Major-General Brunton.

These preparations on the part of the government did not seem to deter the strikers or the mob. On the contrary they expressed the greatest contempt for the military array, and freely mingled with the soldiers. At half-past three in the afternoon, Sheriff Fife, accompanied by a posse of fifteen men, and supported by troops under Major-General Brunton, started for the general rendezvous of the strikers and the mob at the Eighth Street crossing. It had been agreed by the civil and military authorities that the sheriff was to attempt the arrest of those for whom warrants had been issued, and resistance was expected. The sheriff and his men, followed by the military, marched along the tracks to the depot, greeted with the yells and jeers of the crowd.

The military proceeded to clear the track, and the sheriff

to make the arrests. A vast crowd gathered composed of strikers and of citizens in sympathy with the strikers, many of them property holders. The sheriff arrested one man. Accounts differ as to what immediately followed, but it appears that before any act of resistance was made, the officer in command ordered his men to fire upon the crowd. The fire of the soldiers was very destructive; sixteen persons were instantly killed. The whole people were aroused and almost the entire populace was in the streets.

A large body raided the gun-shops and ammunition stores, and it is estimated that they seized over two thousand guns, together with pistols, swords and knives,—in all about $100,000 worth of arms and ammunition. The Philadelphia militia were besieged in the round-house, and were waited upon by a committee of the citizens and requested to leave the city, as their presence only tended to arouse the angry populace.

On Sunday morning, July 22d, the mob fired the trains in some of the buildings of the company. An attempt was made to storm the round-house in which the soldiers were besieged; a breach was made in the walls, but the mob was driven back by the fire of the soldiers. They then retired from that vicinity, the soldiers marching out and proceeding some distance before their departure was discovered. The mob pursued, and severe fighting ensued, until the troops had reached Shaftsburg, beyond Alleghany, from which place they marched twelve miles, to Claremount.

One hundred and twenty-five locomotives and railroad buildings to the value of about a million dollars were destroyed by fire. No private property of any kind excepting arms and ammunition was interfered with during the whole course of the riot. In the end the strikers were forced to give up the fight. Great excitement prevailed at Chicago, where conflicts occurred between the rioters and the police, the women being among the most demonstrative.

Dissatisfaction existed on the Missouri Pacific Railroad, at St. Louis, the wages having been reduced to a point which the men declared was insufficient for the support of themselves and families. A meeting was held by the railroad employees, and it was determined to call upon Mr. Talmage to demand a restoration of the wages paid before the reduction. Mr. Oliver Garrison, vice-president and general manager of the road, readily assented to the restoration of wages to a sum satisfactory to them.

At Kansas City, Mo., meetings of the employees were held on the 24th of July, and all quit work at noon, and no freight trains were allowed to depart. All labor was discontinued throughout the city. On the 29th a consultation was held between the executive committee of the strikers and an arbitration committee on the part of the railroad, and the disagreement was satisfactorily adjusted.

The terrible events at Pittsburgh called forth from representatives of capital, the pulpit and the press such expressions of bitterness, such unreasonable opposition to labor organizations and such demands for the strong arm of the law, as to cause many people to reflect upon the causes which produced these results. It is true that the workingmen all over the country were thoroughly aroused with indignation at the terrible poverty and condition of their fellows employed in the mines and on the great railroads. This feeling extended from Maine to California, and had a deeper root in the mind of what is termed the conservative American element of the workingmen than the public had any idea of. Secret meetings of working were held, and the question discussed in all its bearings. Men were armed, and ready to be armed, in the belief that it might be necessary for self-protection. At one of the meetings held in Boston an address of the Massachusetts labor men to the public was drafted by George E. McNeill, which was adopted and widely circulated. This address acted as a safety valve for the excited feelings of organized labor.

The firemen and brakemen of the railroads centering in Cleveland, Ohio, coopers, iron workers and other craftsmen went on strike.

Organizations heretofore unknown made their existence manifest about this period. Among these were the silver gilders, brush-makers, carvers, confectioners, fresco-painters, pastry-cooks, potters, stationary engineers, and the International Labor Union of America. This last, though never exceedingly large in membership, had branches in seventeen States of the Union. Agitation meetings were held under its auspices in the principal cities, and its declaration of principles and methods of work were extensively quoted. As it has sometimes been confounded with the International Organization of Europe, we give entire its declaration of principles, measures, and methods: —

The safety of society depends upon the equality of rights and opportunities of all its members; and whenever, from any cause, the freedom of a part of the community is endangered, either in their political or economic rights, it behooves the people to devise methods by which the usurpations of the powerful shall be overthrown, and the fullest freedom of the humblest be maintained. The political rights of a people are not more sacred than their economic rights, and to prevent a class from possessing all the material advantages of a progressive civilization is as much an act of tyranny as to prevent them from exercising their right of self-government.

The victory over "divine-right" rulership must be supplemented by a victory over property-right rulers; for there can be no government of the people, by the people, and for the people, where the many are dependent upon the few for an existence. Men will sacrifice their liberties for their lives, and those who control the industries of a people can and do control their votes.

The wage-workers of the world are forced by their poverty into deadly competition with each other. Race is thrown into antagonism with race, and nations of peoples are driven by their necessities to retard the progress of their fellows. In this remorseless warfare upon human welfare, the holiest ties of life are destroyed. The girl of sixteen is made to compete with the woman of thirty; the boy of nineteen against the man of forty. Children are driven from their home and the school, and men are forced to live in idleness upon the paltry earnings of their wives and little ones.

The achievements of liberty are the epochs of history. Villainage, serfdom and chattel slavery — the past systems of labor — have forever disappeared. The laborers of the civilized world have gained the right to starve. It now rests with them to secure the right of possession to the products of their labor.

The liberty of labor is the hope of the world, and that liberty can only be obtained by the solidarity of laborers upon labor measures. We therefore, in the interests of a common brotherhood, declare: —

1st. That the wage-system is a despotism, under which the wage-worker is forced to sell his labor at such price and such conditions as the employer of labor shall dictate.

2d. That political liberty cannot long continue under economic bondage; for he who is forced to sell his labor or starve, will sell his franchise when the same alternative is presented.

3d. That civilization means the diffusion of knowledge and the distribution of wealth; and the present system of labor tends to extremes of culture and ignorance, affluence and penury.

5th. That as the wealth of the world is distributed through the wage system, its better distribution must come through higher wages, and better opportunities, until wages shall represent the earnings and not the necessities of labor; thus melting profit upon labor out of existence, and making co-operation, or self-employed labor, the natural and logical step from wage slavery to free labor.

6th. That all attempts to anticipate co-operation in advance of societary conditions are exotics or mere hot-house growths that are kept alive for a time through the sheer force of character and self-sacrificing leadership attempting them, and are as foreign to an atmosphere of cheap labor and a world of wages as the plants of the tropics in a northern clime.

7th. That the first step, towards the emancipation of labor is a reduction of the hours of labor, that the added leisure produced by a reduction of the hours of labor will operate upon the natural causes that affect the habits and customs of the people, enlarging wants, stimulating ambition, decreasing idleness, and increasing wages.

We, therefore, believing that the emancipation of labor can only be achieved by the organization of the laborers into a great protective propaganda of the principles enunciated in the foregoing declaration of principles, and in response to a demand made upon us by various labor organizations and wage-workers in all parts of the United States, severally agree to form ourselves into a committee, known as the Provisional Central Committee of the International Labor Union, whose objects shall be to secure the following measures:—The reduction of the hours of labor; higher wages; factory, mine, and workshop inspection; abolition of the contract convict labor and trnck system; employers to be held responsible for accidents by neglected machinery; prohibition of child labor; the establishment of labor bureaus.

Labor propaganda by means of a labor press, labor lectures, the employment of a general organizer, and the final abolition of the wage system.

The methods by which we propose to secure these measures are:—

1st. The formation of an Amalgamated Union of laborers so that members of any calling can combine under a central head, and form a part of the Amalgamated Trades Unions.

2nd. The establishment of a general fund for benefit and protective purposes.

3d. The organization of all workingmen in their trade unions, and the creation of such unions where none exist.

4th. The National and International amalgamation of all labor unions.

In this hour of the dark distress of labor, we call upon all laborers of whatever nationality, creed or color, skilled and unskilled, trades unionist, and those now out of union, to join hands with us and each other to the end that poverty and all its attendant evils shall be abolished forever.

The Central Committee was to be composed of one member from each State, and in any State where ten branches were formed they were to elect a member of the committee. No person could be admitted who had acted contrary to the interests of the labor movement or had been excluded from any other labor organization for misconduct, until such satisfaction be given to the injured parties as might be ordered by the Executive Council. Workmen who refused to join the organizations of their trade or calling, provided such organizations existed and were recognized as *bona fide* societies, could not be admitted into membership. Persons who were not wage-workers, but who were in full accord with the letter and the spirit of the organization, and who would agree to be governed by the code of laws, could be admitted by a unanimous vote of a branch meeting and the consent of the Central Committee. This organization had an employment committee for the purpose of procuring employment for its members, and propaganda contingent, out-of-work, travelling, and sick and burial funds. The special organ was the *New York Labor Standard*, edited by J. P. McDonnell of Paterson, New Jersey. The headquarters of the order, and of the paper, were afterwards removed to Paterson. The most effective work was accomplished in 1878. It was during the last-named year that the order of the Knights of Labor became known to the public.

In 1878 the Forty-fifth United States Congress adopted a resolution appointing a committee of seven members of the House to ascertain the causes of the general depression of business, especially of labor, and to devise and propose measures for relief. Hendrick B. Wright was chairman of the committee. Testimony was taken in Chicago, San Francisco, Des Moines, New York, and Boston, principally on the contraction of the currency and land monopoly. The committee reported the testimony in full.

In 1878 and 1879 the Fourth of July was made an occasion of public demonstrations in the advocacy of the Labor movement. In 1878 George E. McNeill, of Boston, was the orator of the occasion at Chicago, and in 1879 Mr. Ira Steward, of Boston, was the orator in that city, and in St. Louis Jonathan C. Fincher was the principal speaker.

In the fall of 1879 a young man, then confined in the hospital in Paterson, N. J., being treated for malarial fever, wrote an open letter for publication and addressed it to the *Labor Standard*, published in that city. The letter was published over the signature of its author, and at the next session of the grand jury the author of the letter and the editor of the paper were both indicted for libel and brought before Judge Dickinson, tried, convicted, and sentenced to sixty days imprisonment in the Passaic county jail. The letter referred to described the condition of the people working in a brick-yard at Mountain View, N. J. He said the hours of labor were from four in the morning till six at night; at seven o'clock the men were called to breakfast, which he said consisted of a pitcherfull of hot water which the cook called coffee, but which the men called "strike water," which means the water used for washing the strikes which clean off the bricks; that the food consisted of salt pork and bread and butter; complaint was made that the bread was sour and that the butter was more like axle-grease; that the bread was baked hard on the outside and was underdone on the inside; that the dinner and supper were of about the same description; that men were forced to lodge in shanties through the roofs of which the rain flowed in torrents at times; that the beds were unwashed and the place filled with vermin. He also referred to the treatment he had received while sick there before going to the Sisters' hospital. The evidence at the trial strongly sustained the charges made by the writer of the letter, and the conviction and punishment called forth a storm of indignation, not only in Paterson, but throughout the length and breadth of the country. Trades assemblies, labor councils, trades-unions, and all kinds of workingmen's organizations, passed resolutions severely criticising the action of the court and sustaining the editor, J. P. McDonnell, and the writer, Mr. Michael Menton, as martyrs to the cause. On the day of their release a public reception was given to the imprisoned men, the streets were thronged with a crowd never equalled in that city. This was the second time that Mr. McDonnell had been convicted for rendering service to the cause of Labor.

In 1879 some excitement was caused by the exodus of the colored people from Mississippi to Kansas. The Commissioner of Labor Statistics of the latter State, in treating this question, says: "Dismal forebodings were expressed by the papers and echoed by many citizens of Kansas regarding the future of these sojourners from the sunny South as they camped upon the bleak prairies of Kansas, and doubtless there were ample grounds for this apprehension." It is estimated that about two thousand people thus emigrated. An investigation has been made into their condition, which shows that as a rule they were very much better off in their new homes. The commissioner says:—

When these people first landed they were, as a class, utterly destitute. They had exhausted their last cent in reaching the land of promise, and they had no food to save them from starvation and no roof to shelter them. Many were shipped to Topeka. They have managed to erect small shanties in the ravine where they first landed, and have managed to subsist, some of them say, better than they did in their Southern homes.

The cause of the exodus was poverty and bad treatment. An investigation into the average daily wages showed the average daily earnings to be $262.75 against $333.09 earned by white laborers in a like column, given in the report.

Numerous strikes occurred in 1880. The drivers of the Third Avenue line of horse-cars in New York City struck on Sunday, June 27th, against the wages and the long hours. The police were called out and held in readiness. The strike was a failure. Strikes also occurred among the ribbon-weavers of Paterson, New York and Philadelphia, against a reduction of twenty per cent. There were strikes among furniture workers in different parts of the country, among the cotton-yard men in New Orleans for an advance of wages, among the stable-men of New York for an advance of wages, in San Francisco, New Jersey, New York, and other places, for the abolition of Sunday work. Strikes occurred in Louisiana among the colored men for an advance to one dollar a day, in which instance the military were called out. The ship-butchers' union, of New York, struck for less hours of work. Gingham weavers and cotton and woolen operatives struck in the New England States, where in some cases, notably that of the gingham-weavers, dividends of from twenty to forty per cent. had been paid, and at the time of the strike fifteen to twenty per cent. had been paid, and the stock had gone up to double its par value. In Omaha, Neb., the men in the smelting works struck. At Cohoes, N. Y., cotton operatives struck for a ten per cent. advance. In Barberville, Va., there was a strike of colored laborers. The barbers and journeymen of New York organized against five-cent shops. The stock-yard men in Chicago denounced the interference of the police in their strike. The men employed on the Hoosac Tunnel struck for eight hours a day and were defeated. Wages were increased in some of the cotton and woolen-mills. Among cabinet and desk-makers wages were advanced. Strikes occurred on some of the railroads; wages were advanced on the Lake Shore & Michigan Southern. A general advance in wages was granted to miners. Fifty cents per day was granted as the result of a strike of some of the stone masons in New York. The strike fever spread among the boys, and at Cohoes, N. Y., two hundred boys employed in the cotton-mills struck, many of them being under twelve years of age. They had banners inscribed "United we stand, divided we fall," "Good news from Fall River," "Ours is a hard fate—all work and no time to play in God's sunshine," "Pity us poor children who have to work," etc. The State of Vermont was also invaded by this spirit; the boys in a carding-room of a woolen-mill struck; some of them were receiving four dollars a week for doing men's work. A newspaper at the time reported that the superintendent shook one or two of them and the rest went to work. From the *Labor Standard* of March 20, 1880, we copy a list of the strikes and meetings reported in that issue. Strikes were reported of potters at Green Point, L. I.; puddlers of Johnstown and Columbia, Penn.; and at Buffalo, N. Y., over seven thousand men involved; journeymen tailors of New York; train and track-men of the Baltimore & Ohio Railroad, at Piedmont, W. Va., struck for a ten per cent. advance; boys engaged in a rope-walk in Brooklyn, N. Y., woolen weavers in Glenham,

N. Y., iron-workers in Pottstown, Penn., and shoemakers at Greensburg, Ind., were on strike.

The National Labor Congress convened at Pittsburgh, Penn., 125 members being present at the opening, representing a constituency of 222,856. The Congress demanded a repeal of the conspiracy acts, abolition of the contract convict labor system, passed resolutions in sympathy with the suffering in Ireland, advocated the establishment of a national bureau of labor statistics, favored the abolition of the truck system, passed resolutions in favor of compulsory education of all children fourteen years of age, the ventilation of mines and work-shops, the providing of fire-escapes, the mechanics' lien law, the incorporation of trades-unions, and the prohibition of Chinese immigration.

At Paterson, N. J., a movement was made by the workingmen to prevent the employment of labor on Sunday, and the announcement of the meeting contained this statement: "Another mill started on Sunday; almost as large an attendance as can be found in some of our churches. Business is booming, though religion and good morals suffer. The Almighty Dollar must be worshipped."

The Central Trades and Labor Assembly of New Orleans is an association of all the labor organizations of the city. This fraternization was brought about by a movement inaugurated in the summer of 1881 by the Typographical Union, and especially by its president, Mr. William J. Hammond, the first president of the new association.

This Union appointed a committee to bring about a meeting of accredited persons from different labor and trades-unions of the city, in order to amalgamate all men who earned their living by labor into a compact combination, for the purpose of mutual aid and support in all controversies between labor and capital, and issued a circular calling a meeting for Sunday evening, August 2, 1881, to appoint an executive committee to supervise the organization of an amalgamated trades and labor union for New Orleans, and for putting it on a working basis.

At this time there were in existence in that city several

organizations, already strong in numbers; but it was thought that the interests of the working classes could best be subserved by such a consolidation as was proposed, and, as a result of this, a confederation was formed by the organization of a Central Assembly or Council, composed of three delegates from each of the associations admitted to the union, and vested with general legislative and executive powers over matters of the assembly.

By this alliance the strength, influence, and financial resources of the thirty odd labor organizations in the city, embracing almost every branch of mechanical and industrial pursuits, were combined. Any one of the constituted bodies could strike, if it saw fit; but it could receive the support of the entire body only after the complaints had been considered by the central body and approved as sufficient grounds for a strike.

The success of the organization was such that in 1883 the total membership was about fifteen thousand. In November of that year there was a parade of the bodies composing the assembly, ten thousand men being in line, representing all countries, colors, and industries. The parade was a brilliant success, and was repeated on November 25, 1884, and on the same date, 1885. John Delaney was Grand Marshal in 1883; in 1884, R. F. Gray, of the Typographical Union, was President of the Assembly, and acted as Grand Marshal in the parade; and J. H. Connors was Grand Marshal in the parade of 1885.

The formation of this association of trades and labor unions is confessed to have done more to break the color line in New Orleans than any other thing that has been done since the emancipation of the slaves; and to-day the white and colored laborers of that city are as fraternal in their relations as they are in any part of the country, — the negroes, especially, taking great pride in their loyalty to their organizations.

In 1882 strikes again multipled. Extensive strikes occurred in some of the iron districts. A strike occurred in the stock-yards at Chicago, Ill., the principal firms demanding a promise from employees that they would not belong to any union. The

First Regiment was held in readiness to assist the Sheriff in maintaining peace.

Coke employees at Mansfield, Penn., struck, and complaint was made by the working people of Pennsylvania against the importation of Hungarians; circulars were issued by the men stating their claims and that women and children were doing work fit only for the stoutest men. Women were found at work with infants lying promiscuously on the ground, and girls under ten years of age were drawing coke. There was extreme filthiness in their houses and habits, some of them carrying on an illicit whiskey traffic, while there was extreme promiscuity in their marital relations.

In 1880 a convention of some of the leading national and international trades-unions was held, and an organization was formed under the name of the Federation of Organized Trades and Labor Unions of the United States and Canada. This Organization was to do the work of former labor congresses. The preamble declares that because of the struggle going on between oppressors and oppressed, capitalists and laborers, in all countries, which was growing in intensity and working disastrous results to the toiling millions of all nations if not combined for mutual protection and benefit, and whereas even a minority thoroughly organized might avert much danger and organize relief, this federation should be formed. The platform demands the enforcement of the existing labor laws and the enactment of others, and recommends all trade and labor organizations to secure proper representation in all law-making bodies by means of the ballot. We quote from the report of the secretary, Frank K. Foster, in 1884.

Under the head of "Organization" he says: "Each trade is groping blindly after results, with more or less defective machinery and imperfect perception of methods and issues. Low dues, partial organization and neglect of business principles have hitherto proved insuperable obstacles to the full measure of success."

He speaks of the nominal triumph of Jay Gould over the Telegraph Brotherhood, the defeat of the Fall River operatives and the bitter contest raging in the Hocking Valley as arguments, not against the principle of organization or the spirit of resistance, but for the more perfect unity of wage-workers. He records, as the result of four months' investigation ninety-eight strikes, involving fifty-three thousand work-people; fifty of them against reduction of wages, seven for an increase, three to establish a scale of prices, five against non-union men, three for less hours, four for back wages, two against signing contracts, three against shop exactions, and twenty-two cause not given. The trades involved in these strikes were miners, printers, metal workers, leather workers, building trades, railroad employees, textile operatives, laborers and miscellaneous. Thirteen were successful, fifteen failures, fifteen were compromised, and sixty-five not recorded.

Under the head of the "Eight Hour Question" he says, "It appears to be the generally expressed desire of the societies represented in this association that it assume the initiative in a movement for the reduction of the hours of labor." He reports the opening of fraternal relations between the trades-unions of France and America, and mentions the delegation of fourteen French brothers visiting this country, sent by syndical chambers comprising sixty-eight of the mechanical arts in the municipality of Paris. A resolution was adopted asking the co-operation of the Knights of Labor to establish the eight-hour reform.

This society has continued its organization up to the present time, doing effective work in the amalgamation of labor societies. Demands for labor legislation and in the National Congress are continually made, and from its formation up to 1886 the work of organization has been carried on quietly but effectually.

The Order of the Knights of Labor began to manifest itself as a potent factor in 1885, and the strikes that occurred under its auspices are matters of recent history, and require no space in this chapter.

The year 1886 will be known as the year of the great uprising of labor. The future historian will say: Trades-unions increased their membership and their powers as never before.

The Knights of Labor, who had for seventeen years struggled against all adverse influences, added to their membership by tens of thousands weekly. Trades and occupations that had never before been organized joined the mixed assemblies or trade assemblies of the order. Hope seemed to have entered the heart of the most oppressed. It was the very dawning of the day when the term "dignity of labor" meant something. Laboring men who had heretofore considered themselves as scarcely more than serfs, without rights or privileges, fearing to organize, or failing to do so because of the hopelessness of their condition, seemed to be inspired with a new spirit. So great was the increased membership that even the largest cities were unable to provide hall capacity for the meetings of organized labor. The horse-car employees, whose long hours of labor and barbarous conditions had been the shame of our civilization, obtained in all the principal cities, a reduction in their working time and an increase of wages. Strikes prevailed everywhere. Thousands of grievances were settled by peaceful arbitration. Every branch of labor was affected. Heretofore there had existed a feeling of caste, even among the laboring men; the skilled mechanic had looked down upon the unskilled, the well-paid considered the ill-paid as hardly worthy of recognition. The skilled and the unskilled, the high-paid and the low-paid, all joined hands. The color line had been broken, and black and white were found working together in the same cause. During the winter months lectures had been delivered and eight-hour agitation meetings held at frequent intervals. The press was filled with labor news. The clergy opened the doors of their associations to labor men for the discussion of labor measures or methods. The great strike on the Southwestern railroad system called attention anew to the giant monopolies that controlled these great interests. The movement for less hours of labor was partially successful, some gaining the eight-hour and some the nine-hour day, while an advance in wages was gained in many industries.

CHAPTER VI.

LABOR LEGISLATION.

A General View — States Legislate for Chief Industries — Legislation for Children — Protection for Mechanics and Other Workmen — Regulating the Hours of Labor — States with an Eight-Hour Law — Short Hours for Women and Children — Children must be Educated — Fire-Escapes on Factories — Other Aids to the Employees — Protection for Miners — Arbitration of Disputed Points — Provided in New Jersey in 1880 — The Law of Pennsylvania — Similar Laws in Other States — New York's Law — The Law of Massachusetts — Bureaus of Labor.

THE progress of agitation upon labor questions and the advance thereon from year to year is easily traced through the statutes of the various legislatures of the country. And yet there has undoubtedly been much agitation in many States, which show no real progress by enacted laws. In them the leaven is surely — even though slowly — working. When they do appreciate the importance of the subject, they will probably go beyond the point reached by their sister States, profiting wisely by their experience, and learning wherein to avoid their mistakes. It is hardly practicable, within the compass of a book of this nature, to state in detail the laws of the States upon the important branches of the labor problem. Only a general view will therefore be given, the minor details being necessarily omitted. Each State naturally has legislated with particular reference to those departments of labor that are most prominent within its own borders. The mining States have their own special laws, with hardly a reference to manufacturing interests; the States where the factory operatives are most numerous have legislated largely in their interests; while the great agricultural States have enacted but little, if any, legislation on these subjects. In considering this subject, it will be most practicable to divide it into its natural departments, even as we find the States themselves have done in their legislation.

Many of the States have laws limiting the hours of labor of children to ten per day. It has become a well recognized truth that the interests of the State demand this care of its children. The laws relating to apprenticeship are of the same general nature, providing for the indenture of children during their minority, after they become of an age when their work is of value, to persons who stand to them in the relation of parents. These laws cover orphans and children in asylums. In most States the consent of the children themselves must be obtained if they are fourteen years of age or over. The details of laws on this topic vary considerably, but all are based on the same general principle. Many States also attempt to guard the interests of the mechanics and all persons performing labor on, or furnishing materials for, any building, by giving them a lien on the structure itself and on the interest of the owner of the lot on which it stands. Many of these laws have been so amended as to make them practically inoperative. They give to employees on railroads and steamboats, and to persons furnishing them supplies, a lien on the franchise, on the gross earnings and real and personal property of the companies operating them; and this lien takes precedence of all other claims. Workmen upon vessels have liens that have the precedence of all others except those for mariners' wages. Lumbermen have liens on the lumber for services or supplies furnished. Farm laborers have a lien on the crops he has helped produce, to secure compensation for his labor. These liens are of more or less limited duration, varying with different States and with the nature of the object the lien is put upon. Miners also have protection by a per diem penalty and other compensations for failure of the companies to pay them within certain regular intervals.

California, Connecticut (except on farms and where otherwise agreed), Illinois, New Mexico (in the mines), Pennsylvania and New York (except for farm labor and weekly, monthly or yearly contracts), have come down to the limit of eight hours as a legal day's work, and most States, however, leave it to be understood that ten hours constitute a day's work unless it is otherwise stated. Various States also have special provision as to the hours of labor for women and children. Massachusetts forbids the employment of minors under eighteen, and women in all corporations for more than ten hours per day, except where the hours are differently apportioned so as to secure a shorter working day each week; but no week shall have over sixty hours of work. Rhode Island provides that minors between twelve and fifteen shall not work more than eleven hours per day, nor before 5 A. M., nor after 7.30 P. M. Vermont limits the hours for the work of children under fifteen to ten daily. Wisconsin and Dakota provide that minors under eighteen, and women, shall not work over eight hours per day in manufactories, workshops or other places used for mechanical or manufacturing purposes. These laws are of little or no effect where organized labor can not compel the standard thus fixed to become the custom. California allows children to work only eight hours daily, except in vinicultural or horticultural pursuits.

In Connecticut children under fifteen can work in mechanical or manufacturing establishments not more than ten hours a day or fifty-eight hours a week. Indiana allows no minors under eighteen to work more than ten hours a day in cotton or woolen factories; and children under twelve must not be employed over eight hours per day. Maine and Maryland say no minor under sixteen shall work over ten hours a day. In Michigan children under eighteen and women can work only ten hours a day or sixty hours a week, and one hour must be allowed for dinner. Minnesota limits the hours also to ten, and New Hampshire fixes that limit for minors under fifteen, New Jersey for those under sixteen, Ohio for those under eighteen, and Pennylvania for those under twenty-one. Several States absolutely prohibit the employment in factories of children under a certain age, as follows: Indiana, none under twelve in the manufacture of iron, steel, nails, metals, machinery or tobacco; Colorado, none under twelve in the mines; Connecticut, none under fourteen, unless having had twelve weeks' schooling; Illinois and Indiana, none under fourteen in the mines; Iowa and Kansas, none under twelve in the mines; Maine, none under twelve, except having had four months' schooling in year previous; Massachusetts, none under twelve during the hours when the public schools are in session; Michigan, none under fourteen, unless with three or four months' schooling in previous years; Missouri, none under twelve, and none under fourteen, unless he or she can read and write, in the coal mines; New Hampshire, none under sixteen, unless attended private or public school at least twelve weeks in preceding year; New Jersey, no boy under twelve, and no girl under fourteen, during school hours; New York, none under fourteen, except with fourteen weeks' schooling in previous year, and none under eighteen more than sixty hours per week; Ohio, none under twelve; Pennsylvania, none under twelve in the coal mines, and none under thirteen in factories. In Georgia the hours of labor for persons under twenty-one in all manufacturing establishments and machine shops, are from sunrise to sunset.

Besides providing that children shall be prohibited from working in factories, except under certain regulations, the State insists that its children shall be educated to a greater or less extent in their early years. Some States in the Union do not make special laws upon this subject, although more or less legislation tends in that direction, while some have very definite statutes upon it. Connecticut requires all children between eight and sixteen, of good physical and mental condition, to attend school while it is in session.

The need of protection from fire has caused legislation requiring factories and large buildings, used either as tenements or for work-rooms, to be provided with fire-escapes. Massachusetts, which is dotted all over with factories, and whose cities are thronged with working people, has as complete laws on this subject as any State, and much more complete than most. It has inspectors of factories and public buildings, who may enter all buildings used for public or manufacturing purposes, examine the methods of protection from accident, the means of escape from fire, and make investigations as to the employment of women and children. The law provides that all factories and manufacturing establishments, three or more stories in height, in which forty or more persons are employed, unless supplied with a sufficient number of tower stairways, shall be supplied with sufficient fire-escapes, properly constructed upon the outside thereof, and connected with the interior by doors and windows, with suitable landings at every story above the first, including the attic, if the same be used for work-rooms. Cities may provide that this provision shall apply to all buildings three or more stories in height. Every building, three or more stories in height, in whole or in part used, occupied, leased or rented for a tenement to be occupied by more than four families, or a lodging-house, shall be provided with a sufficient means of escape in case of fire. Outside or inside doors of buildings where operatives are employed shall not be locked, bolted, or otherwise fastened during labor hours, to prevent free egress. Every room above the second story in factories or work-shops in which five or more operatives are employed, shall be provided with more than one way of egress by stairways on the inside or outside of the building, and such stairways shall be, as nearly as practicable, at opposite ends of the room. Stairways on the outside must connect with each story by doors or windows opening outwardly, which must at all times be kept clear of obstruction. All main doors must open outwardly, and each story must be amply supplied with means for extinguishing fires.

Other States have provisions very similar to those of Massachusetts. Connecticut requires fire-escapes to each story above the second for buildings used for work-rooms, factories, lodging or tenement-houses. Delaware says escapes must be provided for the third story and those above. Illinois requires metallic fire-escapes on all buildings of four or more stories, except exclusively private houses. Maine provides that every building in which trade, manufacture or business is carried on must have fire-escapes from each story above the ground. Michigan requires suitable escapes from similar buildings over two stories high, and New Jersey does for such buildings where thirty or more operatives are steadily or casually at work. Ohio compels convenient exits from the upper stories of such buildings, easily accessible in case of fire. Pennsylvania provides for fire-escapes similar to those in States already mentioned; and also, as an additional safeguard, provides that in each room in such buildings on the third or higher floor there shall be a chain securely fastened to at least one window, not less than ten feet long, to which shall be attached a rope not less than an inch in diameter and long enough to reach the ground. These ropes and chains are to be kept in an unlocked box near the inside sill of the window. The halls and head and foot of the stair-ways in such buildings must be lighted with a red lamp, and alarms and gongs easy of access must also be kept.

In some of the States there are laws requiring that suitable seats shall be provided for females in manufacturing, mechanical and mercantile establishments, which they can use when not engaged in the active duties of their employment. Employers are required to give due notice before discharging an employee. Railroad companies are forbidden to exact any part of the earnings of the employees for any hospital, reading-room, library or gymnasium. Work-shops must be kept in a cleanly condition and free from noxious effluvia from any source, and must be well lighted and ventilated. Elevators and machinery must be properly guarded to prevent accident. The formation of corporations in the interest of trade and labor, for the improvement of the social and material interest of their members, is authorized and encouraged. Corporations must give thirty days' notice of a reduction of wages, specifying amount of same. New Jersey has prohibited employers from attempting to compel their employees to purchase at stores they may own. Ohio has a similar law. New York says operatives may assemble and use all lawful means to induce employers to pay a just and fair compensation for services rendered. Pennsylvania requires persons controlling coal mines to keep at each mine a suitable ambulance and stretchers to carry injured persons to their homes.

The States in which mining is a prominent industry, have

enacted laws to protect the miners from accidents by fire and otherwise. Colorado prohibits the employment of more than fifteen workers in mines where 15,000 square yards have been excavated, unless there are two separate outlets to every seam, separated by natural strata, not less than one hundred feet in breadth, by which distinct means of egress and ingress are always available. To all other mines worked by shafts, slopes or drifts, there must be two openings twelve months after 15,000 square yards are excavated, provided more than fifteen persons are employed. Communication with contiguous mines must be constructed in connection with every vein or stratum of coal worked. Metal tubes or telephones must be provided, so that conversation may be had all over the mine. Safety lamps must be provided. The owner or agent of a mine working ten or more men close to an abandoned mine containing inflammable gas or fire-damp, must bore holes twelve feet in advance of the coal face of the working places. An examination of them must be daily made and a record kept. The fire-boss must make a daily record of defects in ventilating apparatus, etc. The provisions in regard to hoisting apparatus, gang-ways on which cars are moved, ventilation, etc., are very complete. Illinois provides that copper needles must be used in preparing blasts, and not less than nine inches of copper on iron bars used for tamping blasts of powder. Indiana requires an inspection each morning of the wire ropes used for lowering and hoisting in coal-mines, which must be of wire. When gas is known to exist the mine must be properly examined each morning. Not more than ten persons are allowed to work in any mine until a second outlet is completed. Iowa also requires two outlets to all mines, and Kansas requires them when more than twenty-five men are employed. Kansas also requires escapement shafts to be provided with ladders securely fastened so as to bear at least ten men, or other safe means for hoisting miners independent of the regular hoisting machinery. Missouri has laws similar to those of Colorado, as also has New Mexico. Ohio provides that all doors, to assist in ventilation of mines, must shut of their own accord and not be able to stand open. It also requires morning inspection of mines where gas exists, and means of conversation from top to the bottom. The provisions of Pennsylvania are very similar to those already quoted. Tennessee requires machinery in and about mines and tops of shafts to be properly fenced off. Most of the mining States provide for inspectors, appointed by the Governor, with full powers to see that the provisions of the laws are properly enforced.

The question of arbitration for the settlement of controversies between employers and employees has become very prominent within a few years. Several States have already taken action in the matter. In the Legislature of New Jersey, of 1880, provisions were made for the arbitration of labor disputes before an arbitrator selected by employers, another by employees, and a third by the other two. Arbitration is voluntary, but after submission the award is binding. Pennsylvania provides that presiding justices of common pleas courts, upon petition or agreement, shall issue license for the establishment of tribunals to settle disputes in iron, steel, glass, textile fabrics and coal trades. Petition must be signed by fifty workmen or five separate firms, individuals or corporations, within the county of the petitioners, or by five employers, each employing at least ten men, or by the representatives of a firm, individual or corporation employing not less than seventy-five men, and the agreement shall be signed by both of said specified numbers and persons; *provided*, that if there be a strike or dispute at the time, and suspension exists, or is probable, the judge shall require testimony as to the representative character of the petitioners, and if they do not represent, at least half each party in dispute, license may be denied. Workmen signing must be resident of a judicial district one year, engaged in the branch of trade they represent two years, and be citizens of the United States. Employers signing must also be citizens and engaged in some of the branches of business mentioned for one year, must each employ ten workmen in such branch, and each may be a firm, individual or corporation. Petition must be sworn to by at least two signers. After the arbitrators on each side have chosen their umpire, the license may issue, fixing time and place of meeting. One tribunal may be created in each judicial district for each of the trades named, to continue for one year. The position of umpire can only be filled by the mutual choice of all the representatives of both employers and workingmen, and he acts only after the failure of the tribunal to agree in three meetings. His award is final only upon what is submitted to him in writing signed by all members of the tribunal, or by parties submitting the same, and upon questions affecting the price of labor. It shall in no case be binding upon either employer or workmen, save as they may acquiesce or agree therein after such award. The tribunal shall receive no compensation from city or county, but expenses may be paid by voluntary contributions. No lawyers or agents are to appear on either side, and the proceedings are voluntary.

Iowa has a law very similar to that of Pensylvania, but the awards are conclusive and final, and when the award is for a specific sum of money the award may be made a matter of record in the district court of the county, and the proper court may issue final and other process to enforce the same. Tribunals must sit at the county seats, but disputes in one county may be referred to a tribunal sitting in another.

The law of Kansas is nearly in the exact words of that of Iowa. It provides, however, that members of the tribunal shall draw two dollars each from the county treasury for each day of actual service. The award of a tribunal may be impeached for fraud, accident or mistake. Ohio has a law closely similar to those of the above States.

New York provides for local boards of five arbitrators, two to be chosen by the employer and two by the employees, they to choose the fifth, who shall act as chairman. A decision by such a board is final, unless an appeal is made to the State Board. This latter body is appointed by the Governor, and holds office for one year. One member must be taken from each of the two leading political parties and the third from a *bona fide* labor organization. Two of the three make a quorum to transact business, and may hold meetings at any time or place in the State. Each arbitrator is entitled to a salary of

NATIONAL LABOR LEGISLATORS.

$3,000, payable quarterly, while the clerk has $2,000. The duty of the State Board is to consider appeals from the local boards, and its decision is final and conclusive on both parties. This law was passed May 18, 1886, and section 9 provides that it shall make a report to the next Legislature of such statements, facts and explanations as will disclose the actual working of the Board, and such suggestions as to legislation that may seem conducive to harmonizing the relations of, and disputes between, employers and the wage-earning masses, and the improvement of the present system of production.

The Massachusetts Legislature had much debate in the session of 1886 over the question of arbitration, and finally passed a measure known as the Douglas bill, because it was especially in charge of Senator W. L. Douglas, of Brockton, who was on the Committee on Labor, which reported the bill. This provides that the Governor shall appoint one member of a State Board, who shall be an employer or selected from some association representing employers of labor; a second, who shall be selected from some labor organization and not an employer of labor; and a third, who shall be appointed on the recommendation of the other two. If they cannot agree, however, on this third man, within thirty days, then he shall be appointed by the Governor. This Board holds office for one year, or until their successors are appointed. The decision of the board is to be binding for six months, or until either party has given the other written notice of his intention not to be bound by the same at the expiration of sixty days therefrom. The bill further provides for local boards of arbitration with powers equal to those of the State Board, which may ask and receive advice from that Board. The pay of the arbitrators is to be five dollars per day for actual service, and necessary expenses, all to be paid from the State treasury.

The provisions and scope of the national law upon this matter are fully discussed by Hon. J. J. O'Neill, member of Congress from the city of St. Louis and chairman of the House Committee on Labor, in his chapter on "Arbitration," in another part of this book.

Not only have many States created Bureaus of Labor, but

Congress has established (June 27, 1884) a National Bureau, of which Hon. Carroll D. Wright, of Boston, is the chief. The State Bureaus have been established as follows and in the following order: Massachusetts Bureau of Statistics of Labor, 1869; Pennsylvania Bureau of Industrial Statistics, 1872; Connecticut Bureau of Labor Statistics, 1873 (discontinued 1875, re-established 1885); Ohio Bureau of Labor Statistics, 1877; New Jersey Bureau of Statistics of Labor and Industries, 1878; Missouri Bureau of Labor Statistics and Inspection, 1879; Illinois Bureau of Labor Statistics, 1879; Indiana Bureau of Statistics and Geology, 1879; New York Bureau of Labor Statistics, 1883; California Bureau of Labor Statistics, 1883; Michigan Bureau of Labor and Industrial Statistics, 1883; Wisconsin Bureau of Labor Statistics, 1883; Iowa Bureau of Labor Statistics, 1884; Maryland Statistics of Labor, 1884; Kansas Bureau of Labor and Industrial Statistics, 1885. These bureaus are located at the capitals of the States named, and their publications are becoming widely known for the valuable contributions which they make to economic science and literature. They are bureaus distinctly American in their character, although some of the European governments are now contemplating the establishment of kindred offices.

CHAPTER VII.

PRINTERS AND THEIR UNIONS.

First Local Union in America — Rules for Forming New Societies — Demanding a Government Printing Office — The National Typographical Union Formed — Chartering Subordinate Unions — General Laws Formulated — Strong Fraternal Feeling — Conditional Membership — Another Name Adopted — Women's Typographical Union No. 1 — Pressmen's Union Permitted — Federation of Trades-Unions — Experience in Strikes — Important Questions the Union has Discussed — Summary of General Laws — Sessions and Officers of National and International Typographical Unions.

THE International Typographical Union had its origin in the "National Convention of Journeymen Printers," which assembled at Stoneall's Hotel, Fulton Street, New York City, on December 2, 1850. The convention assembled under a call made by printers' societies in New York, Boston and Philadelphia, and comprised delegates from the States of New York, New Jersey, Pennsylvania, Maryland and Kentucky. A permanent organization was effected by the election of John W. Perejoy, of Maryland, as President; George E. Greene, of Kentucky, and M. C. Brown, of Pennsylvania, Vice-Presidents, and F. J. Ottarson, of New York, and John Hartman, of New Jersey, Secretaries. The plan of organization adopted was so well conceived and far-reaching in its aims that substantially the same course of action in respect of the management of the trade throughout the whole country is paramount to-day. How well these pioneer organizers of the printing trade laid the foundation of a stable, well-disciplined and intelligent national craft organization can readily be seen from an address to the journeymen printers of the United States, issued under authority of the first convention, in which are set forth the following guiding modes of action in the formation of societies: —

1st. An understanding in the regulation of scales of prices in different localities, so that those in one place may not be permitted to become so comparatively high as to induce work to be sent elsewhere.

2d. The enforcement of the principle of limiting apprentices, by which measure a too rapid increase in the number of workmen, too little care in the selection of boys for the business, and the employment of herds of half men at half wages, to the detriment of good workmen, would be effectually prevented.

3d. The issuing of Traveling Certificates, by which the distresses of brother craftsmen, incurred in journeying from one place to another in search of work, might be relieved.

4th. Measures to prevent disgraced members of the profession enjoying, anywhere in the United States, those privileges which belong exclusively to honorable printers. These consisted in keeping a registry of "rats," to be sent by the Executive Committee to every Union in the country for reference, and admitting to membership no stranger who did not produce evidence of his having been a member in good standing of the printing society (if any existed) in the place from whence he came.

5th. The gradual collection of a sum of money by each Union sufficient to enable it to hold out successfully against the employers, in the event of a contention for higher wages.

The address, which is generally conceded to have been written by Hon. M. F. Conway, of Baltimore, presented the relations of capital and labor in as clear a light as any later labor monograph on this vexed question, and undoubtedly its free circulation among the craft in the larger cities of this country gave the project of national organization a successful impetus.

Prominent among the subjects discussed at this first session was reform in the public printing, and a resolution was passed recommending Congress to withhold the government printing from all persons not practical printers. The agitation for the establishment of a government printing office through memorials and committees, and the demand for the imposition by Congress of a protective duty on imported stereotype plates, held leading places in the legislation of the national and local unions, year after year, until both measures received the sanction of Congress.

The second "National Convention of Journeymen Printers" assembled in Baltimore, Md., on September 12, 1851, and comprised delegates from seven States. J. L. Gibbons, of Louisville, Ky., was elected President. A select committee was appointed to frame a constitution for the permanent organization of a National Union, which, after slight amendment, was passed, and the new organization took to itself the title of "THE NATIONAL TYPOGRAPHICAL UNION."

The Constitution was signed by all the members of the convention, and afterwards sent to the several subordinate unions for their ratification, the agreement being that when unions in five different States ratified the proposed Constitution, the Executive Committee should order the convening of the National Union in Cincinnati, Ohio, on the first Monday in May, 1852.

The subordinate or local unions were prompt to accept the constitution and new form of government, and the first session of the National Typographical Union was held at the above place and date.

It is noteworthy, and indicative of keen foresight on the part of the founders of this great labor union, that, first, they soon cut loose from the entanglements of State or district unions in even the classification of subordinates by arbitrary or geographical lines, and recognized the unit of organization wherever found; and, second, that initiation ceremonies, melo-dramatic oaths, passwords, signs, grips, etc., though advocated by many worthy representatives, and repeatedly considered by the National Union, never found a place in the national or subordinate constitutions. The healthy growth and life of trade organizations are conserved by maintaining a wise mean between secret and open sessions. Free discussion in meeting-rooms of workingmen has a tendency to evolve measures and legislation able to stand the test of public opinion, when that opinion is invoked.

The issuing of charters by the national body to subordinate unions was commenced at this session. It was found impossible to settle definitely the question of seniority in respect of date of organization of several societies represented, and the matter was finally settled by drawing for numbers, with the following result: Indianapolis, No. 1; Philadelphia, 2; Cincinnati, 3; Albany, 4; Columbus, 5; New York, 6; Pittsburgh, 7; St. Louis, 8; Buffalo, 9; Louisville, 10; Memphis,

11; Baltimore, 12; Boston, 13; Harrisburg, 14. The result of the drawing caused great dissatisfaction in the older societies; Baltimore, especially, at the succeeding session at Pittsburgh, formally protested against her charter assignment as No. 12, claiming that the Baltimore society was organized in, and had remained in continued existence since, 1831.*

The Pittsburgh session (1853) was largely devoted to general legislation; important amendments to the constitution were proposed, a body of general laws was formulated, and a minimum standard of type measurement adopted.

No very marked features in legislation or growth characterized the succeeding sessions at Buffalo, Memphis, Philadelphia, New Orleans, Chicago, Boston, and Nashville. At the last-named (1860) the union adjourned to meet in New York City, in May, 1861; but before the time of meeting, the great Civil War had commenced, and it was judged prudent by a majority of the National officers to postpone the session for one year, which was done, against the earnest protest of the president, who probably shared the optative views of Secretary Seward as to the duration of hostilities. The tenth session, however, was held in New York in May, 1862, but no delegates from the Southern unions put in an appearance, unless St. Louis might be placed in that category. But it would seem that, whether spoken of love or crafthood, absence makes the heart grow fonder, because annually from 1862 to 1866, when the absentees from the South again answered roll-call, the national minutes contain expressions of hearty good-will, which even war could not impair, entertained by the Northern Union printers toward their Southern brethren.

At the Louisville session (1864) a "conditional membership" measure was adopted in the hope of drawing within the scope of union influence that class of young men commonly known as "country printers." Many strikes had been lost to the union cause by the importation into cities, during trade troubles, of callow craftsmen and "two-thirders," and the conditional enrollment of this class in the union ranks, it was

---

* The printers of Boston, Mass., took part in a labor procession in 1834.—[Ed.

expected, would imbue them with the spirit of unionism and increase the number of subordinate unions. At the Memphis session (1867), President Oberly reported: "The conditional card system has proved impracticable, and I therefore recommend that it be repealed." Why did so excellent a measure fail of success? Because, like scores of similar good measures in the history of all trades, it was born before its time. For the past twenty years there have existed conditions conducive to the successful adoption of a nine-hour working day. What has been the cost to workingmen, in lost wages and lost situations alone, of the eight-hour agitation? There is a clever *mot* current among *doctrinaires*, but which does not apply to the practical concerns of men, that "it is well often to aim at the unattainable, as we thereby make attainable what would otherwise be unattainable." On the contrary, no measure of labor reform can be vitalized in the absence of conjunctive conditions and reciprocal relations. Strong unions are slowly built up, step by step.

At the Albany session (1869) the National Union became "The International Typographical Union, of North America," declaring itself to possess "original and exclusive jurisdiction in all matters pertaining to the fellowship of the craft in the United States and British Provinces." This extension of jurisdiction was made at the right time, as immediately four unions in Ontario (Toronto, Ottawa, Hamilton and London), one in Quebec (Montreal), one in New Brunswick (St. John), and one in Nova Scotia (Halifax), joined the international organization. Another step in the right direction was taken at this session, in the chartering of Women's Typographical Union No. 1, of New York City. Plans for regulating female labor in printing offices had been discussed at previous sessions, but no satisfactory conclusion was reached until the Constitution was amended to the effect that "the subordinate unions shall not legislate against women compositors where they conform to the laws and requirements of the International Typographical Union." This wise settlement of the vexed question opened the doors of local unions to competent female compositors and raised their labor to the wage scale of male compositors.

Thus justice at last prevailed over custom, and the old partition wall of restriction, dividing the labor of the sexes, was demolished, it is hoped for all time, in the printing craft.

At the Montreal session (1873) the Constitution was so amended as to permit the formation of pressmen's unions, and two of them (Washington and Detroit) were organized during that year. These unions have materially strengthened the craft in large cities, and wield a power in strikes which cannot well be over-estimated.

It is safe to assert that the International Typographical Union is the oldest national craft-organization in the country, gauged by the standard of continuous existence. Its constitution and rules of government have served as models for other skilled labor unions; and although the Union has been often charged with "selfishness" and "exclusiveness" by sister unions, yet it has generally given its influence and aid, at the proper time, to confederations of skilled labor. During the existence of the first National Labor Union, the union printers were ably represented therein by Mr. Andrew C. Cameron, of Chicago, and others. At the Washington session (1879) the corresponding secretary of the International Typographical Union was directed to correspond with the different "International Labor Unions of North America" on the subject of uniting the trades-unions more closely for mutual defence and support. Notwithstanding many discouragements, the first convention was held at Terre Haute, Ind., in August, 1881, which adjourned to meet in Pittsburgh, Nov. 15th, when one hundred and seven delegates, representing fourteen States, assembled and perfected the organization known as "The Federation of Organized Trades and Labor Unions of the United States and Canada." The platform of the Federation is broad, liberal, practical, and modern; demanding the passage of laws for the incorporation of trades-unions and similar labor organizations (one was passed by the Forty-ninth Congress); advocating State legislation enforcing the education of children, favoring the passage of laws forbidding the employment of children under fourteen years of age, demanding the enactment of uniform apprentice laws, and the enforcement of the national eight-hour law, urging the repeal of laws providing for the employment of convicts under the contract system, favoring the passage of laws to secure the mechanic the first lien upon the product of his labor, demanding the repeal of "conspiracy laws" as applied to organized labor, calling for national legislation to prevent the importation of foreign laborers under contract, etc. As the International Union proudly claims the paternity of this important organization, and its delegates have thus far held prominent place in its management and legislation, the slur of "craft exclusiveness" may as well be dropped by some sister unions.

In the matter of strikes, it is safe to assert that no skilled mechanics in this country have passed through such trying experiences as the union printers. The business history of nearly every prominent newspaper and jobbing establishment has its "strike" paragraph or page. The list of surrendered charters on the records of the International Union only shows the total wrecking of subordinate unions; it does not indicate the great number of crippling compromises, abortive arbitrations, and unsuccessful local strikes, which have marked the history of the printing trade for the past thirty years. And these results are not to be wondered at when we consider that this organization, composed of a remarkably intelligent and independent membership, has been the pioneer in testing and enforcing "usages and customs" in trade-unionism which were neither congenerous to, nor appreciated by, other trades. It has not alone been a series of struggles between capital and labor, about wage-scales and hours of work, but the justice or injustice of craft privileges has held a prominent place in disputes between employers and employees. And in these contentions the union printers have almost uniformly found the whole power of the press arrayed against them; but, even against such great odds, "the men of the stick" have kept their place in the front rank of skilled labor, and are deservedly proud of the acknowledged strength and pre-eminence of their national organization.

Among the general laws governing subordinate unions, is

the following section on strikes, which shows the advanced position held by the craft on this troublesome question: —

The International Union regards the result of strikes as inexpedient, except where the rules or principles of the International or of a subordinate union may have been violated. Recognizing strikes as detrimental to the best interests of the craft, it directs subordinate unions not to order a strike until every possible effort has been made to settle the difficulty by arbitration.

The preceding pages present some of the prominent features in the historical background of the International Union. During the thirty-six years of its existence, scores of important craft questions have been discussed at the annual sessions, such as Sunday work, establishment of a home for superannuated printers, status of subordinate unions in relation to the national body, uniform constitution for subordinate unions, territorial jurisdiction of unions, and the international (strike) fund.

The general laws of the organization have long been considered as models in their way and have proved to be capable of the preservation and promotion of the interest of this great trades-union. These are summarized in the extracts from the first general address quoted in the opening of this chapter. Among other things, the general laws provide that no subordinate union shall admit a person who has worked at the trade for less than five years, or who is under twenty years of age. These general laws also favor admitting employers to membership, when practical printers, if they so desire. One of the most interesting provisions of the general laws is the following: —

Subordinate unions, foremen of offices, and chapels, shall make no distinction on account of sex in persons holding International Traveling Cards. Female compositors holding such cards are entitled to all the privileges and benefits conferred by them, and subordinate unions must recognize that fact. Subordinate unions cannot refuse women admission on account of sex.

Sessions and Officers of National and International Typographical Unions.

Where Held.	When Held.		President.	Vice-Presidents.	Secretary and Treasurer.	Cr. Secretary.
New York	Dec.,	1850	J. W. Peregoy, Baltimore	George Greene, M. C. Brown	F. J. Ottarson, J. Hartman	
Baltimore	Sept.,	1851	J. L. Gibbons, Louisville	W. C. Figner, George Wadman J. R. Lewellen, W. G. Williams	H. A. Guild M. F. Conway, Secretary	
Cincinnati*	May,	1852	M. C. Brown, Philadelphia	S. W. Wilder, E. A. Lewis	G. B. Seig, Secretary J. S. Nafew, Treasurer	 W. A. Baker.
Pittsburgh		1853	Gerard Stith, New Orleans	A. McCoubrey, F. A. Albaugh	H. H. Whitcomb, Secretary M. C. Brown, Treasurer	 J. P. Woodbury.
Buffalo		1854	Lewis Graham, New Orleans	C. Dusenbury, Charles F. Town	H. H. Whitcomb	Wm. T. Yancey.
Memphis		1855	Charles F. Town, New York	F. C. Still, A. Donnelly	" "	Solomon Harris.
Philadelphia		1856	M. C. Brown, Philadelphia	B. C. Sanford, T. F. Hedges	" "	J. H. Blackstone.
New Orleans		1857	William Cuddy, St. Louis	M. C. Misener, E. H. Munday	" "	A. W. Hyatt.
Chicago		1858	R. C. Smith, Philadelphia	W. R. Skelton, M. Dempsey	George W. Smith	E. K. Warren.
Boston		1859	" " "	M. Barrett, G. W. Colby	Thomas J. Walsh	Geo. M. Brisbin.
Nashville		1860	John M. Farquhar, Chicago	Wm. Madigan, S. P. Bassett	" "	I. C. Morgan.
New York		1862	" " "	W. A. Montgomery, J. H. Walker	" "	Theo. Nagle.
Cleveland		1863	Eugene Vallette, Philadelphia	G. McK. Luken, J. A. Spencer	" "	Wm. F. Moore.
Louisville		1864	A. M. Carver, Cincinnati	W. L. Fairchild, C. B. Smith	William F. Moore	M. G. Mason.
Philadelphia	June,	1865	Robert E. Craig, St. Louis	W. Knollin, H. J. Durborow	" "	John C. Frary.
Chicago		1866	John H. Oberly, Cairo	James Risk, J. E. Davis	Alexander Troup	M. J. Divine.
Memphis		1867	" " "	D. C. Morris	" "	W. W. Mayberry.
Washington.		1868	Robert McKechnie, New York	Gerard Stith, G. W. McDonald	John Collins	Wm. Turner.
Albany†		1869	Isaac D. George, Nashville	P. A. Crossby, W. R. Goodnough	" "	Wm. A. Shields.
Cincinnati		1870	W. J. Hammond, New Orleans	T. Willard, John H. O'Donnell	" "	Augusta Lewis.
Baltimore		1871	" " "	M. R. Walsh, J. A. Cushley	" "	Fred. K. Tracy.
Richmond		1872	" " "	E. C. Crump, R. G. Sleater	" "	R. A. Hamilton.
Montreal		1873	W. R. McLean, Washington	Wm. Kennedy, W. G. Johnston	" "	Geo. Hawkins.
St. Louis‡		1874	Wm. H. Bodwell, New York	Henry White, W. D. Redfield	W. A. Hutchinson	W. S. Pride.
Boston		1875	" " "	" " " "	" "	" "
Philadelphia	July,	1876	Walter W. Bell, Philadelphia	James Harper, C. F. Sheldon	" "	" "
Louisville	June,	1877	John McVicar, Detroit	H. Z. Osborne, W. P. Atkinson	John H. O'Donnell	John Armstrong.
Detroit		1878	Darwin R. Streeter, St. Louis	———, Ed. Fitzgeorge	" "	" "
Washington		1879	John Armstrong, Toronto, Canada	O. P. Martin, T. J. Vaughn	William White	Charles Wright.
Chicago		1880	Samuel Haldeman, Washington	Wm. P. Atkinson, C. W. Bovard	" "	Thos. T. Hurdle.
Toronto		1881	Wm. P. Atkinson, Erie, Pa.	H. W. Clayton, Andrew J. Preall	William H. Trayes	Lyman A. Brant.
St. Louis		1882	George Clark, St. Louis	Thomas Wilson, William A. Hovey	" "	John Schley.
Cincinnati		1883	" " "	John F. Clarkson, T. A. Fowler	Mark L. Crawford	John R. Haldeman.
New Orleans		1884	Mark L. Crawford, Chicago	I. N. Jones, M. W. Mathasz	William Briggs	W. A. Wilkinson.
New York	June,	1885	M. R. H. Witter, St. Louis	R. F. Sullivan, P. T. McDermott	" "	" "
Pittsburgh	June,	1886	" " " " " "	Thomas J. Lacey	E. S. McIntosh	H. Thomas Elder.

* National Typographical Union formally organized on third day of session.
† Name changed to International Typographical Union.
‡ Terms of officers extended to close of session.

CHAPTER VIII.

SHOEMAKERS IN THE MOVEMENT.

"Oh! Workers of the old time, styled
The gentle craft of leather!
Young brothers of the ancient guild,
Stand forth once more together!
Call out again your long array,
In the olden merry manner;
Once more, on gay St. Crispin's day,
Fling out your blazoned banner!"
— *Whittier.*

HAND WORK IN THE OLDEN TIME — THE LITTLE SHOP — ITS EDUCATIONAL INFLUENCE — THE NEWSPAPER AND THE DEBATE — COUNTRY WORK — MACHINERY AND CHANGES WROUGHT BY IT — ORGANIZATIONS — THE CRISPINS — THEIR FOUNDER — GROWTH OF THE ORDER — DECADENCE AND MORAL — LASTERS' PROTECTIVE UNION — METHODS AND PRINCIPLES — THE KNIGHTS OF LABOR — LARGE SUPPORT FROM SHOEMAKERS — THE INDUSTRIAL WAR — LYNN IN 1860 — BROCKTON AND THE "42."

THE keen-witted cobbler who made holiday in Roman streets to see and rejoice in Cæsar's triumph, and whose sharp retorts so ruffled the sensitive nerves of Tribune Marullus, was the fitting representative of his craft. A "cobbler's wit" has long been famed; and Shakespeare but used the proverbial aptness of the shoemaker's tongue to spice the opening scene of the great Roman tragedy. The traditions of the craft have been well preserved; and while the shoemaker of the nineteenth century no longer universally "sticks to his last," yet the old-time front rank of comparative intelligence has ever been maintained by the trade as a whole.

The history of organized labor would be really incomplete if the part played by the workers in "the gentle craft of leather" was to be omitted. The cobbler in the streets of Rome, the guild brother in the middle ages, the early New

England hand-worker in the little shop, and the operative of to-day, who guides an ingenious machine in the big factory, have all left their imprint on the era in which they lived.

The leather industry is a typical one in its development from the hand to machine labor; but the shoe factory has been far less potent than the cotton factory as yet, in crushing out the individuality of the people employed in it. This is due to a variety of causes,—among them the comparatively recent introduction of machinery, and superior organization among shoemakers.

The labor question exists in this industry in all its force. Here we find the sharp competition among manufactures for the market, and the still sharper competition among the operators for work. This condition of the latter is interrupted by the constant introduction of new labor-saving and profit-making machinery, and the consequently increased facility with which comparatively unskilled labor may be utilized in the production of shoes. In addition to these drawbacks, shared in common with most of the makers of staple commodities, the shoemaker meets with difficulties peculiar to the craft. Among these may be classed the "farmer and fisherman shoemaker," hard to enroll in the ranks of labor organization, and oftentimes a serious stumbling-block in the way of the union of labor societies in their efforts to control the labor market.

To fully comprehend the work done by shoemakers in organization, in the face of these obstacles, it may be well to glance at the development of the trade itself.

In 1634 Philip Kirtland established a shoemaking shop in Lynn. Kirtland Street, in the west end of that city, is named after him. The trade was not firmly established until nearly a century and a quarter later, in 1750, when John Adam Dagyr, the "celebrated shoemaker of Essex," went to Lynn, laid the foundation of the modern trade. Dagyr was a Welshman, and became successful and famous, although he met with reverses, and finally died a pauper. During the first half of the present century, New England was, even more than at present, the abiding place of the shoemaker. As early as 1812 wagon loads of boots and shoes were sent from Lynn and Haverhill to New York and Philadelphia. These shoes were "hand-welts." The manufacturers cut the stock and then gave it out to be made up in the little country shops. With the coming of canals and railroads, furnishing the manufacturer with means of transportation for the product of his factory, the industry rapidly developed.

Previous to 1857 the wives and daughters of the country shoemakers stitched the uppers at their homes. It was hard and toilsome labor, but labor surrounded by far different influences from those which help to mould those employed in making shoes. It should be pointed out, however, that the date of the organization of shoemakers is nearly identical with that of the establishment of the factory system; that most of the legislation, statutory or to be enforced by wage-workers, aimed at by these organizations, relates to abnormal social conditions brought about by the use of machines, and that possibly the source of the unrest and sense of injustice so largely permeating the wage class of to-day is due as much to the inequitable division of the benefits of machinery, as to any other one reason.

With the machine, in the abstract, the labor reformer can have no contest. The futility of opposing the forces making toward larger industrial development is clearly seen by him. His utmost restrictive effort is to prevent sudden and radical changes with consequent displacement of labor and attendant suffering. The demand of the labor organization is, however, that the machine shall be the servant of the producing masses as well as of the consuming; that its benefits shall be as great to the man who runs as to the man who owns it; that the leisure it creates accrue to mechanic as well as millionaire; that the child and mother be not taken from the home to operate it while the father is made a truant; in short that it be subordinated not alone to the greed of gain and desire for cheapness of production among capitalists, but to the needs, wants and general advancement of the working people. Before machinery made necessary the massing of large numbers of operatives in one factory, it is perhaps not too much to say that almost every New England shoe shop was a lyceum. Not so romantic, possibly, as the academic groves where the Grecian seekers after truth gathered about the old-time philosophers, but quite in harmony with that Yankee combination of utility with a keen spirit of inquiry into all things mundane and celestial. In the little shops of Lynn, Haverhill, Milford and other shoe centres, it was a common thing for the workmen to hire a boy to read to them while they were at work, the contents of the last newspaper; questions public, philosophic and theoretical, were discussed with zest and acumen amid uninterrupted tasks. It may be noted that in Tchernychewsky's "What's to be Done," the Russian reformer describes this method of education as prevailing in the modern co-operative shops directed by the heroine, Vera Parlovnu. To this custom of daily reading and discussions may doubtless be credited the many graduates from the shoemaker's bench to positions of public trust. It was about this date that the Singer sewing machine was introduced. In 1859 Blake brought out his sole-sewing machine. This was remodeled and improved by Gordon McKay, a Lawrence mechanic, and the result was the McKay stitcher, which completely revolutionized one branch of the manufacture of shoes. Previous to the invention of this machine, all the medium and low-priced shoes were pegged, this mode of fastening the sole to the upper being cheaper than the two seams necessary in the welted shoe. The McKay stitcher superseded the hand-welt and turned process, and the large manufactory superseded the small shops of the hand-worker. Soon after this came the pegging machine; then heel trimmers and burnishers, edge-trimmers and setters, bottom-finishers and buffers, heel crimpers, polishers, button fasteners, and scores of other machines followed in quick and bewildering profusion. By 1870 the present factory system was well developed.

It is neither within the scope nor province of this chapter to treat of the effects—physiological, pathological and sociological—of the introduction of machinery upon those improved mechanisms of production. We may, perhaps, be pardoned a memory of regret for that time when the man was more than a tender to the machine, and the military rule of our present industrial system did not oppose a perpetual menace to the individuality of the operative.

The training given its members by the Sons of St. Crispin made them available material for the Knights of Labor, in which society the shoemakers have long taken an active interest. This is especially true of New England, where, until the early part of 1884, by far the greater proportion of the strength of the Order consisted of shoemakers, and even at present nearly fifty per cent. of the members of the Knights of Labor in Massachusetts, Maine and New Hampshire are of the same craft. This being the case, the history of the shoemakers in the Knights of Labor would, so far as New England is concerned, be the history of the Order itself, which is told in detail elsewhere. Chicago, Cincinnati, Rochester, Detroit, Philadelphia, and the shoe towns of Massachusetts, had local assemblies of the society early formed.

The peculiar nature of the shoe industry, with its many branches of labor, formed an excellent field for the practical test of some of the principles of the K. of L. In no other trade, perhaps, has arbitration, in this country, at least, been so thoroughly tried, and in no other trade has it, from the very nature of the case, been so successful. The present system of shoemaking may be compared to a complicated and delicately organized machine, which must be kept in good running order, and in which frictions between the parts must be abolished as much as possible. While arbitration has not proved an infallible lubricating oil, yet it has modified many of the lesser and some of the graver complications arising between employer and employee in the shoe trade. This has been notably the case when the proper machinery for arbitration has been created. In Philadelphia the "Joint Board of Arbitration" brought into being the famous "Philadelphia Rules," which have been adopted in some other sections of the country, and which are referred to elsewhere in this chapter. In Lynn and Beverly a "Municipal Board" serves to form a channel for arbitration; in Brockton a "Joint

Council" and in Haverhill a "Joint Board of Arbitration" serve the same purpose.

The system of organization obtaining in the Order of the Knights of Labor, has also been advantageous to its growth among shoemakers. It was comparatively an easy matter for the trade society to organize the cities, but difficult to get a hold on the country. The local assembly of the Knights of Labor overcame this difficulty by enrolling men of all trades in one branch, where necessary, and developed its greatest strength at first in New England in the shoemaking villages, towns, and smaller cities. Marblehead (L. A. 500) had the honor of the parent assembly, and Lynn, Weymouth, West Quincy, Newburyport, Natick, Milford, and Stoneham are near the head of the list as to priority of organization. Every District Master Workman of District Assembly 30 has been a shoemaker at some time of his life, and most of its executive officers are to-day of the same trade.

Two distinctively trade districts of the Knights of Labor exist at present, — one in Philadelphia (No. 70), an offshoot of District Assembly No. 1, and one in New York, No. 91. New England shoemakers have had the formation of a trade district under consideration for some time, but have, from one cause or another, postponed its construction.

It is as yet a question among the Knights of Labor, and one in which the shoemakers take an active interest, as to whether the purposes of the organization can be best subserved by the system of trade or mixed districts. It is claimed by advocates of the former system that celerity in the doing of business, economy, and greater power can be obtained by first organizing a trade by itself, and then amalgamating in the general body; while the supporters of the latter proposition assert that the trade interest should always be kept subordinate to the general welfare, and that this can only be done by organizing mixed local assemblies. Upon the final decision of this question will largely depend the line upon which future organization of the shoemakers of the country will advance.

Labor organizations among shoemakers may practically be embraced under three heads — the Knights of St. Crispin, the Lasters' Protective Union, and the Knights of Labor. Other organizations of a temporary nature have existed in the trade, and there are at present local unions of edge-setters, trimmers, cutters, etc., here and there. These latter societies are merging, one by one, into the Knights of Labor, and eventually will doubtless become a part of that organization. While the local unions may serve a temporary useful purpose, yet the lesson of the labor organizations of the past seems to be plainly that in the age of collective capital there must be a larger co-operation among the wage-workers than the isolated local union is able to give.

Of the distinctive shoemakers' organizations of America that of the "Knights of St. Crispin" must be accorded foremost mention. The history of the growth and disintegration of this Order makes an interesting and instructive chapter. Here was a powerful combination of intelligent men, extending over the country and numbering at one time many thousand members, practising the virtues of arbitration and co-operation, electing its representatives by scores to the Legislatures, yet without cohesive power enough to hold together to accomplish the purposes for which it was formed.

The Order of the Knights of St. Crispin, like that of the Knights of Labor, was formulated mainly by one man. Newell Daniels, a boot-treer of Milford, Mass., in 1864, first conceived the main points of that organization, drafting a crude constitution, and talking the idea over with some of his fellow-workmen. Daniels went West before his proposed society had taken definite shape in Milford. He finally located in Milwaukee, Wis., and it was not until the first of March, 1867, that his long-contemplated scheme took definite shape in a working lodge of Crispins. The seven founders of the original lodge in Milwaukee were: Newell Daniels, S.; Samuel Wilson, S. K.; W. C. Haynes, K.; Albert Jenkins, I. S.; Thomas Houren, O. S.; F. W. Wallace, Usher; and Henry Palmer. Wallace gave the Order its name, in honor of the patron-saint of the shoemakers, and a ritual had been prepared by Daniels, which was accepted after some modification by a committee of three, appointed for that purpose.

The German Custom Shoemakers' Union, of Milwaukee, soon after this adopted this Crispin plan of organization, and became Lodge No. 2. The Shoemakers' Union, of Chicago, was visited by Daniels in April, but did not at that time accept his invitation to join the Crispins. A circular was drafted by Daniels, setting forth the plans of the Order, and, to use his own words, "sent to every place where we knew there was a shoemaker." Responses were received from various parts of the country, and in September Daniels was sent East to propagate Crispin principles, and to organize societies where possible. Lodges were formed by him in Oswego, N. Y., and in Hopkinton, Milford and Stoughton, Mass. Chicago was the next place to fall into line, and the Knights of St. Crispin may be said to have fairly taken root. In January, 1868, charters were issued and a remodeled constitution printed, the preamble of which was written by Martin Gavin, the former corresponding secretary of the Chicago Shoemakers' Union, who had removed to Milwaukee and become a member of the senior lodge there. Local lodges were now formed quite rapidly. Stoneham, Natick, West Medway, Woburn, Worcester, Upton, Spencer, Danvers, Boston and Webster were among the first towns in Massachusetts to next organize.

The first Grand Lodge meeting was held in Rochester, in 1868, about sixty charters having been issued. Martin Gavin was chosen as the first presiding officer over the Grand Lodge.

The preamble of the constitution, as finally adopted, was as follows: —

The objects of this organization are to protect its members from injurious competition, and secure thorough unity of action among all workers on boots or shoes in every section of the country; claiming, as we do, that labor is capital, and the only capital that possesses power to reproduce itself, or, in other words, to create capital; that labor is the interest underlying every other interest, and therefore is entitled to, and should receive from, society and government protection and encouragement.

Recognizing the right of the manufacturer or capitalist to control his capital, we also claim and shall exercise the right to control our labor, and to be consulted in determining the price paid for it, — a right hitherto denied us; and believe an international organization, embracing all workers on boots or shoes in the United States and provinces of North America, is the only way in which this right can be successfully vindicated.

We believe also in co-operation as a proper and efficient remedy for many of the evils of the present iniquitous system of wages that concedes to the laborer only so much of his own productions as shall make comfortable living a bare possibility, and places education and social position beyond his reach.

We therefore urge all workers on boots and shoes, in every section of the country, to join us in this effort to secure, through the power of organization, both for ourselves and our children after us, a steady demand and fair compensation for our toil, and a position in society, to which, as wealth-producers and loyal citizens, we are justly entitled.

We censure the system of a Crispin making a profit on the labor of a brother Crispin as contrary to the spirit of Crispinism.

The following regulation from a subsequent constitution governing local lodges indicates a vital defect in the Knights of St. Crispin: —

No member of this Order shall teach, or aid in teaching, any part or parts of boot or shoe-making, unless the lodge shall give permission by a three-fourths vote of those present, and voting when such permission is first asked. Provided, this article shall not be so construed as to prevent a father from teaching his own son. Provided, also, that this article shall not be so construed as to hinder any member of this organization from learning any or all parts of the trade.

For five subsequent years, after the Rochester session of 1868, the Order of the Knights of St. Crispin was a power in the land. It made and unmade politicians; it established a monthly journal; it started co-operative stores; it fought, often successfully, against threatened reductions of wages and for better returns to its members for labor performed; it grew rapidly in numbers, and became international in its scope; it is estimated that four hundred lodges and forty thousand members at one time owed it allegiance; it became the undoubted foremost trade organization of the world.

Among the men prominent in its councils and holding positions of high executive trust and responsibility, were Richard Griffiths, since General Worthy Foreman of the Knights of Labor; Ralph Beaumont, "the Elmira shoemaker"; S. P. Cummings, of Lynn; C. C. Mower, of Upton; James P.

Wright, of Baltimore; Robert Schilling, of Milwaukee; Nathaniel Stoddard, of Brockton; Charles S. Goodwin, of Haverhill; B. B. Scully, of Lynn, and scores of others.

The reaction came. The sixth annual session of the Grand Lodge, held in Cleveland, in June, 1873, revealed a deplorable spirit of discord and distrust existing in the organization. The "Report of the I. G. S. K." might contain these words: "Something has got to be done, or this order will be a thing of the past from the adjournment of this Convention." The Convention tried vainly to do this "something." It discussed co-operation and arbitration, and proposed plans to put these principles into effect, but it could find no substitutes for the spirit of confidence and solidarity which had given the order its power and prestige. The subsequent twelve months witnessed the rapid decay of the society, and when a few delegates assembled in Philadelphia, in June, 1874, at the seventh session of the Grand Lodge, as one of them told the writer, they "attended the funeral of the Knights of St. Crispin."

Faith in the Crispin idea was not wholly extinct, however, and a few men, headed by B. B. Scully, of Lynn, went zealously at work to revive the organization. After a year's hard work, in 1875, they succeeded in getting it re-established in some thirty shoe towns of Massachusetts, and it was again pushed westward as far as Chicago. In 1877 the order in Lynn defeated an attempt of the manufacturers to impose an "iron-clad" on employees. For a time the new departure seemed to flourish, but the forces which had shattered the original movement still held powerful, and the revival was but temporary, and by 1878 the order was practically extinct.

Among the causes alleged by old members of the Order, as responsible for the downfall of the Knights of St. Crispin, are interfering in politics, treachery of leaders, high salaried officers, etc. To the dispassionate observer, it would seem as if a deeper reason exists for the failure.

The labor movement, in common with all physical and mental phenomena, is subject to the law of evolution. The Crispin idea of establishing a monopoly in labor on shoes, had in it inherent defects, which brought about its decline

There was much that was practical, much that was good, in the early work of the society. Its base was not broad enough to support the superstructure, and it consequently toppled over of its own weight.

The Crispins failed, not because they were a trade organization, but because, while seeking justice for their own members, they failed to be just to the workers outside their fold. The excessive restrictions imposed by local lodges on their members against teaching any parts of boot or shoe making to others, was as untenable a position as the "iron-clad" of the manufacturers.

In addition to this especial weakness of the Knights of St. Crispin, the order was afflicted with the usual bane of labor societies, diverse theories among those enrolled in its ranks. In the first flush of enthusiasm, its progress was rapid. The mere fact of organization conferred a benefit. After the primary stage had been passed, and expectation had ripened into performance, more or less disappointing, the Order branched out from its original intent, and tried to revolutionize social conditions and qualities of human nature, which are susceptible of modification only after long and persistent effort. It undertook a task beyond its strength, and discord, suspicion and jealousy helped to dig its grave.

The lesson of the Order of the Knights of St. Crispin is not necessarily a dispiriting one. From its ruins, other orders have been evolved; from its mistakes, wisdom may be gained for the future. The band of earnest men who made sacrifices in its behalf deserve all honor and praise as the forerunners of that larger army which is to carry the banner of labor reform to ultimate victory.

The Lasters' Protective Union of New England occupies a unique position among organizations of workers on shoes. In all other divisions of the trade the machine has materially modified the condition of labor; but the laster, with his "jack," hammer and pincers, is yet one of the few handicraftmen of the nineteenth century. Repeated attempts have been made by cunning and inventive geniuses to supplant the lasters with the "iron idol" that never strikes, and is never hungry or tired. Various degrees of success have crowned their attempts, but a complete substitute for the peculiar skill and judgment required to last a shoe by hand has not as yet been found. The secret of the difficulty of the problem is due to the fact that the work of fitting the upper to the sole of a shoe is not automatic. Each pair of shoes, and not infrequently "rights" and "lefts" of the same pair, require a trifle of difference of treatment in order to be a perfect job. This is caused by variation in quality and condition of leather, defects in work done before the shoe reaches the laster, etc. To make a machine which will take account of all these distinctions is apparently as hard as to make one which will set type correctly, and so the laster and the compositor are not yet driven from the field of hand labor by the all-conquering genii of the machine, although the time is doubtless near at hand when the inevitable law of development in the world of production will bring about this result.

The success of the Lasters' Protective Union must, in a large degree, be attributed to the conditions stated in the foregoing paragraph, as well as to its form of organization and excellent administration. As shoes cannot be made without lasting, and as lasting cannot be done without lasters, the problem before the unions has been a simpler one than in divisions of the craft where the machine turns out from fifty to a hundred cases of shoes per day.

After the banner of St. Crispin had fallen and the twin foes of all labor societies, discord and apathy, had done their work in that once powerful Order, the shoemakers of New England went back to the old plan of "every man for himself, and the the devil take the hindmost." It is needless to say that his Satanic Majesty improved the opportunity. The spirit of competition among manufacturers for a market for their shoes brought about the inevitable "bear" pressure upon the market for labor. Yearly reductions in wages in all the shoe-making centres naturally followed. The Order of the Knights of Labor was practically unknown in New England, and once again by sad experience the shoemaker learned the lesson that in an age of associated industry, if he desired a fair return for his labor he also must associate himself with his fellows.

In December, 1869, sixteen Lynn lasters came together and organized under the name of the "Lasters' Protective Union." The lasters were among the poorest paid of any of the operatives in the shoe trade, and had been among the first to feel the effects of the repeated reductions. The Lynn Union was successful in several minor undertakings, and the lasters in other places followed the example of their Lynn brethren and also formed unions. A convention of the various local branches was soon afterwards held and a constitution adopted. The subsequent growth of the Union in New England has been a steady one, and on August 1, 1886, there were in existence fifty-three branches, with an approximate membership of ten thousand individuals. The constitution of the Union sets forth as its objects: "To acquire a thorough understanding of the needs and requirements of each branch; to secure the elevation of our labor and perpetuation of our organization; to render necessary assistance in time of trouble to any branch of our organization which may be engaged in striving to maintain or better the present condition of the labor of its members." This declaration is not so ambitious as that of some other labor societies. There is no indication in it of an attempt to revolutionize society or to overturn the existing order of things, but, measured by the test of real improvement in the wages and condition of its members, the Lasters' Protectve Union may perhaps claim that its work, during the period since its formation, compares favorably with that of any other association of wage-workers.

The various general conventions of the unions have evolved the following plan of government as the most practical and effective in the adjustment of all disputes arising between employers and members of the Lasters' Protective Union. A general secretary is elected annually at a salary of one thousand dollars per year. This officer performs the routine clerical work of the general body, keeps the local branches informed of all difficulties arising in the trade, compiles from the accounts of the local secretaries a statistical account of wages paid in each locality, and in addition acts as traveling executive officer of the unions in all cases of differences with an employer. Those who are accustomed to regard the salaried offices of labor societies as sinecures may possibly exempt the general secretary of the Lasters' Union from the list. The present "Pooh Bah," in the service of the lasters, is Mr. Edward L. Daley, of Lynn, and his conservatism, probity, judgment and ability, are freely conceded by manufacturers and men alike. The general secretary is assisted in his executive work by a general advisory board. This board is made up of one member from each local branch. In cases of dispute requiring the services of the general advisory board, three members of that board act, viz.: the general secretary, the local member, and the representative of the branch situated nearest to the locality of the trouble. This provides for an efficient committee at a small cost.

The Lasters' Union adopted at the beginning, and has maintained until the present time, what may be called an energetic policy; that is, while always practicing conciliation and giving the employer a chance to arbitrate at the commencement of a controversy, yet if other means fail, it has no scruples in using more vigorous methods, believing that the control of the labor market is as essentially the province of the labor organization, as the control of capital is of the capitalist. The Marblehead strike of 1883, embracing twelve shops, and the Brockton lockouts of 1885 and 1886, are among the most notable contests in which the union has been concerned.

The question of merging with the Knights of Labor has several times been considered by the Lasters' Union in their conventions, but while many of its members, probably the majority, are Knights of Labor, yet the Union, as a whole, has preferred to preserve its autonomy as a trade organization.

The various organizations of shoemakers have all had their Sedans and Waterloos, their Bunker Hills and Gettysburgs on the industrial battlefield. Never as yet forced to the starved submission of the cotton-factory folk, shoemakers have always been ready to accept the gage of battle in defence of principle. Organized and unorganized, they have pitted themselves against the "passionless endurance of the almighty dollar," sometimes winning and sometimes losing, in that anomalous strife continually going on between the two factors of modern production. Many of the memorable strikes of shoemakers have been for the recognition of their right to organize. And the tenacity with which the employing classes hold to assumed prerogatives, may be noted in the fact that after a quarter of a century of contention for this right by labor organizations, the Knights of Labor are obliged, in 1886, to fight again over the same ground, and even in the old Commonwealth of Massachusetts to invoke the entire strength of the organization for the exercise of this privilege by its members.

The stories of these contests, their comedies, melodramas and tragedies, would perhaps be as valuable to coming generations as the chronicles of the noisier battle-fields of history; but our space will permit detail in the case of but two typical ones,—the Lynn strike of 1860, and the Brockton strike, or lockout, of 1885.

Lynn early became the "city of shoes," the farmer settlers of the locality turning their attention to this industry. The figures of the trade for 1859, while insignificant in comparison with the immense volume of shoe business transacted in 1885, are yet indicative of the fact that the Lynn of that year was the shoe centre of New England. There were in existence at that period one hundred and thirty-eight small manufactories, with a product of about four million, five hundred thousand pairs of women's and children's shoes. These factories gave employment to eleven thousand persons, over half of whom did the most of their work at home. The leather was first cut by "clickers" in the large shops. The uppers were then turned over to the "binders,"—female workers,—who, at their homes, prepared them for the "cordwainers," and returned them to the factories. The cordwainers received the uppers and soles from the factories and made them up.

Prior to 1860, labor organization was almost totally unknown. The individual looked after his interest as best he could. Wages were low, averaging for male labor not over one dollar a day, and the supply of farmers' sons who were anxious to learn the business was practically unlimited. Trade had not recovered from the panic of 1857, and the winter of 1859 found many manufacturers doing but little work, and privation visited the homes of many of the Lynn cordwainers.

A spirit of unrest and discontent was abroad all over the state. From Milford, Natick and Marlboro came reports of dissatisfaction with the prices paid for labor. Alonzo G. Draper, afterward a brigadier-general in the Union army, and at that time editor of the *New England Mechanic*, for a year had advocated concerted action for increase in prices. The discontent in Lynn gradually took shape. Committees were formed, and the question of wages discussed. On the evening of February 3, 1860, a great mass meeting was held in the old Lyceum Hall, to consider whether a strike was advisable. George P. Sanderson, afterward mayor, was chairman, and addresses were made by Gideon F. Howard, of South Randolph; George Cahill, of Quincy; James Dillon and A. G. Draper, of Lynn. On February 8th a price-list was adopted and resolutions were passed pledging those present to strike unless the list was accepted by the manufacturers. At a subsequent meeting, February 15th, in Lyceum Hall, it was voted that nearly twelve hundred workmen were ready to strike, and it was determined to fix February 22d as the date for the beginning of the contest. Accordingly, on the morning of the birth-day of the Father of his Country, five thousand people, assembled in Central Square, were addressed by speakers, and then paraded through the streets. The great strike of 1860 had begun.

Lynn has seen many strikes since that date, but it is safe to say that in none of them has there been a more determined purpose, more unity of action, or more exciting incidents than in that of 1860, of the cordwainers. The strike is further interesting, as from it resulted the trades organization, which, in one form or another, has since prevailed among the Sons of St. Cripin.

For seven weeks, or until April 12, the struggle continued. All the accompaniments of the modern strike were present, while there were several decidedly unique features peculiar to the time. Oratory, parades, music, banners, etc., abounded. Candy pulls, chopping bees, clam chowders, furnished entertainment to the strikers. Comparatively little suffering is recorded as existing among the families of the participants. The turbulent element occasionally cropped out, and a "scab" was argued with by physical suasion until he saw the folly of his way. Express wagons carrying work into the country were overturned and the cases of shoes taken away.

On March 7th nearly two thousand stitchers joined the strike and a grand procession was inaugurated. The Lynn Guards, with music, headed the column; then came the female strikers, with flags and banners, followed by four thousand workmen, fire companies, etc., ; the whole making an imposing display. A heavy fall of snow commenced, but it did not dampen the ardor of the enthusiastic girls. Each succeeding day brought with it some diversion, and the old Lynn resident has a stock of racy anecdote as a relic of the period. The strikers were organized by wards, and it was customary to gather daily in Central Square, and from thence march wherever the business of the day was to be. One day a trip was made to Marblehead. On another a procession marched to Salem. A clam chowder in Rock's pasture, a tramp to South Reading and Stoneham, a "candy scrape" and dance, were among other notable events. A favorite amusement of the strikers was to escort the fresh converts to the factories, while they formally gave up their jobs. This ceremony was always performed with music and due impressiveness. An illustration of the discipline prevailing among the militia of that time may be found in the following incident: Colonel Coffin ordered Company F to stand guard to quell any possible outbreak. Many of the company were cordwainers, and the organization voted to escort the strikers, which it accordingly did.

After the strike had continued for five or six weeks, the necessity for a permanent organization was seen. The "Journeymen Cordwainers' Association" was formed, and a constitution and by-laws adopted. On the evening of April 12th a big mass-meeting was held, and as the result of its deliberations, it was

Resolved That we now commit our cause, with all its interests, into the hands of the organization known as the Journeymen Cordwainers' Association, whose avowed objects are the protection of labor and the promotion of the welfare of that great branch of industry which has rendered the name of our city so well-known throughout the Union.

The outcome of the strike was a compromise in the matter of prices, and the establishment of a union for future usefulness.

The "Brockton strike" of 1885 deserves more than a passing notice by reason of its bearing upon the recognition of certain principles contended for by labor organizations. Several minor misunderstandings having arising in Brockton during the autumn of 1885, forty-two of the shoe manufacturers of that city associated themselves together to maintain the untenable position that there should properly be but one party to a labor contract, and that party the employer. On November 12th the famous "forty-two" issued a manifesto to the lasters in their employ, stating that on and after November 16th the price for lasting would be fixed at a rate appended. In the manifesto was this paragraph: "We believe in the individual right of all to hire or discharge whomsoever he may choose, as well as the workman's right to work whenever and wherever it is for his interest so to do." As a result of this manifesto, all members of the Lasters' Union were ordered by that body, on the 14th, to stop work, and two days later the finishers followed suit. The Knights of Labor, through their joint board, passed resolutions deprecating the action of the manufacturers in ignoring the labor organizations, and pledged the support of the order in assisting the lasters to win that recognition. A committee of arbitration of nine men, representing all the labor organizations of the shoe trade in the city, waited upon President Geo. E. Keith, of the manufacturers' association, and through him requested that association to meet with them with a view to settling the existing difficulty by arbitration. The request was refused, Mr. Keith stating "that it was no use to talk, as the manufacturers had set their prices." The committee withdrew, feeling they had done all that was possible toward a peaceful and honorable adjustment. On the Wednesday following (18th) the Executive Board of District Assembly 30, Knights of Labor, also endeavored to obtain a conference with the "forty-two," but their communication was ignored. The manufacturers seemed determined to force the contest upon the issue raised, and as the surrender by the labor organizations of the right to be consulted at the making of a price list would have been the virtual surrender of their utility, there seemed to be no alternative except a trial of strength. Consequently the forty-two shops were soon deserted, the amount of their weekly pay-roll of $71,000 was withdrawn from circulation, and 5,755 operatives entered upon a period of idleness.

To this struggle, there could be but one outcome. Public opinion was overwhelmingly on the side of the employees, and was retained by them during the weeks that followed by the sobriety, peacefulness and invariable good order preserved by the strikers. There was a total absence of anything like physical intimidation during the continuance of the trouble, the police record showed a marked decrease in cases of drunkenness, and the whole course of procedure of the operatives was that of a law-abiding, orderly community contending for the recognition of a just and important principle, affecting their industrial welware. One week passed by, two weeks, and the third was drawing to a close. The expected collapse in the labor ranks had not come. The most needy had been assisted from the treasuries of the societies and from individual sources. The outlook was not cheering; winter was rapidly approaching, and the howl of the hunger-wolf could be heard at a distance by anxious parents watching over little ones. On the other hand, the plight of the "forty-two" was unenviable. The smaller manufacturers, especially, were growing restive. Machinery was standing idle, interest on borrowed capital was accumulating, and competitors were encroaching upon their markets.

The Brockton manufacturers, some forty in number, who had not joined the association, were running their shops at full capacity. To the pressure of these circumstances the "forty-two" finally yielded, and on November 30th voted to place the entire settlement of the trouble in the hands of their executive committee. As a result of this step, the committee invited the joint labor board to confer with them, and after repeated interviews a set of rules and regulations was adopted for the government of Brockton factories and the avoidance of future industrial warfare. These rules and regulations were based upon the "Philadelphia Rules," so-called from their previous adoption and use by the Philadelphia shoe manufacturers and operatives. These rules, in substance, embodied: 1. The right of the manufacturer to employ and discharge help, qualified by the specification that no employee should be discharged because of membership or prominence in a labor society. 2. The fixing of the ten-hour day as the standard. 3. The appointment of a joint committee of arbitration, consisting of twelve members, six from each side, with regulations to govern the same. 4. This committee was to settle all difficulties, and no strike or lock-out was to be entered into by either party pending a settlement. 5. The referring of the settlement of wages paid to hands working by the day or week to the manufacturer and individual employee. 6. The payment of standard prices by all members of the association. This agreement was signed on the part of the manufacturers by George E. Keith, Robbins B. Grover, Zimri Thurber, George G. Snow, George Churchill, and D. L. Weeks. For the labor organizations it was signed by James H. Stillman and Jabez Tabor, of the Knights of Labor; Edward Smith and M. J. Dunn, for the Lasters' Union; J. M. O'Donnell and Charles W. Turner, for the Trimmers' and Setters' Union.

The first step had been taken toward a cessation of hostilities, and the community gave a sigh of relief. There was yet much to be done, however, and the joint committee at once met (December 11th) to agree upon a price-list. At the first conference a disagreement arose as to the price to be paid for lasting, and an adjournment of one week was voted before coming to any understanding. Under article nine of the "rules," it was provided that in case of inability to agree in the joint board, each party should appoint one representative, these two the third, and the three were to be the final arbitrators. The claim was made by the lasters that the "forty-two" were trying to reduce prices for lasting. No attempt was made by the joint board to take advantage of the provisions of this article. A feeling of despondency once more settled over Brockton. The law of necessity was stronger than obstinacy, however, and on the 19th three arbitrators were agreed upon. The three men chosen were Mayor John J. Whipple, for the lasters; Walter F. Cleaveland, a city water commissioner for the association, and Charles C. Bixby, as the third member of the triumvirate. On the evening of the 21st the arbitrators rendered their verdict, which was a compromise between the price-list demanded by the lasters and that offered by the "forty-two." Shops were opened on the following morning, and the big Brockton strike was ended.

What was and is the lesson? Simply this, that common-sense and reason in the world of industry are as indispensable as elsewhere, that mutual concession and consideration between manufacturers and operatives is the only solution of "labor troubles," so long as the wage system prevails, and that when the spirit of arbitration is lacking on either side, there will be industrial war useless, bitter and unworthy of our progressive age.

The unfortunate controversy and lockout occurring in Brockton in the July following the adoption of the "Philadelphia plan" but emphasize the fact that rules cannot take the place of mutual consideration, and that fair play between employer and employee is the essence of a just settlement of all difficulties.

In the few pages devoted to the organization among shoemakers, we have deemed it best not to occupy space in recounting trivial details, but rather to outline certain broad phases. The "blazoned banner" of St. Crispin has ever been flung out at the head of the labor column. The organization may come, and the organization may go; but we may have faith that the love of right and liberty underlying all social reforms will in the future, as in the past, give inspiration to the workmen in the gentle craft of leather. Crispin, Unionist, Knight of Labor, have all had for their ideal a better livelihood and larger possibilities for their members, and in this broadening sweep and loftier trend of labor organizations lies the high hope of the days to come and children yet unborn.

CHAPTER IX.

PROGRESS IN THE TEXTILE TRADES.

EARLY ORGANIZATION IN 1850 — A STRIKE IN 1850 — SPINNERS REORGANIZE IN 1858 — PARALYZED BY THE WAR — REORGANIZED IN 1866 — CONVENTION IN 1868 — AGITATION FOR TEN HOURS — FRUITLESS STRIKES — THE UNION BROKEN UP — REORGANIZED — A TEN-HOUR LAW — THE CHOSEN BATTLE-FIELD — OTHER LABOR ASSOCIATIONS FORMED — SUCCESSFUL STRIKE — GREAT STRIKE IN AUGUST, 1875 — UNCONDITIONAL SURRENDER — ORGANIZATIONS BROKEN UP — WEEKLY PAYMENTS — A GLOOMY PERIOD — GEORGE E. MCNEILL TO THE RESCUE — REDUCTION OF WAGES IN 1878 — DEFAULTING TREASURERS — A GREAT DEMONSTRATION — ROBERT HOWARD CHOSEN SECRETARY — ARBITRATION DENIED — A STRIKE ORDERED — JOHN KELLY'S GIFT — THE INTERNATIONAL ASSISTS — STARVED INTO SUBMISSION — AN ADVANCE GRANTED — MORE WEEKLY PAYMENTS — ANOTHER ADVANCE — LEGISLATION REFUSED — STRIKE AVERTED — BLACKLISTING — SPOTTERS — SHORTER HOURS — RHODE ISLAND AND MAINE VISITED — GLORIOUS RESULTS — HARD TIMES AGAIN — ANOTHER STRIKE — AGAIN DEFEATED — BURNING OF SAGAMORE MILL — CURTAILING PRODUCTION — ARBITRATION AND CONCILIATION — GLIMPSES OF OTHER CONTESTS.

THE early history of organization in the textile trades of the United States can be traced as far back as 1844. Strikes had occurred prior to that, and doubtless temporary associations were formed in the thirties, when an agitation was commenced by a small band of earnest men in Fall River, Mass., having for its object a reduction in the hours of labor. A paper was started called *The Mechanic*, to advocate less hours of labor; and about this time, also, a paper was published in the city of Lowell called the *Voice of Industry*, that contributed largely to the advance of the movement. The factory operatives were then working from five o'clock in the morning to seven o'clock in the evening, with but two half-hours of intermission, one for breakfast and the other for dinner, which left the number of working hours thirteen daily. These papers did good service in their own peculiar line towards redressing the grievances of the operatives employed in the textile industries,

It was not until 1850 that anything like a thoroughly organized effort was made to obtain an advance in wages. This occurred in Fall River, where the spinners employed at the Metacomet Mill solicited the treasurer, Colonel Borden, to make a certain alteration in their list of prices. This Colonel Borden refused to do, and, pointing to the sides of his granite mill, he said: "I saw that mill built stone by stone; I saw the pickers, the carding engines, the spinning-mules and the looms put into it, one after the other, and I would see every machine and stone crumble and fall to the floor again before I would accede to your wishes." A strike resulted, which lasted ten months, when the mills started up again, but much difficulty was experienced in finding competent help to fill the places of the strikers, many of them having wandered away and found work elsewhere. Organizations have existed chiefly among the spinners in the textile trade, and no branch of labor has received so many hard knocks, sustained so many crushing defeats, and suffered so much as they have, in defending the rights and dignity of honest labor. It has been so with them all the world over; ever since James Hargreaves, of Oswaldtwistle, England, invented the spinning-jenny, in the year 1767, the spinners' troubles have been going on. Spinning, prior to Hargreaves' invention, used to be performed on the old-time spinning-wheel. The jenny was so constructed that a number of spindles could be driven together, which resulted in throwing many people out of employment, causing great discontent, and leading to troubles of various kinds among the operatives. The spinning-jenny of Hargreaves was improved in 1768 by Richard Arkwright, of Preston, who invented the spinning-frame, and by Crompton, of Bolton, afterwards, who invented the spinning-mule. These inventions, combined with the invention of the power-loom by Cartwright, and the steam-engine by Watts, laid the foundation of the factory system. Those who have been brought up in the cotton trade have often heard their fathers tell, as it had been told them by their fathers before, that the spinners' troubles commenced with the building of factories for manufacturing purposes. Therefore, for years after the failure of the strike of the spinners in 1850, no organization existed outside of that of the Fall River spinners in the textile trade.

The spinners' organization of Fall River, with other friends outside of the trade, kept a running agitation going from the time of their defeat in 1850, in favor of reducing the hours of labor to ten daily for women and minors employed in the textile industries. Their efforts proved unavailing, owing to the lack of support from other manufacturing centres. In 1858 the spinners reorganized their union, with Patrick Carroll as president, and John McKeown as secretary; and immediately began an agitation for an advance in wages. Meetings were held in the fields or behind the mills, where the men thought they would be secure from observation. Finally it was agreed that a petition should be sent to the mill treasurers, asking for an advance in wages.

James Cordinley, one of the members of the organization, invited them to his house to draw up the petition. When the petition was drawn, another obstacle appeared in the way, as no member of the organization dared to place his name first, fearing that he might be singled out as a ringleader, and that his name would be put on the blacklist, which would prevent him from getting work again in the city. Several of their members had been selected as victims after the strike of 1850, and were kept out of employment for years after in the mills of Fall River. However, a woman's ingenuity overcame the obstacle, and Mrs. Cordinley suggested that rings be drawn at the foot of the petition, and she furnished a bowl for the purpose, so that all the rings should be of equal size, and inside of these rings the spinners signed the petition, requesting an advance of wages. The manufacturers, in reply to the request of the spinners, agreed to give one-third of the advance asked for, which was accepted, and the other two-thirds was obtained prior to the outbreak of the war. The union was almost dead during the war, as most of its members had gone to shoulder the musket and to fight

NEW ENGLAND LABOR LEADERS.

for the maintenance of this Union of States, and to strike the shackles from the negro. The books had been closed in 1861, and when they were opened again, at the beginning of 1866, a large number of the old members failed to respond to the roll-call. They had been left behind on the hard-fought battlefields between the Potomac and Richmond, where they had surrendered their lives for their country and freedom.

Shortly after the reorganization of the union in 1866, an agitation, which proved very successful, was begun for advancing wages. Not only in Fall River, but in Lowell, Lawrence, New Bedford, Lewiston, Biddeford, Claremont, and many other cotton districts, the wages were advanced. Print cloths in that year were selling at nineteen and a half cents per yard, which at the present time can be bought at three and one-fourth cents per yard. In the meantime, while wages were being advanced, the members of the union never kept their eyes off that most important question of reducing the hours of labor; and to this end an agitation was started in all the textile districts of New England. Organizers were sent out to preach the doctrine of shorter hours of labor, and point out their advantages to the great army of toilers. These missionaries penetrated nearly every town and city in New England, where the busy hum of the spindle or the merry crack of the shuttle was to be heard, resulting in a convention held in Biddeford, Maine, in 1868. Among those present were Isaac Cartnell, representing Fall River; William Isherwood, Lowell; Patrick McHugh, Lawrence; Wright Beaumont, Lewiston; Richard Barlow, New Bedford; Thomas Lynch, Manchester, N. H., John McLaughlin, Salmon Falls, N. H., and William Green and John Trainer, of Lawrence and Biddeford, respectively. The convention was in session a few days, and it was finally resolved that the efforts of the operatives should not be relaxed, but that they should push forward with new strength and vigor in the hope of having ten hours recognized as a standard day's labor in cotton and woolen mills.

On the return of the delegates, meetings were called to consider the best means to obtain from the manufacturers the concession of ten hours for a day's labor. The manufacturers in some districts agreed to adopt the ten-hour system. Fall River began to work ten hours a day; the Atlantic Mills in Lawrence and the Wamsutta Mills of New Bedford did the same. Several of the districts belonging to the Spinners' National Organization ordered their members out on strike, in the hope of wringing it from their employers, but their hopes were scattered to the winds, for in every instance in the industrial struggles in which they were engaged, they were unsuccessful. Their leaders were blacklisted, and could not obtain employment except in secluded villages where they were not known. New Bedford manufacturers adopted the ten-hour system on the 1st of January, 1868, and went back again to the long hour system on February 1st, the month following. This action of the manufacturers created a strong feeling of distrust and indignation among the operatives, and the Spinners' Union of that city called a special meeting, and before its close a vote was taken and it was decided to strike for ten hours' labor per day. The strike was bitterly contested for ten weeks, when the spinners were defeated, some of them suffering the severest pangs of hunger before they would yield. The blacklist was again brought into force, and all those who had assisted in calling meetings or taken any active part whatever, were compelled to leave the city, work being refused them there. For the unions this was the "winter of their discontent," nearly all of them having fallen through, with the exception of that at Fall River, where the mills engaged in cotton manufacture were still running ten hours per day. Repeated efforts were made between 1868 and 1870 to reorganize the unions outside of Fall River, but they all proved ineffectual, for they had been badly crushed, and their leaders sent away. Still, ten hours for a day's labor was on everybody's lips.

The ten-hour bill in England passed its final stages in 1850, and the great bulk of the textile workers in the United States argued that, living under republican institutions, they were entitled to equal rights and privileges with those living under monarchical institutions.

Fall River still was working its employees in the mills but ten hours per day. In 1870 the spinners asked for a restoration of ten per cent., which had been taken from their wages a short time previously. The manufacturers offered to compromise by giving five per cent., which the spinners refused. A strike was ordered and, after a nine weeks' struggle, the spinners were defeated, and when the machinery was started up again every manufacturer in Fall River went back again to the long-hour system, after working ten hours per day for twenty-two months.

During this nine weeks' strike an effort was made by the Durfee Mill officials to obtain "knobsticks" to take the places of the strikers. Great confusion and excitement prevailed around the mills when the "knobsticks" were put in the mills to work, and several violent assaults were made upon them. Some of them were badly beaten, and it was feared that there would be a riot. The bitter feeling was increased by a mill official's ordering a fire company, which had been summoned, to play upon the excited crowd. This nearly caused a riot, but ultimately wise counsel prevailed and reason triumphed over passion, and the strikers quieted down again.

This strike and its attendant consequences was a severe blow to the spinners of Fall River, for through losing the battle they had to go back to long hours, their wages were reduced, and the backbone of their union broken.

Thus twelve years from the time of the reorganization of the Fall River Spinners' Union, which was in 1858, it had temporarily ceased to exist. The furniture belonging to the union was given to a body of men who had formed a short-hour committee, and who were endeavoring to have a law passed through the Massachusetts Legislature that would restrict the hours of labor to sixty a week for all women and minors employed in textile industries. This band of men were untiring in their exertions, and they could be seen frequently, after their day's work in the mill was over, with a table and a chair at the corners of the principal streets soliciting names to petitions designed for presentation to the Legislature in favor of the passage of a ten-hour law. Among the most diligent workers in this movement were Allen Lockwood and William Isherwood, while Representatives Fairbanks, Davol and Hart supported in an able and effective manner the passage of the bill in the Legislature. The Spinners' Union began to move again 1873, when it was reorganized, and at once took a leading part in the agitation in support of a ten-hour law. The factory hands in Lawrence were working assiduously also to further the ten-hour movement. A demonstration was gotten up on a large scale in Fall River, upwards of fifteen thousand people participating in it. There were bands heading the different divisions of the procession; while banners were carried aloft by little children, with various mottoes inscribed on them favoring less hours of labor. A meeting was held after the procession had marched through the city, and resolutions drawn and approved. They were afterwards sent to the Legislature, and a ten-hour bill was made law for all women and children employed in the textile industries in 1874.

The years of 1872–73, prior to the passage of the ten-hour law, was a very trying time for the operatives employed in the textile industries. The failures of banks and the subsequent financial depression, led to an era of bad trade which continued, with a downward tendency in the price of textile products, and a corresponding decrease in wages, up to the year of 1879. Fall River, having grown into the largest cotton manufacturing city in the country, was destined to play a conspicuous part in the great industrial struggle which took place between employers and employees during this long period of depression, in which there was over forty per cent. reduced from the wages of employees. At the termination of the war, Fall River had 265,328 spindles engaged in cotton manufacture; and ten years after, in 1874, when the ten-hour bill passed both branches of the Legislature, the number of spindles had increased to 1,258,508, and the population increased from 17,525 in 1865, to 43,289 in 1874. No other textile city was growing so rapidly, and none felt the effects of the depressed condition of trade more than this city did, because nearly all its people were dependent upon the cotton industry for a livelihood. In the fall of 1873 wages were reduced ten per cent. In the course of a few months another reduction was made; and, in the beginning of 1874, large meetings of operatives were held in various parts of the city, and resolutions passed protesting against the reductions in wages. The spinners began to fall into line rapidly, leaving no stone unturned to close up and so strengthen their ranks as to be able to not only resist further encroachments upon their wages but to compel a restoration of some of that which had been taken from them the year previously. A convention of delegates from the various spinning districts was convened in Fall River in the spring of 1874, and a system of concerted action was agreed upon; also, that with the first appearance of an improvement in the trade, the spinners of Fall River should throw down the gauntlet and demand an advance in wages or strike for it. Thus Fall River was selected as the battle-field for the textile workers of New England. And it is only fair to say that its working people always proved themselves to be ahead of most of the New England operatives in intelligence, executive ability, perseverance and determination when engaged in industrial warfare. In following the progress of the textile trades organizations through the remainder of this chapter, Fall River will be taken as a suitable type of the cotton-producing districts. Its experience was duplicated with more or less variation in Lawrence, Lowell and similar centers; but it is not essential to detail here the strikes and their results, by which the operatives sought to maintain and improve their condition.

In 1874 the Fall River spinners petitioned the manufacturers for more wages, and were refused. A vote was taken at the next general meeting, and it was decided to defer leaving work until a more auspicious time.

About this time the card-room operatives began to make strenuous efforts to form an organization for the promotion and protection of their interests. After many unsuccessful efforts an association was finally formed, and they commenced to hold their meetings in the spinners' hall. This association consisted chiefly of women, as there are but few men engaged in that branch of cotton manufacturing, and its membership numbered over one thousand at the close of 1874. Simultaneously with the card-room hands, the weavers began to organize also. They formed an association called the Weavers' Protective Association, and before the advent of 1875, that ever memorable year in the history of textile warfare, the number of good members on the books exceeded five thousand. The men who were elected officers of this association were possessed of extraordinary skill and ability as organizers, and they soon began to formulate plans for the organization of the whole of the wage-workers employed in the textile industries of New England. To this end deputations were sent out to do missionary work in the towns and cities of Massachusetts, Rhode Island, Connecticut, and New Hampshire. Several weavers' organizations were formed, and the people were thoroughly aroused to the emergencies of the hour. Promises were made to stand by their fellow toilers in Fall River in defending the rights and dignity of labor. Toward the end of 1874 the spinners, weavers and card-room hands held several joint conferences, with the view of adopting the best possible course to effect a restoration of some of the cut-downs which had been made in their wages during the two preceding years. It was unanimously agreed that mixed deputations, consisting of a spinner, a weaver, and a card-room hand, should interview their employers and request a return of ten per cent. in wages. The request was refused. Consequently the weavers at three mills tendered ten days' notice, prior to going out on strike. In the early part of February, 1875, the notice expired, and the weavers of the Merchants, Crescent and Granite Mills, Fall River, struck work. When the spinners saw the weavers leaving the mills, they struck also; and they were afterwards followed by the card-room hands. Large meetings of the operatives were held, and delegates were appointed to visit all the manufacturing districts to solicit aid for the strikers. The weavers remaining at work at the other mills in the city were levied ten cents per loom to assist those on strike. The card-room hands also taxed each member employed, while the spinners levied a tax of one dollar per head weekly on each member. Considerable money rolled in from outside districts; and what improved the prospects of success was the strengthening of the cloth market, the advance in price of cloth and the appreciation of mill stock. These causes filled the strikers with hope and confidence, and three more mills were ordered to be struck. This action made the total number of operatives on strike between three and four thousand. In the middle of March, negotiations were opened which led to the strikers resuming work on the promise that the ten per cent. advance in wages would be given on April 1st. Shortly after this advance in wages, deputations visited their employers soliciting weekly, instead of monthly, payment of wages. Their request was refused; but this commenced the agitation which resulted in the enactment of the present law in Massachusetts, which compels all corporations to pay their employees weekly.

There was more or less uneasiness evinced throughout the textile districts during the summer of 1875. Strikes on a small scale were very common among the weavers, and much hard feeling was engendered between the employers and the employees. Finally the Fall River manufacturers, taking advantage of a lull in the market and contending that they were paying higher prices than other districts, posted notices to the effect that wages would be reduced on the first of August ten per cent. The embers of discontent, which had been smouldering all summer, burst suddenly into a blaze. Delegates were appointed from the meetings of the weavers, carders and spinners to confer together, to strike out some line of action for the help to pursue. The three separate bodies met in their respective rooms, a few days prior to the notices for a reduction in wages expiring, and delegates were appointed from each body, who conferred together and decided to suspend work for the month of August. Thus on the first of August commenced what is called "The Great Vacation," when 1,269,048 spindles ceased to hum; over 30,000 looms, which manufactured cloth at the rate of 343,375,000 yards per year, or nearly a mile per minute, were silent; which rendered 15,000 people idle, with a loss weekly in wages of $82,973. This was a sad condition of affairs for employers and employees to witness on August 1st, 1875. The breach seemed to widen as the stoppage continued. There did not seem a vestige left of that old friendly feeling which used to exist between employer and employee in the early days of cotton manufacturing in the United States. After three weeks had elapsed, and the help were getting ready to resume work again, it suddenly leaked out that the manufacturers would not start the mills until each operative signed his or her name to an iron-clad document. Some of the stipulations were that only one out of every eight operatives could give notice to leave work at the same time. This was done to prevent concerted action on the part of the operatives. Another stipulation was that no operative should belong to a trades-union in the future. The operatives, after the month's vacation expired, refused to start work under these conditions on the first of September.

Finally hunger and want won the battle, and in the eighth week of the stoppage the various unions voted to resume work unconditionally, accepting the ten per cent. reduction, and signing the infamous document as demanded by the manufacturers. Thus ended the nine weeks' "vacation," which caused a loss of $746,700 in wages alone, while the loss to the manufacturers must have been enormous. With a single exception the conduct of the operatives was praiseworthy all through the strike, and in that one instance it is an open question whether the starving people out of work or the city officials were to blame. Two companies of militia were summoned from Taunton and Middleboro, when a collision between the strikers and the authorities seemed inevitable, and Company M, of Fall River, was also at the service of the authorities. Their services were not needed, however, and the operatives were soon on most friendly terms with them. Those who had acted as leaders in the operatives' ranks, or any of those who had addressed the public meetings, which had been held so frequently during the stoppage of the mills, were all blacklisted, and prevented from obtaining employment at any of the mills in the city. The weavers' organization was completely broken to pieces, and what little money was in the treasury was divided among the members who had been victimized, to enable them to travel and seek employment elsewhere. The card-room operatives' organization went to pieces also, owing to the loss of its leaders, who were all placed under the ban of the blacklist. The spinners' organization still kept its head above the water, and though most of its members signed the "Infamous Document," as did those of other branches, they were no way reluctant in telling their overseers that they did not consider it binding, as it was their starving children that compelled them to sign it against their wills, and that they should still stand by their union.

As a natural result of the fierce industrial struggles between the employers and employees which occurred in the textile industry, and the many defeats the latter sustained, but one organized body of textile workers remained in 1876; that was the Spinners' Union of Fall River. Trade, about this time, took a slight upward movement, and the Fall River spinners, always on the alert, immediately petitioned for more wages. Deputations waited upon the employers at every mill in the city, but the answers received were all unfavorable. Weekly, instead of monthly, payments were granted, however, at some of the mills.

The failure of the chief of the district police to enforce the labor laws caused the adoption of resolutions of censure by the spinners and their remonstrance before the legislative labor committee. A new chief was soon appointed, and the ten-hour law was so amended as to make its enforcement more easy.

During 1876 another ten per cent. reduction was made. This angered the operatives to such a degree that it was only by the utmost efforts of the officers of the union that the spinners were prevented from striking. The union now commenced to lose members. A strike occurred at the Granite No. 1 mill, which ended disastrously to the spinners. An unsuccessful strike in New Bedford at this time was felt so keenly in Fall River also, that many members of the Spinners' Union fell in arrears, and it was with the utmost difficulty that it could be kept together.

For the purpose of stemming the tide of dissolution which seemed to have set in, the veteran labor reformer, George E. McNeill, of Boston, who had in the past given his services to the union, was invited to assist in rallying the men and preserving the Union. Mr. McNeill was highly respected among the spinners, for they knew him to be an earnest, sincere man, who lost considerable time and money through ever being willing to give his services gratuitously to any movement tending to unite and elevate the workingmen. Meetings were held in various parts of the city, which Mr. McNeill addressed. He seemed to inspire new hope and courage into the men. Many of them fell into line again and promised to stand by the Union through "thick and thin," and saying that in it lay their only salvation. Toward the end of 1877 the Spinners' Union was as strong as at any past period in its history.

In 1878 trade gradually grew worse, until there was scarcely any margin for the manufacturer, and the wages of the employees were thirty per cent. less than in 1873. Fall River felt the depression more keenly than any other textile district. Some of the mills were paying twenty per cent. for money, and cloth was down to three cents per yard for prints. On March 12th notices of a fifteen per cent. reduction were posted. A mass-meeting of operatives was immediately held to protest against the reduction. Over twenty-five hundred people assembled in the Academy of Music and protested against their wages being reduced. They said that if the reduction of wages was enforced, it would make forty-five per cent. in the total of reductions in wages sustained in less than five years. Deputations were appointed from the Spinners' Union, to request their employers to run the mills four days per week instead of cutting down wages. The spinners contended that every time wages were reduced the price of cloth fell more proportionately; and, consequently, the reduction was no benefit to employers, while it was a loss to the employees. The only gainers were the consumers. They also claimed that by cutting down wages they were "killing the goose that laid the golden egg," by reducing the purchasing power of the people. The employers insisted on reducing wages, and the reduction went into effect toward the latter end of March. Two weeks after the reduction in wages cloth fell to lower prices than ever known, and a tremendous shrinkage took place in mill stocks. The policy of running the mills on short time, advocated by the operatives but a month before, was resorted to in April by the manufacturers, and the mills were run but alternate weeks for eighteen weeks through the summer months. Hardly had the short time been adopted, when the air was full of rumors that more than two-thirds of the mills in Fall River were on the verge of ruin.

It is hardly necessary here to detail how Treasurer Angier S. Chace of the Union Mill was found to be a defaulter to the amount of about $500,000; Treasurer George T. Hathaway, of Border City, Nos. 1 and 2, and of the Sagamore, to the extent of over $1,000,000; Treasurer Charles P. Stickney, of the Fall River Gas Company, in the sum of $30,000; and how they were sentenced to twelve, ten and five years' imprisonment, respectively, in the State prison. The public has not yet forgotten these crimes and their punishment. The people of Fall River now said that the industrial struggle of 1875 had worked more to the injury of the manufacturers than they had been willing to admit.

About this time the operatives decided to have a public demonstration, expressing dissatisfaction at the low wages they were receiving, at the violation of the ten-hour law, and their contempt for the fraudulent mill treasurers, who, by their dishonesty, had robbed some workingmen of their whole life's savings. The demonstration was on a Saturday afternoon, in the month of May, and the various divisions marched to the city lots in the centre of the city, preceded by bands and commanded by mounted marshals. It was supposed that twenty thousand people participated in the procession, many of them carrying banners and cartoons expressive of their opinions upon the state of affairs in the city, and of their sentiments. Groans were given outside many of the mill-treasurers' residences, but no acts of violence were committed. The procession finally reached the public park, where speeches were delivered from the band-stand by the officers of the day, and the people were advised to go peacefully to their homes, and to respect the law in its integrity and entirety.

There was great misery and distress existing in Fall River during the summer months, owing to the mills running only half time, and to the great reduction which had been made in wages.

The Spinners' Union, the only organization of textile workers in the New England States, could hardly maintain its existence. In the month of June, Robert Howard was appointed secretary, and the association soon began to increase in members and in funds. Every member seemed to have confidence in his ability and strict integrity, and he went to work with a will to help to build up the Union stronger than ever it was before. It had grown so strong by December, 1878, that Mr. Howard was elected permanent secretary, so that he could devote all his time to the interest of the Union and its members. His salary was equal to that of the average spinner. Early in 1879 business began to improve. The members of the Spinners' Union at Fall River thought the time had come for the restoration of a part of the reduction. A meeting of spinners was called, and the condition of trade fully discussed. It was resolved that petitions be sent to the employers, soliciting a return of ten per cent. in wages. The petitions met with a cold and haughty refusal. All argument was of no avail. The spinners, after hearing the reports of the committee, postponed taking action for two weeks. Negotiations were going on meanwhile between employers and employees as to the best and most satisfactory basis on which to effect a settlement of the dispute; but nothing definite was accomplished. When the adjourned meeting came the situation was thoroughly discussed. Finally an informal vote was taken, and the majority voted in favor of striking, in order to to enforce their just demands. The committee, desirous of giving the employers more time for reflection, and feeling opposed to a strike, suggested that the vote be taken by ballot one week hence. In accordance with the laws of the association, a two-thirds vote would be required before a strike could be declared. The taking of the vote was deferred for one week. Efforts were made during the week to bring about a settlement of the troubles by arbitration. To this end the spinners' committee announced publicly that they would submit the whole case for settlement to a board of arbitration. The employers issued a circular shortly after this, stating that they did not propose to allow outsiders to run their business, and that arbitration was not in consonance with the ways of doing business in the United States. The spinners' secretary, Mr. Howard, immediately replied through another circular, showing that arbitration was in consonance with the customs of this country, and that our own Government had set the example by settling with the Government of England the claims arising out of the depredations committed by the "Alabama." All efforts having failed, but two courses were left open to the spinners. One was to entirely recede from their position: the other, to enter into a struggle with their employers, the result of which it was impossible to foretell.

On the 15th of June the spinners decided to strike, and that, instead of leaving work immediately, to give two weeks' notice that unless the advance was conceded by the 26th of June, all hands would leave work. Several meetings were held between the 15th and 26th of the month. But the "die was cast"; neither party would recede from its position. The most that could be gained was a promise from several mills of weekly payments. This did not satisfy the spinners. On the 26th the notice expired, and on the morning following upwards of one thousand spinners and about nine hundred boys, who were employed in the same department, were in the streets. All the money the spinners had in their treasury was fifteen hundred dollars, a sum entirely insufficient to meet the emergencies of the case. Thirty delegates were appointed to solicit aid. Some went to New York, Pennsylvania, New Jersey, Connecticut, Rhode Island, New Hampshire and Maine, but most of them stayed in Massachusetts. A few days after the spinners struck work, most of the other operatives in the mills were compelled to stop for the want of yarn, and other kindred causes, thus throwing over fourteen thousand people on the streets. The cloth trade kept improving, making the manufacturers desirous of getting their machinery in motion. With this object in view, agents were hired and sent out all over the cotton districts to try and obtain spinners. These agents received from three to twelve dollars per head, besides all expenses incurred for every spinner so obtained. Some of these "knobstick" spinners, as they were called, received fifty and sixty per cent. more wages than the spinners on strike could earn, in order to induce them to remain. Every one of them was furnished with a revolver as soon as they entered the mills, to shoot the strikers if they approached them.

Large dwellings were built in all the mill-yards for the knobstick spinners to reside in, because the employers were afraid to have them outside the mill, thinking that the striking spinners would induce them to leave the city. Drink of all kinds used to be carried to the barracks, as their dwelling places were commonly termed, and other various kinds of pleasures were introduced by some of the mill officials, who publicly desired to be regarded among the strongest of temperance reformers.

A great number of the knobstick help consisted of young French Canadians. Circulars and posters in English and French were freely circulated in the regions they came from, stating the cause of the troubles in Fall River, and asking other cotton operatives to keep away. Great meetings were held at Lawrence, Lynn, Boston and Lowell during the strike, all of which were addressed by the secretary of the association. More than ten thousand people were present at the meeting, which was held on the common, at Lynn; and during the strike the shoe-workers of Lynn sent to the strikers in Fall River, $2,300. The cities of Lowell and Lawrence sent $1,400 between them; New York sent $1,500, while large contributions were received from all parts of the States. The Typographical Union, of San Francisco, Cal., sent two hundred dollars by telegraph. It is deserving of mention, as "actions speak louder than words," that two of the delegates who were stationed in New York called upon the late John Kelly, of Tammany Hall fame, who, upon seeing their credentials, immediately gave them one hundred dollars. During the sixteen weeks of the strike upwards of twenty-five thousand dollars were raised from outside sources.

The International Labor Union of America, which the spinners joined a little prior to the strike, rendered them good service, perhaps bringing directly and indirectly about two thousand dollars into the spinners' funds. George E. McNeill was president of this union; John H. O'Connor, of Paterson, secretary; and Carl Speyer, of New York, treasurer. The officers did all that men could do to raise money to enable the spinners to prolong the contest, because nearly everybody was convinced that, if the spinners could only hold out, owing to the great improvement in the market, the manufacturers would eventually yield. The latter, however, determined to starve the spinners into submission. All the relatives of the strikers were prevented from getting work in the city, and such as were working were singled out and discharged. Efforts were made to prevent the storekeepers from serving them with groceries on credit; and many families were put out of their tenements, having to seek shelter where best they could. The spinners, before they struck, passed a resolution to do without any assistance for the first three weeks, and afterwards to be satisfied with such help as the association could render. The relief was doled out in grocery checks, and the amount allowed was one dollar and fifty cents per week for an unmarried man, the same amount to married men, with twenty-five cents additional for their wives and each child unemployed. Before the strike had been progressing many weeks, many of those engaged in it were in an impoverished condition. To make matters worse, the corporation officials had a large number of the strikers arrested on the most flimsy pretexts. So long as the funds of the association held out, none of the strikers were allowed to go to jail, if a fine was the alternative. But this drain on the treasury led to a reduction in the weekly allowance to those on strike. After the strike had continued ten weeks, it was plain to be seen that the employers, despite the advance of three-quarters of a cent per yard in cloth, intended to fight it out to the bitter end. More money was needed by the spinners, or hunger would do its work effectively, and the contest would be lost. A variety troupe was formed from the strikers, which gave several *shows* in the Opera House, Fall River, to good houses, all the proceeds, after paying running expenses, being passed in to the spinners' treasury. So successful was the *troupe* at home, that it ventured abroad, visiting Brockton, Randolph, Holbrook, Lynn, Boston, Lowell and Lawrence. Considerable sums of money were raised by this troupe, all of which were utilized for the benefit of the strikers.

At the end of fourteen weeks from the commencement of the strike, signs of weakness were visible in the ranks. Insufficient food and shoeless feet were telling upon the strikers, and every imaginable kind of temptation was being held out by the superintendents and overseers of the mills, in order to get them to break from the rest and thus hasten the end of the strike. In the sixteenth week a break occurred among the help on strike at the Border City Mills. Several of them, having been filled with drink, returned to work. This was the signal for others to follow. A general meeting was then called, and it was resolved, though not without much opposition, that the help at each mill should make the best possible terms with their employers. Some of the mills promised weekly instead of monthly payments, and other small concessions. Thus ended the most determined and the most bitterly contested struggle that ever occurred in the annals of Fall River industrial history. The strike commenced June 26th, 1879, and ended October 16th. It was lost only for want of money to carry it on with. The strikers were just as determined at the ending as they were at the beginning of the conflict; just as confident that their cause was right.

The spinners, at the first meeting of the association held after the termination of the strike, placed a levy of one dollar and fifty cents per month upon each member to assist those who had been victimized and deprived of their situations.

Trade continuing to improve, the spinners, in November, asked an increase, and two months after the wages were advanced in accordance with the spinners' request; all the mills in the New England States following the example. Thus the persistent and determined action of the Fall River Mule-Spinners' Union secured not only an advance for themselves, but for the whole of the unorganized cotton help of New England. The Union then began to agitate for weekly payments instead of monthly, and before the expiration of March, 1880, nineteen out of the fifty-three mills made the desired change. The power of united action was once more forcibly displayed, as no other cotton mill in the United States was then paying weekly.

The Fall River spinners, in April, 1880, three months after receiving the fifteen per cent. advance, owing to the continued prosperity in trade, voted to strike ten mills out of the fifty-three in the city if wages were not increased ten per cent. The Manufacturers' Board of Trade met on the same day, and it was a surprise on the following morning to find in the same papers two announcements—one, of a threatened strike of the spinners; the other, from the manufacturers, stating that wages would be advanced as desired. The other mills in New England again adopted the example set in Fall River and increased wages. Thus the cotton operatives of New England were once more indebted to the activity of the Fall River Spinners' Union for the increase in wages. From this time until fall the spinners labored zealously for weekly payments and a better enforcement of the ten-hour law. Their efforts were defeated in the Legislature; the mill treasurers were then labored with, and several of them adopted weekly payments. In September, but six months after the last advance in wages, the mill officials notified the help that on account of the fall in the price of cloth, which was then selling at four cents per yard, the wages would be reduced ten per cent.; or, in other words, put back to where they were prior to the first of April of the same year. The operatives were wild with excitement, the storekeepers and other respectable citizens holding with them, because they knew well that during the preceding twelve months the corporations had made immense sums of money, and that many of them, after paying twenty per cent. dividends, had as much money in reserve as would pay dividends for some time to come.

In the face of this extraordinary prosperity, it was no surprise to see the operatives threatening to strike if the reduction should be enforced. Several large meetings of the operatives were held to protest against wages being reduced. It was ultimately arranged for a deputation each of spinners and employers to meet the day preceding the reduction going into effect, to discuss the case on its merits. The Secretary of the Spinners' Association, with five other spinners, met four of the employers. The conference lasted four hours, and then broke up without agreeing to anything. The same night the Spinners' Hall and the stairway to it were crowded with operatives desirous of knowing the result of the interview. It was stated at the meeting that the employers insisted that wages should be reduced, come what might. After a lengthy and heated debate, a vote was taken by ballot for a strike or no strike, and out of 700 spinners 310 voted in favor of striking and 390 against it. A strike was thus averted, and the ten per cent. reduction in wages was accepted under protest. All classes were delighted that there was to be no strike, and many were the words of praise spoken of the officers of the Spinners' Association, especially of the secretary, as it was generally admitted that a word from him could have turned the meeting either way. Another demand for weekly payments was made, and at the beginning of 1882, out of fifty-three mills in Fall River, forty of them were paying weekly—a result reached by the power of organized labor.

About the same time that strikes in Lawrence and Cohoes were progressing, early in 1882, desperate attempts were made by the Fall River Manufacturers' Board of Trade to break up the Spinners' Union. To accomplish this end it was agreed to discharge and blacklist all the members of the committee and the collectors of the Spinners' Union fees. This caused great indignation in the union, and it was very remarkable that every member of the committee was discovered and his name put upon the blacklist, although these members were steady, industrious men, and the very best of spinners. It was discovered about three months after the blacklisting had commenced that a spinner named Wilkinson, who came from the town of Oldham, in England, was attending the spinners' meetings merely to carry away to the manufacturers the names of the committee men and other prominent members, for which services he received ten dollars per month in addition to his wages for spinning. Shortly after Wilkinson was discovered in his nefarious dealings, his goods, himself and family were secretly removed from the city, but to what part of the country it was impossible to find out. He was removed to prevent his making a confession, through the press, of his treachery.

It was a trying time for the Spinners' Union. Many of its members were in favor of striking, while the more conservative were in favor of supporting those who were blacklisted, until work could be found for them. The latter course prevailed, and they were supported at the rate of six dollars per week, and fifty cents for their wives and children not working. Between two and three thousand dollars were paid in this way; but the union was preserved, the Manufacturers' Board of Trade finding themselves unable to destroy it. The spinners who were blacklisted had to resort to various schemes to obtain employment. Many of them began work under assumed names, but when discovered they were immediately discharged. The Board of Trade, in order to checkmate those efforts of the men to obtain employment, hired a clerk, commonly called a "spotter," whose duty it was to visit the mills every month to find out whether any of the blacklisted men were employed. He was furnished with all their names, aliases, descriptions and other particulars, and if any of them were found working they were instantly discharged without any reasons being assigned. Many of the men who were blacklisted had to travel to districts where they were unknown to find employment; and to the credit of the Fall River men it must be said that many of the organizations of cotton operatives now springing into existence in many parts of the New England States are due in no small degree to their efforts.

In the fall of 1882 the spinners of Fall River, Lowell, Lawrence, New Bedford, Manchester, Nashua, Salmon Falls, New Market, Lewiston and Biddeford, held a conference in Codman Hall, Boston, to devise the best means of bringing about a reduction in the hours of labor in the textile trade in States outside of Massachusetts. After a whole day's session one hundred dollars was voted, and Mr. Howard, the secretary, was instructed to commence an agitation for the furtherance of this object in Rhode Island immediately. Early in the following year, 1883, meetings were held in Central Falls, Woonsocket, Rocky Point, and several other places, in favor of a law limiting the hours of labor for all women and minors under eighteen years of age to ten daily. "Ten-Hour Leagues" were established, which worked diligently and faithfully, visiting the representatives in their respective districts, soliciting them to vote in favor of the passage of a ten-hour bill, which was presented by Hon. Hugh Carroll, of Pawtucket. Mr. Howard interviewed Governor Bourne, requesting him to recommend, in his message to the Legislature, a reduction in the hours of labor for women and children employed in textile industries. His Excellency would not give an absolute promise, yet when his message was delivered it contained the recommendation. Mr. Howard in the same year was deputed by the Spinners' Association to appear before the legislative committee on labor in Augusta, Me., where a hearing was being held in the State House, on a bill proposing a reduction in the hours of labor in textile industries. After his return from Augusta he was again sent to Rhode Island, where the seed he had sown a few months previously was now beginning to blossom, The people were awake, and demanded with one voice to be put on a level with Massachusetts in regard to working hours. The first year the bill was defeated; but the year following meetings were held in every village, town and city in the State, hearings were held in the State House and large numbers of operatives appeared before the committee to give testimony in favor of the ten-hour bill. That year (1885) the bill passed both branches of the Legislature, received the sanction of the Governor, and went into force January 1, 1886. As much as the people of Rhode Island were elated over this victory, they were not one whit more so than the spinners of Fall River, who, two years after they sent their secretary to that State to agitate a reduction in the hours of labor, had the proud satisfaction of seeing a law placed on the statute books limiting the working time for women and children to sixty hours weekly.

From 1882 to 1884, the cotton industry was gradually growing worse; goods were being piled up, and scarcely any buyers were in the markets; margins of profits were narrowed down so small that reductions in wages were made in Lowell, Lawrence, Manchester, New Bedford, and, finally, in Fall River. The help in these places were very much dissatisfied, and strongly remonstrated against their wages being reduced. In Fall River the spinners interviewed their respective treasurers, and once more argued against the suicidal practice of reducing wages, and requested that the working time be reduced one-third instead. This proposition was laid before the Board of Trade, composed of manufacturers, and a reply was sent to the Secretary of the Spinners' Association, stating that wages would be reduced first, and that less working time would be considered after. The letter was read to a crowded meeting of spinners, who deemed the answer unsatisfactory, and a strike was finally ordered at ten mills. The Spinners' Union had at this time a fund of over ten thousand dollars standing to the credit of its six hundred members. The spinners entered the contest feeling that right and justice were on their side. They had good reasons for thinking so, for the dividends declared by the fifty-four mills of Fall River averaged a shade over five per cent. for the previous year. The strike began on February 4th, 1884, and was fiercely contested for eighteen weeks. It then collapsed for the want of funds. The mill-owners again imported the obnoxious "knobsticks," in spite of their bitter experience in 1879. The allowance made the strikers was five dollars a week, fifty cents for their wives and twenty-five cents for each unemployed child, while the strike lasted. Large sums were sent from outside cities to assist the strikers. The most notable event of the strike was the burning of the Sagamore mill, which was one where the spinners were on strike. Some of the friends of the manufacturers accused the strikers of setting fire to the mill; but after a most thorough investigation, not a vestige of evidence could be obtained to fasten the crime upon them. The probability was, that one of the "knobsticks," who could do as they liked, was passing through the cotton-room, smoking, and threw a lighted match into a bale of cotton, which quickly took fire, spread with lightning-like rapidity to the other bales, causing the destruction of the mill.

The great curtailment in production caused by the strike did not seem to help the markets as much as was anticipated, and shortly after its termination the mills in Fall River began to stop every alternate week during the summer months, the Lowell and New Bedford mills following the example. This was just the policy the spinners proposed before they went on strike, instead of reducing wages. These stoppages curtailed production to the amount of one million pieces of cloth. But trade still remained dull and unprofitable. In January, 1885, there being no signs of a revival in trade, the corporations of Lowell and New Bedford reduced wages again, which gave the Fall River corporations a good excuse for reducing wages also. Only six months after these reductions, the mills all over New England were compelled by depressed markets to commence working short time again; and in the principal towns and cities of cotton manufacture, from eight to ten weeks' curtailment of production took place in the summer of 1885, which kept more than two million pieces of goods out of the market. This great curtailment of production appeared to be the right remedy for a dyspeptic market, which, for a long time previously, had had more goods forced upon it than it could unload at any price. It soon began to assume a more healthy and profitable aspect. The policy of curtailment of production by running less hours was always advocated by the textile organizations, because their members knew, from close watching of the trade, that the policy which will take from, not that which will add to, is that which is going to bring relief to glutted markets. Reducing the working time lessens the delivery of goods, while lessening the wages, lessens the consumption of goods, owing to the restriction in the purchasing powers of the masses, thus leading to glutted and stagnant markets. The cotton industry is one of the most important of the nation, and no effort should be spared by employers and employees, who believe in doing what is just and right by each other, to settle disputes by some better method than that of brute force.

Over 172,000 people are engaged in cotton manufacturing in the United States, who receive in wages $42,000,000 annually. It seems unwise and unbusiness-like on the part of wealthy corporations, who often allow their employees to go out on strike before they will condescend to consult with them, or take a word of advice from them. The time is coming when employers of labor will find it to their benefit to treat with their employees as equals on questions concerning the welfare of both. Much of the misrepresentation to which both of them have been subjected in the past has been for the want of a better understanding between them; and the best and the only way to bring about a better feeling and a better understanding between employer and employee is to meet together more frequently in friendly conference. A little more of the "milk of human kindness" doled out by employers to employees, the substituting of arbitration for the present methods of settling disputes would enable the manufacturers of the United States to hold the foremost place in the great commercial race now taking place among the most highly civilized and enterprising nations of the world.

It would be extremely interesting to follow the struggles of the cotton operatives in Lawrence, Lowell, New Bedford, Mass., and at Cohoes, N. Y.; but after all it would be mainly a repetition of the story told of Fall River, with the places, names and dates changed. We will just glance at them, however. Lowell saw an unsuccessful strike in 1874, when seventeen hundred dollars was sent the strikers from Fall River. In 1876 there were unsuccessful strikes at Arctic and Aquidneck, R. I., and Clinton and New Bedford, Mass. In March, 1880, a bitterly-contested strike began in Cohoes, N. Y., which resulted in a ten per cent. advance after ten weeks of idleness. After this strike, Secretary Howard, of the Fall River Spinners' Union, visited Cohoes and organized a union there, but it soon went to pieces by reason of blacklisting. In 1882 there was a great strike in Lawrence against a twenty per cent. reduction at the Pacific Mills, which had paid out $9,525,000 in dividends, equal to 381 per cent. on its capital in the nineteen years previous, and had also increased its capital from $2,500,000 to $5,000,000. Public sympathy through the city and State was with the operatives, but they were finally starved into surrender. Contemporaneous with this strike was another, but unsuccessful one, at Cohoes, N. Y., against a ten per cent. reduction. These strikes cost the corporations immense amounts, even though they finally carried their point.

[In the chapter devoted to miscellaneous trades some account is given of the organizations existing in the wool, flax and silk industries.—EDITOR.]

CHAPTER X.

COAL MINERS.

Difficulties of Organization — Farm Laborers as Miners — First Organization, 1857 — Address of Daniel Weaver — National Miners' Association, 1861 — First Miners' Paper — Miners' and Laborers' Benevolent Association — John Siney as an Organizer — Effect of the Panic of 1873 — Repeated Strikes and Defeats — Arrest of John Siney and Twenty-Seven Others — The Union Demoralized — Introduction of the Knights of Labor — Its Rapid Extension Among Miners — Successful Strike in Pittsburgh District — Pit Committees — Movement for Fortnightly Payments, Eight Hours and Abolition of Company Stores — Ohio Miners' Amalgamated Association, 1882 — National Convention at Indianapolis — Organization of National Federation of Miners and Mine Laborers — Its Objects — Arbitration Attempted.

THE coal miners of the United States are, perhaps, more generally misunderstood than any class of laborers in the world. Whenever they have undertaken any step for their industrial advancement it has been in the face of an adverse public opinion, which has been taught to regard them as almost beyond the pale of well-ordered civilization. They have thus failed to receive the moral encouragement and support which has sustained and assisted other wage-workers, especially in their later contests.

But this, serious as it may be, is merely external. Among themselves and in the conditions of their work and life, the miners have had many internal difficulties to contend with — difficulties which have stood in the way of organization and united action. Scattered in remote districts, — frequently many miles away from the towns, — and shut off almost entirely from all social intercourse, the opportunities for the interchange of ideas and the upbuilding of compact, serviceable organizations have necessarily been slight. Nor is this all. The coal miner has been of necessity a bird of passage.

Different seasons have found him in different localities, as the opportunities for work has offered. Coal which depends on river transportation must be mined in the spring and fall, while that transported by the lakes is confined to summer, and only domestic coal can be operated during the winter. These conditions have been serious obstacles to the miners in the labor movement in two ways: first, because they have contributed much to injure the reputation of miners for thrift and stability as a class; and, second, because they have had a tendency to disrupt local organizations and injure their efficiency. It is, however, the first of these two evils that the miners have most deplored. They have felt deeply the injustice of the prejudice existing against them. They trace it to the corporations that employ them, whose interest it has sometimes been to represent them as a class of shiftless laborers, careless of their habits and reputation. These ideas have been sent out especially in times of strikes, the newspaper accounts often giving them free circulation. The public has formed its estimate of the miners' character upon the basis of these unjust assertions, which have taken on a color of truthfulness from the unfortunate circumstances arising out of the conditions of their life. The miner has felt that he could get no fair presentation of his grievances in the newspapers, and that his unequal battle must always be fought in the face of these difficulties. The advent of labor newspapers has done much to change this aspect of the case, however, and gradually the public has been made to see this great body of industrious men in a fair light.

There have been other difficulties in the way of organization, wholly outside of and beyond the prejudice we have noted, and the unfavorable effect of the seasons on mining operations. One of the most serious of these has been the employment of farm-hands in the mines during the winter season. This practice has introduced an element of labor which had nothing to gain by such organizations as the skilled miners were striving to build up. It was an element which had no interest in the permanent welfare of the miners as a class. To them it was of little consequence whether the wages were high or low. Employment in the mines was not their chief dependence. They earned their living by farming, and such few dollars as they could realize in the winter were so much additional income. They were not experts, and their occasional presence among the miners furnished the employers with a pretext for keeping the wages at the lowest point at which men could exist. The effect of this unnatural element of competition on the efforts at labor organization can be readily understood. That the farm-hands were regarded and treated as interlopers coming between the hard-working miners and their just rights, was not much to be wondered at.

In spite of these manifold difficulties, the coal-miners of the United States finally began the work of organization on such a scale that it could not be longer delayed or defeated. It was not until this organization was well under way, that they encountered the last obstacle which the employers had to place in their path, and this was of only temporary and local consequence. This was the policy, steadily pursued by the corporations, of eliminating the leaders from the ranks of the miners by offering them good salaries as superintendents. The plan worked successfully in some localities, and many men, now the bosses of mines, owe their positions to the prominent part they played in the early history of the organization. It is a matter of pride, however, that some of the strongest and ablest leaders were neither to be bought, cajoled, or driven, and that through them the organizations so long desired were finally built up.

In the early history of mining organization the trade was confined to a few States, the anthracite regions and the river coal, as it is called, of the Pittsburgh district, and the block coal of the Chenango Valley being the most prominent. Pennsylvania, the Mahoning and Tuscarawas Valleys, Salineville, Yellow Creek and the Ohio river in Ohio, and eastern and northeastern Illinois, comprising Will, Grundy, Lasalle and other counties, and the Belleville tract, and Eastern Missouri and Maryland. The later efforts took in more territory in Pennsylvania, consisting of the Bartley mountains and Tioga, Huntingdon, Clearfield, Jefferson, and other counties. The great Hocking Valley and its surrounding territory, Guernsey, Jackson, and several other counties in Ohio, were also interested. The whole State of Indiana, part of Michigan, more extended fields in Illinois, Missouri, Iowa, Kansas, Colorado, and the far Western territories, the Virginias, old and west, Tennessee, Alabama, and the Southern coal fields generally joined in the movement. The present efforts that are being made embrace every coal field in the country.

The earliest efforts that we can learn of organization were about 1857 or 1858; but as far as we learn the efforts were confined to districts alone. The condition of the trade at that time was such that it could easily be controlled by such organizations, without calling for assistance from other districts, as each at that time had its own exclusive markets and competition from the others was out of the question. For this reason no efforts were made by the leaders at that time to draw closer together by general organization, and they only lasted for a short time.

The first attempt at national organization was made on the Belleville Track, Illinois, in January, 1861. In the latter part of 1860, Daniel Weaver, Thomas Lloyd, and several others got together and talked up the benefits to be derived from, and the actual necessity for, the general organization, and the result was the following address, prefaced by Mackay's poem, "What Might Be Done?" and signed by D. W.:—

The necessity of an association of miners, and of those branches of industry immediately connected with mining operations, having for its objects the physical, mental and social elevation of the miner, has long been felt by the thinking portion of miners generally.

Union is the great fundamental principle by which every object of importance is to be accomplished. Man is a social being, and if left to himself, in an isolated condition, would be one of the weakest creatures; but, associated with his kind, he works wonders. Men can do jointly what they cannot do singly; and the UNION of minds and hands, the concentration, of their power, becomes almost omnipotent. Nor is this all; men not only accumulate power by union, but gain warmth and earnestness. There is an electric sympathy kindled, and the attractive forces inherent in human nature are called into

HOMES OF THE COAL MINERS.

action, and a stream of generous emotion, of a friendly regard for each other, binds together and animates the whole.

If men would spread one set of opinions, or crush another, they make a society. Would they improve the sanitary condition of our towns, light our streets with gas, or supply our dwellings with water, they form societies. From the organization of our armies, our railroad and banking companies, down through every minute ramification of society to trades' associations and sick societies, men have learned the power and efficiency of co-operation, and are, therefore, determined to stand by each other. How long, then, will miners remain isolated — antagonistic to each other? Does it not behoove us, as miners, to use every means to elevate our position in society, by a reformation of character, by obliterating all personal animosities and frivolous nationalities, abandoning our pernicious habits and degrading pursuits, and striving for the attainment of pure and high principles and generous motives, which will fit us to bear a manly, useful and honorable part in the world? Our unity is essential to the attainment of our own rights and the amelioration of our present condition; and our voices must be heard in the legislative halls of our land. There it is that our complaints must be made and our rights defined. The insatiable maw of Capital would devour every vestige of Labor's rights; but we must demand legislative protection; and to accomplish this, we must organize. Our remedy, our safety, our protection, our dearest interests, and the social well-being of our families, present and future, depend on our Unity, our duty, and our regard for each other.

In laying before you, therefore, the objects of this association, we desire it to be understood that our objects are not merely pecuniary, but to mutually instruct and improve each other in knowledge, which is power; to study the laws of life; the relation of Labor to Capital; politics, municipal affairs, literature, science, or any other subject relating to the general welfare of our class. Has not experience and observation taught us what one of the profoundest thinkers of the present day has said, that "All human interests, and combined human endeavors, and social growth in this world, have, at certain stages of their developments, required organizing; and Labor — the grandest of human interests — requires it now. There must be an organization of Labor; to begin with it straightway, to proceed with it, and succeed in it more and more." One of America's immortals said, "To me there is no East, no West, no North, no South," and I would say, Let there be no English, no Irish, Germans, Scotch, or Welsh. This is our country, and —

"All men are brethren — how the watch-words run!
And when men act as such is justice won."

Come, then, and rally around the standard of Union — the union of States and the unity of miners — and with honesty of purpose, zeal and watchfulness — the pledge of success — unite for the emancipation of our labor, and the regeneration and elevation physically, mentally and morally, of our species.

Yours, on behalf of the miners, D. W.

The result of this address was that on the 28th of January, 1861, a convention was held, consisting of representatives of miners from Illinois and Missouri, and the association known as the "American Miners' Association" was established, and Daniel Weaver was elected president, and Thomas Lloyd secretary. A constitution and laws were adopted and printed. The leaders felt strongly their utter helplessness without organization, and the following verse, quoted at the head of the constitution of this association well expresses the sentiment which ran through all their earlier records: —

Step by step, the longest march
  Can be won, can be won;
Single stones will form an arch
  One by one, one by one.
And by union, what we will
Can be all accomplished still.
Drops of water turn a mill,
  Singly none, singly none.

The preamble sets forth: —

The working miners are, in the prosecution of their labors, subjected to manifold dangers from explosions and insecure roofs; also from fire-damps and other noxious gases, the result of imperfect ventilation, as well as to accidents arising from other causes consequent upon the parsimony of employers, whose objects would seem to be the increase of the volume of their capital, without reference to the fearful loss of life, limb and health, which is the cause of such increase, etc.

The time for organization had come at last. The constitution provided for the formation of members into lodges, lodges to form districts, all of which were under the supervision of a general board of directors or trustees, who, besides exercising general supervision, represented the association in its corporate capacity. The general board consisted of one president, vice-president, financial secretary, corresponding secretary and treasurer, and one delegate from each lodge in the association, who were elected annually by the lodges. The general officers were elected by the delegates, and held their positions two years, or until their successors should be elected and qualified. They were to meet once a year, unless a majority of the lodges determined to call a special meeting of the board. Delegates were allowed a vote for every twenty members they represented. This, in brief, was the form in which the miners finally developed their first national organization.

Daniel Weaver, who laid the foundation of the organization, was an Englishman, raised in the mines, and an old settler in the mining region of the Belleville Tract, to which we owe the first national association. He was, as a matter of course, self-educated. The language of his address betrays the fact that he had taken an active part in the Chartist movement in England, which may, indeed, have hurried his departure. At the time of organizing the American miners he was ripening in years, and was a deep thinker, logical reasoner, forcible in expression, and a plain, energetic speaker, who brought convictions to the minds of those listening to him. Under his guidance the organization could not fail of success.

Weaver was ably assisted in his work by Thomas Lloyd, a Welshman, who came to this country after reaching manhood, and settled on the Belleville Tract. He, also, was a man of mature years, an energetic worker and a forcible speaker, and was the chief support of Weaver in getting the organization established. When the organization was established an Irishman named Martin Burke became one of the most active, eloquent, and successful organizers. These three men were ably assisted by a German named Roeser, who organized and brought into the fold all the German miners in and around that district. Foreigners, it will be seen, were the organizers and officers of the first American association of miners. These leaders finally gave place to younger men. Immediately after the perfecting of the organization, a tailor by the name of John Hinchcliffe started a paper called *The Weekly Miner*, which was recognized as the official organ; and so great was his influence that if any member was behind in his subscription he could not get a clearance card from his lodge. Mr. Hinchcliffe was afterwards elected president of the association. He then read law and was admitted to the bar. In 1871 the miners elected him to the Legislature, where he introduced a law for the proper ventilation of the mines. In 1873 he was chosen State Senator. He died recently, enjoying the full confidence of the leaders and miners generally.

The American Miners' Association was not long confined to the Belleville Tract and Missouri. It made rapid strides eastward. Braidwood and La Salle were soon organized into districts. In March, 1863, a district was formed in the Tuscarawas Valley, under the name of Massillon Miners' Association. The constitution and by-laws of the Massillon Society were very elaborate, and provided for the regulation of work in the mines, and the careful government of the association. A careful examination of the constitutions of the various associations shows us that each was in itself a general organization, though nominally a branch of the Belleville headquarters.

The history of this association, for the few years following that convention, was almost identical with that of every district. Internal dissensions set in among the officers. The result was that with the strikes of 1867 and 1868, the association went down all over the country, and the American Miners' Association passed into history. In 1869, or the early part of 1870, efforts were made to revive it under the old constitution, which was done in some localities; but the efforts were spasmodic, and availed little.

In January, 1871, a convention was held at Bloomington, Ill., which organized the Illinois Miners' Benevolent and Protective Association, providing that five dollars a week be paid to members while disabled from accident in the mines, or while doing business for the association, and forty dollars were paid on the death of a member. It did not long exist.

In the anthracite regions of Pennsylvania, the first organization that attracted national attention and became of national importance was the Miners' and Laborers' Benevolent Association, better known to miners of the present day by its initials, M. & L. B. A. This was organized in Schuylkill County, and soon spread to western Pennsylvania, and, about the time the American went down, this took its place among the miners of Ohio. It took in men of every trade employed in and around the mines. The local lodges were called subordinate; the District, Grand; the State, Grand Council; the National, Right Worthy Grand Council of the United States.

These names were taken from the constitution of Ohio, but in this, as in the American, while the Grand Council of the United States is spoken of, there was no provision made for the recognition of it or its officers, or support to be given to it. Thus, again, each State or territory was a general organization in itself making no provision for representation in, or support of, a higher body. But at this time the States were well able to care for their own trade, and, though no provision was made, a mutual understanding existed between the States for voluntary support and encouragement to each other.

As in the case of the organizations which had gone before it, the constitution of this association was carefully drawn, and provided elaborate rules for the government of the members and the attainment of the ends desired. Its objects were strictly in the line of its comprehensive name.

This association was the strongest the miners ever had in Pennsylvania, Ohio, Maryland and Indiana, though the miners of Illinois and the Western States did not organize under it. Their own was so near like it that cards were exchanged and accepted between them. From the time the association was organized and took the place of the American, it flourished with varying success until finally it was absorbed by the National Association of Miners, organized at Youngstown, Ohio, October 14, 1873.

It was the Miners' and Laborers' Benevolent Association that brought the late John Siney to the front and proved him a successful organizer, although his services in it were mostly confined to the anthracite regions. It lived through the long and bitter strikes of 1869 and 1870, and in 1872 it existed in all or nearly all the bituminous coal fields, and in Schuylkill and several other counties of the anthracite coal fields of Pennsylvania. The same may be said of Maryland, while in Ohio there was not a coal field but was covered with lodges. Indiana was well organized, as were also the coal fields of Michigan, West Virginia and Kentucky. The Western States, as before stated, although not under it, were fairly organized, so that it might be said that the miners of America were better organized in the spring of 1872 than they ever were before or since, up to the time the present National Federation of Miners and Mine Laborers was organized at Indianapolis, September 12, 1885.

In 1873 new conditions were apparent in the coal trade. Prices were falling, new fields were being opened, railroads were extending, and competitors were being drawn more closely together in general markets. The miners saw in this changing situation the need of a new form of organization, and in September, 1873, in response to a call issued by the officers in various States and districts, a convention assembled at Youngstown, Ohio, and organized the Miners' National Association. It was at this point that John Siney came prominently upon the stage. He was chosen president, with a salary of one hundred dollars a month and traveling expenses. John James, of Illinois, was chosen secretary; George Archibald, of Pittsburgh, vice-president, and David M. Davis, of Mineral Ridge, Ohio, treasurer. Headquarters were established at Cleveland. Four nationalities were represented in the chief officers of the association.

The association started with good prospects and a large membership, fully sufficient to pay salaries of officers and all running expenses. But the panic of October of that year blighted its prospects somewhat, and the strikes of 1874 retarded the growth of the organization. Nevertheless, Siney and the general officers persevered, and with assistance of the representatives to the Youngstown convention, and the officers of the local and district organizations already in existence, the work progressed favorably. At the second annual convention, held at Cleveland, O., October 27th to 29th, 1874, there were present thirty-eight delegates, representing 224 lodges and branches in seven States and one Territory. The total membership then numbered 21,200. At this convention provision was made for the publication of an official paper, known as the *The Miners' National Record*. It enjoyed a brief but useful existence. In 1874 the Schuylkill branch of the Miners' and Laborers' Benevolent Association carried its twelve hundred members into the national organization, and, though the Belleville people were not wholly in sympathy with this policy, there was a general movement in the same direction everywhere among the miners' organizations.

The year 1875 saw the Miners' National Association in the zenith of its power. The same year witnessed a crisis in the affairs of all the organizations. It brought anxiety and grief to the heart of John Siney and his brave colleagues, who put forth every effort to check the disintegration going on around them. As the organizations waned, wages fell, and they have yet to be restored to the standard then lost. Everywhere there were strikes, and nearly everywhere defeats. The arrest of Siney, Parks, and twenty-six others, in May, in the Clearfield region, had a very dampening effect upon organization all over the country, and particularly in Pennsylvania. Some of them were sentenced to one year in the penitentiary, with twenty-five dollars fine; more got off with six months' imprisonment and a fine. Siney and Parks were put under five hundred dollars bail to appear at the following September court, when Siney was acquitted and Parks sentenced one year to the penitentiary and one dollar fine. By the fall of that year every district was demoralized.

About this time the Order of the Knights of Labor was spreading rapidly among the miners, and early in 1875 some of the lodges were organized into local assemblies of that Order. The trial of the Osceola men had the effect of driving men to secret organization, and in the winter of 1875 and 1876, such was the excitement in the Pittsburgh district, along the rivers and railways, that a man must have been dull indeed not to know that some kind of a secret organization was being organized, and very rapidly, too, though nothing could be really found out about it. Miners organized very generally into it for a while, in localities, but as it never seemed to show, on the surface, of anything being done to raise the price of mining, they fell off about as rapidly as they organized; but on going to other places, they carried it along with them, thus keeping up a steady growth of the order among the miners, though it never reached sufficient force to make its power felt by any concerted action,—Maryland, of all the States, making an effort to organize the miners thoroughly into the order. The years 1877 and 1878 passed without any success at organization, although several conventions were held in Ohio, and organizations were started, but they went down without getting established, as the spirit of lethargy and indifference seemed to have control of miners generally. It remained thus until the winter of 1878 and 1879, when miners along the Monongahela and Youghiogheny Rivers, of the Pittsburgh district, with District Assembly No. 9, as a nucleus of an organization, determined to ask for an advance in the price of mining when the spring run opened. They were out several weeks to enforce their demand, and were about to go to work without it, when some information imparted to them by D. R. Jones, who was then reading law in Pittsburgh, and had overheard it from the Coal Exchange, caused them to hold out long enough to get the increase demanded.

This success emboldened them, and they at once made up their minds to put some one in the field to look after their interests. As the miners of Haye's Six-mile ferry had taken Jones from the school he was teaching and more than doubled his salary to check weigh for them, the miners took him up, as the most available man for them, and made him president, to look after their interest. They had no regular form of organization except through pit committees, who elected a president and secretary from their number.

The position which Mr. Jones was called to occupy was one of extraordinary power and responsibility. Established in his headquarters at Pittsburgh, he had neither secretary, treasurer, nor executive committee to consult. He was accountable to no one. Each miner paid him five cents a month for his services, and he ran the office as he pleased. The association prospered amazingly under his management, and was an example and an inspiration to other miners in all parts of the country. The success of the Pittsburgh experiment aroused them to action. They met in that city in March,

1880, and decided to make a concerted move for "uniform, or no screen work, fortnightly payments, eight hours' work, and the abolition of company stores." August 1, 1880, was fixed upon as the date on which the decisive step should be taken. The 1st of August found the miners of the Tuscarawas Valley and of Salineville prepared for the struggle. The former stood out for nine months and the latter four months; but, being unassisted and unsupported by the other bodies, the strike was a failure.

A call issued for a meeting of delegates at Columbus, April 22, 1882, resulted in a large representation of the miners, and the formation of the Ohio Miners' Amalgamated Association. This organization has proven a great success, having been tried and proved by the fire of experience. In the fall of 1882, Mr. Jones retired from the management of the Pittsburgh association, which was then thoroughly organized on a new basis.

During 1883 and 1884 the miners became aware of important developments in the coal trade, which they foresaw must, sooner or later, have a serious effect on their wages. Railroads and telegraphs had annihilated space and time until the East was no longer the market of Eastern coal-fields, nor the West of those in its section. The same was true of the North and South. Competition entered fiercely into the price of coal, and wages were endangered as never before. At the same time electricity and natural gas had come in to reduce the demand in that direction, and improved machinery had developed a tendency to reduce the demand for manufacturing purposes. In view of these facts the leaders issued a call for a great national convention, to be held at Indianapolis, September 12, 1885. The representatives of every form of coal miners' organizations were invited to be present. Out of this convention came forth the present great association, known to the country as the National Federation of Miners and Mine Laborers of the United States and Territories. This memorable convention was called to order by J. J. Sullivan, of Iowa. John McBride, of Ohio, was made temporary chairman, and permanent officers were elected as follows: President, Daniel McLaughlin, of Illinois; Secretary, J. B. Fleming, of West Virginia; Assistant Secretary, J. J. Sullivan, of Iowa; Executive Secretary, Christopher Evans, New Straitville, Ohio; Treasurer, Daniel McLaughlin, Braidwood, Ill. The Executive Board consisted of Christopher Evans, Ohio; Daniel McLaughlin, Illinois; John H. Davis, Pennsylvania; J. B. Fleming, West Virginia; J. J. Sullivan, Iowa. Members at large: George Harris, Pennsylvania; John McBride, Ohio; David Ross, Illinois; Patrick McAdams, Indiana; T. P. Gray, West Virginia; A. M. Reid, Iowa; James Smith, Kansas.

The purpose of the organization is well stated in the following preamble to the constitution:—

As miners and mine laborers, our troubles are everywhere of a similar character. The inexorable law of supply and demand determine the point where our interests unite. The increased shipping facilities of the last few years have made all coal-producing districts competitors in the markets of this country. This has led to indiscriminate cutting of market prices and unnecessary reductions in our wages, which for some time have been far below a living rate. Our wages are no longer regulated by our skill as workmen, nor by the value of the products of our labor, but by competition with cheaper labor. Our standard of workmanship is fast being lowered by the present method of screening coal before weighing, and of the practice on the part of our employers of importing foreign cheap labor to their mines. In many localities free speech has been effectually suppressed. That monstrous swindling machine, the "truck system," which was banished from England by legislation, has been transplanted, and is now flourishing in our midst. Our ills are many and our privileges few; all can be attributed to the lack of organized effort on our part. Our failure to act in concert when contesting for principles and rights has brought about the demoralization and degradation of our craft. Local, district and State organizations have done much towards ameliorating the condition of our craft in the past, but to-day neither district nor State unions can regulate the markets to which their coal is shipped. We know this to our sorrow. Hence, while approving of local organizations, whether secret or open in character, we are convinced that by federating under one general head our powers for good would be increased and a speedy betterment of our common condition follow. In a federation of all lodges and branches of miners' unions lies our only hope. Single-handed we can do nothing, but federated there is no power of wrong that we may not openly defy. Federation will act as a stimulant, and infuse new life into all the different local, district and State organizations. It should do so. The cry of distress which arises from members of our craft in all sections of the country demands us to act, and act at once. Then let us organize and agitate for liberty and living mining rates—for justice to our craft.

TRADES UNION LEADERS.

The objects of the association were declared as follows:—

1. The objects of the association will be to promote the interests of miners and mine-laborers morally, socially, and financially; for the protection of their health and their lives; to spread intelligence amongst them; to remove, as far as possible, the cause of strikes, and adopt, wherever and whenever practicable, the principles of arbitration and restriction; to urge upon all miners and mine-laborers the necessity of becoming citizens, that we may secure, by the use of the ballot, the services of men friendly to the cause of labor, both in our State and National legislative bodies; to create a fund for the support and protection of the members of this association.

2. To obtain legislative enactments for the more efficient management of mines, whereby the lives and health of our members may be better preserved.

3. To shorten the hours of labor to eight hours per day.

4. To secure the enactment of a law for the weighing of all coal before being screened, and to prevent operators and miners from contracting to waive or modify the said law.

5. To protect all members who are unjustly dealt with by their employers while endeavoring to carry out the behests of this confederation.

6. To assist all similar organizations which have the same objects in view, to-wit: mutual protection, and the protection of labor against the encroachments of capital.

7. The total abolition of the system of contracting convict labor in any mines, manufacturing establishments, or any other institutions, when brought in contact with free and honest labor.

8. The adoption of the two-weeks' pay system, and the abolition of the truck-store system in all its forms, and to secure to its members justice and equality in every legitimate way.

Having seen, from past experience, the futility of strikes, it was thought best to adopt some method to avoid them, and settle all differences in the future by a mutual understanding with employers. With this end in view a circular letter was addressed to all mine operators in the United States, inviting them to a conference with the miners' executive committee to adopt some method to settle difficulties in the future without recourse to strikes. The result was that several operators met with them at Chicago in October, 1885. There not being operators enough present to guarantee unity on their part, they could enter into no agreement; but a committee representing both sides was appointed to issue an address to all mine operators and miners, showing them the necessity for united action between them to prevent the cutting of prices in the markets, and thus reducing the rate of miners' wages to below the actual cost of living, thereby degrading their manhood. The convention, or conference, adjourned to meet at Pittsburgh, Penn., December 12, at which there was a better representation of both sides. A committee was appointed at that conference to draw up a scale of prices to be paid for mining in the different districts represented, and let the operators into the different markets on an equality in regard to prices paid for mining. A scale was partially agreed upon by the committee and submitted to the conference, and after a great deal of discussion it could not be finally agreed to by all operators present, and the conference again adjourned to meet at Columbus, February 23, 1886, when the following scale of prices submitted was adopted with but one dissenting vote, and signed on behalf of the miners and operators to go into effect May 1, 1886, for one year: —

Pittsburgh	2¾ cents per bushel, or 71 cents per ton.
Hocking Valley	60 " " "
Indiana Block	80 " " "
Indiana Bituminous, No. 1	65 " " "
Indiana Bituminous, No. 2	75 " " "
Wilmington, Ill.	95 " " "
Streator	80 " " "
Grape Creek	75 " " "
Mount Olive	56½ " " "
Staunton	56½ " " "
Springfield	62½ " " "
Des Moines, Iowa	90 " " "
Reynoldsville, Fairmount, screen coal	71 " " "

At West Virginia, the Kanawha district reduced prices to be restored to 75 cents per ton.

In order to settle any disputes that might arise on other questions, and prevent the mines from stopping work, a board of arbitration was appointed for each State, consisting of representatives of each side. In case they could not settle a difficulty arising in their own State, a national board was elected, to whom all cases that could not be settled in any district or State should be referred for final adjudication, and whose decision should be binding upon the parties interested, until May 1, 1887.

So far, there has only been trouble between the miners and

those represented at the different conferences, in one general and one or two local matters. The operator who refused to agree to the scale of prices was McClure, of Grape Creek, Ill., who has locked his men out for not working below the scale of prices, and then endeavored to import colored men from the South to take their places. Trouble has arisen in other places, where the operators declined to attend the conferences and refused to be governed by the scale. The spirit shown by the representatives of miners in inviting employers to counsel with them, and impartially doing all in their power to avoid conflicts, is having, and will have in the future, a good effect, as many operators, who in the past looked upon their employees as something about whom they should have no concern, readily correspond with the executive officers in regard to disputes and differences that are likely to arise.

STRIKES IN THE MINING REGIONS.

There is no industry under the sun that has such a record for strikes as the coal mining industry. The partial cause of this has been stated at the commencement of this chapter. The recklessness of miners is derived from their calling, which also gives them a spirit of independence such as cannot be found among the workmen of any other trade. They do not cringe or fawn to authority. Many of them left their native land because of the oppressions there, and in the hope of obtaining a larger share of liberty here. Hence they resist every imposition placed upon them, and resent every intrusion on their rights; and the stubbornness shown by them in many of their strikes, in which they suffer hunger, cold and hardship, often evicted from their homes in the depth of winter to seek the friendly shelter of the woods or tents, shows how dearly they love justice, and how hard they are willing to fight for it. If the workmen of the shops and factories of the cities and towns of the United States had shown the same spirit at the ballot-boxes for the last twenty years, the mis-legislation that now curses the laboring man would have been wiped out.

In giving a synopsis of the strikes in this trade, a general glance will be sufficient, as the causes that led to them in one district were the causes in another, and generally the result in one place was the same as in another.

The first strike of which we have record occurred in the Belleville Tract, in 1862–3. This was a strike for an advance of wages. After several months, the companies imported a number of Belgians to take the places of the strikers. Many of these new-comers were sent away, their expenses being paid by the Miners' Association. After a nine months' struggle, they gained a victory, their stubborn resistance being aided by the upward tendency of prices. This strike was followed by others in other parts of the country for an advance, all being successful. In some places advances were given without strikes. The prices thus advanced went on with the increased volume of currency, until coal that was mined for $1 a ton paid $2.30 per ton when the volume of currency was greatest.*

The contraction of the currency in 1866–7–8 brought down the prices in proportion, and the miners who fought for the advance did not feel like submitting to a reduction without an effort all over the country. Many of those who had followed the campaigns of the war, and who had come back to the trade they had left, did not feel as though they ought to give up what was theirs by right, and were ready to live again on soldiers' fare rather than yield. In many places the very men whose shackles they had broken were imported to take their places. Particularly was this the case in mining regions in the South and Southwest and along the Ohio River. In Braidwood, during the strikes of 1867 and 1868, Bohemians and Italians were imported into the mines. In the Eastern Pennsylvania regions, in some localities, after over one year's strike, the miners were defeated by imported labor. While the valleys of Ohio did not suffer much from importation, the miners, after several months' struggle, were defeated.

* The present price is seventy cents a ton, with the screen-bars increased in size and width one-fourth of an inch, making it at least equal to another ten-cent reduction.

These strikes were spasmodic from that until the strikes of the anthracite regions in 1869 and 1870 ended them.

While many local strikes took place, most of them of short duration, the next of any importance was the strike of the Tuscarawas and Mahoning Valley, of 1873, against a fifteen cents' reduction on the ton, which lasted for six months, and was compromised at the end of that time in the Tuscarawas; but in the Mahoning it lasted three months longer, when importation of Swedes and Italians into the mines, and the using of cheaper coals for making iron defeated the men, and they went to work in the fall for what they could get. Before this it was thought that the block-coal of the Mahoning and Shenango Valleys was the only coal that would make No. 1 iron; but during the strike of that year, Pittsburgh and other cheaper coals were experimented on, and with success, and proved a very severe blow to that trade and to those valleys.

Then came the strike of 1874 in the anthracite regions of Pennsylvania, in which the men were starved out by imported labor, and the tyranny of the coal, iron and railroad corporations of the State, who owned the legislature, governor and judges, thus controlling the government of the State, and from whose control the workingmen of the State, to their everlasting disgrace, have never wrested it.

These strikes continued until 1875. In that year a coal operator having mines on the Baltimore & Ohio Railroad, from Pittsburgh to Connellsville, imported a number of Italians, arming them with breech-loading rifles and warning them to shoot every English-speaking white man who came near them, informing them that unless they did so they would receive injury. The result was that a riot ensued, in which the Italians used their rifles, killing two men and wounding others.

This created terrible excitement, miners, farmers and business men entering their protest against the action of the coal operator, and declaring that if the law did not restrain these armed Italians, they would. A warrant was sworn out against the operator, Mr. Armstrong, and his Italian employees, and the sheriff of Westmoreland county, assisted by a number of volunteers, arrested them.

The grand jury found a true bill of murder in the second degree against the Italians who used the rifles and against Armstrong and the chief of the Italians as accessories before the fact. The chief and the Italians were sent to the penitentiary, and Armstrong was fined five dollars and costs.

In that same year, at a place about sixty miles distant, John Siney and twenty-six others were arrested for attempting to induce imported men not to take the places of strikers. Among those who were arrested with Siney were J. J. Maloney, John R. Joyce, and Zingo Parks. The two former were forty miles from the place at the time of the alleged offence. Joyce and Maloney were sentenced to one year's imprisonment, because they were president and secretary, respectively, of the Union. Zingo Parks was also sentenced for one year, although he was in another county at the time of the trouble. Six others received sentences of six months each.

Strikes continued through the year, imported labor everywhere taking the places of the strikers. In some places it was colored men; in others, Germans, Italians, Swedes, Polanders, Hungarians, and everything else they could employ, who took the places of the miners. It was only the coolness, fortitude and sagacity of the leaders that prevented bloodshed in every coal-mining district.

The military were called out to serve the purpose of the operators in Indiana, Illinois and Iowa, and every effort was made to incite the men to some rash act, to give the authorities an excuse for the arrest of the men or an attack of the militia. In April, 1876, a small riot occurred in the Tuscarawas Valley, in which one man was shot and a building burned. Several miners were arrested and sent to jail. One man was sent to the penitentiary for three years, who was pardoned out in a few months.

In 1880, a strike occurred in the same valley against the introduction of screens, and was finally defeated by the importation of colored men. Colored men were also introduced in the Mahoning Valley and in the Panhandle district of Pennsylvania. In 1882, in the Pittsburgh district, miners who had been put out of their houses were camping in tents, Hungarians were imported, and men, women and children put to work in the coke regions. The same class were introduced into the soft-coal fields of Clearfield.

The miners of Maryland, having been crushed down by and through the strikes of 1875, quietly submitted without a murmur to all the impositions placed upon them. They organized local assemblies of the Knights of Labor until they had sufficient locals to organize a district, when they organized District Assembly No. 25. They then persevered, and got every mine and mining locality in the State thoroughly organized, and built up a good treasury in the district. When the season for work was about to open, they presented a bill of grievances to their employers, which was indignantly rejected. Knowing they were living up to the Constitution of the Knights of Labor, and would be supported by it, they made every effort to reason with the employers and effect a settlement; but every advance was spurned, and the ones offering them treated with contumely. But it did not end here. The employers, backed and supported by the Baltimore & Ohio Railway, assumed the aggressive and demanded concessions from the men. After four months' struggle the men had to yield, and many of them were prevented from obtaining work elsewhere.

THE GREAT HOCKING VALLEY STRIKE, 1884 AND 1885.

No battlefield was ever better contested than was the strike in the valley during that time; no better generalship was ever shown than was shown by the leaders of the workingmen in that battle. It was a battle of dollars and cents of great capitalists, backed by armed force, against poverty, hunger, cold and want, backed by the support and sympathy of their fellowmen the world over. The same tactics of capital were used armed thugs and imported labor were transported into the valley. Men who preached and taught temperance had barrels of beer and whiskey rolled among their hirelings to make them fighting mad. In their hurry they sometimes shot down each other, and the coroners rendered a verdict of accidental shooting. When arrested the judge and jury set them free. For nine months the contest waged, ending in defeat. They were defeated by circumstances, and they accepted the inevitable with a determination, if ever they had to fight again, they would go through the same thing for the same cause. The Hocking Valley syndicate won, but lost over four million dollars, millions of dollars of credit in the commercial world, and millions of dollars of trade that they have never got back, — and never will, as it has gone elsewhere, — and won nothing but the ill-will of the men.

In January of the year 1884, the syndicate asked the men to accept a ten-cent reduction. The men asked them to appoint a committee to meet in conference, and show cause why they should accept it. The request was granted, a conference was held, and the men demonstrated to them fairly that to accept a reduction would not benefit them in the markets, and they saw it, and did not insist. In March following they offered a twenty cents a ton reduction. The miners accepted ten, and offered to take the other ten if they would give them reasons for doing so. Another conference was held, which resulted the same. This did not suit the syndicate; they wanted a reduction, and to crush out the union, so they could run their own business to suit themselves. So they laid their plans and made up their minds to show the Miners' Association that they would crush it out. They tried, but failed, and after losing millions of dollars as above stated, they are now ready at any time to consult the officers of the Ohio Miners' Association, which is stronger now in the great Hocking district than it has ever been.

A short strike took place in the Third Federated District for the Columbus scale, which was too hasty and ill-advised to be a success, the miners of that district being yet unorganized, and were not prepared, nor had they confidence in the hastily chosen leaders of that movement, or in themselves. There is now, April 15, 1886, a strike existing at Grape Creek, Ill., over the Columbus scale, and the same old tactics, — armed thugs and imported labor.

The Miners' and Laborers' Benevolent Association was successful in securing the appointment of mine-inspectors in the anthracite coal regions and the enactment of laws giving proper ventilation to the mines, with penalties attached for violation. These laws give the inspectors power to bring suit to enforce the law. A law was also passed making the area of screens in the bituminous regions uniform in size, the miners to be paid for all merchantable coal. This law, together with laws with regard to company or "pluck-me" stores, as they are called, are a dead letter.

Coal miners also took part in the general agitation of the movement, electing delegates to various labor congresses and labor conventions, and helped to secure the establishment of the Pennsylvania Bureau of Labor. Some of the most earnest and able advocates for justice to labor were educated in the meetings of the miners. This organization also assisted in securing legislation in Ohio, establishing mine-inspectors. The miners of Ohio have as yet failed to secure legislation regulating the size of screens. A commission was appointed to investigate the question, and two reports were presented, the committee not being able to agree. Laws have also been passed in Ohio, abolishing the "pluck-me" stores and the scrip and check systems; but these laws are not wholly enforced. The miners in this State have also taken an active part in the general movement, signing petitions for the better treatment of girls and women in stores, workshops and factories.

In Illinois, the miners of St. Clair county held a convention, and voted to support only candidates in favor of their interests. This resulted in the election of John Hinchcliffe, as before mentioned, who introduced the legislation.

Among the papers which have been of great assistance to miners are the *Workingmen's Advocate*, of Chicago, Ill., edited by A. C. Cameron, established in 1864, — one of the ablest labor papers ever published; *The Workingman*, of Pottsville, Penn., the official organ of the miners of that State; the *Weekly Record*, of Mahoning City, Penn., edited by a miner; and the *National Labor Tribune*, of Pittsburgh,

Penn., started in 1872. This last-named paper has stood by the miners through sunshine and cloud, and is now the official organ of the Federation.

PINKERTON'S DETECTIVES AND MOLLY MAGUIRES.

These two subjects cannot be treated separately. Of late years it has been the custom of corporations, whenever there was a dispute between them and their employees, to send to the Pinkerton detective agencies for assistance. These agencies have furnished men to any required number, and have armed them with rifles, revolvers, and other deadly weapons, presumedly to guard property and to protect the men who take the place of those on strike. They have awakened the hatred and detestation of the workingmen of the United States; and this hatred is due, not only to the fact that they protect the men who are stealing the bread from the mouths of the families of strikers, but to the fact that as a class they seem rather to invite trouble than to allay it.

The editor of this work has had occasion to review much that has been said and written upon this question, and is convinced that the full truth cannot be written, at least so as to be believed, until some years have elapsed from the time of the occurrence of the scenes that have been and are being enacted. How far the detectives were instigators and abettors in the Molly Maguire difficulties is not generally known. But the editor, at least, is convinced that many innocent men suffered death in consequence of the Pinkerton exposure rather than as a result of crimes committed.

The author of this chapter charges the Pinkerton force with being recruited from "the lowest beings in human society,—thieves, pickpockets, and penitentiary refugees."

With this statement, we give the following story as it comes to us: The Pinkerton detectives are employed to terrorize the workingmen, and to create in the minds of the public the idea that the miners are a dangerous class of citizens that have to be kept down by armed force. These men had an interest in keeping up and creating troubles, which gave employers opportunity to demand protection from the State militia at the expense of the State, and which the State has too readily granted. This additional expense of a coal and iron police is added to the cost of mining, and comes out of the men working in the collieries.

With the going down of the open organizations in 1879, the detectives came into play in a very prominent manner. Unless some sensational plot or conspiracy was discovered, their services would not be required. They were compelled to do something that they might continue in service at good wages.

A class of men gathered around the mining regions, sometimes working, and always drinking, boasting that they belonged to the Molly Maguires in the old country. Some of these men were the terror of the region, dangerous to property and to human life. That they held meetings and denounced not only some of the employers, but some of the workingmen, is a well-known fact. It is claimed that the detectives, coming amongst these men, representing themselves to be miners from other parts of the country, and setting themselves up as martyrs to aristocracy and respectability, gained considerable influence, and that the Molly Maguires, as an organization, were organized with their connivance and assistance.

When the meetings were held whiskey flowed freely. As no business could be done or speaking indulged in unless the members were half or wholly drunk, meetings were generally held convenient to a saloon or bar-room. The very worst men were put into official positions; every virtue was crushed out, and vice was instilled into the minds of the men; manhood and morality were totally tabooed.

If there was an honest man on the police force in these localities who did not agree with them and their methods, he was marked; if there was any business man who was not liked, or any boss they could not freely bleed, no matter how valuable he was to the company, he was put out of the way, and sometimes the more valuable he was, the better the plea to put him out of the way, thus giving the company a greater reason to believe that it was done through retaliation,—the detectives claiming to be on the track of the assassins.

The members not being able to fully realize their positions, would sit and listen to the blackening of the characters of good men that all the subtleties of a fiendish imagination could bring forth or the eloquence of demons inspire. The necessity for their destruction was painted in vivid colors, so that the allusion to their taking off was greeted with applause. By the time the meetings closed there were often volunteers to carry out the work. If volunteers were not forthcoming, as men, sometimes, drunk though they were, were appalled at the thought of taking human life, they drew lots and fixed upon the man to do it. The deed was done, and then the detectives had the task of hunting down the assassins, knowing very well who they were.

If there was a sober, industrious man who had the courage of his convictions, and by expressing them had made himself obnoxious to the Pinkerton men or to the company by whom they were employed, that man was selected, and step by step he was dogged and hunted down. Juries were packed and judges selected to give sentence. Men were paid to swear his life away for some offence of which he was innocent, the real murderer generally being away.

This evidence only educes the fact of the power of a few men to terrorize a community and to bring disgrace upon a movement that seeks the elevation rather than the degradation of mankind. The miners' organizations and miners generally have been made to suffer under the burden of the terrible accusations against them, while stories fully as tragic have been repeated of border life and of murders committed in the open streets by gamblers and blacklegs, without any special effort on the part of any corporation of employers to bring such men to justice. All that the miners and mine laborers ask of the general public is to investigate into the real facts and into the conditions under which they labor, and to assist them rather than to hinder them in their efforts at improvement. They point to the arrest of John Siney, Parks, Joyce, Maloney, and twenty-six others, in 1875, and the cases of William

Walton, Johnson, and twenty-six others in the present year, who were guilty of no like offence, but whose every effort has been to bring peace and justice to all.

The future prospects of the coal miner are anything but encouraging. The consumption of coal is daily being displaced with gas and electricity. The mines are now overcrowded with men who find that every day not only increases the efficiency of coal-producing machinery, but adds to the producing power of labor in the mines; thus increasing the hardships of the miners, many of whom, ere long, will be forced to seek other occupations to procure a living for themselves and their families. Organization, thorough and complete, may give temporary relief; but the fact cannot be denied that there are too many mines and too many miners, and to afford means for all to live and prosper, new fields of labor must be found.

CHAPTER XI.

THE STORY OF THE IRON WORKERS.

THE FIRST UNIONS — A STRIKE IN 1850 — THE WORKMEN DEFEATED — UNITED SONS OF VULCAN — THEIR GROWTH, SUCCESSES AND DEFEATS — ASSOCIATED BROTHERHOOD OF IRON AND STEEL WORKERS — IRON AND STEEL ROLL HANDS' UNION — A NOTABLE STRIKE — THE UNITED NAILERS — THE AMALGAMATED ASSOCIATION OF IRON AND STEEL-WORKERS — HOW IT WAS FORMED — ITS PURPOSES — CO-OPERATION FAILS — RAPID GROWTH OF THE ORDER — PERIOD OF STRIKES — A TARIFF QUESTION — STRIKE AT CINCINNATI — 1882, A YEAR OF STRIKES — GREAT STRIKE AT PITTSBURGH — WORKMEN DEFEATED — TESTIMONIAL TO PRESIDENT JARRETT — NAILERS LEAVE THE ASSOCIATION, MEET REVERSES, AND RETURN — REASONS FOR PROTECTIVE TARIFF — PRESENT CONDITION OF THE ASSOCIATION — ARBITRATION AND CONCILIATION — THE LATTER PREFERRED — STRIKES — CONCLUSION.

THIRTY years ago no labor organization or union of any kind existed among the iron and steel-workers of the United States. The first union of which we have any authentic information connected with the iron trades in this country, was that known as the "Sons of Vulcan," the membership of which was composed of boilers and puddlers. The next union was that of the "Associated Brotherhood of Iron and Steel Rail Heaters of the United States." This was followed by the "Iron and Steel Roll Hands' Union," and this again by the "United Nailers." These different unions were federated in 1876, forming the present great organization known as the "Amalgamated Association of Iron and Steel-Workers of the United States." In tracing the history of the trades-unions of the iron workers, we will give a brief outline of each of the unions in the order in which we have here enumerated them. It would be extremely interesting to trace the growth of the iron industry here, but it can be only briefly touched upon. Iron was first manufactured in this country in Lynn, Mass., in 1645, the works consisting only of a blast furnace and refinery forge. Iron was not manufactured in Pennsylvania until early in the eighteenth century, when Thomas Rutter built, in 1716, a blomary on Manatawney creek in Berks county, about three miles above Pottstown. A blomary is the place in which the iron is produced directly from the ore. But Pennsylvania rapidly took the lead in this industry, and in 1759, Acrelius says: —"Pennsylvania, in regard to its iron works, is the most advanced of all the American colonies." Early in the seventeenth century, improvements in the manufacture of iron were invented in England, and they were soon adopted in America. In 1790, Jacob Perkins, of Newburyport, Mass., invented and patented the first nail-cutting machine. About the same period, also, important inventions in this line were made in England. The iron industry grew most rapidly under the stimulus of these inventions. In 1817, the first rolling-mill proper in the United States, where puddling and rolling of bars was done, was built by Colonel Meason, at Plumsock, Fayette county, Penn. Edward Nock, an Englishman, introduced the process of pig-boiling in this country, at the mill of Lorenz & Cuddy, Pittsburgh, Penn., November 16, 1837. Boiling soon superseded puddling, and but little puddling is now done in this country. The price paid for boiling in 1837 was $7 per ton; for puddling, $4.25. By 1842 boiling was reduced to $5, and puddling to $3.50. The first strike of the boilers was caused by a reduction from $5.50 to $5 per ton, in February, 1842. The strike was ended July 9th, by the surrender of the strikers, and $5 was paid until 1845. In May of that year an advance of one dollar per ton was demanded and refused. A strike followed, which ended successfully in the latter part of August, and $6 was paid until January, 1850. Early in 1848, the puddlers at thc Phœnixville Rolling Mills, Chester county, Penn., struck against a reduction from $5 to $3.50 per ton, but at the end of April they accepted the reduction and returned to work. In conducting these strikes some form of organization must have been created. It is through such experiences as these that the wage-workers learn the need of trades-unions.

On January 12, 1850, a strike of the iron workers of Pittsburgh commenced, against the following proposed reduction in wages: —

Puddlers, from	$4.00	to	$3.50	per	ton.
Boilers, "	6.00	to	4.50	"	"
Refiners, "	1.00	to	.80	"	"
Scrappers, "	3.75	to	2.50	"	"
Heaters, "	1.37	to	1.00	"	"

This strike was a remarkably bitter one. For the first time in the iron mills, the manufacturers resorted to the tactics of importing foreign workmen to take the places of workmen on strike. On February 18th, they had succeeded in getting a sufficient number of hands from the East to start four mills at the reduced rate of wages. This caused very bitter feelings on the part of the strikers, their wives and children, against the manufacturers, and particularly against the imported workmen. A few attacks were made upon the mills and the workmen operating them at the reduced wages, in which the women were by far the boldest and most aggressive; but the total damage done amounted to but a few hundred dollars, and the injury of one or two workmen. Several arrests were made of those who had taken part in these attacks. They were put on trial, and two men and four women found guilty in manner and form as indicted. Three of the men were acquitted. The male defendants were sentenced to pay a fine of six and one-fourth cents, with cost of prosecution, and undergo imprisonment for eighteen months in the penitentiary. The women were each sentenced to pay a fine of fifty dollars and costs, and imprisonment for thirty days in the county jail. They were subsequently pardoned, and the fines remitted by Governor Johnson, upon petitions of eight of the jury that convicted them and a large number of citizens. The strike ended in favor of the manufacturers; but the result left the workmen greatly depressed and discontented, and many scattered to new fields of operations throughout the West. The next ten or eleven years witnessed many petty strikes, as the men, at every available opportunity, would seek redress for some real or imaginary wrong, while the manufacturers, in times when the prices tended downward, in an effort to save fleeting profits, would retaliate through a reduction of wages. Rules and regulations were adopted in the several mills by the manufacturers which were very obnoxious to the workmen, and which they resisted in every possible way, strikes and losses to both sides generally being the result. To add to the misery, the condition of trade was very dull, business was demoralized, and a more deplorable condition of affairs was hardly conceivable. Wages kept going down, money was growing more scarce and of less value every day, until in 1858 boiling was down to $3.50 and $4.00 per ton, and in some of the Eastern mills boiling was below $3.00 per ton, and puddling, in some instances, down as low as $2.20 per ton, and we have an instance in which $1.90 was paid for puddling at Danville, Penn. The pay in those days was generally in store-orders. During these dark and dismal years it might truthfully be said that upon the whole the workmen, notwithstanding their occasional turbulence, were as completely subjugated to the will of their employers as it was possible for men to be in this free and rapidly-growing country. It was in the midst of these dark years that a trades-union was formed, under the name of the

"UNITED SONS OF VULCAN."

On the 12th day of April, 1858, a few of the men connected with the boiling department of the iron mills of Pittsburgh held a meeting at the "Our House," on Diamond street, and organized the above-named trades-union. Among the boilers who were early pioneers of trades-unionism present at this meeting were Patrick Graham, Matthew Haddock, James Davies, Joseph Mellard and Hughey Hagan. A few others were present, whose names are not known.

The inactivity of business and consequent scarcity of employment, together with the supposed hostility of the mill-owners, caused the membership to keep the fact of organization a profound secret. Through fear of hostile action by the employers, but very few names were added to the list of members. In the fall of 1858, the members, impressed with the perils incident to an effort to extend the organization, concluded to suspend further operation.

A favorable opportunity presented itself to reorganize on a firmer basis, in 1861. The members assembled and a platform of principles and a constitution were adopted. The growth of the organization was very slow for some time, as the members realized that their object required quiet yet earnest labor; hence great precaution was taken as to who should be admitted to membership.

In August, 1861, Miles S. Humphreys was elected Grand Master of the organization. The breaking out of the War of the Rebellion and the passage of the tariff of 1861, was followed by a revival of business and greater activity in the trade. Through this, together with the energy thrown into the work by Grand Master Humphreys, the organization rapidly increased in membership. The National Forge was organized in Pittsburgh, September 8, 1862. The first officers elected were: President, Miles S. Humphreys; Vice-President, Patrick Graham; Treasurer, H. Thompson; Vice-Secretary, M. Grogan. By this time the organization had gained position and influence, which it immediately began to exert, culminating in a full and complete recognition of its rights by the manufacturers, early in 1873. Nearly every demand made by its members upon the manufacturers was conceded, and its growth became very rapid.

In the second annual session, held in Wheeling, W. Va., a general constitution was adopted. This provided that only good, practical workmen should be admitted to membership, and that the objects of the organization should be to maintain the best interests of the craft, to aid sick and distressed members and to do all other things pertaining to the business of the forge. By this time President Humphreys had organized forges in Pennsylvania, Ohio, New York, New Jersey, West Virginia, Kentucky, Illinois and Maryland. At this time demands for increasing wages were usually acceded to, or were granted after short strikes. Difficulties of this kind frequently occurred and a conference of representative men from each side was chosen to adjust them. The plan worked well, but necessitated so frequent meetings that a general plan was sought which would fix wages justly commensurate with the price of iron. This gave birth to what is known as the "Scale of Prices" system in regulating wages among the iron and steel workers. The first scale adopted will be given under the heading of "Arbitration and Conciliation." This was the first graduated scale of wages based on the price of the product of the workman that we have on record. The system was first suggested by Mr. B. F. Jones, of the firm of Jones & Laughlin, Pittsburgh, and afterwards worked out by President Humphreys, who is the acknowledged founder of the scale system. Mr. Humphreys served in the capacity of President up to 1866. He was succeeded by Joseph Chiverton.

No official record of the proceedings of the annual meetings of the National Forge were published until 1867, hence we have no data of the number of forges previous to the assembling of the National Forge in Pittsburgh, in August, 1867. At this convention there were fifty delegates present. The number of forges was forty-seven. Twelve forges were not represented. The organization was divided into districts, and placed under the charge of district deputies. Five heats double, and six heats single turn was fixed as the limit of a day's work at a puddling furnace. The attempt was made, but failed, to organize a helpers' union, making it subordinate to the local forge. It was decided that the Grand Forge should issue a pamphlet on the same plan as the first *International Journal of the Moulders' Union*. This was afterwards changed, and a very good and useful little pamphlet, called *The Semi-Annual Vulcan Record*, was issued. Resolutions were unanimously adopted, in which they pledged themselves to spread the seeds of union zealously until the iron boilers and puddlers of every locality should be under the jurisdiction of the union; demanded through the simplicity of justice fair remuneration for their arduous toil, and the elevation of labor; pledged themselves to support the laws enacted at this session, and to support the *Daily and Weekly Advocate*, of Pittsburgh, which they practically adopted as the official organ of the union; condemned the statement of A. S. Hewitt, of New Jersey, relative to the moral standing of the organization, made before the Royal Commission of England, as a base calumny, holding him up to contempt; thanked Hon. W. C. M'Carthy, mayor of Pittsburgh, for the courteous manner in which he tendered the hospitality of the city to the union; and thanked the *Daily Evening Advocate* and the *Commercial* for publishing reports of proceedings, etc.

Internal dissensions, however, had already sprung up in the organization, local forges were behind in their dues, petty jealousies existed, and there was a stormy time over fixing the compensation of the Grand Secretary, which was finally made $700 a year. After this convention, the organization became more demoralized, and less than half the members remained at the time of the next convention, held at Buffalo, August 5, 1868, when only fourteen forges were represented. At this time the treasury of the Grand Forge showed a deficit of about $800. The Grand Master's address at this convention was a remarkable document, full of wise advice, sound argument and excellent counsel. The constitution was largely reconstructed at this convention, and the question of making the organization a beneficial one was referred to the sub-forges for consideration. Hugh McLaughlin, of Chicago, offered a resolution relative to forming an association for the purchase of public lands. It was adopted, but no further action on it was taken. The offices of Grand Master and Grand Secretary were consolidated, and John O. Edwards chosen to fill it. He was a man of great energy and perseverance, and a good financier. He freed the Grand Forge from debt. Under his administration the organization gained new life, energy and strength; and it kept growing larger and stronger until it was merged into the Amalgamated Association.

At the convention in Wheeling, W. Va., August 3, 1869, the constitution was remodeled. A strike at Clifton, W. Va., had taken place during the year, caused by a failure of the employers to pay wages as promised. A committee from the men waited on the manager; hot words ensued, and the manager ordered the discharge of the committee. The forge took the matter up, and sent resolutions to the office demanding the payment of wages due, the reinstatement of the discharged committee, and the removal of the manager. The Grand Master sustained the men in the first two demands, but strenuously opposed the last. He urged the men to strike only for principles, and not against men. He said it was "presumption in us to dictate to our employers whom they shall or shall not hire to manage their affairs. I think the gap between us and our employers would be lessened, as they could see that we were led by reason, and not by prejudice." The men, however, refused to accept his advice. The convention indorsed the sentiments of the Grand Master, but quietly passed over the refusal of the men.

During the following year, several small strikes in the Eastern mills against a reduction of wages were settled by compromise. At the convention of 1870, held at Harrisburgh, Penn., resolutions, prepared by ex-Grand Master Humphreys, were adopted. In them the policy of importing of Chinese labor was deprecated as derogatory to the best interests of the free and intelligent labor of the country; the selfishness characterizing the actions of capitalists was condemned, as incompatible with American patriotism; and the importation of contract labor, which "piled the wealth of our country into heaps, making the rich richer, and the poor poorer," tending to unduly depreciate the value of all labor, was stigmatized as not being in the spirit of the policy of inviting immigration to the United States. These resolutions are among the first blasts of organized labor against the importation of foreign labor under contract. The Sons of Vulcan were opposed to the free importation of the products of foreign labor in competition with those of their own labor. It needs no argument, therefore, to prove they were, as all iron workers now are, consistent protectionists.

In August, 1871, the Grand Forge met in Chicago, and twenty-one new forges were reported. Grand Master Edwards, after serving the organization for several years most faithfully and efficiently without compensation, was succeeded by Hugh McLaughlin, of Chicago, who served very acceptably for two years. In 1872 a salary of $1,200 dollars was voted the Grand Master, as the duties of that office now occupied all his time. An epidemic of strikes broke out, and when the Annual Convention met in Troy, N. Y., in August, 1873, he seemed to have lost proper control of the organization. During his two years of service, however, it almost doubled its membership. At this convention the Committee on the Good of the Order advised most patient and careful consideration of evils proposed to be remedied before a strike was agreed on; and that strikes should always be made for the removal of evils, not against managers.

During President McLaughlin's term, efforts were inaugurated to form an alliance with the Amalgamated Iron Workers' Union, of Great Britain. But up to this time nothing had been accomplished, because the communication from the Sons of Vulcan to the union, relative to such a federation, was not intended to be official. The union was heartily in favor of the principle of federation.

David Harris, of Pittsburgh, Penn., was chosen as the successor of Hugh McLaughlin. He was remarkably well fitted for the office in all respects, and his selection was most opportune. The panic of 1873 had already set in. Prices tumbled, wages went down, mills stopped, and strikes seemed to be the order of the day. The depression in trade, and dearth of work and scarcity of money, demoralized matters generally, so that the opening of the year 1874 found the forges almost totally poverty-stricken, and many of them unable to pay their National Forge dues. In that year of severe troubles, President Harris organized twenty new forges, and the organization steadily increased in membership. Towards the end of October, 1874, the manufacturers notified the union that they desired a change in the base of the scale from $6 to $5.50. This was, after several conferences, finally rejected, and thus occurred the trying strike of 1874-75. No organization was ever more severely tried than were the Sons of Vulcan during this strike. Both officers and men fought bravely through that dark and dreary winter. It was during these times that the question of a more perfect organization, or, more properly speaking, the amalgamating of the several iron workers' unions into one grand organization was talked of in a general way. It was the time of seed-sowing. The strike of the winter of 1874-75 made it highly apparent that such an organization was necessary. President Harris served two years in office, and was succeeded by Joseph Bishop, of Pittsburgh, who was the last President of the Sons of Vulcan. He was elected at the Philadelphia Convention in August, 1875, and served for one year. Under his leadership the organization flourished remarkably well. Nothing of particular importance took place during the year. The time was chiefly spent by the president in preparing the groundwork for the new organization, the Amalgamated Association.

ASSOCIATED BROTHERHOOD OF IRON AND STEEL RAIL HEATERS.

This organization was formed in the latter part of August, 1872. Several local lodges had been organized previous to this date, but it is impossible to get at the exact dates of their formation. That of Friendship Union Lodge, of Chicago, Ill., is the earliest on record. The organization of this lodge took place some time in 1869. It was this lodge that took the initiative steps to bring about the organization of a National Association, by issuing a circular calling a convention of the craft at Chicago, August 30 and 31, 1872. Delegates from the following mills met at the hall of the Association, 358 Milwaukee avenue; Bridgeport, Alleghany, Penn.; Joliet, Ill.; Bethlehem, Penn.; Wyandotte, Mich.; Wheatland, Penn.; Decatur, Ill.; Bay View, Wis. Thomas P. Jones was chosen President, and E. B. Evans Secretary of the Convention. A constitution and by-laws were adopted, and such other measures were enacted as were necessary to perfect the organization. A strong feeling existed among delegates that a clause should be placed in the constitution to make provisions for the support of families of sick or deceased members, but the question, when put to a vote, was lost. The word "rail" was ordered stricken from the title of the Brotherhood; and bar-mill, plate-mill and guide-mill heaters were made eligible to membership. A motion was made to have the word "white" inserted in the clause on eligibility of membership, but it was lost. The following were elected officers of the Grand Lodge: W. G. S., Thomas P. Jones, Chicago; W. V. G. S., E. B. Evans, Bay View; W. G. I., John Rees, Bridgeport; W. G. B., Morgan D. Davies, Alleghany, Penn.; W. G. Sc., James D. Kelly, Joliet, Ill. The Grand Lodge of the Associated Brotherhood met annually after this up to the date of its being merged into the Amalgamated Association. Its second convention was held in Alleghany City, in May, 1873. The first year had been a prosperous one, the organization having increased from nine to twenty-two lodges.

The reports of subsequent conventions show that internal dissensions soon crept in. The nature of the depressed period of trade following the panic of 1873 also worked serious injury to the success of the organization. At the Third Annual Session of the Grand Lodge, in Covington, Ky., July, 1874, it appears that the total number of lodges represented was 18, with a total membership of 459; not reporting, 10. Total membership, 700. Much of the increase in membership was due to making "rollers" and "roughers" eligible to membership; but from this date the organization gradually lost strength. It is a singular fact that even to the present time no class of iron and steel workers are so badly disorganized as are the heaters, rollers and roughers of the large rail-mills of the country.

President Jones was an able and well-informed man, bold and impartial. He was succeeded in 1874 by Adam W. Schada, of Bethlehem, Penn. In 1875, there was no regular meeting of the order, and the final meeting was at Pittsburgh, in August, 1876. For the two preceding years neither the president nor treasurer had attended to their official duties. Vice-President Sullivan and Recording Secretary Spangler attended to the executive business of the organization, for which they deserve the highest praise. At the Pittsburgh Convention only 13 delegates were present, representing 14 lodges, having a membership in good standing of 412. There were 18 lodges having no delegate present. These lodges had about 650 members. Much credit is due to Samuel Rowley for his good services to this organization.

IRON AND STEEL ROLL HANDS' UNION.

This organization was composed of practical rollers, roughers, catchers and hookers, thus making it the second organization composed of what are termed, in rolling-mill phraseology, "finishers." It will be observed that the Associated Brotherhood of Heaters, Rollers and Roughers made no provision to admit to membership a large portion of finishing hands, hence the necessity of this organization. Local lodges were organized as early as 1870. The roll hands of the North Mills, Chicago, were the first to form a local lodge. Springfield, Ill., and other places soon followed. The organization of the National Union took place at Springfield, Ill., June 2, 1873. The first National Convention was held at the same time. Nineteen delegates, representing fifteen lodges with a total membership of 473, were present. The National Union officers elected were as follows: President, Alfred Sowers, Springfield, Ill.; Vice-President, John W. Fultz, Indianapolis, Ind.; Secretary, Robert F. Williams, Springfield, Ill.: Financial Secretary and Treasurer, Richard Brunt, Chicago, Ill. During the convention R. F. Williams resigned, and William Houston was elected in his place as secretary. The business of the convention was of the usual formal character incident to organization. The most striking feature was a seeming opposition to any affiliation with other organizations. This feeling was carried so far as to culminate in a motion "That our union have nothing to do with the Heaters' or Puddlers' Union." The vote on this motion was a tie; but the president, casting his vote in the negative, the motion was lost. A motion then prevailed "That no roller go to a heaters' union, but let us have an understanding between both grand bodies to assist each other in a legal strike, or in any dispute that may arise." Later, this union became the most zealous advocate of amalgamation. Buggymen were made eligible to membership, and later, during the convention, a motion prevailed "That all workmen in the mill who are capable of working around the rolls be taken into the union." The limit of a day's work was fixed at six rounds. The first year of the existence of the Roll Hands' Union was fraught with difficulties throughout. It was a common thing for employers to have a "black-list."

The following short history of a strike at Carondelet, Mo., very clearly shows the disposition of employers and employees at this time. The company had notified the workmen that a reduction of fifteen per cent. in wages was to take place. New rules for the government of the works were put up by the company. These rules, it appears, were very obnoxious to the men. We have failed to get a copy of them. However, the workmen refused to accept the reduction offered, or to abide by the new rules. The reply of the workmen to the company was as follows: —

1. We agree to accept the same reduction as Chicago, viz.: nine and one-half per cent. (said reduction to come off our old scale), and no other.

2. We agree to sign said scale for one year, or longer if required; either party wishing a change to give thirty days' notice of their intentions.

3. We refuse to sign any agreement to forfeit money due for quitting work without giving notice.

4. We demand the abolishment of the "black-list" forever.

5. No prejudice to be held against any one for any part taken by them; we, leaving here, have no objections to any one going to work in our places, if they do so on conditions required above. Any one going to work in our stead, and signing conditions required of us by the company, we shall consider them doing an injury to the cause of labor, and unworthy of being a citizen of the great Republic.

In reply to this, the following is the only agreement the company would make: "We hereby pledge ourselves that we will not 'black-list' any person in our employ, providing he works the usual notice, and leaves the company in an honorable way."

In this case the workmen were defeated, by parties accepting the terms of the company. The Roll Hands' Union suffered a period of decadence from the date of its second annual convention, up to the time the Amalgamated Association was brought about.

The President and Recording Secretary of the National Union were both men of broad views, and well informed on general topics. They were succeeded by David A. Plant as President and William Martin as Recording Secretary. No two men did as much as they in bringing about the unification of the iron and steel workers of the United States. They served in their official capacity for two years. No annual convention was held by this organization in 1875. The postponement of this convention and that of the heaters' organization was brought about by correspondence carried on by Mr. William Martin with the subordinate lodges of both organizations, which culminated in an agreement to meet in joint session in Indianapolis, Ind., for the purpose of drafting a code of laws to govern them as an amalgamated body. Thus practically the unification of the workmen of the finishing departments had been consummated in advance of the more general unification of all iron and steel workers in the Amalgamated Association.

THE UNITED NAILERS.

This organization was composed of only a few local lodges. A national lodge had never been formed. These lodges were in existence at the date of the organization of the Amalgamated Association, one of which was represented at the convention, and admitted to membership in the Amalgamated Association.

THE AMALGAMATED ASSOCIATION OF IRON AND STEEL WORKERS.

The first official action taken towards bringing about the consolidation of the preceding organizations was by the Iron and Steel Roll Hands' Union, at its convention at Columbus, O., in April, 1874. A motion was carried "That this convention use every honorable means to get the Roll Hands' Union, the Heaters' Association, and the Boilers' Union confederated, and that a delegate be elected by this convention to confer with the heaters at their next convention." Mr. David A. Plant was elected to attend to the duty. He at once opened correspondence with the President of the Heaters' and Boilers' Union, and received a reply stating that personally he heartily favored the movement. In July following, Mr. Plant attended the Heaters' Convention at Covington, Ky., before which he laid the action taken on the question of amalgamation by the Roll Hands' Union, and also read the communication he had received from President Harris. After a lively debate upon the subject by the representatives present, it was

Resolved, That there be a committee appointed from this body to confer with a like number from the Rollers' and Boilers' Union, looking to the consolidation of the three in one.

The committee selected was composed of Thomas P. Jones, Richard Sullivan, and John Schreyer. Mr. Plant addressed the Boilers' Union in August, 1874, in favor of the proposed federation. The convention took favorable action, but in the haste of legislation the appointment of the committee was overlooked. In the Annual Convention held at Philadelphia, in August, 1875, President Harris in his report urged very strongly the advantages of a union of all the various branches of iron workers.

This question was again referred to the Committee on Good of the Order. In the meantime arrangements had been made by the Heaters' and Roll Hands' Union to dispense with holding the regular annual convention, and instead to meet in joint convention for the purpose of consolidating. This joint convention was held in August, 1875, at the same time the Boilers' Convention was in session in Philadelphia. Favorable action was again taken on the question of amalgamation. Shortly after the adjournment of the Philadelphia Convention, President Bishop, of the Boilers' Union, opened correspondence with the representatives of the Heaters' and Roll Hands' Union It was arranged that the committee of the several organizations meet in Pittsburgh Penn., December 7, 1875.

The meeting was held on this date. The following are the names of the respective committees: —

Iron and Steel Roll Hands: David A. Plant, Grand President; William Martin, Grand Recording Secretary; John W. Fultz, Grand Treasurer.

Associated Brotherhood of Iron and Steel Heaters, Rollers and Roughers: Richard Sullivan, Vice-Grand Sire; Benjamin F. Spangler, Grand Scribe; James Penney, Central Lodge No. 10, Pennsylvania; James T. Clites, Wheeling Lodge No. 1, West Virginia.

United Sons of Vulcan: Joseph Bishop, President National Forge; Elisha H. McAnincle, Deputy, first district; David Reese, Deputy, second district; John Jarrett, Deputy, sixth district.

The above committee formed a constitution and by-laws for the government of the proposed amalgamated society. The laws thus provided, together with a number of suggestions, were published and submitted to all the lodges and forges throughout the country for their inspection. It had been arranged that the several conventions of the Heaters', Roll Hands' and Boilers' organizations should meet in Pittsburgh, on the first Tuesday in August, 1876, and, after disposing of such business as pertained to their respective bodies, take up the subject of amalgamation. Each convention favored the formation of the amalgamated society. Arrangements were then made by the representatives of the several conventions to enter into joint convention on Thursday, August 3, 1876. At the hour appointed, the Boilers' committee met the representatives of the Heaters' and Roll Hands' organizations, and escorted them to the hall of the United Sons of Vulcan.

The work of organization was at once entered into by the election of James Grundy, of Covington, Ky., as chairman of the convention, and William Martin, secretary. The number of representatives present was 68, divided as follows: Representatives from the Sons of Vulcan, 46; Heaters' Association, 15; Roll Hands, 6; Nailers' Association, 1.

The constitution and by-laws drafted by the committee at Pittsburgh, in December, and which had been submitted to the various lodges and forges, were adopted, with a few alterations. The most important and vital question brought before the convention was that of arbitration. After a lengthy debate the convention decided against arbitration by a vote of fifty majority. The prevailing sentiment of the delegates present was one of caution in the question of strikes, as is evidenced by the following: —

Resolved, That every representative to this convention be instructed to impress upon the minds of the members of their respective lodges the necessity of using every precaution in guarding against strikes or any other troubles that may arise during the first year.

The preamble to the constitution expressed the views and causes that led to amalgamation. It quoted from a writer on association, setting forth "that labor has no protection; the weak are devoured by the strong; all wealth and all power centre in the hands of the few, and the many are their victims and their bondsmen." It set forth the necessity of having the most perfect and systematic arrangement possible to attain the highest degree of success in any undertaking; that to acquire such a system requires that the business should be controlled by one mind, if persons so controlling were actuated by pure and philanthropic principles; that in the formation of a national amalgamated association, embracing every iron and steel worker in the country lay their only hope, concluding as follows: —

We ask, is it charitable? Is it humane? Is it honest? To take from the laborer, who is already fed, clothed and lodged too poorly, a portion of his food and raiment, and deprive his family of the necessaries of life — by the common resort — a reduction of his wages? It must not be so. To rescue our trades from the condition into which they have fallen, and raise ourselves to that condition in society to which we, as mechanics, are justly entitled, and to place ourselves on a foundation sufficiently strong to secure us from further encroachments, and to elevate the moral, social and intellectual condition of every iron and steel worker in the country, is the object of our National Association, and to the consummation of so desirable an object, we, the delegates in convention assembled, do pledge ourselves to unceasing effort.

Section 2 of the constitution stated that the objects of this association shall be to obtain by conciliation, or by other means that are fair and legal, a fair remuneration to the members for their labor; and to afford mutual protection to members against broken contracts, obnoxious rules, unlawful discharge, or other systems of injustice or oppression.

The National Lodge officers elected by the convention were: President and Secretary, Joseph Bishop; Treasurer, Edward McGinness; Trustees, David A. Plant, William Martin, and John Jarrett.

The salary of the president was fixed at $1,500 for the year.

The choice of Mr. Bishop for the presidency was a very happy one, as subsequent events clearly proved. The conditions surrounding the new organization were fraught with difficulties of every description. The most dangerous of these were the antipathies of the different trades towards each other, especially between the puddling and finishing departments. This was handled in a masterly way by President Bishop, and to all appearances, at the end of the first year of the existence of the association, seemed to be almost entirely obliterated. Fortunately, the first year was in a general way of a peaceable character; but very few strikes occurred, and what did were of minor importance; consequently it was a prosperous year, but not so much in the material growth of the organization as the advancement in thought and progressiveness of the membership. A change for the better was taking place; the impulsive, hasty sentiment was being superseded by the calm and dispassionate. Indeed, so great were the strides in progress and intelligence, that the convention which met at Columbus, in 1877, has been looked upon as the most progressive and successful ever held by the iron and steel workers of this country. It was also beyond a question the most harmonious.

Nothing more clearly defines the position of the membership at this time than the resolutions passed in reference to the serious railroad troubles of that year. They declared: That it is thé duty of workmen to combine for their common protection; that the demand for a restoration of the late reduction and the modification of tyrannical rules and orders was just and proper; that all violations of law tended only to injure the cause and those engaged therein; that they were ready at all times to co-operate with other organizations to resist oppression and an unnecessary reduction of wages; that the acts of lawlessness, the destruction of property, bloodshed and riotous demonstrations were to be condemned; that the arbitrary power assumed by corporations demanded serious and careful reflection in order to strip them of some of their unlimited powers and to better reward labor; and that disagreements between employer and employee should be settled by representatives of both sides meeting together.

The second year brought about somewhat of a reaction in the growth of the organization, due to the depression in business. This condition of affairs continued until early in 1879. Prices kept steadily going lower up to October, 1878, and remained almost stationary for four months. For the year ending August, 1878, eleven new lodges were organized, and ten became defunct. Strikes now began to multiply. Several of these were against reductions in wages. Others were against what was known as the "contract" system, which was a kind of co-operation offered by the company, in which were certain conditions, the principal of which was that the men agreed to allow the company to retain the first four weeks' wages in hand, and also twenty-five per cent. of all wages earned thereafter, the same to be paid to men at the end of the year, if the profits of the business would justify such payment. It is needless to add that the reserved wages were invariably lost by the men. Another drawback was the failure, on the part of the officers, to enforce the law on the protective fund. This law provided that twenty-five cents per month should be paid by each member for the purpose of providing a fund to pay members on strike. Up to this time this law had not crystallized. This was a source of annoyance to the president, and of disaffection among the members who were so unfortunate as to find themselves on strike. The duties of the president, in serving as secretary, were too onerous. It was therefore enacted that he should be an organizer, and attend to executive duties only, at a salary of

$100 per month. He was also empowered to appoint a secretary at a salary of $50 per month. Mr. William Martin was selected by the president to serve as secretary.

The "old rail" question at this time became a source of great annoyance. These rails were largely imported. Besides this, the tin-plate mills were closed down in 1878. This brought forth an expression, as the sentiment of the Amalgamated Association, in resolutions, passed at the Third Annual Convention, held at Wheeling, in August, 1878. These resolutions set forth that the iron manufacturers had introduced the custom of making finished iron out of old rails, thereby depriving a large number of men of employment; and a committee of seven was appointed in each congressional district to personally visit or communicate with representatives to Congress, showing the evil effect of admitting old rails under the existing duties. The resolutions also demanded two and a half cents duty per pound on tin and tern-plate. The Amalgamated Association, and the other iron and steel workers' unions before it, have always been in favor of a high protective tariff; but it was seldom that such emphatic action as this just referred to was taken. Mr. Bishop and his committee went to Washington, and to them is due much of the credit of defeating the Wood Tariff Bill.

Early in 1879, trade began to revive somewhat, and with it the organization revived. During the year ending at the session of the Fourth Annual Convention, held at Youngstown, in August, 1879, twenty-seven new lodges had been organized. During the same year President Bishop, in his annual report, said: "The history of the Associations furnishes no parallel to the past year for strikes and disputes. We have not been without a strike a single day during the year." These strikes were chiefly in the East. For certain reasons, the East had never been successfully organized. Special efforts were at this time put forth to establish unionism in the eastern mills; these were partially successful. But the resulting strikes seemed to have a paralyzing influence on the movement, which necessitated a temporary suspension of operations. Much dissatisfaction was created about this time with the

National Lodge President, and his methods of transacting the financial affairs of the organizations. This also caused a temporary set back, but it was of brief duration. The president's salary was reduced to one thousand dollars per annum. No change was made in that of the secretary. The secretary was, however, made an elective officer. This action on the part of the convention could be nothing but displeasing to President Bishop; for, on the 1st of January, 1880, he resigned his position as president. He resigned chiefly on account of the reduction of his salary thirty-three and one-third per cent. in two years. He said the men themselves would be justified in complaining at any such reduction at the hands of their employers; that a strike would be ordered, and thousands of dollars spent to support the men. He thought the men should apply the same principle to those they chose as officers to work for them. If it was wrong for their employers to reduce wages, it was just as wrong for them also to reduce the pay of their own officers.

The author of this chapter was elected president on the 10th of January, 1880, and at once entered upon the duties of the office. This was the most remarkable year the association ever experienced in material growth. Mr. Bishop had, from the date of the convention, in August, up to the 1st of January, organized thirty new lodges. In the same period of time five became defunct. From the 10th of January to August, 1880, forty-three new lodges were organized, and three became defunct.

The iron boom which started in 1879 reached its highest point in February, and continued at this point until early in the following April, when suddenly a collapse took place, followed by one of the most remarkable episodes that ever transpired in the history of the iron trades. In the short space of four weeks, dating from the 8th of April to the 5th of May, prices fell from the highest point reached in the boom to the lowest point, a fall of about fifty per cent. Under the scales of prices wages fell in the same proportion; and yet, sudden as this reaction in wages was, everything passed of as quietly and smoothly as though nothing extraordinary had happened. Under other circumstances, serious strikes would unquestionably have prevailed. This is a clear proof of the advisability and utility of the scale of prices system of regulating wages.

Notwithstanding this sudden reaction in the iron trade, the association kept on improving. It was, however, becoming more apparent, as time passed on, that new evils were making themselves felt. The National Lodge President, in briefly summing up these in his annual report, at the convention in Pittsburgh, August, 1880, said: "Great care must be taken, or our growth may be a source of weakness to us. Let us not trust in our strength; the stronger we grow the more care we need to exercise."

Strikes were very prevalent this year, especially in the Eastern mills. In this year the Philadelphia workmen demanded a scale of prices to govern wages. The manufacturers refused, but after a strike of nearly two months a compromise was effected, by which the employers agreed to a scale which provided no fixed minimum. Later, however, came the successful termination of the strike, by which the manufacturers conceded a fixed minimum of wages, based on a manufacturers' card of two cents per pound for bar iron. The majority of strikes ended in the defeat of the men. The places that suffered defeat were Valley Falls, R.I., Columbia, Birdsboro, Catasanqua, Manayank and McKeesport, Penn., and Richmond, Va. All of these are Eastern mills, excepting McKeesport. The few Western mills that engaged in strikes were generally successful.

The convention that met in Pittsburgh, August, 1880, was by far the largest in the history of the organization. The number of officers and representatives was 192. The question of the importation of old iron rails and scrap was still a source of annoyance, and called forth the following resolution, instructing

The President of the National Lodge to call a meeting in each district comprising the members of this Association, for the purpose of selecting one representative from each district to visit Washington, D. C., and there lay before Congress our grievance on the above, and such other subjects, as we may deem of interest to the industries of our country.

The members of this convention seemed to realize the importance of paying their officers a decent salary. The salary of the president was fixed at $1,200, and that of the secretary at $1,000 for the next year.

This was a year of trials. Strikes of greater magnitude had to be met, and some of these were of such serious proportions as to entail much suffering and loss on both employees and employers. The most important of these was that of the Harrison Wire Mill, St. Louis, the Steel Works, Pittsburgh, Chattanooga and Knoxville, Tenn., Atlanta, Ga., Springfield, Ill., and the Cincinnati mills, including Wyandotte, Mich., Janesville, O., Portsmouth, O., and Aurora, Ind. Those of Pittsburgh, Knoxville and Janesville ended in the defeat of the men. The Cincinnati strike was caused by the employers refusing to sign the scale of prices presented by the men.

Large advances in wages had been demanded by the workmen of the different branches of the finishing departments, ranging from ten to thirty-six per cent., against the advice of the National Lodge president. In answer to this, the employers presented a scale of prices which was practically the Pittsburgh scale. Several conferences were held between the employers and the workmen, the last of which was on June 16, 1881, when the men presented their ultimatum, which was the usual prices, viz., ten per cent. above Pittsburgh. This the employers refused.

The Cleveland Convention, held the following August, heartily concurred in the action of the president at that place, and maintained that the condition of affairs there was entirely due to the hasty and unwise action of the brothers of the Third District.

This strike is referred to here because of the influence it had on subsequent events. It cost the organization a vast sum of money, and eventually nearly every lodge in the district became defunct. Not a single mill ever regained its lost trade, several have been shut down ever since, and those that are operated are run only part time; and this, too, in view of the fact that the manufacturers succeeded in establishing Pittsburgh prices as the rates. The strike thus ended with disastrous effects to both sides.

The President of the National Lodge, in his annual report at the time, after referring to the general and serious aspect of affairs, said: —

But let us not be deceived, for we are now on the eve of troublous times. There are a few things that I desire to present to you for your consideration. In the first place, I find much discontent, perhaps jealousy, existing between some of our trades. A feeling is prevalent that because one department may be a majority in numbers, that this majority is against the minority exercising their legitimate rights. This feeling is especially suspicious on the wages question. It has caused me much anxiety, from the fact that *internal* dissension is much more hurtful than any external influences, and requires much sacrifice and patience to control. What remedy have we for this growing evil? I answer, the cultivation and fostering of a greater degree of love and charity for each other, more confidence in the integrity and honesty of each other, more self-denial, and desire for the *general* welfare of our membership. To assure the success of our organization, we must lay by small bickerings, and keep in view the fact that *individual* benefit depends upon the *general* good.

The convention did all that possibly could be done to prevent any further spread of these feelings, but it only succeeded in postponing the trouble.

At the Cleveland Convention, Canada was added to the jurisdiction of the National Lodge. It made colored men eligible to become members, as well as quite a number of trades, such as engineers, boiler-tenders and firemen directly connected with mills, and steel-converting men and others in Bessemer steel mills. Blast-furnace men petitioned for admission, but their petition was refused to the lodges. The convention adopted the eight-hour law in Bessemer converting and rail mills, and raised the president's salary to $1,500, and the secretary's salary to $1,300 per annum. Thirty new lodges were organized during the year, and eighteen lodges became defunct.

The iron and steel workers had for several years advocated a federation of trades. Indeed, it may be said that they were the pioneers of the movement in this country. The Amalgamated Association of Iron and Steel Workers were represented at a labor congress, held in Pittsburgh, November

15-19, 1881, by the National Lodge president, and Secretary Martin. This was the only year the association was represented. The cause of future non-attendance was the striking out of resolution 11 of the platform, which provided for "Protection to American Industries." The year 1882 was the most remarkable and critical in the history of the association. The predictions of the president were fully verified. Strikes of the most crucial character took place. Still, the association continued to prosper, forty-six new lodges being organized. The convention which met in Chicago, in August, 1882, was the largest ever held, the number of officers and representatives present being 213. It required a session of nine days to accomplish its work. Many important changes were made in the constitution and by-laws, among which was that providing for district conventions for the purpose of acting on the scale question. Provision was also made for a general scale convention, to which the action of the several district conventions would be submitted for ratification. This law is still in force, and seems to work remarkably well.

The refusal of the President of the United States to appoint a labor representation on the Tariff Commission called forth a resolution condemning the action of the President in so completely ignoring the desires and interests of the producing classes in the formation of said committee.

The strike at Homestead, the only one settled among those on in August, 1882, was to all intents a victory for the association. No more justifiable strikes ever took place than those of Newburgh, Erie and Phœnixville. Each of these was a struggle for the maintenance and recognition of the association. Both Newburgh and Phœnixville were strategetic points, the former for the Western and the last for the Eastern mills. While they were at this most critical period, the great strike of Pittsburgh and the Western iron mills was inaugurated, thus drawing away the support of these two important points, resulting in the defeat of the men and of the association.

Much speculation exists in outside circles as to the wisdom

TRADES-UNION LEADERS.

or folly of the "great strike" of 1882. It was brought about by the workmen in all departments making a demand for a general advance in wages of ten per cent. Speaking of this strike in his annual report, the President of the National Lodge says:—

> The prevailing opinion existing among the men of the First District prior to the 1st of June was that prospects for trade were good; that the state of the markets was favorable, and everything, in fact, in favor of making a demand for higher wages a question of but a few days before it would be decided in our favor. So unanimous was this sentiment, that upon a final vote being taken, it was almost altogether in favor of striking. I most earnestly and heartily fought against the movement. I explained that stocks were very heavy on the market; that the market was fairly glutted with iron, and that prices had a downward tendency, and from these facts I tried to show that I believed the present time rather hazardous to engage in a strike. I further argued that the result of the Cincinnati strike was yet fresh before us, even staring us in the face; that serious strikes already existed at Phœnixville and Newburgh.

It may be well to state here, that in 1880 the minimum of the boilers' wages had been increased from $5 to $5.50 per ton on a two and a half cent manufacturers' card, and in 1881 the minimum of the wages of most of the finishing departments now had been advanced ten per cent., thus equalizing the advance in wages to all the several departments. As these advances had been attained with but little effort, a general feeling existed in 1882 that if the demand only was made, concession on the part of the manufacturers was sure. Then again the great strength of the association was too largely relied upon. Subsequent events, however, proved that a serious mistake had been committed. The strike was fully ratified by the Chicago Convention, and this at a time when the strike had been in existence for over two months. Still, after a brave struggle of over four months, there being but little sign of an advance in prices of iron in the market, the association withdrew the demand for the ten per cent. advance in wages, thus ending the strike. Work was resumed in the mills at the old rates. The influence of this strike was very damaging, especially upon the *morale* of the membership. The antipathies between the boilers and finishers broke out with greater violence than ever, and internal dissensions became so rife as to put the association to the severest tests. To add to the confusion, the Bessemer steel rail manufacturers notified their workmen of a reduction in wages of twenty per cent. This was in December, 1882. The price of rails had decreased from $59 to $45 per ton during the year. The men refused to accept this reduction, but finally offered to compromise at twelve and a half per cent. This was rejected. The price of rails was still going lower, and quoted at $43, when the National Lodge president advised the acceptance of twenty per cent. reduction in wages. This the men refused to do. A few days later the manufacturers withdrew the proposed reduction of twenty per cent., and instead proposed thirty-three and a third per cent. reduction. A bitter struggle followed, lasting in most of the works for fully four months, when the workmen agreed to accept thirty-three and a third per cent., and in some cases even a greater reduction in wages. The organization thus received a severe set-back.

The number of lodges instituted during the year ending at the convening of the Philadelphia Convention, in August, 1883, was 34. The number of defunct lodges was 48,— a net loss of 14 lodges. Nineteen of these were, however, connected with closed works, and quite a number of these works are still idle. The number of officers and representatives present at the Convention of 1883 was 153. At this time there were 183 lodges in good standing. This convention was the last one at which the author of this chapter presided. He had notified the association of his firm determination to retire from office. This determination was formed simply because he believed a change would be beneficial to the welfare of the organization. The true relationship between the retiring president and the association is shown by the following, taken from the Journal of Proceedings, Philadelphia Convention, August, 1883:—

The next business that came before the convention was the most touching of any during the entire session. It was that of presenting a testimonial, procured by the delegates, to President Jarrett, on his retiring from the office of president. It consisted of a beautiful gold-headed cane, and an elaborate and handsome silver set of seven pieces, the inscription on which read: "Presented to Mr. John Jarrett, by the Delegates to the Eighth Annual Convention, A. A. of I. & S. W., August, 1883." It had been quietly arranged to surprise President Jarrett, and it was carried out to the letter. During the presentation speech it was an affecting scene to see the commotion among the delegates, but few dry eyes being in the audience.

Vice-President John I. Davis had been chosen to make the presentation speech, and in it he spoke in the highest terms of the retiring president, extolling his wisdom, integrity, fidelity and efficiency in the highest terms, and claiming him as one of the most consistent, fearless and foremost champions of labor. The presentation was a complete surprise to the president. His response expressed his appreciation of this expression of esteem for him, and a recognition of his earnest labors in behalf of the association. Deafening cheers from the delegates, as he closed his speech, testified further their regard for him.

William Weihe was elected president at the Philadelphia Convention, and he still retains that position. He has proved himself an admirable leader. Under his leadership the association, though under adverse circumstances, still maintains its lead among the trades-unions of the country. The first and second years of his incumbency in office were a period of decadence, but the last year is one of growing prosperity and rapidly returning strength. The decadence referred to was partly due to the strikes that had previously taken place. But new elements of discord were forcing themselves forward, breeding discontent and animosities. Secretary Martin, in referring to these at the Wheeling Convention, in 1885, said: —

Internal dissensions, stoppage of mills in whole, or in part, depression in trade almost bordering on a panic, and the withdrawal of the nailers and nail-feeders, mainly brought about by a cowardly, cringing, vacillating minority, have all combined to reduce the numerical strength of the organization in the past year.

The withdrawal of the nailers was due directly to two causes: first, dissatisfaction with the way the apprentice rules were enforced by President Weihe; and, second, difference of opinion as to the propriety of demanding extra price for cutting steel nails. At the Scale Convention, held in Pittsburgh, April 5, 1884, it was resolved to demand twenty per cent. extra for cutting steel nails, when harder than iron. The Wheeling nailers did not, it appears, enforce this demand. The question was brought up before the Pittsburgh Convention, in 1884, when it was

Resolved, That the vice-presidents of the districts be instructed to compel all nailers in this association to enforce the provisions of the scale in relation to steel nails.

In the attempt to carry out his resolution, it was discovered that the nailers, or at least eighteen out of twenty, in their testimony before the investigating board, said, "that the steel they were working was equally as soft as iron," and some said "that they would prefer steel to iron at the same prices." This testimony was not kindly received by the membership in general, they failing to conceive how steel could be as soft as iron. Still the matter was allowed to drop. Early in 1885, the National Lodge officials issued a circular bearing on the wages question, and the prospects of a reduction in wages. A few of the nailers took umbrage at this circular, and presumably for the purpose of protecting themselves, issued a call for a delegate meeting of nailers, to be held in Wheeling, February 5, 1885. At this meeting it was resolved to withdraw from the Amalgamated Association, and to form a new organization, to be called "The United Nailers of America." All the lodges composed of nailers at once withdrew from the Amalgamated Association, and formed themselves into the new organization. The action of the nailers in withdrawing in a body from the association, together with the loss in membership, did not have the demoralizing effect anticipated, but proved in many ways to be extremely beneficial. Internal and personal bickering dissensions gave way to a desire to build up the organization.

In the adjustment of the annual scale of wages in June, 1885, the association agreed to a reduction of ten per cent. in all departments except that of the sheet-mills. This reduction was based on a reduction of the base of the manufacturers' card from two and one-half to two cents. This conciliatory spirit on the part of the workmen was very discreet. Nothing more clearly demonstrates this than the result of the nailers' action. They refused to accept any reduction, the manufacturers having proposed a reduction from twenty-one cents to seventeen cents. A strike ensued, which continued throughout the year, resulting in disaster to the nailers, though the year has been one of upbuilding to the Amalgamated Association. At the last convention, the nailers petitioned the association to allow them to return. The petition was, after a lengthy discussion, conceded.

In a general way but very few strikes of importance, outside of that of the nailers, have taken place in the last three years. It has been a period of comparative peace. The changes in the laws have been of but a moderate character. The stoppage of the third turn in sheet-mills was one of the most important. This third turn in sheet-mills was one of the few instances in which the eight-hour system has been tried among the iron workers. In some few mills it seemed to work very satisfactorily; but, as it could not be applied satisfactorily to the workmen in all the mills, it was decided to discontinue the system altogether in sheet-mills. The eight-hour system is still carried on in the Bessemer converting, and in some cases, finishing mills. The association is in full accord with the general eight-hour movement, and favors the system in all instances in which it can conveniently be administered.

The association seldom takes any action on questions of a political character. It is severely non-political. It never referred to party politics but in one case, and that in connection with the appointment of a labor representative on the Tariff Commission. Though always an ardent advocate of a protective tariff, it was such from an economic standpoint only. The following is a close expression of its sentiments on this subject: —

That all producers and manufacturers should bear alike equal burdens of taxation, and foreign producers and manufacturers should not be exempted therefrom. Our tariff should at all times be so adjusted as to, at least, tax them the like amount of tax paid by home producers and manufacturers for the support of local, State and National governments, as well as the amount of difference in the wages of labor and cost of manufacture, and the ruling rate of interest in this country, so that American capital and labor invested in the productive industries of the land shall be placed upon an equal footing in our own home markets with foreign capital and labor, and not discriminated against by national legislation. Our government has neither the moral nor political right to discriminate against home capital and labor in its tariff legislation, and against any such policy we are unalterably opposed. We therefore favor a tariff so adjusted as to give to our people, who pay the taxes and support the government, adequate protection against foreign competition, and place them upon, at least, an equal footing with foreign competition, in our home markets. We also favor the abolition of internal revenue taxes, and if, after their abolition, further reduction of taxation by the National Government shall be desired at any time, it shall be done by placing on the free list such articles as do not enter into competition with home productions and manufactures; but in no case should the tariff upon such articles as do enter into competition with them be placed at lower duties than shall be required to maintain and keep them upon a footing with foreign competitors.

In the former part of this chapter, reference is made to the iron workers as being the pioneers of the "Federation of Trades." At their last convention, it was determined to have nothing to do with the movement. We cannot give the reasons for this, unless it be that the Amalgamated Association expect that the Knights of Labor will eventually represent, or, what is more proper, actually be the "Confederation of Trades." The question of affiliation with the Knights of Labor was submitted by the convention to the subordinate lodges for their consideration. The next convention will take action on the subject.

The association is not a beneficial order, in the sense of providing for sickness and death among its membership. In the case of disabled members, the result of serious accidents, in the mills voluntary subscriptions are generally taken up — a plan that has always worked very successfully. Sums of from $1,000 to nearly $3,000 have been realized in this way, and the disabled member would be started in a lucrative business. It can be said of the iron and steel workers, that, as a rule, they are generous and charitable towards a brother who happens to be so unfortunate as to meet with serious bodily harm, and become unable to follow his occupation, or perform other manual labor to earn a living. The *National Labor Tribune* has been the official organ of the association for over ten years.

Mr. Martin, the secretary of the association, has served in that capacity for nine years. He is a man of rare ability, and for care and fidelity, unsurpassed. The whole office work of the association is conducted on strictly business principles; and to the credit of Mr. Martin, it may be said that no serious error ever occurred in the financial affairs of the association during his official career. The salary of the secretary, at present, is $1,170 per annum, and that of the president is $1,350 per annum.

ARBITRATION AND CONCILIATION.

The Amalgamated Association never advocated arbitration as a means of settling disputes, or regulating wages. It is somewhat singular, too, to observe that though a strong sentiment in favor of arbitration existed among the iron and steel workers up to the period of the organization of the Amalgamated Association, since then it has steadily been growing weaker, until at the present time the feeling is one of strong opposition. The association is, however, heartily in favor of conciliation. By conciliation is meant the right to settle or prevent labor differences by conferences between the parties interested, or their authorized representatives, these conferences having no power to reach a decision only as the result of mutual agreement. But arbitration provides for a third party to pronounce judgment, should the interested parties or their representatives fail to reach a settlement. It is not, however, so much the third-party idea as other matters that cause the association to oppose arbitration. They maintain that arbitration does not and cannot protect the workingman: because, first, there is no fixed amount that can be considered as fair profits to the employer; second, no provision is made to provide a fixed minimum in wages or prices, and consequently under the laws of free competition it is possible that prices may go so low as to make reasonable wages an impossibility. As an illustration of this fact they point to the operation of arbitration among the iron workers of the North of England, where prices of iron have become so low as to leave the wages of the workmen so meagre that respectable living is out of the question. Under arbitration in England, the price of puddling is reduced to six shillings and three pence, or $1.50 per ton, with the possibility that it may be yet further reduced; when with conciliation, in this country, the price of puddling is $5.00 per ton, which is the minimum, based on a two cents manufacturers' card.

The Amalgamated Association place a great deal of importance on the fixity of a minimum in wages. The principle is, beyond question, a correct one; for the argument involved is that the first consideration to be accepted is of greatest importance in the laws of production — is reasonable wages to labor. It is a common saying among iron workers, "let us take care to secure fair wages, and prices may take care of themselves." They, however, while professing to be a combination to maintain reasonable wages, also advocated combinations among manufacturers for the purpose of maintaining prices at a reasonable level. The idea of the manufacturers, by so doing, becoming a monopoly, is absurd and ridiculous, because the scales of prices provide that the wages paid are based on the selling prices of iron, whatever that may be; but wages are not affected when iron sells below the minimum price recognized by the association.

Conciliation, as a means of settling labor disputes between the iron manufacturers and their employees, has been in operation for nearly twenty-two years. The appointment of conference committees representing each side, dates back to January, 1865. The result of this — the first meeting of what, as many term, the Conciliation Board — was the adoption of the following scale of prices: —

Memorandum of Agreement,

Made this 13th day of February, 1865, between a committee of Boilers and a committee from the Iron Manufacturers, appointed to fix a scale of prices to be paid for boiling pig iron, based on the manufacturers' card of prices, it being understood either party shall have the right and privilege to terminate this agreement by giving ninety days' notice to the other party, and that there shall be no deviation without such notice. When the manufacturers' card of prices are at the rate named below, the price for boiling shall be at the prices opposite, per ton of 2,240 pounds: —

Manufacturers.	*Boilers.*
8½ cents per pound	$9 00
8¼ " " "	8 75
8 " " "	8 50
7¾ " " "	8 25
7½ and 7¼ cents per pound	8 00
7 and 6¾ " " "	7 50
6½ and 6¼ " " "	7 00
6 and 5¾ " " "	6 50
5½ and 5¼ " " "	6 00
5 and 4¾ " " "	5 75
4½ and 4¼ " " "	5 50
4 and 3¾ " " "	5 00
3½ and 3¼ " " "	4 75
3 and 2¾ " " "	4 50
2½ cents per pound	4 00

The adoption of this scale was hailed by all as an era of peace; but, as subsequent events showed, they were disappointed. Iron declined from seven and one-half cents in February, to four cents in July; and, as a consequence, the price for puddling declined in the proportion stipulated by the scale. Impressed with the belief that the basis of the scale was too low, the puddlers gave the required ninety days' notice, in the summer of that year, to terminate the agreement. At the expiration of the notice, the price of iron had advanced slightly, giving the puddlers $6.00 per ton, whereupon they demanded and received $2.00 per ton of an advance, making the price $8.00 per ton. The latter figure prevailed as the price for puddling from October, 1865, to October, 1866, when the puddlers, believing that the price of iron justified their action, demanded an advance of $1.00 per ton, which was, with considerable reluctance, conceded by the manufacturers. About two months later, the manufacturers gave evidence of an unwillingness to continue paying the prices, and finally served notice of a reduction of $2.00 per ton. This the workmen promptly rejected, when a general lock-out resulted in all the Pittsburgh and adjacent mills. The lockout lasted from December, 1866, to May,

1867, when it terminated by the manufacturers paying the old price of nine dollars per ton. At the close of the lock out, the Boilers' Union, with the view of cultivating a better feeling between the workmen and the manufacturers, and to prevent the possibility of further strikes, resolved to ask a conference with manufacturers, for the purpose of adopting a scale of prices. A committee was appointed to negotiate with the manufacturers. They at once prepared and addressed a circular to the employers, in which they favored the establishment of a rule fixed upon the average price of the different grades of manufactured iron, as a basis by which the wages of labor should be governed. They allowed a reasonable time for the consideration of the proposition, and asked for a conference between a committee of the employers and a committee of the men.

The manufacturers, in due course of time, responded affirmatively to the above circular, when conference committees were selected by each side, who convened and after several meetings, agreed "That nine dollars per ton shall be paid for boiling iron, until the 17th day of August, 1867. From that date until the 15th day of September, eight dollars shall be paid;" and a regular scale of prices was provided after the latter date, it being twenty-five cents per ton reduction or advance, in the price of boiling, for each change of one-quarter of a cent per pound on card rates. Either party to this agreement could terminate it by giving thirty days' notice to the other party. In 1871, by mutual consent, slight technical change was made in the scale. It was arranged that the manufacturers' card rates should rise and fall by tenths in place of by one-fourths; the price of boiling to advance and decline ten cents on each one-tenth manufacturers' card.

For a period of seven years following the adoption of the foregoing scale, the relations of employers and employees were uninterrupted. The gradual decline in the price of iron from five cents per pound in January, 1873, to two and one-half cents per pound in the fall of 1874, together with a falling off in the demand, caused the manufacturers, in October of the latter year, to request a conference with the workingmen. At this meeting, the manufacturers gave the required thirty days' notice to terminate the scale. They also demanded the following change in the "Scale of Prices;" viz.: a reduction of one dollar per ton for puddling on the basis of the present scale; that is, when iron is selling at three cents, boiling shall be $5 per ton, and $4.50 on a two and a half cent card. It will be observed that this was a reduction in the base of the scale. Several conferences were held between the committees of the Boilers' Union and the manufacturers, but no decision could be reached. Finally, as trade was depressed and wages generally were low, the workmen's committee proposed to knock off the limitation, and allow the card to drop to two and a half cents, boiling at that rate to be $5.50 per ton. But the manufacturers would not deviate one iota from the stand they had taken. A lockout followed, which lasted for five months. On the 14th day of April, 1875, the Association of Iron Manufacturers held a meeting, and resolved to accept the terms of the boilers, and resumed operations by signing a scale of prices which was ten cents' advance or reduction for each change of two dollars per ton on card. Either party to this agreement could terminate the same by giving thirty days' notice to the other party.

The continued depression in business, and consequent decline in prices of iron, kept matters in a very discouraging condition, with no immediate hope of relief; the manufacturers contending, in the meantime, that they were losing money, and justly unable to continue paying the wages, according to the scale.

In October, 1875, the scale was again set aside by the action of the manufacturers, and committees were called together to consult over a reduction. The price-list of iron had fallen to two and a half cents per pound, while large quantities were being sold at a much less figure; in fact, everything became confused, and all, apparently, sold at prices best suited to themselves. The subject for consideration before the conference committee was not so much the adoption of a scale of prices as the devising of some means and the adoption of a rate of wages as would enable all to tide over the difficulties that oppressed them. The manufacturers insisted that boiling should be reduced to $4.50 per ton. A compromise was at last effected, early in December, providing that wages, up to December 13th, should be at the rate of $5.00 per ton, and from December 13th to February 14, 1876, the wages were to be $4.75 per ton. After the expiration of the above date, the committees again convened, but failed to effect any definite arrangement, and finally separated with the understanding that each and every firm was at liberty to act as they thought best. The boilers, however, resolved to accept no further reduction, so that $4.75 continued to be the price paid till May, 1875. Early in May, the committee again met, but failed to arrive at any agreement. The men had observed that up to this time the manufacturers had always made their attempts to reduce the scale in the winter. To obviate this in the future, it was determined to make the scale of prices operative for one year, dating from June 1st of each year. Having failed in agreeing upon a scale with the manufacturers, the boilers presented a scale, being a reduction of fifty cents per ton for boiling on a two and a half cent card. The scale was accompanied with the notification that, unless agreed to by the manufacturers, they (the boilers) would cease working after the 31st of May. The manufacturers refused to sign this scale, and as a result the mills stopped. The suspension, however, lasted only about two weeks, when the manufacturers signed the scale, and for the first time work was resumed, with the assurance that for one year at least the wages question was settled. Upon the recurring month of June, 1877, the same proceedings were enacted; also in June, 1878, and June, 1879. In June, 1880, a demand of fifty cents per ton advance was made by the boilers on the two and a half cents card, and, after a stoppage of a few days over a week, it was conceded by the manufacturers. The scale of 1880 was operative for five years, when the base was reduced to $5.00 per ton on a two cent card.

The only scales of prices adopted previous to June, 1880, to govern the finishing departments were those of the Guide

Mills, made on the 2d day of April, 1872, and the Bar Mills, made on the 17th day of October, 1879.

The agreement was entered into between the committee of the Manufacturers' Association and a committee of the Amalgamated Association of Iron and Steel Workers, at Pittsburgh, Penn., June 25, 1886. This scale of prices covers every possible detail of boiling, muck or puddle mill, bar and nail-plate mill, guide, ten-inch, hoop and cotton-tie mills, with its different departments of nut iron, channel iron, "T" iron, angles, clip, or wagon strap, hame iron, ten-inch mill, and hoop and cotton-tie mills; also plate and tank mills, sheet mills, Birmingham wire-gauge, and nail-cutting. The space of this chapter will not permit of the introduction of the figures. The following table, however, will be of interest, as showing the wide range in prices: —

AVERAGE PRICES OF THE FOLLOWING ARTICLES FOR THE LAST TWENTY-FIVE YEARS.

Dates.	Anthracite Foundry Iron, Philadelphia, per ton.	Refined Bar Iron, at Stores, Philadelphia, per ton of 2,240 lbs.	Bessemer Steel Rails, in Pennsylvania, per ton.	Cut Nails, per keg.
1860	$22 75	$ 58 75	....	$3 13
1861	20 75	60 83	....	2 75
1862	23 87	70 42	....	3 47
1863	35 25	91 04	....	5 13
1864	59 25	146 46	....	7 85
1865	46 12	106 38	....	7 08
1866	46 87	98 13	....	6 97
1867	44 12	87 08	....	5 92
1868	39 25	85 63	$158 50	5 17
1869	40 62	81 66	132 25	4 87
1870	33 25	78 96	106 75	4 40
1871	35 12	78 54	102 50	4 52
1872	48 87	97 63	112 00	5 46
1873	42 75	86 43	120 50	4 90
1874	30 25	67 95	94 25	3 99
1875	25 50	60 85	68 75	3 42
1876	22 25	52 08	59 25	2 98
1877	18 87	45 55	45 50	2 57
1878	17 62	44 24	42 25	2 31
1879	21 50	51 85	48 25	2 69
1880	28 50	60 38	67 50	3 68
1881	25 13	58 05	61 13	3 09
1882	25 75	61 41	48 50	3 47
1883	22 35	50 30	37 75	3 06
1884	19 87	44 05	30 75	2 39
1885	18 00	40 32	28 50	2 33

STRIKES.

The story of the iron workers would be quite incomplete without reference to their strikes. And yet these contests, so important to the manufacturers and so vital to the workmen, had a similarity of cause, progress, and result that would render their history much alike to the general reader. This topic, therefore, through lack of space to present the interesting and instructive details, must be treated in the briefest manner. Strikes and lockouts were known forty years ago, or more. The Sons of Vulcan had few strikes, the sentiment of the workmen being conservative. The revival in the iron business, after the breaking out of the war, caused the workmen to be more aggressive, and they gained about all the advances they asked. Finally, a conference committee, suggested by Mr. B. F. Jones, adopted a scale of prices in February, 1865. This caused a rapid reduction in wages, corresponding, of course, with the rapid fall in the price of iron. Then followed strikes and lockouts, generally favorable to the workmen, until a new scale of prices was adopted in July, 1867. During a lockout, from December, 1866, to May, 1867, an attempt was made to employ workmen brought from Europe, but they proved incompetent. There were few strikes until 1869, but from that year until 1874 was a period of bitter conflicts. Most of the strikes and lockouts were over wages, but some were simply contests for supremacy. In the winter of 1874, a big strike occurred at Pittsburgh against a reduction in the base of the scale and in wages in general. This was the bitterest and most hotly-contested lockout in the history of the iron workers. The men were in destitute circumstances, and ill-prepared for a lockout at such a season. They believed that it was a crusade against their organization, and they had good reasons for such a belief. During this lockout the workmen refused arbitration, believing it impossible to secure fair, impartial arbitrators, as public opinion was against them. Finally, the manufacturers agreed to start their works on the terms demanded by the workmen.

It appears, from the records of the Sons of Vulcan, that from 1867 to 1875 there were 87 legalized strikes within their jurisdiction, of which 69 were for rates and payment of wages, 16 for administration of works, and two for miscellaneous reasons. As near as can be learned, 28 terminated in favor of the workmen, 22 favorable to the employers, 21 were compromised, and 16 are doubtful. The Amalgamated Association had few strikes in its first and second years, and generally succeeded in those few. In its third year, the Pennsylvania manufacturers attempted to destroy it by discharging its leading men. During the next year, the fight was kept up by the Eastern manufacturers. Many strikes occurred in both these years; and the men were, as a rule, defeated. Wages were increased in some places in 1880 and 1881, and this increase caused strikes in other places for a like advance. Some of these were successful, while others failed. Other strikes followed, aimed directly at the association, and then came the great strike known as "the Pittsburgh strike of 1882." A reckless desperation seemed to prevail everywhere among workmen and employers. At the Chicago Convention the author, hoping to bring about sober second thought, discussed the situation at length, urging the men to cultivate a higher moral tone, and to act only from principles of right, as well as impressing upon them the injury done themselves and their cause by unjustifiable strikes. But there seemed to be no abatement of the striking spirit. The great strike of Pittsburgh ended in favor of the employers. In the latter part of 1882 and the first seven months of 1883, twenty strikes and one lockout occurred, nearly all of which were precipitated by the workmen, and ended disastrously. In my last annual report, I said: —

Strikes have their causes, and these causes exist either on the part of employers or employees. Every opposition to wrong is a strike; but a strike is not always an opposition to wrong. Thus it is that strikes are sometimes a mistake, and become an absolute wrong in themselves. Such strikes, when entered into, usually terminate against the aggressive party, but not always so; for we have to admit that *might*, not *right*, is often the deciding factor in these questions. Yet, notwithstanding this fact, too much care cannot be taken to prevent unjust and uncalled-for strikes. Full and justifiable cause should exist.

and every recourse exhausted before the final step is taken. It is very wrong to assume that all strikes emanate from the workingmen; for the facts teach us, in our departments of labor at least, that the employers are very often the instigators of strikes.

Early in 1884, all the strikes of any consequence had been settled, with the exception of that at Birmingham, Ala. In the case of this one, the reaction following all spasmodic movements now set in. A sudden and violent revulsion of feeling and sentiment manifested itself against strikes; and, from that time to the present, no strikes of any magnitude have occurred.

The total number of legalized strikes entered in the records of the association from 1876 to 1885, inclusive, was 93, the causes of which were as follows: Wages, 61; Unionism, 17; Signing of Scale, 3; Miscellaneous, 12. Of these 28 were successful; 61 were unsuccessful; 4 were compromised. Startling as these results appear to be, it does not necessarily follow that no good has been accomplished by strikes. We may yet discover that these are side-lights by the way, leading us to a higher state of intelligence. To the association they may prove to be the "baptism of fire" in preparing it for more useful work in the future issues of the labor problem.

CONCLUSION.

The most important inventions affecting the iron industry since 1840 were the "Bessemer" and "Open Hearth" processes for manufacturing steel, and it was not until 1858 that Mr. Bessemer finally succeeded in producing cast steel from cast iron. The first Bessemer steel rails made in this country were rolled at the North Chicago rolling-mill on May 24, 1865. But not until 1867 was there any quantity made to order. From 2,550 net tons in 1867 the production rose to the highest point in 1882, when the tremendous total of 1,438,155 net tons was reached. The new processes referred to above have made great changes in the manufacture of iron and in the number of hands employed in the various departments. Many improvements have also been made in the manufacture of rails, by which a large amount of labor has been saved. The vast displacement of manual labor caused by these improvements has completely changed the relations between employers and employees; and to this is due, more than anything else, the failure of strikes in the large Bessemer works, and, as we find in most of the Eastern works, the complete subjugation of labor to the will of the employers. I believe that the inventive genius of man in bringing about those vast improvements, is the unseen hand of the Almighty preparing the way for the higher industrial conditions awaiting us in the near future, where the benefit of all this genius will be enjoyed by all men

It may well be asked, What is the difference between labor owned by the capitalist, in the form of labor-saving machinery, and the laborer himself, as a slave owned by his master? We need some system whereby the great improvements brought about by man's ingenuity will both lighten the arduous tasks imposed upon the laborer and also shorten his hours of labor. The great task before the labor organizations, in the first place, is to secure fair wages to the laborer. The idea embodied in the scale of prices of the Amalgamated Association, that of the fixity of a minimum of wages, is, to my mind, the most feasible. It is no use wasting time *talking* co-operation, —we must *act* co-operation; and the first thing to co-operate in is the fixing of a minimum of wages of labor. The wages of the workman should never go below the point that would make it hard for a frugal, industrious man to live and maintain a family. Common day-labor, for instance, should never be below one dollar and fifty cents per day. There is no necessity that I should go on enumerating a whole list of occupations; the principle I advocate is easily understood. But the question may be asked, How is this to be accomplished? I answer, by co-operation of employers and workmen. But I must not be understood as saying that this co-operation is possible without organization. Not at all. Such an assumption would be preposterous. There must be organization of workmen, and there must be organization of employers. Instead of being constantly in conflict, there should be,—there must be,—harmony between these two factors. Employers should combine to pay good wages. They will then have to fix the price of their products, if they are producers, or whatever their position in the social and industrial world may be, in proportion to the wages paid.

There is no reason why women should be paid such low wages as thirty-five and fifty cents a day making shirts. Let them be paid, at the lowest, one dollar per day, though to do so would make the shirt that we can now get for seventy-five cents cost us twenty five cents more. Of course, in this large increase in price, I would include better wages to the labor employed in making the linen, or cotton cloth, or whatever it may be, out of which the shirt is made. The advocate of free competition, and the survival of the fittest, would call this an infringement of personal rights. I am not a believer in the everlasting cry of cheapness. We demand good wages first; and if the business men who attend to the distribution of the products of labor want to charge exorbitant rates, we must then combine to attend to the business ourselves. It is well for workingmen to observe that some of the richest men are to be found among the merchants,—the distributing class.

Again, there must be some means adopted of finding employment for all. There must be employment, or there cannot be any earning of wages; and when there is no receiving of wages there is no money to spend in buying food, clothing, and the other necessaries of life. To this end the Amalgamated Association advocate a protective tariff. They do not believe in buying abroad such products as should be produced at home. Every ton of iron and steel brought here from abroad means that amount less work for our iron and steel-workers to do, and the loss of that amount of wages. It is therefore a double loss—a loss not only to themselves, but to all dependent upon them. They believe, too, that they must have the work to do, or they cannot be in a position to command good wages, or, indeed, any wages at all. It is but fair to state that the iron and steel-workers advocate a tariff on all products of foreign labor that are brought here in competition with those of home labor, even to prohibition, if necessary, believing that the more complete is the control of the market, the easier it is to regulate wages; and on precisely the same grounds as those on which they advocate tariff, they advocate the prohibition of the importation of foreign labor under contract, and the regulation even of foreign immigration. Though prison-contract labor, or the products of the labor of the convicts, do not enter into direct competition with the products of our iron and steel mills, still the workmen are strenuously opposed to it. They are also opposed to the system of letting work out on contract, which is now so general. A contractor is nothing more or less than an overseer, or boss, and for his services should be paid reasonable wages; but he should never be allowed to carry on his business at a profit squeezed out of the daily wages of the operative. They also believe in equal pay for men and women, and for white and black. The measure of wages must be in proportion to the work done or labor performed, and not whether it be a man or a woman that does it.

Notwithstanding the action of the last convention in deciding not to affiliate with the "Federation of Trades," I know the iron and steel workers are in hearty accord with all the great questions of the day, as advocated in the platform of the "Federation," and the declaration of principles of the Knights of Labor. They are especially in favor of the compulsory education of children, and forbidding the employment of children under fifteen years of age, and the reservation of the land for actual settlers. The only essential point of difference is on that of arbitration. The association attach much importance to the question of temperance. It regards intemperance as a prolific source from which spring many of the evils which the workingman have to endure. Great care has always been taken to impress upon the minds of the members the necessity of properly husbanding their resources. It is not only necessary that the workmen should receive good wages, but also necessary that they judiciously spend them. In brief, the sole aim of the association is the social, moral, mental, and financial improvement of its members.

CHAPTER XII.

THE RISE OF RAILROAD ORGANIZATIONS.

THE ENGINEERS FIRST ORGANIZE — FIRST CONVENTION, 1855 — THIS ASSOCIATION SHORT-LIVED — ORGANIZED AGAIN IN 1863 — PURPOSES OF THE NEW BROTHERHOOD — RAPID GROWTH OF THE ORDER — LIMITING MEMBERSHIP TO ENGINEERS — ATTEMPTED DESTRUCTION OF THE ORDER — PRESENT NAME ADOPTED — ORGANIZATION IN NEW ENGLAND — OFFICIAL JOURNAL ESTABLISHED — CHIEF WILSON'S RESIGNATION DEMANDED — CHIEF ARTHUR ELECTED — STRIKES OF THE BROTHERHOOD — COLOR-BLINDNESS — DISCUSSION OF THE LABOR PROBLEM. THE BROTHERHOOD OF LOCOMOTIVE FIREMEN — ORGANIZED IN AN OLD CAR-SHED — ANNUAL CONVENTIONS AND RAPID GROWTH — ITS BENEVOLENT WORK — STRIKES UNKNOWN — ITS CHIEF OFFICERS. BROTHERHOOD OF RAILROAD BRAKEMEN — ORGANIZED, 1883 — PHENOMENAL GROWTH — PRINCIPLES OF THE ORDER — IT IS OPPOSED TO STRIKES. THE SWITCHMEN'S MUTUAL AID ASSOCIATION — ORGANIZED, 1877. ORDER OF RAILWAY CONDUCTORS -- ORGANIZED, 1868. MASTER MECHANICS' ASSOCIATION.

THE idea that in union of like interests there is strength comes sooner or later to those most concerned therein. Oftentimes its full force is not felt until some pressure from without drives it home. The Brotherhood of Locomotive Engineers is a conspicuous illustration of this truth. Almost as soon as the railroads of the country became sufficiently numerous and centralized to make it practicable, the engineers began to move towards an organization for mutual aid and assistance. As early as 1854, it appears that the engineers on the Baltimore & Ohio Railroad joined in a strike, on account of some difficulty with the officers of the company, in which sixteen of them lost their situations. The rapid extension of railroads, the consequent great demand for engineers, and the evils resulting from the employment of inexperienced, incompetent, and intemperate men for this work caused the older and more thoughtful engineers on that road to discuss means of mutual protection, and the improvement of their fellow-craftsmen.

It was decided to call a convention of locomotive engineers to consider the subject more fully. Accordingly, a circular was sent to the men on all railroads through the country, asking them to send delegates to a convention in Baltimore, November 6, 1855. About 70 delegates responded to this call, representing 14 States and 55 railroads. An organization was effected under the name of the "National Protective Association of the United States," and the following officers were chosen: President, Benjamin Hoxies, of the Delaware and Eastern Division of the New York & Erie; Vice-President, J. R. Smith, of the Baltimore & Ohio; Secretary, William D. Robinson, of the New York Central; Corresponding Secretary, Christian Smith, of the Baltimore & Ohio; Treasurer, Henry Brown, of the Hartford, Springfield, & New Haven. A constitution and by-laws were adopted, and resolutions setting forth the wants, aims, and objects of the association were passed. The convention adjourned to Columbus, Ohio, on the first Tuesday in October, 1856. It had failed, however, to adopt certain measures necessary for the successful continuance of such organizations; and, after meeting at Columbus, pursuant to adjournment, when no important business appears to have been transacted, it never again assembled. Some subordinate associations were formed during the first year, and maintained their organization in a more or less demoralized condition for a few years. Some may even have been in existence in 1863, when the present Brotherhood was founded.

The engineers were now rapidly becoming more and more numerous; and the necessity for combination for mutual protection against the growing disposition of railroad officials to encroach on the compensation of the engineers, and many other rights and privileges they considered themselves entitled to, became correspondingly apparent. At this time, little thought was given towards an association for the improvement of the character of those in the service. The need for mutual protection was more keenly felt in the West than in the East. The course of the officials of the Michigan Central, in the fall of 1862 and the following winter, aroused much indignation among the engineers, caused a general discussion of the situation, and led the more zealous to earnest efforts for organization. W. D. Robinson, of Marshall, and George Q. Adams, of Detroit, were especially prominent in this work. In the meantime an association of employees of the Michigan Southern had been started at Adrian, and the men on the Central were invited to join. Messrs. George Q. Adams, Samuel Keith, and M. Higgins, representing the engineers on the Central and the Detroit & Milwaukee, went to Adrian and joined the organization to learn its purposes. They found it was designed to include all railroad employees in the mechanical departments, and reported unfavorably on the movement, believing the best interests of the engineers could be served by an association which would include only engineers and firemen.

Soon after this, on a Sunday early in the following April, several engineers met at the engine-house in Marshall, as engine-men were in the habit of doing. Among them were Messrs. Robinson and Adams. Conversation naturally turned on their grievances, and some plan to remedy them. While they were talking they discovered the division master-mechanic of the road watching them; and so, on the invitation of Mr. Robinson, they withdrew to his house, where they might be more secure in the expression of their opinions. The situation on the Central was only a type of that through the country generally. The railroad officials were constantly encroaching on the compensation and accustomed privileges of the employees, and the latter were becoming more and more discontented in consequence. This gathering of the engineers was the first formal expression of discontent. They met as friends to talk over their grievances; but before they separated, they planted the germ of a brotherhood that soon grew and extended until its branches had reached the furthermost parts of the country. It was here decided to open correspondence with engineers on different roads running into Detroit, looking toward the accomplishment of definite terms of co-operation. An agreement was also drawn up that, if any one should be discharged from the service of the company for any action in the contemplated movement, the rest of the engineers would notify the company that, unless he was reinstated, they would quit work in a body. Copies of this agreement were circulated among the engineers on the road, and was signed by all but four. This correspondence resulted in calling a convention in Detroit, May 5, 1863. Engineers on only the following roads were asked to attend this first convention: Michigan Central, Michigan Southern & Northern Indiana, Detroit & Milwaukee, Grand Trunk on the American side, and the Detroit branch of the Michigan Southern. A goodly representation of the engineers on these roads appeared at the appointed place. The Michigan Southern and Northern Indiana were represented by F. Avery, Frank Wheeler and John Kennedy; the Detroit branch of that road, by T. Wartsmouth and E. Nichols; the Detroit & Milwaukee, by M. Higgins; the Grand Trunk, by B. Northrup; the East Division of the Michigan Central, by George Q. Adams; the Middle Division of the same road, by W. D. Robinson. The West Division of this road was not represented. These men, with the advice and counsel of several engineers on these roads, who were not considered delegates, entered on their duties with praiseworthy zeal. A constitution and by-laws, embodying the fundamental principles of the Brotherhood as it exists to-day, were adopted, as was a form of obligation as a bond of union. On the 8th of May, 1863, twelve engineers, including the delegates, joined hands in a circle, repeated the obligation, which was read by George Q. Adams, thus pledging themselves to support the constitution and by-laws then adopted. Officers were at once selected, and Division No. 1, Brotherhood of the Footboard, was fully organized, and stood forth as the pioneer in the great work of regeneration and elevation of the locomotive engineers on this continent, eager to extend the hand of fellowship to all worthy members of the craft who had any faith in their rights as a class, and a belief that in organized action alone rested a hope of their vindication. In a general way, it may be said that the idea most prominent in the constitution, and which is repeated with emphasis in every annual address of the Grand Chief Engineer, is that members of the Brotherhood shall aim to reach a high standard of ability as engineers and of character as men, well fitted to the important and responsible nature of their occupation, thus entitling them to liberal compensation, which should be insisted upon by all legitimate means. Argument, the true worth of able and competent men, and the highest and best interests of the companies themselves, rather than strikes, were at first, always have been, and are now, the means on which the Brotherhood has relied to maintain the justice of its requests at the hands of the railroad companies.

Immediately after the adjournment of this initial meeting, the organization of other divisions in the West and Northwest was rapidly prosecuted, and sub-divisions had been formed before the leaders of the movement could pause to organize a Grand Division. This was done at Detroit, on the 17th of August, 1873, and the component parts of the Grand Division then established their location and date of organization were as follows: Division No. 2, at Marshall, Mich., June 4; Division No. 3, at Michigan City, Ind., June 16; Division No. 4, at Adrian, Mich., about June 16; Division No. 5, at Norwalk, O., July 5; Division No. 6, at Chicago; Division No. 7, at Lafayette, Ind.; Division No. 8, at Crestline, O.; Division No. 9, at Laporte, Ind., and Division No. 10, at Chicago, followed in close succession. The first meeting of the Grand Division was held in the room of Division No. 1, 23 Merrill's Block, corner of Jefferson and Woodward avenues, the same room occupied by that division to-day, and which they have held continuously. All ten divisions were represented at this convention, when the constitution and by-laws were somewhat modified and improved. The Grand National Division was here organized. William D. Robinson, who has been called the Father of the Brotherhood, was chosen Grand Chief Engineer; Charles Steele, of Division No. 5, First Grand Engineer; George Q. Adams, of Division No. 1, Second Grand Engineer; O. T.

Johnson, of Division No. 7, First Grand Assistant Engineer; Frank Wheeler, of Division No. 4, Second Grand Assistant Engineer, and E. C. Redfield, of Division No. 6, Third Grand Assistant Engineer. This convention adjourned to meet in Indianapolis, August 17, 1864.

The burden of the work fell on the Grand Chief, who was regularly employed on the middle division of the Michigan Central. His increasing work in this office compelled him to obtain leave of absence from his post, and his prominent connection with the Brotherhood finally culminated in his discharge from the road, about the middle of November. Finding it difficult to obtain employment on other roads, for similar reasons, he resigned his office of Grand Chief, November 17, 1863; but his resignation was not accepted. It was soon decided that he should devote his whole time to the interests of the Order. The treasury had become empty, and printed copies of the constitution and by-laws were nearly exhausted. These difficulties were finally overcome, and on December 14, 1863, he started on his mission. In just one month he visited fourteen divisions, organized divisions in Milwaukee, Zanesville, Cleveland, Cincinnati, Covington, Ky., and Columbus, and granted charters for Nashville and East St. Louis.

Early in 1864 Division No. 12, at Fort Wayne, became involved in a dispute with the officers of the Pittsburgh, Fort Wayne & Chicago Railroad. Chief Robinson visited them, and left them apparently in good condition. They soon became demoralized, however, and destroyed their charter. The division was soon reorganized. It is needless to say that these engineers were worsted in this the first conflict of the Order. It had now become evident that changes must be made in the constitution, and a special convention was called at Detroit, February 23, for that purpose, when this work was satisfactorily accomplished. The original constitution allowed any engineer of good moral character to become a member, and some divisions sought to gain in numbers by admitting any one who could run an engine, and some firemen and machinists were admitted; but at this special session an amendment was adopted excluding firemen and machinists.

In consequence of grievances at the hands of the Chicago & Galena Union Railroad, a special convention, or union meeting, was held in Chicago, March 10, 1864. Evidence was produced showing positively that a conspiracy on the part of certain superintendents and master-mechanics to destroy the Brotherhood in detail, and that Division No. 6, at Chicago, had been selected as the first victim. At this meeting resolutions of the strongest and most able character were passed, amounting to the Brotherhood at large as a declaration of rights and the vindication of the legitimacy of combination for protection, or other purposes, so long as such combination possessed no unlawful or treasonable features. This movement was premature, the organization being yet too imperfect, and the minds of the men not prepared to act in concert in any movement of such magnitude. The superintendents and master-mechanics also denied being concerned in an attack on the Brotherhood, although there was sufficient proof that the above road was joined with others in some kind of a movement in which they gave it valuable assistance at this time. After this convention the Grand Chief started East, organizing divisions at Altoona, Penn., Philadelphia, Baltimore, and Port Jervis; at this last place completing the organization of the engineers on the Erie Railroad. He was then called West, and was never able to visit the East as an organizer.

During the remainder of this year, nothing of special consequence to the Brotherhood transpired, except its rapid growth, by which it reached a total of fifty-four divisions, scattered over the country from Chicago and St. Louis to Albany and West Lebanon, N. H., and as far south as Nashville. The finances of the Grand Division were now in a flourishing condition.

At the Second Annual Convention, held in Indianapolis, August 17, 1864, all the grand officers were present. There were thirty-eight of the fifty-four divisions represented. Chief Robinson reported at length on the work done in the first year, and suggested many needed changes in constitution and by-laws, which were made. The name and title was changed to the Grand International Brotherhood of Locomotive Engineers. The form of initiation was changed, and made more impressive. The office of Guide in sub-divisions was created. At this convention the doctrine or improvement in ability and character of the members was made specially prominent. Charles Wilson, of Rochester, N. Y., was chosen Grand Chief, — an office he held for over ten years. Robert Laughlin, of Hornellsville, N. Y., was chosen First Grand Assistant Engineer, and that office was made the only salaried one of the Brotherhood, the compensation being fixed at $125 per month. It was voted to adopt the *Trades Review*, of Philadelphia, as the official organ of the Brotherhood.

It happened that a lot of Confederate prisoners were confined near Indianapolis at this time, and the appearance of the engineers there caused many to think they were connected with a reported scheme for the release of these prisoners. The delegates were consequently followed to and from their hall by a file of United States soldiers, who also guarded the hall while they were in session. As yet the order had no permanent headquarters. The new Grand Chief soon decided that, in consequence of the hostility among railroad officials to the Brotherhood, to remain at home and do the work of organizing as best he could by correspondence. This policy proved a wise one. Doubting and suspicious railroad officials were hardly able to understand the quietude, while the Brotherhood used every effort to win their confidence on the merits of their order. As yet there was only one division in New England, No. 13, at West Lebanon, N. H., which was organized by engineers on the Northern Railroad, December 28, 1863. H. A. Cheney was a leading spirit in its organization, the preliminary meetings being held at his house, while he went to Detroit to obtain the work and authority to organize. Soon after the Indianapolis Convention, the engineers of the East began to realize the importance of associating themselves with this movement, and those running out of Boston were the first to fall into line.

About December 1, 1864, a meeting was held in the Olympic Theatre building, corner of Washington and Howard streets, to consider the question of organizing a division. Maynard Banister, Samuel Hobart and J. M. Alger, of the Boston & Worcester road; James H. Prince and L. Cole, of the Boston & Providence, and John T. Otis, of the South Shore, were present. It was decided to organize, but adjournment for one week was had without definite action. In the following week, the engineers of all roads running out of Boston were interviewed and invited to participate in the movement. The next meeting was held in Hospitaller Hall, on Washington street. After full discussion, John T. Otis was appointed a delegate to secure the work and a charter, with authority to organize. He went to Rochester, N. Y., and joined Division No. 18 there, December 17, 1864. He then secured a charter from the Grand Chief, and authority to organize. At the following meeting, Friday evening, December 30, at Hospitaller Hall, five members were initiated, as follows: Maynard Banister, S. B. Hobart, J. H. Prince, L. Cole, and W. E. White. One week later they initiated fourteen more. Permanent officers were chosen, as follows: John T. Otis, Chief Engineer; S. A. Bragg, First Assistant Engineer; M. A. Banister, Second Assistant Engineer. Division 63 was organized at Springfield, Mass., March 3, 1865, and Division 57 was organized at Providence, R. I., April 27, 1865.

These first few months, closing with the organization of the divisions in Boston, Springfield, and Providence, practically cover what may be termed the formative period of the Brotherhood. Its growth since then has been steady, but not uniform. It now has a membership of 20,000 in round numbers, divided among 319 divisions. Various causes, from time to time, tended to delay its development. The chief officers, however, in the face of all difficulties always insisted upon using every possible argument before authorizing a strike, and continually urged upon the members to attain so high a degree of excellence as to command the highest wages without objection by the companies. The annual conventions

TRADES-UNION LEADERS.

were held in prominent cities through the country, and were frequently attended by prominent city and State officials. These conventions were generally held in October. At the Convention of 1866, the *Locomotive Engineers' Journal* was established, which has since reached a very general circulation through the Brotherhood. Its pages each month were filled with topics of general interest to the members, — special correspondence from brothers, communications from various officers and editorial comments on current topics of particular interest to engineers. It has been a great power in building up the Brotherhood. This convention also established the Widows', Orphans', and Disabled Members' Fund, of which P. M. Arthur, Anson Gustin, and J. H. Prince were the first trustees. This fund was subsequently, after it reached the sum of $14,639.48, transferred to the General Charity Fund. On the 3d of December, 1867, the Locomotive Engineers' Mutual Life Insurance Association was established, and it has proven a source of great benefit to the members.

In 1868, trouble arose between the engineers at St. Louis and the roads, when the right of the Brotherhood to strike on all roads because of trouble on one came up. Chief Wilson claimed that as the companies combined to help each other, so their employees had the same right. His own plan, however, was to have each road settle its own difficulties independently. In 1870, it was voted to establish headquarters in Cleveland for the following ten years, and there they have remained ever since. An order of burial-service was also adopted at this convention. In 1871, it was determined to procure an international act of incorporation, if possible; if not, then a charter from the United States, so that the Grand International Division might be recognized as a legal body. It was proposed to incorporate the chief officers and one delegate from each State. An act of incorporation was drawn up, but it died in Congress. Division 33 was incorporated in Tennessee in 1870, but as the division died a natural death in 1877 the brotherhood is not now incorporated in any State. In 1872, the convention voted to expel all members engaging in strikes without the direction of their divisions. The grand officers were also unanimously instructed to do all in their power to induce the companies to discontinue Sunday trains.

A special convention was held at Cleveland, February 25, 1874, when the resignation of Chief Wilson was asked for and received. His successor was P. M. Arthur, who had been prominent in the Brotherhood almost from its inception, and who has held that place ever since. The cause for this convention was as follows: In November, 1873, the engineers learned that the railroad officials throughout the country had combined to reduce their wages, on account of alleged decrease of business and earnings. The engineers did not believe the reasons given were the true ones, and successfully resisted the attempted reduction on one principal road, and checked it on many others by timely remonstrances. An attempted settlement with the Pennsylvania road and leased lines failed. Chief Arthur claims the road did wrong in posting a ten per cent. reduction while it still had a written agreement with the engineers that they should receive a stipulated sum for certain services. The reduction was made on a day's notice. The engineers thought such action arbitrary and unjust. They claimed they should have been consulted, and that they would cheerfully have submitted to a reduction, had a good reason therefor been shown. Failing to secure a restoration of wages, they struck at an appointed hour, first having given due warning of their intention. For this Chief Wilson denounced them through the public press, although he did not condemn the officials of the road. His action caused an immediate demand for his resignation, which was given, as stated above.

Many chapters could be written simply upon the strikes in which the Brotherhood has been engaged, although they have been comparatively few. But they vitally concerned the general public, and were followed with the closest interest while they lasted. In general, it may be said that they were all, or nearly all, caused by attempted reduction of wages and attempts to break up the organization. The Brotherhood, as its records abundantly show, first exhausted all pacific means, in accordance with their principles, and then stopped the trains at such hours as to cause as little inconvenience as practicable to the travelling and business public. The Brotherhood was generally successful in securing a compliance with their requests without much delay. Sometimes the struggle was more protracted, the officials refusing at first to even recognize the Brotherhood, or Chief Arthur as its representative. But they were eventually compelled so to do. In a few instances the strikes were unsuccessful, owing usually to the assistance rendered by other companies. The companies always paid much more, in the long run, to fight the Brotherhood than it would have cost to have acceded to its requests. In commenting on the result of one strike, which cost the company at least half a million dollars, Chief Arthur said:—

It is not the money that has been paid the engineers that has bankrupted so many railroads. It is the peculation, fraud, and mismanagement of those high in authority. If all the legitimate earnings of the railroad companies found its way into their treasury, they could afford to pay their employees liberal wages and declare a fair dividend to their stockholders.

About 1879, the question of color-blindness became prominent, and had reached such importance by the time of the annual convention in 1881, that Chief Arthur gave considerable space to it in his annual address. He referred to the discharge of experienced engineers, especially in Massachusetts, for this cause. He charged the examining board of that State with seeking more to enrich themselves than to promote the safety of the travelling public, and urged that common sense would show that self-interest would cause the companies to employ only men who would not cause them serious loss by mistaking the color of signals. He urged the Brotherhood to use its influence to prevent similar legislation in other States to that of Massachusetts and Connecticut on this subject.

In the tenth annual address of Chief Arthur, he dwelt at length upon the labor problem, and some of his most striking ideas are quoted, as follows:—

Labor needs unity in its ranks, honesty and intelligence in its leaders, and wisdom in its councils. * * * * Employers should rise above their narrowness, and endeavor to work, as far as possible, to the interest of their workmen, and create more kindly relations. If this were done, there would be fewer strikes, and capital would be benefited in a corresponding degree. * * * * The great mistake some employers make is in refusing to recognize the committees sent to them by their workmen to present their grievances. It was the refusal to receive our committees that led to all the trouble we have had as an organization. The best method to settle the difficulties that arise between employer and employee is for the representatives of both sides to come together and talk them over in a friendly spirit, each one making concessions whenever the nature of the case would seem to warrant it. * * * * There is no occasion for this constant warfare between capital and labor; both have rights that each other are bound to respect; their interests are identical; the one is indispensable to the success of the other; and the sooner men realize that fact the better it will be for the whole country.

THE BROTHERHOOD OF LOCOMOTIVE FIREMEN.

This brotherhood was founded December 1, 1873, by nine locomotive firemen. They met in an old car-shed at Port Jervis, N. Y., on that day, and organized Deer Park Lodge, No. 1, of the Brotherhood of Locomotive Firemen. The purposes of the Order, as stated in the preamble to its constitution, are for effecting a unity of the locomotive firemen of North America, and elevating them to a higher social, moral, and intellectual standard; for the promotion of their general welfare and the protection of their families, and for bringing into perfect harmony the firemen and their employers, since their interests are identical, and for aiding the families of its members.

The first Grand Master chosen was J. A. Leach, and he held that office until September, 1876. The first Grand Secretary and Treasurer was G. S. Murray. So zealously did the founders of the Brotherhood labor, that twelve subordinate lodges were the fruit of the first year's work. These lodges sent two delegates each to the first annual convention, at Hornellsville, N. Y., December 15, 1874. At this convention, H. W. Plummer was chosen Vice-Grand Master, the first to hold that place. In December, 1875, the Second Annual Convention was held in Indianapolis, and it was then found that the Order had grown to 31 lodges, and over 600 members. At this convention it was voted to issue the *Fireman's Magazine*, in the interests of the Brotherhood; and it has now become one of the finest journals of its class, with a very large circulation. The Annual Convention, in St. Louis, in September, 1876, showed 53 lodges and over 1500 members. The Convention of 1877, in Indianapolis, showed 78 lodges and 3,500 members.

In 1877 came the great railroad troubles of the country; and the Brotherhood, whose growth naturally depends upon a healthy state of railroad interests, felt a check in its growth, which continued even through 1880. But by the time of the Annual Convention of the latter year, which was held in Chicago, in September, it was evident that the Order was again advancing, for it reported 98 lodges and a membership of 4,500. The Convention of 1882, at Terre Haute, Ind., showed 124 lodges and 5,000 members, which were increased during the next year to 178 lodges and 7,337 members. This was the remarkable growth of only ten years, during three of which the Order was comparatively at a standstill. The Eleventh Convention was held in Toronto, Can., September 23, 1884, and by this time the lodges numbered 240, and the membership over 12,000. At the last Annual Convention, which was held in Philadelphia, September 21, 1885, the grand total of 290 lodges and 15,000 members had been reached. On January 9, 1886, at Saginaw City, Mich., was organized Harbor City Lodge, making a round 300 lodges and a membership of over 16,000. Thus is sketched the foundation and growth of one of the most successful fraternal organizations among railroad men.

This order is truly a "brotherhood" in all that the name implies. Its last report shows that it has paid out of its beneficiary fund $271,764, and to members who have been totally disabled $44,000 more, making a grand total of $315,764. This has gone to those whose extra hazardous calling does not allow them the advantages of ordinary life and accident insurance; and yet these premiums have not cost the members over twelve dollars each per annum.

The Order is wholly fraternal and benevolent. It has an insurance system, under which it pays $1,500 to the family of a deceased member. In this way it has already paid out over

$600,000. Its motto is, "Benevolence, Sobriety, and Industry." As an organization it has never seen a strike, having always been able to adjust its grievances by arbitration, which is one of the fundamental principles of the Order. Although its membership is more largely in the North, it has representatives in every State and Territory in the Union, and in Mexico and every section of Canada.

The chief officers of the Brotherhood, from its founding, have been as follows: Grand Masters—J. A. Leach, W. R. Worth, F. B. Alley, W. T. Goundie, F. W. Arnold, Charles Pope, and Frank P. Sargent; Vice-Grand Masters—H. W. Plummer, H. H. Clapp, John Broderick, W. T. Goundie, J. M. Dodge, J. E. Briggs, W. E. Burns, F. P. Sargent, and J. J. Hannahan; Grand Secretary and Treasurers—G. S. Murray, W. N. Sayre, Eugene V. Debs; Grand Organizer and Instructors—S. M. Stevens and J. J. Hannahan; Grand Trustees—A. H. Tucker, W. F. Hynes, and C. A. Cripps. At the Toronto Convention, in 1884, E. B. Mayo, W. E. Burns, S. Vaughan, F. W. Dyer, and C. A. Wilson were chosen as Grand Trustees to serve for two years, Mr. Mayo being chairman and Mr. Burns secretary. Mr. Mayo has, however, been succeeded as chairman by Mr. H. Walton, of Philadelphia. W. N. Sayre was first editor of the *Fireman's Magazine*, which is now most ably conducted by E. V. Debs, Grand Secretary and Treasurer, assisted by W. F. Hynes as associate editor.

BROTHERHOOD OF RAILROAD BRAKEMEN.

This brotherhood is one of the youngest of the organizations of railroad men. It was organized at Oneonta, N. Y., September 23, 1883, when nineteen brakemen employed on the Albany & Susquehanna Railroad assembled, and, with much misgiving and fear of its success, sent out a constitution and by-laws. But the growth of the Brotherhood has been remarkable. At its First Annual Convention, held at Oneonta, October 20, 1884, there were 37 lodges reported, with a membership of less than 2,000. The Second Annual Convention met at Burlington, Ia., October 19, 1885, when

161 lodges were reported, with a membership of nearly 7,000. It now numbers over 230 lodges and about 12,000 members, while it is confidently expected that at the Third Annual Convention, which will be held in San Antonio, Texas, in October, 1886, fully 250 lodges will be represented, and a corresponding number of members. Two organizers are constantly on the road organizing new lodges, and instructing those already organized. The growth of the Brotherhood has, indeed, been phenomenal. Its officers expect to see it become in a short time the strongest railway organization in existence, as there are two, and in some cases three, brakemen to one conductor, engineer or fireman. Already the members enjoy many privileges which were considered beyond their reach three years ago, and these are but a small part of what may readily be obtained by united effort. The Order enjoys friendly relations with all railway companies, and its future looks very bright.

The Brotherhood has been, on the whole, especially fortunate in its choice of officers, and is to-day exceedingly well supplied in that respect. The preamble of its constitution states the purposes of the organization to be: To unite the railroad brakemen of the Western hemisphere; to promote their general welfare, and advance their interests, social, moral and intellectual; to protect their families by the exercise of a systematic benevolence; and to establish mutual confidence, and create and maintain harmonious relations between the members and their employers.

Unlike some other organizations of railroad men, the Brotherhood never had a strike. Secretary O'Shea, of the Grand Lodge, says: "Our Brotherhood has never had a strike; we are opposed to strikes as a means of settling disputes and differences between employer and employee. A strike should never be engaged in until all means of arbitration have failed, and then only as a last resort."

On May 24, 1886, there were twenty-six members expelled, and thirty suspended for inaugurating and conducting a causeless strike on the Union Pacific Railway.

The brakemen, like all other railroad men, are very charitable towards their fellows; and this Order has already paid out nearly one hundred thousand dollars in benefit-claims alone to the families of dead and disabled members.

The Grand Officers for 1885–86 are as follows: Grand Master, S. E. Wilkinson, Peoria, Ill.; Grand Vice-Master, Neil Sullivan, Binghampton, N. Y.; Grand Secretary and Treasurer, Ed. F. O'Shea, Galesburg, Ill.; Grand Organizer and Instructor, L. C. Foster, Jr., Ithaca, N. Y.; Board of Trustees — S. E. Wilkinson, Chairman, Peoria, Ill.; Daniel L. Cease, Secretary, Phillipsburg, N. J.; Daniel J. McCarty, Oneonta, N. Y.; T. J. Shehan, Denver, Col. Editors of Magazine — J. P. Bledsoe, Rock Island, Ill., and Ed. F. O'Shea, Galesburg, Ill.

THE SWITCHMEN'S ASSOCIATION.

The first Switchmen's Association was founded in Chicago, August, 1877. It was a local society, chartered by the State of Illinois. The charter-members were: Edward W. Jennings, Thomas Griffin, James Cullerton, William Hopper, Thaddeus Boyd, Thomas Green, Edward Scanlon, John Kenny, William Short, Charles Richardson, William Rosencrause and John Reily. The first officers were: William Hopper, President; Thaddeus Boyd, Vice-President; Thomas Griffin, James Cullerton and Edward W. Jennings, Trustees. Little was done but maintain the organization until 1884, when the spirit of the times and new officers of unusual energy, ability, and enthusiasm infused new life into the association. Many new associations were formed, and the need of a national organization became manifest. In response to a call, a large number of representative switchmen met at 112 East Randolph street, Chicago, February 22, 1886. The meeting lasted eight days, and was very harmonious and enthusiastic. Mr. John Drury, of Chicago, called the delegates to order, and was chosen as chairman. The other officers were: James A. Healey, of Chicago, Secretary; Joseph D. Hill, of Kansas City, Reading Clerk; M. J. Keegan, of Chicago, Sergeant-at-Arms. A constitution and by-laws were adopted, and these officers chosen for the current year: James L. Monaghan, of

Chicago, Grand Master; John Drury, Vice-Grand Master and Instructor; John Downey, of Chicago, Secretary and Treasurer; M. J. Keegan, James A. Kelly, W. A. Simmons and James A. Healey, all of Chicago; Joseph D. Hill, of Kansas City; J. L. Hyer, of Rock Island, and W. R. Davison, of Joliet, Board of Directors. A uniform price was adopted, and it was voted to aid in the publication of a monthly journal, devoted to the interests of the Order. The full title of the association is, "The Switchmen's Mutual Aid Association of the United States of America." Its purposes are mutual advancement, mutual protection, and mutual good, especially caring for its members who may be injured in their dangerous calling, and those dependent upon them.

ORDER OF RAILWAY CONDUCTORS.

The Order of Railway Conductors of North America was organized at Mendota, Ill., in 1868. Its records, however, have been very imperfectly kept, and a consecutive history of its growth is impossible. It is fraternal and benevolent in its objects. C. S. Wheaton, of Chicago, is Grand Chief Conductor; W. P. Daniels, of Chicago, Grand Secretary and Treasurer; J. R. Robinson, of Milwaukee, Hiram Hurty, of Elmira, N. Y., and E. H. Belknap, of Galesburg, Ill., Executive Committee; C. S. Wheaton, W. H. Ingram, of St. Thomas, Ont., and W. S. Sears, of Adrian, Mich., Insurance Committee: W. P. Daniels, of Chicago, Editor of the *Railway Conductors' Monthly*, with C. S. Wheaton, E. B. Coman, of Kansas City, Orange Sackett, of Avon, N. Y., and J. B. W. Johnstone, of Corsicana, Tex., Associate Editors.

MASTER-MECHANICS' ASSOCIATION.

The First Convention of the American Railway Master-Mechanics was held at Cleveland, O., September 30, 1868, some fifty or sixty prominent mechanics being present, and "The American Master-Mechanics' Association" was then and there formed. H. M. Britton, of the Indianapolis, Cincinnati & LaFayette was chosen President; N. E. Chapman, of the Cleveland & Pittsburgh, Vice-President;

Frederick Grinnell, of the Atlantic & Great Western, Secretary; S. S. Hays, of the Illinois Central, Treasurer. A constitution was adopted, and signed by thirty-eight members, representing Eastern and Western roads. The Association, as formed, admitted to membership master-mechanics, those in charge of the mechanical departments, general master-mechanics, and master-machinists. The officers are chosen annually.

CHAPTER XIII.

THE BUILDING TRADES.

"Good now, sit down and tell me, he that knows,
Why this same strict and most observant watch
So nightly toils the subject of the land;
And why such daily cast of brazen cannon,
And foreign mart for implements of war;
Why such impress of shipwrights, whose sore task
Does not divide the Sunday from the week,
What might be toward, that this sweaty haste
Doth make the night joint laborer with the day:
Who is't that can inform me?"

Hamlet, Act I, Scene I.

Ship-Building the Earliest Industry — Employers' Liability, 1631 — The Luncheon Privilege — A Most Remarkable Race — Work from Sun to Sun — Demand for Less Hours — The Black-List — Failure of the First Strike for Ten Hours — Captain Richard Trevellick's Statement — Unique Description — Ten-Hour System Gained on Old Work — Thirty Years' Advance — Mechanics' Bell — Ten-Hour Bell — The Bell Disappears — Brought Back with Great Rejoicing — Statement of an Old Ship-Carpenter — Agitation for Eight Hours — California Ship-Builders — Strike for Eight Hours, 1853 — Strikes in New York and Philadelphia — Organization of House-Carpenters' Association — Eight-Hour Movement in California — Meetings in New York and New Jersey — Horace Greeley before the Building Trades — The Amalgamated Society of Carpenters and Joiners — Brotherhood of Carpenters and Joiners — Objects, Methods and Benefits — Nine Hours on the Pacific Coast — P. J. McGuire's Reports — Strikes for Eight Hours.

SHIP-BUILDERS.

FROM Shakespeare's time to 1835, the shipwright's work could well be described as "sweaty haste," with the night made "joint laborer with the day;" yet the shipwright, in spite of hard physical labor and wearing hours, was a thinker as well as a worker, and to him is largely due the direction of the labor movement toward less hours of toil.

The annals of the building trade are meagre. A careful examination of the local histories of the old seaport towns of New England furnishes us, however, with many interesting details. The inquiry has also been productive of results of a moral and intellectual character, and broad, historical tendencies have been discovered, which it is hoped will prove of sociological values to the student of that science.

Ships were built in Boston as early as 1642, and a map dated 1743 shows twelve ship-yards located in the city proper. The same number is contained in the map of the siege of Boston, dated 1775. This industry was of sufficient importance to excite the opposition of the merchants and shipbuilders of England; for the London master-shipwrights, in an address to the Lords of Trade, in 1724, said that in the eight years ending in 1720, there were seven hundred sail of ships built in New England. Many of these vessels were of large size, even for our own times.

Governor Winthrop, the royal governor of New Hampshire, wrote to the Lords of Trades, at the same time, that a ship was building in Massachusetts of one thousand tons, to mount seventy guns.

On May 28, 1629, the Company's Court wrote Governor Endicott a letter, in which reference was made to a bark already built in the country, from which it appears, as Mr. Felt says, in his "History of Salem," that a vessel had been built, most probably at Naumkeag, and that the "Desire," afterwards launched at Marblehead, was not the first vessel built in the colony.

In those early days, a sense of justice and equity seemed to provide for that which the workmen are now seeking to cover by the employers' liability law; for, in 1631, while Richard Hollingsworth was engaged in building a large vessel, one of his workmen was killed, and Hollingsworth was required by the Court of Assizes to pay ten pounds sterling to the wife and children of the deceased, because they thought that sufficient care was not taken to have his tackle strong enough.

In 1631, the bark, "The Blessing of the Bay," built by

Governor Winthrop, was launched at Mystic. The cost of this bark was said to be £145, being of thirty tons' burthen.

The colonists were evidently determined to have good work, as on October 7, 1641, it was ordered that, when any ship was to be built within that jurisdiction, it should be lawful for the owners to appoint and put in some able man to survey the work and workmen from time to time, to see that it be performed and carried on according to the rules of their art; and, on May 29, 1644, the General Court proposed the formation of a company of ship-builders, with power to regulate the building of ships, and to make such orders and laws amongst themselves as might conduce to the public good.

In the early part of the present century, the town of Medford, Mass., carried on quite an extensive ship-building business, the Middlesex Canal giving them facilities for getting their timber. From 1803 to 1855, 232,206 tons of shipping were built at this place, at an estimated cost of $10,449,270, or $45 per ton.

It had been the custom in this industry, as well as in others, to furnish drink or grog at various intervals in the day. In 1817, Thacher Magoun, a ship-builder, determined to abolish the grog privilege. The ceremony of laying the keel, and of commencing each part of the work, as also the christening or naming of a vessel, was always accompanied with the use of ardent spirits. Upon Mr. Magoun giving notice that no liquor could be used in his ship-yard, the words "*No Rum!* No RUM!" were written upon nearly every clap-board of the workshop, and on each timber in the yard. Some of the men refused to work, but finally all gave in, and a ship was built without the use of liquor in any form.

The hours of labor at that time were from sunrise to sunset, and all employers were obliged by custom to furnish liquor free at least twice a day. These two periods for drink were really periods of rest, and were called luncheon times, the men having an opportunity to eat as well as drink, and Mr. Magoun's no-rum movement meant no luncheon time, and was practically an increase in the working time, the employer thus saving the cost of time as well as the cost of the rum. The hours of this luncheon privilege were eleven o'clock in the forenoon, and four o'clock in the afternoon.

Many of the workmen who were temperance men were indignant at the action of their employer, as they felt that the luncheon times were as oases in the desert of unremitting toil.

Drinking habits continued, in spite of this innovation; and it is a matter of record that the agitation for temperance in drink coincides, in point of time, with the agitation for temperance in labor, — that is, for shorter hours.

Richard Henry Dana, in his "Two Years Before the Mast," gives considerable space to the introduction of this reform, and charges some of the reformers with the most selfish motives. It is not to be wondered at that neither the sailors nor the workingmen were very favorably impressed by the penurious manner in which the change was brought about. Mr. Dana, in the book referred to, says: —

This was a temperance ship, and, like too many such ships, the temperance was all in the forecastle. The sailor, who only takes his one glass as it is dealt out to him, is in danger of being drunk, while the captain, who has all under his hand and can drink as much as he chooses, and upon whose self-possession and cool judgment the lives of all depend, may be trusted with any amount to drink at his will. By seeing it allowed to their officers, they will not be convinced that it is taken from them for their good, and, receiving nothing in its place, they will not believe that it is done in kindness.

By the local decay of ship-building on the south shore early in the nineteenth century, this force of shipworkers was diffused, carrying with them certain steady tendencies toward industrial progress, as far as the city of New York on the one hand and the city of Bath, Me., on the other. None of the towns on the south shore obtained the size and importance of the ship-building localitied on he north shore. It thrived in many of them until the exhaustion of timber and the demand for large vessels transferres the industry to various points on the north shore of Massachusetts Bay.

A most remarkable race and local development presents itself here, calling for a notice, which must be much briefer than its importance demands. The inhabitants of the towns of Scituate, Marshfield, Pembroke, and Hanover, and the region thereabouts, were, and are to this day, distinctively marked by the mental and physical characteristics of the Roman people. One cannot be familiar with them without noticing the Roman cast of countenance, and the prevalence among the women of Latin names, such as Julia, Marcia, Sylvia, etc. This is accounted for by the fact that the first settlers of these localities came from the south-east portions of England. That part of our mother-country was the first that was occupied by Julius Cæsar, and the last to be abandoned by the legions. Rome held possession of the island more than four hundred years, and it was never abandoned by those descended from the Romans. They retained their local authority and customs, especially in the city of London, as late as the Danish invasions in the ninth century. The Anglo-Saxons, though nominally in authority, were glad to make common cause with them in resisting the Danes. It is in consequence of the discovery of these facts that the theory of the exclusively Saxon character of English civilization is now repudiated by some able scholars.*

The influence of this Roman element in forming the character of New England has been, as in old England, entirely overlooked; but it has been of great value. Deane's "History of Scituate" speaks thus of the original colonists:—

> Previous to 1640, most of the population was from the county of Kent, in England. Many of them were from London.

After giving a list of names, it says:—

> The above-named gentlemen, and others, were called "men of Kent." * * * * It was a natural and unavoidable consequence, that in this wilderness a less polished race should succeed; yet many of their fathers survived the darkest period of the colony, and gave a lasting impression of their manners upon posterity. * * * * The North River was celebrated for its ship-building in the early annals of the colonies, and it has held its ascendancy until late years [written in 1831]. It has been famous for the education of shipwrights, *who have emigrated, and established their business along the whole coast, from New York to the furthest boundary of Maine.* Scarce a ship-yard or navy-yard can be visited in this whole range of coast, without meeting many workmen who, themselves or their fathers, were educated on the North River.

---

* See "The Romans of Britain," by Henry C. Coote.

Here it is necessary to glance at some of the main currents of history, in order to explain fully the tendency of the preceding statements.

Of all the people of the ancient world, the Romans had the fiercest contest over the social question, and the empire fell because of their failure to adjust it. The uprising of the peasantry of Essex and Kent, in 1381, — the two counties of England the most deeply impressed by the Romans through marriage and the irregular intercourse of the soldiers, — was a reappearance of the old Roman spirit of agrarianism in their descendants. London, even, had not entirely lost its Roman character, as is shown by the ready union of its lower classes with the insurgents under Wat Tyler. The insult to the girls, and the swift uprising of the people which followed, was substantially a repetition of the scenes connected with the assassination of Virginia by her father, and the meeting of the Roman army at Mons Sacer.

The strongly marked character of the immigration into Scituate and the adjoining towns brought the seeds of the social question in its highest form to our shores. By all the circumstances of their origin, these humble but energetic people were fitted to revive it at the right time and in the proper manner.

As the Dutch man-of war which carried the first Africans into James River contained the seeds which were to ripen in the tremendous struggle which has just ceased, so the conflict of ideas was inaugurated by the "men of Kent" in the strike of 1832, by the south shore ship-carpenters, laboring at Boston and New York. They triumphed by united action and peaceful discussion. *They proved that daily labor may be limited without reduction of production or wages, or injury to society;* and in doing this they were the first to lay a broad and firm foundation for the elevation of the working classes of the earth.

The story of the struggle of the ship-workers and building trades in the early days of the Republic has been told in Chapter IV, "The History of the Movement Before the War." It is evident that they were among the first to organize their craft into unions, and that they jealously guarded its interests, bringing their apprentices into the rules and customs of the craft on the completion of their apprenticeship. They seem to have been the first to bring the question of the hours of labor to a direct issue. The journeymen mechanics and master-mechanics of 1825 and 1830 were the employees of the merchants, so that the contest of the ship-workers of that time was with the merchants rather than with their direct employers.

Calkers, from the painful positions of their labor and other causes, were especially prominent, if not really in advance of the ship-carpenters in matters of organizing. They were a set of rough and ready men, interested in public affairs, and from the date of the agitation against the oppressive acts of Great Britain convened together, often in a social manner, and it is claimed that the word "caucus," now so much out of repute, and yet a necessity for political methods, was first derived from the words "calkers' meeting."

The New York Society of Journeymen Shipwrights was incorporated on April 30, 1803, and the house-carpenters of the city of New York, in 1806. We have not records of these societies, — no account of their objects or methods.

The resolutions adopted by the merchants at that time against reducing the hours from fourteen to ten are very similar in their character to the position taken by them in the recent demand of the mechanics of the country for eight hours. The merchants of that day said to their fourteen-hour workmen, "No unreasonable service is expected or required;" but the ship-carpenters and caulkers still continued to think it unreasonable service, and continued their struggle, often at great sacrifice of time and money.

We give the following resolutions, adopted by the merchants, entire: —

Resolved, That we view with deep regret the course that some of our fellow-citizens, journeymen ship-carpenters, caulkers and others, are pursuing in the adoption and maintenance of a system of measures designed to coerce individuals of their craft, and to prescribe the time and manner of the labor for which they are liberally paid.

Resolved, In our opinion, the tendency of this combinatiou of ship-carpenters, caulkers and others, instead of benefiting them, has a direct tendency either to put their business into other hands or seriously to injure it by inducing ship-owners to repair their vessels elsewhere rather than submit to the inconveniences, delays and vexations to which they would be exposed when they can obtain labor only at such times and on such conditions as the folly and caprice of a few journeymen mechanics may dictate, who are now idle two or three of the most valuable hours in the day.

They then proceeded to declare their intention to blacklist all persons who belonged to the association.

In an appeal of the ship-workers to the merchants of Boston, dated May 21, 1832, the grievances of which they complained, in addition to the long hours, were, that if a vessel had to be moved from one part of the city to another, they were compelled to assist in doing it; that after getting the vessel in place, if the weather was unfavorable, they had to wait, and were sometimes detained three or four days before they could commence work on her; that they were compelled to be at the yard in the morning by sunrise and labor until sunset of the longest days, with hardly time to get their meals, and if anyone happened to be tardy, the finger of scorn was pointed at them, and the employer would say, "Where have you been?" or, "If you don't come earlier, I will not employ you any more." They complained that it was but few of them that could make both ends meet at the end of the year. They also complained that sometimes it happened that it would commence to rain after they had been at work two hours, and that they would not be paid for their two hours of work.

The statements in respect to overwork have an important bearing on the question of the adaptation of reduced hours of labor to exceptional trades, such as moulders, who must attend to furnaces, etc. It was quite properly asserted, by the employers, that as many of the jobs called for early and late labor on account of the tides, the reform was inapplicable to the repairs of shipping. The men claimed that they would cheerfully meet this objection by extra hours when the exigencies demanded it. The event has justified their position, as there is at present no friction from this cause, nor has there been during all the thirty years or more in which eight hours has been established.

It is worthy of further note, as bearing on other callings, that the extraordinary demand for ships during the California emigration in 1850, and thereafter, was met without overwork, and without breaking down the ten-hour day, which had by that time extended to the ship-yards.

The demand was so sudden and imperative that ships of two thousand tons, and more, were contracted for under penalty of a heavy daily forfeiture if they were not alongside of a wharf, ready for their cargo, in ninety days. The contracts were met; thus proving the existence of a flexibility in the conditions of toil, of which we had been previously ignorant.

That the same result would happen in the case of the great manufacture of boots and shoes, is believed by those most conversant with the facts. It is claimed by the employers that the hours in that business do not admit of a reduction below ten, on account of the necessity of filling orders rapidly, but the mistakes and misapprehensions of the past on this subject are too evident to give the claim much value. It may be safely inferred that the piece-working shoemakers of the country will inaugurate the change when its merits are fully understood.

A very large sum of money was subscribed by the merchants to defeat the ten-hour movement. A meeting of the ship-workers was held shortly afterwards, at which resolutions were adopted indicating that they were willing to work more than ten hours a day for additional pay; and it was further resolved by them

That we think it an unreasonable representation to make towards the society of which we are the members, to state in public print that we are vexatious, and that we refused to work any more than ten hours per day. We are willing to receive any communication or meet any committee in a fair and honorable way.

Resolved, That, from and after the 20th of March until the 1st of September, we will not labor more than ten hours per day, unless being paid extra for each and every hour; and that we are willing, if requested, to begin at half-past four in the morning, and labor not exceeding ten hours, or we will work later in the evening, if requested, not exceeding ten, by being paid therefor.

The following extract from a communication published in one of the Boston daily papers will show the feeling which existed against the objects and organization of the men:—

Had this unlawful combination had for its object the enhancement of daily wages, it would have been left to its own care; but it now strikes the very nerve of industry and good morals, by dictating the hours of labor, abrogating the good old rule of our fathers, and pointing out the most direct course to poverty; for to be *idle* several of the most useful hours of the morning and evening will surely lead to intemperance and ruin.

That our readers at a distance may know the truth of their "oppression," we state that the hours of labor are from sunrise to sunset, allowing two hours for meals; and for this service a journeyman, who is a *tolerable* workman, gets two dollars and fifty cents. Thus, for one good, old-fashioned day's work, enough is paid to defray the board of a whole week. The vicissitudes of weather may occasion, at times, the loss of a day; but the shipwright is no more exposed to this casualty than is the mason, carpenter, painter, or many other tradesmen, who work as many hours as they can see for much less pay than the complaining ship-wrights get. The truth is, that such combinations never take place but in times of great depression, or, the reverse, of extreme prosperity, as is now the case with all whose labor depends upon the shipping interest. The course which the persons alluded to are thus pursuing will tend to lose them the respect not only of the merchants, their direct employers, but of all members of the community, and finally of themselves.

The journeymen carpenters and calkers failed to secure what they sought; but, through July and August, 1832, they were allowed two hours at noon, because of the extreme warmth of the weather and the fear of pestilence.

The defeat of the first strike for ten hours appeared at the time to be disastrous and humiliating. It is probable, however, that the moral effect of the repulse was more beneficial than victory would have been. Sympathy was aroused, the interests of cultivated circles were enlisted, and yet when the ten-hour day was gained, it was gained as the result of a strike.

While the merchants of Boston were saying that it was impossible to conduct their business on the ten-hour system, the system was adopted in New York and Philadelphia, after a struggle, of which mention will be made hereafter, and it was working satisfactorily.

The arguments adduced by the representatives of labor

in favor of the ten-hour movement did not fail to have their effect upon the thoughtful minds in the community. An article in the *New England Magazine* — a magazine of high rank in that day (1835) — spoke in no uncertain terms. It charged that the employing class was so exclusively engaged in its own affairs that the laborer was not only greatly neglected, but constantly liable to have his rights trampled upon, and to be injured by the competition of foreigners, whose increase ought to be checked by legislation. The writer says: —

> Is there no duty to be discharged? Is there nothing to be apprehended from the great mass of uneducated minds whose restless heavings are felt in every part of the land? Is there no danger that this chaos of intellect may, ere long, break forth like the rushing storm, and cover the country with desolation far and wide?

Public sentiment grew stronger in favor of the ship-workers, and the boon gained by New York and Philadelphia in 1832 or 1833 spread along the coast, and culminated in the proclamation of President Van Buren, fixing the hours of labor for persons employed in the navy-yards.

Captain Richard Trevellick, now of Detroit, Mich., who was a ship-carpenter in New York in the early days of the movement, thus describes the conditions under which the men worked, in letters to *Fincher's National Trades Review:* —

> Everywhere, from the Government ship-yards down to the ten-ton sloop set up in the woods miles from any place, the rule holds good. Hurrah! hurry and hiring men to-day; to-morrow, or day after, or next week, the place is as quiet as a grave-yard; the crisis is passed, hurry is over, the craft launched and gone, and so all the craftsmen — scattered in as many directions, perhaps, as there are men, in search of some other three-weeks' job.
>
> In some four or five of our larger cities ship-work is something more continuous and reliable; but even they are by no means exempt from depressions and sudden fluctuations; and whenever the "slack time" comes if the ship-carpenter, caulker, joiner, etc., is not absolutely discharged, his wages are reduced until he finds himself wondering "what he will do with it," his remuneration, at the highest figure, being no greater than that of some half a dozen other classes of mechanics, whose employment is constant and always under shelter, so that whatever time they may lose is voluntary.

He speaks thus of the regulation of the day's work: —

> As the order of labor in those days was to fall to in the morning at the first glance the bosses could catch at a sunbeam gilding the tallest spire in sight,

— there being no steeple in sight from the "Hook," bosses used to catch their matin sunbeams from the vane of the 170-foot Liberty-pole over in Grand street, below Lewis, — the stretch during the summer solstice, from "commencement" to twelve o'clock, was rather a long and tedious one. It would have been far more tedious but for an indulgence that custom had made as much of a necessity in a New York ship-yard as a grind-stone.

In our yard, at half-past eight A. M., Aunt Arlie McVane, a clever, kind-hearted, but awfully uncouth, rough sample of the "Ould Sod," would make her welcome appearance in the yard with her two great baskets, stowed and checked off with crullers, doughnuts, ginger-bread, turnovers, pies, and a variety of sweet cookies and cakes; and from the time Aunt Arlie's baskets came in sight until every man and boy, bosses and all, in the yard, had been supplied, always at one cent apiece for any article in the cargo, the pie, cake and cookie trade was a brisk one. Aunt Arlie would usually make the round of the yard and supply all hands in about an hour, bringing the forenoon up to half-past nine, and giving us from ten to fifteen minutes' breathing spell during lunch; no one ever hurried during "cake-time."

After this was over we would fall to again, until interrupted by Johnnie Gogean, the English candy-man, who came in always about half-past ten, with his great board, the size of a medium extension dining-table, slung before him, covered with all sorts of "stick," and several of sticky, candy, in one-cent lots. Bosses, boys and men — all hands, everybody — invested one to three cents in Johnnie's sweet wares, and another ten or fifteen minutes is spent in consuming it. Johnnie usually sailed out with a bare board about eleven o'clock, at which time there was a general sailing out of the yard and into convenient grog-shops after whiskey; only we had four or five men among us, and one apprentice — not quite a year my senior — who used to sail out pretty regularly ten times a day on an average; two that went for whiskey only when some one invited them to drink, being too mean to treat themselves; and two more who never went at all.

In the afternoon, about half-past three, we had a cake-lunch, supplied by Uncle Jack Grider, an old, crippled, superannuated ship-carpenter. No one else was ever allowed to come in competition with our caterers. Let a foreign candy-board or cake-basket make their appearance inside of the gates of our yard, and they would get chipped out of that directly.

At about five o'clock P. M., always, Johnnie used to put in his second appearance; and then, having expended money in another stick or two of candy, and ten minutes or so in its consumption, we were ready to drive away again till sun-down; then off home to supper.

Captain Trevellick, the same writer, thus describes the methods of settling difficulties in 1835: —

Thirty years ago the mechanics of the country had no other resource, no available means of coping with and conquering capital, whenever it began to inflict upon us its more objectionable features of serfdom, than by prompt and absolute defiance in refusals to labor until demands that we believed to be just were complied with. In those days there was little of tact, diplomacy, or spirit of concession manifested in any of our strikes. They were crude in conception, stubbornly contested, and resulted always in something of humiliation to the conquered party, — a sentiment never conducive to cordiality in the future. Besides, our early strikes almost always resulted in pecuniary loss to ourselves, whether we conquered or not.

Nevertheless, firmly imbued with the belief that our strikes being justifiable, would result in something better eventually, in some form that was all vague and indefinite to us then, we persisted in our strikes, improving their features always as time went on, doing the best we could, under the circumstances, to protect ourselves and prepare the way for future mechanical organizations more perfect in their moral and social economy.

Mechanical mankind had labored from sunrise to sunset, with only the hour of intermission at dinner-time, so long that, at the beginning of my apprenticeship, New York mechanics of all classes had no idea of a briefer term of labor; and one night, when some premature philosopher and philanthropist (I have forgotten who he was), preached *ten hours* to eight or nine hundred of us in the old Broadway Tabernacle, telling us earnestly that the time for a reduction of the hours of labor was close at hand, we laughed at his absurd theories, ourselves convinced that the advent of a ten-hour system of labor was ten times more remote than that of the millennium. This was, notwithstanding an honest, earnest and most eloquent appeal to our sympathies from Mr. James Harpier, then, as he has ever been since, the firm, fast, and consistent friend of mechanics. When the hats were passed around to take up a collection for the benefit of the first champion of the reduction of the hours of labor, so little did we understand our rights and necessities, and so ungrateful were we for the stout battle done in our behalf, that in every hat that went up to the speaker's stand there were infinitely more of Mrs. Miller's "fine cut," "old sojers," eyeless brass buttons, and "bungtown" coppers than silver quarters, shillings and sixpences.

I remember distinctly the inimitably droll, sarcastic manner in which we were reproved; it made many of us hang our heads in shame, and sneak off out of the Tabernacle as though we had been detected thieves.

At this time the general term for a strike was "turn out;" so when, some time after this, Mr. Trevellick was informed that they were going to "strike" the bosses, he supposed that they were going to do personal violence, and he protested; but, when it was explained to him that they were to "turn out" for hours, or going to "strike" for hours, he joined issue with them. This was at the time of one of the great ship-carpenters' strikes for the ten-hour system, and the one which proved successful. He writes: —

I think the strike continued ten days, during the whole of which time our bosses came and went about their business, just as if there was no difficulty anywhere; and when, at length, our rebels returned, saying that the bosses up the "island" had agreed to the ten-hour regulation and all hands were going to work again, the bosses said, "Very well, you can come on whenever you like." Thus was the ten-hour rule of labor inaugurated among New York ship-mechanics, and again all went on quietly as before.

Immediately after the adoption of the ten-hour system, a code of labor regulations was adopted, in which it was agreed that all the work performed on any craft afloat, whether new or old, was to be considered "old work," on which the day's work was to be *nine* hours, and if they worked till bell-time it was to count an extra eighth. So, also, if they went to work on any hurrying old job at six in the morning, that hour was to be another eighth of a day to them. He continued: —

The educational advance made by the mechanical and laboring classes in the United States since the inauguration of the ten-hour rule of labor has been more than equal to every step taken in that direction since the days of John the Baptist, and, for all that any of us know to the contrary, a thousand years previous to that era. Add the other two hours to the liberty term, and we shall increase the ratio of progress threefold, with the certainty of knowing that, with the generation next following, we or our country shall have, as a rule, mechanics and all classes of laboring men and women educated to a standard of physical, mental, moral and social excellence that will be its own security against idleness, vice, degradation and misery.

Comparing the advancement made in different sections, Mr. Trevellick writes: —

The mechanics of New York, Philadelphia and Baltimore have made, I think, about five times the progress towards moral and social respectability within the last twenty-five years that the Bostonians have, simply because twenty-five years ago Bostonians had five times fewer steps to climb up the moral and social ladder than the mechanics of her three sister cities above named. While a mechanical apprentice or journeyman mechanic of Boston was just, and as justly proud of being a respectable member of society, and a gentleman in general deportment twenty-five or thirty years ago as they are to-day, with us in New York, boy or man, we were rather proud to be known as one of the infamous "Chichester Gang," "Sons of Harmony," or a "Butt-Ender." Philadelphia mechanics of that day — boys and men, or those who ought to have been men — knew no more coveted distinction than that of a "killer" or a "Moyamensing Ranger." While Baltimoreans were prouder of the titles of "plug uglies," "blood-tubs" and "roughs" under half a dozen other distinctive names than they were of being good citizens or skilful mechanics.

He claims that the reduction of the hours of labor tended greatly to the overthrow of all these brutalisms, and that they rapidly came up from the depths, and contributed such examples and instructions to their provincial brethren all over the country as would develop their ambitions, energy, and determination not to be left behind in the mechanical reform race.

He concludes :—

> The constantly accumulating power of multiplied trades-unions throughout the length and breadth of the land, and the great eight-hour Magna Charta of emancipation for the American people from excessive labor are now becoming everywhere popular. Our march is shoulder to shoulder, in solid phalanx towards a common goal, that thirty years ago was beyond the orbit of Mars to the operative mechanics and workingmen of this country.

THE MECHANICS' BELL.

The story of the "Mechanics' Bell" is the story of the first victory won on this continent for less hours of toil. As the "Liberty Bell" rang out the proclamation of liberty from monarchical control, so the "Mechanics' Bell" proclaimed the liberty of leisure for the sons of toil.

The old "Mechanics' Bell" hangs in its skeleton tower at the East River, foot of Fourth street, New York, directly opposite the spot where once "Skinny" Beadle's cottage stood. Beadle was a watchman for Smith & Dimon, ship-builders, whose yard, more than sixty years ago, was on the territory where now stands the tower of the old bell. Old "Skinny" died during the campaign of "Buck. and Breck." in 1856. For a long time his old cottage was untenanted, and was said to be haunted. Men could be found who were positive they saw old "Skinny" long after he was buried.

The original "Mechanics' Bell" was erected in 1831. It first stood in a coal-yard, and afterward found a resting-place in Bishop & Simonson's yard. Its first ringer was a man named McCoy, who died more than a quarter of a century ago. When the bell was first erected, there were no regular hours of labor, and the mechanics worked from sun to sun. It was no unusual sight to see men working in the ship yards and along the wharves at four o'clock in the morning. For the ship yard men, life was simply work and sleep, recreation being almost lost sight of. Many efforts were made to change this state of things, and strikes were resorted to after arbitration had failed. At first the strikes were for regulating the hours of eating, sleeping, and working, and they were resisted by the bosses, who would not listen to this new idea. The strikes broke out periodically. At length the bosses divided on this question, and an unkindly feeling sprang up between a majority of them on one side, and the remainder and the mechanics on the other. After a bitter struggle, the mechanics carried their point. They then demanded ten hours a day, without naming the particular hours. Against this the bosses struck, but gave in after a short struggle.

The mechanics, proud of their victory, determined to have a new bell, to be known as the "Ten-hour Bell." They took the old bell, which was small, and had it recast into the new one, dropping gold, silver and copper coins into the furnace. The new bell was raised with appropriate honors in 1844, and "Old Baxter," a veteran of 1812, was appointed bell-ringer. The bell was now placed on a new skeleton tower on the top of a blacksmith's shop in Webb's shipyard, on Lewis street, between Fifth and Sixth streets. On one of the cross-pieces of the tower was placed a golden sign, with the words, "Mechanics' Bell."

The first ten-hour day was from 6 A. M. to 8 A. M., when an hour was given for lunch. The bell rang again five minutes before nine, and rang five minutes while the men proceeded to work. It rang again at noon, when an hour was given for dinner; at 1, when the men returned to work, and again at 6, when the day's work ended. The bell, at five minutes of 9, also served as a school-bell for the old Fifth-street School. After about ten years of this arrangement, the ten-hour day was regulated as at present. Matters thus continued until the eight-hour strike, during the war. The mechanics who then owned the bell ordered that it should be rung at 8 A. M., 12 M., and 1 and 5 P. M.; and it continued thus to ring during that strike. After the failure of the strike, the bell was rung as previously. For many years, however, on Saturdays the bell has rung at 4 P. M., instead of 6, work then stopping. On Monday, May 17, 1886, the bell began to ring at 7, 12, 1 and 5, making only nine hours a day, and the ship-joiners of the Eleventh Ward are now working under that system.

Webb's shipyard, where the "Mechanics' Bell" stood, changed hands, and the decay of ship-building, the last ship having been built in New York during the eight-hour strike, having driven the mechanics away from their old stamping-ground, an effort was made by Webb's successors to seize the bell. Their excuse was the damage to them by having boys throw stones at it. The old bell had not rung for a long time, and they thought no one would bother their heads about it. They intended to sell the old bell to pay for damages. But one day William Douglas, a veteran shipwright and president of the Shipwrights' Association during the eight-hour strike, made his appearance at the old bell-tower, and, to the astonishment of the neighbors, proceeded to take down the bell. The news spread like wildfire, and an excited crowd soon gathered, demanding the reason of this action. Douglas explained; and, instead of being mobbed, he was loudly applauded. By adroit talk, Douglas secured the confidence of the owners of the yard, and when the bell was down a cart was handy, on which the old bell disappeared. For a long time its whereabouts were unknown, except to a few devoted men sworn to secrecy. At length, it was determined to raise it again. The old stock wished it replaced in the Eleventh Ward, the shipyard district, while others wished it taken to Greenpoint, on the ground that the bell should follow the ship-building business, which had left New York City. At an exciting meeting the New Yorkers won. A new tower was erected, and the old bell was raised, amid the most intense enthusiasm, where it now stands, at the foot of Fourth street, East River. There it remained until October, 1880, when it cracked and ceased ringing.

It was recast about a month later, and was again hung on the day of President Garfield's election, and has never ceased ringing regularly since.

It now rings four times a day; ringing at 7 A.M. for the men to go to work, again at 12 M. for dinner, at 1 P.M. for the return to work, and at 5 P.M. to finish,—thus making a nine-hour day. It has rung under this system only a few months, an agreement between the mechanics and the "bosses" having brought this about.

The ten-hour system did not extend outside of the "old workers" of Boston for several years. It was first adopted on new work in the shipyards of Medford, Mass., — at that time the chief ship-building centre of the New England States, — in 1840, as will be seen by the following statement of Mr. John Stetson, an old ship-carpenter, now living in that town: —

MEDFORD, MASS., *July* 19, 1886.

* * * * Early in the spring of 1840, namely, April 14th, the day of my marriage, I, with a gang of six other men, under a written contract made by me, commenced a job of ceiling and putting in lower deck of a ship in the yard of Jotham Stetson, in Medford. The men engaged with me were Benjamin H. Sampson, Luther Turner, Amos Hutchings and others. Before commencing the job, we took a vote to do it on the ten-hour plan. This was the first work done, I believe, on this system in private yards, although it had been to some extent adopted in government yards.

At the same time Mr. Hutchings had made a contract for the same gang to plank a ship for Mr. James O. Curtis. Mr. Curtis' opposition to the plan was so great that he would not allow the work to be done by us.

Mr. Stetson was extremely indignant, and opposed us bitterly; but was obliged to submit, as we had a written contract with him. He contented himself with announcing that in future he should reserve the right of employing men who would do as he wished. I told him he always had had that privilege, as I had the right of working for whom I chose.

Public sentiment, as well as the ship-builders, was strongly opposed to the ten-hour plan. The builders sent to other places for men, who, on arriving and learning the state of affairs, refused to go to work on the old plan. Several public meetings were held in the town hall.

However, we did that job on the new time-table, and I never did a day's work on the old plan after that. Mr. Curtis' opposition was such that the gang all but myself went to Haverhill, where they built a ship on ten-hours' time, and thence they went to Newburyport to plank a ship, — the first ten-hour work done there, as I believe.

At the beginning of this movement, business was very dull; but soon after all the builders made contracts to build, and business reviving, all fell into line, and the system was established. Yours truly,

JOHN STETSON.

This coincides with the experience in Bath, Me., as given to us by Mr. Henry T. Delano, an old ship-carpenter, now living, who introduced the ten-hour system in that city, in

1847, as related in the chapter on the "History of the Movement," page 96.

It will be noted that the proclamation of President Van Buren, establishing the ten-hour system in all public establishments, was issued on April 10, 1840.

The ship-carpenters and calkers continued their organization, and the workers on old work soon commenced the agitation for the eight-hour day, gaining it in 1849; and the agitation for shorter time continued among the other building trades, notably the stone-workers, who probably were second only to the ship-workers in their movement in this direction. Strikes occurred for less hours of work on Saturday, for advances in wages, and against proposed reductions. Great carelessness existed then, as now, in the preservation of the records of the labor associations, and little is known of their individual efforts. It was not until the national and international organizations came into existence that much information could be obtained; and, even in the case of many of these, the records have been lost by the secretaries, especially where an organization has disappeared for a time, to be revived and controlled by new men.

The discovery of gold in California revived the ship-building trades, and many of the ship-workers themselves were among the emigrants to California. They proceeded to organize as soon as work in their craft demanded. Isolated unions of house-carpenters, painters, roofers, bricklayers, stone-masons and stone-workers generally, existed.

In the spring of 1853, there was an extensive simultaneous movement in the building trades, the principal demand being for an increase of wages. The Boston ship-joiners on repairs made an unsuccessful strike for eight hours, which they succeeded in gaining the next year. The movement for an advance of wages was especially strong in Philadelphia, and many strikes occurred. A Philadelphia correspondent of the New York *Tribune*, in 1853, confessed that an advance of wages was absolutely necessary in order to enable the workingmen to support their familes under the burdensome prices.

House-carpenters, shoemakers and riggers held meetings and adopted resolutions expressing a determination to obtain an advance. The metal-workers of New York City and Brooklyn held a meeting in April of that year, and organized by the selection of Mr. A. B. Smith as chairman, and Mr. William Caldwell as secretary. They voted to demand an increase in wages, their present rates being from ten to twelve shillings a day, and they concluded to demand two dollars. The ship-joiners resolved to demand $2.50 per day.

During the summer months, the journeymen house-carpenters of Boston held a meeting for the organization and government of the Carpenters' Association. They voted to adopt a ten-hour system, and to raise a fund for the benefit of those persons whose employers should not accede to their demands.

A Board of Trade report of about 1853 says, that in Boston there was a scarcity of men; that there was much repairing going on, and not more than half the number of men to be obtained that might work conveniently on vessels.

The report of the second commission on the hours of labor, Massachusetts House Document 44, 1867, says: —

> Those who are familiar with the former condition of the workmen in this business know that it is much elevated in consequence of a reduction of the hours of labor and associated effort in trades-unions. They are remembered as working in 1835 thirteen or fourteen hours a day for $1.50 per diem. They lived, for the most part, in the city near their work. The younger portion formed the nucleus of the Fort Hill rowdyism. It was a period when, in connection with fire department, they kept the city in constant alarm. From 1853 to the present time, the same class of labor, and some of the same individuals, are found in possession, as we have shown, of the eight-hour day, — the president of the association stating that at least one-third of them are owners of property.

In 1856, the ship-carpenters of California had organized and moved, with other trades, for the eight-hour day; for it must be remembered that the eight-hour system was gained only for workers on old work. Continued efforts were made to secure the same privileges for new work among the house-carpenters and other building trades, but little was gained. Constant demands were made, and in 1866 the ship-carpenters employed in the various yards in Greenpoint, L. I., went on strike for the eight-hour system.

This movement extended to other trades, and on April 5th a mass-meeting of the workingmen of New York, Jersey City and Brooklyn in favor of the eight-hour system was held in Union Square. Four stands were erected in the vicinity of the Maison Doree; and in consequence of the mildness of the evening, as well as the interest taken in the subject, the attendance was very large. About eight o'clock delegations from the different trades-unions, with banners, music, torch-lights, and transparencies marched into Union Square, and took up their positions around the several stands. Mr. John Reed, the president of the Workingmen's Union, was chosen chairman, and H. A. Whitfield secretary.

Mr. Reed made a very able speech, in which he referred to the fact that they were not aware of their strength physically and politically, or of how it might be effectually used. He said: "It is our glory and boast that we have reached a higher standard. We can afford to put this question on the very highest grounds." He said that the system of co-operation, or self-help, was the great and only solution of the labor problem, but that it was not available at present; that the great mass must get along on the old wage-system for some time to come. A series of resolutions were adopted, regretting the defeat of the Eight-hour Bill in the Assembly, and asking the adoption of the ordinance by the common council of the city.

Horace Greeley was introduced, and was received with tremendous cheering. He said it appeared to him a desirable, natural and proper arrangement, that they should have one-third of their time for sleep, one-third for labor, and one-third for all other employments; it seemed to him a beneficial result, at which they should all aim, and to which he believed and trusted they would ultimately come. He said: —

The fault of this age is that workers, whether with hand or brain, labor too hard and too long. We have too many idlers, and too many who do a great deal more than one man's part. In this city we employ more than a hundred thousand persons, who add nothing to the wealth of the world; they are mere distributors.

He had but little faith in legislation for reducing the hours of labor, but he was willing to see the experiment tried. He thought labor should take a little more responsibility upon itself. Addresses were made at the other stands by prominent labor men.

On April 17th, the ship-joiners of New York and vicinity held a mass-meeting, and adopted, among others, the following resolution: —

Resolved, That we, the ship-joiners of New York and vicinity, in mass-meeting assembled, do hereby announce through the city press that we boldly sustain and heartily co-operate with the following trades in the movement to reduce the hours of labor: New York caulkers, ship-wrights, riggers, house-carpenters, and ship-painters.

The master-shipwrights and caulkers of New York published an article against the movement, which aroused the indignation of the men, who claimed that the names subscribed to the article represented only one-fifth of the capital invested. The ship-workers proposed to do the work themselves, without the aid of the master ship-wrights, agreeing to do it as quickly and as perfectly, at less cost. They also published a card, correcting various statements made by the master ship-wrights in their article, in which they solicited work.

The New York *Tribune*, of May 10th, reports a meeting of the ship-carpenters and joiners on the preceding evening to take action in reference to a strike, which had then been continued six weeks. The movement was controlled by the Workingmen's Union, which consisted of the various trades of the city.

The *Tribune* said: —

There are nearly ten thousand mechanics now out of employment by reason of the strike, whose united earnings would have amounted to nearly one hundred and fifty thousand dollars per week.

At the meeting, the president denounced the manner in which the press had spoken of the strike.

On May 15th, the New York papers announced the failure of the strike. The *World*, referring to the matter, said: —

He is not a friend of American workmen who does not tell them plainly why, in the struggle which they have sought, justice is not on their side. As for legislating eight hours to be a day's work, it is contrary to the true interests of the workingmen that government — city, State or federal — should meddle with the matter at all. No number of hours can hereafter, any more than now, be the measure of a day's work in the various industries of different men.

The *Tribune*, while agreeing with the *World* in respect to legislation, said: —

But the *World* fails to take into account the counteracting influences, the continual progress and important results of labor-saving inventions, of railroads and canals. Between 1850 and 1860 the population of this country increased but little over thirty per cent., while the increase of our natural wealth was over one hundred per cent., and that of our efficiency as producers of wealth was fully as great, so that it by no means follows that we must work harder for a given result in 1870 than we did in 1860.

A large and enthusiastic meeting of the workingmen of Boston was held in that city, on July 2, of the same year, to hear a true statement of the calkers' lockout, and to tender aid. Colonel C. E. Rowell presided. A speech was made by Mr. C. E. Turner, president of the Boston Calkers' Association. He stated that this was not a strike, but a lockout, and that the lockout was caused by the fact that the ship-calkers of Boston would not work on ships forwarded from New York. He said: —

We were obliged to assist our fellow-craftsmen. We have worked for fifteen years on the eight-hour system, and want not only to continue it, but to help others to it.

It seems that a vessel, which was chartered in New York, was forwarded to Boston for repairs, and the men refused to work, unless New York calkers could come and assist on the work on the eight-hour system.

It was these strikes and lockouts and the previous agitation which led to the eight-hour law being passed in 1868, which was inaugurated in the navy-yards, shortly after the Fourth of July, of that year.

In the spring of 1869, workmen in the yards received official notice that their pay would be reduced one-fifth. Opportunity was afforded them to labor ten hours at the usual rate of wages. The government was desirous of increasing its force at the time, but found it impossible to obtain men who would comply with the terms imposed, and many of the employees withdrew. This led to the proclamation of General Grant, as published in Chapter V. From this time the depression in the ship-building industry has seriously affected the men, and very little has been attempted in the direction of organization.

In Philadelphia, they were the first to organize under the Knights of Labor after its formation by the garment-cutters. Strikes have occurred in the ship-building centres during this time,—some of them for higher wages, some against reduction, and some for less hours of labor.

The craft has lost its prominence in the labor movement, probably to revive with power on the revival of their industry.

AMALGAMATED SOCIETY OF CARPENTERS AND JOINERS.

This organization was founded in England, in June, 1860, but there are several branches in the United States. Candidates for admission must be in good health, have worked at the trade five years, be good workmen, of steady habits and good moral character, and not less than 20 nor more than 45 years of age. The scale of entrance-fees varies from 7 shillings and 6 pence at 25 to 1 pound and 15 shillings at 45. In 1860, it had 618 members and £321 assets; but at the end of 1885 it had 25,781 members and £50,850 assets. Its average annual membership was 12,180. The total amount of benefits paid out per member for 26 years was £46 10*s.*

It appears that on the 31st of January, for the last eleven years, the number per one thousand members unemployed was as follows: 1876, 16; 1877, 26; 1878, 42; 1879, 187; 1880, 181; 1881, 191; 1882, 68; 1883, 81; 1884, 77; 1885, 108; 1886, 180. The most severe season was 1879, when the cost for unemployed benefit per member was £1 12*s.* 9*d.* per member; and 1885 came next, with £1 7*s.* 3*d.* The depression of 1879 came after several years of fairly good trade; but that of 1885 came after losses in preceding years, and was most severely felt. The annual report for 1886 says:—

During the year we have only made one serious resistance to a reduction of wages, viz.: at Sunderland, and in this case the men fortunately sustained their point. The struggle, however, was so prolonged and costly that both sides agreed and have succeeded in forming a Board of Conciliation and Arbitration, to which all future disputes shall be referred.

The branches are now distributed as follows: England, 338; Ireland, 20; Scotland, 15; United States, 25; Canada, 6; New Zealand, 10; Australia, 22; South Africa, 4; total, 440. There is kept in the treasury a balance equal, at least, to two pounds per member. The society publishes an annual report,—that for 1886 making 366 pages,—which is mostly filled with statistical information as to the state of the order, as a whole, and of the branches in particular.

THE BROTHERHOOD OF CARPENTERS AND JOINERS.

The Brotherhood of Carpenters and Joiners was organized at a Convention of Carpenters' Unions held in Chicago, Ill., August 8, 1881. Prior to this organization, many local unions had existed, and efforts had been continually made for the formation of a national organization. The first attempt was made in 1854, and the second in 1867. The preamble to the constitution sets forth the objects to be

To rescue our trade from the low level to which it has fallen, and, by mutual effort to raise ourselves to that position in society to which we are justly entitled; to cultivate a feeling of friendship among the craft; and to elevate the moral, intellectual and social condition of all journeymen carpenters. It is furthermore our object to assist each other to secure employment; to furnish aid in cases of death or permanent disability, and for mutual relief, and other benevolent purposes.

The officers consist of a general president, eight vice-presidents, a general secretary, treasurer, and an executive board. The executive board is composed of five members, elected from the union or unions within a radius of ten miles of the city selected as headquarters. This board has power to decide all points of law, settle all grievances, and to authorize strikes in conformity with the constitution.

The constitution provides that whenever a dispute arises between an employer or employers and members of the

Brotherhood, the members shall lay the matter before the local union, which shall appoint an arbitration committee to adjust the matter; then, if the members of the committee cannot settle the dispute, the matter shall be referred to the union. If a two-thirds vote of secret ballot shall decide that the members shall be sustained, then they shall be authorized to strike; which strike shall take effect immediately whenever the demand is refused by the employers the following day.

The organization provides a funeral-benefit of $250 if a member dies, and $50 in case of the death of the wife of a member. It also provides a disability benefit. Any member in good standing, who becomes permanently disabled by accidental injuries received at his work, which incapacitates him from again following the trade, shall be entitled to $100 for a six months' membership, and $200 dollars for a two years' membership. The majority of the local unions have weekly sick-benefits, ranging from $3.00 to $3.50 per week.

The organization favors the establishment of building leagues; is opposed to piece-work and convict labor, and desires uniform lien laws throughout the United States and Canada.

The First Convention of the Brotherhood after the organization was held in Philadelphia, in 1882. The Second Convention was held in New York, in 1884. The Convention of 1883 was postponed, in order to place the unions on a better foundation, giving them more opportunity to ascertain the actual requirements of the organization, and become more familiar with the constitution.

The struggle during the first year or two of the organization, as of all other workingmen's societies, was a difficult one; but at this convention the general secretary was able to report that the association was out of debt, and that a surplus of funds was on hand. During the preceding year, twenty-one new unions had been formed, — an increase of 1,866 members in good standing. The secretary reported that strikes had occurred in Chicago and New Orleans, and had succeeded in fixing the standard rate of wages at three dollars per day.

The strike lasted three weeks, and resulted in partial success. A strike occurred in Canada for nine hours per day, lasting two months and a half; but, owing to the influx of immigration, a compromise was made upon eight hours as a day's work on Saturday. The secretary says: —

> The successful movements for nine hours in the spring of 1885 on the Pacific Coast, in San Francisco, San Rafael, Oakland, and Alameda, has had a salutary effect in those localities, and it is due to the example of our Brotherhood that other trades are falling into the same line all over the country. A reduction of the hours of labor on Saturday in St. Catharines and Hartford, and Philadelphia, and Boston, has been accomplished, an agitation has been created, out of which has grown a strong central organization of various trades in Philadelphia, known as the Short-Hour League. The usual custom of reducing the wages in winter and payment by the hour has ceased to be the rule where the union has any power. The rates of wages have become firmer, and all men less exposed to reduction of wages; and on organization they have been able to save themselves from any imposition.

He favors the forming of trades-assemblies central councils, and calls upon the members to secure a close co-operation of the bricklayers, plasterers, and laborers of each city, and refers to the fraternal feelings existing between the organizations and the Knights of Labor in several cities. At this convention, a Declaration of Principles was adopted, containing these salient points: That as the average laboring man expends his entire earnings immediately, every dollar added to his wages adds to every market he patronizes; and, therefore, that every reduction of wages immediately cripples all markets; that a reduction of hours of days' work increases the opportunities and intelligence of the laborer, as well as increases the demand for labor in price for a day's work; that it is ruinous to reduce domestic wages to enable our country to compete with foreign markets; that as the laboring classes are united all over the world, and regard it as nationally as well as morally due of all for the interest of all to stop this ruinous competition of wages; that all protected productions are protected at the expense of citizens, and that such industries have no moral right, and should have no legal right, to employ foreign labor, or persons who send or carry their earnings out of the country; that all aliens shall be employed by self-sustaining industries, and not by those receiving support by tax upon the citizens; that protected industries should have no legal right to reduce, or aid in reducing, wages from any standard. They object to prison-contract labor, because it puts the criminal in competition with honorable labor. They hold that voting is better than striking, but that both are right and necessary, and that no wage-worker should vote for any man or any party that does not directly support the labor cause by thought or argument and action; nor should any wage-worker vote for any man or party who has, does, or will oppose any man opposed to the party.

The next biennial convention was held at Buffalo, N. Y., August 3d, and continued four days. The general secretary, in his report, congratulates the members upon the great growth of the organization. One hundred and forty-eight new unions had been formed, and six unions reorganized. The general secretary, in his report, says:—

This convention marks the entrance into the sixth year of our history as an organization; and in that time a work has been accomplished that, when we contemplate its magnitude, our hearts swell with a modest and exultant pride in the results achieved.

As the humble founder of this Brotherhood, it affords me the immense pleasure to predict that, from present indications, our society, before many years, will be one of the most powerful trades organizations in America, and second to none in point of members and financial standing. For that object I have labored and struggled for many a long and weary day; and I take this occasion to thank the delegates here assembled for their presence, and the officers and members of the local unions, for their faithful aid and co-operation in this noble and exalted work.

Referring to the condition of trade, he said:—

The past year has not been as brisk for carpenter-work as was anticipated in the early spring, though in some locations it has been fairly good. The railroad strikes in the Southwest had a very depressing effect on speculative capital, and it shrank from contemplated investment in real estate, causing quite a depression in the building trades. As a consequence, the movement this spring for shorter hours among the workmen in the building trades were thereby much embarrassed. Trade has improved considerably of late; wages and prices, however, are by no means commensurate to the work, while in the majority of cities the labor market is constantly overcrowded with carpenters. In the two years that had intervened the Association had increased its membership over seventeen thousand, making a total membership of 21,423. The financial affairs were in a prosperous condition. He reported eight unions working eight hours per day, seventeen working nine hours per day, and twenty-one working shorter hours on Saturday. Seventeen thousand nine hundred and fifty dollars had been paid in benefits. In relation to the standing of the Brotherhood with other societies, he reports that the Carpenters' Assembly, Knights of Labor, of Troy, N. Y., refused to work with members of the Brotherhood, and struck against them.

He adds: —

I wrote, on March 18, 1886, to the General Secretary of the Knights of Labor, proposing a mutual interchange of cards between our respective organizations. To this I received a promise that the subject would be referred to the General Executive Board of the Knights of Labor, but up to date nothing has been done in the premises.

He refers to the meeting of the representatives of the thirty-two national and international unions to bring about harmonious relations between the unions and Knights of Labor. He called the meeting because, as he says, "I discerned a secret and formidable movement of a certain element within the Knights of Labor bent upon hostility to trades-unions, and aiming to attack them singly, and, if possible, encompass their destruction." "Friendly relations," he said, "are maintained between the Brotherhood of this country and the carpenters' unions of Great Britain, Germany, France and other European countries.

Referring to the strikes for eight hours on May 1st, he says: —

In twenty-one cities our local unions have gained twenty-five cents per day advance in wages, making in all fifty-three cities where our local unions have made gains the past year, either in more wages or in reducing hours, while only in nine cities have our local unions failed to secure their demands, and in these cities they demanded the eight-hour system last May. A resumé shows that 2,486 of our members are working eight hours per day, 5,824 are on nine hours per day, and 1,118 are having shorter hours on Saturdays. This makes a total gain to these members of 65,894 hours per week, adding to the gains on the Pacific Coast, which amount to 6,540 hours per week, makes a sum total of 72,434 hours per week gained to our members through organization. It now remains with this convention to take wise and judicious steps, whereby a reduction of the hours of labor may be more universally established in the trade.

At this convention, W. J. Shields, of Boston, was elected general president, and P. J. McGuire was re-elected general secretary.

From 12 local unions in 1881, the Brotherhoood has increased to 214 local unions, at the present writing, and from a membership of 2,042 it has grown to 42,521 members, — a gain of 18,481 members the past two years. Its jurisdiction stretches from Union No. 83, of Halifax, Nova Scotia, to San Francisco, Los Angeles and British Columbia, with 11 local unions in Canada, and more than a score of unions in the Southern States, as far south as New Orleans and Galveston. In the Southern States the colored men working at the trade have taken hold of the organization with avidity, and the result is, the Brotherhood embraces 14 unions of colored carpenters in the South.

It is by no means unusual to see colored delegates in attendance at the conventions of the Brotherhood; for the organization recognizes no distinction on account of color, race, nationality, religion, or politics, — its members recognizing each other only as American workingmen. Its constitutions and documents, however, are translated and printed in the German, French, Bohemian and Scandavian languages.

CHAPTER XIV.

MISCELLANEOUS TRADES.

Trades Organizations, Past and Present — Their Influence on the Labor Question — Axe-makers' Unions — Panic, 1873 — Reduction in Wages — Forty per cent. Reduction in 1880 — Strikes — Axe-makers Affiliate with K. of L. — Journeymen Bakers' National Union — Nationality of its Members — Early Attempts to Better their Condition — Employers Make Concessions — Unions Formed in all Large Cities—Boilermakers and Iron Shipbuilders' First Organization — Branches in U. S. and Canada — Opposed to Strikes — St. Paul Strike — Union Victorious — Bricklayers and Masons — An International Organization — Annual Convention — Demoralizing Effect of Panic, 1873 — Union both Benevolent and Protective — Barbers Organize a Protective Union — Druggists' Ware and Glassblowers Organize, in 1874 — Improved League — Men Imported from Germany — Manufacturers Attempt to Break Up the Organization — Flourishing Condition of the Organization — Amalgamated Engineers — Its Membership — Painters' Union — Organized, 1856 — International Furniture Workers' Union — Attempts to Enforce the Eight-Hour Law — Granite-Cutters — National Union Organized — Discharges and Lockouts — Combination of Employers to Reduce Wages — Horse-Railroad Men — Strikes on the New York City Horse-Railroad Lines — National Silk and Fur-hatters — National Association Formed — New York Stereotypers' Association — Journeymen Tailors' National Association — The Telegraphers — Their Strikes — Wood-Carvers — Wool-Hat Finishers.

NEARLY every trade and occupation has had in the past, as most of them have in the present, some form of a trades organization. Each one of these crafts or callings has its own peculiar history. As a rule, these organizations have had but short existence, taking new forms and new names and adopting new methods, as the exigencies of the times demanded. They have tended very much to the development of the labor question. One by one they join some federation, either in their town or city, under the name of central trades and labor unions, or by uniting with other unions, and, after a time, form a national organization of their trade. Since the organization of the Knights of Labor, trade assemblies have been organized, and some unions have received charters from the General Assembly of the Order as Trade Districts. Notably among these is the Miners' National Assembly, of which William H. Bailey, a member of the Executive Board, is District Master Workman.

In this chapter we give, in their alphabetical order, a brief abstract of the history of some of the labor unions not included in the foregoing chapters. We are obliged to omit from this list some of the organizations of the glass industry; also the horse-shoers, iron-moulders, metal-workers, piano-makers and plasterers. The glass-workers, in some of the branches, have had organizations in this country as far back as 1848 or 1850.

The glass-blowers' organizations at one time held an almost complete monopoly of the skilled craftsmen, and the price-lists of the union were accepted by the manufacturers without question; and, in conversation with some of the manufacturers years ago, we found them favorable to the organization: yet the glass-blowers have had many and fierce struggles as an organized body and as individual craftsmen. In New Jersey, the truck system prevailed to a great extent; and it was the custom of the manufacturers to issue a "currency" of their own, contrary to law. The organization succeeded finally in electing one of their prominent members to the New Jersey legislature, and by public agitation succeeded, through the combined efforts of the State Conventions of the unions, in securing some beneficial legislation.

The window-glass blowers, having a charter from the Knights of Labor, hold a complete monopoly of their craft. The story of some of their contests to gain this desired end reveals the utmost heroism and devotion to their cause. Their motto is, "Never surrender!" and since they have come under the shield of the Knights of Labor, they have sent their agents to Europe and organized the workers there, — Isaac

Cline, whose picture appears elsewhere in the work, being at one time their agent.

The horse-shoers now have a national organization, with James Rafferty, of Pittsburgh, as president. This was a difficult craft to organize, on account of the numberless small shops, where one or two men were employed; but, as the horse-railroads and other great enterprises tended to congregate these workers in large bodies, they succeeded first in forming local organizations, and then bringing them together into a national body.

The Iron Moulders' Union for a time was one of the great leading unions of the country. It has had some of the ablest leaders of the movement as its officers, and covered the principal points of its industry from East to West. The national organization has its headquarters at Cincinnati, Ohio, with Mr. T. S. Fitzpatrick as its president.

Of the Metal Workers' National Union, we have no information at hand. W. M. Schultz is the general secretary, with his headquarters in New York City.

The piano-makers commenced to organize shortly after that industry was introduced, and have had many hardly-contested struggles for advanced wages and for lessening the hours of labor. Their headquarters are in New York City.

The plasterers, as a class, were especially prominent in the struggle for eight-hours, presenting, in the great processions which took place in the principal cities in 1872, a fine appearance. Many plasterers' unions have existed outside of the national organization, and some of them are now organized under the Knights of Labor. The general secretary of the national organization, James Murphy, has his headquarters at Buffalo, N. Y.

The plumbers were among the first of the trades to gain the eight-hour system, which they succeeded in holding for a number of years. All efforts to secure information from the officers of these organizations having failed, we but thus briefly refer to them. In all cases where the history of a trade has been given, we have obtained the information from the leading officers of the several unions.

THE AXE-MAKERS' UNIONS.

The first Axe-makers' Union was formed at a recent period, compared with the organization of unions in other trades. This was largely because, up to about thirteen years ago, axe-makers were very well satisfied with their lot. Till then they worked less hours a day, and received much better compensation, than other mechanics. Five or six hours a day was considered a day's work, for which the axe-maker received $5.00 or $6.00 per day, his helper $3.00 or $4.00, while the unskilled laborers about the shop received $2.00 or $2.50 per day of eight hours. Then, also, they used to be at liberty in the afternoons, and people would wonder if they worked at all. Of course, such a state of affairs did not incite the axe-makers to any action for bettering their condition, or for even preserving the existing conditions. When a member of the craft proposed forming a union, he was cried down as a "crank," and was told there was no need for a union.

At this time the axe-makers were chiefly American and Irish. Each bit-drawer had a helper, who served an apprenticeship, and became an axe-maker in turn, as a locomotive fireman learns to become an engineer in time. An axe-maker named Horrigan introduced French Canadians into the trade at cheap prices, whose competition had the usual result of lowering wages.

The first union was formed in Lewiston, Penn., in 1869, more for fraternal purposes than anything else. It existed only nine or ten months. Branches were started at Lockhaven and Millhall, Penn., and Cleveland, Ohio, and an unsuccessful attempt was made to organize at Rochester, N. Y. These unions did not live to see the necessity of wider organization.

During the panic of 1873, a general reduction of wages took place throughout the country, averaging from ten to twenty per cent. The workmen now made more axes per day, and made the old wages. Then there was another cut, and the daily production was again increased, until where, formerly, an axe-maker would make 100 bits per day, the limit of 200 per day was finally reached; and where the wages had been $4.75 and $3.75 for 100 drawn bits, over-coat steel, they are now about $1.10 for the helpers, and $1.50 for the bit-drawers, making the present daily average earnings in the vicinity of $2.20 and $3.00, respectively, except in Massachusetts and New Hampshire, where the wages fall somewhat below this standard.

After the above-mentioned unions had died out, no organization existed until the formation of a union in Pittsburgh, Penn., in 1877. The first work of this union was to strike against a reduction of wages. This strike lasted four months, and was successful. About the same time, a union was organized in Cleveland by Thomas B. Barry, then working at that trade. This union succeeded in obtaining a ten per cent. increase of pay, and the institution of a "draw-pay," whereby, two weeks after the regular monthly pay-day, they could draw fifteen dollars on account. The members, having accomplished thus much, became careless, owing to the opposition to unions, and allowed the union to go down.

Up to 1880, the Knights of Labor had worked secretly. Some few axe-makers had joined them, and were hoping to see their craft generally become Knights. In that year came a forty per cent. reduction of wages, and agitation was begun to secure an advance. In Pittsburgh, Beaver Falls, Lewiston, Tyrone, Millhall, and Cleveland the shops had been organized into the Knights of Labor. A strike was inaugurated in November, 1880. Mr. Barry was then Master Workman of District No. 47 and of the Axe-makers' Assembly. He was requested by the men in Pittsburgh to move for an increase of wages. He felt that the Order was yet young, and that if it met with defeat it would help to sustain the reputation of Cleveland as the graveyard of trades-unions. He sought to secure the increase by peaceful methods. The chairman of the shop committee at Pittsburgh agreed with him. They thought the vast difference in prices paid in the shops was good reason why the company should not refuse, and so asked for an advance. The Cleveland axe-makers desired a twenty per cent. advance, with or without a strike. Mr. Barry tried to avoid a strike, and was called a "scab" for his pains. He replied that, as for himself, having other resources, he was prepared to go into a strike and carry it through, and never go into a shop again if he did not get the advance. A committee of the best men in the shop waited on the officials of the company, and requested an advance; but the officials refused to negotiate or talk with them. The committee returned to their respective departments, and in a short time the arms of the hammers were thrown up, the dampers of the fires knocked down, and the "heats" taken out of the fires, and thrown on top of the "caps." The strike lasted nine months; and, while it was not a complete success, it probably cost the company $200,000 to carry on the fight. They were obliged to employ unskilled men, in consequence of which they lost, never to regain, their trade and standing in the market.

The workmen were scattered, but Mr. Barry was the only victim. When the strike terminated he had exhausted his means, and become somewhat involved in debt. He then learned that he could not get work at his trade in the United States or Canada. The doors of sixty-two shops had been closed against him as a dangerous man. The Association of Manufacturers by vote debarred him from working at his trade. He went to work on the Cleveland Breakwater at $1 per day. Finally a shop in Saginaw, Mich., not in the association, offered him work, and he removed there with his family. Later, this company joined the association, and was obliged to discharge him, in July, 1882. The man who notified him expressed his sorrow at it, but said he must go.

The unions were all connected with the Knights of Labor at this time, but were broken up as a result of the strike. At present they are forming other assemblies of the Knights, secretly in some places, but openly in others.

JOURNEYMEN BAKERS' NATIONAL UNION.

Prior to January 13, 1885, when the first convention was held, the various bakers' unions amounted to but little. Most bakers are Germans. Their excessively long hours and the high temperature of their shops, and other abnormal influences caused them to be indifferent to the great questions of the day. Here and there they tried to better their condition,—organized, went on strike,—but in almost all cases failed, either by treachery of their own men or of their bosses. In almost all cases, after such failures, those bodies, or rather their remnants, were turned into benefit societies, of which almost every large city had one or more. The first great strike that occurred took place in June, 1880, after the bakers of New York had been organized. On that occasion, the New York union numbered about twenty-five hundred members. All of them quit work on one day, and assembled at Irving Hall, where the employers had to call, and sign an agreement, wherein they pledged themselves to have their men work no longer than twelve hours, and fifteen on Saturday; to abolish board, *i. e.*, give their men the liberty to board where they chose; and to employ their new hands from the Labor Bureau of the Union, instead of at the various lager-beer saloons, which figured up to that time as bakers' labor exchanges, to the detriment of the pockets and the morals of the journeymen bakers. After the men had returned to work, unexperienced as they were in the labor movements, they thought they would not require a union any more. They became negligent, and abandoned the union, which soon dwindled down to almost nothing,—just having enough of principled men to uphold the remnants for a few years; sometimes even not having the necessary quorum to transact their business.

As a consequence of the movement in New York, the bakers in Chicago, New Orleans, St. Louis, and a number of smaller cities, such as Newark, N. J., New Haven, Cleveland, etc., also formed unions; but the downfall of the New York union caused them to collapse and to remain idle, as such, for a period of years. For three years following 1881, nothing was done among the bakers. In April, 1885, Secretary Block started a weekly paper for bakers solely, with the view to establish thereby a National Union, and at the same time educate the men up to the principles of trades-unions, and social questions in general. The New York union, or rather the remnants thereof, consisting of about twenty-five members, laughed at the idea; but they were soon convinced of the probability of success. The paper was intended, from the beginning, to be the property of the union. The union assisted him, and, on May 2, 1885, the first number of the *Deutsch-Amerikanische Backer Zeitung* (*German-American Bakers' Journal*) made its appearance. It at at once spread like a prairie-fire through the whole country, and found its way into every German bakershop throughout the land. All leading cities at once went to reorganize their forces. The secretary's first attempt was directly towards a National Convention, and his efforts were so far crowned with success, that on January 13, 1885, twenty delegates from seventeen cities gathered in Pittsburgh, Penn., to lay the foundation-stone for the Journeymen Bakers' National Union, of the United States, of which he was elected national secretary. At that convention, of course, the leading question was, how to act to accomplish an improvement in the condition of the men in the trade. Mr. Block advised them not to follow the policy of strikes, if it could be helped, but in all cases to apply the "boycott" if a struggle should ensue. The delegates approved of his suggestion, and later events proved its efficacy. In New York, Chicago, St. Louis, Brooklyn, Cleveland, Buffalo and Detroit, a great change was accomplished in the trade. The hours of labor, which up to that time ranged from 13 to 18, and on Saturdays, with Sunday, from 15 to as much as 25 in some cases, were reduced to 12, and 14 on Saturdays; in Chicago, even to 10 and 12; and the fight is still going on, on the whole line, without strikes of any account, simply by the aid of "Saint Boycott." The National Union numbers to-day 38 local unions, from Boston to San Francisco. Its paper is a complete success,—a thorough educator and organ, and a medium of exchange of thoughts among the German bakers of this country. The union has accomplished a great deal in one year. It is about to gather statistics to show, beyond question, how far it has benefited the men. It has elevated a great number of the men intellectually, has sown the seed of true republicanism into their minds, has elevated them to be men who are ready to fight for their rights, has taught them that they are not born to remain willing slaves. The bosses display antagonism against Secretary Block, and have gone so far as to establish a weekly trades-paper in New York City, to counteract his efforts.

BOILERMAKERS AND IRON-SHIP BUILDERS.

The International Brotherhood of Boilermakers' and Iron-Ship Builders' Union was first formed by the boilermakers of the city of Chicago, in 1880. In that year, they sent a delegate as an organizer all over the country, and in one year he organized sixty-four branches of this union. There had been local unions in some cities he visited. In New York, there has been a local union for over thirty years, but this is the first international union ever organized by boilermakers in this country. It now numbers 108 branches in the United States and Canada with a membership of over 8,000 in good standing. It extends from Maine to California, and from Canada to the Gulf of Mexico. The first convention was held in Chicago, and there were 23 delegates present. The next was held at Boston, and there were 68 delegates present. The next convention was held at Cincinnati, and the iron-ship builders from the Delaware River were admitted into the organization. The number of delegates present at this meeting was 82. The next convention was held in New York, and there were 97 delegates present. Three of these were from England to represent the boilermakers and iron-ship builders of that country, where it is one of the strongest and richest of the trades-unions. At this convention the organization joined hands with the boilermakers of England, and became part and parcel of that union. It claims that it is the only trades-union in this country whose organization extends over the New and the Old World. The Convention of 1885 was held in Milwaukee, Wis., in September, and that of 1886 in Reading, Penn., also in September.

This organization never allows a strike in any branch of the Brotherhood. It always claims the right of a conference between the employer and the members of the union. If all fails, and it has no other remedy, it reserves the right to strike. Since the organization has been in existence, it has had some very hard strikes to handle.

The St. Paul, Minn., strike lasted six months, and the Brotherhood won. The Brotherhood has never lost a strike. It is not organized for strikes. It has a far higher calling and duty to perform, as it is a chartered body under the laws of the State of New York, for benevolent and charitable purposes. This charter is given to all branches of the organization. There are very few trades-unions in the United States that have the same advantages as the branches of this organization on this question. This organization also advocates the principle that every national or international trades-union should regulate its own affairs; for a man from another trade or calling does not know the needs and grievances of the men in a different trade. It believes that each trade should preserve its own distinct individuality and autonomy.

BRICKLAYERS' AND MASONS' INTERNATIONAL UNION.

For some time previous to the late Civil War, bricklayers' unions of a local character were organized and thrived in several cities of the Union; but until 1865 there was no effort made by any of the craft to institute or perfect a national organization. The agitation of such a movement, however, between the bricklayers of Philadelphia, Baltimore and New York City resulted in a conference of delegates from the unions of those cities, which was held, October 16, 1865, in "Painters' Hall," Philadelphia. Mr. John A. White, of Baltimore, was called to the chair, and Jared A. Bitting, of Philadelphia, was made secretary. After adopting the name, "International Bricklayers' Union of North America," and a constitution, the conference, having issued an address to the bricklayers' unions of the country, adjourned, to meet in

NEW YORK LABOR LEADERS.

their first annual session, which was held in Baltimore, Md., in Royston Hall, Monday, January 8, 1866.

This convention was attended by delegates from Philadelphia, Baltimore, New York City, Brooklyn, Williamsburgh, Jersey City, Richmond, Va., St. Louis, Mo., and Cincinnati, O. The convention lasted five days, resulting in perfecting a permanent organization, establishing a code of laws for its government, and perfecting its constitution. Its first national officers elected were: John A. White, of Baltimore, president; J. Edward Kirby, of Baltimore, secretary; Joseph Hackney, of Philadelphia, treasurer.

The following year the second annual session was held in Cincinnati, O., when delegates from twenty-five unions attended, representing the States of New York, New Jersey, Massachusetts, Connecticut, Pennsylvania, Maryland, Ohio, Missouri, and Indiana. From that time to 1874, the organization grew rapidly, having sixty-nine unions on its roll, and embracing a membership of near ten thousand. In the meantime, the title of the Order was changed to "National Bricklayers' Union," and it continued under that name until 1883, when it was again changed to its present form, that of "Bricklayers' and Masons' International Union of America." The reasons of changing the title first adopted to that of "National Union," was that the Order did not at the time deem it advisable to take in unions of its craft in the Dominion of Canada; therefore, they deemed its title of "International" did not hold good. Since then, events which were proving to the contrary, the old title was renewed, and the word "Masons" added; and the Order now reaches from Providence, in the East, to Denver, Col., in the West; from Toronto, Canada, in the North, to Galveston, Texas, in the South.

During the depression of business, occasioned by the financial panic of 1873, and which extended to 1880, the Order decreased in unions and membership until, in 1879, but three unions sent their delegates to represent them in annual convention. Those there were No. 1, of Cincinnati, O.; No. 1, of Indianapolis, Ind.; and No. 2, of Covington, Ky. A reaction in business caused a reaction in organization. Union after union reorganized, and reported for admission; and now the Order is stronger than ever before. It has on its roll 103 unions, with a membership of about 16,000; and charters for new unions are being granted almost weekly.

The Order is a purely protective one in a national sense, though all of the subordinate unions have benevolent features combined. Should any unions encounter any difficulty or have trouble with "master-builders," which would result in causing a strike, such union will have to present a bill of grievances, which will be submitted to all the subordinate unions before they can be allowed the permission to strike, so as to procure the necessary relief and assistance from the International Union.

The International Union reserves the right, in all such matters as those, of establishing regular hours of labor; and any subordinate unions which take any of these measures upon themselves without the necessary permission do so upon their own responsibility, and receive no countenance from the Order.

The union is now in the twenty-first year of its growth, and has held its annual conventions in Baltimore twice, in Cincinnati three times, in New York twice, in Washington, Chicago, Pittsburgh, Albany, Indianapolis, Louisville, Brooklyn, Quincy, Ill., Covington, Ky., Buffalo, Providence, Jersey City and St. Louis. The next place of meeting will be Washington.

At the last convention in St. Louis, Mo., the Order decided to enforce the nine-hour system, to go into effect on the 1st of May last. This demand was readily and generally acquiesced in, being regarded by the capitalists of the country as the most conservative demand made by any organization relative to the question of the hours of labor, and, therefore, the least open to objection. The union believes in slow, but sure, methods of conducting business, and always strives to act intelligently on any subject before adopting it. Patiently it waits for the time to come when, to belong to a labor organization is not to be considered a reproach, but to be accorded the same recognition and respect as is given to those of the wealthier class, who belong to the so-called boards of trade, exchanges, etc. The objects of both elements are the same, the only difference consisting in "the name."

BARBERS, OR HAIRDRESSERS.

This branch of industry is different from the others, in that there are more proprietors of shops to the number of journeymen than in any other occupation. The subject cannot, therefore, well be considered from the employers' stand-point. While it would be interesting to trace the progress of this trade from "ye olden tyme," when the same person was barber and surgeon, we must come at once to 1878, when some of the members of the trade saw that a halt must be called to stop ruinous competition, and the "Barbers' Protective Union" was formed, with headquarters at Philadelphia, and a national organ, known as the *Barbers' National Journal*, was started. The organization did not grow very rapidly, and it is dying from inactivity. Various papers were started in favor of the trade, among which may be mentioned the *Barbers' Gazette*, of New York; the *Tonsorial Clipper*, of Chicago; the *Hairdressers and Perfumers*, of New York; and *The Shaver*, of Holyoke, Mass., the latter being really an ideal paper for the trade. Until recently, the various unions had done comparatively little that was really beneficial to the craft. But since the birth and general development of the Knights of Labor, there have been formed in nearly all the principal cities assemblies of that order, composed exclusively of barbers, and much good has been done. In many instances Sunday-work has been abolished, and there is a general move in this direction in the larger cities. The five-cent shaving has, to a great extent, been done away with. The fight has been hard and bitter, but much good has been done.

Seeing the necessity of united action, the Boston barbers have called upon their brothers throughout the country to assist in forming a national organization. It is hoped that this will soon be accomplished, and that the condition of the trade will be kept up to its standard. The union in Boston has been the cause of many being formed in the United States, and has performed a great deal of active work.

IMPROVED DRUGGISTS' WARE GLASSBLOWERS' LEAGUE.

This organization, as at present constituted, dates from 1874. Previous to that time, there had been a union that had gone to pieces in 1867, and glass bottle-blowers in the interim were in a badly demoralized condition. In 1873, just after the "panic," manufacturers took advantage of the situation, and commenced reducing wages. A union of glass bottle-blowers, called the "Improved League," had been started east of the Alleghany Mountains several years previous to its introduction in the West. The first branch in the West was organized at Pittsburgh, and was known as Branch 14. The new union very soon extended throughout the West. William Campbell, of St. Louis, was elected the first manager of the Western district, which embraced Pittsburgh, and all places west of it. In Pittsburgh, in 1876, the manufacturers demanded a further reduction of ten per cent, to which the League refused consent, and the factories lay idle the most of that year. A few were running with men who were not members of the League; but all those who were gallantly held out, and in the spring of 1877 went to work, the winners of the contest. In that year the St. Louis manufacturers demanded a reduction, which was refused, and the men went out on strike. The manufacturers went East for men, and brought back a full set to take the places of the strikers. But they did not remain long in St. Louis, as they were prevailed on to go home upon having their fares paid by the strikers. It was a bitter struggle, but resulted in a triumph for the League. In 1877, William Simpson, of Pittsburgh, was elected Manager of the League. In 1878, with an improvement in trade, the League rapidly gained strength and cohesion, gathering in all the stray workmen who had held aloof during the dull times. In 1880, Louis Arrington was elected manager. That summer a demand was made for a ten per cent advance, which was granted without any trouble. In 1881, the De Steiger Glass Company, of La Salle, Ill., discharged all their blowers, and sent to Germany and imported a full set of men, to work for but little more than half of the current rate of wages. The League tried all manner of inducements and explanations with these imported men to show them where their true interests lay, but could make no impression on them. In 1883, the manufacturers complained of the low prices, principally caused by La Salle cutting under the market, and demanded a reduction of ten or twenty per cent. This was refused, and the factories lay idle, generally until February of the following year, when they resumed at the old rate. But, in the fall, they came again with the same demand. It was still refused, as the League could not see that it would improve the condition of the trade a particle. The majority of the factories did not run more than half-time that season. In the meantime, the De Steiger firm at La Salle had failed. Several other firms had tried the German workmen, who were offering themselves on any terms; but they were found to be both unprofitable and unsuitable. In the fall of 1885, the Pittsburgh manufacturers, doubtless expecting that the League treasury and men were impoverished, made the old demand, and refused to start. A number of other places followed their example, so that only about one-third of the men got to work. There was, undoubtedly, a deep-laid plot to break up the League; but it was entirely unsuccessful. It has now 670 members, divided into 15 branches. Last season, it distributed $30,000 in relief to its needy members; and to-day it is numerically and financially stronger than at any period of its history.

AMALGAMATED ENGINEERS.

This organization of machinists was established first in England, but it has numerous and powerful branches on the continent and in America. It is one of the most powerful labor organizations. Many years ago, it succeeded in fixing nine hours as the standard for a day's work. It has a large benefit-fund, and never carries in its treasury less than an allowance of $15 for each member. It now has about 52,000 members, and about $1,000,000 in its treasury.

INTERNATIONAL FURNITURE WORKERS' UNION.

The oldest union now belonging to the International Furniture Workers' Union is Union No. 7, of New York City. It was organized in April, 1859, under the name, "United Cabinet-makers of New York." This union made an attempt to enforce the eight-hour work-day in 1872. It only partially succeeded, and had to give up after a strike of eight weeks. They claimed that the failure was due to the inactivity of the workmen in other cities. Unions were at that time organized, or reorganized, in several cities, which communicated with each other, and arranged the First Convention of Furniture Workers, which met in Cincinnati, O., July 7, 1873. A national organization was effected, under the name, "Furniture Workers' Association of North America." Unions from the following cities were represented: New York, Philadelphia, Cincinnati, Chicago, Evansville, Ind., Louisville, Ky., Rochester, N. Y., St. Louis, Mo., and San Francisco. The constitution provided for a central committee as the head of the organization. The central committee had to elect a corresponding secretary, treasurer, and financial secretary, who were the general officers of the organization. There being no president, the executive committee had to elect a chairman for each session. The constitution provided for mutual assistance in strikes, but had no benevolent features. The following resolutions were adopted:—

The Congress declares the establishment of the eight-hours' normal working-day to be indispensably necessary, and demands the union to begin a lively agitation for its introduction by legislation. The Congress also advocates the abolition of piece-work.

The Congress recommends to all workingmen's organizations to agitate for the following points:—

That no master shall employ children under fifteen years of age; that public school instruction should be obligatory until the age of fifteen years; that school instruction should be gratuitous up to the highest degrees.

The Congress recommends to the workingmen to organize their trades-unions in the first place, and then to form an independent workingmen's party, to elect only representatives of the working class to the highest legislative bodies of the country.

The Congress advocates the mutual co-operation of the workingmen of all countries, and directs the central committee to enter into relations with their respective central bodies.

The Congress recommends to the local unions the establishment of labor bureaus.

The Congress demands that employers shall be responsible for all damages to workingmen from accidents arising through any negligence on the employers' part, especially by machinery.

Considering that the present economical circumstances force the workingmen to the practice of unlimited solidarity; that secret organizations are an obstacle to the labor movement, the Congress recommends to the unions "unrestrained" publicity in their meetings.

The first central committee was located in New York City, with Karl Speyer as corresponding secretary. The next convention was held in Baltimore, September, 1874. Eleven unions were represented,—among which were one of upholsterers and one of wood-carvers, both of New York,—from the following cities: New York, Baltimore, Philadelphia, Chicago, Providence, R. I., St. Louis, San Francisco. The number of members had decreased since the previous convention, on account of the business depression which ensued in October, 1873. The members in Cincinnati went on strike without the consent of the Executive Committee, and were defeated. This broke up their union.

The next convention was held in Indianapolis, in September, 1876. B. Kaufmann was secretary at the time. The number of local unions had at that time, in consequence of the business crisis which wiped so many organizations out of existence, dwindled down to nine. Some of them ceased to exist soon afterwards. At this convention, it was resolved to institute a tool-insurance, for the benefit of the members in case of fire. Such an institution had to a great extent benefited the members of Union No. 7, New York, where it was started in 1860. Many thousands of dollars have been paid to members who lost their tools by fire. This insurance is about one-half cheaper than in capitalistic companies. At this convention, it was resolved that the central committee should be located in Chicago. Up to that time, no strike of any importance, as far as the national organization was concerned, had occurred. The central committee had expended hundred of dollars in agitation, without much success, besides keeping the organization in existence. After this, no convention was held for four years. The central committee remained in Chicago for two years. H. Stahl, and after him G. Hocrist, was elected corresponding secretary. By a general vote in 1878, the central committee was again located in New York, and L. Zetsche elected secretary. The central committee then began a lively agitation for eight hours, and issued a pamphlet in favor of the movement.

The Fourth Convention was held in Chicago, in 1880, and eight of the local unions then existing were represented. Some changes of minor importance were made, and resolutions were adopted, declaring

> That it is the duty of all the unions to take in hand, without delay, a reduction of the work-day, so as to hasten the advent of the normal work-day of eight hours, which alone can render an equipoise of production and consumption possible, and a lack of employment avoidable.

New York was again selected as the place for the central committee. The Fifth Convention was held in Cincinnati, where changes of great importance in the constitution were made. A "strike-fund" was established, in order to abolish assessments in cases of strikes. Into this strike-fund, which is under the control of the executive committee, which name was substituted for central committee, each local union has to pay its monthly dues for each of its members. A death-benefit fund was also instituted, out of which, up to the present day, $4,450 have been paid to twenty-eight families. It was further resolved to issue a journal every two weeks, to be edited by the corresponding secretary. A sick-benefit fund was also established, out of which, during the three and a half years of its existence, $6,488.29 have been paid to sick members.

These new institutions in the organization required, of course, higher dues. The executive committee again came to New York, and H. Emrich was re-elected secretary. Two months after this new constitution was enforced, four unions ceased to exist. The number of members of the International Furniture Workers' Union—which was the name adopted at Cincinnati—was only 1,300. But through the influence of the *Journal*, it soon commenced to grow again, and has to-day 26 local unions, with over 6,000 members, after several thousand new members have been lost, and after the failure of the eight-hour movement in May last, in which 14 of the local unions were engaged, and over $30,000 paid out on strike-benefits by the local unions.

The Sixth Convention was held in Alleghany City, 1884. No great changes were made there, but an important declaration of principles was adopted. It affirmed that there was antagonism between the proprietary and the working-classes, the interests of the former being to keep wages as low as possible; "that the laboring class must emancipate itself from all influences of its enemy, the proprietary class, and organize locally, nationally, and internationally, to set the power of the organized masses against capitalism; and that it must see that its interests be represented in the shops, in the different branches of the local, State, and national administrations and government."

Since then, the executive committee has been in New York, with H. Emrich as secretary. The main object in view is still the shortening of the hours of labor.

THE GRANITE-CUTTERS' NATIONAL UNION.

The first conception of this union was at Clark's Island, Me., January 2, 1877. The union was started with a view, if possible, of combining every granite-cutter in the United States in one general union. A temporary organization was formed at Clark's Island, a board of officers was elected, and communications entered into with Carver's Harbor, Hurricane Island, Spruce Head and Dix Island. Committees were sent to each place, the result of which was the formation of organizations or branches, and a convention was held in Rockland, Me., by delegates selected by Clark's Island, Carver's Harbor, Spruce Head and Hurricane. A constitution was drawn up, which was submitted to the branches for adoption. The branch at Spruce Head announced on March 6, 1877, that N. C. Bassick had been elected president for one year; N. S. Fales, Thomas Fahy,

P. H. Cooney, I. P. Clay and William K. Smith, standing committee, and T. H. Murch, secretary. The first meeting of the National Board was held March 10, and the union duly organized as a National Union, and from that time the union has steadily advanced. The secretary, T. H. Murch, having been elected to Congress in the place of Eugene Hale, J. B. Dyer was elected his successor. The first convention of the union was held in Evans Hall, Boston, Mass., February 5, 1878, with twenty-four delegates present, representing twenty-two branches. The first strike of the union was at Vinalhaven, April 6, 1878. Mr. Wharf, the agent of the Bodwell Granite Company, having discharged thirty of the most prominent members of the union, the other members struck, and presented a bill of prices. Since then, the union has been engaged in several strikes and lockouts, the most notable being the lockout in Quincy, Mass., lasting nearly nine months. The union, being conducted on a conservative policy, has gained the approval of the majority of large employers in the trade, and nearly every branch has its bill of prices to govern its locality, preventing considerable trouble, which previously occurred; and many of the employers, who were first antagonistic to it, are now its advocates, and prefer union to non-union men. Previous to the organization of the National Union, several places had attempted local unions, but they had fallen through, owing to their isolated condition. Among those were New York, Westerly, Philadelphia, Washington, Boston, Richmond and Baltimore; but they are again organized as branches of the National Union. The headquarters of the union is changed every two years, and has been located in Rockland, Me., Boston, Mass., Westerly, R. I., Quincy, Mass., and is at present located at 1907 Market street, Philadelphia, Penn. The President is John G. Laycock, and the secretary Josiah B. Dyer. The union publishes a trade journal monthly, which is acknowledged to be a credit to the craft.

In the spring of 1885 a combination was formed, composed of the Smith Granite Co., Rhode Island Granite Works, the Chapman Granite Works of Westerly, R. I., A. G. Crumb, of Niantic, R. I., Charles F. Stoll, Merritt Gray & Co., of Groton, Conn., Gates & Park, and Booth Bros., of Millstone Point, Conn., to cut down prices fifteen per cent., and efforts were made to get all the New England manufacturers to join with them. The men employed on the Rhode Island Granite Works, at Westerly, Gates & Parks, and Booth Bros.' works at Millstone Point, and Merritt, Gray & Co., of Groton, struck against the reduction; and, after a protracted struggle, the men were successful, the other firms not enforcing the reduction when the time came. The Rhode Island Granite Works held out until February, 1886, when both parties agreed to leave the question in dispute to the arbitration of the Executive Board of District Assembly 99, Knights of Labor, who, having decided in favor of the union, the works were opened to union men and declared a union job, and on March 8th a social reunion was held in Westerly, in which all parties engaged in the dispute and settlement had a "good time," and "buried the hatchet." As an offshoot of this trouble, the manufacturers of Barre formed a combination to crush out unionism in Vermont, and on a branch being formed in South Ryegate, they sent to the Ryegate Granite Works, at South Ryegate, and the other manufacturers of that place, inviting them to join their combination. As a consequence, the following notice was issued by the Ryegate Granite Works:—

South Ryegate, April 8, 1885.

Dear Sir:—We are informed that something is being done with reference to the formation of a stone-cutters' union in this place. We have seen much of the trouble and disturbance arising from such unions, and are satisfied that they are neither an advantage to workmen nor contractors. We prefer and propose to deal with every man in our employ as an independent individual, capable of managing his own contracts. We allow none of our co-contractors to dictate to us as to what terms we shall employ you upon. And we want no one to dictate to you as to the terms on which you shall work for us. In this view, we have decided to employ no one who is engaged in the enterprise first named.

An immediate reply, stating what action you intend taking in the matter, is requested.

We are, yours very truly,

Ryegate Granite Works,

Sellick.

The men who organized the branch, on being thus locked out, inserted an advertisement in the Boston *Herald* to keep men away, and the works were declared "scabbed." Carter, who ran the works, threatened legal proceedings if the advertisement was not withdrawn, and an humble apology inserted. The men refused to do so. They were arrested and taken to St. Johnsbury, charged with conspiracy, and thirteen were bound over for trial under $300 bail each. The citizens of South Ryegate promptly came to the rescue, and bonds to the amount of $250,000 were ready if necessary. At the June term of court, the grand jury having found a true bill, the case was continued until the May, 1886, term, when the judge took the case under advisement to search up authorities cited by Bates & May, the attorneys for the so-called "conspirators," and it still remains unsettled.

Trouble has also been caused by convict labor on the new capitol at Austin, Texas, which was therefore declared a "scab" job. The contractor endeavored to get granite-cutters from Aberdeen, Scotland, and had some success. On Monday, April 26, 1886, his agent landed at Castle Garden, New York, with seventy-eight granite-cutters and eight tool-sharpeners, under contract to go to Burnet, Texas, to work for him. An effort was made to prevent their proceeding any further in violation of the contract-labor law; but owing to its defects the attempt was unsuccessful, and the agent and the imported aliens were allowed to proceed by the United States authorities, but twenty-four decided to remain in New York. Those remaining having the proofs of the contract made in Aberdeen with them, and their passage-money advanced them, an affidavit was made before the United States Commissioner, and all the necessary documents forwarded to Texas for the purpose of testing the law. Suits have been entered against the contractor and the syndicate for the full penalty of one thousand dollars for each man imported, and nineteen additional affidavits have been forwarded to Austin. The trial is expected to come on in the August term of court, and the case is being watched with much interest, as it is claimed to be the clearest case of violation of the law yet discovered. The proofs of contract and of payment of passage-money are so clear, that it appears an impossibility for the contractor and the syndicate to evade the full penalty of the law. D. A. 78, at its last meeting, decided to push the matter to the utmost extent, and a committee was appointed to secure all legal assistance necessary. In this fight the Granite Cutter's National Union and D. A. 78, Knights of Labor, are standing shoulder to shoulder, recognizing fully that "an injury to one is the concern of all," in the ranks of labor's army.

THE HORSE-RAILROAD MEN.

The first horse-railroad employee to join the Knights of Labor in New York was initiated in a printers' local assembly. A printer riding up and down on the cars entered into conversation with the driver, and showed him the advantages of being a Knight. The driver was convinced, made application, was initiated and finally persuaded thirteen more drivers to join. They then obtained transfer-cards, and started the first local assembly of horse-railroad employees in September, 1883. Owing to the opposition of the railroad officials, great caution at first was necessary. By December, the membership was increased to about five hundred, and another local assembly was formed, in East New York. Then assemblies were formed in Flatbush, in January, 1884; and in Greenwood and at Green Point in February. A traitor to the cause obtained entrance to the first assembly organized, and gave to the company's officials a copy of the constitution, the names of the officers of the assembly, and of those most active in its interests. Soon after this information was given, three of the officers and about twenty members were discharged by the company. This caused a panic in the organization; and the railroad employees feared to visit any assembly, knowing they would be discharged if such visits were found out. The company's inspectors and superintendents followed the men after they were through work for the day to see where they went, and where the meetings were held, and those seen attending the meetings were discharged. This caused the assembly, which numbered six hundred, to drop to thirteen members in good standing in three months. These, however, determined to carry on the cause they had espoused, and to form a district assembly of their own. In July, 1884, a district charter was procured from the Knights of Labor. At first it was impossible to procure members, owing to the terrible boycott of the companies. But in September, eleven men were secured to start the first assembly in New York. This assembly prospered until January, 1885, when forty of its members were discharged by their employers, and the work of organization was checked.

The next attempt was made on the "East Side" where three drivers met in a basement, knowing well what would become of them if the company knew they had joined the Knights of Labor. Working cautiously, they secured three more within a week. In another week, these six secured twenty-two, who started the assembly which conducted the strike on the Third Avenue line. The second assembly on the "East Side" started with nine members, who worked so carefully that none were discharged for being members of the Order. Another assembly was formed on the "West Side," in July, 1885. These four assemblies initiated some two hundred members each weekly, until, by January, 1886, nearly all the horse-car drivers in New York had been initiated. After this was accomplished, they began to initiate the conductors, and in a few weeks succeeded in getting all of them.

On the 18th of December, 1885, the first list of grievances was submitted to the Third Avenue Company, which asked time to consider it. This was given, and the answer was satisfactory to the men. A list of grievances was then presented to the Sixth Avenue Company. This was entirely ignored, the company refusing to recognize the organization. After three weeks, the company failing to come to any settlement, a strike was ordered. After five hours, the company consented to sign the agreement, and the men returned to their places. The Broadway line was next in order, and after a two weeks' delay a strike was ordered. It lasted only ten hours, the company then signing the agreement. A strike on the Fourth Avenue line then followed. The company soon signed the agreement, but broke it in two weeks. After consultations for five days, it refused to make another agreement.

The men gave up their cars, and after sixteen hours they made the first agreement that has been made with any railroad company in Brooklyn or New York. The smaller companies readily complied with the demands of the men.

The Dry Dock Company was considered by the men the hardest and most selfish corporation in New York city, and they therefore left it until the last, believing that others who had been helped by the Order would stand by it in the trouble expected with this company. Being unable to secure even recognition from the company, a strike was ordered, which resulted in a settlement at the expiration of five days. The committee from the Knights then waited upon President Jacob Sharp, of the Bleecker Street and Twenty-third Street Railroad. He said he understood how to run a railroad, and that he did not propose to allow any labor organization to dictate to him how much he should pay his employees, nor how many hours they should work. A strike was ordered, which in one day brought Mr. Sharp to an agreement. This was to take effect in ten days. He failed to keep it, saying he was making only ten per cent. profit, and that he would work his men as he pleased, without regard to any organization, etc. The police commissioners and superintendent of police had been witnesses to the first agreement, and they were now appealed to by the committee. After some discussion, the original agreement was renewed.

Little or no trouble was experienced in Brooklyn until the Broadway Company was reached. Its president refused to answer verbally the questions of the committee, but wrote on a sheet of paper that his men were satisfied, and that he would stand no interference. A strike was therefore ordered, which, in twenty hours, caused the president to send for the committee, with whom he made a settlement. After some three weeks of hard work, an agreement was also made with the Atlantic Avenue Company.

During all this time, the companies were doing all they could to weed out the Knights from their employees. One company had its men take an oath that they would not belong to any labor organization. The Third Avenue Company failed to keep the agreement made in December. In January and February, they agreed to right the grievances complained of, but failed so to do. The men presented another list, April 15th. The company then refused to treat with the men at all, and the latter appealed to the executive committee, who tried to make a settlement; but the president said his board of directors had passed a resolution not to increase wages, nor to have anything to do with the Knights of Labor or any other organization. There were fourteen grievances presented to him,—thirteen relating to hours of labor, and one asking for the discharge of six men. He gave only the last to the representatives of the press, saying the company had granted all else the men asked, and that now the men were determined to strike, because the company would not discharge their old and trustworthy employees. This strike, after lasting several weeks, was settled.

During these months of conflict, the companies have discharged about one hundred men, and blacklisted them, so that some had to change their names in order to get work. The assemblies have become so large that they have been split up into twenty-three, with a membership of about 15,000, including all classes employed by the companies.

In all of the cities and large towns, the employees of the horse-railroad companies flocked into the Order of the Knights of Labor. Strikes were entered into by the men before they had learned anything of the objects or methods of the Order. The student of the labor question will understand why these men, who had been brutalized by long hours of labor, should so suddenly order strikes, and that these strikes should be followed by acts of violence. In large cities, like New York, Chicago, and St. Louis, there is a large class of men ready to join in any tumult, and to such men much of the blame of unlawful deeds is due.

PAINTERS' UNION.

Since 1856, the painters of this country have been struggling to bring about an organization of the craft that would place them as artisans in a position to command that consideration and recognition from the employing class that at this time many of the other branches of labor have arrived at.

Previous to this, scattered associations existed throughout the country, and these only numbering from one-third to one-half of the men working at the trade; the same state of affairs existing to-day, with the exception of a few of the larger cities, where more perfect organization can be found.

In 1859, John Siney travelled through the country in his work of establishing and building up the Moulders' International Union, and to his strong appeals to workingmen, urging them to action, was largely due the impetus given to many of the trades in forming new unions and organizing old ones that were drooping.

At this time an effort was made to found a national union of painters, and the members of the Philadelphia association took a lively interest in the matter. A convention was called and formulated laws; but after a brief existence the movement perished, — it being found impossible to persuade the scattered bodies to come together and contribute to the sustenance of a national body.

In 1871 the New York Operative and Benevolent Union, the oldest and best-governed union of the trade now in existence, came to the front, and the Painters' Grand Lodge was formed. This organization extended into several States, and held four annual conventions, — three in New York and one in Baltimore.

At this period, the International Workingmen's Association was making rapid strides, and many of the branches affiliated with that body. It was at this time that the eight-hour agitation was made. The painters entered into the movement with great zeal; and the first demand made and the first victory won for shorter hours, both in the North and West, entitle the craft to the honor of claiming to be "the pioneers of the eight-hour movement."

The grand lodge, as far as its means would warrant, made every effort possible to extend its influence, and at one time things looked quite cheering; but the great panic that came upon the country at this time — causing the overthrow of so many labor organizations, among which was the young and struggling association of the painters — seemed to put a damper upon them, from which they are just beginning to recover. In a great many localities, the Knights of Labor have succeeded in annexing the local painters' unions; but it is very generally urged that that organization, while having noble aims, is, with its complicated machinery and its thousands of inexperienced members who have been (contrary to its principles and the object of its founders) admitted to its folds, quite too tardy in action, and too unwieldy to properly legislate for any single craft.

The hope is now revived that a national brotherhood of painters and decorators will at once be instituted, with some twenty to twenty-five States to begin with. A provisional national committee has been formed, and communication opened with all parts of the country; letters are reaching us from all points, and we may safely promise that, after May next, will be found a new army of workmen organized and in the field.

NATIONAL SILK AND FUR HAT-FINISHERS' ASSOCIATION.

Hatters' guilds were established in England, many years ago; from them the trade in this country derived its fundamental laws. The first association in this land was established in Philadelphia, in 1836; in New York, in 1845; in Boston, in 1850. The National Association was formed in 1854. All "locals" have their own laws, subject to the Central or National. They have no strikes, and, as their work is piece-paid, they have no stated hours of labor. Their relations with employers are amicable. Any difficulty arising in "locals" is referred, with evidence sent, to the National Board of Directors. Instructions are then sent. If they fail, an officer is sent to interview the parties, and he reports to the board. The decision is final. In the principal cities, the associations are protective as well as benevolent. A strict discipline is enforced among them regarding their duties. Apprentices are registered, and serve four years prior to being 21. They must learn, at least, two of the three branches, and must maintain good moral character. The mission of the association is to assist all legitimate trades-unions with material aid when struggling for a principle; to carry comfort and aid to our distressed, medicine and proper attendance to the sick; and to furnish burial to the dead wife or husband. This free land never need be ashamed of such men in trades-unions. In fact, they consitute a bulwark of its ablest defenders.

NEW YORK STEREOTYPERS' ASSOCIATION.

This union was instituted September 8, 1863. It was started with about forty men. The trade at that time was not very extensive, stereotyping being used exclusively on book-work and occasionally on jobbing. Now all the daily papers are stereotyped, and books are electrotyped. From its organization up to the present day, it has been one of the most successful trades-unions in New York, seldom if ever having trouble in the shops, free from strikes, and commanding the highest wages, beside having an admirable apprenticeship law, which is vigorously enforced. The union numbers about 125 members. Wages are, for day-hands, $4 per day; for night-men, $4 per night. As a general rule, the men are seldom out of employment, the periods of trade depression lasting but a few weeks. The organization has no connection with any national or international union. Many of this trade are members of the Knights of Labor, and a movement is being made to found a National Trade District.

JOURNEYMEN TAILORS' NATIONAL UNION.

The Journeymen Tailors' National Trades-Union was organized in Philadelphia, in 1865, and continued in existence till 1886, when the last convention was held in that city. It collapsed in consequence of the depression of business, and its resisting reductions during those years; also the treasurer, John T. Walsh, absconded with the entire funds, of which he had complete control in 1885. He disappeared just previous to the convention, which was held in St. Louis, in August, 1885, taking with him about $3,000. During the union's existence, J. Worstadt, of New York, was president, and S. C. Hougendobler, of Philadelphia, was secretary. In 1885, the National Union was composed of thirty-five locals and about 4,000 members. The monthly dues were ten cents, and it paid $9 per week in case of strike.

The Journeymen Tailors' National Union was founded at Philadelphia, at a conference called in the fall of 1883. In August, 1884, at the convention held in Chicago, the present constitution was adopted. It provided for the appointment of an executive board of seven, who should have a supervision over all strikes, declared in favor of arbitration, and selected for officers John B. Lennon, of Denver, Col., president; Joseph Wilkinson, of New York, secretary, and Fred Werner, of New York, treasurer. It also provided for the appointment of three trustees to guard the funds, together with a bond from the treasurer. In 1885, the convention was held in Baltimore, and elected for officers, Charles H. Sharp, of Philadelphia, president; Joseph Wilkinson of New York, secretary; Fred Werner, of New York, treasurer.

The National Union, during its existence, has engaged in a number of strikes, in most of which it has come out victorious; but its chief good has been in preventing strikes and reductions,—because being composed of most all the first-class tailors in the United States, an employer will think twice before he will encounter such a body in an unjust demand.

THE TELEGRAPHERS' NATIONAL UNION.

The telegraphers, as a rule, situated as they are, with their fingers on the arteries of intelligence and news, have been very susceptible to the agitation in the labor movement and its consequent organization. After the war, a great number of military telegraph operators were thrown into the ranks of the commercial operators, causing disarrangement in wages and competition for places. This, in connection with the then existing labor agitation, led to the formation of a Telegraphers' National Union, in 1870, and a strike of short duration in 1871, which resulted unsuccessfully, many of the best men leaving the profession, as it is termed by operators, for more lucrative methods of earning a livelihood. This was followed by a short local strike of the unions in San Francisco and Sacramento, Cal., which comprised nearly all the operators in the State. After the unsuccessful termination of this strike, organization slumbered till the fall of 1882, when a few operators in Pittsburgh, Penn., formed an assembly of the Knights of Labor, and bore the expense of sending organizers to the principal Eastern cities. At about the same time another union, called the "Brotherhood of Telegraphers," modelled on somewhat the same principles as the Brotherhood of Locomotive Engineers, was formed in the West, and the various local bodies soon after amalgamated, under the name of the Brotherhood of Telegraphers, District 45, Knights of Labor. In May, 1883, the question of whether a strike should be ordered on the lines of all the telegraph companies was sent to all the local bodies, to be voted upon, the result being an overwhelming vote in the affirmative. Accordingly, July 19, 1883, the word was sent over the wires in cipher from Pittsburgh, by John Campbell, District Master Workman, and at noon all the commercial operators, all over the United States and Canada, left their keys, and marched out in a body when the whistle—the signal agreed on—was blown. Offices everywhere, in large cities and in country hamlets, were left silent and deserted. The press operators and the broker operators were left as the only means of furnishing telegraph accommodations, and perhaps for the first time the public realized its dependence on this means of swift intercommunication. From July 19th to August 17th, nearly a month, the contest was waged between the men and the companies, with varying success, two of the companies, the American Rapid and the Bankers' and Merchants', having acceded to the demands of the men, which were a general fifteen per cent. advance and the abolition of Sunday-work without pay, and of other minor grievances. On the latter date, August 17th, the strike was declared off and the men ordered back to work in a body, by an order from the same source which brought them out. This was generally obeyed, and the men went back in a body, most of them obtaining their old positions. The companies abolished the Sunday-work without pay; and, as all were paid by the month, the month was reckoned at 26 or 27 days, when formerly it was estimated at 30 or 31 days. Where a man was paid $60 for performing 30 days' work, he now receives $60 for performing 26 days' work. It cost the Western Union Telegraph Company $500,000 extraordinary expenses and an estimated loss of receipts of nearly $1,500,000 more, and the company has never fully recovered from the blow, — followed, as it was, by the active competition of the Baltimore & Ohio Telegraph Company and other companies. There were some individual cases of hardship among the men, but they were comparatively few when the vast aggregate of cases, about 67,000 in all, is considered. It being in the summer, many took it as a summer vacation, which few had enjoyed, owing to the great rush due to the opening of summer offices in beaches and watering-places. The companies, since this strike, seeing that the men had not preserved their organization, displaced as rapidly as possible the higher-paid men by a cheaper grade, until the average was brought very low. The operators have at last, however, plucked up courage, and have secretly reorganized, until they have an organization called the "Telegraphers' Protective Union," which is said to number 8,000 operators in all.

THE NATIONAL WOOD-CARVERS' ASSOCIATION.

This association was organized in Philadelphia, in January, 1883, by delegates from local associations in New York, Boston, Philadelphia, New Haven and Cincinnati. The New York association was quite an old organization, and had passed through many vicissitudes; the others were comparatively young. A convention was held in October of the same year at Cincinnati, when the original constitution was thoroughly revised. The next convention was held in New York, October, 1884, and the last in Boston, October, 1885, when the plan of holding biennial conventions was adopted, instead of annually, the organization having become so perfected that annual conventions were deemed unnecessary.

At the present time, there are two associations in New York, and one each in Philadelphia, Boston, New Haven, Cincinnati, St. Louis, and Grand Rapids, Mich. The association has a central committee, composed of the recording and corresponding secretary in one person, a financial secretary, treasurer and three trustees, elected by the "local" in the places elected by the convention for the location of the committee; and this committee carries on the business of the National Association, and also has a board of supervisors, located in another city, composed of five members, elected in the same manner as the central committee, who have a certain control over the central committee, and power to suspend any member of the whole central committee for cause, and order a new election. The association has had several strikes, and been successful in all until, the recent eight-hour strikes, which were not entirely successful. It adopted the principle, on the start, that a strike should not be entered into except for good and substantial cause, and after all other means had been exhausted for an adjustment, and then only if there was a reasonable certainty of being able to carry it through successfully. In pursuance of this policy, it has been successful when the power of the association was concentrated upon a single individual or corporation. The present central committee is located in New York, where the next convention is to be held in October, 1877, and the board of supervisors in New Haven, Conn.

WOOL-HAT FINISHERS' ASSOCIATION.

The date of organization of this association, or, as it used to be called, "Hatters' Society," is unknown to any of the oldest hatters living. The old hatters say they have never heard of the time that it was not a trades-union. It was a well-organized society in olden times; and, in fact, up to 1840, all hats were made by hand. When a boy was put to the trade, he had to serve so long a time at each branch of the business that when out of his time he could take the fur or wool and turn it out a hat. In a large number of the shops, they made fur and wool-hats. These they called "costume shops," where a man would go in, and leave his order for a single hat of whatever style he wanted. At this time, the makers, blockers, and finishers were all in one society, and the fur and wool-workers recognized each others' card. The first introduction of machinery in hatting was got up by Mr. Messer, one of the oldest hatters now living, being now eighty-seven years of age. He got up a lathe for finishing hats, and sent the papers and a model of the lathe to Washington, for the purpose of obtaining letters-patent on his invention. But, unfortunately for him, the Patent Office was burned down, and with it the model and paper. Shortly after this, the demand for hats increased, so that the Taylor sizing-machine and fulling-mills took the place of hand-work. A man sizing or making hats by hand would average two dozen and a half per day, while a fulling-mill would do twenty-four dozen, — thus driving all hand-made work out. Probably there is no wool-shop to-day where they make hand-sized hats. There are still a few of the Taylor machines used for fine vitriol-hats.

With the introduction of machinery, hand-blocking has in a great measure passed away.

There is no class of workmen more zealous in upholding trades-unions than hatters. The first employer that tried to break up the union was James H. Prentice, of Brooklyn, in 1863. He fought them until he became a bankrupt. The second strike of importance to the trade was in John T. Waring's shop, in Yonkers, N. Y., in 1866, for prices. This was a hard fight on both sides. John T. Waring succeeded, with the help of a number of non-union men from Prentice's shop, in Brooklyn, in making his shop "foul," or independent. In 1868, the independent men of Waring's shop became dissatisfied at the task imposed on them for a day's work; and, when one of the men remonstrated to one of the employers, he was discharged. The other men — about fifty finishers — left the shop in a body. The "fair" hatters in Baldwin & Flagg's tried to help them secure a fair settlement; but some of the strikers turned traitors, and Waring was again able to run his shop. About twenty-five of the strikers joined the Hatters' Union, in Yonkers. At that time, local societies were wholly independent. Several old journeymen at Yonkers—among whom were Robert Savage, Patrick Curran, Thomas Davis, Thomas Daley, and Thomas Nevins—met, and advised the forming of a national organization.

Letters were sent to all local secretaries, asking them to take action on bringing all local associations under one national association. All the associations were in favor of it, and on the 7th day of April, 1869, delegates from every "fair" shop in the State met in Danbury, Conn., and organized the National Association, by electing Mr. F. A. Lewis, president, and D. F. Nolan, national secretary, with a supervising committee as a board of arbitration.

A preamble was adopted, urging the necessity of organization to elevate the trade, and to protect the workmen against the encroachments of employers. The delegates pledged themselves to strive "to secure to us our rights as journeymen hatters, and to our employers theirs as capitalists."

The growth of the business soon caused independent or "foul" shops to start up, and there was more or less antagonism between the "fair" and "foul" hatters. In 1876, an organization was affected among the independent men, who joined the "fair" association as fast as they proved themselves worthy and so desired. At the Annual Convention, in New York, May 12, 1884, it was voted that every hat-shop in the country be made "fair," and all under the jurisdiction of the United States Wool Hat-Finishers' Association, with C. Oatman Osborne as president, and Archibald M. Taylor as national secretary. This consolidation pleased the employers, for their interests are guarded as well as the journeymen's. Two important strikes occured in 1884. Lewis Tompkins, of the Dutchess Hat-Works, at Fishkill Landing, found fault because his shop was made "fair," and gave his men notice that he should employ only non-society men. His men declined, with a few exceptions, to work on those terms, and have been out ever since. The other strike, the last of any importance, was in W. B. Thom's factory, at Haverhill,

Mass., on December 9, 1884. Mr. Thom notified his finishers of a ten per cent. reduction, to take effect on the 15th. He was then paying ten per cent. less than union prices, and monthly payments. When he advanced money to his help before pay-day, he charged five per cent. a month interest. This trouble is still unsettled.

CHAPTER XV.

HISTORY OF THE KNIGHTS OF LABOR.

Cause for Founding the Order—Garment-Cutters' Association—Need of Secrecy—First Meeting—Names of the Founders—Taking the Obligation—Name Adopted—Uriah S. Stephens—Election of Officers—First Officers—Purveyor Appointed—First Annual Address of Uriah S. Stephens—Ship-Carpenters and Calkers Join the Order—The First Twenty Locals—District Assembly, No. 1, Founded—General Assembly Formed, 1878—Officers Elected—Second Session of General Assembly—Address of Grand Master Workman—Profound Secrecy—The Five Stars—Making the Name Public—Third Session—Address of the Grand Master Workman—Election of T. V. Powderly as Grand Master Workman—Fourth Session—Address of T. V. Powderly—Abolish the Wage-System—Co-operation—Fifth Session—Sixth Session—Attempts to Create Division—The Boycott—Blacklisting—Brutal Treatment—Death of Uriah S. Stephens—Seventh Session—Address of the Grand Master Workman—Strikes Discountenanced—Political Action—Hungarians in the Coke Regions—Trade-Mark or Label adopted in 1884—Ninth Session—Pinkerton's Detectives—Question of Education—Address of the General Master Workman—Special Session—Relations of Trades-Unions—Strikes—Arbitration—Co-operation—Rapid Growth of the Order.

PHILADELPHIA, the City of Brotherly Love, the home of Lippard and of the Brotherhood of the Union, has the honor of being the birth-place of the Noble Order of the Knights of Labor.

In 1862 or 1863, the garment-cutters of Philadelphia organized an association, and, desiring to obtain a charter from the State, added to the usual features of such associations that of co-operation. It was, practically, a trades-union, and had for a time considerable influence in the trade.

After the ups and downs, failures and successes, incident to such organizations, it was finally decided to dissolve and divide the fund among the members, which amounted to $89.79. This action was finally taken on December 9, 1869.

For a year and a half prior to this time, the formation of a secret society had been frequently discussed.

Every movement of the union was known to the employers, and members were constantly in danger of discharge; and, hence, it was very difficult to find earnest and active members who were willing to serve on committees. The attendance at the meetings was necessarily very small at times, not even a quorum being present to transact business.

On November 25, 1869, a committee had been appointed to prepare a plan of reorganization. This committee made a partial report at the meeting on the evening of December 9. The report provoked much discussion, the committee favoring the formation of a secret society. It was during this discussion that the motion to dissolve was made and carried.

Immediately upon the dissolution of the meeting, those who were in favor of forming a secret society remained. Mr. James L. Wright, as president of the former association, called the meeting to order, and appointed Robert C. Macauley secretary, he having occupied that position in the old association.

The following-named persons then agreed to form a secret society: James L. Wright, Robert C. Macauley, Joseph S. Kennedy, William Cook, Robert W. Keen, U. S. Stephens, James M. Hilsee, David Westcott, W. H. Phillips, Washington Shields.

The chair then, on motion, appointed Robert W. Keen, U. S. Stephens, David Westcott, Joseph S. Kennedy, James M. Hilsee as a committee to prepare a secret work. Mr. Wright, the chairman, and Mr. Macauley, the secretary, were added to the committee. The meeting then adjourned to meet at the same place, — America Hose Company's House, Jane street, below Seventh, — on December 23, 1869.

During the interval between the time of adjournment and the time fixed for the next meeting, the committee met at the house of Mr. Joseph S. Kennedy, on Green street, above

Ninth. On December 23d, they met according to adjournment. No business of importance was transacted, except that they resolved to meet at the house of Mr. Kennedy on December 28th. On that date it was announced that they had secured a hall in the United States Fire-Engine House, Fourth street, above Vine, for $1.50 per night. The Committee on Ritual made a partial report, and the following persons being present subscribed their names to the obligation: —

Uriah S. Stephens, James L. Wright, Robert C. Macauley, James M. Hilsee, William Cook, Robert W. Keen, Joseph S. Kennedy.

At this meeting, upon motion of Mr. Wright, the new organization was named the "Knights of Labor." And, from this humble beginning, in the house of a garment-cutter, within sound of the old "Liberty Bell" that rang out the war against the monarchical system of government, and proclaimed liberty to the people, there went forth a new declaration of war against the monarchical system of labor, and the proclamation of a new era of liberty, of peace and plenty.

Here, in this house, these seven men founded an organization in whose power now rests, perhaps, the destinies of the Republic. Under the standard that they lifted at this Christmas season of 1869, — a standard of peace and good-will to all good-willing men, — a peaceful army of a million workers now rally. These heretofore unknown men, who stood the jeers of their fellows in the early days of the organization, now bear modestly the accumulating honors due their long-continued years of honorable service. One of them, the first Grand Master Workman, whose words were of wisdom, unswerving fealty, and untiring effort, has passed away, his body lies in an unmarked grave in the Odd Fellows' Cemetery in Philadelphia, near the last resting-place of George W. Lippard, the founder of the "Brotherhood of the Union." Uriah S. Stephens is not forgotten. His pictured face looks down from the walls of the assembly-rooms upon the thousands who are building a monument of gratitude to his memory, not in crumbling granite, but in the building of an organization seeking the ends he sought, and that shall, if true to its mission, witness the culmination of his hopes; but, as the heart-love of the people seeks expression by outward signs, the day is not far distant when the small contributions of the many shall lift a shaft ever pointing upward, on whose entableted sides the people of the future shall read the story of a peaceful revolution.

The next meeting convened in the new hall, on Thursday, December 30th, — Thursday having been chosen as the regular meeting night, from which custom Local Assembly 1 has never departed. At this meeting, six candidates were proposed and elected.

At the meeting of January 6, 1870, David Westcott, who was present at the first meeting, subscribed to the obligation, and the titles of the several offices were fixed, and five more candidates were elected. At this meeting, Mr. Stephens took the chair for the first time, Mr. Wright having served in that capacity up to this date.

On January 13, 1870, the following officers were elected, and took their several positions for the ensuing term: Venerable Sage, Past-Officer, James L. Wright; Master Workman, U. S. Stephens; Worthy Foreman, Robert W. Keen; Worthy Inspector, William Cook; Unknown Knight, Joseph S. Kennedy. On January 27th, the following additional nominations were made: for Recording Secretary, John W. Breen; Financial Secretary, G. W. Cook; Treasurer, Joseph S. Kennedy. On February 3d, the office of Statistician was created, and Robert C. Macauley was elected to that position. The officers nominated at the previous meeting were elected, and took their respective stations.

The affairs of the assembly ran along smoothly, working in the utmost secrecy, — the name of the organization or its object never being divulged. It was the habit of the assembly to meet immediately after working-hours, — a custom that still prevails in some garment-cutters' assemblies at this date. It was this practice that led to the establishment of the office of purveyor, so that refreshments might be served to the members; and, as it was the custom of the purveyor to carry a large teapot always in the same direction and on the same

WILLIAM COOK. JAMES L. WRIGHT. R. C. MACAULEY. VACANT CHAIR OF U. S. STEPHENS. J. M. HILSEE. R. W. KEEN. J. S. KENNEDY.

THE FOUNDERS OF THE KNIGHTS OF LABOR.

Photographed July 7, 1886.

evening of the week, the assembly became known as the "Teapot Society." This pot was carried to the meeting-room for the purpose of preparing coffee; for these men were not addicted to the use of intoxicating liquors.

The dissolution of the old society created quite a commotion among the garment-cutters of the city, who immediately set about reorganizing their association. They were quite successful, attaining a membership of seven or eight hundred. Those who joined the Knights of Labor did not again join the Garment-cutters' Association. A rivalry sprang up among the garment-cutters; and the reorganized association passed a resolution forbidding any of its members joining any other association, open or secret, of their branch of trade, under pain of expulsion. Hence, when one of their number absented himself from the meetings and neglected to pay his dues, he was suspended, and an obituary notice inserted after his name in the records, "Gone to join the Teapot Society." The rival association continued in existence for four years, when it finally collapsed, and to-day is known as a local assembly of the Knights of Labor.

The little band continued to initiate members, and from time to time added to its ritual, which was not completed for a long time afterwards.

The first quarterly report showed a membership of twenty-eight, with the finances in a flourishing condition.

In the early part of May, 1870, public meetings of the garment-cutters were inaugurated, for the purpose of increasing the membership, by discussing questions of interest to the trade; but the name of the new Order was carefully kept secret.

These meetings had a beneficial effect, as the membership at the time of the second quarterly report was forty-three, an increase of fifteen; and the finances were still in good condition. The third quarterly report showed an increase of nine, — fifty-two members then being in good standing.

On October 5, 1870, occurred the first death, — that of Henry A. Senning, he having died on that day, aged 35.

On December 29, 1870, the second election occurred, and

all the officers were re-elected. The first annual report, of January 5, 1871, showed a membership of sixty-nine in good standing.

At the meeting of January 12, 1871, Mr. Stephens, Master Workman, made the following address to the Assembly: —

A cycle has ended, — the first in our history, — and bears its record of labors and toils to the dead sea of the past. During the year God's toilers have worked and wept as of yore; the brain has throbbed and the heart has beat for wrongs they were powerless to right. Busy industry has struggled to heap in the lap of the world's commerce the usual amount of values, —

> "Rich in model and design;
> Harvest-tool and husbandry,
> Loom and wheel, and engin'ry,
> Secrets of the sullen mine,
> Steel, and gold, and corn, and wine,
> Fabric rough or fairy fine,
> Sunny tokens of the line,
> Polar marvels and a feast
> Of wonders out of West and East."

And while the toiler is thus engaged in creating the world's value, how fares his own interest and well-being? We answer, "Badly," for he has too little time, and his faculties become too much blunted by unremitting labor to analyze his condition or devise and perfect financial schemes or reformatory measures. The hours of labor are too long, and should be shortened. I recommend a universal movement to cease work at five o'clock Saturday afternoon, as a beginning. There should be a greater participation in the profits of labor by the industrious and intelligent laborer. In the present arrangements of labor and capital, the condition of the employee is simply that of wage-slavery, — capital dictating, labor submitting; capital superior, labor inferior.

This is an artificial and man-created condition, not God's arrangement and order; for it degrades man and ennobles mere pelf. It demeans those who live by useful labor, and, in proportion, exalts all those who eschew labor and live (no matter by what pretence or respectable cheat — for cheat it is) without productive work.

Living by and on the labor of others is dishonest, and should be branded as such. Labor and capital should treat each other as equals.

Let us hint to the world, in broad and unmistakable terms, our demands.

Where lies the fault that this condition of things exists? Mainly with ourselves. Disjointed and inharmonious, no concerted action, not even much mutual respect. Prone to defer to wealth, to respect pretension and bow to assumption, instead of boldly stripping it of its mask and exposing its hideousness.

What is the remedy? Cultivate friendship among the great brotherhood of toil; learn to respect industry in the person of every intelligent worker; unmask the shams of life by deference to the humble but useful craftsman; beget concert of action by conciliation, confidence by just and upright conduct toward each other; mutual respect by dignified deportment; and wise counsels by what of wisdom and ability God, in his wisdom and goodness, has endowed us with.

In our own sphere and circle much has been done in the year that is passed; much preparation before the foundation could be laid, much material to be gathered. A retrospect of the year is satisfactory. Several have been steadied in their situations, some have been changed to better, and many have been assisted to vacancies they would not have known of. All this, and more, has been done, and all has tended toward the central point of keeping the remuneration up to a satisfactory standard. Influences are at work to reduce the standard. This must be watched vigilantly, and, if necessary, an effort must be made to counteract the evil, by public open work, by blows in the right place, that will tell and hurt; for all evils have their vulnerable points, and can be reached. There is work for the ready hand and willing heart; an abundant harvest awaits the reaper.

Let us be aroused. Labor's interests have suffered long enough, because the interested ones have neglected to take care of them; unwise counsels have too long prevailed; suspicion and distrust have too long kept us apart. Let us reason together, and let our reasonings bear the fruit of action.

Knighthood must base its claims for labor upon higher grounds than participation in the profits and emoluments and a lessening of the hours of toil and fatigues of labor. These are only physical effects, and objects of a grosser nature, and, although *imperative*, are but stepping-stones to a higher cause, a nobler nature. The real and ultimate reasons must be based upon the more exalted and divine nature of man, — his high and noble capabilities for good. Excess of labor and small pay stunts, and blunts, and degrades those god-like faculties, until the image of God, in which he is created and intended by his great Creator to exhibit, are scarcely discernible, and ignorance boldly asserts that it does not exist.

Time will not permit us to reason out the details, or enforce them by argument, but we must leave their development to your own thought and investigation. To God and your own best judgment I leave the cause. Prophecy and inspiration assert the ultimate triumph of the principle.

In March, 1871, Messrs. Stephens and Breen began a correspondence with the coal-miners and nail-cutters of Pennsylvania, — this being the first outside work. At the beginning of 1872, Robert C. Macauley was called to the chair, as Master Workman, Mr. Stephens declining a nomination for a third term. The ship-carpenters and calkers employed in Cramp's ship-yard, on the Delaware, true to the traditions of their craft as pioneers, organized the first local assembly, outside of Assembly No. 1, in 1872. Prior to this, Assembly No. 1 had initiated some plumbers, paper-hangers, and painters, admitting them into the original assembly. They, however, were termed "sojourners," not paying any dues nor being allowed to vote. They were initiated, that they might work for organization in their respective crafts; but, up to the organization of Local Assembly No. 2, attempts at organization outside the original assembly were unsuccessful. After Local Assembly No. 2 had been organized, the Order spread rapidly, — no less than twenty assemblies being organized in Philadelphia during that year, as follows: No. 3, Shawl-weavers; No. 4, Carpet-weavers; No. 5, Riggers; No. 6, Carpet-weavers; No. 7, Stone-masons; No. 8, Bag-makers; No. 9, Machinists and Blacksmiths; No. 10, Stone-cutters; No. 11, Wool-sorters; No. 12, Machinists and Blacksmiths; No. 13, Tin-plate and Sheet-iron Workers; No. 14, Steel-makers; No. 15, Pattern-makers and Moulders; No. 16, Shopsmiths; No. 17, Machinists, Blacksmiths, and Boiler-makers; No. 18, House-carpenters, Ship-joiners, Millwrights, and Cabinet-makers; No. 19, Bricklayers; No. 20, Gold-beaters.

The first local assembly to be organized outside of Philadelphia was No. 28, composed of gold-beaters of New York City. The second local organized outside of Philadelphia was No. 30, Ship-carpenters and Calkers, of Wilmington, Del. The third was No. 31, of the same craft, in Camden, N. J. This assembly is now known, however, as a shoemakers' assembly.

Up to this time the ritual was neither written nor printed, the officers of Local Assembly No. 1 being compelled to found new locals, and fill the offices until their own officers had acquired a sufficient knowledge of the secret work to conduct the meetings. The organization spread so rapidly that the Committee on Ritual was appointed Committee on the Good of the Order, and to them all matters of dispute arising in the local assemblies were submitted for final adjudication. This committee was practically the first district assembly in the Order, performing all the functions of a district assembly. This work, however, became too arduous, and the committee began to construct a ritual for a higher body, to be known as a "district assembly."

A communication was sent from Local Assembly No. 1 to the various locals then in existence, notifying them to send delegates for the purpose of founding a district assembly. These delegates met on Christmas Day, 1873, and founded District Assembly No. 1. The committee of Local Assembly No. 1 thereupon surrendered all its powers to the district assembly. This district assembly did not receive a charter, however, until August 19, 1878, when all district assemblies formed prior to that date received charters from the General Assembly. The charter of District Assembly No. 1 is dated back to Christmas Day, 1873, to legalize what had been done by that body up to the foundation of the General Assembly.

The following local assemblies composed District Assembly No. 1 at the time of its formation: No. 1, Garment-cutters; No. 17, Blacksmiths and Boiler-makers; No. 23, Carpet-weavers; No. 31, Ship-carpenters and Calkers, Camden, N. J.; No. 53, Cigar-makers, Philadelphia; No. 64, Shoemakers, Philadelphia; No. 84; No. 116, Stove-mounters, Philadelphia; No. 131, Bolt-makers, Philadelphia; No. 260, Train-hands, Philadelphia; No. 262, Philadelphia.

The continued increase in membership and in the number of local assemblies was such, that before the end of the year 1877 new district assemblies had been organized, as follows: District Assembly No. 2, in New Jersey; District Assembly No. 3, in Pittsburgh; District Assembly No. 4, in Reading, Penn.; District Assembly No. 5, in Charleston, S. C.; District Assembly No. 6, in New Haven, Conn.; District Assembly No. 7, in Akron, O.; District Assembly No. 8, in Pittsburgh, Penn.; District Assembly No. 9, in West Elizabeth, Penn.; and others, to the number of at least fifteen.

Up to the beginning of the year 1878, the various branches of the Order had, by tacit consent, regarded District Assembly No. 1 as the head of authority; and that district assembly, by its officers, issued a call for a convention of delegates from the several district assemblies, which was accordingly held at Reading, Penn., January 1, 1878, and a General Assembly of the Order was formed, with a constitution, and three salaried officers.

Uriah S. Stephens was chosen temporary chairman, but was called away by business before the end of the session, which lasted four days, yet in his absence he was chosen Grand Master Workman. Ralph Beaumont, of Elmira, N. Y., was chosen Grand Worthy Foreman; Charles H. Litchman, of Marblehead, Mass., Grand Secretary; John G. Laning, of Clifton, West Va., Grand Assistant Secretary; and Thomas M. Gallagher, of St. Louis, Mo., Grand Treasurer, for the ensuing year.

Among the delegates to this First General Assembly was T. V. Powderly, representing District Assembly 5, of Scranton, Penn. The number of this District Assembly was afterwards changed to 16. There were present, delegates from seven States, representing the following trades, viz.: Garment-cutters, miners, shoemakers, machinists, locomotive engineers, stationary engineers, glass-workers, moulders, printers, coopers, blacksmiths, boiler-makers, nail-packers, teachers, and carpenters.

The Declaration of Principles adopted at this convention contained fifteen planks, which are the first fifteen in the present Declaration of Principles.

The chairman of the Committee on Constitution, who probably had this in charge, was Robert Schilling, of Ohio, who was president of the Labor Congress at Rochester, N. Y., in 1874. The convention adopted a constitution for the General Assembly, District Assemblies, and Local Assemblies.

A special session of the General Assembly was called to meet at Philadelphia, Penn., June 6, 1878, an emergency having arisen demanding consideration. There were present delegates from six States, and they were in session two days.

The next session of the General Assembly was held January 14–17, 1879, at St. Louis, Mo., at which delegates from thirteen States were present. The Order had spread into the Southern States, and as far as California,

The Grand Master Workman, U. S. Stephens, referred to the fact that great political elections had recently been held, but no real politics had been settled. He said: —

The *few* are millionaires; the *many* struggle for bread. Where, if not here in this Western World, shall the patriotism and statesmanship be found to preserve the race from destruction? Neither the bayonet, nor bullets from Gatling-guns, can save it. Justice to all alone can do it.

Failing in that, these American governments will fail; and over our institutions the dust of ages will fall like Pompeian ashes, and we shall live only in the misrepresentations of history. But your presence here gives us life and hope. It means a waking up to the historical facts: that great wealth means certain corruption at the fountain of law; that limited intelligence is suborned to villany, and the best genius of our time is perverted to the baseness of unprincipled, and yet, after all, *bankrupt* greed. Coming, as you do, from all over this continent, shows the magnitude of the awakening. It foretells the blessing of Heaven upon those who help themselves. It secures the coming "to the fore" at an early day, in industrial, commercial, political and social life of those principles and legal enactments that shall secure the physical well-being, the mental development and the moral elevation of mankind.

He continued: —

During the year that is past, a large increase and prosperity have attended our efforts to spread our already widely-extended Brotherhood, when we take into consideration that the means we had at our command were so limited, and the work to be accomplished scattered over a whole continent.

Concerning the amalgamation of entire callings, he said: —

During the year, some trades and callings have so nearly accomplished the complete organization of their entire branch all over the continent, within our fraternity, that but little remains for them to do in the work. The callings named are now in condition to maintain the standard of wages, and the standard amount of work or production that constitutes a fair and just day's work (this latter, in many trades, often entailing greater evils and engendering more dissatisfaction and bitterness than the former), or of restoring standards that have, through cutting-down, been lost, or by the adoption of machinery unreasonable enlarged.

He suggested the issuing of an address to the trades associations of the continent, calling their attention to the benefits of amalgamation and affiliation with their great brotherhood, and the evils of isolated effort or association. He continued: —

We must show ourselves mightier than the difficulties confronting us; and, when we succeed in doing that, the *world* will respect us, and we shall respect *ourselves*.

He suggested that the ensuing year be especially devoted to welding all labor organizations into one grand consolidated body, and also called attention to the importance of teaching and organizing co-operation by the district assemblies.

The secretary, in his report, called attention to the necessity of taking some action to preserve a history of the origin of the Order, as from this history an address could be prepared for the members of the Order, and be the means of adding largely to the membership.

At this session, district assemblies were granted the privilege of making the name of the Order public, upon a vote of two-thirds of the delegates of the district.

Mr. Stevens was re-elected Grand Master Workman; Mr. Litchman, Grand Secretary; James McGinness, of Kentucky, was elected Grand Assistant Secretary; and William H. Singer, of Missouri, Grand Treasurer.

The third regular session of the General Assembly convened at Chicago, Ill., September 2, 1879, and continued in session five days.

In his opening remarks at this convention, Grand Master Workman Stephens said: —

The entire history of the world, in every age and in every country, as unvarying as the laws that govern the universe, demonstrates the fact that the physical, intellectual, and moral condition of mankind is governed entirely by the conditions that surround the productive toiler, and marks the progress of a people, or indicates, unerringly, the downfall of a nation. This should be the only criterion of a statesman, the guide of the political economist, and the inspiration of the philanthropist. Sad experience assures us no relief can be expected from those elevated by the polluted channels of party politics to positions that should be held by patriotic and enlightened statesmen; or the stilted ignorance of political economy, as usually taught in the schools; and even the philanthropist is more or less blinded by the glamour and misrepresentations promulgated by concentrated wealth. If ever relief is had, or simple justice secured to the masses, it will have to come through the efforts of themselves alone. To this fact is owing the existence of Knighthood. As nature abhors a vacuum, so at the call of the strongly-felt want of a working world's saviour, this brotherhood sprang into existence, and espoused the cause of oppressed humanity. No other organization in existence proposes to meet this great want, or directs its efforts to this mighty work. To this session all eyes are turned in expectant hope, and upon it mainly depends the issue of an upward trend of the toiling millions towards a higher and a better plane of existence, as "God, the Father of all," intended should be the condition of His children, or a downward drifting toward a fathomless abyss of pinching poverty, and to the untold millions hopeless, unrequited toil and serfdom to combined wealth, — the landless, disinherited life of the Eastern pariah. Let us, therefore, give a calm consideration, a cool, collected wisdom, and the very best efforts of our united intellect, to each measure presented, so as to perfect the best methods possible for advancing the objects we desire and humanity so much needs.

He again called attention to the unification and extension of the labor movement. In correspondence which he had with labor men, he says: —

The fact appears to be established tnat all the leading minds and close thinkers among the union men in all branches are ready for the consummation, and that nothing really beneficial can be accomplished until a complete unification is had. The time has fully come when *all* trade and labor organizations of every description should be united. The interest of each would be greatly enhanced thereby.

He calls attention to the frequent attempts being made all over the country to break down the ten-hour standard, and enforce longer hours, which he claimed was done to affect the eight-hour movement, to which he gave encouragement, and urged active exertion and agitation to bring public sentiment up to a point that would successfully carry the principle of eight hours through the ballot-box.

He concluded his remarks as follows: —

The moment has come to say farewell, and to surrender into the hands of others the trust you have confided to me since the organization of the General Assembly. May I not embrace the opportunity to say that my heart and soul are bound up in the success of that which has been so ably planned, so patiently cultivated, and so zealously defended. And when the closing years of my life are passing away, it will cause my pulses to beat with a quicker throb to recall the duties of this trust, and to reflect that perhaps, in some small degree, the manner in which those duties were performed aided in gaining the success which I know will surely come.

Up to this time, 700 local assemblies had been organized, but only 102 reported. There were about 5,000 members in good standing, according to the reports, but there was probably a very much larger membership.

At this session Mr. Powderly was elected Grand Master Workman, Richard Griffiths, of Illinois, Grand Worthy Foreman, Mr. Litchman was re-elected Grand Secretary, Gilbert Rockwood, of Boston, Mass., was elected Grand

Assistant Secretary, and Dominick Hammer, of Ohio, elected Grand Treasurer.

The fourth session of the General Assembly was held at Pittsburgh, Penn., September 7–11, 1880. Forty delegates were present.

Grand Master Workman Powderly, in his address, said: —

The quicksands which have swallowed up many a noble organization in the past are many, and still exist; they are ever present, and, unfortunately, keep pace with our organization. Could men learn and profit by the dread experience of the past, instead of groping blindly into the future, we would fare far better.

He spoke of strikes as one of the evils which beset trades-unions, and which now and then come to the surface in this organization. He said: —

We are the willing victims of an outraged system that envelopes us in the midst of the ills of which we complain. We should not war with man for being what *we* make him, but strike powerful, telling blows at the base of the system which makes the laborer the slave of his master. So long as the present order of things exists, just so long will the attempt to make peace between the man who sells and the man who buys labor be fruitless.

He said the only way to prevent strikes was to abolish the wage-system. He further said: —

This is the system which carries with it into the workshop, the mine and the factory a host of evils, which, to repeat, would completely exhaust the whole vocabulary of murmurings which fill the complaint-book of labor.

This is the system which, serpent-like, pushes itself along wherever those bands of commercial iron and steel are laid, carrying discontent and misery in its train.

This is the system which enables half-a-dozen men to sit at their tables in any of our large centres of trade, and, without any thought of the welfare of the country, issue the imperial mandates which direct the movements of the whole industrial population of the United States.

This is the system which makes every railroad superintendent, every factory or mine superintendent, an autocrat, at whose nod or beck the poor unrequited slave who labors must bow the head and bend the knee in humble suppliance.

To point out a way to utterly destroy this system would be a pleasure to me. I can only direct your attention to it, and leave the rest to your wisdom; and I firmly believe that I have pointed out the most vicious of all evils which afflict labor to-day.

But are we prepared to lay siege to this bulwark of oppression? Remember that for centuries it has been slowly, yet steadily, creeping onward, making, each year, new and deeper inroads upon labor, until to-day it stands so well established and powerful that even the staunchest heart in the ranks of labor's defenders almost sinks in despair at the thought of breaking down the barriers of fear, ignorance and superstition, to which its existence has given birth.

The wage-system, at its inception, was but an experiment, and doubts were entertained as to its adoption; but the avaricious eye of the Shylock of labor saw in it a weapon with which he could strike the toiler to the dust, and to-day that system has so firm a hold upon us that every attempt at shaking off the fetters by resorting to a strike only makes it easier for the master to say to his slave, "*You must work for less wages.*"

We must teach our members, then, that the remedy for the redress of the wrongs we complain of does not lie in the suicidal strike; but it lies in thorough, effective organization. Without organization, we cannot accomplish anything; through it, we hope to forever banish that curse of modern civilization, — wage-slavery.

But how? Surely not by forming an association and remaining a member; not by getting every other worthy man to become a member, and remain one; not by paying the dues required of us as they fall due. These are all important factors in the method by which we hope to regain our independence, and are vitally important; they are the elements necessary to a complete organization.

Organization once perfected, what must we do? I answer, study the best means of putting your organization to some practical use by embarking in a system of co-operation, which will eventually make every man his own master, every man his own employer; a system which will give the laborer a fair proportion of the products of his toil.

It is to co-operation, then, as the lever of labor's emancipation, that the eyes of the workingmen and women are directed; upon co-operation their hopes are centered, and to it do I now direct your attention. I am deeply sensible of the importance, of the magnitude of the undertaking in which I invite you to engage. I know that it is human nature to grow cold, apathetic, and finally indifferent, when engaged in that which requires deep study and persistent effort, unattended by excitement; men are apt to believe, that physical force is the better way of redressing grievances, being the shorter remedy; but even that requires patience and fortitude as well as strength. I need but point out to you the war of the Revolution, which took nearly eight years of hard fighting and persistent effort upon the part of men who fought for a principle. Had these men fallen into the same error which labor has so often fallen into, there would be no independence; had they gone to their homes after the battle of Bunker Hill, there would be no Bunker Hill Monument erected, even though the result of that battle was encouraging.

To the subject of co-operation, then, do I invite your attention, and I liken it unto the Revolutionary war. If you decide upon carrying it out at this convention, it will be the Bunker Hill of Industrial Independence; but you must also bear in mind, though the longest term allotted to man be yours to live, you will not see during that term the complete triumph of your hopes. The war for American Indedendence had its Bunker Hills and its Washingtons, but it also had its Valley Forges and its Benedict Arnolds. The enthusiasm of the hour will avail us nothing, and co-operation requires every Washington of labor to be up and doing. The laboring man needs education in this great social question, and the best minds of the Order must give their precious thought to this system. There is no good reason why labor cannot, through co-operation, own and operate mines, factories and railroads. By co-operation alone can a system of colonization be established in which men may band together for the purpose of securing the greatest good to the greatest number, and place the man who is willing to toil upon his own homestead. Through co-operation alone can the people reclaim the land, the heritage of the Universal Father. Millions of acres have been stolen from the people, and while we may think that that question is of no interest to us here to-day, I sincerely believe that for every acre of land which God designed for man's use and benefit that is stolen, another link is riveted to the chain with which the land bond-lords hope to finally encircle us. A few short years ago, if the representatives of labor had met in convention such as this is, the land question would not necessarily have intruded itself upon them; but during those few short years we have slept, and to-day, whether we will or not, it is thrust upon us.

Our Order has within its folds some of the best minds of the country; and, recognizing the fact that this body of men cannot, at this session, perfect the best means of embarking in co-operative or colonization enterprises, yet we can discuss this question, and frame such laws as to us seem best.

On the eight-hour law, he says: —

A reduction in the hours of labor is a necessity, to which we can no longer close our eyes. To the inventive genius of the mechanic and laborer are due the new and varied improvements in machinery of all kinds. The man who sits comfortably clipping the coupons from his bonds, never invents anything, unless it be a new way to squeeze more labor out of the toiler for less money. He must depend upon the man who labors for everything, including the wonderful inventions in the way of improved machinery. Does the improvement of any of the machines in use, or the invention of a new one, add to his labors? No. On the contrary, he is enabled thereby to reap a greater profit; for, if an employer, he discharges the man who invents the machine, and hires a boy to run it for less money.

The wonderful machinery of to-day renders it possible for man to perform tenfold more labor than a century ago. Have the hours of labor been reduced accordingly? On the contrary, men are obliged to work longer in proportion to-day than they did in the past.

If to the workman's brain is due these wonderful inventions, then to his body should come the rest made necessary by such drains upon his mental system, and the only way to give that rest is to reduce the hours of labor, and every opportunity should be improved looking to that end; but a mere request to lend assistance in reducing the hours of labor will not avail. Men *must be compelled to help themselves*, and a law should be passed at this General Assembly, requiring each member to assist by voice and pen, by petition and means, every honest effort looking towards the amelioration of the condition of the wage-slave by reducing his hours of labor.

On the subject of child-labor, his remarks were:—

Does not every thinking man tremble when he gives a moment's thought to the future of this great nation; when he considers that the children of to-day will be the men who will govern the nation, or be governed by tyrants themselves? If they are to govern the nation, is it not a terrible, a sad commentary upon our institutions, that the future governors are to-day receiving the training necessary for such an undertaking in our county jails and prisons? If, on the other hand, they are to be governed, what a hopeless, dreary, drudging life is opened up to men, who, knowing but little of their rights, will never dare to ask for them! Either of these pictures is an unpleasant one to contemplate. Our Order can be made an engine of destruction to the system which drives the child of tender years into competition with its parent or parents. It is our duty, then, to do something here, to-day, for the good of humanity in the future, by beginning an agitation upon this question, which will end in its disappearance from our country.

The Grand Secretary made an exhaustive report to the convention, devoting considerable space to the Eight-hour law. Up to this time, the *Labor Tribune* had published a column under five stars, (*****) which meant the Knights of Labor.

The fifth session was held at Detroit, Mich., March 6–10, 1881.

In 1880, the Order did not increase much in membership, and the desire to make its name and principles public had increased. Some of the district assemblies were working openly, while others worked secretly.

At this convention, Mr. Litchman declined to be a candidate for the office of Grand Secretary, and Robert D. Layton, of Pittsburgh, Penn., was elected.

The next session was held in New York City, September 5–12, 1882.

During the preceding year, an effort had been made by certain parties to create division in the ranks of the iron and steel workers, with a view to their joining the Knights of Labor.

The General Assembly, at this convention, deprecated any efforts of this kind, and passed resolutions giving the Amalgamated Association of Iron and Steel Workers their moral support, and expressed their opposition to any movement tending to weaken the position assumed by the Amalgamated Association.

Some changes were made in the secret work of the Order during this year, and considerable insubordination was aroused.

Strikes had multiplied from year to year. The General Master Workman, in his address, said:—

> One cause for the tidal-wave of strikes that has swept over our Order comes from the exaggerated reports of the strength of the Order, numerically and financially, given by many of our organizers. Such a course may lead men into the Order, but by a path that leads them out again; for, as soon as they become convinced that they were deceived, they lose confidence in the Order.

Many misrepresentations had been made in reference to the objects and name of the Order, and the General Master Workman was quoted as saying that he would "*vote a rifle and Gatling-gun to each member of the Order.*"

The great boycott of the Duryea Starch Company attracted considerable attention at the time, seriously affecting the credit of the Grand Statistician of the Order.

The Order increased in membership. Workmen in many places were blacklisted for belonging to it. Many complaints were entered of overbearing and tyrannical treatment by employers. Coal-diggers were said to be treated like slaves; from another place the complaint was made that workmen were treated in a brutal manner; if one became sick, he was discharged. It was reported from another place that the utmost tyranny prevailed in most of the shops and factories; that efforts to organize were punished by dismissal.

We quote a few more complaints: "Treated with harshness;" "the treatment is insolent, arrogant and oppressive;" "we are treated the same as any other piece of machinery;" "frequently threatened and victimized;" "treated like dogs, and have to sign an agreement not to belong to the Knights of Labor, if we want to get employment;" "employers around here never concede anything without a strike;" "horses are treated better than men in this region.;" "we are forced to trade at the 'pluck me'" (meaning a truck-store).

After the organization of labor in certain localities, the treatment seems to have improved, one assembly reporting: "The treatment was arbitrary and unjust before we were organized: now it is courteous;" another, that "they (the employers) have simmered down since the Order was established here," while another report was: "The treatment has gradually improved since the labor agitation in Chicago brought about laws in our own interests and sanitary inspection in factories and dwellings."

The death of the founder and first Grand Master Workman of the Order, U. S. Stephens, was noticed by fitting resolutions.

The seventh session convened at Cincinnati, O., September 4, 1883, and was in session eight days.

The Grand Master Workman, in his address at this convention, referred to the strike of the Telegraphic Brotherhood, District Assembly 45, Knights of Labor, and said:—

> The failure of the strike may be attributed to the same cause as of old,—a lack of funds and a lack of knowledge of the principles involved; men who had large families dependent on them, and were otherwise burdened, were the last to return to work, while those that were younger, and had no one to care for but self, were the first to forget their allegiance to principle.

The change was made in the title of the officers of the General Assembly, from "Grand" to "General." Some changes were made in the officers, Frederick Turner being elected General Secretary, and Mr. Powderly being re-elected General Master Workman.

During the preceding year, there had been formed an organization under the name of the "Improved Order of the Knights of Labor."

Referring to this Order, General Master Workman Powderly wrote for the Pittsburgh *Times*, of July 16, 1883, as follows:—

> A great deal has been said of late concerning the dismemberment of the Knights of Labor, and the forming of the federation of trades. The principal reason given for the proposed action, summed up in a few words, is, that each trade or craft in being organized for itself can more easily and successfully engage in a strike. There are other arguments made use of to bolster up the "federation" idea, but that appears to be the principal one; at least, it is the one to which most prominence is given in the Eastern press. One thing is certain: the originator of that idea was neither a Knight of Labor nor a member of a trades-union, for members of these associations know that the tendency of the times is to do away with strikes; that remedy has been proved

by experience to be a very costly one for employer and employee. The trades-union does not favor a strike; it is regarded as a *dernier resort* by every labor association in the land, and no good can come of the dismemberment of an association, which, among other things, aims at the perfecting of a system by which disputes between the laborer and capitalist can be settled without resorting to so costly an experiment as the strike is acknowledged to be. Why, the Knights of Labor and the various labor associations of the country are in no great danger of being disbanded. I called the strike an experiment, and I would have every advocate of such a measure note these words. Strikes have been resorted to for centuries; and to-day, after hundreds of trials have been had, men cannot embark in a strike with any assurance of success, based upon a former precedent. Every one must be decided upon its own merits. I will never advocate a strike, unless it be a strike at the ballot-box, or such a one as was proclaimed to the world by the unmistakable sound of the strikers' guns on the field of Lexington. But the necessity for such a strike as the latter does not exist at present. The men who made the name of Lexington famous in the world's history were forced to adopt the bullet, because they did not possess the ballot. We have the latter; and if the money of the monopolists can influence us to deposit our ballots in favor of our enemies, — if we cannot be depended on to go quietly to the polling-booth, and summon to our aid moral courage enough to deposit a little piece of paper in our own interest, — how can it be expected of us to summon physical courage enough to do battle for our rights, as did our fathers at Lexington? And if we do go to the tented field, will not the same agency that induced us to vote against ourselves, induce us to thrust our bayonets into the hearts of our friends instead of our foes? I answer, "Yes; for a faithless citizen never made a faithful soldier." What, then, is the duty of the hour?

Men may argue, from what I have said, that I believe our cause to be hopeless, and, did I not have faith in the Knights of Labor, I would say, "Yes; the cause is lost." Other men entertain different opinions, and positively assert that the panacea for all the ills we suffer will come through the adoption of such advice as they have to offer; for instance, "Democrat" says in his letter of July 4th, that, in order to secure the blessings we seek, we have only to merge ourselves into the great Democratic party, and help to swell the triumph of the plain people in 1884! I must be pardoned for differing with him. I do not believe that it lies within the province of any party to protect the many against the unjust encroachments of the moneyed few, unless the many are properly instructed in the science of government. The party is the concrete man. If the individuals comprising the party are ignorant of their rights, and must trust to the wisdom or discretion of the party leaders, they either follow in the wake of blind leaders, or permit themselves to be blindly led along by their leaders. In either case, it will not be the intelligence they display, or the instructions they give that will urge their leaders forward in an honest groove, and under such circumstances as these the duty of the citizen ceases so soon as he casts his vote. Will "Democrat" assure us that if each of the associations he names (the Grangers, the Knights of Labor, the Amalgamated Association, and the various trades-unions) should cease to work, and "merge into the Democratic party," that they would not be obliged to reorganize again in a few years to protect themselves from the Democratic party? Will any Republican assure members of these associations that a general reorganization will not be necessary, should they merge into the Republican party? Remember, I am not assailing parties; the party is good or bad, as the majority of its members determine. Who is to blame for the misdeeds of a party? The majority. Who comprise the majorities in the Democratic and Republican parties? Why, "the plain people," of course. I believe that there is no man so good that he will not bear watching. What is true of man is true of party; and, in either case, the watchers must be educated — they must be actuated by one common impulse; in other words, they must be organized. That there are men who believe that political parties require both watching and teaching, I am positive. Let me quote the words of a man whose fidelity to the Democratic party cannot be questioned, but whose love of justice is stronger than his regard for party. In his letter to the Constitutional Club, of New York, Judge Jeremiah S. Black says: —

"What is the remedy? No enforcement of the Constitution and laws, which command what is right and prohibit what is wrong; for that cannot be effected without officers that are faithful. As it is, our Governors do not govern, and legislators laugh in your face when you tell them of their oaths. Shall we turn them out and fill their places with true men? That is easier said than done. Monopoly has methods of debauching party leaders, cheating voters, and deceiving the very elect, which perpetually defeat our hopes of honest government. If the power of the corporations increases a little more, they can put their worst rascal into the highest office as easily as Caligula's horse was elected consul by the people of Rome.

"You will infer from this that I am somewhat discouraged; and it is true that very recent events here in Pennsylvania have much disappointed me. But that is no reason why you should despair. You have what we have not, — an organization to make your grievances known; and I hope that from your meeting the truth will go forth to rescue and rouse up like the sound of a trumpet."

It may be inferred, from the position I have taken in the foregoing lines, that the mission of the Knights of Labor is to become a political party, and that it is intended to take precedence of the Democratic party. The inference would be wrong. The Order of the Knights of Labor is higher and grander than party. There is a nobler future before it than that which clings to its existence amidst partisan rancor and strife. The Order is a friend to men of all parties, and believing that the moment it assumes the role of a political party its usefulness would be destroyed, it has refrained and will refrain from doing so. The moment we proclaim to the world that our Order is a political party, that moment the lines are drawn, and we receive no more accessions to our ranks from the other existing parties, with the exception of here and there a member who becomes a convert through conviction that we are right. We have political parties enough. Every one of them in its early days was honest and gave promise of good results; but the moment that success perched upon its banners, the vultures who feed upon spoils also perched upon its body, and to a certain extent frustrated the designs of its organizers. The same would be true of the Knights of Labor. One reason why political parties degenerate is because the masses of the common people are not educated. We may be able to read and write, but we are not educated on the economic and social questions with which we are brought in contact every hour. If we were, we could more easily discern the difference between good and bad legislation, and we would not be clamoring so often for the repeal of bad laws. The chief aim of the Knights of Labor is to educate not only men, but parties; educate men first, that they may educate parties and govern them intelligently and honestly. Ralph Waldo Emerson gave this advice before leaving us. He said:—

"Let us make our education brave and preventive. Politics is an after-work, a poor patching. We are always a little late. The evil is done, the law is past, and we begin the up-hill agitation for the repeal of that of which we ought to have prevented the enacting. We shall one day learn to supersede politics by education. What we call root and branch reforms of slavery, war, gambling, intemperance, is only medicating the symptoms. We must begin higher,—namely, in education."

"To supersede politics by education," it first becomes necessary to organize the masses into an association where they can be educated. Take fifty men of one calling and place them in a room organized under the laws of a distinct trade society, and they will discuss nothing but such matters as pertain to their trade. If they do not mingle among those of other trades, they will grow indifferent to the wants of others; they will remain in ignorance of their own rights through the ignorance of the rights of others. Selfishness will be the rule, and "the up-hill" agitation for the repeal of that which we ought to have prevented the enacting, still stares us constantly in the face. I am aware that the Knights of Labor meet with opposition from the leaders of some labor organizations. They anticipate that in the event of their associations becoming a part of the Knights of Labor, their occupation, like Othello's, will be gone; but they entertain groundless fears. We seek the co-operation of every labor society, the dissolution of none. We seek and intend to enlist the services of men of every society, of every party, every religion and every nation, in the crusade which we have inaugurated against these twin monsters, tyranny and monopoly, and in that crusade we have burned the bridges behind us; we have stricken from our vocabulary that word "fail"; we aim at establishing the complete rights of man throughout the world; we take as our guide no precedent ever set by mortal man, unless it be right; we tolerate no dissensions, and will have no disbanding, save as is ordained by the Great Master Workman, when He calls from our ranks each individual member, and bids him join that silent majority, whose votes upon the questions of this world find voice only on the pages of the recorded past.

The eighth session of the General Assembly was held at Philadelphia, September 1, 1884, and continued in session eleven days.

General Master Workman Powderly referred, in his address, to the growth of the Order since its inception, and said that up to that day it had been sowing the seed, and that in the future members must bend their energies to gathering in the harvest.

Speaking on the subject of political action, he severely criticised the course of politicians, saying: —

Nominate a man for the legislature in any of our large cities to-day, and, unless he buys his way into office, he stands a good chance of being defeated.

In regard to misrepresentations as to the doctrines, objects and purposes of the Order, he said: —

Such doings have retarded the progress of organized labor as much as the opposition of capital. * * * We have had too much trouble from members advancing their own ideas, or the theories of some other organization, and palming them off as declarations of the Knights of Labor.

The importation of laborers under contract was commented upon at some length by Mr. Powderly, at this convention. His remarks were, in substance, as follows: —

One of the evils of which we complain at the present day is the manner in which unfortunate men and women are brought to this country under a contract to work for a master for from two to five years. This is slavery in its worst form. Not only does it enslave the unfortunate immigrant, but it also enslaves the men and women with whom he is brought in competition on our shores.

In the June previous to this convention, Mr. Powderly had published a letter in the Scranton *Truth*, with reference to the working of Hungarian women at the coke-ovens. In this letter, he wrote that he had spent a good share of a week in investigating the conditions and surroundings of the wage-workers of that section. He had ample opportunity afforded him of viewing the details. He referred incidentally to the misrepresentations made to these people by the agents of monopoly, and continued: —

The opposition to the Hungarians in the coke regions amounts to hatred, — a hatred which is liable at any time to burst forth in a blaze which may sweep them entirely out of that country. This antipathy is not confined to the workingmen alone: it is shared in by *business men and workingmen alike*; and they all unite in cursing the advent of the Hungarian to the coke region. Last Monday, the largest firm engaged in the manufacture of coke sent a force of Hungarians down into the mines, and the men employed in the mines immediately quit work. There was no meeting called for the purpose of coming to an agreement; but just as soon as it was ascertained that a Hungarian was entrusted with a lamp, the other men employed there quit work. I asked some of the men why they would not work with the Hungarians, and the answer was, "We don't care whether they pay these men more wages than they do us or not. It is not a question of wages. We might as well commit suicide as to go into the mine with them. They don't understand the manner of handling the safety-lamp, and may set off the gas at any time, and burn us all to death. They don't know how to read, and cannot tell when they see the danger-signs."

At the request of the men, I remained in Connellsville last Wednesday night, for the purpose of visiting an assembly. Shortly after the meeting opened, a message was handed in to the chairman, asking whether the doors could not be thrown open to the public. The request was granted, and the hall was soon filled by business men and farmers. They said that they all suffered through the evils of Hungarian labor, and wished to take counsel with the workingmen as to the best steps to take in removing this curse from the country. They work for little or nothing, live on fare which a Chinaman would not touch, and will submit to any and every indignity which may be imposed on them. In a word, they are utterly devoid of the spirit necessary to make them good and patriotic American citizens.

The following day, I spoke at an outdoor meeting at the mine where the strike occurred. At the meeting it was resolved to inaugurate a series of meetings throughout the entire coke region, and enlist the sympathy of every interested person in the valley. I had often heard of the *employment of women* at the coke-ovens, but never had an opportunity of seeing it before. The women are not employed by the corporations, but they accompany their husbands and fathers to the ovens early in the mornings and assist in drawing and forking coke. At six o'clock in the morning, I went to the coke-works, and saw for myself that the stories that I had been told were not exaggerated. At one of the ovens, I saw a woman drawing the hot coke from the chamber. She had no covering on her head, and very little on her person. Her only attire consisted of a short, coarse chemise and a pair of cowhide boots. In a freight-car close by stood another woman forking the coke as it came to the car. Forking is the term used to indicate the disposition of the coke when it is thrown into the car. The person who does the forking throws the coke to either end of the car as it is wheeled in. This woman stood in the doorway, and was dressed in a coarse, loose-fitting outer garment and an apron. Her person from the waist up was exposed. When she stooped over to handle the coke, she caught her hair between her teeth in order to keep it out of her way. Her feet were incased in a pair of heavy shoes; her legs were exposed from the knees down. Her babe, which she had brought to the works with her, lay in front of the car, with scarcely any covering except the shadow of a wheelbarrow which was turned up in order to protect the child from the rays of the sun. Many more such scenes as these met my view,—some of them even worse than the ones I have described. These will, however, suffice to give your readers an idea of *what imported contract labor really means.*

Before the Hungarian was imported, the task for an ordinary man was to

GENERAL EXECUTIVE BOARD, KNIGHTS OF LABOR.

draw five ovens; but the Hungarian takes the contract for six ovens for less money than the American formerly received for five. He compels his wife or grown-up daughter to accompany him to the ovens in the mornings and assist in the work until about noon; after that, she may go home.

While the owner of the works does not employ the women, he is responsible for the crime of permitting them to work there, and should be held up to public execration and scorn.

If it were possible to make good and useful citizens of these men, I would never raise my voice against them. But that seems impossible. They will not adopt our manners and customs, except in rare instances. I have seen nine of them—eight men and one woman—occupying two small rooms; have inquired into their mode of living, and ascertained, beyond the shadow of a doubt, that the store-bill for the nine persons for the previous month was but twenty-seven dollars. Show me an American who will live like that, and I will show you a being who was born in vain. He may be fit to work—so is a mule. He may know enough to go in when it rains—but that is all. I believe that the claims to American citizenship should be based on intelligence, not wealth. To the exile from every land, who comes to us with the intention of staying among us, adopting our manners and customs, and assisting in protecting our institutions, I extend the open hand of welcome; but to the creature whose highest ambition is to work,—work, without knowing whether he receives adequate compensation or not, I have no welcome, and would prevent him from landing if I could. I believe that this country was intended for a race of freemen, and, believing that, I will always oppose the introduction of such men as are not capable of enjoying, appreciating, defending and perpetuating the blessings of good government.

The increase of the Order in the preceding year was steady and healthy. Statistics were presented to this convention, consisting of a table of wages, a table of ages, and a table of the hours of labor per day. Reports from every part of the country, save two, told tales of hardships suffered by the wage-workers.

A Knights of Labor trade-mark or label was adopted in 1884; but it was impossible to get it registered, owing to the fact that it was impossible to designate the character of the goods upon which it was to be used.

T. V. Powderly was again elected General Master Workman, Richard Griffiths was elected General Worthy Foreman, and Frederick Turner re-elected General Secretary-Treasurer. The ninth regular session of the General Assembly convened at Hamilton, Ont., October 5, 1885, and was in session eight days.

The General Master Workman's opening address has been

published within a year in the public press, and consequently we give only the salient features.

He spoke of the serious disturbances in the labor world, saying: —

> Men have grown restive under the treatment they were receiving, and have struck against impositions being practiced upon them. It has become fashionable of late to refuse to treat with workmen while they are on strike. In some cases, violence was practised; in others it was hinted at, and in others roughs were bargained for to disturb the peace, in order that the militia could be called out. Had the employers and employees come together, either through their agents or principals, all the things that have occurred could have been avoided. I am not prepared to say that the workers had justice on their side in every instance; but I am positive that the introduction of the Pinkerton detective as an agent in the settlement of disputes is entirely foreign to the letter and spirit of the Constitution of our common country. The men who make up the Pinkertons aregathered in from the brothels, gambling-dens and slums of our large cities, — composed of creatures who are outcasts from decent society. Their introduction for the purpose of settling disputes through force of arms is an insult to society everywhere. The employer of labor who calls to his aid a body of hired assassins — and the Pinkerton thugs can be called by no more appropriate name — must have a poor estimate of his own abilities and intelligence, when he lets such delicate and important work as the regulation of his business with his employees out to a human brute, devoid of intelligence, manhood, self-respect and decency.

He quoted from the Declaration of Independence as follows, referring to the complaints against the King of Great Britain: "He kept among us in times of peace standing armies without the consent of the legislature. He has affected to render the military independent of and superior to the civil power."

He spoke of the political power of the masses, when rightly directed and of the evils of convict labor on national work. He favored the incorporation of trades-unions and labor associations, called attention to the employment of foreign labor, gave considerable attention to the question of land legislation, recommended the appointment of a committee to look after necessary legislation, recommended trade industry, and spoke in his usual emphatic way against drunkenness. He also recommended co-operative efforts.

Important legislation was enacted at this session, and general lecturers appointed. As a result of this convention,

George E. McNeill was appointed by Mr. Powderly to represent the Order at Washington, he having no authority to appoint a committee.

In the winter of 1885 and spring of 1886, the Order grew with unprecedented rapidity. Never in the history of the world were the workingmen everywhere, of all trades and callings, so aroused to the needs of organization. Local assemblies were multiplied by hundreds, and thousands of men were enrolling their names daily. With this influx of new members, undisciplined and ignorant of the failures of the past, strikes multiplied as though a contagion spread from one end of the country to the other. This wonderful and unnatural growth led the Executive Board to place a check upon further organization, and in District 30 (Massachusetts,) led even to the suspension of the initiation of new members. In this last-named State, instructors were appointed to visit the local assemblies, and instruct them in the principles and work of the Order.

A special session of the General Assembly was convened at Cleveland, O., May 25, 1886, and was in session until June 3rd. At this session, a committee was appointed to look after legislation, and six auxiliary members of the Executive Board were elected, consisting of James E. Quinn, New York, W. H. Mullen, Richmond, Va., Hugh Cavanaugh, Cincinnati, O., D. R. Gibson, Hamilton, Ont., Joseph R. Buchanan, Denver, Col., and Ira B. Aylesworth, Baltimore, Md. Much time was consumed in discussing the relations of the Order to trades-unions; a circular address to the trades-unions was adopted, and a committee of five authorized to confer with the trades-union organization. The circular was as follows: —

To the Officers and Members of all National and International Trades-Unions of the United States and Canada, Greeting: —

BROTHERS IN THE CAUSE OF LABOR: — We, the Knights of Labor, in General Assembly convened, extend our heartiest greeting to all branches of honorable toil, welcoming them to the most friendly union in a common work.

This organization embraces within its folds all branches of honorable toil, and all conditions of men, without respect to trades, occupations, sex, creed, color, or nationality. We seek to raise the level of wages, and reduce the hours of labor; to protect men and women in their occupations, in their lives and limbs, and in their rights as citizens. We seek, also, to secure such legislation as shall tend to prevent the unjust accumulation of wealth, to restrict the power of monopolies and corporations, and to enact such wise and beneficent legislation as shall promote equity and justice, looking forward to the day when co-operation shall supersede the wage-system, and the castes and classes that now divide men shall be forever abolished.

We recognize the service rendered to humanity and the cause of labor by trades-union organizations; but believe that the time has come, or is fast approaching, when all who earn their bread by the sweat of their brow shall be enrolled under one general head, as we are controlled by one common law,— the law of our necessities; and we will gladly welcome to our ranks, or to protection under our banner, any organization requesting admission. And to such organizations as believe that their craftsmen are better protected under their present form of government, we pledge ourselves, as members of the great Army of Labor, to co-operate with them in every honorable effort to achieve the success which we are unitedly organized to obtain; and to this end we have appointed a special committee to confer with a like committee of any national or international trades-union, which shall desire to confer with us on the settlement of any difficulties that may occur between the members of the several organizations.

We have received a communication from a committee of some of the National and International Trades-Unions, requesting certain specific legislation at our hands; but as we believe that the object sought and stated in the preamble to the communication above referred to, can best be accomplished by a conference between a committee of this association and a committee of any other organization, and as the propositions contained therein are inconsistent with our duty to our members, we therefore defer action upon said propositions until a conference of committees can be held.

The basis upon which we believe an agreement can be reached would necessarily include the adoption of some plan by which all labor organizations could be protected from unfair men,— men expelled, suspended, under fine, or guilty of taking places of union men, or Knights of Labor while on strike or while locked out from work; and that as far as possible a uniform standard of hours of labor and wages should be adopted, so that men of any trade, enrolled in our Order, and members of trades-unions may not come in conflict because of a difference in wages or hours of labor. We also believe that a system of exchanging working-cards should be adopted, so that members of any craft, belonging to different organizations could work in harmony together, — the card of any member of this Order admitting men to work in any union shop, and the card of any union man admitting him to work in any Knights of Labor shop.

We further believe that, upon a demand for increase of wages, or shorter hours of labor, made by either organization, a conference should be held with the organized labor men employed in the establishment where the demand for increase of wages or reduction of hours is contemplated, — action upon a proposed reduction of wages or other difficulty to be agreed upon in like manner; and that, in the settlement of any difficulties between employers and employees, the organizations represented in the establishment shall be parties to the terms of settlement.

Trusting that the method proposed herein will meet with your approval, and that organized labor will move forward and onward in harmony of effort and of interest, we are yours fraternally.

The members of the committee recommending the above circular to the General Assembly were Frank K. Foster, chairman; Henry Mente, William H. Smith, P. H. Cummins, J. J. McCartney, Robert Schilling, Oliver Otis, L. L. Conaway, and George E. McNeill.

Among the cases settled by arbitration, under the auspices of the Order, in 1885, was the great Dueber Watch Company lockout, which lasted many months, and was finally settled by the reinstatement of the men. The strike on the Wabash system of railroads, after a large amount of correspondence, was settled by the following agreement: —

That no official should discriminate against the Knights of Labor, or question the right of the employee to belong to our Order.

That all employees locked out June 16, 1885, or who came out in their support since that date, should be reinstated as fast as possible.

That no new person should be put to work by the officials of the company until all the old employees locked out, or came out since the lockout, who desire employment, are reinstated.

KNIGHTS OF LABOR STRIKES.

Reference to the chapter on the Preamble and Declaration of Principles of the Knights of Labor will show that it is the desire of this Order, as it is of all labor organizations, to do away with strikes. They have made the principle of arbitration especially prominent, — not only asking of legislative bodies that courts of arbitration may be established, but that the members themselves may seek a settlement of all disputes by this means. The largest part of the time of the General Executive Committee, as well as that of the district and local executive boards, have been given to attempts to settle disputes in this way. Under the laws of the Order, every possible effort must be made to avoid strikes. When a grievance occurs in any establishment, it is referred to the local assembly having jurisdiction; or, where more than one assembly exists, and persons employed in the establishment are members of more than one, joint boards of arbitration are established, a committee of the board presents the grievance to the employer, and many difficulties have been settled by these local boards without the knowledge of the general public. In case of the refusal of the employer to meet the committee, or if a satisfactory arrangement cannot be reached, the case is referred to the District Executive Board; and, in case of a failure on their part, a statement of the case is presented to each local within the jurisdiction of the district, and the members are requested to vote upon the question of whether or not a strike shall be ordered. Neither the local nor the district board has the right to order a strike where more than twenty-five persons are involved. If a strike is ordered by a local assembly on the vote of its members, they have no right to the assistance fund; and where the district orders any strike without first obtaining the sanction of the General Executive Board, no assistance can be claimed outside of the district. Every effort is made to conserve the strength of the Order. Many of the local district strikes have been forced upon the men by attempts of the employers to break up the organization by the discharge of its members.

The space for this chapter will not allow even a summary of the strikes that have occurred. At certain periods strike-epidemics prevail, and the organization is no more responsible for their breaking out than the Government is for any epidemic which science fails to prevent or check. It is true that the Government is responsible for the conditions which furnish opportunities for epidemics and contagions. Lack of sanitary laws, as well as a failure of enforcement of such laws as exist, have much to do with the existence of these monster evils; but the poverty of the masses is the prime cause of pestilence, as of most of the vices and crimes that afflict mankind. As the Order grows in wisdom as well as in power of numbers, strikes will become less frequent.

The history of some of the labor organizations prove that strikes can be averted. When an employer knows that to reduce wages without first consulting with the organizations represented in his establishment may cause him such a lengthened period of inaction as not only to destroy his profit, but diminish the value of his plant, he will hesitate before action. So, too, the employees will hesitate to enforce their demands for an advance of wages, when they have a sufficient knowledge of the condition of the markets, as well as of the individual enterprise, and know that a strike at such a time would jeopardize their own interests.

The Knights of Labor, while attempting peaceful settlement of the inevitable difficulties under the wage-system, use every effort to inculcate the principles of co-operation, and give encouragement to co-operative enterprises. The General Assembly have established a co-operative board, whose reports contain not only an account of the co-operative efforts coming under their observation, but they also publish able and earnest arguments in the direction of co-operative effort. The most remarkable strikes of the Order, having occurred during the present year, are fresh in the memory of the people; and, while those that have attracted the most attention — like the great South-western Railroad strike — have proved failures, others have proved remarkably successful. But the proudest claim that the Knights can make is in the advance of wages and the improved opportunities that have been gained through the numerical and moral force of the organization, whether secured through the use of the boycott, as in the Dueber Watch-Case Company, or by conciliation, as in the case of the horse-railroad employees of Boston.

The boycott against the Dueber Watch-Case Company was justified by the act of the proprietor, — he having discharged all the members of the Order in his employ, and refused to treat with the General Executive Board. It is only just to say of Mr. Dueber, that, when he finally decided to retrace his steps, he was as emphatically conciliatory as he had been determinedly aggressive. The success of the horse-car employees of Boston was largely due to the wisdom of the president of the Metropolitan Railroad. But for his genial acceptance of the situation and ready compliance to the wishes of the men, every horse-car running in Boston would have been tied up. The men on this and other roads acted with commendable patience; and their thanks are due more to T. C. Thompson, Master Workman, Local Assembly 2898, than to any other person. The editor, as a colleague of Mr. Thompson in this work, feels that historical accuracy demands this statement; and special attention is called to this case, because an advance of wages and a reduction of hours were gained without the stoppage of a car or the loss of a day's work.

The local assemblies of the Knights of Labor, counted by the thousands, furnish the wage-workers of the continent with opportunities of association and advancement never before enjoyed. From Maine to California, from Canada to the Gulf, in all the States and Territories, in the lumber regions and in the mines, amidst the fluff of the textile industries, amidst the din of the iron hammer, in workshop and store, wherever men and women are congregated, — in the village and upon the plantation, — the Knights of Labor are marching on to ultimate victory.

CHAPTER XVI.

THE CHINESE AND THE LABOR QUESTION.

China the Reservoir of Cheap Labor — Condition of the People in China — Their Habits and Customs — Opinions of W. W. Stone — Caucasian and Mongolian — Expenses of Civilization — The Six Companies — Seeking the Cheapest Labor — Female Slaves — The Christianity of the Chinese Exemplified — The Nobility of Gold — The Gathering Pagan Host — Capturing the Trades — The United Workmen — The Chinese Taxes — Legislation in Respect of Chinese Immigration by Congressman Morrill — The Building of a State — Legislative Discussion in California, in 1882 — The Monthly Tax — Act of 1862 — The Burlingame Treaty — Appeal to Congress — The People of One Mind — Treaty of 1880 — Restrictive Legislation — American Interest in China.

CHINA is the reservoir of the cheap labor of the world. Her centuries of growth have been followed by centuries of reaction. Walled in by laws, customs and religion, her people have crowded against each other until her civilization has become stunted, her people pygmies and her women slaves. With wonderful skill in handicrafts, and imitative power unequalled, she has wrought no wonders and performed no service to humanity. Her mountains are full of ores, unworked; for man-power is cheaper than horse-power, and machinery is practically unknown. Her economy of living is but another name for starvation. Her people being unread in the history of the outer world, unused to travel, and without the inspiration of hope or the knowledge of better opportunities, emigration is practically a banishment. That this people should flow over to the land where the highest wages were paid, and the highest conditions of life were enjoyed, is a wonder of the nineteenth century, if the artificial causes that operated to produce this result were not known. The discovery of gold in California tempted not only the mechanics and farmers of the States and of Europe, but tempted the avarice of the capitalists at whose bidding the Six Chinese Companies were formed. Gold flowed from the mines into the hands of the miners; but also into the hands of the speculators. Land-steals were common, not only under the old Spanish land-grants, but by processes of surveying and forced titles, evicting squatter and farmer; and because of the high price of food, rendering the cultivation of large farms profitable, more money was to be realized by the importation of cheap labor than from almost any other source. Farm-laborers and servants were needed, and the wages of mechanics were necessarily lifted to something near the earnings of the miners.

The secret history of the Six Companies may never be written; but the accomplished fact stands out before the world that these companies brought over to California hordes of "cooly" laborers under contracts and conditions more baneful to our civilization than the importation of the African slave. The story of the mid-passage has been told; the story of the importation of the Chinese "cooly" is unwritten.

That conflicts should occur between the white miner and the Chinese was but natural; for the miner, coming from the centres of civilization, had become somewhat brutalized. His home was a cabin, without the refining influences of mother or wife or child. But it was not until the demand for craftsmen in the realms of organized industry that the contest between the two races reached its highest point. From the high-tide of unexampled incomes, white labor was crowded down to its lowest ebb. The Chinaman could live as he lived in China, while the emigrant from other lands was soon brought up to American habits and customs. From the crowding out of the workman, they soon found it practical and possible to crowd out the employer; for no manufacturer employing white labor could compete with the Chinese employer having his own countrymen as employees. Their habits, their language and their religion necessitated a crowding together until they covered street after street with their workshops, gambling-saloons, houses of prostitution, tenements and joss-houses. Every part of the building from cellar to attic is crowded full of human life, and furniture and the usual appliances of civilization are unknown. Their beds are bunks, built on the sides and in the centres of the rooms; their furniture, a board table; their cutlery, chop-sticks. They make no demand for the products of other labor. These habits are not only common to California, but wherever these people settle in numbers. In the report of the Massachusetts Bureau of Statistics of Labor for 1871, a description is given of the Chinese "cooly" laborers employed at shoe-making at North Adams, from which we quote:—

We found there seventy-three men, clad in cotton cloth, with cheap Chinese hats and shoes. Their dining-tables were made of pine boards, without covering; their chairs were wooden benches; their sleeping-places bunks on the sides of the room, with thin mattresses and scant bedding. The dinner-set for every six persons was a bowl for each, a platter with boiled pork and potatoes cut into bits, a tin pan filled with boiled rice, with ladle to dip it into each man's bowl, and their table-cutlery a pair of chopsticks for each, what tea they took being taken in the same rice-bowl.

And the Bureau asks this question: "What industrial production is stimulated by such a laboring population?" and then gives this answer:—

The woollen and cotton-mills of Lowell and Lawrence, of Fall River and Salisbury, the cutlery-works of Shelburne Falls, the furniture-factories of Essex and Worcester counties, the hat-factories of Methuen, the boot and shoe-factories of Milford, the Bridgewaters and Lynn — nay, more, the authors and publishers, the newspapers and expressmen, the railroads, all the varied industries of the Commonwealth, would be brought to ruin under such a method of "breaking down the nuisance of trades-unions," the accomplishment of which is the declared intent of this cheap and ignorant labor.

At first, the Chinamen were laughed at by some; but they were welcomed by the controlling classes. In the public procession in celebration of the admission of California into the Union, Chinese were a conspicuous feature. They were spoken of as "our elder brothers." Their presence was welcomed as affording opportunity of doing them good, and influencing their native land. History had given its warning of the threatened danger. Every writer conversant with the habits and customs of the race, and every experiment of their settlements had proved that this people were moral and spiritual lepers. Before the settlement of this continent, they had been ordered to leave Manilla; and such was the hatred engendered by their habits that over fifty thousand of them were massacred by the Spaniards within fifty years. In 1740, twelve thousand were massacred by the Dutch.

[We herewith present the views of W. W. Stone, of California.]

THE CHINESE-LABOR PROBLEM.

In considering the effect produced by the presence of the Chinese in the American world of labor, writers may be pardoned if they take rather extreme views. The manufacturer, as an employer, rushes to the conclusion that he is obliged by some arbitrary power to go out in diligent search of the very cheapest producing material that can, by any possible combination, be seized upon. The laborer, naturally, *per contra*, views the Chinaman as a mere labor-machine, devoid of intelligence, utterly destitute of ambition and reason, and willingly working for the mere purpose of existence. Here is an antagonism, but it is artificial, — not natural. The manufacturer produces for the love of gain. His masters are the laboring consumers; and the more well-to-do the master, the greater the consumption. On the other hand, the consumer patronizes, not for any regard for the manufacturer, but in obedience to the law of necessities. The manufacturer, therefore, is the agent or servant of the laborer, and has no rights or standing over or above any other equal factor. Extremes here meet; and, instead of standing on neutral ground, sound results can be best attained by reasoning from the stand-point of the general welfare.

It is the basic principle of this government that every citizen has a right to enjoy and to exercise the various faculties of mind, soul and body, as long as that enjoyment does not infringe upon the rights of others. In the exercise of these rights, a man may not store explosives in the midst of a community, because of the danger to others; he may not amputate a sound limb, because he is liable, by so doing, to become a burden on the community; he is restricted in the use and sale of poisons to mind or body; he is morally and often legally obliged to educate himself up to a proper knowledge and appreciation of his rights and duties as a citizen. We thus see that the purer the democracy, the nearer we approach to a grand co-operative, mutually protective association. Here is where the Chinese-labor question enters as a discordant element. From his cradle, the Chinese serf is disciplined in the doctrine of nonentity. He was born under a government having a spiritual and a temporal head; and he is, therefore, mangled body and soul. His temporal government is of the patriarchal type, and the sins of one of a family are visited upon the heads of the remainder.

It does not require much knowledge of human nature to arrive at the inevitable conclusion that an element trained in such a school cannot possibly sympathize with our plan of co-operation. Every item in such a training is only another barrier to assimilation. Properly apply all these conditions in the consideration of the labor problem, and the gravity of the situation will be fully appreciated.

The manufacturer of to-day, rejecting the co-operative plan of our governmental system, goes into the labor market and calls for the lowest bidder. In answer to the call, the Caucasian and the Mongolian commences to figure upon the basis of living prices. The Caucasian must add to his own individual needs the cost of maintaining a wife and family. There is rent to pay, clothing to be provided, books to buy, and, added to all this, the many little wants that arise out of the conditions of a Christian civilization. The Mongolian comes much closer to the wind. He is a mere servile unit in one of the Six Companies. He has a merely nominal rent; for he is content with a little shelf in a barrack-structure, fashioned after the forecastle of a sea-going vessel. He is not burdened with the cares and expenses of family, because he is content with a fractional interest in the body of a female slave; his food and clothing, imported almost entirely from his native country, cost him about $7 per month. The maintenance of a Caucasian family ranges from $40 to $50 per month. Figuring from these bases, can it be otherwise than inevitable that Caucasian labor must go to the wall? The uninitiated declare that this in time will be righted; that the laws of trade will equalize and adjust conditions and rates, making eventually a satisfactory equilibrium. It must be borne in mind that the entire population of the United States is 50,000,000, while just outside of the portals of our Golden Gate 400,000,000 Mongolians are engaged in a desperate struggle for existence. The insignificant fraction of this overwhelming host now swarming on the Pacific coast have not gained any individuality by migration. The presidents of the Six Companies know that Chinese labor is accepted, not because it is better, but because it is cheaper. As fast, therefore, as the rate of wages for white labor falls, these serf-owners lower their scale, always underbidding the Caucasian rates. In this way the Christian, with his helpless family, is jostled aside, and the pagan slave fitted in his place.

A year or so ago, the writer was talking to a well-informed Chinaman on the question of American toleration. "You will live to see the day," said the Chinaman, "when we shall control the labor-market of the whole of this country." It is an inexorable fact that this country must be either all Caucasian or all Mongolian. Are we ready to submit to absorption? I think that the patriotism and intelligence of the American people rise to a higher plane. An eminent authority has said that if American muscle cannot compete with Mongolian labor, then *the American must go to the wall!* Can we afford the price? To compete with success, we must cut down all expenses outside of the bare items of animal existence. We must shut up our schools, for these institutions cultivate a craving for a living above the mere animal. We must close up the churches, because the Chinaman has no day of rest. We must sweep away a thousand and one products of Christian civilization, because Christianity, in its essence, elevates mankind above the groveling instincts of the animal of the field, and encourages a life of intelligence and self-improvement. Surely no just student of industrial economy will deny the fairness of these conclusions. The conditions of the problem are justly set forth, without exaggeration. The cold-blooded query is, Shall the area of the United States be a vast auction-block, on which labor is to be offered up at lowest prices? If so, then civilization must step down to give room to barbarism. To compete successfully under such a system there must be an intelligent sacrifice of every want above the mere animal necessity; and, as such a sacrifice carries with it a loss of mentality, there must survive a class whose province would be to maintain the level. We hold that the American Union is based on business principles of mutual co-operation. Every individual of the firm has a duty to perform in contributing to the industrial welfare, and in return is entitled to compensation on a scale that shall enable him to maintain his standing as an intelligent factor. Proceeding on this basis, the manufacturer has asked for protection against the importation of the product of pauper-labor. The request has been complied with. Now, the laborer raises his voice, and asks for protection *against the pauper himself*. We do not ask for a sweeping restriction that shall prevent the incoming of intelligent and assimilative toilers. We ask this protection, not only for the same reasons urged by the manufacturer, but on broader grounds. We ask protection from an element that, in coming, receives, but does not give; makes, but does not use; enjoys advantages, but does not return benefits. That this antagonism is not trivial or imaginative, we have only to point to the industrial history of the Pacific coast. We find the Chinaman controlling the boot and shoe-trade, and yet, without exception, he sends to China for his shuffling slipper. He supplies the trade with cigars, and yet smokes nothing but an opium-laden pipe. He entirely usurps the making of underwear, he throws thousands of female washers and sewers out of employment, and, without a thought of reciprocity, he bands with a number of his fellow-countrymen and sends to China for a female slave to be farmed out as a satisfaction to the vile lust of the community. He is a pagan and a monarchist, and leaves behind hostages for his allegiance. He cannot become either an American citizen or a Christian. No Christian will sacrifice his loved ones for commercial advantages; and, therefore, paradoxical as it may seem, tne more consistent the pagan, the better the Christian!

I do not know that I violate any confidence in narrating a conversation between a so-called Chinese Christian and Mr. J. G. Kennedy, ex-Superintendent of Schools, of San Jose, California. A lady belonging to the San Jose Christian Chinese Mission had recommended Ah Wow as an excellent Christian. In course of conversation, after the introduction, the question of Christianity was alluded to, Ah Wow speaking of it rather slightingly. I give the rest verbatim: —

MR. KENNEDY: I thought you were a Christian, Ah Wow!

AH WOW: No! I no such ting. I allee same Chinaman.

MR. KENNEDY: So you do not believe in Christ?

AH WOW: No, no! d——— Clist! I no flaid. Chinaman go mission, gettee little jobs. Ole women play and men pleach. Velly good for Chinaman wantee work. Plenty work, 'legion go to h———

This is about the sum and substance of the Chinese creed.

Here on the Pacific coast, we may see every day the evidences of human skill and energy in the tearing down of mountains and filling up of swamps. Apply this energy to the leveling of the field of labor by the introduction of an element such as we have pictured; throw open our groaning Gate and let the surplus of 400,000,000 roll in from the overladen West, and you will have such a leveling as was experienced when the Zuyder Zee burst over its boundaries and engulfed the cities and towns of Holland, leaving nothing visible above the sullen waters but an occasional church-spire that stood as a mournful evidence of an engulfed civilization. How much more consistent with the principles of co-operation and Christianity is the system that comprehends the establishment of a board of arbitration that shall so regulate the rate of wages that the humblest citizen may not only satisfy the wants of the mere animal, but that he may possess means by which he may maintain the dignity of an American freeman! This leads on to the deprecatory exclamations adopted by a few who are temporarily benefited in a pecuniary way by the employment of Chinese labor. We sometimes hear these people say: "We cannot rely upon our white help! We are compelled to use the Chinese, because we find them obedient, submissive, tractable, and cheap." All this was urged by the Southern planter, when he drew upon Africa for a contingent labor fund. The sturdy yeomanry who landed upon Plymouth Rock, or who braved death under a hundred guises in the wilds of a new world, were not the men to tamely submit to the imperious exactions of petty landholders, who wanted labor-machines, and not men. The ignorant and submissive son of the Dark Continent has been eagerly seized upon as an available substitute. The student of American history need not have pointed out to him the instructive *tableaux-vivants* furnished in the progress of our experience in the use of submissive and tractable labor. The Missouri Compromise, the Mexican struggle, the Kansas–Nebraska warfare, and the Great Rebellion are pictures not forgotten. The fact is, there is a class rapidly growing up in America, who believe in the nobility of gold. This class act upon the assumption that the acceptation of wage-money carries with it a forfeiture of manhood or womanhood. To this class the advent of mere labor-machines is a godsend.

That Chinese labor comprehends a system of slavery is a fact that it is idle to deny; and to invite immigration is only to welcome a repetition of our past experience. It should be understood that we have here the flower and the cream of the Chinese working-world,—the young, the ambitious, the strong and energetic of the race; and yet, withal, the Caucasian rejects this infusion for the pure blood of the manly American. Look at the history of the many islands of the Pacific Ocean, wherein these heathen have gained permanent footing! Without exception, the progress of the invader has been marked by outbursts of volcanic wrath, deluging the devoted territories with fire, blood, loathsome diseases and unbridled lust. We sometimes come across some short-sighted writer, who, having availed himself of the services of one of these servile, obsequious, and apparently self-sacrificing pagans, instantly institutes a comparison between this specimen and some degraded sample of Caucasian he has chanced to meet, and concludes from this comparison that the Asiatic race is the superior element in the field of labor. To such, we would suggest a visit to the cities of the "more favored nation." There he would find the brute slave, without the the first instincts of the freeman. Our sturdy forefathers of Revolutionary times never dreamed of the introduction of such an element into our body politic, when they threw open the ports of the country to the oppressed of the world. We of a more enlightened age see this in the light of experience, and view with alarm the danger of deterioration by reason of non-assimilating material. It must not be taken for granted that this feeling of antagonism is a short-lived or a newly-awakened sentiment. When, in 1849, the news of the discovery of gold startled the laboring world, there came an irresistible rush from all quarters of the globe. The Chinaman was not absent from the current. He came by twos and by threes at first; but gradually the number increased, until, in 1854, the gathering had so enlarged that the subject was made a matter of official investigation by a committee of our State Senate. Senators Ralston, Frey, Soule, Estelle and Warner composed this committee; and, after a thorough analysis of the industrial situation, they presented a report, containing a forecast that shows that the Labor Question is a mathematical rather than a dogmatic problem, and as such is capable of easy demonstration. Read this in the light of to-day's experience, and mark the justice of the committee's conclusions:—

> The Chinese are destructive to the best interests of the State, and dangerous to its peace. They come, not as freemen, but as serfs and hirelings of a master. It needs no Solomon to predict the result; disputes will take place, and blood will flow, to be followed by the expulsion of a population who will be driven from the State by violence instead of law.

Here is a horologue cast, not by demagogues and time-servers, but by grave and reverend seignors, learned in law, and living in an atmosphere far removed from idle clamor. These Senators recognized the fact that free, intelligent and well-remunerated labor is one of the important elements of a republican government.

The greater the remuneration for labor, the better the patronage from the laborer. Some of our near-sighted manufacturers could not see this. They looked around with longing eyes for cheap labor. In 1872, a cigar firm in San Francisco concluded that it was for their interest to employ Chinese help. A few were taken on, and taught the mysteries of the trade. At that time, cigar-manufacturers were growing rich; dealers were doing well, and cigar-makers prospered. To-day, we find 8,000 Chinamen controlling the entire trade. Here, as in other branches, the manufacturer has been "hoist by his own petard," for the factory-hand has assumed the *role* of manufacturer. It has been estimated that about five millions of dollars are annually sent to China by the cigar-trade alone. So independent and arrogant had the Mongolian become, that, in 1885, the guild-leaders ordered out the Chinese hands from a white employer's factory, because the owner attempted to use the services of a few white men. In 1870, a shoe-firm taught a few Chinamen to make shoes. One after another followed. Wages for good workmen in 1870 averaged about $20 per week. To-day, some 6,000 Chinese are employed in the one industry, at wages ranging from $20 to $30 per month. Out of the sixty boot and shoe-factories of the city, the Chinese own forty-eight; while of the fifty slipper-factories, *every one* is owned by Chinamen.

It is pleasant in this desert of industry to record an oasis. As I write, I hear the carpenters' hammers ringing merry changes in the morning air. I look out, and see workmen busily engaged in adding a story to the factory of the United Workmen. The history of this company is instructive. In 1870, a few shoemakers, indignant at the influx of Chinese, left the bench in a mixed factory, and started out in business on their own account, on a co-operative plan. They were paralyzed by earthquakes, benumbed by serf-competition; but they persevered. They turned out nothing but first-class goods; they starved themselves to buy all the modern improvements in the mechanical line. Public confidence was gained; and to-day the poor shoemakers of old are growing rich, with more orders than they can fill, and giving employment and fair remuneration to a hundred hands.

I should like here, parenthetically, as a Christian and patriot, with all due reverence, to remark that we have even in this country two classes of Christians, for whom the remainder of this chapter can have no charms. I allude,—

1st. To the gentlemen who claim that the Almighty created human workers and human drones.

2nd. To the enthusiasts who believe that souls are embodied merely for the work of salvation. To these theorists the question of wages is an idle incident. I desire to call the attention of patriots and humanitarians to the fact that, as countries emerge from the cloud of barbarism, the condition of the humble toilers rises in full proportion, the scale of wages being a kind of civilometer, by which we can estimate the full measure of elevation. In 1870, the Chinese commenced to pay attention to the manufacture of ladies' shoes. At that time, workmen were paid $18 per dozen for a department in that trade. In 1872, the price fell to $15.00; in 1874, to $14.00; in 1876, to $10.00; in 1878, to $9.00; in 1880, to $7.00; to-day, it is $6.00. In 1876, skilful tailors received $25.00 per week; in 1878, $20.00; in 1881, $15.00, with still a downward tendency. In 1872, sempstresses could make from $15.00 to $20.00 per week. To-day, the entire trade of underwear is absolutely under the control of the Chinese, and women have been forced out of that avenue of employment. This may be called a dispensation of Providence for them; for we find them appearing in the counting-house, at the printers' font and on the keys of Morse's telegraphic instrument. Fortunately for them, the instincts of barbarism are not in the ascendancy, or they would have been relegated to the seclusion of the hut to act in the capacity of drudge, as chattel appendages in the menial retinue of lordly masters. It would consume too much space to enumerate the many particulars of our down-sliding. A brief summary only can be given. We have 8,000 Chinamen in the cigar-trade to 600 whites; 10,000 Chinese in wearing-apparel; 8,000 laundrymen; 4,000 prostitutes, making a grand total in all branches of about

32,000 non-affiliating, non-consumers, paying taxes on less than a million dollars on real and personal property, and draining the country of $8,000,000 annually.

I am proud to be able to say that the Knights of Labor are fully alive to the danger of the situation. As secretary of the District Assembly of California, I called the attention of General Master Workman Powderly to our efforts here, and received a reply, concluding in the following words: —

> The men of the West must not be allowed to fight the battle single-handed and alone. The evil they complain of is no longer confined to one section of this country. It is spreading, and its evil influences are being felt in all our industrial centres, and if a desire to assist our brethren in a righteous cause is not sufficient to animate us and spur us to action, then self-interest will soon prompt us to bestir ourselves. The Order must act as a unit in this matter.

We frequently hear this great Republic spoken of as the "Great Giant" of the Western World. We speak of the Chinaman as "the little brown man." We are thus furnished with material for a Gulliver romance. Our "Giant" has been hitherto sleeping in conscious strength. One by one the little threads of industrial degeneration have been thrown around the quiescent limbs, until a cable-like bond has fastened itself about our body politic, and we awake with a start to find ourselves enmeshed in barbaric thraldom. Go down to the "Chinatown" of San Francisco, and you will see a forecast of the condition of this whole city before the close of the present century, if this evil is not immediately checked. You will find crime in its most hideous aspect; disease in its most loathsome form; vice, ignorance and brutality in the most disgusting shape. Here, filth and utter depravity hold high carnival, with surrounding horrors beyond the possibility of pen to picture. The helots of ancient times were held up to symbolize purgatory; we point out the "Chinatown" of our fair city as a materialized Hell. We are too intelligent and progressive a people to allow this industrial tumor to spread. The great Fathers of the Revolution produced a nation of freemen; and the gallant army of veterans, gathered this year in San Francisco, fought to perpetuate that birth-right. Time may be required to eradicate this evil; but I feel certain that the wisdom and patriotism of the people will to serve redeem the land, so that, by the time our children shall have assumed our positions in the walks of life, they will not be compelled to struggle with ignorance and brutality for the mere right to live.

LEGISLATION IN RESTRAINT OF CHINESE IMMIGRATION.

[The important subject of legislation upon this question is admirably treated in the following contribution from the Hon. W. W. Morrow, of California. — Ed.]

The immigration of Chinese into the United States commenced soon after the discovery of gold in California, in 1848, and was part of the large population suddenly attracted to that section from all parts of the world in the hasty pursuit of wealth. At first, the effect of the strange and unassimilating "little brown man" in our body politic was, perhaps, not generally considered, — for the reason, doubtless, that but few people went to California in early days seeking a permanent home. The difficulties, therefore, whatever they might be, arising out of the presence of large numbers of Chinese in the new fields of industry were, to most of the Argonauts, as temporary as their intended stay in the country was uncertain; but as soon as it was discovered that the resources of the newly-acquired territory invited permanent residence and occupation, and the people undertook the building of a State on the principles of modern civilization, it occurred to men of intelligence that the increase of the Chinese population, to any considerable extent, would certainly make it a disturbing element in the industrial and social organization of the Commonwealth.

As early, therefore, as 1852, we find the question of Chinese immigration a subject of discussion in the Legislature of California. In April of that year, the Committee on Mines and Mining Interests of the Assembly presented a report, in which attention was called to the evil arising from the concentration within the limits of the State of vast numbers of the Asiatic races, and of the inhabitants of the Pacific Islands, dissimilar from ourselves in customs, language and education. The committee stated, among many other reasons, why an indiscriminate immigration of this class of foreigners should not be permitted, that "most of them arrive here, not as freemen seeking liberty and the pursuit of happiness, but are brought as absolute slaves by their foreign masters, and by foreign capitalists, and are held to labor under contracts which our laws do not recognize, and whose penalties are revolting to our sympathies." Governor Bigler also sent a special message to the Legislature, in which he urged upon that body the necessity for action concerning the wholesale importations into this country of immigrants from the Asiatic quarter of the globe. He stated that he was deeply impressed with the conviction that, in order to enhance the prosperity and to preserve the tranquillity of the State, measures should be adopted to check this tide of Asiatic immigration, and prevent the exportation by them of the precious metals, which they dig up from our soil without charge, and without assuming any of the obligations imposed upon citizens. The Governor submitted two propositions for the consideration of the Legislature:—

1st. Such an exercise of the taxing power by the State as would check indiscriminate and unlimited Asiatic immigration.

2nd. A demand by the State of California for the prompt interposition of Congress, by the passage of an act prohibiting "coolies," shipped to California under contracts, from laboring in the mines of the State.

The first recommendation took form in the enactment of a law imposing a monthly tax of $4 upon all foreigners taking gold from the mines of the State.

The first Legislature, which met at San Jose, in December, 1849, and prior to the admission of the State into the Union, had imposed a monthly tax of $20 upon foreigners engaged in mining; but this tax was not specially directed against the Chinese. There were other foreigners swarming into the State at that time, of a highly objectionable character; and it was to restrain this undesirable immigration that this law was passed. The act, however, yielded but little revenue; and, in 1851, it was repealed. It was substantially this law that was revived in 1852, when the immigration of coolies became alarming. The reduction of the tax to $4 per month was, doubtless, for the purpose of making the law effective as a revenue act. This license-tax was declared constitutional by the Supreme Court of California, and was continued until the year 1871, when John Jackson, the sheriff and tax-collector of Trinity County, was indicted and convicted in the United States Circuit Court, sitting at San Francisco, for the offense of collecting the tax from a Chinaman, contrary to the provisions of the Act of Congress approved May 31, 1870. The prohibition of the Federal statute against any person within the jurisdiction of the United States being subjected to the deprivation of any right enjoyed by white citizens, and against the imposition of any different punishment, pain or penalty, by reason of such person being an alien, was held to operate against the foreign miners' license-tax, and its collection was at once abandoned.

In 1855, the Legislature of California passed an act which subjected all ships and masters, owners and consignees thereof to a tax of $50 a head on every person imported by said ships into the State, who was incapable of becoming a citizen thereof or of the United States. An attempt was made to collect from the owners of the ship "Stephen Baldwin" this tax on two hundred and fifty Chinese passengers, brought on that ship to San Francisco from Hong Kong; but the Supreme Court of the United States declared the law unconstitutional on the authority of the passenger cases, decided by the Supreme Court of the United States, in 1848. Meantime, the act was repealed by the Legislature of 1856. In 1858, the Legislature passed an act prohibiting the entry into the State, or the landing at any port thereof, of persons of the Chinese or Mongolian races. This act was also declared unconstitutional by the Supreme Court of the State.

The next effort of the State to restrain the increasing flood of Chinese immigration was the Act of April 26, 1862, imposing a Chinese police-tax of $2.50 each month upon all persons of the Mongolian race of eighteen years and upwards, residing in the State, except such as should take out licenses to work in the mines, and excepting also those engaged in the production and manufacture of sugar, rice, coffee and tea. The power of the State to prescribe terms upon which Chinese should be permitted to reside in it was very ably discussed before the Supreme Court of the State upon the hearing of a case arising under this law; but the Supreme Court, in a very elaborate opinion, decided the law unconstitutional. It would be unprofitable to refer to all the measures adopted by the people of California to protect themselves against the evils of Chinese immigration. Accustomed to rely upon their own ingenuity and will in the solution of difficulties pertaining to their new society, the Californians undertook to legislate upon this subject with a view of discouraging an increase in this class of population. They accordingly provided statutes against the importation of certain objectionable classes, and imposed penalties against many of the evil practices common to the Chinese habits of life; but this method of procedure, being restricted under our form of government to police regulations, the legislation proved ineffectual to restrain the Chinese invasion. That the State has, however, gone to the full extent of its sovereign power in this direction by constitutional and legislative enactments, is fully attested by the large number of cases brought to the Supreme Court of the United States, wherein that authority is questioned as infringing upon Federal jurisdiction.

An appeal was accordingly made to Congress to interpose its unquestioned power and authority in this behalf. Prior to 1868, no right of emigration of Chinese subjects to the United States existed by reason of any formal treaty stipulations with China; and, in fact, no such stipulation was necessary. The country had always been open to immigration, without condition as to the nationality of the immigrant. The generous declaration that this country is the asylum for the oppressed of every nation, had been sufficient for all purposes in the encouragement of foreign immigration to our shores, and it did not exclude the Chinamen. In the year 1868, Mr. Burlingame negotiated a treaty with China, in which free immigration was for the first time established as a treaty-right. But the ink with which this treaty was written was hardly dry when an unsuccessful effort was made in Congress to restrict Chinese immigration. In 1870, Mr. Fitch, then a representative in Congress from Nevada, in a speech in the House of Representatives, concerning Chinese immigration, said: —

> Only here can this tide be stayed. The States of the Pacific are powerless to legitimately resist it. It is no act of statemanship to burn a steamer or mob a Chinese factory. The Chinese who are here under existing laws and treaties, are entitled to be protected in their persons and property; and the Pacific coast cannot resist the power of Federal government. We cannot offer isolated, ineffectual opposition to the incoming of these Asiatics. We must appeal to the wisdom and justice of Congress, from being over-run and devastated by these Asiatic locusts; and if we appeal as one people, without seeking to make it a partisan question, we may not appeal in vain.

In 1872, the legislature of the State of California adopted resolutions setting forth the evils of this immigration; and, through its Senators and Representatives, urged upon the Federal Government the adoption of such treaty regulations and legislation as should discourage its continuance. A like appeal was also made in 1874. During this time, numerous memorials, resolutions of public meetings and petitions, — one of which numbered over sixteen thousand signatures, — were presented to Congress, asking for relief from the growing evil.

In 1877, an address was prepared and issued by a committee of the senate of the State of California, to the people of the United States, upon the social, moral and political effect of Chinese immigration. In this address, the whole question was ably discussed, and an earnest appeal was made to the country to come to the aid of the Pacific coast in its effort to secure a restriction of Chinese immigration through the peaceable means of legislation or treaty stipulations.

In 1878, the legislature of the State of California again appealed to Congress to take action upon this vital question, and recommended the modification or abrogation of the Burlingame Treaty.

In 1879, at a general election held for State officers in California, the question of Chinese immigration was submitted to the voters of the State for an expression of sentiment as to whether or not such immigration was desirable.

For Chinese immigration, there were cast 883 votes; against Chinese immigration, 154,638, — showing a majority of 153,755 against such immigration. This popular verdict in favor of protecting American labor against foreign invasion came alike from the employee and the employer, the laborer and the capitalist, the miner and the banker. It came from the school-room, the pulpit and the public press. It represented all classes, and for all practical purposes was the united voice of the free, law-abiding, patriotic people. And it secured attention; for, in this same year, Congress finally passed an act limiting the number of Chinese passengers that should be permitted to come to the United States on any one vessel, to fifteen. This bill, however, failed to receive Executive approval, on the ground that it was in conflict with the treaty obligations then existing between the United States and China.

A commission was thereupon appointed to proceed to China and negotiate a new treaty, having in view the declared purpose of Congress to prohibit the further influx of Chinese subjects into this country.

The result of this action is to be found in the present treaty with China, dated November 17, 1880.

From this statement, it will be seen that the opposition to Chinese immigration is by no means a new sentiment on the Pacific coast, and that party bias has had nothing whatever to do with it. It is a question upon which the political parties are agreed; and, in every instance where popular expression has been sought in the various stages of the agitation, the two great parties have been united in their influence and efforts in favor of peaceful and conservative methods, as distinguished from violent demonstrations and lawless conduct.

The first article of the Treaty of 1880 provides as follows: —

Whenever, in the opinion of the Government of the United States, the coming of Chinese laborers to the United States, or their residence therein, affects or threatens to affect the interests of that country, or to endanger the good order of the said country, or of any locality within the territory thereof, the Government of China agrees that the Government of the United States may regulate, limit or suspend such coming or residence, but may not absolutely prohibit it. The limitation or suspension shall be reasonable, and shall apply only to Chinese who may go to the United States as laborers, other classes not being included in the limitations. Legislation taken in regard to Chinese laborers will be of such a character only as is necessary to enforce the regulation, limitation or suspension of immigration, and immigrants shall not be subject to personal maltreatment or abuse.

In accordance with this stipulation, Congress, on the 6th day of May, 1882, passed an act suspending for the period of ten years the coming of Chinese laborers to the United States.

By its terms, the act went into effect on the 5th day of August, 1882. Questions at once arose as to the status of various Chinese persons, claiming the right to come into the United States, under some exception or omission in the law. Some of these questions came before the Executive department of the Government for determination, while others were taken into the United States courts for decision. Whether the ruling of the departments was correct or not, it is not necessary at present to inquire. It is enough to say, that, under one pretext and another, Chinese laborers were permitted to come into the United States in such numbers as to excite alarm on the Pacific coast, and give the impression that the Restriction Act was a failure.

This state of affairs led to the passage of an amendatory act, dated July 5, 1884, which had for its purpose the curing of certain serious defects developed in the former act. The anxiety of the Chinese to come to this country had become so strong under the flattering inducements offered by their masters, that they immediately proceeded to test the provisions of the amendatory act, and it became the subject of construction in the departments of the government and in the United States courts. The purpose of the law was again evaded in its execution, and large numbers of Chinamen obtained admission into the country upon artful claims of prior residence, transit privileges, and other pretences.

The people of the Pacific coast naturally became exasperated over this condition of things, and demanded that something should be done to put a stop to this immigration. Accordingly, the delegation from California in the present

Congress made a very careful investigation as to the practical operations of the law. The Chinese restriction acts of the Australian colonies, British Columbia and the Sandwich Islands were examined, and information obtained as to their value for the purpose intended. Amendments were thereupon prepared to the present law, and submitted to persons well informed as to the technical and legal deficiencies of the statute. The result of this work may be found in the bill introduced in the House of Representatives, in December last, amending the Restriction Act. A copy of this bill was introduced in the Senate, and referred to the Committee on Foreign Relations. After very careful examination of its provisions by that committee, it was reported favorably to the Senate by Senator Sherman. It passed the Senate without serious opposition, and in the House was referred to the Committee on Foreign Affairs, where it still remains.

The House bill had been referred to this committee long before, where it was considered, amended and reported to the House.

As amended, the bill was objectionable, and would be of but little value as an amendment to the Restriction Act. The original bill provides for the extension of the Restriction Act to a period of twenty years; limits the life of a return-certificate issued to a departing Chinaman to two years; perfects the details of the return-certificate in the identification of the person to whom it is issued, and limits the number of Chinese passengers that can come to the United States on any one vessel to one for every fifty tons of the registered tonnage of the vessel.

Such amendments to the Restriction Act would undoubtedly cure many, if not all, of its serious defects.

The difficulties, however, in the way of an effectual enforcement of the present law are so numerous that the sentiment of the Pacific coast is favorable to an abrogation of so much of the Burlingame Treaty as relates to the immigration of Chinese subjects to the United States. If Congress would provide for the abrogation of all treaty stipulations with China relating to immigration, and exclude all classes except ambassadors and officials representing the Chinese government, the question would be settled at once.

As an indication of the profound sentiment prevailing in California upon this subject, it will not be inappropriate to notice the petition presented to Congress, in June last, from the Knights of Labor. The petition contained nearly 50,000 names, and was one of the most formidable documents of the kind ever presented to Congress. It represented the views of the people engaged in every profession, trade and calling in the State, and called upon Congress to take such action, either by appropriate legislation or by a change in the present treaty with China, as might be deemed necessary to forever prohibit the further immigration of Chinese to the United States. It is difficult to understand why such urgent and continued appeals for relief should go unheeded by Congress.

But it is urged that there are commercial reasons why such extreme measures should not be adopted. A careful examination of our relations with China will show, however, that there are no such benefits derived from our trade with that country as to warrant us in leaving our doors open to Chinese immigration.

The Chinese population in the United States, according to the census, was, in 1860, 34,933; 1870, 63,199; 1880, 105,465. Much reliance cannot be placed on the census report in a matter of this kind. The experience on the Pacific coast, and particularly in San Francisco, shows that the usual appliances for enumeration are insufficient to determine, with any degree of accuracy, the population of an ordinary "Chinatown." The figures above given will, however, do for comparison. The census of 1880 was of the date of the treaty with China, providing for the restriction of immigration. Had the purpose of this treaty been promptly and effectually carried out, the number of Chinese in the United States would necessarily have been less now than in 1880. But what is the fact? The number is now not much less than 200,000, or nearly double what it was at the date of the treaty. Is it any wonder that the people are restless under this state of affairs? The marvel is, that they are as patient as they have been.

In the face of a rapidly-increasing and absorbing competition in every department of labor and every line of industry, these people have said that Chinamen who are here shall be protected in all their rights; but, in the name of everything that is near and dear to them, they demand that this invasion shall cease. Is there anything extraordinary in this demand?

The President has called the attention of Congress to the fact "that the exclusion of Chinese labor is demanded in other countries where like conditions prevail, is strongly evident in the Dominion of Canada, where Chinese immigration is now regulated by laws more exclusive than our own." Now, what was the condition of affairs in Canada that induced its parliament to pass laws more exclusive than our own? The immigration has been into British Columbia, on the Pacific coast, where, in 1883, the total population was 49,459, of which only 4,350 were Chinese, or less than one-tenth. The building of the Canadian Pacific Railway brought a large, but temporary, increase of the Chinese population; and at one time (in 1885), it was estimated that there were 18,000 Chinamen in British Columbia. The people of that section protested against this immigration, and demanded it should cease, whereupon the government at Ottawa passed a restriction act, dated July 20, 1885, section 5 of which provides: —

No vessel carrying Chinese immigrants to any port in Canada, shall carry more than one such immigrant for every fifty tons of its tonnage; and the owner of any such vessel who carries any number in excess of the number allowed by this section, shall be liable to a penalty of $50 for each person so carried in excess.

In other sections, further penalties are provided for evasions of the act, and the exclusion is perpetual, and not temporary; but notwithstanding the effective terms of the act, it is announced that it is to be further amended, so as to enlarge its penalties, and make the exclusion more rigid and certain.

The seven colonies of Australasia contain a population of a little over 3,000,000 of people, with a Chinese population of less than 50,000. Some years ago, it was determined that a restriction should be placed on the further immigration of Chinese; and, accordingly, laws were passed having this object in view. The last statute on this subject which has come under my notice limits the number of Chinese immigrants that can be carried on any one vessel to one for every one hundred tons of the tonnage of the vessel.

In the Hawaiian Islands, the Chinese population increased from 5,116 in 1878 to 17,937 in 1884, at which last-named date the total population numbered 80,578. The process of Chinese absorption had commenced, when the government interposed and put a stop to the immigration.

In the face of such examples, showing the action of other countries in dealing with this question, ought the Government of the United States further to hesitate in this matter? The situation is far more serious on the Pacific coast than is generally understood, and invites the attention of the country to the careful consideration of this question. The successful method adopted in other countries for restricting Chinese immigration has been to limit the number that may be carried on any one vessel. This was the restriction first proposed by Congress; and it would have been the law to-day, and this question settled, if it had not been for the Burlingame Treaty. The present treaty, however, permits a restriction of this character; and, accordingly, it is proposed that vessels shall not bring to this country a greater number than one Chinaman to every fifty tons of the tonnage of that vessel. This is the present limitation in Canada, and half what it is in Australasia. It cannot be said, therefore, to be unreasonable. The argument is made, however, that there are Americans in China whose interests would suffer from any aggressive action on our part; but, when we inquire how far our American energy and enterprise have been invited in that direction, we find that there are only 621 Americans in the whole Chinese empire, including men, women and children, and comprising in occupations missionaries, students, merchants, mechanics, engineers, bankers and ship-owners. What interests can these few adventurers have in China, as compared with the interests of 60,000,000 of people at home, to preserve the peace and good order of the thousands of industrial communities scattered all over this land? It is absurd to seriously discuss measures for the protection of American labor and American industries, and imperil the whole principle under some vague impression that 621 Americans in China have acquired rights that can only be preserved by a submission to the tyranny and demoralization of Chinese labor, habits and morals.

It is a further fact worthy of special attention, that under our present treaty stipulations with China, neither the handful of Americans who are now in China, nor any number who may choose to go there, have any such rights as the 200,000 Chinese have in the United States. The Chinaman in this country may go where he pleases, and trade and labor in any community he likes, enjoying the same privileges as our own citizens. But not so with the American in China; he is restricted in his residence and trade to certain ports, called "treaty-ports," which number twenty-two in all; but only twenty ports are in fact open to foreign trade and commerce. In these "treaty-ports," the Americans, like other foreigners, are even there subjected to restrictions as to residence, business and travel, not imposed upon Chinese subjects; and hence, it is urged, that our relations with China are in no sense reciprocal or just to our own people, and we ought not to hesitate in imposing whatever restrictive measures may be necessary to protect our laboring classes against the evils of Chinese immigration.

CHAPTER XVII.

THE PROBLEM OF TO-DAY.

Equity between Men — The Complaint of Labor — Partisan Statesmanship — Contrasts — "The City Streets" — Despotism of the Wage-System — The Responsibility — War Relations — The Duty of Government — A Permanent Class — More Time, More Wages — The Learned and Powerful — From Villanage to Co-operation — Civilization is Common Property — Private Ownership and Public Interests — Levelling-up — No Bloody Reprisals — The Army of Peace — God and Mammon — The New Pentecost.

THE problem of to-day, as of yesterday and to-morrow, is, how to establish equity between men. The laborer who is forced to sell his day's labor to-day, or starve to-morrow, is not in equitable relations with the employer, who can wait to buy labor until starvation fixes the rates of wages and hours of time. The labor movement is the natural effort of readjustment, — an ever-continued attempt of organized laborers, so that they may withhold their labor until the diminished interest or profit or capital of the employer shall compel him to agree to such terms as shall be for the time measurably equitable. These are the forceful methods of all time, and may continue to develop manhood and womanhood by peaceful revolution, as laborers advance their line, or may cause a social earthquake, and become destructive by the organized repression of labor's right. Before the solution of the labor problem can be reached, the nature of the complaint must be understood. The author, in 1877, attempted a diagnosis of the disease, which was given to the public in the form of an appeal; and, as it voices the complaint of labor to-day, it is here reproduced: —

"Primarily, the responsibility for strikes and outbreaks rests upon the wage-labor system, — a system that encourages cunning above conscience; that robs the producer, and enriches the speculator; that makes the employer a despot, and the employee a slave,—a system that shortens life, engenders disease, enfeebles the mind, corrupts the morals, and thus propagates misery, vice and crime.

"We complain, that whereas labor produces all the wealth of the world, the laborer receives only as much as will keep him in the poorest condition of life to which he can be crowded down, for the shortest number of years; that he makes civilization possible, and is reduced to barbarism,—building houses not to own them, carriages not to ride in them, growing food he may not eat, and weaving raiment he may not wear; that all of the arts and comforts that lift human life above the brute are present to tantalize, and not to encourage him; that steam, electricity, chemistry and productive machinery are competitors, and not co-operators, with him; that the conditions of his employment are debasing, and not elevating,—demoralizing, and not self-controlling; and that, whereas he is the most important factor, he is treated as the least; that his home is in the tenement-houses, back-slums and alleys of the city, or the unhealthy lowlands of the suburbs; that his wife is forced from home, and his children from school; that he cannot, as a laborer, hope for thanks, honors or positions of trust; that he is practically debarred from representation or the public expression of his complaints. When at work, he belongs to the lower orders, and is continually under surveillance; when out of work, he is an outlaw, a tramp,—he is a man without the rights of manhood,—the pariah of society, homeless, in the deep significance of the term.

"The laborer's complaint is not that brains rule, or that culture leads, but that conscienceless cunning and miserly acquisitiveness are rewarded better than constructive ability or open-hearted integrity. We complain that culture busies itself upon immaterial subjects,—conning the olden lore, not delving for the unrevealed treasures that lie embossed in humanity; that learning interests itself with the science of things, and not with the science of men; that philanthropy is the maudlin moan over the needs of the beasts, and a scoffer at the woes of humanity; that cats, dogs and horses are better cared for than the children of the poor; that there are societies for the prevention of cruelty to animals, and none to prevent cruelty to humanity.

"We complain that our rulers, statesmen and orators have not attempted to engraft republican principles into our industrial system, and have forgotten or denied its underlying principles.

"We complain that statesmanship is narrow and partisan, the pulpit blind and ignorant, and the press the advertising channel of wealth; that the spirit and power of our institutions are being subverted from the high positions attempted by the Fathers, by gradual limitation of the power of the ballot, making elections less frequent, appointments more numerous, terms of office longer, by decrease of opportunity for the intelligent comprehension of the rapidly-increasing political duties, by the teachings of a false and pernicious system of political economy, that has no logical rule or law of action, or systematic arrangement of data,—a system that, up to this time, has taught that the production, and not the distribution, of wealth was the greatest factor in civilization.

"We complain that the courts are administrators of estates, and not of justice; that the weight of wealth, and not of testimony, wins the case or decides the penalty.

"We complain that the jurors are chosen from the traders and speculators, and not from the wage-laborers.

"We complain that the poor can be distressed by trustee-processes, while the merchant and banker can be released from his indebtedness by bankruptcy; that we are wholly in the hands of our employers,—serfs of the mill, the workshop, and the mine,—subjects of the railroad kings and the cotton lords, who know no divided allegiance.

"Such are a few of the complaints of labor; and, while we thus suffer, fortunes are accumulated, wealth and power are centralized.

"And while our masters are revelling in luxury, excelling the nobility of Europe in extravagant display, aping their manners and imitating their follies, we are becoming crowded down to the level of the 'pauper' labor of the monarchical countries."

These contrasts of conditions have aroused not only the angry hate of the desperate poor, the saddened thought of the philosopher and philanthropist, but have furnished a theme for the poet's pen * : —

A city of palaces! Yes, that 's true;
  A city of palaces built for trade;
Look down from this street — what a splendid view
  Of the temples where fabulous gains are made.
Just glance at the wealth of a single pile,
  The marble pillars, the miles of glass,
The carving and cornice in gaudy style,
  The massive show of the polished brass;
And think of the acres of inner floors,
  Where the wealth of the world is spread for sale;
Why, the treasures enclosed by those ponderous doors
  Are rich as an Eastern fairy tale.
Pass on to the next, it is still the same;
  Another Aladdin the scene repeats;
The silks are unrolled and the jewels flame
  For leagues and leagues of the city streets.

Now turn away from the teeming town,
  And pass to the homes of the merchant kings;
Wide squares, where the stately porches frown,
  Where the flowers are bright, and the fountain sings.
Look up at the lights in that brilliant room,
  With its chandelier of a hundred flames.
See the carpeted street where the ladies come,
  Whose husbands have millions, or famous names;
For whom are jewels and silks: behold,
  On those exquisite bosoms and throats they burn;
Art challenges Nature in color, and gold,
  And gracious presence at every turn.
So the winters fly past in a joyous rout,
  And the summers bring marvellous cool retreats:
These are civilized wonders we 're finding out,
  As we walk through the beautiful city streets.

A city of palaces, — hush, not quite!
  A city where palaces are, is best;
No need to speak of what 's out of sight;
  Let us take what is pleasant, and leave the rest;

* "The City Streets," by John Boyle O'Reilly.

The men of the city who travel and write,
Whose fame and credit are known abroad,
The people who move in the ranks polite,
The cultured women, whom all applaud.
It is true, there are only ten thousand here;
But the other half-million are vulgar clod,
And a soul well-bred is eternally dear —
It counts so much more on the books of God.
The others have use in their place, no doubt;
But why speak of a class one never meets?
They are gloomy things to be talked about, —
Those common lives of the city streets.

Well, then, if you will, let us look at both;
Let us weigh the pleasure against the pain,
The gentleman's smile against the bar-room oath,
The luminous square with the tenement lane.
Look round you now: 't is another sphere,
Of thin-clad women, and grimy men;
There are over ten thousand huddled here,
Where a hundred would live of the upper ten.
Take care of that child: here, look at her face, —
A baby who carries a baby-brother;
They must learn to be helpers in this poor place,
And the infant must often nurse the mother.
Come up those stairs where the babies went;
Five flights the little one climbed in the dark;
There are a dozen of homes in the steep ascent,
And homes that are filled with children. Hark!
Did you hear that laugh with its manly tones,
And the joyous rings of the baby voice?
'T is the father who gathers his little ones,
The nurse and her brother, and all rejoice.
Yes: human nature is much the same,
When you come to the heart and count its beats;
The workman is proud of his home's dear name
As the richest man in the city streets.

* * * * * * * * * *

'T is civilization, so they say,
And it cannot be changed for the weakness of men.
Take care, take care; 't is a desperate way
To goad the wolf to the end of his den.
Take heed with your civilization, ye,
On your pyramids built of quivering hearts;
There are stages, like Paris in '93,
Where the commonest men play most terrible parts.
Your statutes may crush, but they cannot kill
The patient sense of a natural right;

It may slowly move, but the people's will,
  Like the ocean o'er Holland, is always in sight.
We have churches enough, and they do their best,
  But there's little of Christ in our week-day laws;
The Gospel is taught, but the gain is test;
  We punish the sin, while we cherish the cause.
Not gold, but souls, should be first in an age
  That bows its head at the Sacred Word:
Yet our laws are blind to a starving wage,
  While guarding the owners sweat-wrung hoard.
"It is not our fault," say the rich ones. No:
  'T is the fault of a system, old and strong;
But men are the judges of systems; so
  The cure will come if we own the wrong.
It will come in peace if the Christ-word lead;
  It will sweep in storm if it be denied;
The right to bring justice is always decreed;
  And on every hand are the warnings cried.
Take heed with your progress. Its feet have trod
  On the souls it slew with its own pollutions;
Submission is good, but the order of God
  May flame the torch of the revolutions.
Beware with your classes. Men are men,
  And a cry in the night is a fearful teacher;
When it reaches the hearts of the masses, then
  They need but a sword for a judge and a preacher.
Take heed, for your Juggernaut pushes hard;
  God holds the doom that its day completes;
It will dawn like a fire when the track is barred
  By a barricade in the city streets.

These extremes of wealth and poverty are threatening the existence of the government. In the light of these facts, we declare that there is an inevitable and irresistible conflict between the wage-system of labor and the republican system of government, — the wage-laborer attempting to save the government, and the capitalist class ignorantly attempting to subvert it.

The strike of the trainmen on the Baltimore & Ohio Railroad was the serving of a notice upon the people of this nation that wages could not be further reduced, — a protest against robbery, a rebellion against starvation. The trainmen were under despotic control. To leave their employ was to become tramps, outlaws; to submit was to starve in serfdom. They knew that the power of the railroad oligarchy exceeded and superseded that of the national and State governments. The railroad president is a railroad king, whose whim is law. He collects tithes by reducing wages as remorselessly as the Shah of Persia or the Sultan of Turkey, and, like them, is not amenable to any human power. He can discharge (banish) any employee without cause. He can prevent laborers from following their usual vocations. He can withhold their lawful wages. He can delay trial on a suit at law, and postpone judgment indefinitely. He can control legislative bodies, dictate legislation, subsidize the press, and corrupt the moral sense of the community. He can fix the price of freights, and thus command the food and fuel-supplies of the nation. In his right hand he holds the government; in his left hand, the people. And this is called law and order, — from which there is no appeal. It is war, — war against the divine rights of humanity; war against the principles of our government. There is no mutuality of interests, no co-operative union of labor and capital. It is the iron heel of a soulless monopoly, crushing the manhood out of sovereign citizens.

The subjects of this power, overworked, underpaid, underfed, and uneducated, — are asked to be wiser than the statesmanship and culture of the nineteenth century.

In this war between the master and his vassal, property was destroyed, and men were prevented from taking the places of the strikers. Whoever is responsible for the cause is responsible for the effect. Men respect property only as it represents the public good, and hate it whenever it becomes typical of wrong and oppression. The crown, the Bastile, the slave auction-block and the lash earned the hate of those who destroyed them.

The bell that calls the weary, half-paid worker from his needed rest, taunts him with each resounding stroke. The machinery that renders his skill and time of less value to himself and more to his master, becomes the hated instrument of torture; its monotonous hum keeping time to his groans and curses. The mill, the mine, the foundry and the round-house stand like giants, ever ready to swallow up his substance. With such feelings constantly present in the hearts of the laborers, unused to thought, disciplined only to act, what wonder that violence should spread like an epidemic from station to station, from mine to mine, and from factory to factory. What wonder that in this war life was destroyed? The man who, for his class, dares death for freedom's sake, must needs look upon the man who takes his place as giving aid and comfort to the enemy. It is war, and cries of "peace, peace," when there is no peace, will only lull the thoughtless into treacherous sleep.

The laborer and capitalist are living in war relations; and the sooner this fact is acknowledged, the better for the adjustment of differences.

The mob can be put down for a while; but the spirit of hate that now centres upon the great monopolies will soon extend to the government that acts as their protector.

Men love the government under which they can enjoy the largest prosperity, and hate that under which they are being crowded back into barbarism.

The existence of a million tramps is a standing threat against the stability of our institutions. They are the unorganized militia of incipient rebellion; and the attempt to suppress them by violent measures will fail in the nineteenth as well as it did in the sixteenth century.

The demand for a stronger government is the demand of deadened consciences and enfeebled brains. Strength will not be found in a standing army; for, when our internal commerce and manufactures are protected by armed men, the Republic is dead. "Righteousness alone exalteth a nation."

The crisis that we are rapidly approaching is not local. No Mason and Dixon's line, no color-tests divide North, South, East and West; wherever laborers congregate, whether in the factories of New England, or the sunless mines of Pennsylvania, one chord of sympathy unites them all.

No demagogue's cant of race or creed will hold them from their purpose to be free. In that coming time, woman will teach her children the lesson of her hate and wrong. Already a generation has arisen, schooled in the great moral agitation for public good.

Justice demands that those who earn shall receive; that no one has a right to add cost without adding value.

Recognizing that the steps toward the attaining of the end must be slow, we demand, first, legislative interference between capital and labor; restraining capital in its usurpations, and enlarging the boundaries of labor's opportunity.

The Constitution of the United States demands that each of the sovereign States shall have a republican form of government. A greater power than that of the State has arisen—"a State within a State,"—a power that is quietly yet quickly sapping the foundations of the majority-rule. The law of self-protection is greater than constitutions, and legislative bodies are bound to interfere to protect the sovereign citizen against the insidious inroads of the usurping power.

Monarchal governments rest upon the ability of the ruler to maintain order by physical force. Republican institutions are sustained by the ability of the people to rule. The government has the right, and is bound in self-defence to protect the ability of the people to rule. It has the right to interfere against any organized or unorganized power that imperils or impairs this ability. Upon no other argument can the free-school system be maintained, institutions of learning, of science, and art be endowed by the State or exempt from taxation. It is the policy of the government to protect, not only her domain from monarchal interference, as set forth in the Monroe doctrine, but to protect her citizens from the influence of cheap labor and over-work. For cheap labor means a cheap people, and dear labor a dear people. The foundation of the Republic is equality.

The cheap laborer is an irresponsible agent; the dear laborer, an independent citizen. The Mason and Dixon line was the attempted wall of defence against the cheapest laborer in the world (the chattel-slave). The protective tariff was the pretended wall of defence against the competition of the monarchal serf (European wage-slave). The cotton oligarchy South, and their tools, defied the theory and policy of the government, by making the boundary-line of slavery (cheap labor) of no effect. The cotton oligarchy

North (lords of the loom) defeated the purpose of the Government to protect the laborers, and made the tariff a wall of protection to invested wealth, without giving ample protection to invested time and skill.

They placed a tariff upon things, the product of New England cheap labor, thus commanding their own price for home production; and, by forcing an unnatural immigration of cheap laborers to our shores, commanded the wages of home-producers; bringing the condition of labor in this country nearer to that of the lowest and most neglected classes of Europe, — thus amassing princely fortunes, and creating in our midst a vassal or permanent wage-labor class.

Chattel-slavery died at its own hand, — the suicide of secession. The cotton-lords and their tools have increased productive capacity, and decreased distributive ability, until it has met with the natural stagnation that foreshadows death.

The equilibrium between production and consumption must be adjusted; and that can only be attained by the better distribution of wealth in the process of production.

The demand of labor is for more wages and more time, — more wages to obtain more comforts, and more time wherein to enjoy them.

The measure that will soonest lift the laborer to a higher level of manhood, and will at the same time tend to the employment of more laborers, will inaugurate a less spasmodic system of industry, and will set more "idlers to working, and more workers to thinking," is a reduction of the hours of labor, — a measure that is based on sound economic principles, as well as sustained by the most humane considerations.

We demand that the policy of the government shall be declared as against cheap labor, and that all encouragement and aid shall be withheld from all forms of monopoly that endanger the ability of the people to rule.

The statesmanship of the nation and the world is summoned to the solution of this problem. The theory that mental force has any diviner right to rob and oppress than brute force is false. Labor will not step down another inch without revolting. Concessions must come from those who have.

The labor movement appeals to the learned and powerful to waste no further time in the conceits of an unwieldy culture. Take lessons in humility, and be wise in time. Civilization, in its onward march, forces concessions from those who have. The Magna Charta was the concession of the power that made all powerful. Art, science and machinery, when made to serve all the people, will accomplish miracles that the power of kings cannot evoke. The movement pleads for the protection of all the past achievements of labor. Through the system of wage-labor, humanity is marching from villanage toward co-operation. If its progress is aided by timely concession, its steps shall keep time with law and order. But if stubborn power resists its progress, history will repeat itself. The product of the world is man, not classes,—humanity, not race.

Civilization is measured, not by the wealth, power or culture of the few, but by the quantity and quality of the opportunities possessed by the many. Civilization is common property. The institutions that enable the many to read and write and speak their native language amply and correctly are communistic institutions, inasmuch as the results are common property, even when the buildings are under private ownership. So, to-day, the advantages of transportation of persons or commodities by steam or the transmission of intelligence by electricity are of common benefit in the saving of time to all. The demand for their common or public ownership is based on the theory and fact that private ownership gives private control over vast public interests.

Economic equity demands the elimination of waste as a great step in the direction of the abolition of the poverty of the world. Whoever makes it possible to travel one thousand miles at an expense of ten days' where it formerly cost thirty days' wages, has conferred a benefit on the public; but to pay $200,000,000 to the organizer of this benefit is an extravagance the public cannot afford.

Under the present system of wages for laborers, and profits

upon labor for capitalists, the natural tendency is toward the establishment of permanent classes; the wage-receiving class becoming more and more permanent, and hence less and less hopeful and intelligent, — continually forced to be smaller consumers of products, until their condition forces the reaction of bloody revolution, or degrades them to the "cooly" level. The theory and fact of the constant change of classes is based and founded on the accidents of fortune rather than upon scientific development. Panics in trade, stagnation in industries, stock and all other gambling, intemperance, extravagance and imbecility of children, wars, convulsions of nature, and, to a certain extent, fires and strikes, all act as ministers of change from class to class. Social as well as physical upheavals always change the order of classes. The negro, in rising from his chains, overturned private ownership in the black man's public and political rights; and, in that overturning, the class of masters was changed.

The statement that the rich man of to-day may be the poor man of to-morrow, and that the poor man's children may be the employers of the rich man's progeny, is a confession that bankrupts, failures, panics, industrial stagnation, speculation, gambling, and wars are the proper methods by which wealth should be redistributed. As the labor problem is a question of civilization, and the movement of the laborers toward equity is not that individuals should be thereby made rich, while the many are made poor, but that wealth should be distributed in the process of production. The demand of the laborer is for a change of conditions; and the solution of the problem will show that the extremes of wealth and poverty are curses, not benefits. The thoughtless opponent of the labor movement flies at once to the conclusion that the satisfying of the demands of the laborers would necessitate leveling down instead of leveling up. They say, "If all men are wealthy, there would be no motive for labor." The changes which will be wrought in the future in the leveling-up process will reveal the wonderful change of motives. The motives of the chattel-slave are buried with his chains; new ambitions are aroused, new hopes give strength to new demands; education, culture and opportunity are ever beckoning to new energy. The wage-worker is, by the law of necessity, an eye-servant, — as a rule, perhaps, rendering grudgingly his services; when he becomes an employer or co-operator, he works as never before. As the laborer receives more and more for his earnings, abolishing the need of overseers and middle-men, as well as the further use of capitalists and speculators, as worse than useless factors in society, more and more labor-saving machinery will be introduced, the hours of labor being continually decreased, and the buildings devoted to work so improved that labor shall become a blessing instead of a curse, a pleasure instead of a pain. Instead of, as now, the poor, ignorant, physically and mentally, and sometimes morally, deformed, unskilled worker leaving the stifling, sunless room of the crowded tenement, or the cabin of the unsanitary lowlands, by early morning-light, to eke out, at the risk of health and limb, and perhaps life, the mere pittance that shall give him the poorest food and poorest shelter, and none of the advantages of civilization (excepting that of the poison-draught which science has developed to his destruction),— instead of this, the now-dawning day shall witness a well-built, fully equipped manhood, using the morning hours in the duties and pleasures of the sunlit-home; taking his morning bath before his morning work, reading his morning paper in the well-equipped reading-room of the manufactory, or, if perchance, handling the cruder tools of a harder and less-skilled occupation, he shall have the stimulant of being equally honorable and equally remunerative with the more easy methods of gaining a livelihood. With the hours of work reduced to the minimum, the profits of his work increased to the maximum, he will be a man upon whom the honors and duties of civilization can safely rest. The new revolution that shall bring about these changes shall evolve the dude out of existence; the rot of a false-named culture shall be of the past. The pretended fear that this will make all men alike in ambitions and tastes, is born of ignorance and cowardice. Varieties multiply under the best cultivation. The common weeds may look alike, but the plants and flowers are of endless variety. It is the very poorest men and races who look alike, think alike, and act alike, — whose thoughts and actions are controlled by one instead of the many. The physical transformation of races under the influences and opportunities of republican institutions is marked, and can be read of all men. The poor, over-wrought worker of the Old World, stunted in growth, with marked physical characteristics of expression, and of almost physical deformity, and made a subject because of this, to caricature and ridicule, finds under our institutions such opportunities of development as shall cause his children to be born, not only under better opportunities, but under better physical conditions, until the wonderful transformation of a generation shall witness the glistening eye, the well-formed mouth and chin, as the result of the change in habits, thoughts and actions, consequent upon his environment. A retired capitalist once informed the writer that the labor movement would develop the beauty of the race. He might have added, "the beauty of the world."

The real problem of to-day is, the true and practicable steps by which equity between men can be administered? As the sick man, struggling with disease caused by the violation of the laws of nature, grasps for remedies and seeks immediate recovery from his self-inflicted ills, so the system which is corrupting mankind to-day cries out for instantaneous cure. As common sense in medicine has developed the fact that pure air, pure water, sunlight, and careful attention to the laws of hygiene are the best remedies in many instances, so the labor movement needs to-day the light of a most thorough and unprejudiced investigation. It calls for the purest thought, the purest men and women; it calls for the healthy exercise of the noblest sentiments; it calls for treatment commensurate with its importance. While nature calls for natural remedies, the angry clamor and fear of some monopolists, and of desperate, unthinking men, calls for blood, forgetting all past history, and all logical deduction from causes. The hanging of seven anarchists, at Chicago, after a hasty trial and conviction, will not remedy the evil nor wash out the stain of anarchy with the blood of men hastily condemned. The organized labor movement of the age looks to no red-handed or bloody reprisals of its wrongs. To-day, the disciplined ranks of all divisions of the Grand Army of Labor march to the music of liberty and law. The flag they carry is the white flag of pure, enduring peace; and as long as they can freely gather in their union-halls and assembly-chambers to discuss with freedom the questions of the day,— so long as the press is free and speech remains untrammeled, organization unforbidden, and our moral, social and political influence remains intact,— he is an enemy to the labor movement who seeks to hasten the liberation of the poor by the force of dynamite or of arms. The danger comes, not from labor associations, from their methods or their measures, from strikes or boycotts, but from the concentrated power of those who, holding the supplies of life, the opportunities of labor, command such conditions as the price of employment as shall turn the manly effort of the present into the cowardly method of other climes. When men cannot speak, they will think; when they cannot act publicly, they will act secretly. The hope of the peaceful solution of the problem of to-day rests in the Christianizing influence of our free institutions. The Pilgrim leaven still works, true to the fundamental principles of the great Leader of men, who walked the earth "with not where to lay His head," despised by the wealthy, hated by the powerful, and beloved by the poor. The influence of the teachings of the carpenter's Son still tends to counteract the bad influences of Mammon. In this movement of the laborers toward equity, we will find a new revelation of the old Gospel. When the Golden Rule of Christ shall measure the relations of men in all their duties towards their fellows, in factory and workshop, in the mine, in the field, in commerce, everywhere the challenge will go forth as never before, "Choose ye this day whom ye will serve,—God, or Mammon." Though the Mammon-worshippers may cry, "Crucify! Crucify!" the promise of the prophet and the poet shall be fulfilled, and the glad evangel of the Christmas morn shall sound again in the glad ears of all; and peace on earth shall prevail, not by the subjugation of man to man, or intellect to superstition, but by the free acceptance of the Gospel that all men are of one blood. Then the new Pentecost will come, when every man shall have according to his needs.

CHAPTER XVIII.

THE HOURS OF LABOR.

LESS HOURS OF LABOR FOR THE EMPLOYED MEANS MORE HOURS OF WORK FOR THE UNEMPLOYED — THE LABORER'S RIGHT TO SELL HIS TIME AT THE HIGHEST PRICES — RAPID PRODUCTION — EVILS OF MONOTONOUS LABOR — OBJECTIONS TO THE EIGHT-HOUR SYSTEM ANSWERED — THE MARKET FOR THE PRODUCTS OF LABOR DEPENDENT UPON THE CONDITION OF THE MASSES — THE EARNINGS OF LABOR DEPENDENT UPON THE HABITS AND CUSTOMS OF THE PEOPLE — THE BEST MARKET WHERE THE SHORTEST WORK-DAY PREVAILS — STRIKES — LEGISLATION — FREEDOM OF CONTRACT — DEMAND AND SUPPLY — PROFITS AND WAGES AFFECTED BY LESS HOURS OF LABOR — THE UPLIFTING INFLUENCE OF LEISURE.

MEN who are compelled to sell their labor, very naturally desire to sell the smallest portion of their time for the largest possible price. They are merchants of their time. It is their only available capital. They feel that, if they flood the market, — that is, sell more hours of labor than the market requires, — stagnation will follow.

The growth of population, greatly enhanced by artificially stimulated emigration from the long-hour and cheap-labor countries of Europe, tends to crowd the streets with unemployed men. Men out of work will underbid the men at work, and so wages are affected and sometimes governed, not by the value of the service rendered in time or skill, but by the number of the unemployed.

The instincts of the wage-workers are wiser than the philosophy of the schools. The demand for less hours of labor for the employed means more hours of work for the now unemployed. It is the demand for a better distribution of work, as well as a demand for an increase of value on each hour's service. The rapidity of production consequent upon the introduction of labor-saving machinery has made an hour of time more valuable to the world than ten hours were twenty-five years ago. The intelligent wage-worker recognizes this fact; and, feeling that as the demand for hand-skill is being diminished, and opportunity of advancement continually lessened, he turns to his only remedy,—a refusal to oversell the market.

The fact that men who ask for less hours often ask for increased wages at the same time, is because they have prized the value of their time at a higher rate than formerly.

The objections to the reductions of the hours of labor now made are of the same character as the objections that were raised to the shortening of the day's work to ten hours of labor. Among these objections may be named the objection that a reduction of hours would necessarily reduce the wages of the employees, and thus tend to injure the very persons who are making the demand; second, that the reduction of the hours of labor would tend to an increase of intemperance, vice and crime; that it would tend to discourage enterprise and increase the cost of production; that it would lessen the profit upon capital invested; that capital would seek investment in those localities where the longer work-day existed; that it would encourage foreign competition.

On an examination of these objections, it will be found that some of them are self-contradictory. If wages are reduced, as a consequence of a reduction of the length of the work-day, then certainly the cost of the product could not be enhanced, because the price per hour would remain the same, and certainly the product of one hour in eight would not be less, but in some cases would be greater than the product of one hour in ten. It will be still further agreed, that to produce the same amount of product as is now demanded, one-fifth more employees would be required, thus creating or awakening a new market of consumers.

This statement of the inevitable consequences of the reduction of hours, without an increase of wages, shows conclusively that the wages would be increased; for the employment of more men to produce the same amount of product would necessarily quicken the demand in the labor-market. Lessening the number of unemployed would give the employed the opportunity to demand more wages.

To the claim that less hours of labor means less wages to the employee, we point to all past experience as the answer. The history of the labor movement shows that, from 1832 to 1853, a reduction of three hours per day had been made in many of the employments, and that this considerable reduction of one hour every six and a half years was followed by an increased purchasing power of the day's labor. The experience in this country is the same as that in England. For, while the workingmen were commencing the agitation in the council chamber of Boston, Mass., in 1832, the same agitation had reached the Parliament of Great Britain; for it was in that year that Michael T. Sadler introduced the ten-hour bill, and by his enthusiasm and energy calling into the advocacy of this measure the Earl of Shaftsbury, John Fielding, and William Cobbett, who were supported by Lord Macaulay, the Bishops of Manchester and Oxford, and Earls of Ellsmere and Fersham.

Experience has not only proved in England that wages were not reduced, but were advanced, so that more than twice as much flour could be purchased by a day's work in 1850 than could be purchased in 1804.

The oft-repeated statement, that less hours of labor means less wages, is historically untrue and theoretically unsound, and is based upon a false theory of the law governing wages. If wages were regulated by the number of hours of work, then among those classes or communities where the day's work was longest, wages would be highest, and where a day's work was shortest wages would be lowest. The reverse is true. Civilization follows the line of less hours of daily work; and civilization simply means, materially, the highest purchasing power of a day's labor.

The great governing law of wages rests upon the habits of thought and feeling, customs and manners of the masses. Where the level of thought is purely physical or animal,—groveling with the swine it feeds, occupied in discussing the fighting merits of game-cocks or men, and where the custom exists of working at all hours possible, occupying the hours of holidays and other periods of rest in filth and drunkenness,

— there wages will be paid to the level that will enable the laborers to enjoy themselves in their own low condition. To disturb this class of men from their sottish contentment by an agitation for more wages or less hours, is to lift them up in the level of their manhood to thoughts of better things, and to an organized demand for the same.

The school-taught American boy, compelled by the customs of his village to be neatly dressed, and competent to hold his own with his fellows in matters of literary attainment, will not rest satisfied with wages that compel him to forego the appetites that the school-room created. His wages must give him opportunities of association, of travel, of reading; and these are among the most expensive habits incident to a shorter work-day, as is evidenced by the fact that the lyceum, debating-school, lecture-room and library received its impetus when the hours of labor were reduced to ten. The mammoth and wonderful circulation which the daily papers of the large cities have obtained is due to the fact that the common people are considering the questions of public moment. The fact that space is given to sports and to crime, and to those things which appeal more to the physical man, is not so much due to the demand of the working people for this kind of reading as to the fact that a large portion of the community — not wage-workers — are interested pecuniarily in these games, and to the existence of a large criminal gambling class, as well as to the fact, as far as athletic games are concerned, that in all periods of time physical sports have been looked upon as a proper physical recreation; and those who cannot enjoy themselves by participation enjoy, at least, the pleasure of reading accounts of them.

James Hole says: "Inferior habits of living are as much the cause as they are the result of low wages;" and John Stewart Mill says: "No remedies for low wages have the smallest chance of being efficacious, which do not operate on and through the minds or habits of the people." Reducing the hours of labor acts more directly on the habits and thoughts of the people than any other measure heretofore proposed.

It is true that those who have acquired bad habits under the old system are in danger of continuing them through the momentum already gained; but the fact that the larger proportion of the working classes are as measurably correct, and that opportunities heretofore given have been opportunities improved, and that leisure operates upon the home, stimulating home influences for good, — lessening the hours of household drudgery, and giving the husband and wife opportunities of improvement heretofore unknown, is evidence that less hours of wage-service yield more hours for individual and public good. The claim that to lessen the hours of work would tend to increase intemperance, vice and crime is answered by the undeniable fact, as testified to by men of large experience and observation, who unite in their testimony that the intemperate and the vicious habits in England and America — the drunken Monday, as well as the debauched Sunday — have been partially remedied, and that the halls of meeting and reading-rooms have multiplied by the thousand wherever the short work-day has been generally introduced.

The claim of the manufacturer and capitalist, that this system would tend to lessen the profits upon the capital invested, is well made. The inevitable tendency is in the direction of reduced profits, and the hope of the future rests upon these two facts: that while profit upon capital is being diminished, profit upon labor is being increased, and the capitalist and the middle-man classes are being ground to powder between this upper and nether millstone of progressive civilization. It is said that, if profits are reduced, capital will not seek investment, and hence enterprise will be checked. Capital is soon consumed when not recuperated by interests, rents or profits. It will be forced to accept such percentage as the civilization of the times will permit it to have; and the insecurity of the capital itself, when invested in speculative and gambling enterprises, will always tend to force the conservative possessor to seek safe investment, however small the rate of interest.

The demand of our time is for the rapid production of things. The stage-coach is superseded by the steam-engine, and steam gives way to electricity. The price of the product of the manufacturer is governed largely by the quantity it is possible for him to produce in a given time. Not many years ago, the manufacturer who turned out a few score of cases of shoes a week was considered fortunate; but to-day, more shoes are turned out in a day by our manufacturers than were turned out in a month, or many months, thirty years ago. An investigation of the causes for this rapid production brings us back again to the wage-question. The larger the demand, the larger the means of supply. The demand determines the amount, the market determines the demand, the condition of the people determines the market, and the rate of wages determines the condition of the people. High wages under short hours mean that a large share of the products of wealth are being distributed among the earners of wealth; and capital will be forced, finally, to consider the question of offering to the laborer a genuine partnership, in which the elements of common risk and common profit shall enter. The individual employer, when forced to meet this question of reduced hours, looks naturally and properly to his own immediate profit; but, to be successful in the future of our manufacturing industries, he must consider the man, not only as a producer, but a consumer. To reduce wages is to turn civilization backwards; to advance wages is to lift civilization to a higher level.

The argument which has the most powerful influence against the demand for less hours of toil is, that to grant this demand would necessarily increase the cost of production. The elements of cost in any enterprise are, first, the ruling rate of interest upon the money invested, the price of the raw material, the cost of labor, and the cost of placing the goods upon the market. We have seen that the cost of the article is regulated more by the number of the article demanded — that is, by the condition of the market — than from any other cause; that to make one chair would cost, first of all, more than to make one of a thousand chairs, and so of all other products of hand or machine-labor. Labor-saving machinery is never introduced until it pays; and it never pays until wages have advanced to that point that it is cheaper to have the work performed by machinery than by hand. High wages, then, invite more and more machinery, demand more and more goods, call for more rapid production, lessen profits, and increase the purchasing power of labor. That this will ultimately revolutionize the whole system of employers and employees, is as inevitable as it is desirable; and no man will be necessarily rendered uncomfortable because of the fact that the many may have been rendered more comfortable. The extremes existing in society will be abolished, and with these extremes the curses and crimes incident to poverty and extreme wealth will disappear. If the world is too poor to provide mausoleums worth from $100,000 to $250,000 for dead capitalists, neither civilization nor the decaying bones of the departed monopolist will suffer. If the fewer cannot make their semi-annual trips for extravagant display in foreign countries, the many will be able to make trips of recreation and of observation to their benefit, and the general advancement of society.

The claim that the stimulant to labor would be overcome, if getting a living were made easier, is not sustained by experience. Men who think they can retire on fifty thousand dollars, when they attain that sum, are more anxious to double the amount; and contentment in one's position is unknown, except among the most degraded and depraved. Men will be stimulated but by higher motives; and stimulated, not so much from the desire of individual aggregations as for public aggregations, because he and all others will be benefited therein. The demand for public parks in our great cities, although, perhaps, fostered in a measure by speculators and contractors, has its firm footing upon the common impulse for opportunities for public possessions for general enjoyment.

Of the evils of over-work, or of the "long-hour system," as well as of the moral, educational and physical influences of a shorter work-day, much has been said and written. The space allotted to this chapter can only permit a reference to the history of the movement, as evidence that the working people themselves have continually pointed out the physical and moral degradation of over-work, and have exemplified the benefits of leisure.

In the days before the introduction of labor-saving machinery to any extent, every craftsman became a skilled workman in a sense that is now but little understood; each workman turning out a completed article; and the work upon these different parts called into requisition not only different muscles of the body, but different faculties of the mind, form, shape and color, as well as something of the imaginative and poetical nature of man, in giving finish to the constructive whole. The visitor to the workshop or shoe-shop of forty years ago would witness the craftsman turning over in his hand, and looking with something of pride and admiration at the finished work of the hand and brain.

The reduction of the hours of labor to eight will tend very much to remedy the evil effects of the present system of the division of labor. Less hours of application to the production of a fractional part of a product will give more hours to the development of those muscles of the body in the self-employment at the home, and more time for the development of the moral and mental qualities through opportunities of civilization, observation and association.

Under the present system, in many places, and especially in the large cities, the hours of labor are practically from twelve to thirteen per day. Forty years ago, the laborer lived near his workshop or factory; now, the enhanced cost of land forces the laborer to the extremities of the city, or the suburbs, and to-day many a skilled workman, working ten hours per day in the shop, is forced to eat his breakfast at half-past five in the morning, that he may reach his work at seven. He is compelled also to take with him a cold lunch for the mid-day meal, or buy his dinner at a convenient restaurant, — the former course being the most prevalent; he returns from his work, arriving at home at seven, or half-past, in the evening, exhausted physically by his work and the lack of a hearty warm mid-day meal, as well as by a much too early breakfast, demoralized mentally by his constant application to the repeated operation of but few faculties. To take two hours off his working-time would then leave his hours of labor, or hours occupied in the necessity of earning a living, over ten; but would enable him, in many cases, to remove his family still further away from his work, into more healthful surroundings, and to resort to steam facilities for travel.

Two methods have been attempted to secure this boon for labor: one, the strike; the other, legislation. Strange as it may seem, the strike has won the most in this direction. It was the organized movement in Australia that won the eight hour system for the trades there. It was the strike of the ship-builders and calkers, and of the building-trades, that won the ten-hour day; and, certainly, it was the strike which forced public attention to the consideration of the question and directed to the advocacy of this measure men outside of the wage-earning classes. Factory operatives, and others of the most helpless classes, — those who have been ground down by factory discipline and corporate greed, where the largest number of children and women are employed, and where every effort has been made and is being made to drive intelligent laborers out of the industry, to be supplanted by the cheapest foreign element, — for them legislation is a necessity. But when these women and children, without votes and without wealth or influence, ask for legislation, they are met by the so-called political economists, whose theories agree with their pecuniary interests, with the statement that such legislation would destroy the great right of freedom of contract.

FREEDOM OF CONTRACT.

It is the old, old story of those who oppose legislative interference against pecuniary interests. The criminal and vicious classes ask not to be interfered with. Rumsellers oppose interference, either by license or prohibition; they say the people have the right to drink, or to let it alone. The builders of the great tenement-houses, whose imperfect walls threaten human life, doubtless object to the legislative interference which provides inspectors of public buildings, and forces them to build the walls of a certain thickness, and to make the structure safe. So, too, when this same greed crowds hundreds of families into crowded rooms, damp cellars and leaky attics, where neither sunlight nor pure air can penetrate,—these owners, doubtless, object to legislative interference, that in the name of public safety and public health requires the fulfillment of certain prescribed sanitary conditions. Hackmen cannot have the freedom of contract to charge the passenger who arrives at the railway-station such price as the driver may dictate; the maximum amount he shall receive for the carriage of passengers is fixed by law. The butchers and bone-boilers, the managers of obnoxious trades, and proprietors of establishments devoted to the manufacture of explosives, do not have the freedom to contract to manufacture where they will, but must be assigned by government officials, or obtain permission, before they can locate their factories.

Legislative bodies have the right to interfere, as they shall judge to be for the good and welfare of the Commonwealth,—not as shall serve the good of the few, but of the many.

A contract supposes *two* parties,—one with something to sell, and one wishing to buy. Whatever tends to put one of these parties under the power of the other, destroys the freedom of the act. Under the wage-system, no congregated form of labor is conducted on the theory of freedom of contract. At a recent hearing before a legislative body, the treasurer of a large manufactory was asked if he ever consulted with his help in reference to the matter of wages. His answer was, "Do you suppose I run my establishment on the town-meeting plan?" In other words, he confessed, as all employers confess, that they do not propose to allow any freedom of contract as between them and their employees. The contract, so-called, is an agreement that the employer or corporation shall name all of the conditions to the bargain. The only opportunities for the nearest approach to the freedom of contract, is when a powerful labor organization has practically obtained a monopoly of their craft,—that is, that a manufacturer cannot employ help, unless they are members of the Union. In this case, the manufacturer and the representatives of the employees meet on equal terms, provided that the organization is strong enough to remain from work for such a length of time as shall so diminish the capital invested in the enterprise as to cause bankruptcy. No one is better acquainted with these facts than the distinguished representative of the non-interference political economists, who, failing to find a remedy for the evils that affect mankind, has gone back to the propositions advanced by a distinguished Englishman in the last century,—that the people "must be educated to live cheaper,"—and has followed the example of Sir Frederick Eden, in giving to the world receipts showing how to cook shin-bone soup. The remedy will not come through making people live cheaper, but by making them live dearer. Shin-bone soup may prove nutritious, and would be found beneficial as a diet to the apoplectically inclined, but would not answer as a sustenance for those who by their labor produce the wealth of the world.

The old cry of the partnership between labor and capital has finally awakened in the minds of the silent partners in the concern a demand for an examination of accounts, as well as a more equitable division of the profits. Heretofore, the laborer, having no right of free contract, sold his labor at such terms and for such time as the proprietor or employer should fix; and if, at any time, the laborer asked for higher remuneration, he was informed that the interests of the enterprise would not permit an advance, and that, as one of the partners in the labor and capital combination, he must waive any right to increased payment, lest he should hazard the existence of the enterprise.

Another so-called "argument" against either legislation or strikes for shorter hours of labor is based on the "demand and supply" theory.

It is true, that if laborers are plenty, and opportunities of labor few, and the laborers are compelled to sell their labor or starve, then wages will fall to the level of the barest existence upon which the poorest of their number can live; and if laborers are scarce, and opportunities of labor plenty, wages would be naturally advanced; but it will be noted, that the reduction of wages, in the first instance, is due to the fact of the inability of the worker to sustain himself until the opportunities for labor are improved. If a merchant or manufacturer finds that his merchandise is not salable, he does not necessarily continue in multiplying the product; nor does he force his product upon the market at the declining price, or sell it at all, excepting under the same conditions that the laborer sells his labor,—fear of bankruptcy. Under *that* fear, he may sell the product at much less than cost, as the least of the two evils; as the laborer will sell his labor for a mere loaf of bread for himself and family, if that is the best he can obtain.

Mr. Ira Steward, who gave great thought and consideration to this question, and who was, perhaps, the deepest thinker which it has produced, used these words, in referring to the law of supply and demand: "The employer is the master, and the employee is the slave, of this law." The organization of laborers will free the laborer from these slavish conditions. He will deal with his commodity,—selling as much of it, or withholding it, according to the market; and, as capitalists have heretofore imported cheap laborers to take the place of the higher-paid, so labor will restrict the importation of cheap labor, and thereby inaugurate a protective tariff, which will protect the wages of the laborer, as it now protects the profits of the capitalists.

The eight-hour movement is the movement of the laborer toward higher wages or higher profit on his investment of time. When a man invests his past accumulations in any enterprise, he not only seeks the security of his investment, but such remuneration for his services as shall permit him to live according to the custom of his class, and in addition to this payment for services, a payment for the investment in the shape of interests or profits,—such interests or profits to cover not only the necessary growth of the enterprise, but its insurance against loss by fire, or against loss by any stagnation of industry or financial panic that may arise. Under the present system, he is justified in taking all these precautions; but the laborer is compelled under the wage-system to sell his commodity to-day, or not sell it at all. A day's opportunity to labor lost is never regained, and the laborer is forced to sell his skill and time without any reference to the security of his investment. He may jeopardize his health, his limbs or his life; the margin of his wages will not cover these elements of risk, nor will it guarantee provision against the stagnation of industry, fires, panics or the failure of his immediate employer. Neither has he any provision by which he can provide for himself or family, in case of the ordinary casualties of life, or when he is unable to labor. The eight-hour movement seeks to remedy this by giving to the laborer under the wage-system, first, the advantages now possessed by the capitalist until the profits upon his labor now obtained by the employer and middle-man shall so diminish and his own increase, that finally the profit upon labor shall cease, and co-operative labor be inaugurated in the place of wage-labor.

The great uplifting influences of leisure are manifest everywhere. The busy man, devoting no time to the obtaining of a broad knowledge of the things of this life, or of the physical, mental or moral laws of our being, or of the universe, is but a narrow man; and, however much he may accumulate wealth, he will still be looked upon by the cultured wealthy as a boor, unfit for their society. The reduction of the hours of labor is placing the lever of civilization under the humblest man, and lifting him up to the enjoyment of all the opportunities of civilization, making him a better man in this world and in the world to come.

CHAPTER XIX.

DECLARATION OF PRINCIPLES OF THE K. OF L.

UNJUST ACCUMULATIONS — MORAL WORTH OF THE INDIVIDUAL — FOXCRAFT — ONE GREAT SOLIDARITY — NATURAL LAW OF DEVELOPMENT — THE DEMAND FOR LEISURE — NATURAL WEALTH — NATIONALIZATION OF LAND — GIVING AWAY EMPIRES — PUBLIC OWNERSHIP OF RAILROADS — CONSPIRACY AND BOYCOTTING — CHIEF-JUSTICE SHAW'S DECISION — EMPLOYERS' LIABILITY LAW — ABOLITION OF THE CONTRACT SYSTEM — ARBITRATION — CONVICT LABOR — GRADUATED INCOME TAX — FINANCE — NATIONAL BANKS AND BANKERS — PROHIBITION OF THE IMPORTATION OF FOREIGN LABOR — ARTIFICIALLY STIMULATED EMIGRATION — CO-OPERATION — THE OLIVE BRANCH OF PEACE.

CIVILIZATION is but another name for progress in the direction of the better distribution of the material comforts and mental and moral opportunities of mankind. Whatever tends to assist in the equitable adjustment of the relations of laborers and capitalists tends to the public good. The Preamble to the Constitution, or Declaration of Principles of the Knights of Labor, which was adopted at the first session of the General Assembly, in 1878, seeks these results; and it is the embodiment of the measures formulated by experience and observation of the organized labor movement from 1825 to the present time. It is the same in scope, and nearly the same in language, as that adopted by the National Labor Congress of 1874, as given in Chapter X.

This Preamble demands, not the division of past accumulations, however unjustly accumulated, but rather that measures be provided for the distribution of products and opportunities in the future, by and through the wage-system, until the moral and social wisdom and the increased wealth of the masses shall ultimate in co-operation.

An examination of the Preamble in detail shows a desire to check unjust accumulation and the power for evil of aggregated wealth by perfectly legitimate means. Building up from a firm foundation of the moral worth of the individual, it enlarges gradually and symmetrically, first in the direction of material wants,—better wages or a more equitable share of the wealth created; then reaching out toward the intellectual and social opportunities which come from less hours of employment for gain, and more time for the employment of their faculties for the greater gain of their moral and mental growth. It cannot be gain-said that as material wealth increases, the share of each should increase, and that the tendency toward the aggregation of wealth into the hands of those whose faculties of absorption have been unduly stimulated, furnishes a power to the few, which makes the possessor a dangerous factor to society.

Men wholly developed in all the attributes of manhood cannot become accumulators. It is only toward those possessing special qualifications of management, of speculation and of foxcraft that the flow of accumulated wealth centres. That these giants of the industrial system have served as treasurers of the common fund, and that their services under the competitive system have been of value in the development of vast enterprises, will not be denied; but that they are unduly paid and unjustly rewarded, is generally conceded. Vanderbilt's two hundred millions of dollars were not the result of his executive ability, but the result of the conditions existing in consequence of the distribution of wealth which had already been accomplished. The system of railroads which rendered it possible to carry a barrel of flour from the West to the East for seventy cents was possible because of the population upon the line and at the termination of these railways, over whose power of demand and consumption he had not been the controlling factor. He found the demand, the steam-power and the railway service already inaugurated. The principles of the Knights of Labor makes no war upon Vanderbilts, but upon the system which makes Vanderbilts possible.

The Knights of Labor believe that a thorough investigation of the conditions now existing will develop methods out of which the results achieved by Vanderbilts can be attained without the depression of the many, and the rich rewarding of the few. None of these mammoth enterprises were possible, even to these giant organizers, but for the standard of living which had been attained through our free political and educational systems and the higher moral attainments of our people, as well as the great help rendered them by legislative enactments or legislative interference with the operations of natural law.

This preamble well says, that "The alarming development and aggressiveness of great capitalists and corporations, unless checked, will inevitably lead to the pauperization and hopeless degradation of the toiling masses." The demand of the Knights is, then, that this development shall be checked, not only because of the danger to our institutions from the power of these great monopolists and monopolies, but because of the pauperization and degradation of the workers in consequence thereof. The method of checking and remedying this evil is, first, the organization of all laborers into one great solidarity, and the direction of their united efforts toward the measures that shall, by peaceful processes, evolve the working classes out of their present condition in the wage-system into a co-operative system. This organization does not profess to be a political party, nor does it propose to organize a political party; but, nevertheless, it proposes to exercise the right of suffrage in the direction of obtaining such legislation as shall assist the natural law of development. It is true that the demands are revolutionary, as it is the purpose of the Order to establish a new and true standard of individual and national greatness.

To-day the possession of wealth is the great factor that is recognized as the standard of power, and, too often, of worth. The Knights of Labor seek to make industrial and moral worth the standard, — giving honor to those who work in any of the fields of labor, whether of the hand or of the brain, and relegating the possession of wealth back to its true position.

The first step in the direction of this change "is to secure to the workers the full enjoyment of the wealth they create, sufficient leisure in which to develop their intellectual, moral and social faculties, all of the benefits of recreation, and pleasures of association; in a word, to enable them to share in the gains and honors of advancing civilization." To ascertain as nearly as possible how much of the wealth of the world is created by labor, as well as to expose the true condition of the workers, it desires the establishment of bureaus of labor statistics.

Natural wealth, although at present in the hands of individual proprietors, was originally common property, and was first obtained by physical power, by robbery or fraud. The driving of the native from the land of his fathers, — the common property of all, — to make way for a newer and grander civilization, cannot be justified if these possessions are to remain in the hands of the individual proprietors, and not as the common property of all. If the natives were driven away from their possessions in the name of civilization, then in that name their possessions should be common property.

The first step in the immediate direction of the possession of wealth by its producers, is by the conferring of sufficient leisure upon the masses for their development. The argument to sustain this claim is contained in another chapter. In this place we can only add, that this demand is the ever-rallying cry of organized labor everywhere. The demand for legislative interference in the direction of shortening the hours of labor has stamped itself upon the statute-books of all civilized nations. It is not merely a coincident of history, that, to the demand for shorter hours of labor, or more leisure, is added the demand that the public lands be reserved for actual settlers. In the history of the movement in this country, these two great measures have kept step together. The early leaders of the labor movement, before the great West was opened up to civilization, and when our public lands were public empires, greater in extent than the whole of continental Europe, foresaw the dangers that threatened the Republic through the powers of speculators, corporations and unscrupulous legislators, and sought to remedy the evil. Since their day, we have witnessed the giving away of empires from the public land to aid and assist corporation enterprises and individual efforts; we have witnessed systems of stock-watering and bribery, the corruption of public offices and courts of justice of these same mammoths of capital. Hence, the Knights of Labor demand the reservation of all lands not already disposed of, and the reclaiming of such as can be legally reclaimed.

The great common public have given away their inheritance to railroad corporations; and the acts of Congress, in thus conferring these great estates on individual enterprises, have been justified under the supposition that the public would thereby be benefited by bringing the Atlantic and Pacific coasts into closer relations with each other. We have no desire to dispute the claim that the building of these great roads has worked a public benefit; but, as the government furnished the land and the credit or capital necessary for the enterprise, we know of no good reason why the property and the profits, if any, should be divided among the few patrons of the Government,—the railroad magnates; nor do we know of any reason why this profit and property should not be possessed by the government,—its creator. The argument, that the people are not competent to select the managers of these vast enterprises, comes with poor grace from the classes who have controlled the legislative functions of the government since its foundation. But few wage-workers or wage-earners, by hand or brain, have ever been called into these important positions; and it is a sad confession for wealth and culture to make that they dare not trust their own classes in the administration of internal commerce. That the Post-office Department has been conducted measurably safe and prompt, and thorough and cheap, is evidence that other steps may be taken in the same direction. This preamble also demands the abrogation of all laws that do not bear equally upon capital and labor, and the removal of unjust technicalities, delays and discriminations in the administrations of justice. All well-meaning people sustain this demand of the organization; but the question comes: Do the laws that we have tend to bear equally upon capital and labor? And the answer to this query would in itself necessitate a chapter; for the vast tomes in the National and State capitols show that the great bulk of legislation has been directly in the nterest of capita or investment; and it must be acknowledged that legislation has been founded upon the theory that, "if you protect capital, capital will protect labor." For the past half-century, the statute-books are but the records of the demands of capital for the advancement of proprietary interests. Tariffs have been established, subsidies granted, and special privileges accorded, that individual stockholders might have the fullest opportunities of accumulation. The burdens thus imposed upon the common people have been borne by them; for they are the tax-payers,—paying interest and taxes on all things consumed by them, as well as furnishing the incomes of all middle-men, and by the defense of property in time of war. Many of the laws thus enacted bear heavily upon the laborer; an'd the Knights of Labor, as an organized expression of the will of the people, demand their abrogation. So, too, in the administration of law or the judiciary of the Republic. The courts are open to the humblest; but the power of capital comes to the court-room, in spite (if need be) of judge and jury, and makes the administration of justice impracticable and often impossible. Delays in trials, inability, because of poverty, to procure witnesses and learned counsel, make it often better for the poor man to suffer "the ills he has rather than to fly to others he knows not of."

Recent decisions of judges upon the question of conspiracy and boycotting are new revelations of an old fact, that the interpretation of law rests largely upon the public sentiment of the wealthy part of the community. The Dred-Scott decision was declared infamous by those who were lifted to the level of the spirit of our institutions; yet, nevertheless, that decision was a confession that the controlling classes were under the subtle influence of the slave-power. The continued peaceful agitation of the slavery question, uninterrupted by war, would have rendered such a decision impossible; so, too, the attempts now made to prevent the working people from using the great power of the boycott will be found to be in contradiction, not only of individual, but of constitutional rights. A man has not only the right to buy where he pleases, but he has the right to advise another man to buy or not to buy of friend or enemy; and whether the exercise of the boycott is judicious or injudicious, justifiable or unjustifiable in certain instances, the innate right of man to the privilege of exercising his moral power and social influence in the direction of trade, or to withhold trade, cannot be safely denied.

Chief-Justice Shaw, in his decision of the celebrated case of the *Commonwealth* vs. *Hunt et als.*, as given on page 95, says: "Associations may be entered into, the object of which is to adopt measures that may have a tendency to impoverish another, thus to diminish his gain or profits, and yet so far from being criminal or unlawful, the object may be highly meritorious and public-spirited."

The denunciation of the boycott comes with ill grace from a class who have ever exercised the infamous power of the blacklist against their workmen for no palpable cause. The history of the labor movement is a continued chapter of the boycotting of members of committees and leaders of labor organizations. T. V. Powderly, the General Master Workman of the Knights of Labor, was thus blacklisted. As a rule, the efforts to crush the life out of trades-unions and other associations have produced the opposite result. Men and women, thus driven from their homes, have been the unpaid messengers of the Gospel of organized efforts. The great Order of the Knights of Labor was founded largely because of the employers' system of boycotting.

Many of the measures of relief included in the preamble have already so far commended themselves to the public as to have forced legislative acquiescence in some of the States. Among these measures may be mentioned laws providing for the life and safety of those engaged in mining, manufacturing and building industries. Factory and mine-inspectors have been appointed, and protection against fire and against accidents by uncovered belting and dangerous machinery has been provided. Trades-unions have been incorporated, weekly payments in lawful money have beer gained for the employees of corporations in the State of Massachusetts, and must soon be conceded by all employers of labor. The truck, or "pluck-me" system of payment, still prevalent in many States and Territories, and especially among miners, has secured legislative attention, and must soon give way to the frequent payment of wages in lawful money. The old-time system of payment, in goods instead of in cash, is a relic of the chattel-system.

The demand for an employers' liability law will still continue to trouble the legislators, and should trouble them, that the scandal may no longer continue that a man is pensioned for wounds received in the destruction of property and life, but must be pauperized when receiving injuries in the peaceful pursuits of life.

The preamble demands the abolition of the contract system on National, State, and municipal works. Under the contract system, two monster evils have come into existence: one, the mammoth robbery of the treasury; the other, the mammoth robbery of the workers. This system, as conducted on the aqueduct-works of New York city, and exposed by the New York *Sun*, render argument useless, when we know that this is not an individual instance of the oppression of the poor by the contract system, but is only one of the numberless instances of the same iniquitous system.

The demand for laws providing for arbitration between employers and employees has been conceded in some instances, as will be seen by referring to the Chapter on Legislation; but the value of this system of settling disputes between the two classes is very much weakened, not by the decisions of the arbitrators, but from the many failures of the employing class to keep faith with their employees.

Constant approaches are being made in the direction of prohibition of the employment of children under fifteen years of age in the workshops, mercantile establishments, mines and factories. But this movement is altogether too slow. Children are being employed at eight years of age and upwards in the workshops, mines and factories. In some States, the law fixes the limit of years at ten,—some at eleven and twelve.

And yet these little ones are found in our manufacturing centres as well as in the mining and coke regions, dragging their weary bodies to unwelcome work in unseasonable hours, in heat and cold, denied the pleasures of the play-ground and the benefits of the school-room, robbed of all the educational influences of home, rendered desperate and ungovernable, and made old before their time. The Knights of Labor, worthy of the loftiest chivalry of the nineteenth century, demand that this shall not be, but that the place for the child is at the home, in the school-room, and upon the play-ground, and that when the child enters the mill as a child to help eke out the miserable pittance of the family earnings, he or she enters as a competitor against the older brother and the father, reducing their wages so that the grand total of the family earnings shall be but bare enough for the family's existence. Civilization is drunk with greed, when it drags the child from the enjoyment of childhood, and makes him a bread-earner, when he should be merely a bread-eater. The republican institutions are not safe under such conditions. In the days of old, when the child worked with the father and the mother on the farm or the homestead in the healthful pursuits of agriculture, men and women could be grown worthy of the age. But factory discipline, however kindly it may be administered, is not the discipline for childhood. We are demanding that the discipline of the school-room shall be relaxed for the younger children, and that the hours of school-time shall be reduced. The Knights of Labor demand for the children of the unfortunate all that shall be demanded for the most fortunate.

The hiring out of convict labor, and the whole system of convict labor, needs remedy. The preamble emphatically demands the prohibition of the hiring-out system, and this prohibition is demanded in the name of justice to labor. The convict is restrained from liberty as a punishment for criminal acts done, and as a restraint or protection against his opportunity of committing other crimes. That the health and discipline of the convict demands his employment, no one denies; but all organized laborers protest emphatically against his entering the market as a competitor with them. The convict is a slave,—the slave of the government, — and his labor is slave-labor; he having no control over the price or quantity, or his freedom of action. The defence of the present system, on the plea that the product of this labor is such a small amount as not to become a factor in the wage-market has little force. Ira Steward once said that wages, like water, always seek the lowest outlet. If a case of convict-made shoes can be sold for twenty-five per cent. less than free-made shoes, the convict-made shoes tend to the reduction of the selling-price of the free-made article, if of nearly the same quality. Organized labor does not attempt to prohibit labor in the prisons and other correctional institutions; it only asks that this labor shall be organized in such a way as not to become a competitor. Therefore, they demand the abolition of the contract or hiring-out system. The convict may well be employed at hand labor in the manufacture of such products as are needed in the correctional, reformatory, and charitable institutions; by being compelled to work without the use of labor-saving machinery, they become better accustomed to the handling of tools. They would then become more interested in their work; above all, they would be released from the enervating and demoralizing tendencies of monotonous labor. The free workman engaged upon machinery, constantly repeating his part of the work, suffers morally and physically, but is relieved somewhat from the evil effects of the system by the social intercourse, and by the opportunities of leisure and change of scene. Monotonous labor within prison-walls is in itself a punishment greater than should be inflicted upon any man. The statistics of convict-life give evidence of the need of a reform that goes to the root of the difficulty. That they are not graduated first-class mechanics or first-class men is not a surprise. As a rule, they graduate poor mechanics as well as poor men. The measures hereinbefore enumerated as a part of the preamble under consideration have been uniformly demanded by all branches of organized toil. The next demand is of a more radical nature, although finding many advocates outside of the wage-labor class.

The question of taxation is one that constantly demands the attention of all organized bodies of men. The question of "What shall be taxed, and how much?" sometimes creates, sometimes divides, and sometimes destroys parties. If governments have any rights, they have the right to tax property to any extent that their necessities may require. Policy demands that this tax shall not be such a burden upon enterprise as to compel stagnation. The theory of taxation has been largely in the direction of obtaining the revenue of the government from those articles of least importance to the community at large. It is safer to tax the surpluses than the necessities of society. Wines, spirits, cigars and other luxuries are taxed on the theory that civilization can continue without their consumption. Upon this theory and fact, the Knights of Labor ask that a graduated income tax be levied; in other words, they ask that the surpluses of past accumulations be taxed out of existence; that small enterprises and property-holders be practically exempt, while the mammoth fortunes from the investment of incomes be taxed in increasing ratio to their amounts. This is considered by some as agrarian legislation; and yet, as will be noted, it is not the taxation of a necessity, but the taxation of a kind of luxury that threatens the existence of the Republic, — the luxury of a monopoly.

The Knights of Labor, in common with the old National Labor party, deal not only with the question of industrial reform, but place two planks in their platform of principles bearing upon the question of finance. This work has been devoted wholly to the consideration of the question of the industrial movement and industrial reform. The question of finance in itself has found many powerful writers of pronounced views. The space of this article will not warrant any discussion of the merits of the different systems. The demand of the Knights in this direction is patriotic, and measurably practicable. National banks and bankers have little favor with the Knights of Labor. The present system of filtering the national currency through the national-bank sieve to the profit of the banker, and the loss to the people, has few friends in this organization. They demand "a national monetary-system, in which the circulating medium, in necessary quantity, shall issue direct to the people, without the intervention of banks, and that all the national issue shall be full legal-tender in payment of all debts, public and private, and that the government shall not guarantee or recognize any private banks of credit, or any banking corporations, that interest-bearing bonds, bills of credit or notes shall not be issued by the government, and that when any emergency shall arise, shall issue a non-interest-bearing money." As the national banks are founded upon the national debt, wisdom demands, and statesmanship should provide, some method by which the bills and coin should serve their purpose without giving power to chartered corporations to interfere with the control of the currency, or to receive undue payment for any service rendered. It is not expected that the people can receive printed national legal-tender notes for the asking. But that some system can be devised, better than the present, and more in accord with our republican institutions, is believed by many, not only within, but without the organization.

That the demand for the prohibition of the importation of foreign labor under contract is a just one, is now confessed; but, though "confession" may be "good for the soul," the reiteration of the sentiments against this importation will not restrain unscrupulous contractors and employers from bringing into the country, from the most pauperized and degraded of the human race, laborers contracted for under misrepresentation of facts and conditions, and bringing them here as enemies to our high-wage civilization. This requires not only legislation, but enforcement; and such enforcement as shall absolutely protect the American wage-worker from this danger. And it is even a question if legislation will not be demanded by other than wage-workers to prohibit, for a time at least, the importation of the cheaper class of laborers, whether under a contract or not. If protective tariffs can be advocated as a means to uphold the wages of American labor, whether truly made or not, labor and all lovers of republican institutions have the right to demand that this artifi-

LEADERS OF THE KNIGHTS.

cially stimulated immigration, largely consequent upon the misrepresentations of the protectionists themselves, shall be absolutely prohibited. The defence of such a course must be founded upon the right of self-protection belonging to classes and communities and governments. To enact such legislation is a confession of the failure of our statesmen to anticipate societary effects from societary causes. As the physical man is strengthened by what is digested rather than by that which is consumed and undigested, so nations grow in strength as fast as the immigration from other lands is assimilated to the native institutions. The necessity for immediate attention to the prohibition of Chinese labor is set forth in the chapter devoted to that subject. As the first sentence of the preamble calls attention to the alarming development and aggressiveness of great capitalists and corporations, so the last demand upon the government refers to the same question, and demands of the government the possession, by purchase under the right of eminent domain, of telegraphs, telephones and railroads.

In the days of the struggles of the abolitionists, propositions were made for the purchase of the slaves by the government, and then their emancipation; so now the Knights of Labor, witnessing, as we have described, the power of these corporations over the government, and over their employees, equalled only by the power of the Czar, propose their purchase,—not their seizure, but their purchase and control; and the question will soon force itself upon the republican citizens in this form: "Shall these great corporations control the government, or shall they be controlled by the government?" The terrible condition of servitude into which the employees of these vast enterprises have been forced, and the endangering of the public peace, caused by the natural and proper unrest of the wage-workers, as well as the danger to traffic and the numberless industries dependent upon uninterrupted transportation and communication, is the warning-cry that justice must be done to the poorest, and that this justice cannot be expected under the present system of greed. The control of railroads, telephones and telegraphs, and their operation by the government, is as feasible, and will prove to be as beneficial, as the present post-office system, which, perfect as it is, needs enlargement in the direction of making them safe deposits, as is the system in England.

In addition to the demands made upon the State and National governments, hereinbefore enumerated, this organization proposes to its members to associate their own labors for the establishment of co-operative institutions, believing that through experiments in this direction, and that by reduced profits upon labor and increased remuneration to labor, consequent upon advancing civilization, that the co-operative system will supersede the wage-system. They also pledge themselves to secure for both sexes equal pay for equal work, and supplement their demand for legislation in the direction of less hours of labor by instructing their members to prepare for a general refusal to work for more than eight hours per day.

This preamble, which commences with the warning-cry against the power for evil of great corporations and capitalists, concludes by holding out the olive branch of peace, desiring that no unnecessary antagonisms may be created, — using the power of organization not to force, but to "persuade employers to agree to arbitrate all differences which may arise between them and their employees, in order that the bonds of sympathy between them may be strengthened, and strikes may be unnecessary."

CHAPTER XX.

ARBITRATION.

Disastrous Strikes — Losses and Consequences thereof — Dealing with Human Beings — Workmen Favoring Arbitration — Employers Ignoring the Humanities of Life — Discussing Differences — Opinions of George Odger, Professor S. Waterhouse, Professor J. B. Clark, Professor Henry C. Adams, Professor E. J. James, John Jarrett, D. H. Donelly, Conseils des Prud'hommes — Arbitration in Belgium, Austria, and Great Britain, and in the United States — Arbitration Law of the Last Congress — The Labor Parliament — Organization Essential to Arbitration.

"Come now, let us reason together." — *Isa.* 1 : 18.

A FEW months ago, dense clouds lowered upon the fields of industry. Disastrous strikes then prevailed throughout the South-west, threatening at one time to involve the entire railroad system of the United States, — a misfortune which was alone prevented by the good judgment and firmness of the leaders of the Knights of Labor and Locomotive Engineers; while, during the same period, other strikes were pending, involving thousands and thousands of workingmen in various factories and workshops. These have all passed away, and to-day witnesses comparative peace throughout the length and breadth of the land. At such a time, it is peculiarly opportune to appeal to the intelligence of the country, — workingmen and employers alike, — to devise some better plan of adjusting differences than by strikes on the one hand and lockouts on the other, with their concomitant train of disaster, ruin, and frequently crime.

The losses sustained by workmen and employers, together with incidental injuries to the people at large, in the disastrous conflicts of the last few years, would present a frightful spectacle of the absolute waste of hundreds of millions of dollars. For while the loss of the strikers from their enforced idleness, and the loss to employers from injury to property and the unproductiveness of their investments, amounts to millions of dollars, the greater loss is borne by the entire country from the loss of the wealth produced by employed labor, from the increased cost of all articles involved in the controversy, and, in case of a railroad strike, from the increased cost of fuel and food to the people, from the difficulty and delay in obtaining supplies; resulting, also, in the enforced closing of workshops and factories, through the inability of employers to obtain necessary materials, thus swelling the ranks of those thrown out of employment by additional thousands, who are in such cases the unfortunate victims of a controversy in which they are not directly interested.

These reasons justify every citizen in carefully studying the question of the relations of capital and labor, and endeavoring to bring them together as friends and allies by guaranteeing that peace and prosperity which flows from continued industry. Is it not the part of every good citizen in all disputes to advise their fellow-men, whether workmen or capitalists, to come together and reason like men?—to meet at the same table for a mutual interchange of views,—an honest and frank statement of his grievances by the workman, and an equally manly and honorable consideration, and, when necessary, concession by the capitalist?

Employers must understand by this time that, in dealing with human beings, they cannot successfully apply the rule that the only thing necessary to be considered, when engaging in any enterprise, is to ascertain how great they can make their profits, and how low they can make the wages. If the promptings of humanity will not induce them to act fairly and honorably by their workmen, the disastrous experiences of strikes should by this time, at least, have been sufficient to convince them that from a purely selfish standpoint they can accomplish far more and achieve greater success by pursuing such a course as will prevent strikes, and enlist the sympathy of the workman in the success of his employer,—adopting the humane maxim, to "live and let live."

Workmen, as a rule, have always favored arbitration, and the submission of their differences to an impartial tribunal; and history shows that, in almost every instance where they have succeeded in obtaining an impartial hearing of their grievances, they have loyally and honorably abided by the result. Employers, as a rule, have been slow in recognizing the right of workingmen to even a hearing,—ignoring the humanities of life, and placing workmen on the same footing with their merchandise. Such a position, whenever a dispute occurs, has invariably resulted in a conflict, for the reason that workingmen will not submit to being ignored by an enterprise in which they believe that their labor and genius are as much the mainsprings of its success as the capital invested.

It is the same old story, repeated with slight variations, since civilization began, of the weak fighting the strong. In many cases, the weak may win by persistence in suffering; but, in the meantime, men and women will go hungry, and children will cry for bread. This continual clashing, involving so much suffering and loss of money, is unavoidable, unless both parties seek for and adopt a better system of adjusting differences. That such a system can be found in arbitration, based on principles of equity between employer and workman, has been amply shown in individual shops, and in whole communities in the Old World. So far as it has been tried in this country, it has proved far superior to any other method of settling differences. In no other way can the correlative interests of both labor and capital be so effectively guarded.

The principle of appealing to facts and reason, instead of to brute force, is rational, and at once commends itself to the judgment of every right-minded man. When workmen and employers meet together and discuss their differences and try to adjust them, they give evidence of the nobler qualities of their manhood.

Strikes and lockouts are characteristics of the Feudal Age, when might was right, and every dispute was settled by a resort to force. Arbitration will be characteristic of the age of reason and law.

George Odger, in 1866, at a large meeting in Sheffield, England, expressed the opinion "that strikes were in the social world what wars were to the political world: they became crimes, unless they were prompted by absolute necessity." When men of labor and capital meet together as men of business should meet, and discuss their differences in a friendly spirit, the chances are that they will reach an amicable settlement. Their success runs in parallel lines. Their interests are identical. Labor is capital, and capital is labor. They suggest the remedy for the conflict,—the remedy that civilized nations are now substituting for war; the influence of reason and voluntary arbitration of labor's troubles and capital's claims trusting to the enlightened public opinion to sustain their awards. Arbitration means education, and education means a proper maintenance of just principles. Education, arbitration and humanity are the triple link which will unite labor and capital.

The utterances of prominent men on the subject of arbitration, which I append, are evidence that the demand for arbitration must be conceded.

Professor S. Waterhouse, of the Washington University, St. Louis, says of arbitration, that

> It would settle disputes by the awards of reason, allay the unfriendly feelings which now exist between workmen and their employers, save the time and money which are now wasted by the arbitrary closing of manufactories or the ill-advised withdrawal of operatives, and prevent the scenes of violence and outrage which so often disgrace strikes.

Professor J. B. Clark, Smith College, Northampton, Mass., says: —

> Arbitration is, in itself, an appeal to equity, and a departure from the competitive principle.

Professor Henry C. Adams, Lecturer on Political Economy in the University of Michigan and Cornell University, says: —

> Arbitration is not the missing coupling between labor and capital, but it is the thing for which, at the present time, it is practical that workingmen should strive. Its establishment is the first step towards the overthrow of the wages system.

Professor E. J. James, of the University of Pennsylvania (Philadelphia), says:—

Arbitration has the great advantage of subjecting the acts of the parties to it to the efficient and powerful control of an energetic public opinion. It recognizes indirectly what is too often overlooked,—that the interests at stake are not merely those of the laborer and employer, but also those of the community at large. The latter has such a great stake in the contest that it cannot afford to stand idly by, and permit the former to disturb society to its foundations, and destroy in their struggle the very conditions of sound economic progress.

P. H. Donnelly, Esq., Secretary of the Illinois Miners' Protective Association, says:—

Arbitration means a stop to those prolonged and ruinous struggles between employers and employees,—a shaking of hands across the bloody chasm.

Fred Woodrow says:—

To-day there is no question, even in national politics, so vital in its import or so grand in its issues as this self-same idea of arbitration. It is at the causes of strikes and lockouts as an axe at the root of a tree, and a knife at a cancer. Of its adoption there is no doubt, though its details and methods may be matters of experience and time. It has its enemies, as had the act of emancipation.

John Jarrett, Esq., Secretary of the American Tinned-Plate Association, says:—

I know of no better remedy, in the adjustment of all differences that may arise between employers and employees, than arbitration and conciliation.

Hon. E. R. Hutchins, Commissioner of Labor Statistics, State of Iowa, says:—

Wherever it is tried honestly, it is successful.

This is true in this and in the old countries. But it must be honest. It must be entered into with sincerity on the part of both sides, and its results must be as binding as any law upon a statute-book.

Hon. Joel B. McCamant, Chief of Bureau of Industrial Statistics, State of Pennsylvania, says:—

Arbitration, in my opinion, is the only reasonable coupling between labor and capital.

Hon. Oscar Kochtitzky, Commissioner of Bureau of Labor Statistics and Inspection, of Missouri, says:—

A Board of Arbitration, composed of persons capable to judge clearly between right and wrong, possessing in every respect the confidence of the community, and who are not directly interested in the dispute to be settled, would, in nearly every case, present a plan of settlement acceptable to both parties. Any proposition made by a board so composed would be supported by the moral force of public opinion; and the refusal by either party to the dispute to accept the plan of settlement proposed could only be fatal to the interests of the party so refusing.

Industrial arbitration originated in France, in 1806, when the first Napoleon, at the request of the workingmen of Lyons, caused the creation, by law, of boards of arbitration and conciliation. These, with but slight changes, have continued until the present time under the title of "Conseils des Prud'hommes." They are judicial tribunals, established at the important trade-centres of that country, and are composed of an equal number of employers and workingmen, each class electing its own representatives, and the president and vice-president are named by the government. Their authority extends to all questions that can arise in the workshop between the employer and his workmen, and also between the workmen and apprentices or foreman. Arbitration is compulsory upon the application of either party, and the decisions of the board can be enforced the same as those of other courts of law. There are now about one hundred and fifty such councils established in France, and of the many thousands of cases brought before these courts it is claimed that ninety-five per cent. have been settled. The influence of these councils in removing causes of difference, and preventing disputes, has been of incalculable benefit, and greatly contributed to the industrial prosperity of France.

In Belgium, the French system is adopted, and under the same name, with the exception that the Belgian "Conseils des Prud'hommes" have a criminal jurisdiction, which has seriously impeded their usefulness.

In Austria, in 1859, arbitration courts were established in every important town and district. The jurisdiction of the arbitration courts extends to the usual subjects of dispute between employers and workmen, and their awards have the force and effect of judgments of courts of law.

In Great Britain, a law similar in its character to that of France was placed on the statute-books in 1824; but its compulsory features were so obnoxious to both employers and workingmen that very little was made of its provisions. A similar fate befell two subsequent enactments.

In 1860, Mr. Mundella, a member of one of the largest hosiery firms in England, conceived and put in practical operation the first attempted voluntary arbitration in England. The trade with which he was identified had been severely injured by strikes and lockouts. He brought about a conference between the employers and workmen, which resulted in the institution of the "Board of Arbitration and Conciliation in the Cloth and Hosiery Trade." Ten years later, Mr. Mundella, reviewing his work, stated that

Strikes are at an end. Levies to sustain them are unknown, and one shilling a year from each member suffices to pay the expenses. That he had inspected a balance-sheet of a trades-union of 10,300 men, and found the expenditures for thirteen months to amount to less than £100. The success of this Board of Arbitration, known as "the Nottingham Board of Arbitration and Conciliation," attracted public attention, and workingmen and employers hailed with enthusiasm this application of new principles to industry. Three years later, it was adopted by the building-trades (Wolverhampton system), and at a late period by the iron trade (North of England system); it also extended to the pottery and other industries.

The following statements will furnish conclusive evidence of the benefits arising from the application of this principle:—

For thirty years, strikes have been almost unknown in the pottery trade. Since 1869, when the "Board of Arbitration and Conciliation for the Manufactured Iron Trade for the North of England" was established, it has proved a blessing to employers and workmen. Strikes are unknown; whereas prior to that time, that district was in a continual state of anarchy, resulting from the social struggles of labor and capital, frequently causing destruction of property and loss of human life. In an address by Frederick Harrison before the Trades-union Congress, at Nottingham, in October, 1883, he stated that ninety-nine per cent. of those societies' expenditures were for benevolent and provident purposes, and only one per cent. for strikes, showing the great value of trades-unions in preventing trade disputes. The almost unanimous voice of the trades-unions of England, which to-day number over 800,000 members, is for arbitration in industrial pursuits. And it is a fact, in the history of arbitration, that the first steps toward the adoption of this method were inaugurated by the trades-unions.

In the United States, the growth of the principle of the application of arbitration as a means of settling disputes between employers and workmen is due mainly to the efforts of this same organization, which has at all times strongly favored arbitration. Over twenty years ago, arbitration became one of the demands of the Trades-union Congress. The Knights of Labor, who constitute to-day the greatest labor-union in the country, have embodied in their platform the following, among other aims:—

22. "To persuade employers to agree to arbitrate all differences which may arise between them and their employees, in order that the bonds of sympathy between them may be strengthened, and that strikes may be rendered unnecessary."

In 1883, legal arbitration was first presented in this country. In that year, the Wallace Act was passed by the Pennsylvania Legislature, and is the first piece of legislation in this country practically indorsing the principle of voluntary arbitration. In Ohio, a law was enacted in February, 1885, to "authorize the creation and to provide for the operation of tribunals of voluntary arbitration, to adjust industrial disputes between employers and employed." In Massachusetts, Iowa, New York and New Jersey, bills for the creation of arbitration boards have either become laws or are now pending.

The House of Representatives of the Congress of the United States passed a so-called "labor-arbitration bill," at the present session, which is now pending in the Senate. Every reader of this article understands the narrow field to which the Federal Constitution restricts Congress, and that many of the most important industries, employing millions of our citizens, are beyond the reach of the power of legislation vested in Congress.

The narrow orbit within which Congress is compelled to revolve appears from the first section of this bill, which reads as follows: —

That whenever differences or controversies arise between railroad companies engaged in the transportation of property or passengers between two or more States of the United States, between a Territory and State, within the Territories of the United States, or within the District of Columbia, and the employees of said railroad companies, which differences or controversies may hinder, impede, obstruct, interrupt or affect such transportation of property or passengers, if upon the written proposition of either party to the controversy to submit their differences to arbitration, the other party shall accept the proposition, then and in such event, the railroad company is hereby authorized to select and appoint one person; and such employee, or employees, as the case may be, to select and appoint another person, and the two persons thus selected and appointed to select a third person, — all three of whom shall be citizens of the United States, and wholly impartial and disinterested in respect to such differences or controversies. And the three persons thus selected and appointed shall be, and they are hereby, created and constituted a board of arbitration, with the duties, powers and privileges hereinafter set forth.

It is evident from this section that the occasions for appeal to this species of arbitration must, in the nature of things, be few; that the subjects embraced are limited in number, and that the system of arbitration intended to be established is absolutely voluntary; inasmuch as both parties to the differences or controversies must concur before the tribunal can begin to exist.

That it is wholly intended to rely upon moral means to enforce the awards rendered under the act, is manifest from the concluding paragraph of the third section, which reads as follows: —

And after concluding its investigation, said board (of arbitration) shall publicly announce its award, which, with the findings of facts upon which it is based, shall be reduced to writing, and signed by the arbitrators concurring therein, and, together with the testimony taken in the case, shall be filed with the Commissioner of Labor of the United States, who shall make such award public as soon as the same shall have been received by him.

Another section of the bill provides that the entire expense of an arbitration conducted under this bill shall be paid by the United States, provided such expense does not exceed one thousand dollars.

The bill is pre-eminently conservative, and devoid of all legal enforcements. It passed the House by a vote of 195 to 29, and manifests the good-will of the majority of the House of Representatives toward the class of laboring men intended to be included within its provisions, and is an evidence that the National Legislature is no longer indifferent to their cause.

The disadvantages under which the wage-earner is placed in the struggle for subsistence is well understood. One of the first steps to be taken to remove these disadvantages is to place labor, in cases of contest, on equal terms with capital. This can be greatly promoted by the aid of the State and Federal governments. Establish by legislative authority tribunals of arbitration and boards of conciliation, and useful progress will be made in the right direction.

Combination, union and harmony are power. In the Middle Ages, the societies of tradesmen, by combination and concert of action, overcame the robber-baron and the feudal lord, and wrested from them their rights long denied. Mechanical industry was essentially of a democratic character; and between it and the feudal system there was an "irrepressible conflict." Small bodies of organized mechanics existed as early as the twelfth century. Labor is the working man's capital. Let him combine it by organization. The small beginnings of the twelfth century have grown to enormous proportions in the nineteenth. We have witnessed its growth in this country. But look abroad. The Labor Parliament (or Trades-union Congress) held in England, in 1876, represented 113 societies and 557,488 members. The same convention held at Leicester, in 1877, represented 112 societies and 691,089 members.

Every intelligent man knows that some disease lurks in the body politic, when, as now, in a short life-time, a single individual can accumulate a fortune of a hundred millions.

This disease should be cured. The laboring man, mechanic or farmer has furnished, in times past, the great world-teachers and benefactors.

If the labor organizations shall succeed in establishing peaceful methods of solving, not only how to prevent strikes and lockouts, but how to prevent the growth of monster monopolies of wealth on the one hand, and monster deformity of poverty on the other, then will history speak of them as among the most beneficent instances of justice.

CHAPTER XXI.

CO-OPERATION.

Opinions of John Stuart Mill and George Jacob Holyoake—Antiquity of Co-operatve Forms—Profit sharing in Agriculture—Reorganizing Society—Rochdale Pioneers—Profit-sharing in France—Co-operative Credit in Germany, Russia and Italy—Raw-Material Supplies Societies—Co-operation in America, in 1830—New England Protective Union—The Granger Movement—Sovereigns of Industry—Industrial Society of Philadelphia and Trenton—Co-operative Society—Co-operative Credit in the United States—Co-operative Productive Enterprises—Official Statistics—Co-operative Coal-Mining—Tendencies of Co-operative Experiments—First American Attempts at Profit-sharing—More Wealth Divided—Interest and Faith—Net Profit—Plans of Division of Profit—The Chief Defect—The Immediate Need—Industrial Federation—Competition—Co-operation and Socialism—The Duty of the State—Just Legislation and the Control of Monopolies in the Hands of Voters.

ONE of the purposes of the Knights of Labor, as set forth in the preamble of their constitution, is: "To establish co-operative institutions, such as will tend to supersede the wage-system by the introduction of a co-operative industrial system." This statement contains the true co-operative idea. Co-operation is industrial reorganization. At present, the chief efforts of organized labor are directed toward securing amelioration of the wage-system. Arbitration, a shorter working-day, restriction of the labor of children and married women, are the immediate demands. Beyond these a majority of workingmen have as yet no definite plan, save, as they hope, by limiting the competition for employment, to get better wages. The leaders of the co-operative movement go farther, and attack the present basis of distribution; it is better not to say the wage-system, because the regular payment of stipulated wages, at frequent intervals, is a necessary feature of any practicable co-operation.

They assert that the arrangement by which profits are distributed, — solely on the basis of capital, while labor, having no control of the means of production, is bought at the lowest market-rates, — is wrong. They claim that labor, including brain-labor, should receive its wages at market-rates, and capital its interest at market-rates, and that whatever profit then remains should be divided among all parties having anything to do with the product, from the workers to the consumers. John Stuart Mill said: —

Co-operation is where the whole of the produce is divided. What is wanted is that the whole working class shall partake of the profits of labor.

And George Jacob Holyoake's definition of co-operation is: —

Co-operation is a scheme by which profits can be obtained by concert, and divided by consent, including with the producers the indigent consumer. The original and defensible purpose of co-operation is the better distribution of wealth throughout the whole community, including the consumer. Co-operation to benefit the capitalist at the expense of the workman, or to benefit the workman at the expense of the consumer, still maintains a virtual conspiracy against the purchasing public. Such co-operation leaves the third and larger class unprotected and unbenefited, save indirectly or temporarily.

This scheme is nowhere completely realized as yet. Distributive co-operation divides the profits of retail trade among consumers. Co-operative banks and building associations divide the profits of the money-lender and the landlord among home-owners. The industrial arrangements variously known as productive co-operation, profit-sharing and industrial partnership, distribute the profits of production among workers in proportion to their services. While all these last-named arrangements are co-operative in principle and profit-sharing in practice, and all are therefore in a broad sense industrial partnerships, it is convenient to distinguish by these terms three different types of co-operation, according as one or another feature predominates. In productive co-operation, then, the workers own the business and choose the managers, who are responsible and accountable. In the usual forms of simple profit-sharing, the business is owned by a firm or corporation, in which the workmen, or the majority of them, at least, are not legal partners or stockholders, but are allowed a dividend, or bonus, from the profits. The perfect industrial partnership is a more complex organization, uniting the business talent, enterprise and resources of one or two chief partners, holding a controlling interest, with the fidelity and industry of interested workmen, who not only receive a dividend on their labor, but are encouraged also to become stockholders, and thereby to share in the dividend to capital and in the control of the business. Profit-sharing concerns, when they develop in a natural way, without interference or mishap, tend to become industrial partnerships. Co-operative companies would undoubtedly do the same, but for the limitation of individual stockholding, which prevents any one member or minority of members from acquiring a controlling interest.

Most of the co-operative producing companies in this country and abroad are but imperfectly co-operative in actual organization and practice. The workmen organize as a joint-stock company or corporation, paying in their capital, and electing a treasurer, clerk and directors, who elect a president and other executive officers. The management hires and discharges help, giving preference to stockholders, but not usually under any obligation to retain an incompetent man because he is a stockholder. The workers are paid wages at regular intervals, just as if they had no ownership in the concern, and at the end of the year receive the profits, if any, in the form of dividends. Where the co-operative idea is strictly carried out, only a part of the profits is divided as a dividend on capital. Another part is divided as a dividend on labor, and apportioned among the workmen, according to their wages, or the number of days each has worked. A third part is divided as a dividend on purchases, the chief customer, in this case, being a co-operative store, which is a stockholder in the producing company. When the entire profit is divided on the shares of capital, the company is still in a degree co-operative, inasmuch as the workers own the capital, usually in nearly equal amounts. The profit contains an increment created by the superior zeal of the working owners as self-employers; and the dividend each receives under these conditions must be approximately proportional to his services.

Co-operative and fraternal forms of industrial association are as ancient as society itself. The joint undivided family, from which grew craft-guilds and brotherhoods, and the village communities, from which sprang the English parish and the New England town, were to a great degree communistic in their industrial affairs. From time immemorial, profit-sharing has existed in agriculture and fisheries, and it is probably older than the wage-system as a method of rewarding labor. The earliest industrial institutions of the New World were largely co-operative in principle and practice. But the forms and applications of co-operation that we are here concerned with, had their origin in that quickening of humanitarian thought and zeal which was started by the speculations of St. Simon and Fourier, in France, and Robert Owen, in England. They are the tangible results of the united efforts of those who looked forward to a speedy reconstruction of society as a whole, and of many others who cherished no such dreams, but had faith, nonetheless, that something could be done by personal effort and voluntary association to ameliorate the condition of labor. The different plans have been developed, and have flourished best in as many different countries, each proving to be specially adapted to certain social conditions and types of character. The co-operative association and training of workmen in production and distribution, without the intervention of the employing capitalist, has been carried farthest in England. Profit-sharing, as a voluntary concession by employing capitalists, has had its best development in France, and co-operative credit has succeeded best in Germany and the United States.

Of the more than three hundred co-operative societies started in England, Scotland, Wales and Ireland, between 1820 and 1830, when faith in the possibility of reorganizing society was strong, some were thoroughly communistic, dividing profits equally among members, without regard to capital invested or value of services. Others divided on capital only. Nearly all were short-lived; and it was not till 1844 that the idea which was to afford to distributive co-operation a substantial basis and ensure its growth — that of dividing profits in proportion to purchases — was successfully worked out by the Rochdale Pioneers. From that time on, the movement had able business direction, and the sympathetic aid of such leaders of opinion as Charles Kingsley, Frederick D. Maurice and Thomas Hughes; and, during the last twenty years, British workingmen co-operators have done a business of £250,000,000, on which they have made a profit of £20,-000,000. Methods have been reduced to system, and a secure foundation obtained in statute-law. On the Continent, both distributive and productive co-operation have been extending, and at present seventy productive societies in France have a membership of 4,920, and a capital of about 5,000,000 francs.

Meanwhile, profit-sharing by the employer with wage-earning employees, first successfully attempted in 1831, by Vandeleur, on his estate in Ireland, and then tried in France, where it found favorable conditions, by the Parisian house-painter, Leclaire, in 1842, and by the Paris and Orleans Railway Company, in 1844, has been so steadily growing in favor that at the close of 1885, there were ninety-eight profit-sharing houses on the Continent, of which forty-nine were in France and twelve in Switzerland. Some convert the dividends to labor into shares of stock; and in the two most perfectly organized industrial partnerships in the world, — those of the Maison-Leclaire and M. Godin's Familistere, at Guise, — not only may the workers become, through their profits, shareholders, but shareholding workmen may become directors and managers, — the way being open for the humblest worker, if he has ability and character, to rise to the highest place.

The earlier forms of co-operation revealed the need of co-operative credit; and this was organized by Dr. Schulze, at Delitzsch, in Germany, in 1850. The Schulze-Delitzsch credit-unions, now known by the simpler name of people's banks, which he founded, enable the poorest persons not only to save, but to borrow small sums on such security as wages due, merchandise, or chattels, or to secure any other common banking service. They have multiplied rapidly in Germany, Russia and Italy, and have accomplished an immense amount of good, enabling the workman or small tradesman to buy tools or enlarge his business without ruinous resort to Shylocks and pawn-brokers. There were 1,965 of these banks in Germany in 1884, 879 of which reported loans amounting to 1,516,952,618 marks. Dr. Schulze also founded the raw-material supply societies, which enable handicraftsmen to buy material at wholesale rates. These, with the co-operative magazines, or selling-houses, — another class of societies peculiar to Germany, — do much to enable independent producers on a small scale to maintain themselves in competition with large manufacturing establishments.

This glance at the progress of co-operation in Europe shows us the antecedents of co-operation in America, and affords a basis of comparison for estimating American results. As early as 1830, co-operation began to engage the attention of the workingmen in New England, and isolated experiments in co-operative distribution were here and there made. Most of them were short-lived, and even the record of their names seems to be now beyond recovery. The New England Association of Farmers and Mechanics discussed the subject at Boston, in 1831, and appointed a committee to investigate it; but no report was ever made. A decade of feeble attempts and failures followed; and then, in 1845, — a year after the successful organization of the Rochdale Pioneers in England, — a dozen members of the Workingmen's Protective Union opened a store, consisting of a box of soap and half a chest of tea, in a room over the Boylston Market, at Boston. In less than five years, the union had built up an annual trade of $500,000. Its organization consisted of a central-supply agency and local divisions or branches. The name was changed, in 1849, to the New England Protective Union. Growth and prosperity continued until 1853, when the union was ruptured by a personal controversy. It was then doing a business of probably $2,000,000, or more a year, — 165 of its 403 divisions reporting sales of $1,696,825 for 1852. The new branch called itself the American Protective Union. For a few years, it did an annual business of $1,000,000 to $1,-500,000. The older branch did almost as well. But by 1859 decline set in, and the outbreak of the war brought an end to both branches as general organizations. Some of the local divisions survived, and are still in existence. One of these, the Natick Protective Union, with a capital at present of $6,000, and carrying a stock worth $6,000 to $7,000, is twenty-five years old, and prosperous.

During the ten war-years, no general society for co-operative distribution was in existence; but local societies continued to multiply. Thirty-six stores in ten States were counted in 1866; a wholesale store at Boston was projected, and a conference of New York and Massachusetts stores was talked of. In that year, there was a marked revival of co-operative interest, and a rapid multiplication of co-operative undertakings began, which has continued to the present time. In Massachusetts, they were given the benefit of a general law, under which seven or more persons could become an incorporated association, enjoying all the powers and privileges, and subject to all the duties and liabilities of corporations in general, except that no member could have more than one vote, nor hold shares amounting to more than $1,000, and that the maximum capital-stock was fixed at $50,000. This limit was extended in 1879 to $100,000.

In 1867, the great Granger movement began, and the Patrons of Husbandry quickly became an organization of national extent. The secretary of the National Grange reported, in November, 1875, 24,290 local granges, with a membership of 763,263. A year later, the Order owned or controlled twenty-two warehouses for storing goods, thirty-two grain-elevators, and five steamboat or packet-lines. Its co-operative methods were of an imperfect kind at first, — the local granges being a sort of purchasing-clubs, employing general agents to buy and ship goods in quantity, at a liberal discount. This plan worked well at first, but later led to heavy losses, and the Rochdale system was afterwards quite generally adopted. The greatest success of granger co-operation has been in Texas, where the Patrons have a State co-operative association, with a wholesale agency, and one hundred and fifty stores.

The Sovereigns of Industry, founded at Worcester, Mass., in January, 1874, by William H. Earle, as a secret order, with co-operation as one of its principal objects, had a phenomenally rapid growth for a few years, and then as rapidly went to pieces. Councils were formed in eighteen States within forty days. The Rochdale plan was generally followed in the Sovereigns' stores. These were most numerous in New England, and the largest ones were in Springfield and Worcester, Mass. In the former city, the Sovereigns' block was erected at a cost of $35,000, and the store did a business in one year of $110,000. The Order failed in 1880; but numerous stores in Massachusetts and other States continue to perpetuate its name.

The greatest successes in co-operative distribution have been in cities and towns of Massachusetts, New Jersey and Pennsylvania. In the former State, there are twenty-five or more stores, each having a capital stock ranging from $1,000 to $15,000,—$2,000 to $5,000 being the usual amount. The Industrial Co-operative Society, of Philadelphia, has over 2,000 members, who are mill-operatives, $21,000 capital-stock, and annual sales of $250,000. The Trenton Co-operative Society, of Trenton, N. J., with 200 members and annual sales of $15,000, is organized on a model basis,—the division of profits including interest on capital and a dividend to the labor employed, as well as to customers. A granger store and bank at Olathe, Kan., started ten years ago, has a capital of $40,916, has made sales in nine and a half years to January 1, 1886, of $1,706,110, and, after paying to stockholders ten per cent. on capital, has divided $99,278.83 in dividends. At present, the Knights of Labor are the active organizers of co-operative effort; and, while there are no statistics of the number, trade and profitableness of distributive co-operation in the country at large, it is probable that there is not a State, and perhaps not a Territory, in which successful stores may not be found.

Co-operative credit in the United States dates from 1831, when the Oxford Provident Building Association was founded at Frankfort, near Philadelphia. To-day, there are nearly two thousand such associations in Pennsylvania; and the saying that they have created for workingmen in and around Philadelphia a hundred thousand homes, tells very nearly the literal truth. Within ten years, they have been multiplying under various names in other States, especially in Massachusetts, New Jersey, Ohio and Illinois; and it is safe to estimate the total number at not less than 4,000, with a membership of more than 500,000, and an aggregate capital of $1,000,000,000. The plan is substantially the same in all, and may be understood from a summary of the excellent Massachusetts law for their incorporation, enacted in 1877. They were then called co-operative saving-fund and loan associations; but the name was changed, in 1883, to co-operative banks. The membership must comprise at least twenty-five persons. The capital is limited to $1,000,000; and no member may hold more than twenty-five shares of the par value of $200, or have more than one vote. The shares are sold, to members only, in series, to be paid for by installments. On each share that he buys, the purchaser must make a monthly payment of one dollar, until the sum of these payments, plus the profits accruing on the share, amount to its nominal value, $200. The time varies from eight to ten years. The money in this way accumulated is loaned, from time to time, to members, the loans being made at auction, to the bidders of the highest rates of interest. Loans must be secured by real estate mortgage, and by the borrower's shares as collateral. No member has more than one vote.

By means of the co-operative bank, its members may become house-owners in a few years, through monthly payments, little, if any, greater than they would pay for rent. With the strongest inducements to save, they are encouraged to save in the easiest way, — by regular installments of moderate amount. As borrowers, they can obtain small sums as readily, and on as favorable terms, as large ones. There is ample time for payment, and the debt is all the while undergoing extinction. In some States, there have been heavy losses through bad management; but in Massachusetts, these banks are subject to the inspection of the savings-bank commissioner, and their shares are as safe as any investment can be. The advantages of this free State oversight may be inferred from the fact that in California the co-operative building associations find it worth while to employ expert accountants, at their own expense, to examine their books, and prepare elaborate statements for the stockholders. The Pennsylvania associations are allowed to invest in real estate and engage in building operations, and some of them find it advantageous to do so when the demand for loans is slight. Some of the Western associations have enjoyed remarkable prosperity. The Quincy Building and Homestead Association, of Illinois, has 5,750 shares in force, on which the annual profit is thirteen per cent., and in twelve years it has paid out $70,930.64 in profits on matured stock and withdrawn shares.

Productive co-operation is co-operation in its most difficult form, and its development has been correspondingly slow; yet it has been substantial. In such industries as iron-founding, wood-working, boot and shoe-making, glass-making, hat and cigar-making, production by associated workmen is well established in the United States. The earliest co-operative productive enterprise of which we have any record was that of the Boston Tailors' Associative Union, of 1849, which divided profits among its members in proportion to the labor they performed. It did not long survive. Scarcely anything was done until after the war, when the Iron-moulders' International Union became interested in the subject, through the efforts of its founder, William H. Sylvis, who made a report in 1864, urging the advantages of co-operative foundries. Several foundries were soon after started, in accordance with his ideas, three or four of which are yet in existence. The oldest is the Troy Co-operative Stove Works, established in April, 1866. This was, for a time, a true co-operative company. No member had ever more than one vote, and all earnings in excess of ten per cent. were divided on the basis of labor. The co-operative features have disappeared, and it has become a stock-company, with thirty shareholders. In 1867 were started the co-operative foundries at Rochester, N. Y., Cleveland, O., and Somerset, Mass. All the employees of the former, at first, were stockholders, and profits in excess of twelve per cent. were divided according to the earnings of labor; but, after a few years, the initial dividend on capital was advanced to seventeen and a half per cent., then to twenty-five per cent., and before long the bonus to labor was discontinued altogether. Now, not more than one-fifth of the employees are stockholders. The Somerset foundry, which had been a failure in private hands, was bought by a company of working moulders, who brought it up to a high degree of prosperity. Profits are paid on capital only, but other co-operative features have been retained. By the law of the State, no member can hold stock in excess of $1,000, or have more than one vote; and the by-laws give a preference to stockholders and their sons in employment and apprenticeship, and require members wishing to sell their shares to offer them first to the company. There are successful co-operative foundries of later establishment at Cincinnati and St. Louis.

Though most of the co-operative producing companies in the United States are so imperfectly co-operative, being little more than joint-stock associations of workmen, they are, nonetheless, as such, of no little importance in the growth of co-operative methods; for they are affording to their members the training and business experience which co-operation will demand. The history of nearly every one is the record of a brave struggle to accumulate a sufficient working capital and an assured credit. Yet these obstacles have not only been overcome in scattering individual instances, but in some places by considerable groups of co-operative undertakings. Conspicuous among such are the co-operative enterprises at St. Louis, Minneapolis, and Stoneham, Mass.

At St. Louis, besides the foundry already mentioned, there are four prosperous wood-working and furniture companies. The oldest, the Mechanics' Planing-Mill Company, was founded in 1874. The nominal capital was $50,000, but there were only $10,000 paid in and available. The members accepted the smallest cash payment for their labor that they could live on, and took the balance due them in certificates of stock. At one time, the company had not credit enough to buy ten feet of belting, and in the second year the works were totally destroyed by fire, at a loss of $8,000. But in 1884, the capital-stock was all paid up, and a surplus of $35,000 had been accumulated; and the shares, of the par value of $500, are now held at $1,000. The Furniture Workers' Association, started in 1878, with almost no capital, has accumulated one by funding a percentage of wages, and has become prosperous. This company is, to a considerable degree, truly co-operative, — no person being permitted to own more than twenty of the twenty-five dollar shares, and pains being taken to keep the stock in the hands of working members. The Central Furniture Company, organized in 1881, has a paid-up capital-stock of $30,000; and the Mechanics' Furniture Association, incorporated in 1885, has a capital-stock of $25,000, one-half paid up. The former accumulated its capital largely from its earnings, dividing one year a stock dividend of thirty-five per cent., and another year twenty per cent., and the latter withholds ten per cent. of wages, and declares stock dividends.

Among the coopers of Minneapolis, American co-operative production has attained its highest success. There are seven co-operative shops, employing four hundred and fifty workmen, most of whom are stockholders, and doing a business of $1,000,000 a year. The oldest, the Co-operative Barrel Association, was organized in the fall of 1874, with a capital-stock of $15,000. Each member paid fifteen dollars at first, and a weekly assessment of five dollars until the whole amount was paid in. The second was organized in 1877, the third in 1880, and the fourth and fifth in 1881. The largest has a capital-stock of $75,000. All are purely co-operative in plan and operation. All the stock is held by actual workmen, and each stockholder has but one vote. Capital receives only a fixed rate of interest, and profits are divided among the workers according to their wages. The men are described as "a mixed multitude of Swedes, Norwegians, Irish, Germans, Italians and Americans; yet they consult dispassionately, vote fairly, submit without hesitation, work faithfully, choose their best men always, obey implicitly, and have unlimited faith in co-operative effort." Before they became co-operators, they had a bad reputation on the score of sobriety and order; they now stand high in the estimation of the community as good citizens.

The four co-operative boot and shoe companies at Stoneham, Mass., are co-operative only to the extent that each stockholder can own but $1,000 of the capital-stock, and have but one vote; but as stock associations of workingmen producers, they have been remarkably successful. The Stoneham Co-operative Shoe Company was organized in 1872, by men temporarily unemployed, who subscribed a capital-stock of $10,000, which was increased to $15,000 in 1880, and to $20,000 in 1881. Its stockholders are of all nationalities, and have always worked together harmoniously. The value of its annual product is $150,000; and its dividends, from 1879 to 1884 inclusive, were seventeen, fifteen, fifteen, twenty-one, twenty and six per cent. The Middlesex Co-operative Boot and Shoe Company, organized in 1875, with a capital-stock of $10,000, increased in 1883 to $15,000, has paid dividends of ten per cent. in 1880 and 1881, twenty per cent in 1882 and 1884, and twenty-five per cent. in 1883. The shares of both these companies have been transferred at $400, the par value being $250. The value of the annual product of the Middlesex is $90,000. The American Co-operative Boot and Shoe Company was organized in 1882, with a capital of $10,000, which was increased to $20,000 in 1883, and to $30,000 in 1884. It does a business of $50,000 a year. There is not much mixture of nationalities among stockholders, and stock is regarded as an investment merely, giving no claim to any other advantage. The Franklin Co-operative Boot and Shoe Company dates from 1883, has a capital stock of $20,000, and does a business of $50,000 a year. It started with $7,000 paid in. In this company, stockholders have the first right to employment, and the expectation is that they will be given employment when possible. These four shops gave employment in 1885 to 185 workers, of whom 97 were stockholders. One hundred and four of the employees were females, and twenty-five of the female employees were stockholders.

Massachusetts is the only State which has yet published official statistics of the co-operative production within its territory. These were included in the report on "Profit-Sharing," prepared by the present writer for the Seventeenth Annual Report of the Bureau of Statistics of Labor. From 1867 to 1875, fifteen co-operative manufacturing companies were organized in that State, and only three of them are still in existence. Five of the defunct companies were boot and shoe-manufacturers, and of these three were at Lynn. The other two were at North Adams and Truro. The other seven extinct companies were cigar-manufacturers,—six at Westfield and one at Springfield. At Lynn and Westfield, therefore, co-operative production has been a failure. Insufficient capital and disagreements among the members were the chief causes of disaster. In the ten years, 1875 to 1885, thirteen more companies were organized, six of which were short-lived. These were two cigar companies at Westfield, two boot and shoe companies at Marlborough, a furniture company at Orange, and a hardware company at Greenfield. There were left ten companies in operation in 1885, besides two or three small printing and publishing companies. The five besides the Somerset foundry and the four Stoneham shoe companies, were the Kingston Co-operative Foundry at Kingston, the Leonard Co-operative Foundry at Taunton, the East Templeton Co-operative Chair Company, the Athol Co-operative Furniture Company, and the Wakefield Co-operative Shoe Company. The ten had an aggregate capital-stock of $191,900, an annual business of $605,000, and gave employment to 264 men and 83 women, of whom 186 men and 26 women were stockholders. The average dividend of the ten companies for ten years had been four and six-tenths per cent.; but there had been in two cases heavy losses by fire, and two companies had so recently started that no dividend had been declared. The Knights of Labor have recently established co-operative shoe companies at Lynn and Spencer.

Among the scattering enterprises in productive co-operation may be mentioned the Flint-Glass Works, at Beaver Falls, Penn., established in 1879, which have paid large dividends; the Co-operative Iron-Moulders, at Nashua, N. H.; the hat-makers, at South Norwalk, Conn.; Co-operative Granite works, at South Ryegate, Vt., and Quincy, Mass.; Co-operative Carpenters, at Decatur, Ill.; Expressmen, at Detroit; a co-operative coal-mining company, at Peoria, Ill.; a nail mill at Carmi, Ill.; and co-operative manufacturing companies at Easton, Penn., and Richmond, Va. The Kentucky Railroad Tobacco Company, at Covington, Ky., is unique in its method of dividing profits, and claims to be the only factory in the United States that recognizes the equality of labor and capital. Each workman is supposed to represent a labor-capital, on which his wages, at the current rates of the vicinity, are a six per cent. dividend. If his wages are $9 a week, he represents a labor-capital of $7,500; since $7,500 at six per cent. would yield $450, his actual wages being $468. Each workman, then, is paid his wages weekly. Money-capital, in like manner, receives six per cent. interest. If, after making these payments, any surplus profit remains, it is divided *pro rata* on the money and labor-capital. Thus the man whose wages are $468 a year, will have his dividend computed on his $7,500 of labor-capital, not on his $468 of wages. It will be seen that the dividend to labor is much larger in proportion to the dividend to capital, under this plan, than it is when computed as a percentage on wages. Every stockholder in this company is required to be a worker, and every worker to be a Knight of Labor.

A comparison of records shows that a large percentage of co-operative enterprises have been started by men temporarily out of employment, and in the midst of dull times. This fact accounts for many of the discouragements they have had to contend with, and for many failures. When employment is abundant and wages good, men are satisfied with their lot.

They think of co-operation when reverses come; and it is then that co-operation is exceedingly difficult to establish. Another cause of failure has been the lack of sufficient capital, and a third one the failure to pay wages regularly, at frequent intervals. Men immediately dependent on the fruits of their labor cannot wait to an indefinite future for an uncertain and indeterminate profit. It is true that several highly successful companies, starting with little, have accumulated capital by regularly withholding a percentage of wages. But, when this has been successfully done, it has been done under a perfectly definite arrangement, faithfully lived up to. The wages to be paid have been paid regularly, and the percentage to be deducted, as regularly withheld. The vital importance of sufficient capital in co-operative production led Dr. Schulze to entertain the belief that the firm establishment of co-operative credit was the first thing to be looked after. Undoubtedly, the two are destined to aid each other.

There has been a decided tendency to drop the co-operative features, and degenerate into a mere stock association. Up to a certain point, the subordination of the labor relation to the stockholder relation seems to be necessary; but this ought not to go to the extreme of eliminating co-operation altogether, and it need not. In Massachusetts, the law under which the companies are incorporated prevents the complete over-riding of the individual by the capitalist, by limiting the amount of the capital-stock that any member can own, and allowing to each stockholder but one vote. Probably, before true co-operation can be firmly established in productive industry, it will be necessary to include in the law of incorporation a provision that the division of profits shall be, in part, on the basis of labor.

The men who have succeeded in co-operation have been men of superior character and energy, of good business sense, willing to defer to each other, and to trust large powers of management to their directors, under responsibility, and as ready to obey orders as to help make them. The best thing about co-operative production, in its present stage of development, is its educative value. It is teaching men to regard the problems of labor and production in the right way,— training them in prudence, economy and business affairs, and disciplining them in mutual action for a common end.

Where co-operation initiated and controlled by workmen fails, co-operation initiated and controlled by capitalist employers finds its great opportunity. We need not linger over the simple forms of profit-sharing familiar in the fisheries and in agriculture, in which a share of profits is substituted for wages, but will glance briefly at what has been done in such highly organized industries as manufacturing, in profit-sharing as supplementary to the wage-system. It is not very much,— only a beginning has been made; but it is an encouraging beginning, showing that there are great possibilities in this method of identifying the interests of capital and labor.

The first American attempts of this kind appear to have been those of A. S. Cameron & Co., manufacturers of steam-pumping machinery, at New York, and Brewster & Co., carriage-builders, in the same city. A. S. Cameron & Co. began to divide profits with their employees in July, 1869, and continued the practice with marked success for eight years, when it came to an end by Mr. Cameron's death. The method of division was to set aside annually ten per cent. of the company's net profit, as a dividend to labor, which was divided among the men on the basis of their wages. The bonus was four and a half per cent. of the total wages each year, and it did not operate to reduce wages. It had a salutary effect on the men, morally and economically, and on the success of the firm. The industrial partnership formed by Brewster & Co. with their employees, in 1869, was like the Cameron arrangement in the division of profits, save that the dividend to labor was ten per cent. of gross profits,— there being no deduction first of any salary or interest on capital for any member of the firm. The employees were also given representation in a general board of governors, and in boards of control for the several departments of the work. The former had power to make all rules and regulations for the shop, and to hear and investigate complaints. The boards of control enforced the regulations made by the board of governors. This arrangement gave entire satisfaction during the two and a half years of its continuance. It came to an end through the excited action of the employees in joining the eight-hour strike, when they had it in their own power, through their board of governors, to make eight hours their working-day, if they had chosen. They forfeited a dividend of $11,000 and $8,000 in wages.

An experiment begun at Peacedale, R. I., in 1878, by the Peacedale Manufacturing Company, has been a remarkably interesting one, as showing the educative power of the profit-sharing arrangement. This firm, manufacturing shawls, coatings, cassimeres, and other woolen fabrics, employs about four hundred and fifty persons, — men, women and children, of all nationalities. It has had no serious labor trouble in twenty-five years. No salaries are paid to the officers, who are the principal stockholders; and, after a fair dividend, is paid on capital, the remaining profit is divided with the employees, and distributed on the basis of wages. The bonus has not been large at any time, owing to the depressed state of the woolen manufacture since profit-sharing was commenced, and some years there has been no bonus; yet the effect of the arrangement, as the firm testifies, has been to develop diligence, care-taking, fidelity and interest in the general welfare to a remarkable degree. The case strikingly exemplifies the whole theory of profit-sharing. The bonus is not a gift, taken from the employer's share of the product, to be added to that of the employee, but it is paid out of additional wealth, created by increased industry and saving, and the more perfect co-operation between labor and management.

Lister Brothers, manufacturers of agricultural chemicals, at Newark, N. J., divided $15,000 of their profits among their 500 employees, in 1882. They made the mistake of dividing by classes, without reference to individual worth, as measured by wages; and the inevitable consequences of misunderstandings and jealousies terminated the experiment. The Pillsbury Flour-mills, at Minneapolis, have been dividing profits with employees for four years, with such excellent results that a member of the firm says that the arrangement will not be willinglv discontinued, so far as the firm is concerned. To participate, an employee must have worked for the firm five years. Three years ago $25,000, two years ago $25,000, and last September $32,000, were divided among upward of 100 of the 1,100 hands. The five-year limit is now bringing in a large additional number of participants. The dividends to labor have been twenty-five to forty per cent. of wages.

The Century Company, of New York, and the *Staats-Zeitung* Company, are profit-sharing publishing companies. In the former, the heads of departments and their principal assistants own stock of the corporation to a limited extent; and, in addition, the dividend on certain other shares of the capital-stock, after interest on the cost has been deducted, is divided among all employees of the company, in proportion to their salaries. Mr. Roswell Smith, the principal capitalist, limits his ownership to three-fifths of the stock; so that, in general terms, it may be said that capital owns three-fifths of the Century Company, and labor two-fifths, except that all the capital employed is represented by active workers, there being no outside investors. The *Staats-Zeitung* has, for several years, shared profits with its employees, at the rate of ten per cent. on their salaries. As much as $20,000 has been distributed in this labor-dividend in one year. The paper has been very successful in securing continuity and fidelity of service.

In no case of true profit-sharing are wages ever reduced to meet the dividend to labor. These American attempts have shown that the dividend is earned by the increased interest and efficiency of the employees. The arrangement benefits all. More wealth can be divided, for more is produced to divide. It is a potent educative influence, bringing employer and employee into such humane relations as can never exist when one is a mere buyer of the physical and moral powers of the other, considered as merely so much merchandise.

Interest and faith in the plan are rapidly growing, and within a year as many as ten or twelve large firms and cor-

VETERAN CORPS, KNIGHTS OF LABOR.

porations, in various parts of the country, have adopted it. The most noteworthy of these is the New England Granite Works, of Hartford, Conn., and Westerly, R. I. The arrangement there is to divide the net profits remaining after wages, interest and all other necessary expenses have been paid, into three parts, — one-third to be set aside as a reserve against loss and depreciation, the other two-thirds to be distributed *pro rata* on capital and labor.

If the net profit were $25,000, the capital employed $100,000, and the entire amount paid for labor during the year $150,000, the guarantee-fund would be $8,333.33, the dividend to capital two-fifths of the remainder, or $6,666.67, and the dividend to labor three-fifths, or $10,000. The dividend to labor is distributed *pro rata* on wages among the men, — salaried officers, contractors and men discharged for cause not participating. Wages are fixed by mutual agreement or by arbitration, and the employees have a voice in choosing the auditor to examine the accounts, and certify that the profits have been fairly determined. Mr. J. G. Batterson, president of the company, says that, with the results of a long experience before him, he is convinced that the payment of fixed wages to a large number of men carries with it no inspiring motive to the attainment of a high standard of excellence, either as to quantity or quality of production; and he believes thoroughly in the efficiency of individual interest as the only available stimulant to natural ambition. He also makes the exceedingly important statement, that it is his purpose to claim no more for capital than is sufficient to hold it in the business, giving the balance to labor. This is a direct reversal of the common rule of the industrial world, to buy labor at the lowest competitive rates, and give the balance to capital.

Ara Cushman & Co., shoe-manufacturers at Auburn, Me., after paying interest on capital and other expenses, divide the remaining profit between labor and capital in proportion to the amount of capital and the annual value of labor. Three representatives of the employees who are allowed a confidential knowledge of the business, confer with the firm in regard to details of the plan. Employees are encouraged to convert their dividends into shares of stock. The firm of Rogers, Peet & Co., clothiers, at New York, convert an unspecified percentage of their net profit into a labor-dividend. The Union Mining Company, at Mt. Savage, Md., pays to labor a dividend equal to ten per cent. of the dividend paid to stockholders. Welshaus & McEwan, of Omaha, Neb., allow ten per cent. to capital, and divide any remaining profit equally between capital and labor. The N. O. Nelson Manufacturing Company, of St. Louis, and the Hoffman & Billings Manufacturing Company, of Milwaukee, allow seven per cent. to capital, and divide the remaining profits equally between capital and labor.

The variety of plans of division shows the experimental nature of all these attempts, and reveals the total lack of agreement as to what is the most equitable basis. Nevertheless, there are a few business principles of profit-sharing that may be considered established. The first condition of success is, that the employer shall have full faith in the system, and not be impatient for quick and showy results. The identification of interests aimed at cannot be achieved in a day or a year; it must be a process of growth. The ideas and sentiments that years of antagonism between labor and capital have generated, have all to be remoulded; and that means a long course of educative work, under conditions of friendliness and confidence. The second condition is, that the absolute confidence of the employees must be secured and held. It may not be thought best to make them all acquainted with every detail of the business; but they must be allowed to know, through a committee or auditor chosen by themselves, that everything is as represented. If the confidence of the employees is held, the question, What will happen when there are no profits to divide? will answer itself. When they know that the employer is doing the best he can by them, they will submit to loss and sacrifice without complaint.

The chief defect of American plans of profit-sharing so far, is, that they are not systematic and constructive enough. They offer an immediate reward for increased diligence, but fail to build for the future. In this respect, the prevalent French method of converting the labor-dividend into an accumulating fund, is better. The dividend that each individual receives from year to year is small; but, capitalized from year to year, it would become a handsome fund. But the logical carrying-out of profit-sharing really requires the conversion of the annual bonus into certificates of stock. The worker would then become a full legal partner in the company. He would receive increasing dividends on his increasing stock, as well as on his labor, and every year his interest in the business would be growing larger. This arrangement, moreover, would fully meet the objection of those who claim that profit-sharing should be offset by loss-sharing. As a stockholder, the worker would, of course, share in any loss incurred, and he could afford to. The new Massachusetts law, enabling corporations to designate and set aside a certain portion of their stock as employees' stock, offers an excellent opportunity for trying a thorough-going plan of industrial partnership.

The immediate need of American co-operation is a central organization, like the Central Co-operative Board of England, and something corresponding to the English Co-operative Congress. Co-operators and profit-sharing companies are working with little reference to each other, and with little knowledge of each other's methods and results. Central organization would speedily reduce the results of experience to something like system, and enable new co-operative undertakings to avoid causes of failure. A promising effort to bring this about is now being made by the Sociologic Society of America,—an organization aiming to further the development of a civilization based on co-operation instead of competition.

With a central organization established, a movement toward industrial federation, which is the co-ordination of co-operation, and its goal, would begin. Short of this, the highest purpose of co-operation, which, as was said at the outset, is industrial re-organization, with the preservation of what is best in the competitive system without its evils, cannot be achieved.

Competition fosters invention and enterprise, and tends to reduce the price of goods to the cost of production. This is a good when the degradation of labor is not an element in the reduction of cost. But this degradation unrestricted competition often produces; and it results, also, in enormous wastes of wealth. The unnecessary paralleling of railroads in the United States, according to Professor Richard T. Ely, has consumed capital enough to provide a comfortable house for every family in the United States that does not already own one. The federation of co-operative enterprise offers a way for placing goods with consumers at the lowest cost consistent with the liberal reward and gradual uplifting of labor, and without unnecessary duplication of plant, risk, superintendence and work. All these conditions would be fulfilled, if a group of co-operative stores, giving their patrons the profits of distribution, took all the products of a group of farms, manufactories, etc., under agreement that the stores should have the goods at the lowest prices consistent with the payment of certain specified dividends on capital and labor. Undivided profits, accumulated by stores, might or might not, constitute the capital of the manufactories; the arrangement could be the same in either case. In England, federation has been attempted on an altogether inadequate and inflexible plan, with the unfortunate result of dividing co-operators into antagonistic parties of "federalists" and "individualists." The "federalists" would have all productive establishments owned by the stores in their corporate capacity, individual stockholding being disallowed, the stores to have the goods at actual cost, — labor getting nothing beyond wages, except through the store dividends on purchases. No such narrow system will ever prevail widely. A federal co-operation capable of universal extension must be a broad scheme, with a place in it for the store, the individual stockholder and the profit-sharing capitalist employer; a "bottom" price for the purchasing co-operative store, and dividends for the customer, stockholder and worker. It must be also progressive, — all the while expanding and building for the future by carrying out the sound advice of M. Godin, to capitalize and maintain undivided a portion of the profits, so as to have at all times the resources for developing new opportunities, and providing employment for labor that might otherwise seek it in vain.

Co-operation differs from socialism in its reliance on the vitality, adaptability and growing power of voluntary association. It does not ask the State to take possession of all capital, and manage all industry, and order all men in their industrial life as it orders regiments of soldiers. If the worker got more wealth under a socialistic system than he does under such employers as he serves now, which is not probable, he would at least not be more free. There are those who favor socialism, because they despair of the possibility of improving social arrangements by any other means. William Morris, the English poet-socialist, who has long been a profit-sharing employer, holds that, short of socialism, co-operation stands no chance against a crushing competition. This is to overlook the vitally important truth, that there are monstrous evils associated with competition at present, which have grown up through the shameful neglect of the government to fulfill its primary functions of protecting equal rights and enforcing justice. The privileged corporations and monopolies, which exact tribute of all industry, are the creatures of government, and should be brought by government within proper limits of privilege and action. If this were done, and certain other wrongs, as those connected with unjust land-laws, were remedied, there would be no need of revolution and State socialism for the realization of the co-operative ideals. The remedy is through wise legislation and honest administration, and it is in the hands of voters.

CHAPTER XXII.

INDUSTRIAL EDUCATION.

INDUSTRIAL EDUCATION A FACTOR IN THE INDUSTRIAL PROBLEM — OUTLINE OF GENERAL SYSTEM OF INDUSTRIAL EDUCATION — I. KINDERGARTEN: FOUNDATION OF SYSTEM — II. THE PUBLIC SCHOOL: DRAWING; MODELING; SEWING; ELEMENTS OF SCIENCE; SCHOOL WORKSHOP; EXPERIMENTS IN — III. EVENING CLASSES: EUROPEAN EXPERIMENTS; AMERICAN EXPERIMENTS — IV. TRADE SCHOOLS: SCHOOLS FOUNDED BY PRIVATE PHILANTHROPY; BY BUSINESS HOUSES AND COMMUNITIES; BY THE STATE — V. HIGHER TECHNICAL SCHOOLS — VI. POLYTECHNIC SCHOOLS, IN EUROPE AND AMERICA — VII. HIGH SCHOOLS OF INDUSTRIAL ART — VIII. A CENTRAL MODEL SCHOOL OF INDUSTRIAL SCIENCE AND ART — IX. INDUSTRIAL MUSEUMS: SOUTH KENSINGTON MUSEUM, ETC. — X. COST OF SUCH A SYSTEM OF INDUSTRIAL EDUCATION.

EDUCATION is a factor, and a very important one, in the equation of a higher industrial order. Of the various aspects of education in its bearings upon the labor problem, the most urgent is that which is known as an industrial education, — the instruction and the training which develop directly the dispositions, the knowledge and the powers which make the successful handicraftsman. Accepting the fact that our country urgently needs such a system, and that other countries have proven its practicability, let me try to sketch the outlines of a true industrial education, illustrating the subject from the experiments made in Europe and in our own country, and thus indicating the progress made in this direction.

I. THE KINDERGARTEN. — The foundations of industrial education are of the utmost importance to the superstructure. The kindergarten forms a most wise system for culturing the dispositions and knowledge and powers which lay the foundation for industrial skill. The natural instinct of childhood to busy itself with doing something, its spontaneous impulse to be making something, is in the kindergarten utilized for the purpose of education. Pricking forms of geometrical figures and of familiar objects on paper, weaving wooden strips into varied designs, folding paper into pretty toys and ornaments, plaiting variegated strips of paper into ingenious and attractive shapes, modeling in clay, — these, with other kindred exercises, "pretty plays," as they all seem, constitute a most real education by and for work. By means of these occupations, the eye is trained to quickness of perception and accuracy of observation, the hand to deftness of touch and skill of workmanship, such as the child may win; the sense of the beautiful is inspired, the judgments exercised and strengthened, originality is stimulated by often leaving the children to fashion their own designs, while habits of industry are inwrought upon the most plastic period of life, and the child is accustomed to find his interest and delight in work, and to feel its dignity and nobleness.

As to how far the kindergarten fulfills practically such expectations, let Miss Blow testify, — who should know whereof she speaks, since she was at the head of the kindergarten department of the public-school system of St. Louis for several years: —

> In the Des Pères Kindergarten, predestined engineers have built bridges as remarkable in conception, as clever in execution; little mathematicians have discovered, rather than learned, all the simple relations of numbers; tiny fingers have guided the pencil to trace beautiful decorative designs, and soft clay has been fashioned into flowers, fruits and animals, by the dextrous hands of embryo sculptors.

The National Teachers' Association, in convention at Saratoga, last summer, expressed the hope that "the time is near at hand when public sentiment and legislative enactment will incorporate the kindergarten into our public-school system."

The kindergarten is already being adopted as the sub-primary department of our public-school system in a few of our cities. St. Louis was the pioneer in this direction; and to Miss Blow's able and enthusiastic labors we owe the splendid pattern set by this city, with its thirty-three kindergartens, gathering 5,000 children under its beautiful culture. The expenses of these kindergartens are provided from the school taxation. Philadelphia has a sub-primary school society, incorporated in 1881. In 1885, it had twenty-nine free kindergartens under its care, enrolling a thousand pupils. The expenses of the society amounted to nearly $11,000, for which the city of Philadelphia appropriated $7,500. In Boston, the splendid liberality and far-seeing wisdom of one lady has provided some twenty free kindergartens. San Francisco has a kindergarten association, which carries on a number of free kindergartens; and, in various cities, churches and philanthropic societies support local kindergartens.

II. The Public School. — Upon the kindergarten, as the foundation of industrial training, there must be reared in the public-school system the next stone in the superstructure of manual training. Of course, it is out of the question for the public schools to undertake to turn out carpenters or other craftsmen. Experience, however, shows that a proper proportion of manual training furthers mental training; that to a true education of the head an education of the hand is essential.

The following branches would seem to be entirely practical in the public schools, and eminently serviceable to the cause of industrial education: —

Drawing. — Drawing, freehand and mechanical, chiefly with relation to industry, — industrial drawing, as it has well been called, — should plainly constitute an integral part of our system. In many forms of scientific industry, it is of great importance to every workman. In all forms of artistic industry, it is absolutely essential. In all handicrafts, it proves eminently useful. The value of drawing, as a foundation of industrial training, is clearly recognized by all who have studied the subject.

Philadelphia claims to have made the first experiment of a branch-school of industrial art in connection with its public-school system. Boston appears to have been the first to introduce the elements of drawing into the public schools generally. In most of our cities and large towns, drawing is now taught as a part of the course. The results attained are sometimes very striking. I visited lately one of our ward-schools in New York, in which the specimens of drawing shown greatly surprised me. The Royal Commissioners on Technical Instruction reported that they were "of opinion that sound instruction in the rudiments of drawing should be incorporated with writing, in all primary schools, both for girls and boys."*

Massachusetts has led off in our country in making drawing compulsory. We have now twenty-one cities, each having a population of from 50,000 upwards, representing schools with an average daily attendance of 386,200 pupils, and fifty-eight cities having a population between 10,000 and 50,000, with an attendance of 116,000 pupils, wherein drawing is compulsory. The use of industrial drawing is rapidly spreading through our public schools.

Modeling. — Modeling is of great value in industrial education. All that has been said of drawing holds true of modeling; while it is to be added that the latter work, dealing with plastic material, has certain beneficial influences of its own. The child is busied in shaping a thing, and not merely in making a picture of a thing. The sense of touch is educated. The average child finds greater interest in modeling an object than in drawing any form. There is a realism in the work of the miniature sculptor which the embryo artist does not find. The Royal Commissioners reported that they were "of opinion that more attention than has hitherto been devoted to it should be directed to the subject of modeling in the elementary school. * * * * Modeling is an exercise of great importance to the future workman, and its rudiments can well be taken up, as in Continental schools, at the earliest age."* Modeling is slowly coming into use in our schools.

Sewing. — Sewing can readily be taught in our public schools. For a long time, it has been taught in the so-called industrial schools connected with our churches and charitable organizations, — the practical experience of workers amongst the poor having taught them the necessity of training the girls under their care in this simple feminine craft, since a large proportion of women earn their livelihood by some use of the needle. The trouble with the charitable work in this line has been that the instruction given has been largely superficial and unsystematic. Only the elements of needle-

* Second Report of the Royal Commissioners on Technical Instruction. Vol. I., pp. 519–520.

work have been taught, and these in far from a businesslike manner. What is needful is that a well-graded system of instruction shall be carried out, and thorough training be given through all the stages. Several cities have already introduced instruction and training in sewing, among them Baltimore, Newark, Boston, Providence and Philadelphia. In Baltimore, one afternoon each week is devoted to instruction in sewing, knitting, embroidery and kindred useful branches. In the public schools of Boston, two hours a week are set aside for instruction in sewing.

Science. — The rudimentary elements of scientific knowledge bearing upon industry could be given in our public schools. The children need to get peeps into the marvels of nature, which open everywhere beneath the common products of mill and factory and workshop. How greatly life would grow in interest, and what zest the daily tasks would yield, were there any such training from childhood upward! Hosts of men are doing mechanical tasks which open to them no springs of pleasure; whereas they might find in those labors a bubbling-up of the waters which make life beautiful in the commonest surroundings. Once started upon the track of observation and thought in connection with the daily work, a bright lad would push on unaided and educate himself through his tasks, while many a time lighting upon the trail which leads up to some great discovery. As a mere matter of doing his work well, every workingman would be aided by some knowledge of the processes amid which he is busied daily. Such simple elementary instruction in science could readily be embodied in our public schools, in a manner to bear directly or indirectly upon the industrial life. The average boy ought to pass out from the public school with a good knowledge of the rudimentary principles of the sciences which underlie our great industries. A thorough grasp of any of these sciences, of course, can only be obtained in more advanced schools or colleges.

Workshop. — The workshop should be connected with the school in some way. There is an education to be effected in the use of tools, — a science and an art of handiwork to be mastered. The Russian system has scientifically graded exercises in the use of tools.

One very important advantage of such a connection of the workshop and the school would be that the boys who look forward to manual labor would have the opportunity of trying their hand in different lines of work, thus finding out their natural tastes and aptitudes. This would prevent the serious mistakes so often made in the choice of a trade,—diminishing the number of incompetent hands in each craft, and adding to the general wealth of the people.

Experiments in School Workshops.—Experiments have been made in this direction quite extensively, apart from State initiative. The Washington University, St. Louis, was one of the first institutions in the country to lead off in blending the workshop with the school-room. Without attempting to teach any trade, it provides training in carpentry, blacksmithing and turning.

The Commercial Club, of Chicago, has lately illustrated very happily the power of our great business associations to foster the cause of industrial education. As an outgrowth of a discussion upon industrial education, the Manual Training School, of Chicago, is now in a prosperous existence, housed in an admirable building, having ample appointments for its work, at a cost of $100,000. This school is open for boys of fourteen years of age, who have passed through the grammar schools. Its course of study comprises mathematics and some of the literary branches of the ordinary high school, together with drawing, freehand and mechanical, carpentry, joinery and turnery, pattern making, modeling and casting, forging, machine-shop work and the study of enginery, including the management of steam-engines and boilers.

Two of the most valuable private experiments in this direction in our country are comparatively late essays, each being the result of a carefully worked out theory of education on the part of an enthusiast; each also aiming to lead children on from the point where the kindergarten leaves them. The Grammercy Park Tool-House is an adjunct to a fashionable New York school. Its founder, Mr. Von Taube, is an enthusiast upon the question of blending manual training with general education. The school-course comprises, in addition to the usual literary department, a tool-house, in which instruction in the principles and training in the methods of wood-work, metal-work, printing, applied chemistry and general workshop practice is given.

The Workingman's School, founded and sustained by the Society for Ethical Culture, of New York, presents a peculiarly interesting attempt to shape a complete system of education for children, in which general intellectual cultivation shall be allied with manual training. The foundation of the school is a free kindergarten. The school proper assigns four hours weekly to instruction in the use of tools. As the softest wood is too hard for the delicate fingers of children of seven years old, clay is used in the earlier series of lessons; for which a complete series of patterns have been devised, in reproducing which the children are familiarized with various mathematical forms, and are taught the fundamental principles of geometry. With the work of the second school-year, object-lessons are given, in which all the forms hitherto taught appear in the most various combinations. When the children have reached the age of nine, and have already worked for two years, it is assumed that they possess enough strength and skill to work in wood, and to manage a simple saw. With unbarked wood as a material, and a saw, knife, hammer, nails and a little glue as tools, the children make photograph-frames, match-boxes, savings-boxes, four-footed garden furniture, etc. When the pupil has attained his eleventh year, and entered his fifth school-year, he is given a scroll-saw to work in wood, and, later on, also, to work in zinc. Here, for the first time, the pupil learns to work after a drawing, which drawing must be thoroughly understood. He is then led on to design patterns, which, of course, tends to develop the imagination. The simplest house and kitchen utensils are manufactured, — such as pot-covers, spoons, frying-pans, strainers, pots, salt-cellars, etc. The carpenter's bench becomes the pupil's true work-table, while various planes, drills, saws, constitute the necessary tools. Articles.

manufactured at first are limited to the most simple household utensils; but the pupils speedily advance to more complicated work. When this branch has been thoroughly pursued for the period of two years, carving and turning offer very few difficulties to the worker. The last stage in the system, as at present developed, consists of instruction in turning and in the locksmith's craft.

The Workshop in the Public School.—What, then, has the State done in this line? The State's action, in some parts of Europe, has been very statesmanlike. The Royal Commissioners state that the "system of school workshops, inaugurated by the Austrian Government, is probably the most complete in Europe, and the results so far appear to be most encouraging." Austria has already one hundred *Fach-Schule*. These schools sometimes develop into what are practically trade-schools. The Innsbruck school provides class-rooms for freehand drawing, geometrical and mechanical and modeling; a physical cabinet and a rudimentary school museum. The modeling-school has a graded series of studies for those who are looking forward to metal-work, and a similar graduated series of stages is employed in the carving-shop. There are about two hundred students in the school. These State schools are periodically visited by a staff of inspectors, who report to the minister. The articles made in the school workshops are sent to Vienna for sale in a special show-room that has been opened.

In our own country, a number of essays have been made toward combining the workshop and the school,—notably in Gloucester, Boston (Mass.), Hoboken, Montclair (N. J.), New Haven, Jamestown (N. Y.), Philadelphia, Baltimore, Toledo, Peru and Moline (Ill.). The courses of instruction provided in these cities are as follows: Hoboken provides industrial drawing, clay-modeling and sewing; Montclair, sewing, embroidery, carpentry and wood-carving; Moline, industrial drawing and carpentry; Peru, carpentry, use of wood-working tools, object and mechanical drawing, clay-modeling and casting in plaster, needle-work and plain sewing. Jamestown has established a very carefully graded course of industrial work, kindergarten-work, sewing, embroidery, crocheting, cooking, cutting and fitting, printing, carpentry, industrial drawing and design, typewriting, shorthand and microscopy. Toledo, Baltimore, Philadelphia and Boston have established manual training-schools in connection with their public-school system. Philadelphia, in addition to its kindergarten sub-primaries, teaches sewing thoroughly through all grades, and then provides the Industrial Art-School, which supplies instruction in freehand drawing and designing, modeling in clay, wood-carving, carpentry and joinery, and metal-work, and the Manual Training-school, which adds wood-turning, pattern-making, forging, bench-work and fitting, proper care and use of tools, and study of the steam-engine, including the management and care of steam-engines and boilers.

III. Evening Classes.—For a long time to come, there will remain in large numbers those whose existence compels as early a resort to work as possible. Children of this class will drop attendance upon the school as soon as the law allows. During the years that must elapse before a thorough system of manual training shall be engrafted upon our public schools, there will be pouring forth from them each year hosts of lads who have had either no training at all, industrially, or only a very slight amount thereof. These lads will need some means of supplementing the defects of the present school-course. Their needs will demand some instrumentality for developing industrial education beyond the point which the public school can reach. The high school can take up the incomplete courses in industrial education, and lead them on higher,—as it should, by all means, do. But only exceptional youths go into high schools,—those, upon the whole, who are looking forward to some professional or semi-professional career. The bulk of our boys and girls will not go beyond the grammar grades. What, then, can be done for this majority of our youths, with reference to their higher education in scientific, artistic and practical industry? The answer is being given in the evening schools. In the Old World, they are successfully supplementing the instruction and training of the elementary schools; and in our own land they have been making encouraging experiments toward the same end.

As to what is being done in this line in Europe, let the English "Blue-Book" speak: —

There are also in all large towns in France, and to a more limited extent in other countries, numerous evening *conferences* and *cours*, on almost every subject of interest in art, science and literature, which workmen have the opportunity of attending, as they are entirely gratuitous. Amongst these, the most remarkable are the lectures given by eminent men at the *Conservatoire des Arts et Metiers*, of Paris. Most of these institutions are of the nature of lectures rather than of classes for practical instruction. There are, however, in many places, excellent and numerously attended evening and Sunday technical classes, more especially in Belgium and Austria; and there can be no doubt that the instruction thus given is already exerting a considerable influence on the capacity and intelligence of the workmen, and that this influence will be increasingly felt in the future.

For instruction in drawing, as applied mainly to decorative work in France, and to both constructive and decorative work in Belgium, the opportunities are excellent. The crowded schools of drawing, modeling, carving and painting, maintained at the expense of the municipalities of Paris, Lyons, Brussels, and other cities, — absolutely gratuitous, and open to all comers, well lighted, furnished with the best models, and under the care of teachers full of enthusiasm, — stimulate those manufactures and crafts in which the fine arts play a prominent part, to a degree which is without parallel in this country.

In our own country, as usual, the lead has been taken by private philanthropy. We have had, for many years, most valuable provisions for evening-work in some of our leading cities. The Franklin Institute, in Philadelphia, founded in 1824, has, during sixty years, provided evening-classes, securing instruction in drawing on three evenings in each week. A progressive course, covering mechanical, architectural and topographical drawing, both freehand and instrumental, has been laid out, reaching through a period of three years. Special classes in machine-drawing have been lately started. The institute also provides courses of lectures on subjects connected with the callings of its members,— geology, the rise and progress of manufactures, the microscope and its wonders, engineering, mechanics, chemistry, astronomy, machine-design and construction, silk and its culture, photography, etc. The institute has a valuable library, containing upwards of 15,000 volumes, which is said to embrace one of the most valuable collections in the country upon science and art. There is a membership of 2,000. Its income is $15,000 per annum, largely from invested funds. Another excellent Philadelphia institution of a similar nature is the Spring Garden Institute.

One of the best-known institutions in the country is the Cooper Union, for the advancement of science and art. Its instruction consists of a free library and reading-room, free lectures during the winter, an evening-school of science, and an evening-school of art. There are also, in addition, a day-school of art for women, a school of art for amateurs, a school for wood-engraving, and a school for telegraphy. The evening-school of science embraces fifteen classes, developing the ordinary common-school education in the direction of mathematics, mechanics, engineering and chemistry. The night-school of art embraces classes in drawing, — rudimental, mechanical, architectural, form and figure, perspective and ornamental,— decorative designing, and modeling in clay. Lectures to the classes are also given. The science-classes were attended in 1882 by nearly a thousand students, and the art-classes in the same year by upwards of twelve hundred students. This institute, as everyone knows, is the princely benefaction of Mr. Peter Cooper. The Mechanics' Institute, of Cincinnati, established in 1829, has similar aims, and pursues similar methods. It sustains a reading-room, courses of lectures, evening drawing-schools, evening-classes in geometry and mathematics, and in elementary physics and mechanics, lectures, and meetings for the discussion of questions in science. Such institutions indicate the natural tendency of general industrial education to reach out into more specific technical training, — a training which will fit pupils for practical success in special crafts and trades.

The Women's Institute of Technical Design, New York; the Society for Decorative Art, New York; the Young Women's Christian Association, New York, — and other similar associations, present interesting experiments towards supplying the need of advanced industrial training for young women.

These private philanthropies have had a sufficient length of life, and have secured sufficient results to call for the State's action in this direction. The State has, some time since, moved tentatively towards the taking up of evening instruction. Night-schools of one kind and another have been for many years a recognized branch of the work of our boards of education in many cities. For the most part, however, these night-schools have aimed at supplementing the work of the day-schools foı a lower class of children than these schools reached, — the waifs of our great cities. The instruction offered has, therefore, been rather of the nature of a rudimentary general education than of an advanced industrial education. In a number of instances, however, night-schools have been provided for this need which we are now considering, and their result has been fairly encouraging.

In two of the evening-schools of St. Louis, in which there is an average attendance of about 200, the branches taught are such as form an elementary polytechnic course of studies. Boston had six evening drawing-schools in 1880, with an average attendance of about 300. The instruction that it offered gave a choice of four courses, — freehand design, machine-drawing, building construction and ship-building. Worcester reports evening drawing-schools, consisting of beginners and advanced classes in both freehand and instrumental drawing, — the students being, for the most part, young men and women engaged in mechanical or artistic callings, or in teaching.

IV. Trade-Schools. — When all such general instruction and training has been secured, there will still remain the need of yet more specific technical education, for the best success of individual handicraftsmen and for the general prosperity of an industrial people. Trades must be thoroughly taught, at once as to the principles involved and the methods used in them. Trade-schools may be supplied in many ways. Workingmen themselves, when they have awakened to the importance of such schools, may provide them. As the old-time guilds supplied such trade-training, so our modern trades-unions might supply it, partially, at least. They have among them the men who are competent to act as instructors in such trade-schools. The means also need not be lacking, as such schools could be made, from the start, either partially or wholly self-sustaining. By founding such schools themselves, our unions would secure the control of the supply for their several trades, and thus would win a power far superior to that which they now possess. There are, however, as yet very few indications that workingmen are awakening to the importance of such action. An association of clockmakers in Paris provides for the technical training of apprentices; and a plumbers' union in our own country arranges for the instruction of lads who are looking forward to becoming plumbers; but there are not many examples of this wise action discernible.

Trade-Schools Founded by Private Philanthropy. — Private philanthropy has already moved to supply such schools, especially in our own land.

The Hampton Normal and Agricultural Institute, Hampton, Va., is a practical demonstration of the possibility of combining general education with industrial training, carried to a point of thorough technical mastery. It owes its foundation to the large-minded and large-hearted idea of General Armstrong, who, when his duties in the War of the Rebellion were ended, looked about him for the next great work to be done for the country, and singled out the education of the race just emancipated in the South as his mission. The problem was that of giving the blacks a general education, and of training them in habits of work, while teaching them the mastery of trades in which self-support might be won. From this germ-thought there has slowly grown the splendid institution which, by the shores of the Hampton Roads, practically solves the problem of industrial education. In this school, Negroes and Indians of both sexes are well grounded in a general education, and effectively trained in various crafts. Students are admitted between fourteen and twenty-five years of age. The time devoted each day to manual work is arranged according to occupations. Those engaged in farming are employed either half-time or wholly for four days, with two whole days for their studies. The departments cover farming, wheel-wrighting, saw-mill and wood-working, engineering, the work of the machine-shop, knitting, printing, shoe-making, carpentry, turning, harness-making, sewing, tailoring, cooking and household-work. The work of these various shops is made to contribute substantially to the support of the institution,—thus insuring sufficiently good workmanship to command a market for the products of the institution. Pretty much all the work required for maintaining and adding to the institute is done on the ground by the students. The school numbers about one thousand officers and students. The success of the work in the general development of manhood and womanhood is best indicated by the constantly increasing demand for its graduates as teachers; thus effectively and practically disproving the prejudice that so much training of the hand interferes with the best training of the head. The support of the school is provided for in part by grants from the State of Virginia, but chiefly by the philanthropic contributions of its Northern friends, filled out by the income from the trade-shops of the institution.

One notable feature of the schools is the fact that the youths who are found indisposed to more purely intellectual studies have their energies turned into practical channels. The greater part of their training is made industrial.

Of trade-schools pure and simple, the New York Trade-School presents a fine illustration. This was founded five years ago, by the wise philanthropy of Colonel R. T. Auchmuty. His aim was to secure, through day and evening-classes, thorough instruction in the principles, and as thorough practice in the methods, of some of the more important trades; and, while not making the school a charity, to put the cost of its education at a figure low enough to enable any average young man to avail himself of its advantages. Evening instruction is offered in plumbing, gas-fitting, brick-laying, plastering, stone-cutting, fresco-painting, wood-carving and carpentry. Day-classes are open for instruction in plumbing, brick-laying and wood-carving. The instruction is at once scientific and practical. Skilled workmen in the various trades are the instructors. The school-shops provide every facility for the work carried on in them. The full course in plumbing and gas-fitting, for example, which includes the day-school and evening-classes, reaches over three months, and can be had for $35.00. The evening-school in carpentry, which has three sessions a week, from October 25th to April 6th, charges $15.00 for the full course. The attendance of the schools has steadily increased from 30 in the first year to 88 in the second, 207 in the third, 298 in the fourth, and 304 in the fifth year. The results, according to the latest report of the school, "have proved the success of what was at first an experiment in industrial education. Many young men who came to the schools without knowing how to work are now skilled mechanics, receiving high wages." Perhaps the best testimony to the success of the school is the changed attitude of some of the trades-unions towards it. How widespread a want is met by such a school is sufficiently indicated by the fact that its students have come not only from surrounding towns, but from distant States. No one fact could more strikingly illustrate the appreciation shown towards this school than the statement of the founder of the school, that, at the end of five years, it can be said that "there has not been a bit of wanton injury done to the building or its tools,—not even a pencil-mark on the walls." Mr. Auchmuty speaks in private with the greatest satisfaction of the practical success of the work. He says: "I have now a record of many young men, who, to use the expression of more than one of them, owe their success in life to the school."

Trade-Schools Founded by Business Houses and Communities.—In nearly all the great industrial centres of Great Britain,—London, Glasgow, Manchester, Liverpool, Oldham, Leeds, Bradford, Huddersfield, Keighley, Sheffield, Nottingham, Birmingham, etc.,—more or less flourishing schools of science and art, of various grades, together with many art and science-classes exist; some of these schools developing into genuine trade-schools. Such, for example, are the schools established by Sir W. Armstrong, at Elswick, by the London & Northwestern Railway Co., at Crewe, and those of Messrs. Mather & Platt, Salford, in connection with their engineering works. This latter serves as a specimen of these schools. It is a private technical evening-school, established and supported by the firm for the benefit of their apprentices. The drawings are of work actually in progress in the establishment. The teacher lectures upon them, explains them, and makes calculations concerning them; and the boys, the next day, at the works, see the very things which they have been hearing about in the shop. Everything required, patterns and models, is here shown in full size. The teachers are the draughtsmen in the establishment. The boys are not allowed to copy drawings, everything being drawn on a different scale from a flat copy. The heads of this establishment consider that this school has been "an incalculable advantage."

The Bradford Technical College is an illustration of wise action on the part of an industrial town. Its foundation was the result of the public sentiment in the business community of Bradford, as to the necessity of greater technical knowledge in the various industries on which the prosperity of the district depends. The college was founded to secure such instruction in the principles underlying these industries. It has developed into departments for pure art, designing, weaving, chemistry and dyeing, mechanical engineering, and the sciences connected with the building and other mechanical trades. There are mechanical and dyeing laboratories, weaving-shops, and mechanical workshops. There is also a handsome lecture-hall, capable of holding six hundred persons, and a large museum for textiles, raw materials, natural objects, etc., and, finally, a large, well-furnished reading-room. The art department is under the charge of Mr. Walter Smith, well known to us in our country as the art-director of the State Schools of Massachusetts and of the Normal Art College, in Boston. The textile department covers instruction in the manufacture of textile fabrics of every description, including the nature and properties of the raw material, and the application of design to woven fabrics. Few weaving-schools in any country are so well equipped with all the best appliances of instruction, or so largely attended. Nearly three hundred students attend these classes. The majority of those who come in the evening are workingmen or over-lookers, while the day-classes are attended by the sons of manufacturers. In the chemical and dyeing departments, students are grounded in the principles of chemistry, which they apply to the investigation of the properties and uses of the various dyeing materials, by analysis and by practical experiments. In the engineering and machine departments, the theory of the class-room is united with the practical experience of the bench, lathe and forge. It is questionable whether there is any school-workshop in any country—so say the Royal Commissioners—as well fitted up with modern mechanical tools and appliances. In the general science department, there are classes in practical, plane and solid geometry, mathematics, physics, chemistry, steam, applied mechanics and machine instruction. The especial feature of the college is the day-school, in which there are one hundred and thirty pupils, whose ages vary from twelve to seventeen. This department acts as a feeder to the college, preparing the students for the technical classes. The curriculum of the school covers: (1.) a general course, including English, mathematics, mechanics, chemistry, physics, drawing (freehand, model and geometrical), and machine instruction; (2.) a technical course, in which the pupil may select a line of study from the following branches: mechanical engineering, art, pattern-making, designing, weaving and dyeing; (3.) languages, including French, German and Latin. The pupils who are studying technological subjects receive one or two lessons a week from the various specialists, and spend, in addition, several hours each week in the weaving-shops, workshops, dye-houses or art-rooms, as the case may be. An important feature in connection with the day-school is the scholarship scheme, whereby, from a fund subscribed by manufacturers, merchants and others, about sixty boys of the artisan population are taken from the elementary schools of the town, by competition, and receive two years' instruction in the school, free of charge. All the instructors in the college and school are of recognized eminence in their departments. In the several departments, there are altogether nearly nine hundred students.

On the Continent, there are many similar institutions. One of the best illustrations of private sagacity in this respect is the *Ecole professionnale*, of the printing establishment under the management of Messieurs Chaix et Cie. This school was founded by the heads of the establishment, to train skilled workmen for that establishment. The foundation of the school is laid in a special primary course, for those whose previous schooling had been insufficient. Upon this foundation, there is laid a technical course, which covers grammar and composition, reading proofs and correcting for the press, the study of different kinds of types and engraving, and the reading and composing of English, German, Latin and Greek,—in the latter case, from a purely typographical point of view, without any attempt to understand or translate. Finally, it completes a supplementary course, which includes the history of printing, simple notions of economics, a little mechanics and physics and chemistry. In the latter field, the materials dealt with in the business are specially considered,— such as acids, oxides, oils, carbons, soda, etc. This school has some thirty apprentices connected with it. The apprenticeship lasts four years.

In Germany, we find schools for miners and for workers in iron and steel, founded or maintained by business associations. In several of the more important industrial centres of the Continent, there exists societies, such as the *Societes industrielles*, of Mulhouse, Rheims and Amiens; the *Societe d'enseignement professionnel du Rhone*, which has its head quarters at Lyons; and the *Niederoesterreichischer Gewerbe-Verein*, of Austria. These associations are supported mainly by the merchants and manufacturers of the district to which their operations are restricted. They are also further aided from the municipalities, and sometimes from the State. The society in Lyons has established numerous evening-classes for elementary and technical instruction. The South Austrian Trade Society, which has its central office in Vienna, has organized technical day and evening-schools for operatives of every grade. These have now passed under State control, and receive subventions from the government. Chemnitz, in Saxony, has achieved an enviable reputation for its large-minded and large-hearted public spirit in connection with industrial education; and the results have been full of encouragement, — Chemnitz having been rapidly built up, in consequence of these schools. Crefield is another town which has followed a similar policy, with similar results.

Our country furnishes some examples of the same wise policy on the part of individual employers and business corporations, — though, as yet, we have scarcely any parallel case of a municipality devoting itself to statesmanlike measures on behalf of industrial education. The establishment founded by Mr. Richard M. Hoe, so widely known through the country, has sought a high degree of skill and intelligence and of conscientious work, such as is not easily secured in these days of nominal apprenticeships. It has need of men who, beginning early, purpose to devote their whole lives to the acquisition of technical skill, and to its broadening by a liberal intellectual training. Two or three hundred boys are required in the establishment. These have been carefully selected with reference to their capacity and dispositions. As soon as secured, the firm begins to educate them. It provides an evening-school, where the common-school education is supplemented, with special reference to the practical needs of life. Everything is provided by the firm, — rooms, teachers, books and materials; but attendance is compulsory. The boys are chiefly trained in mathematics and mechanical drawing. Each boy's special capacity or tendency is considered in determining his particular course. If he has a gift for mechanical drawing, it is specially cultivated to fit him for work in the designing department; and thus with other faculties; the aim being so to train each lad that he shall have a

VETERAN CORPS, KNIGHTS OF LABOR.

chance to make the most out of himself, and thus the most for the firm. Advancement is made wholly upon merit,—no time being fixed for continuing in any stage of work. A practical application of the principles inculcated in the night-school is secured in the work of the establishment by day. As most of the boys live far from the factory, the firm provides them with a plain, plentiful and wholesome supper.

The Carriage-builders' National Association has established a technical school for carriage-mechanics, which was opened in the fall of 1880. It is located at 214 East Thirty-fourth street, in connection with the Metropolitan Museum of Art-Schools. Three evening-lessons are given each week. In addition to the class-instruction, it provides lectures upon mechanical topics, a technical library and museum. It gives students who have shown special aptitude and application a printed certificate,—a sort of diploma,—which must be invaluable as a security of work. Its pupils have come from a wide area,—from Ohio, Kentucky, Iowa, Massachusetts and Canada,—and have represented the various departments of work in the industry. The tuition-fee is placed at the nominal rate of five dollars for the season.

Trade-Schools Founded or Supported by the State.—Paris has thirteen technical schools, which turn out young men possessing sufficient knowledge of a trade, both theoretical and practical, to enable them to earn their livelihood. Pupils must be thirteen years old, and must pass an examination in order to enter. The period of training extends over three years. During the first twelve months, the pupil remains a certain time in each of the different workshops representing the respective branches of trade. Thus an insight is obtained into each craft, and the disposition of the student is developed, while his abilities are being educated. Four hours a day are spent in the different classes, where French, English, history, grammar, chemistry, geography, drawing, etc., are taught. In the first division only four hours daily are devoted to manual labor in the workshops, and two hours to books. The schools have half a dozen shops, under the superintendence of able, technical men. There is a modeling-room, a blacksmith-shop, a fitting-room, wood and metal-turneries, and several carpenters' and joiners' shops, where every branch of these trades can be learned. It is proposed to open a practical college in each *arrondissement*, and workshops are to be attached to each of the municipal schools. France has developed complete apprenticeship schools, as notably those of La Villette, in Paris, and Havre. The National Government and various municipal authorities have combined in founding these schools in different towns of France. The government commission, appointed in 1881, has drawn up a programme for handicraft-schools through the country.

Objections have been raised against such apprenticeship-schools by practical men in England; but the French appear to be, upon the whole, satisfied with the progress that has been made through them.

In our own country, there is not a single trade-school for the rank and file of labor which owes its existence to any municipal or State government, or to the National Government. Congress has indeed made large land-grants in aid of industrial education; but, whatever may have been its intentions, these grants have practically resulted in building up agricultural schools and schools for higher technical training in a few semi-professional lines. This has been quite natural, under the circumstances, since agriculture and engineering have been the most imperative necessities of our new country; but, nonetheless the fact remains that we have not a single State trade-school for the average workingman.

V. Higher Technical Schools for Foremen and Managers.—A higher grade of technical schools for the training of lads fitted to become foremen, becomes a necessity in the development of industrial education. Europe has recognized this need, and taken steps to meet it.

France made experiments in this direction some time ago; but these experiments amounted to little until their reorganization within the last generation. Among the good examples of schools for foremen are those of Winterthur, in Switzerland, Chemnitz, in Saxony, and Komotau, in Austria, and the *Ecole des Mines*, at St. Etienne. The theoretic instruction in these schools is similar in character and also in grade to that of the great polytechnic schools. Great attention is paid in them to practical instruction in laboratories and workshops, which is not always the case in the polytechnic schools. A beginning has been made in Prussia toward the establishment of such secondary technical schools. The *Industrie Schulen*, in Bavaria, corresponds to this second grade of technical high schools, giving both theoretical and practical instruction in some cases,—the latter being highly specialized, as a preparation either for direct entrance on an industrial career or for further study in the polytechnic school. France is establishing technical schools of this type all through the country, a good example of which is found in the school at Rheims.

This school was established in 1875, as the result of the investigation of a municipal commission, composed of the leading business men of the city, concerning the need of higher industrial education. The school is housed in a building which has cost $120,000. Boys enter at about thirteen, and continue for three years. During the fiist two years, all the pupils pass through the same course of theoretical and practical instruction. In the third year, boys are divided into sections, according to the aptitude displayed by them during the previous years. The classification is made according to the different pursuits carried on in Rheims and the neighborhood, — manufactures, mechanics, commerce, agriculture, etc.

The workshops and laboratories are large, airy and well-lighted; and their character will be sufficiently indicated by a description of one of the workshops.

The weaving and spinning-sheds contain a carding-engine, a drawing-frame, a spinning-frame with forty spindles, a warping-machine, nine small pattern-weaving looms, four jacquard looms, a punching and card-cutting machine, and four power-looms, each of a different type, and of the most recent construction. In this department, the student is able, practically, to apply his theoretical instruction to the production of the various textile manufactures of Rheims. He can, in fact, spin and weave the wool he has himself washed, carded, dyed and prepared; and can, moreover, practice each operation in the school with similar plant to that which he would find in the regular factory. This department is provided with a large collection of woven fabrics and samples of raw materials.

The school also provides thorough instruction in drawing, and, yet further, has an admirable school-museum. It has about two hundred pupils, and has a large number of free studentships.

The schools of which the Rheims school is a type lead up to the *École des Arts et Métiers*, at Châlons-sur-Marne, or the *École Centrale*, or the *École Polytechnique*. Such technical high schools for foremen are practically provided in some parts of England, in the schools of art and science which have of late grown into such large proportions in certain industrial centres, — of which examples have already been given in other connections.

VI. Polytechnic Schools. — There will still remain the need of yet higher technical schools, for the instruction and training of those who expect to become heads of industrial establishments, superintendents, managers, etc., and for the education of men for the professional branches of business, industrial chemistry, engineering, etc.

Such colleges have existed for some time in Europe, in the well-known Polytechnique Schools, to which she owes so much of her industrial prosperity.

As already indicated, greater provision has been made for such higher technical training in our country than for any other department of industrial education. We have begun at the top instead of at the bottom, and have put a roof on a structure that has no foundation.

The Massachusetts Institute of Technology, Boston, in addition to teaching mining, mechanical and civil-engineering, provides instruction in the mechanic arts to students who come from the ordinary public schools at sixteen years of age, and secures them a two years' course in technical training. This institution, one of the most completely appointed in the country, offers for this class of students courses in machine-construction, pattern-making, moulding, forging, etc. But as the fees are $200 per annum, the average workingman's son is practically shut out from the benefits of this admirable institution. The Worcester Free School confines its education principally to the theory and practice of mechanical engineering.

The Stevens Institute, of Hoboken, was founded by Mr. E. A. Stevens, as an institution for thorough technical and scientific training in mechanical engineering, in which it stands very high. The Cornell University provides, in addition to a general liberal education, technical schools in agriculture, mechanic arts, civil engineering and mining engineering. The mechanic arts are taught experimentally, by the aid of a brass and iron-foundry, blacksmith-shop and shops for pattern-making. Purdue University, Indiana, supplies another excellent illustration of a high school of industrial education, as does the Kansas University.

VII. High Schools of Industrial Art. — So many industries really enter the field of applied art, that it is becoming increasingly necessary to foster a higher development of artistic tastes and powers than the lower-grade schools can secure. Every country is feeling the need of increasing the supply of industrial artists.

The provision made for this need, in the great art-schools of Europe, is comparatively familiar to us in this country; and, as space is shrinking, no detailed reference to it will here be made. We are naturally backward in this respect. Such high schools of art can only be expected to arise in sufficient numbers as our general system of education increasingly emphasizes industrial art. We have, however, a few such schools already; as, *e. g.*, the Philadelphia School of Design for Women, the Normal Art-School of Massachusetts, in Boston, the Fine-Art School connected with the Gallery of Fine Arts, in Boston, and the Metropolitan School of Art, in New York.

The constant tendency in these schools is for pupils of any ability to become ambitious of turning out artists, of whom there is already quite an ample supply, of one sort and another, in the country. These schools should keep strenuously before them that nobler aim, with reference to the country at large, of imbuing the artisan with the spirit of the artist.

VIII. A Central Model-School of Industrial Science and Art. — What is needed, over and above such scattered local efforts, is a largely conceived and thoroughly planned and amply endowed system for stimulating and guiding the scientific and artistic departments of industrial education in their higher stages. As already indicated, the Continental States direct, from a central ministry, their systems of industrial education, — thus securing the thoroughness which otherwise might be lacking. What needs to be done, and what it is possible to do, is best seen in the case of the South Kensington Museum, of England.

This famous institution, as every one knows, was the outgrowth of the first World's Fair, in London. That international exhibition revealed so clearly the inferiority of England in all artistic industries as to lead to this attempt to educate the nation's workers. It includes a vast national industrial museum, central schools for scientific and artistic instruction, and local branches in various towns, through which it guides the industrial education of England. The results of this wise action, in one generation, have been astonishing. Whereas, in 1851, England had found herself at the bottom of the list of nations engaged in art-manufactures, as soon thereafter as 1867, in the Paris Exhibition, she found herself in the foremost rank, having in some lines distanced the most artistic nations.

There is no question that the chief factor in this astonishing change was the influence of the South Kensington Museum. Professor Dresser is the authority for the statement that —

> Our art-schools and this museum have exerted a more and more powerful influence over the manufacturers, the designers and the native buyers of our productions; and the result has been such as to cause the late Emperor of the French to say, after the International Exhibition of Paris, in 1867, that while the French had made little progress during the ten preceding years, the advancement of the English in art, as applied to industries, had been so rapid that England must be regarded as a dangerous rival.

How such an industrial revolution could be brought about by the founding of one national institution, let the following facts as to its progress tell. In 1851, there were nineteen schools of art in the United Kingdom; now there are over one thousand schools of art and art-classes, and of a much higher standard of success than in 1851, while industrial drawing is now taught in the national schools.

IX. Industrial Museums.—Such a large and thorough system of industrial education needs to have provided the adjunct of industrial museums. The need of such museums is obvious. Seeing is understanding, as well as believing. Description never makes the clear-cut impression that the sight of an object and the handling of it creates. The tools and machinery used in an industry should be somewhere open to examination; the materials used in that industry should be arranged in the order of their use, and the articles produced in the various stages of production should be on exhibition; while models for the young student and workman should be conveniently accessible. Mr. William Morris is as capable of giving an able and authoritative judgment upon this matter as any living man, and he testified before the Royal Commissioners that he considered it an absolute necessity that there should be a collection of examples of the manufactures of each district, accessible in that district; and not only specimens of that special manufacture, but selections of beautiful objects in other manufactures, which the workman might thus study. In his judgment each locality should, therefore, establish its own museum. In addition to this, he regarded it as necessary that there should be a great central museum, to which visits could be made, and wherein some thorough study could be carried on by workmen from different parts of the country,—a museum which should really furnish all needful illustrations in the various departments of scientific and industrial art.

The South Kensington Museum well illustrates what such a great central national museum should be:—

The collections at South Kensington Museum now comprise: (1.) Objects of ornamental art, as applied to manufactures; (2.) The National Art Library; (3.) British pictures, sculptures and engravings; (4.) The Educational Library, with appliances and models; (5.) Materials and models for building and construction; (6.) Substances used for food; (7.) Reproduction by means of casting, electrotype, and photography, of objects displaying the art-manufactures of all nations; (8.) Naval models.

The Museum of Ornamental Art comprises upwards of 20,000 objects. *The National Art Library* contains about 33,000 volumes. *The Collection of British Pictures* now numbers 585 oil-paintings, and 1,005 water-color drawings,—specimens of the best British masters, nearly all contributed by private individuals for the advancement of the public art-education of this country. *The Department of Sculpture* is very large and valuable, and consists chiefly of decorative sculpture of the Renaissance period, in marble, stone and terra-cotta, including numerous specimens of glazed terra-cotta of the fifteenth century, known as Della Robbia ware. *The Educational Collection* has now, by means of voluntary contributions of the publishers of educational works, and by the aid of the State, become a very important branch of the South Kensington Museum; seeing that its library contains upwards of 20,000 volumes of educational books, while the collection of models and appliances for educational purposes numbers some thousands of specimens. *The Department of Materials for Building and Construction* comprises samples of building-stones, cements, terra-cottas, brick fire-proof floors, ornamental tiles, enameled slate, specimens of woods for construction, etc.

As an evidence of the popular appreciation of this museum, one fact will suffice. The attendance at the museum increased from 104,832 in 1854 to 914,127 in 1874. In three years, between 1869 and 1874, the attendance averaged over 1,000,000 per annum.*

A fine example of the local industrial museum is found in quaint old Nuremberg. Edinburgh has also a fine science and art museum. The Industrial Society of Mulhouse has established such a local museum, and the leading manufacturers of the place testify that it has exerted a most beneficial

* The above statements are drawn from the "Memorandum on the Formation of the South Kensington Museum," by P. Cunliffe Owen, British Commissioner to the Centennial Exhibition, Philadelphia, 1876.

influence upon the industry of the district. Some go so far as to say that they cannot see how the trade can prosper without it. To the designer, it is a constant source of instruction,—his library. It cultivates and raises the taste of the working-man, sharpens the wits of the manufacturer, and is a constant register of the relative progress of the competing countries. It gives invaluable assistance in such lines as the application of historic styles to current wants.

In our own country, the only serious attempt at providing for this need in any local centre of industry grew out of the Centennial Exhibition in Philadelphia. The beautiful Memorial Hall, then erected, was subsequently set aside as an industrial art-museum, under the auspices of the Pennsylvania Museum and School of Industrial Art. The museum is, however, but poorly supplied with objects, and seems to languish for want of any real interest on the part of the city or the State. The foundations have not as yet been laid for our future National Museum of Industrial Art.

Such museums should themselves form a graduated series. There should be small school-museums attached to our public schools, each city having a central museum, from which the different ward-schools could be supplied by loan collections. Around these museums the industries of each great city might gather; each industry having its own department. The various States should then have their central museums, and the National Government its museum for the common country.

X. Cost of Such a System of Industrial Education.—The chief difficulty in the way of such an elaborate system of industrial education is, of course, its immense expensiveness. It is obvious, without entering into any detail, that for the development of such a large system, vast sums of money will have to be expended; yet this should not stand in the way of such a beneficent reform. Chemnitz, in Saxony, which has developed, perhaps, more extensively than almost any other Continental town a local system of industrial education, is taxed more heavily than any city of Germany, with one exception; yet the burden is cheerfully borne, because the people have learned the pecuniary value of their system of industrial training. Situated amid great natural resources, its life was sluggish and its prosperity scant, until the foundations of this system were laid. Now it teems with schools of industry, in which weaving, architecture, agriculture, mechanical arts and miscellaneous crafts are thoroughly taught, — each one contributing directly to build up the town. It flourishes upon this basis of wise outlay for educational purposes. The manufacturing cities of other countries are discovering that their specialties are being produced cheaply and artistically in Chemnitz. Already Nottingham has yielded to it the front rank in the production and sale of gloves. Taxation for pauperism, disease and crime is reduced proportionately to the increase of taxation for education; and the citizens, upon the whole, believe that they make by the exchange. We have only need in this country to examine the statistics of public taxation and of private charity, necessitated by our problems of pauperism and vice and crime, to realize that such an outlay as would be necessitated for a thorough system of industrial education would be most economical. It is a notorious fact that a large portion of our criminals are generally uneducated, and that a still larger portion of them have lacked any adequate training whereby they could secure their self-support. Dr. Wines reported that in Baden, while only four per cent. of prisoners are unable to read when received, fifty per cent. have not learned a trade. Such a system would also develop the resources of the country in a manner transcending our present imagination; and, in the aggregate wealth thus created, the expenditures for industrial education would be amply compensated. A nation which, while paying off its national debt in a manner absolutely unprecedented in history, is yet accumulating a surplus revenue which its statesmen (?) do not know how to use, cannot well plead poverty as the excuse for not laying the foundation of a system of industrial education commensurate with its destined greatness. Better far such a system of fortification than the most elaborate coast defences.

CHAPTER XXIII.

THE LAND QUESTION.

Magnitude of the Question — First Principles — The Land-Owner the Absolute Master of Men who must Live on his Land — The Order of Nature Inverted — Equal Rights to the Use of the Earth — Selfishness, the Evil Genius of Man — The Irish People Forced to Beg Permission to Till the Soil — Appropriation of the Church-Lands — Land in Itself Has No Value — The Great Cause of the Unequal Distribution of Wealth — No Hope for the Laborer, so Long as Private Property in Land Exists — Nothing Mysterious about the Labor Question — The Difficulty in Finding Employment — Nature Offers Freely to Labor — Natural Means of Employment Monopolized — Speculation in the Bounties of Nature.

BENEATH all the great social questions of our time lies one of primary and universal importance, — the question of the rights of men to the use of the earth.

The magnitude of the pecuniary interests involved, the fact that the influential classes in all communities where private property in land exists are interested in its maintenance, lead to a disposition to ignore or belittle the land question: but it is impossible to give any satisfactory explanation of the most important social phenomena without reference to it; and the growing unrest of the masses of all civilized countries, under conditions which they feel to be galling and unjust, must at length lead them, as the only way of securing the rights of labor, to turn to the land question.

To see that the land question does involve the problem of the equitable distribution of wealth; that it lies at the root of all the vexed social questions of our time, and is, indeed, but another name for the great labor question in all its phases, it is only needful to revert to first principles, and to consider the relations between men and the planet they inhabit.

We find ourselves on the surface of a sphere, circling

through immeasurable space. Beneath our feet, the diameter of the planet extends for eight thousand miles; above our heads night reveals countless points of light, which science tells us are suns, that blaze billions of miles away. In this inconceivably vast universe, we are confined to the surface of our sphere, as the mariner in mid-ocean is confined to the deck of his ship. We are limited to that line where the exterior of the planet meets the atmospheric envelope that surrounds it. We may look beyond, but cannot pass. We are not denizens of one element, like the fish; but while our bodies must be upheld by one element, they must be laved in another. We live *on* the earth, and *in* the air. In the search for minerals men are able to descend for a few thousand feet into the earth's crust, provided communication with the surface be kept open, and air thus supplied; and in balloons men have ascended to like distances above the surface; but on a globe of thirty-five feet diameter, this range would be represented by the thickness of a sheet of paper. And though it is thus possible for man to ascend for a few thousand feet above the surface, or to descend for a few thousand feet below it, it is only on the surface of the earth that he can habitually live and supply his wants; nor can he do this on all parts of the surface of the globe, but only on that smaller part, which we call land, as distinguished from the water, while considerable parts even of the land are uninhabitable by him.

By constructing vessels of materials obtained from land, and provisioning them with the produce of land, it is true that man is able to traverse the fluid-surface of the globe; yet he is none the less dependent upon land. If the land of the globe were again to be submerged, human life could not long be maintained on the best-appointed ships.

Man, in short, is a land-animal. Physically considered, he is as much a product of land as is the tree. His body, composed of materials drawn from land, can only be maintained by nutriment furnished by land; and all the processes by which he secures food, clothing and shelter consist but in the working up of land or the products of land. Labor is possible only on condition of access to land, and all human production is but the union of land and labor, — the transportation or transformation of previously existing matter into places or forms suited to the satisfaction of man's needs.

Land, being thus indispensable to man, the most important of social adjustments is that which fixes the relations between men with regard to that element. Where all are accorded equal rights to the use of the earth, no one needs ask another to give him employment, and no one can stand in fear of being deprived of the opportunity to make a living. In such a community, there could be no "labor question." There could be neither degrading poverty nor demoralizing wealth. And the personal independence arising from such a condition of equality, in respect to the ability to get a living, must give character to all social and political institutions.

On the other hand, inequality of privilege in the use of the earth must beget inequality of wealth and power, — must divide men into those who can command and those who are forced to serve. The rewards which nature yields to labor no longer go to the laborers in proportion to industry and skill; but a privileged class are enabled to live without labor by compelling a disinherited class to give up some part of their earnings for permission to live and work. Thus the order of nature is inverted, — those who do no work become rich, and "workingman" becomes synonymous with "poor man." Material progress tends to monstrous wealth on one side, and abject poverty on the other; and society is differentiated into masters and servants, rulers and ruled.

If one man were permitted to claim the land of the world as his individual property, he would be the absolute master of all humanity. All the rest of mankind could live only by his permission, and under such conditions as he chose to prescribe. So, if one man be permitted to treat as his own the land of any country, he becomes the absolute sovereign of its people. Or, if the land of a country be made the property of a class, a ruling aristocracy is created, who soon begin to regard themselves, and to be regarded, as of nobler blood and superior rights. That "God will think twice before he damns people of quality," is the natural feeling of those who are taught to believe that the land on which all must live is legitimately their private property.

Here is the explanation of the main facts of human history. In the land question, we find the great key to the differences of political, social, industrial, and even religious development, —the reason of the growth of monarchies and aristocracies, of the degradation of base and servile classes, the cause of wars and tumults and social conflicts. The equality of men is not a dream of latter-day visionaries. It is the order of nature. Men come into the world of like shape, with like members and like wants; and the differences of physical and mental power among them are but individual variations from a common standard, which, comparatively small in normal humanity, are largely, if not entirely, offset by compensations. And nature treats all men with strict impartiality. She will give to the noble no more readily than to the serf. Fire will burn, and water will drown, the king as surely as the peasant. The sun shines and the rain falls on the just and the unjust alike. The first perceptions of man are always those of human equality.

> "When Adam delved and Eve span,
> Who was then the gentleman?"

The man of gentle or noble blood,—the man entitled to reap without sowing, to consume while others produce, to command while others obey,—never could exist where the equal rights of men to the use of the earth were acknowledged. He is the product of a system that makes the land on which a whole people must live, the property of a portion of their number. For they who thus become earth-owners are enabled to levy a toll for the use of nature's bounty, to prescribe terms on which alone other men can live. They become the land-lords, or land-gods of these other men,—beings who deem themselves of superior mould, and who look down upon their fellows as born to a life of toil for their pleasure.

"He that will not work, neither shall he eat." This is the decree of nature, that with every human mouth brings two human hands into the world, and ordains that human wants shall only be satisfied by labor. But that selfishness which is the evil genius of man, has always prompted the strong and cunning to endeavor to escape the necessity of laboring by compelling their fellows to do their work for them. Of the devices to this end, the two most important have been that of making property of men, and that of making property of land. Chattel-slavery, however, is but a rude and primitive method of systematically robbing labor, profitable only in countries of sparse population, or when it is desired to remove the laborers to another place. Where the population is dense enough, the easier and more convenient way of enslaving a whole people and of more conveniently appropriating their labor, is to appropriate their lands, since they can in this way be compelled to yield their labor or its produce in return for the mere privilege of living. Thus the Norman Conqueror did not distribute the people of England among his freebooters: — he distributed English land. Thus, the adventurers who, at subsequent times, passed over into Ireland, did not seek to enslave the Irish people, but to secure Irish land. Once masters of Irish land, the Irish people were forced to beg permission to till it for them; and, instead of having to chase runaway slaves, they had, in the power of eviction, a means of coercion by which they could extract from the laborer all he could possibly give.

The natural perception of mankind is that of the equality of rights to the use of the earth; and it is probable that private property in land, like chattel-slavery, has nowhere originated save in war and conquest. But when this means of appropriating labor once obtains a footing, it becomes a potent means for the enslavement, by the cunning of men of their own blood. This process, of which the history of ancient Rome gives us a complete example, has been going on in England and Scotland for some centuries, in the appropriation of the church-lands, the changing into individual property of the land held on feudal rents by tenants of the State, the enclosure of commons, the conversion of the tribal holdings of Highland clans into individual property of the chiefs, and the substitution of large proprietors for small freeholders. It is going on to-day in the United States, in the fencing in of the public domain, and the steady relative decrease of the land-owning class. That a man can draw an income of so many thousands of dollars from the ownership of American soil, means that so many American citizens must yield up to him the produce of their labor, — are virtually his slaves.

Land in itself has no value, and can yield no revenue, for land is only the passive factor in production. Labor is the active factor, by whose exertion upon land all wealth is produced. The owner of the richest land could get no revenue from his ownership; all that he could get from it would be what his own labor produced, until some one else was willing to pay him for the privilege of living on it, or working it. The moment this becomes the case, — the moment others will consent to give the land-owner a portion of the produce of their labor for the privilege of using his land, — his ownership will yield him a revenue independent of his own labor, — a revenue derived from the labor of others. Thus land acquires a value, — a value which increases just as the growth of population and improvement increases the amount of the labor-produce which permission to live on or work land will command.

Where population increases, or is expected to increase, the growth of the selling-value of land, however, may to some extent precede the growth of the power of obtaining revenue from its ownership, for the same reason that in the days of slavery, a negro child had a value before it could work, and, as the proverb ran, "A nigger's worth a hundred dollars as soon as he hollers." So, around growing cities, and in countries where population is rapidly increasing, land is held and sold at prices higher than the owner could now obtain for its use. But as in the case of the value of a slave-child, this speculative value of land arises from expectation of the revenue which it will in future yield, — the basis of all land-values, actual or prospective, being the amount of labor or labor-produce which its owner may obtain without labor on his part by permitting others to use his land. This, it is to be observed, is invariably true, — as true in the case of the little piece of land owned by the man who uses it himself, and whose income is derived from his labor upon it, as in the case of the great proprietor, whose income is derived from the labor of those whom he permits to use his land. For, so long as the owner can only get an income from his land by using it himself, the land has no value. It is only when, if he were to stop using it himself, he could, by selling it or renting it, get the produce of other people's labor, that land has a value. The value of land, where land is made private property, always means, therefore, the ability of the non-producer to live upon the producer, — the power, actual or prospective, of the land-owner to compel labor to pay him toll.

Increase of land-values, where land has been made private property, means simply that a larger and larger amount of the produce of labor goes to non-producers; that labor must pay more and more for being permitted the use of natural facilities indispensable to its exertion. For though the giving of labor, or the produce of labor, for the use of land has the semblance of an exchange, the transaction is in reality on the one side an appropriation, and on the other the payment, of a tribute. It is precisely such a transaction as that in which the fisherman is required to give up fish, which he has taken at the cost of labor and privation, in return for the privilege of using the ocean.

Here we have the great cause of that unequal distribution of wealth, which is apparent throughout the civilized world, and which increases with material progress. Low wages, pauperism, laborers who cannot find employment, goods which cannot be sold; a marvelous increase in the power of supplying human needs, yet great masses of human beings suffering from want; poverty seeming to spring from the very excess of production; monstrous fortunes accumulating in the hands of a few, while among the many the struggle for existence grows harder and more bitter, just as the discovery of better methods and the invention of better machinery make easier the production of the things necessary for the maintenance of existence, — all these phenomena, with all their social, political and moral consequences, spring from one fundamental maladjustment universal throughout the civilized world, — from a primary wrong, which destroys equality by dividing men into two classes: those who own the world as their private property, and those who, having no legal right to the use of the world, must buy the privilege of living and of working.

It is not in the relations of labor and capital; it is not in the greed of employers or the shiftlessness or intemperance of workingmen; it is not in interest, or currency, or profits, or in monopolies, such as those of railways and telegraphs, nor yet even in public debts, or the waste of standing armies, — it is not in any nor in all of these things that an explanation can be found of the fact that the workingman is everywhere the poor man.

All these are effects, or at most secondary causes. Given a country where there were no railroads, no government, no machinery, no currency, no capital; where there were no employers and employed, but where each worker obtained subsistence from nature as directly as do the birds; yet if the land of such a country were treated as throughout the civilized world land is treated, and were made the private property of but a part of the people, — should we not see essentially the same phenomena that to-day we see in the most highly civilized societies, — non-producers enjoying the fruits of labor, and producers in poverty; men, possessed only of the power to labor, compelled, in return for permission to exercise it, to give up the larger part of all they produce, — retaining for themselves only enough to support life? Why, if the very birds could so far pervert their instincts as to treat the earth as the private property of some birds, so that others did not dare to peck fruit, or catch worms, or build nests, without purchasing permission of some feathered earth-owner, should we not see among birds just what we see among men, — a few fat and lazy birds, deeming it beneath them to catch a worm or carry a straw, sitting amid great piles of wasting food, painfully gathered and brought to them by miserable, winged wretches, half-starved amid abundance?

Or, on the other hand, imagine civilized society in its highest development, with all wrongs abolished, save the primary wrong involved in private property in land. Let there be no standing armies, no public debts, no wars nor preparations for war. Let the railroads be run under the most perfect system, and with sole regard to the interests of the public; let the wasteful "protective" tariffs, which beget monopolies and hamper the trade of the world, be swept away; let perfect purity obtain in politics, and governments be carried on with absolute honesty and at the minimum of expense. Imagine, if you please, all taxes abolished, and public expenses met by the contributions of public-spirited citizens. Imagine employers to share their gains equally with their workmen, and co-operation so general that it should do away with the middle-man's profits; let there be a perfect currency; and imagine, if that be imaginable, all interest abolished. Imagine everybody prudent and honest, the craving for liquor a forgotten taste, and the making of intoxicating beverages a lost art. Yet if private property in land be retained, — if one set of men must still pay another set of men for the use of the planet, — what would be the gain to the mere laborer? All these social improvements would, by diminishing waste, add to the wealth of society. But all the other classes that prey upon labor being eliminated, the result would be that the land-owners could get all the more of this wealth. Good government, cheap railroad-fares, free trade, a perfect currency, the abolition of the profits of middle-men, temperance and thrift, would not enable men to live without land or to work without a place to work on, and something to work up. And, this being the case, all these improvements could make no improvement in the condition of the masses. Laborers of more than ordinary skill or ability might, as now, get more than a bare living; but men of only ordinary abilities and skill, possessed only of the power to labor, and with nothing to use that power upon, must still, by the inevitable law of competition, be driven to give up all their labor could produce above a bare living, for the sake of getting permission to live at all.

This impossibility of relieving poverty and securing an equitable distribution of wealth, while the land on which all must live is made the private property of some, arises from the very constitution of man, — from the fact that he is a land-animal, who must live on and from land, if he lives at all. This being the case, there is no possible reform, no possible improvement, no possible discovery or invention, which can permanently raise the lowest class of society above the verge of starvation, so long as private property in land exists. The failure of the great improvements and discoveries and inventions of the nineteenth century to eradicate want; the fact that poverty seems to deepen with material progress; that the most wonderful multiplications of the productive power of labor seem, instead of lightening the toil of the laboring class, to compel even women and children to work; and that, amid the greatest accumulations of wealth, human beings die of starvation, does not arise from the fact that these inventions and discoveries and improvements have not yet gone far enough, but from that fundamental law of his being, which makes it impossible for man to live, save on and from land, — from that fundamental limitation of his power which makes it impossible for him to create something out of nothing, and restricts all his production to the utilization of the pre-existing matter and force of the universe.

And in this absolute dependence of labor upon land, we may see the explanation of the paradox that poverty seems to spring from the very excess of the production of wealth, and that the increase which improved processes and inventions give to the productive power of labor make the mere laborer more helpless. For it is manifest that, were invention and discovery to go so far as to dispense with labor in the production of wealth, all the wealth that they could desire could be obtained by land-owners without the employment of labor, and that mere laborers would become but cumberers of the land-lord's ground, and could only escape starvation as paupers, supported by his bounty. This is the direction in which labor-saving discovery and invention must tend, wherever land is private property. And thus it is, that want seems to arise from the very "over-production" of things that satisfy want, and that as the productive power of labor increases, the struggle for existence becomes more bitter, and the number of men for whom there seems to be no place and no need in this world becomes larger and larger.

That what is called the labor question is simply another name for the land question; that all the ills which labor suffers spring from the appropriation as private property of the element without which labor is useless,—becomes evident upon any honest attempt to trace these ills to their source. The trouble with most of the clergymen, and professors, and dilettante philanthropists, who are now directing so much attention to the labor question, is, that they are not honest. They are making believe to look for what they really do not want to find; they are pretending to seek the remedy of a great wrong, with a predetermination to avoid any conclusion which would offend "vested interests," or disturb the "House of Have." They deliberately turn away from the only road which could lead to the explanation they profess to desire, and as a remedy for the most widespread and gigantic evils have nothing better to propose than some canting injunction that everybody should be good; some exhortation to employers to be kind, and to workingmen to be industrious, temperate, and, above all, contented; some two-penny scheme of co-operation or "profit-sharing." There is nothing mysterious about the labor question. The cause of the terrible competition in the labor-market which cuts down wages to the point of bare subsistence, when not restrained by the combinations of workmen, and of all the manifold evils to which this leads, is simply that all the men who want work cannot find work, and that there is at all times a great number, and in times of commercial depression a very great number, who are anxious to earn a living, but cannot get the opportunity.

Now, whence arises this difficulty of finding employment,—this seeming excess of the supply of labor over the demand for labor? With every pair of hands that come into the world, does there not come one mouth? Is there not demand enough for labor in the wants of those whose power to labor is going to waste, because they can find no use for it? Too little demand for labor! when even of those at work so many are under-fed, under-clothed, and not half-sheltered; when the great majority of men in all civilized countries are harassed by wants they are unable to supply!

If there are more men seeking employment than can find employers, what is to hinder these men from employing themselves? Did the first man have to hunt around for some one to hire him before he could go to work? Who was there to hire Robinson Crusoe? Yet did he lack employment? Did the settlers of this country, or the men who ever since have been pushing out into the wilderness, have to get themselves employers before they could make homes and earn a living?

The only indispensable condition to the employment of labor is LAND. Capital in all its forms, wealth in all its forms, is but the produce of labor exerted upon land. Give labor the use of land, and all things that man can bring into being can be produced. If, therefore, labor is going to waste; if men willing to work to supply their needs cannot find opportunity to do so, and must engage in a cut-throat competition with each other for the wages of some employer, it is solely because they cannot avail themselves of the natural opportunities for making their labor available.

But this is due to no lack of natural opportunities. In the most densely-peopled country of the civilized world, there are natural resources which would suffice for many times the population. In our own vast country, we have hardly begun to scratch the surface of nature's store-house. Around every city there are vacant lots, on which labor might find employment in building houses for an over-crowded population. There are millions and millions of unused acres, on which men who are becoming tramps might make themselves homes. There is clay and timber and iron and coal, of which no use is made. Of our agricultural land, that which is cultivated is but an insignificant part of what remains to cultivate. If labor cannot find employment for itself, it is not because of the failure of nature to offer opportunities for its employment. It is simply because we have allowed these opportunities to be seized and held by men who cannot use them themselves, and will not allow others to use them, — because we permit what nature offers freely to labor to be used as a means to extort blackmail from labor. Here is the one great cause of unemployed labor, of depressed trade, of the competition which everywhere tends to force wages down to the starvation point, and of widespread poverty, conjoined with the most enormous powers of producing wealth.

The natural means of employment monopolized, men who have nothing but the power to labor are driven into a cut-throat competition with their fellows to obtain from some other human creature the "leave to toil." Compelled to stint, unable with the produce of their own labor to purchase the produce of other's labor, goods that cannot be sold accumulate in warehouses while thousands suffer from want.

There is but one way of solving the labor question, of preventing monstrous injustice in the distribution of wealth, and substituting just and wholesome social conditions for those which it is now becoming clear must, if unchecked, lead us to anarchy; and that is by securing to all men their inalienable right to live and to work. This can only be done by abolishing the private ownership of land, and making the land of a country the common property of the whole people. The doing of this does not involve any denial of legitimate property-rights, any lessening of the incentive to build, improve or cultivate; any interference with that security of possession which is necessary to all the higher uses of land. It is only necessary to treat land as the common heritage of the whole people, and individual possessors as tenants of the community, paying a just rent for any peculiar privileges they enjoy. And the easy method of accomplishing this is to abolish all the taxes which now oppress labor and hamper production, and by means of a tax, not upon land, but upon the value of land, to collect for common uses that "unearned increment" which now goes to land-owners. Were this done, it would become unprofitable for any one to hold land that he was not putting to use, and the city-lots, the mines, the unused fields, that are now held on speculation would necessarily be thrown open to those who wished to use them.

Thus speculation in the bounties of nature would be destroyed, production would be relieved of all burdens, and that value which attaches to land by reason, not of the exertion or improvements of individuals, but by the growth and progress of society, would constitute a great fund from which all public expenses could be met.

How this simple yet far-reaching reform would secure the farmer his homestead, and give the tenement-dweller a spot he could call his own; how it would relieve the dreariness of country life and the congestion of over-crowded cities; how it would simplify government and purify politics; how it would equalize the distribution of wealth and enormously increase production, I have shown in detail in my books, but cannot dwell upon in the space allotted to me here. But whoever will heed the general principles I have here endeavored to point out, must see that in the divorce which our laws make between men and the natural element from which the means of life must be drawn, lies the cause of that monstrous injustice which piles up wealth in the hands of non-producers, and makes labor a suppliant for the very "leave to toil;" and that, at whatever cost, to conform our treatment of land to the dictates of justice is the only way in which our civilization can escape such wrecking disasters as have overwhelmed civilizations that preceded it.

There is in this world no necessity for poverty, and for the vice and crime that springs from it. That so much of human life is a bitter struggle for mere existence, is man's fault, not God's. The powers with which man has been gifted, the potentialities which exist in nature, are sufficient to give to the very humblest all the real advantages that the richest can now enjoy, to make possible a social state in which men should no more vex themselves about the satisfaction of material needs than do the lilies of the field. But the Creator has annexed to his gifts the inexorable condition that we shall deal justly with our fellows. A system which denies their birth-right to the children who come into the world involves a crime which must bring its punishment.

HENRY GEORGE.

CALIFORNIA LABOR LEADERS.

CHAPTER XXIV.

THE ARMY OF UNEMPLOYED.

The Cincinnati Riots — Labor-Saving Machinery — Less Hours of Toil — Statistics — Flesh-and-Blood Men — Remedies Recommended — The Sin of Cheapness — Too Much Wheat.

IN January, 1884, the following paragraph appeared in one of the daily papers:—

It is estimated, that at the present time, one million and a half of men are out of employment in the United States; it is safe to predict that, if opportunities were offered to these men to drop into useful occupations, a large majority would not avail themselves of them.

Since then, the number of the unemployed must have increased; for nearly every day we read such items as this:—

The worsted-mill connected with the Bigelow Carpet-Mills, which employs about three hundred hands, shut down this morning, for three weeks. This, with the five per cent. cut-down at the Lancaster Gingham-Mills, where two thousand five hundred hands are employed, which also went into effect this morning, makes Clinton's business outlook decidedly poor.

In the two years ending December 1, 1884, those employed in and around the coal-mines worked but a little over half-time, and for the length of time that they were not at work, they must be counted in with the unemployed. If the figures above quoted were correct in January, it is safe to assume that at present, the number will not fall short of 2,000,000. The census of 1880 shows that the number of persons engaged in gainful occupations was 17,392,099. Of this number 3,837,112 were engaged in manufacturing, mechanical and mining pursuits, while 5,183,099 gained a livelihood as laborers (agricultural and otherwise). Thus, in 1880, we had, in the United States, between laborers, mechanics, miners and those engaged in manufacturing establishments, 9,020,211 persons.

From a personal experience, I am led to believe that the greater portion of those who are now out of employment comes from occupations that go to make up the 9,020,211. It is safe to assume, that the 2,000,000 unemployed persons are discontented with their lot; and, not only are they discontented, but those who labor at the same occupations that they previously followed, have every reason to be dissatisfied also. With so many men and women seeking employment, the tendency of wages must be downward. It does not follow, because men are out of employment, that such articles as their fellow-workmen produce should decrease in value, or that the profit on the manufactured article, accruing to the owners of the establishment in which they work, should be any less; on the contrary, the expectation is, that diminished production will increase the price of the manufactured article, or at least prevent its depreciation when thrown on the market. Notwithstanding the reduction in the expenses of the mining company, we pay the same price for coal that we paid a year ago. It matters not that the carpet-mills "suspend three hundred hands," the price of carpeting remains unchanged. The gingham-mills and the cotton and woolen-mills may reduce the wages of employes five and ten per cent., yet the price of gingham and calico continues as before. Whether the manufactured article commands the same price in the market or not, the employer, knowing that he can secure an abundance of help, reduces the wages of his employees. Those who are out of employment are no longer producers, and they certainly are not consumers, to any increased extent. The wages of those employed having been reduced, their powers of consumption are limited. The merchant, whose shelves are stocked with goods, becomes discontented, when he views the rows of men and women that stand in front of his store, peering with hungry-looking eyes through his windows at the goods so temptingly held to view, willing and anxious to buy these goods, but deprived of the means, through enforced idleness or inadequate compensation for services rendered. Ask the business man what the cause of the depression is, and he, parrot-like, will say, "It is all regulated by the law of supply and demand." A moment's reflection would show him that the law of supply and demand, like all other laws, is open to different constructions. On his shelves is a supply of goods; outside of his window is a demand for these goods,—a demand that is at all times equal to the supply. Why is it, that the demand does not reach forth and secure the supply? The answer comes, "Because the medium of exchange is lacking; because labor is too cheap and plenty, and money too dear and scarce." That a deep-rooted feeling of discontent prevades the masses, none can deny; that there is a just cause for it, must be admitted. The old cry, "These agitators are stirring up a feeling of dissatisfaction among workingmen, and they should be suppressed," will not avail now. Every thinking person knows that the agitator did not throw two millions of men out of employment. The man that reads such paragraphs as this, will not lay the blame of it at the door of the agitator:—

Mrs. Sarah Jane Geary, an Englishwoman, residing in this city, committed suicide, a few days since. Her husband is a miner, and, owing to the frequent suspensions of business in the mines during the past winter, his meager earnings were insufficient to support the family. The fact preyed on Mrs. Geary's mind, and she resolved to end her life, that her children might receive her share of the food; otherwise, they would go hungry.

The Cincinnati riots, that occurred less than one year ago, were not brought about through the agitation of the labor-leader. If the demand for "the removal of unjust technicalities, delays and discriminations in the administration of justice," had been listened to when first made by the Knights of Labor, Cincinnati would have been spared sorrow and disgrace, and her "prominent citizens" would not have had to lead a mob, in order to open the eyes of the country to the manner in which her courts were throttled, and virtue and truth were trampled upon in her temples of justice. That the army of the discontented is gathering fresh recruits day by day, is true; and if this army should become so large, that, driven to desperation, it should one day arise in its wrath, and grapple with its real or fancied enemy, the responsibility for that act must fall upon the heads of those who could have averted the blow, but who turned a deaf ear to the supplication of suffering humanity, and gave the screw of oppression an extra turn, because they had the power. Workingmen's organizations are doing all they can to avert the blow; but if that day dawns upon us, it will be chargeable directly o men who taunt others with unequal earnings, and distort the truth, as was done in an interview recently had with Mr. William H. Vanderbilt:—

One of the troubles in this country, just now, is the relation of wages to the cost of production. A skilled workman, in almost every branch of business, gets every day money enough to buy a barrel of flour. I don't refer to ordinary laborers, but to men skilled at their trades. The man who makes the article receives as much wages, in many instances, as the article is worth when it is finished. This is not exactly fair, in my opinion, and must be adjusted. Until wages bear a truer relation to production, there can be no real prosperity in the country

I have seen no denial of the above, and take it for granted that it is a correct report. Mr. Vanderbilt starts out well enough; but he is in error when he says that "a skilled workman, in almost every branch of business, gets money enough every day to buy a barrel of flour." I know of no business in the United States, in which a skilled mechanic, working regularly at his trade day by day, gets money enough for his day's labor to buy a barrel of flour. That they earn the price of a barrel of flour, I do not deny; but that they get it, is not true. It may be that Mr. Vanderbilt refers to superintendents, foremen or contractors; for they are the only ones that receive such wages. The average wages paid to the skilled mechanic will not exceed $2.50 a day. I know of but few branches of business in which men can command that price. The wages of skilled mechanics are on the decline, while the price of flour remains unchanged, from $5.75 to $8.50 a barrel. If Mr. Vanderbilt will demonstrate how one can purchase a six-dollar barrel of flour for two dollars and a half, he will have solved a very difficult problem for the workingman. It is not the labor of the skilled mechanic alone that must be taken into account, in computing the cost of the manufactured article; the average price paid to labor in the establishment should be the standard, if a standard of wages is required. An examination of the last census report shows that the number of manufacturing establishments in the United States was 253,852, and the amount of capital invested was $2,790,272,606; the average number of hands employed was 2,732,595; the value of the raw material was $3,396,823,549; while the product of the manufactured articles was $5,369,579,191. Deduct the sum paid for the raw material from the product of the manufactured article, and we have $1,972,745,642. This sum represents the difference between the price paid for the article when in a raw state and that received for it when manufactured. It is evident that something more than interest on money invested was required to give this additional value to the material. That something was the labor of the hands referred to. The total amount paid in wages, to the employees of these establishments, was $947,953,795. Deducting this amount from the $1,972,745,642, we have left $1,024,791,847. This sum goes to the manufacturer. It is estimated by some that the amount paid for raw material includes taxes, insurances, salaries and repairs; but, in the absence of reliable statistics, I am not prepared to prove that such is the case. By adding the sum paid for raw material to the amount of capital invested, we have $6,187,096,155, the total investment of the manufacturer. From this sum we have, pitted against every one of the 2,732,595 employees, a fraction over $2,264. While the average yearly earnings of each employee were $720, he received in wages but a fraction over $346, or a trifle over one dollar a day for every working-day in the year. Subtract the wages of the employee from his earnings, and we have left $374. The employee receives an average of $346 a year for his labor, while his employer receives $374 on an investment of $2,264. Instead of basing the cost of the manufactured article on the wages given to the highest-priced skilled mechanic, it should be based on the average wage paid to the men in these establishments. It thus appears that a barrel of flour costs several days' labor.

It may be said that many of the employees of the manufacturing establishments are minors, and consequently cannot perform as great an amount of labor as a corresponding number of adults. That argument might have had some weight years ago, but now it is fruitless. The age and strength of the workman are no longer regarded as factors in the field of production; it is the skill of the operator in managing a labor-saving machine that is held to be the most essential. It is true that a child can operate a machine as successfully as a man, and that muscle is no longer a requisite in accomplishing results. It is also true that less time is required to perform a given amount of labor than heretofore. This being the case, the plea for shorter hours is not unreasonable. Benjamin Franklin said, one hundred years ago, that "if the workers of the world would labor but four hours each day, they could produce enough in that length of time to supply the wants of mankind." While it is true that the means of supplying the wants of man have increased as if by magic, yet man has acquired no new wants; he is merely enabled to gratify his needs more fully. If it were true in Franklin's time that four hours of toil each day would prove sufficient to minister to the necessities of the world's inhabitants, the argument certainly has lost none of its force since then. At that time, it took the sailing-vessel three months to cross the ocean; the stage-coach made its thirty or forty miles a day; the electric wire was not dreamed of; and the letter that traveled but little faster than the stage-coach was the quickest medium of communication.

It required six days' labor at the hands of the machinist, with hammer, chisel and file to perfect a certain piece of machinery at the beginning of this century. The machinist of the present day can finish a better job in six hours, with the aid of a labor-saving machine. In a yarn-mill in Philadelphia, the proprietor says that improved machinery has caused a displacement of fifty per cent. of the former employees within five years, and that one person, with the aid of improved machinery, can perform the work that it took upward of one hundred carders and spinners to do with the tools and implements in use at the beginning of this century.

In Massachusetts, it has been estimated that 318,768 men, women and children do, with improved machinery, the work that it would require 1,912,468 men to perform, if improved machinery were not in use. To insure safety on a passenger-train, it is no longer necessary to have a brakeman at each end of the car; the automatic air-brake does the work, while one brakeman can shout, "All right here!" for the whole train. The employee that has had a limb cut off in a collision, must beg for bread or turn the crank of a hand-organ, and gather his pennies under the legend, "Please assist a poor soldier, who lost his leg at Gettysburg." He is no longer stationed, flag in hand, at the switch; the automatic lever directs the course of the train, and renders the one-legged switchman unnecessary. It is said that the iron-moulder recently invented is capable of performing as much labor as three skilled workmen; while the following dispatch to a Philadelphia paper, from Mahanoy City, shows what is being done in the mines:—

For the past three years the reduction in wages has been systematic and steady. When one of the officials of one of the great companies was interviewed on the matter, he replied that the advance in labor-saving machinery had lightened the labor of the men. A miner at one of the Reading collieries says that some months ago he expended a large sum for a patent drill, which enabled him to do five times the usual amount of work. He was employed in driving a gangway, the price paid being $10 a yard; but at the end of the week, when the officials saw the amount of work he had done, the rate was reduced to $4,50 a yard.

Take the iron-moulder as an illustration. Three flesh-and-blood men, who require shelter, clothing, recreation and social intercourse, who must eat or starve, who must pay taxes to support the State, and whose bodies can be taken to defend the State, in case of invasion or rebellion; one iron man, who does not feel, sleep, eat or drink, who never tires and never rests. Three flesh-and-blood men, who have children depending upon them for bread; one iron man, who has no family to support; and the three men whom he has displaced, must continue to support families, or enlist in that ever-increasing army of tramps. Heat, steam, electricity, labor-saving machines pay no taxes, municipal or national; the men thrown out of employment, through the introduction of these agents, are deprived of the means of contributing to the support of the State, and an extra burden is shifted to the shoulders of those that continue to work. The existence of such a state of affairs gives evidence that the introduction of machinery, from which the many should derive an advantage, is being used for the benefit of a few, who already feel the blow given to trade, through the displacement of so many consumers.

A great many remedies are recommended for the ills that I speak of. Let me deal with what seems to be the most unimportant, — the reduction of the hours of labor to eight a day. Men, women and children are working from ten to eighteen hours a day, and two million men have nothing to do. If four men, following a given occupation, at which they work ten hours a day, would rest from their labors two hours each day, the two hours taken from the labor of each, if added together, would give the tramp that stands looking on, an opportunity of stepping into a position at eight hours a day. It is said that a vast majority of those who are idle would not work, if they had work to do. That statement is untrue; but let us admit that five hundred thousand of the two million idle men would not work, and we still have a million and a half who are anxious and willing to work. If but six million of the seventeen million producers will abstain from working ten, fifteen, and eighteen hours a day, and work but eight, the one million and a half of idle men that are willing to work, can again take their places in the ranks of the world's producers. Need it be said, that a million and a half of new hats will be needed; that a corresponding number of pairs of shoes, suits of clothing, and a hundred other things will be required; that the wants of these men and their families will be supplied; that shelves will be emptied of their goods, and that the money expended will again go into circulation. It would entail hardship on some branches of business, to require men employed in them to work eight hours a day. Miners and those working by contract could not very well adopt the eight-hour plan, without lengthening their hours of labor. Before giving the matter a second thought, many of these men look upon the eight-hour agitation as of no consequence to them. If a mechanic is thrown out of employment, and cannot find anything to do at his trade, he turns toward the first place where an opportunity for work is presented. If he is re-enforced by two million idle men, the number that apply at the mouth of the mine, or seek to secure contracts at lower figures, becomes quite large; and the miner and contract-man grumble, because so many men are crowding in upon them in quest of work. Every new applicant for work in the mine makes it possible for the boss to let his contract to a lower bidder; therefore, it is clearly to the interest of the miner to assist in reducing the hours of labor in the shop, mill and factory, to the end that the idle millions may be gathered in from the streets to self-sustaining positions.

The eight-hour system, to be of value to the masses, must be put in operation all over the country; for the manufacturers of one State cannot successfully compete with those of other States, if they run their establishments but eight hours, while others operate theirs ten or twelve hours a day. The movement should be national, and should have the hearty co-operation of all men.

A Scottish clergyman, Dr. Donald Macleod, in a sermon on "The Sin of Cheapness," says that "the craving for cheapness and hunting after bargains, is not only economically false, but a cause of great suffering to thousands of men, women and children." If men worked shorter hours, they would learn that when a man begins to look for cheap bargains, he strikes a blow at trade everywhere. The employer looks for a better bargain in labor, and reduces his force or hires cheaper men. His employee must practice enforced economy, which is no saving; he drives sharper bargains for articles manufactured by others; he cannot purchase so good an article, or in such quantities, as before; and the effect is felt where these articles are made, taking the shape of a reduction, either in the working force or in the wages. When the President of the United States issued his Thanksgiving proclamation, in 1884, there were millions of men and women in want of bread, notwithstanding "the abundant harvests and continued prosperity which God hath vouchsafed to this nation;" and the cry, not of thanksgiving, went up from millions of farmers, of "Too much wheat!" Doubting as to the exact meaning of the Creator in growing so much wheat, they invoked the aid of such institutions as the Chicago Board of Trade, in the hope of thwarting the will of God, by cornering wheat. These men invoked blessings on their Thanksgiving dinners, and thanked God for the turkey, while they hoarded the wheat away from those who asked for bread.

Give men shorter hours in which to labor, and you give them more time to study, and learn why bread is so scarce, while wheat is so plenty. You give them more time in which to learn that millions of acres of American soil are controlled by alien landlords, that have no interest in America but to draw a revenue from it. You give them time to learn that America belongs to Americans, native and naturalized, and that the landlord who drives his tenant from the Old World must not be permitted to exact tribute from him when he settles in our country. T. V. POWDERLY.

CHAPTER XXV.

THE LABOR MOVEMENT IN CANADA.

Early Settlers in Canada — First Labor Organizations — A Typographical Union — Feeling Between Races — First Printers' Union — Other Trade Organizations — First Printers' Strike — The Union Victorious — A Bitter Contest — A Trades Council — Its Candidate Elected — Zeal of Toronto Workingmen — A Trades Congress — Canadian Labor Union Formed — Favorable Labor Legislation — The Knights of Labor Appear — Their Rapid Growth — Advantages of Combination — Successful Coöperation.

UP to 1800, Canada was, comparatively, a *terra incognita*, except to a few. While the Province of Quebec was peopled by the descendants of its early French conquerors and masters, excepting, perhaps, the cities of Quebec and Montreal, and a scattered colony here and there throughout the eastern townships on the borders of the United States, where a sprinkling of English-speaking people were to be found, only the northern banks of the St. Lawrence and the lakes Huron and Erie on the eastern and southern boundary of Ontario had an English-speaking population. In many instances these settlements were long distances apart, and the only means of travel was by water in the summer season, and in the winter by sleighs on the ice. In the Province of Quebec the bitterness engendered by difference of race, and which found vent in many a local and violent struggle, had its effect in preventing for a long time that cohesion of elements in the ranks of those who worked for wages. The rebellion of 1837, and the subsequent burning of the Parliament House in Montreal, years afterwards, tended in no small degree to intensify this feeling between the races, and to its continuance for many years afterwards.

Despite all this, however, labor organizations had begun their work in Lower Canada, as the Province of Quebec was then called; for as early as 1834, and, perhaps, before that period, the shoemakers were holding their meetings regularly in the city of Montreal, and at the same time and to that extent, at least, serving as a model for, as well as in a degree educating, their less fortunate brothers in other callings in the directions in which every calling or trade has, at irregular intervals, drifted since that time. There is no reason to believe that this old and often sorely-tried organization has ever, for a moment, ceased from that time until the present moment to exist in Canada; and to-day it is one of the most conservative as well as one of the most wealthy labor organizations of an international character in the Dominion.

Contrary to the general idea prevalent in Canada, to the French-speaking artisans of the Province of Quebec belongs the credit of originating in Canada the formation of labor "circles" or unions; for we find that as far back as 1827 the printers in the city of Quebec had a local Union, the scope of which embraced, besides the regulation of wages and the care of its members while incapacitated from pursuing their calling through illness, the delivery of lectures, reading of essays, and the holding of entertainments of a musical character. The Union was merged into the National Typographical Union at Cincinnati, in 1852, and that again in the International Typographical Union, at Albany, in 1869.

It has been an unfortunate and too common habit, not yet altogether forgotten, on the part of English-speaking trades-unionists to reflect in no flattering terms upon the manhood of French-Canadian artisans and workmen generally. But ample experience has conclusively proven that where these people have had extended to them that cordiality and fraternal treatment to which as men they were of right entitled, then were they found second to none in battling for justice and right. Before being severely critical as to our fellow-workingmen of French extraction, as to their want of knowledge as to what may be and is expected at their hands, when they find themselves away from their homes and among English-speaking people, it should be remembered that their means of learning of current events in the labor world are very circumscribed and limited; as, outside of the cities of Quebec and Montreal, there are comparatively few, if any, daily newspapers published in that Province in the French language. If trades-unions in the Province of Quebec have not been as successful in the past as in other sections of the Dominion, it is primarily because of want of tact and judgment on the part of the English-speaking section in attempting, in every instance, to have everything their own way, despite the fact of being almost always in a minority.

In Upper Canada, — now Ontario, — as in Lower Canada, we find that the Knights of St. Crispin and printers are the oldest as to organization, for at the present time Toronto Typographical Union No. 91 is in possession of the minute books of the Printers' Union or Society of "Little York," the name by which Toronto was known prior to its incorporation as a city under its present title some fifty-three years ago. The printers of Toronto were the first in Canada to affiliate with the International Typographical Union, their charter number being No. 91 of that body. They were followed by Ottawa, No. 102; Hamilton, No. 129; Halifax, N. S., No. 130; London, Ont., No. 133; Jacques Cartier, Montreal, No. 145; Quebec, No. 159 (French); Quebec, No. 160 (English), Quebec; Montreal, No. 176, Montreal; and later still by those of St. Catherine's and Kingston, in Ontario. To the printers of Canada belongs the principal credit in all that has been done in the direction of organizing and educating the artisan classes of that country. Notwithstanding this fact, however, it is not to be overlooked that other trades were none the less active in the work; for we find the stone masons, the bricklayers and the blacksmiths each organized, at least at Ottawa, in 1868–9, and it may be previously, in Toronto. During the years mentioned, and for many years afterwards, hosts of men were employed directly as well as indirectly in providing materials for, or in the erection of the Dominion Parliamentary and Departmental buildings then being under construction in that city. It is needless to remark that during the many years so many men were congregated at one place, and having to deal with contractors of the usual character engaged in such heavy undertakings, more than one "difficulty" arose; but they usually terminated in favor of the workers; for even if their organizations were not as compact and as well versed in the necessity and advantages of cohesion and unity as at the present day, yet the population from which to supply their places when on strike was not so numerous, nor was the skilled labor market subject to the periodical congestion to be witnessed at a later period.

In the early part of 1866, the first steps were taken by the printers, at Ottawa, to organize themselves into a Union. They met on a Sunday afternoon in a private school-room, the free use of which was kindly granted for the occasion by an old and respected school teacher, whose son was a printer and had served in Colonel Ellsworth's famous Zouaves in the early days of the United States Civil War. Officers were elected *pro tem.*, and steps were taken to secure a charter under the National Union. On the following Monday morning it was announced in some of the printing-offices that the proprietors had determined to raise the current rate of wages one dollar per week. Up to this time wages, such as they were, — for each man made his own bargain, — were paid in such manner and at such times as suited the convenience or the whim of the employer. "Store orders" on advertisers were tendered more often than ready money, and the consequence to the worker was that, besides being often obliged to purchase goods he was in no need of, he was unblushingly "plucked" by the store-keeper. There was no allowance made for overtime, and it was surprising how much of it was exacted. From thenceforward a marked improvement in the life of the printer in that city evinced itself, although the first president elected, — a Mr. Bradford, — and some of the others who took an active part in the formation of the Union, "found their vocation gone," and had to depart for "pastures new." In 1870, the then government printing contractor made the first direct assault on this original Union, No. 102. He imported printers from England, but most of them refused to work against the strikers, who were "out" because he tried to employ non-union men, and he ultimately succumbed. In

1873 the same contractor attempted a reduction of wages, which caused a fight of many weeks. The strikers received financial aid from all over the country. The contractor again imported many men from England. The government itself aided the contractor in many ways. But very few of the new men, on learning how matters stood, would take the place of the strikers. The contractor was unable to comply with the terms of his contract, and it was given to McLean, Rogers & Co., who still hold it. Mr. Rogers, of the firm, was Secretary of the Union during the troubles, and has always kept his office a "union" one.

In this year, 1873, also, owing to the rapid increase in the formation of local trades-unions, a Trades Council was organized in Ottawa, which was of more than passing importance to the cause of labor in Canada in after years; because, being at the seat of the Dominion Government, it was in a position to exercise its functions not only in matters affecting local interests, but also in pressing upon members of Parliament the desires and the views of like and other labor bodies wherever situate throughout Canada. One of the first subjects that engaged this Trades Council after its organization was the necessity existing for direct labor representation in both Dominion and Provincial Parliaments, and it was resolved to seize the first opportunity to make the attempt in Ottawa. This came sooner than anticipated, but the Trades Council was equal to the occasion. The Legislature of Ontario having previously repealed the "Property Qualification" clause in the law governing or respecting candidates for election to that body, and a vacancy arising in the representation of that city in the Provincial Legislature, the then President of the Trades Council was selected and put in nomination as the workingmen's candidate as an Independent, and under the express instruction that under no consideration was he to pledge himself to either of the existing political parties. This unlooked-for and unexpected action on the part of "mere workingmen" was more than a surprise to the old-time political manipulators, as well as to the "shoddy aristocracy" of the Federal capital. An active campaign was entered upon. One political party had its nominee in the field previous to the nomination by the Trades Council. The opposite party offered conditional support to the labor candidate. This was promptly declined. But, despite this, the party making the offer voted unconditionally for the labor candidate, and he was elected by a large majority. He was re-elected in 1874, despite the fact that, having breathing-time to recover from the surprise and result of the previous contest, both political parties put strong and experienced campaigners in the field. In the elections of 1879, he declined to accept a party nomination, and was defeated, not by any defection of former supporters, but by their removal to other fields of labor. His career as a legislator was very creditable, and much favorable labor legislation now in force is due to his efforts.

While the workingmen of Ottawa were thus engaged, their brothers in Toronto and Hamilton were by no means idle. The latter city sent a workingman to the House of Commons, who rendered efficient service to the cause of organized labor. He failed of re-election by reason of not having met the wishes of all his constituents, who did not understand the obstacles in the way of their particular representative.

To the workingmen of Toronto is mainly due the solidity and permanence of labor organizations in Canada. In this city, in 1872, these organizations first determined on a nine-hours day. The effort was only partially successful, but it led to a new era of labor reform through the whole country. By previous arrangement, the Typographical Union led the van in this movement. Organization by the laborers led to counter organization among the employers. The latter invoked the aid of the Government, and caused the arrest of leading members of the Typographical Union on the charge of conspiracy. Without following the extremely interesting details of this contest, conducted on each side with great skill and vigor, suffice it to say that ultimately the prosecutions were dropped, and the Union gained the nine-hours day. No other Union fought for or gained like concessions at that time, although to-day many labor organizations enjoy like hours, while the stone-cutters work but eight. Despite all attacks on them, the Bricklayers' and Iron-moulders' International Unions of Canada are in a flourishing condition. Nor have purely local Unions, such as the Operative Tailors, the Painters, the Stone-masons, the Builders' Laborers, the Plasterers, and the Lathers, in Ontario, as well as ship laborers in the city of Quebec, in the Province of the same name, ever been found wanting in their efforts when called on to assist one another, or to insist upon their rights as freemen and citizens.

As an outcome of the agitations throughout the province of Ontario during the previous few years, and to which great stimulus was given by the printers' strikes at Ottawa and Toronto, already referred to, Toronto Trades Assembly called a convention of organized labor bodies throughout the country to meet in Toronto, September 23, 1883. Although the existence and principles of the Knights of Labor were not even known by this convention, yet it arrived at the same conclusions on many questions as the Knights had already reached, showing how the spirit of education and thought was abroad to a far greater extent than was dreamed of by either party, even at that time. This convention sat for three days, and may be credited with being the first step taken in Canada to give light and direction, as well as oneness of aim to the Trades Unions of Canada. The bodies represented were: Toronto Trades Assembly, Amalgamated Engineers, Toronto; Coopers No. 13, of Ontario, St. Catharine's; Coopers No. 8, of Seaforth; Iron Moulders No. 26, of Hamilton; Coopers No. 17, of Ontario, Bowmanville; Typographical Union No. 91, of Toronto; Bakers Union, Toronto; Knights of St. Crispin, St. Catharine's; Knights of St. Crispin 315, Toronto; Knights of St. Crispin 159, Toronto; Iron Moulders 189, Cobourg; Coopers No. 3, of Ontario, Toronto; Amalgamated Carpenters and Joiners, London; Bricklayers and Masons, Toronto; Knights of St. Crispin, 212, Hamilton; Machinists and Blacksmiths No. 1, of Ontario, Toronto; Bricklayers and Masons, Ottawa; Tailors, Ottawa; Carpenters and Joiners, Ottawa; Typographical Union No. 102, Ottawa; Tailors, St. Catharine's; Operative Tailors, Toronto; Free Stone Cutters, Ottawa; 'Longshoremen, Toronto; Limestone Cutters, Ottawa; Painters, Toronto; Machinists and Blacksmiths No. 2, Hamilton; Knights of St. Crispin 242, London; Amalgamated Engineers, Hamilton, and Iron Moulders Union No. 28, of Toronto. Mr. J. W. Carter, President of the Toronto Trades Assembly, voiced the spirit and views of the Canadian labor reformers of 1873 in his address on the formal opening of the convention. He alluded to the significance of such a convention; said the interests of labor must be taken hold of by the workingmen; urged the identity of interest of Capital and Labor; and advocated laws that should make no distinction of man as man. He said the necessity of establishing a Canadian Labor Union was beyond doubt, and showed how the workingmen by organization could secure representation in legislation. In accordance with his suggestions, the convention resolved itself into the "Canadian Labor Union," electing J. W. Carter, of Toronto, as its first President; D. J. O'Donoghue, of Ottawa, Vice-President, and J. Hewitt, of Toronto, Secretary. A constitution was adopted, the preamble of which indicated in no uncertain language the motives actuating its founders, and which was in the following language:—

Whereas, the workingmen of the Dominion of Canada, in common with the intelligent producers of the world, feel the necessity of co-operate and harmonious action to secure their mutual interests, just compensation for their toil, and such limitation of the hours of labor as may tend to promote their physical and intellectual well-being, and believing that the causes which have operated in the past to the detriment of labor may nearly always be traced to the want of proper organization in the various branches of industry;

Therefore, to unite the energies of all classes of labor in the Dominion of Canada, for the purpose of guarding their inherent rights, we, the representatives of the workingmen of the Dominion of Canada, in convention assembled, do hereby enact and adopt the following constitution.

The committees on "Hours of Labor," "Arbitration," "Organization," "Prison Contract Labor," "Cheap and Imported Labor," "Labor Bureau" and "Legislation," made reports, which were adopted, showing that the pioneers and veterans in the labor cause in Canada in 1873 and of years before had given more than passing attention to these problems, which are not yet solved; that their views were abreast of the most advanced of that time; and that they were such as would be acceptable to the leading labor reformers of to-day.

On the fourth, fifth and sixth of August, 1874, the next sessions of the Canada Labor Union were held in a large committee room in the House of Commons of the Dominion at Ottawa; and in 1875, at the city of St. Catharine's, on the third, fourth and fifth of August of that year. On both occasions the work inaugurated at the meeting held in Toronto in 1873 was furthered and elaborated with vigor, many charters being issued to subordinate and newly organized bodies under the seal of the central body. The executive had worked untiringly and with vigor in bringing to the attention of the Legislatures the questions determined on; and in 1874, being meanwhile elected to the Provincial Legislature, Mr. D. J. O'Donoghue introduced and had passed the bill entitled "An Act establishing Liens in favor of Mechanics, Machinists, Laborers and others;" in 1877, "An Act to amend the Act respecting Master and Servant;" and, again, in 1878, "An Act to amend the Mechanics' Lien Act, 1874;" "An Act exempting $25 of a workingman's wages from garnishee;" and contributed during his term to the enactment of other laws beneficial to wage-earners. During these years was continued a vigorous and healthy agitation in all labor centres and in the House of Commons in favor of, or against, such legislation as had been indicated as beneficial or otherwise by the several sessions of the Canada Labor Union.

In 1873, the criminal law was amended so as not to render trades-unionists liable in certain cases as conspirators; and in 1876, the Masters' and Servants' Act was so amended that breaches of contract under it were no longer criminal, but merely breaches of civil contract. Owing principally to stagnation of business, the Canada Labor Union practically ceased to exist as a body after its session at St. Catherine's, in 1875.

In 1876 came the strike of the locomotive engineers, followed by legislation providing that passenger and mail trains must make their through journey without a strike by the employees. In 1882 came the act to establish a Bureau of Industries, of which Mr. Archibald Blue, a journalist of experience, ability and untiring energy, was made secretary. His reports have already become a valuable aid in determining many important labor questions. In 1881 the twenty-ninth annual session of the International Typographical Union was held in Toronto. The trades-assembly there had ceased to exist; but as a result of this meeting, a trades and labor council sprang into existence, which has had great influence for labor reform ever since. It summoned a Labor Congress in December, 1883, which was very successful. Mr. Charles March was its permanent chairman.

In the fall of 1881 the first local assembly of the Knights of Labor in Canada was organized in Hamilton, the ceremony being performed in the basement of the Canada Life Assurance Building, then in process of construction. Others began their existence in that city in comparatively rapid succession thereafter. The first assembly still exists as a Painters' Assembly. At a subsequent period, District Assembly No. 60 was formed in the city of Hamilton, with delegates from some twenty-five local bodies of the Order. Hamilton was not destined to monopolize the existence of Knights of Labor for a lengthy period, however, for on August 27th of the following year the telegraphers of Toronto were organized as a local assembly of the Order, under the title of "Morse No. 2163." This was the first assembly organized at this date in any part of Canada outside of Hamilton. About five weeks afterwards the factory shoemakers, Local Assembly 2211, were organized; and these were followed in the spring of 1883 by the organization of the first "mixed" Local, being No. 2305, which in after days, although small in its membership, under many difficulties upheld the banner of that Order, when its very existence in Toronto was in doubt.

During the great strike of the telegraphers against the Western Union, which began on July 19, 1883, almost every telegrapher in Canada was found within their ranks, and they did all that was possible to secure a successful termination of the contest. To offset the defeat of this strike, the leaders of Mixed Local Assembly No. 2305, of Toronto, which numbered only about twenty members, introduced public lectures on the principles of the Order. Captain Richard F. Trevellick, of Detroit, was first invited. His first audience numbered only twenty persons. His effort bore abundant fruit, however, and his audiences since have always been very large. General Master Workman Powderly followed Captain Trevellick, and his reception was never surpassed by that of any public personage in that city, many Canadians of note being on the platform with him. Then came a turn in the tide, and assemblies sprang up in a marvelous degree everywhere in Ontario. There are now no less than six district assemblies in Canada; that of Toronto, No. 125, having representatives from some forty local assemblies. The Order has ever been watchful for the interests of Labor. In 1884, it not only prevented the passage of an obnoxious life insurance bill, but secured an amendment making legal the cheap insurance schemes of the labor bodies in Canada, and that its provisions should not apply to bodies doing an insurance business solely within their membership. Mr. D. J. O'Donoghue, representing the Knights of Labor, and Mr. J. W. Carter, representing the Sons of England, were especially instrumental in securing this legislation. The anxiety to have direct representation in both Houses is heightened by the fact that while constantly improving labor-saving machinery, both in factory, workshop and farm, is rapidly forcing host of willing hands into idleness, hundreds of thousands of dollars of the public moneys of the country are being annually voted and devoted to the "assisting" and encouragement of the immigration of British paupers and indigents into Canada. The Dominion Parliament alone, at its last session, voted $300,000 for this purpose, despite the vehement remonstrances of the various labor bodies within the Dominion. Without trenching upon the domain of political party policies in Canada, it may be said that that country presents the anomaly of highly protecting home manufactures and at the same time handicapping home labor by actually expending immense sums of public money in promoting an influx of foreign labor to still further hamper the chances of employment for its own people in the labor market. There is scarcely a doubt but that with unity and tact on the part of trades-unionists and Knights of Labor, a radical change in this and other equally important directions can and will be secured in the near future in the Dominion of Canada.

Nor is Co-operation, both productive and distributive, being neglected, since the existence of the Knights of Labor has become a fixed fact in Canada. Toronto has its co-operative manufacturing and distributing bakery and general grocery store, and its weekly *Labor Record* newspaper; Woodstock has its match-making and lumber-dressing manufactory; and the thriving town of Chatham has just applied for incorporation under Provincial law for its baking and biscuit manufactory. And so this good work will continue doubtless. It is the firm impression of every true labor reformer in Canada that as peaceable agitation and general education progress, the Dominion will not be found second to any country in the world in the good work of remedying the disadvantages under which its wage-earning classes labor, and in securing that ultimate justice for all, which should be the sole aim of every form of government.

APPENDIX.

CIGAR-MAKERS' INTERNATIONAL UNION.

THE history of the Cigar-makers' International Union forms an integral part of the general labor movement. In the earlier stages of its development, numerous mistakes were inevitable. Its growth was of a spontaneous character. From the shop-meeting it developed by successive stages into a union, local in its character; and, finally, it culminated in the National and International Unions.

The first Cigar-makers' Union was organized on May 5, 1851, in Baltimore, Md., at that time one of the leading centres in the cigar-trade. In order to counteract the influence of the union, one Tom Little, cigar-manufacturer, imported a large number of cigar-makers from Bremen, Germany.

Between 1852 and 1853, the cigar-makers employed in Mark Sharkey's shop, New York city, numbering between sixty and seventy, organized a union. The chief promoters of the organization consisted of English and German cigar-makers. Shortly after this, a strike occurred in South Brooklyn, against a reduction of wages on a California cigar. It resulted in a failure. The various nationalities represented in the union did not harmonize. Suspicion and ill-feeling prevented the growth of the organization. Only 160 out of 800 belonged to the union, which, after six months, ceased to exist.

In 1859, another union was organized, in consequence of a strike in Tom Little's shop, — said Little having migrated from Baltimore to New York city. The grievances were of a general nature. The union numbered 250 members, and lasted ten months. It was the means of preventing several reductions, thereby demonstrating its usefulness. Internal dissensions, arising from a diversity of opinion in regard to representation in the board of management, brought about the dissolution of the union. The dues were a shilling a week.

Prior to this, in 1854, the cigar makers of Troy, Syracuse, Rochester, Utica, Albany and Auburn decided in their shop-meetings to call a State convention, which was held in Syracuse, N. Y., on May 10 and 11, 1854. The object of the convention was to establish a uniform bill of prices in the State of New York, and to regulate the apprentice system. Mr. John G. Woodruff, of Troy, presided, and Mr. Theodore Fitzgerald, of Syracuse, acted as secretary. The cigar-manufacturers from Syracuse and surrounding towns were present, and took part in the deliberations. The convention lasted two days; but no permanent organization was formed. Nevertheless, the prices established were generally adhered to. "Scabs" were held in such abhorrence that they could not show themselves in fair shops.

In 1855, a large strike occurred in Suffield, Conn., for an increase of wages. A meeting was held, in which five hundred cigar-makers from Suffield and surrounding towns participated. The strike lasted between six and seven weeks, and was financially supported by the cigar-makers of New York, Albany, Syracuse, Troy, Westfield, Springfield and Fredenhills. The majority of the strikers left in quest of employment. The strike was finally settled by a compromise. In 1860 and the following years, the cigar-makers organized local unions spontaneously all over the country, and the necessity of a closer combination was generally felt among the workers. A preliminary conference was held in the city of Philadelphia, in 1863; and, on June 21, 1864, the National Union was organized in the city of New York.

The delegates to the convention, numbering twenty-three, represented local unions in Pennsylvania, New York, New Jersey, Ohio, Connecticut, Massachusetts, Rhode Island and Michigan. Mr. Thomas Harrock, of Suffield, Conn., was elected temporary chairman, and Mr. Charles Baker, of Philadelphia, secretary.

The following resolutions, explaining the objects of the convention, were adopted: —

"Believing that the time has arrived whereby the more perfect union of all local unions with one grand national union, the object sought to be obtained, viz.: the welfare of the cigar-makers as workingmen, can be better attained by being under one head. Therefore, we, the delegates assembled in New York city, June 21, 1864, adopt the following resolutions: —

"*Resolved*, That we, the cigar-makers' unions throughout the United States, do hereby unite ourselves by forming a national union, for the better protection of our trade, and for the advancement of our craft in general, and under such laws as adopted by this body, and adopted by two-thirds of local unions.

"*Resolved*, That our first object should be to unite the good cause, and earnestly request all unions to organize to aid us in so doing, and extend the right hand of fellowship to them.

"*Resolved*, That we earnestly request all cigar-makers to immediately organize themselves into unions, and when they are not in sufficient numbers to sustain themselves as a union, it shall be their duty to join the union nearest to them, in the county or district in which they work.

"*Resolved*, That no cigar-maker coming from any city, county or district, who is not a member of a union, if any exists, from whence he came, be allowed to become a member of the union where he has come to obtain employment, or be allowed to work in said city, county or district, until he has been admitted as a member in the place from whence he came.

"*Resolved*, That we discountenance the practice of any unions allowing its members to work in a shop or manufactory that employs no union men working for them out of the shop or manufactory.

"*Resolved*, That any cigar-maker having a card from any union acknowledging the authority of the National Union, may, by depositing this card, become a member free of charge, provided he has not violated the laws of said union."

The following officers were elected for the ensuing term: President, A. Zeitler, Albany; Vice-President, D. W. Donaghy, Philadelphia; English Recording Secretary, S. W. Holmes, Newark, N. J.; German Recording Secretary, A. Dans, Cincinnati; Corresponding Secretary, Charles Baker, Philadelphia; Treasurer, J. Bronk, Boston. One of the grievances of cigar-makers was the restrictions imposed upon them by the permit-system in the revenue laws, which was condemned by strong and sarcastic resolutions.

The objects of the National Union are thus stated in the first constitution: "To facilitate the thorough organization of the trade it represents for the mutual benefit and protection; to secure co-operation whenever it may be required, and to decide all differences that may arise between local unions." The Second Convention of the National Union was held at Cleveland, Ohio, on September 5, 1865. The local unions were represented by twenty-four delegates. The secretary in his report said that, since the first convention, the National Union had an increase of five unions; that a number of local unions decreased in membership, because a large number of members had enlisted in the army to battle for the country. A great many had laid down their lives on the altar of patriotism,—among them, Andrew J. Zeitler, president of the National Cigar-makers' Union. The receipts were $191.05; expenditures, $237.67; deficiency, $46.62. The aggregate membership of the National Union was 984. A special committee reported the indictment of a number of members of the local union of Syracuse, under the conspiracy laws of the State of New York. The committee said: "The National Union takes a wider view of the contest than the mere local interest and safety of the Syracuse union, and feels that the whole craft is endangered; that for the bosses of Syracuse to succeed would make the associating together, for protective purposes, both profitless and dangerous." The convention pledged itself to sustain those members before the court. It recommended that the members should subscribe for the following labor papers: The *Workingman's Advocate*, of Chicago; *Fincher's Trade Review*, of Philadelphia; Detroit *Daily Union*, and the *Daily Press*, of St. Louis. The following article, characteristic of its time, was engrafted in the constitution: "No person shall be eligible to membership in this union, unless he be a white male of the age of eighteen years, and has served an apprenticeship of not less than three years." L. C. Walker, of Baltimore, was elected president, and Charles Baker, of Philadelphia, secretary and treasurer.

The Third Annual Convention of the National Union convened on September 4, 1866, at Baltimore. The unions were represented by twenty-nine delegates and thirteen proxies. The following is quoted from the president's report: "The first question that presented itself, after the last convention, was, How to provide for unions on strike? The absence of all laws upon the subject by which we should be governed, was seriously felt at the start. A protracted and lengthy correspondence between the secretary and myself ensued, but nothing definite was arrived at. Finally, the secretary deemed it his duty to visit me for consultation; the result was the adoption of the present system of voluntary contributions. Under the circumstances, this was thought to be the most effectual mode of accomplishing the desired object." The secretary of the National Union, Mr. Baker, reported that, since the last convention, thirty-seven new unions organized, four disbanded, leaving in good standing sixty-two unions. Five unions engaged in strikes against reduction of wages, and other causes, of which three were successful. The assistance rendered in aid of these strikes amounted to $2,618.09. The receipts for the management of the organization from capitation-tax, and charter-fees, amounted to $531.30; the expenditures, $483.83; leaving a balance in treasury of $47.47. The election of officers resulted in the re-election of Mr. L. C. Walker as president, and Charles Baker as secretary. A resolution was adopted directing the officers to communicate with the cigar-makers' unions of Great Britain and other countries, for the purpose of preventing unfair men to join the unions in the United States at the regular initiation-fee, without the payment of fine. The question of obnoxious revenue laws and "permit"-system, came up for discussion, and resolutions were adopted declaring that the only fair way of taxing tobacco was upon the leaf, so that the whole consumption of tobacco will pay equal revenue, and be a sure means of preventing fraud; that, if the tax could not be levied on the leaf, the laws be amended so that the different grades of smoking-tobacco would pay a tax nearly equal to that levied on cigars per pound; that a specific tax would be next fairest; that the "permit and account system," was obnoxious and degrading. A resolution was also adopted in favor of eight hours as a legal day's work.

The Fourth Annual Convention was held in Buffalo, September 2, 1867, and forty-two delegates were present.

Mr. John J. Junio, of Syracuse, was elected president, and Mr. Charles Baker, of Philadelphia, secretary-treasurer.

The name of National Cigar-makers' Union was changed to Cigar-makers' International Union of America.

The convention also took ground in regard to the general agitation for shorter hours of labor, by adopting the following resolution: —

"WHEREAS, The workingmen of the country are, at the present time, advocating an eight-hour law system; therefore, be it

"*Resolved*, That this National Union approves of their efforts in contending for their rights as workingmen, hoping they will be successful without deduction of wages."

The Buffalo *Gazette*, published by Mr. Kernaham, president of the Trades-Association and Eight-hour League, was adopted as the official organ of the Cigar-makers' International Union of America.

The following labor papers were recommended to the craft: *Workingman's Advocate*, of Chicago; Boston *Voice*, *Fincher's Welcome*, of Philadelphia; Troy *Herald*, Baltimore *Laborer*, *Westliche Post* (Post of the West), of St. Louis, and Detroit *Union*.

The words "male" and "white," to be eligible for membership, were stricken out from the constitution, and the words "practical cigar-maker" inserted in their place.

The German cigar-makers of New York and Brooklyn, organized in independent societies, were permitted to organize separate unions under the banner of the International Union, by applying for charters, etc.

The Committee on Officers' Reports stated that the expenditures for strikes during the fiscal year amounted to $1,506.15.

A resolution was adopted demanding again from Congress the repeal of the obnoxious law now enforced, compelling cigar-makers to take out a permit to work at their legitimate business, knowing the same to be contrary to a republican form of government.

The subsequent three conventions were held at Cincinnati, Chicago and Syracuse. At the latter place, a special convention was held. In the call for the same, signed by Fred Blend, president, and Elias Smith, secretary, the object is stated as follows: —

"To take into consideration the past strikes, and to bring about a final settlement of the same; to complete arrangements for future strikes; to take more active measures toward assisting the interest of co-operation; to take into consideration the present revenue laws; and to protest against the importation of coolies.

Two large, protracted strikes and lockouts, which took place between 1869–1870 in New York city and Cincinnati, necessitating heavy assessments, endangered the International Union, which had then reached its highest numerical growth preceding the industrial panic of 1873.

In 1870, the organization had seven strikes, of which only two were successful, the expenditures amounted to $43,017.00.

The two large lockouts brought the International Union into a financial embarrassment, being unable to fulfil its obligations in the payment of the regular strike-benefit. Worthless checks were issued to members in lieu of cash.

This was one of the causes that led to the dissolution of unions, and to the suspension of a large number of members. In 1869, the membership of the International Union was 5,800; in 1873, it had decreased to 3,771. Besides this, the absence of benevolent features was largely felt in a lack of cohesion among the members.

The fight of the unions against the introduction of the moulds, ending disastrously, also assisted in the disintegration of the unions.

From 1871 to 1875, inclusive, there were 78 strikes; 66 of which were unsuccessful, and 12 successful. These cost an expenditure of $24,242.08. Sixty-four of these strikes were against a reduction of wages.

At the convention at Detroit, Mich., in 1873, the following endowment plan was adopted: —

SECTION 1. In case of the death of a member of a local union in good standing, the officers of the union to which the deceased has belonged shall notify the International Secretary, within ten days thereafter, of such death; said notification to bear the seal of the union, and be accompanied by a certificate of the attending physician or health-officers.

SECT. 2. Immediately upon receiving such notification, properly attested, it shall be the duty of the International Secretary to order each union to forward, within twenty days, to the union where such death has occurred, the sum of ten cents per member in good standing, for the benefit of the widow, orphan or nearest dependent relative; *provided*, that in all cases where the deceased leaves no widow, orphan or dependent relative, this section shall remain inoperative.

This endowment plan was supposed to be a substitute for the loaning system to traveling members, which was abolished by the convention.

The abolishing of the loaning system, — a system of support to the traveling fraternity, — was a mistake. Its provisions should have been modified on a sound basis, by which dishonesty could have been checked, and the unemployed in quest of employment retained in the union.

The convention also adopted a system of arbitration as a means of preventing needless strikes.

The disastrous effect which the industrial panic of 1873 had upon the organization is best illustrated in the biennial report of President William J. Cannon, at the Paterson Convention, held in September, 1875: —

"The panic, with all its attending evils, came upon us like a whirlwind, carrying destruction and desolation in its path, — making fearful havoc and ghastly inroads into the prosperous and happy homes of the working people, effectually closing every avenue of prosperity and every channel of industry. It required no foresight to see that the effect on our trade would be disastrous, and that unless wise and judicious councils prevailed among the members of our local organizations, they would embark upon a series of ruinous strikes, which would not only end in their own destruction, but also in the dissolution of the International Union.

"I issued a circular urging the unions to use discretion in acting upon proposed reductions, and to weigh well chances of success against the almost certainty of defeat before launching into a strike. The response came in the shape of applications for strike-benefits from Paterson, Richmond, Cincinnati, St. Louis and Westfield. These were followed by other applications in rapid succession, nearly every mail bringing to my notice either an anticipated reduction or an inaugurated strike.

"It became evident to me that the ability of the International Union to stand adversity as it had prosperity was about to be put to a severe test. Feeling the impossibility of making a successful resistance, I advised to avoid strikes. In a few cases, this advice was adopted; but the great majority claimed as good a right to strike and receive support as any other union, and when they did not receive the support promptly, would return to their work, and the union disband. In this manner, our membership has been largely reduced, as well as the number of our unions, while of those which remain many are weak, only awaiting their death-blow in the form of a reduction or a special assessment of a few cents weekly."

The endowment plan, adopted at a previous convention, proved to be a failure, because the members refused to pay the assessments, and it was repealed by a vote of the unions.

The International Secretary, E. J. Cox, reported that, on September 30, 1873, there were in good standing 84 unions, with a membership of 3,771. On the 30th of September, 1884, there were 54 unions, with a reported membership of 2,167, — showing a decrease in unions of 30, and in membership of 1,604.

Only eleven delegates met at the Paterson Convention. Two important resolutions were adopted, — one authorizing the president to publish monthly the *Cigar-makers' Official Journal*, the other allowing bunch-breakers and rollers to become members. The offices of secretary, treasurer and president were combined in one person. Mr. George Hurst, of West Suffield, Conn., was elected to the position.

The recognition of bunch-breaking and rolling, in localities where the system was fully established, caused a great deal of dissension. Several unions, where that system was unknown, seceded, and divided the funds; others maintained independent local unions.

Between 1875 and 1877, the International Union was in the most critical condition. Members had deserted the ranks, and unions dissolved. Confidence, so essential to the success of a trades organization, was completely destroyed. To see a traveling member in possession of a card was a rarity.

In 1876, there were nine strikes against reduction of wages, which terminated unsuccessfully. Expenditures, $582.20.

In September, 1877, the convention of the International Union met at Rochester. It was composed of seven delegates, representing 17 local unions and a membership of 1,016. This was the lowest point the International Union had reached since its organization. The New York delegate was instructed to introduce out-of-work, sick and traveling-benefits; but was entirely unsuccessful in convincing the majority of the utility of these benevolent features. Mr. A. Strasser, of New York city, was elected president. After balloting twenty times, he received four votes out of seven.

Fortunately for the organization, there was a slight revival of trade in some of the large centres of the cigar industry. The cigar-makers, having been cut in their wages to the minimum point during the period of depression grasped at the slightest opportunity for an advance of wages.

The tenement-house system, the curse of the trade, had assumed gigantic proportions; nearly four-fifths of the cigars made in New York city were made in tenement-houses.

In the month of August, 1877, a strike occurred in the shop of Frederick DeBarry, New York city, for an increase of wages. In the months of September and October, the strike extended to all leading factories and tenement-houses, resisted by a powerful combination of 32 manufacturers. Over 7,000 men and women were affected. It followed close upon the gigantic railroad strike. The strike, although not entirely successful, was a great lesson to the cigar-makers. It clearly demonstrated the necessity of organization and the building-up of a reserve fund. During the strike, which lasted 107 days, over 1,000 families, making cigars in their tenements, were dispossessed from their homes by the sheriff. The total cost of the strike was $48,476.39.

The reason that the expenses of a strike involving so many thousand persons were so low, was due to the fact that the Relief Committee supplied the needy ones with bread, beef and other necessaries of life, which they purchased at wholesale prices. Over 1,000 loaves of bread, each weighing three pounds, and 2,500 pounds of meat were distributed every day. The heroic struggle of the raw recruits engaged in the fight created enthusiasm among the cigar-makers all over the country. Unions sprang up in every direction, and before the strike had ended, local unions had doubled in number. In New York city alone, over 7,000 enrolled in the various unions, of whom, after the struggle was over, only 131 remained true to their colors.

The next convention of the International was held at Buffalo, in 1879. The credentials of 11 delegates were approved. The president reported a net increase of 18 unions since the last convention, while the membership increased from 1,016 to 1,250.

The president recommended, in his biennial report, the federation of trades-unions for the purpose of uniting all trade and labor-unions of America into one grand body; the enforcement of the eight-hour law for all government employees; the employment of a general organizer; the continuation of the agitation against tenement-house cigar-factories; the prohibition of child-labor and enforcement of the school-laws; the regulation of female labor; the prohibition of contract convict-labor; the prohibition of the importation of coolies, and the abolition of the truck system; the introduction of benevolent features; the equalization of funds, and the adoption of equal dues and initiation-fees.

The convention adopted the loaning system for the support of the traveling fraternity, equal dues and initiation-fees for all members, and the equalization of funds. The strike-laws were modified in conformity with the experience of the past, and a sinking-fund of $2.00 per member was embodied in the constitution. The president's salary was $250.00 per annum. Mr. A. Strasser, of New York, was re-elected. The adoption of these new features had a remarkable influence upon the organization; it helped to strengthen the revival of unionism in all parts of the country.

The next convention was held in 1880, at Chicago, Ill., represented by 32 delegates. The president reported an increase of 38 unions in one year, and an increase in membership of 3,159. In his reference to the necessity of connecting additional benevolent features with the organization, the president said: "I do not know of any cigar-maker opposed to additional benefits. The strongest and most powerful trades-unions of the civilized world are those which secure to the members the greatest amount of protection, not only during strikes, but when sick, out of work, in search of employment, and almost in every other station of life where our own resources are insufficient, and we have to depend upon others."

Regarding strikes, the president recommended not to recognize any applications for an increase of wages until the coming spring, and to make "haste slowly."

In 1880, there were sixteen strikes, — five for an increase of wages, one against the truck system, six against reduction, and the rest for maintenance of the union. Of these sixteen strikes, nine were successful, five lost, and two compromised; the expenditures were $6,315.93. The convention adopted, after a prolonged and heated debate, the sick and death-benefit features, and empowered the president to appoint an organizer, at an expense not to exceed $300.00 per annum. The union label, known as *the blue label*, was also adopted. Mr. A. Strasser, of New York, was unanimously re-elected as president.

The next convention, known as the Fourteenth Annual Session, was held in September, 1881, at Cleveland, Ohio. It consisted of 53 delegates. The president reported, in his annual address, an increase of 52 unions, and 8,300 members.

In 1881, there were 69 strikes, of which 49 were for an increase of wages, 10 against reductions, 10 against the truck system, and other causes. Of these strikes, 57 were successful, and 12 lost. The expenditures amounted to $21,058.08. In regard to the evils of making cigars in tenement-houses, the president made the following statement: —

"Eight years have elapsed since the system was first exposed in public meetings, and the board of health requested to recognize them as a public nuisance, dangerous to the health and morals of the occupants. The white-washing report of the board was published in the *Workingman's Advocate*, then the official journal of the Cigar-makers' International Union. The agitation was continued, and carried to the Senate of the United States. In the month of February, 1879, the Senate Committee on Finance adopted a bill to abolish the evil. It was carried through the committee of the whole, by an unanimous vote, in a division of the Senate by a vote of 27 to 4, but ultimately defeated by a vote of 35 to 25. Defeated in the Senate of the United States, the bill was introduced as a sanitary measure in the Legislature of the State of New York, during the winter of 1880. It was carried through the committee, but defeated in the committee of the whole, by a vote of 49 to 40. The bill was again introduced in the Legislature, and defeated by a vote of 45 to 45. This is a brief history of the agitation to the fall of 1881."

The convention again adopted a resolution prohibiting local unions from striking for an increase of wages from November 1, 1881, till April 1, 1882. The sinking-fund was raised from $2.00 to $3.50.

The following section regulating the hours of labor was embodied in the constitution: "Every local union shall have the power to regulate the hours of labor, in its respective locality; but in no case shall they exceed ten per day."

Shortly after that convention commenced an internal conflict in New York city, known as the secession of the so-called progressive cigar-makers, led by men that were only a short time in the country, and not acquainted with the peculiar course of the American labor movement.

The conflict in the ranks of the cigar-makers almost destroyed the usefulness of the organization in New York city. It is a dark episode in the history of the craft.

The next convention was held at Toronto, Ont., in September, 1883. The credentials of 88 delegates were approved.

The biennial report of the president showed an increase of 59 unions, and an increase of 1,291 in membership. A comparison with past years showed the following growth: —

September, 1877	. . . .	17 local unions.
" 1879	. . . .	35 " "
" 1880	. . . .	74 " "
" 1881	. . . .	126 " "
" 1883	. . . .	185 " "

The managing expenses for two years, including eight million labels, twenty-four issues of the journal, and five supplements, amounted to $16,566.70. From the president's report, the following is quoted on strikes: —

"We do not court them, nor do we favor them. They should not be resorted to until all peaceable means have been tried and exhausted. To go out on strike without cool and calm deliberation, where all chances are carefully taken into consideration, is neither heroic nor worthy of imitation. The object of every well-regulated union is to check and to discourage frequent difficulties; to secure an advance of wages whenever the condition of trade is favorable, without the expedient of a strike.

"A revision of our strike-laws is of the utmost importance. The International Union must be enabled to check strikes in time of necessity, restrict and regulate the power of local unions in the inauguration of the same. The welfare of the entire organization is sometimes endangered by a single strike. During the last two years, the number of difficulties has no parallel in the history of the organization. The expenditures were enormous, involving a large portion of our income. We have expended $77,203.47. I can safely say that, outside of regular assessments, over $40,000 have been contributed voluntarily. Within the last two years, the International Union approved 194 strikes. They were inaugurated for the following causes: Ninety-seven for an increase of wages, fifty-two against reductions, and forty-five for various other causes. Of these, 135 were successful, 47 lost, and 12 undecided. I have endeavored to make a careful calculation, from the monthly reports returned, of the amount gained in wages through these strikes, within a period of four years, and have come to the conclusion that it amounts at present to $150,000 per month, or $1,800,000 per annum. It is hard to estimate what has been gained by preventing reductions of wages; but I do not think that it will fall much below $500,000 per year."

In regard to the hours of labor, the president made the following statement: —

"A large number of trades organizations have agreed that the reduction of the hours of labor is a cardinal principle of the labor movement. In the past, the building trades have led in this direction. The time has come when all trades must prepare for some reduction of the working-time. I recommend that steps be taken toward the adoption of the nine-hour system. From the reports returned by local unions, I notice that, in a good many places, the hours of labor do not exceed fifty-four per week. It would, therefore, be an easy step to make them uniform. The following table is copied from the monthly reports of local unions, and shows the average weekly working hours in the several localities: —

13	local unions make report of working	60	hours per week.
1	" " " " " "	59	" " "
22	" " " " " "	58	" " "
32	" " " " " "	57	" " "
18	" " " " " "	56	" " "
26	" " " " " "	55	" " "
12	" " " " " "	54	" " "
1	" " " " " "	53	" " "
10	" " " " " "	52	" " "
3	" " " " " "	51	" " "
8	" " " " " "	50	" " "
4	" " " " " "	48	" " "

"The fact that the reduction of the hours of labor has been followed by an increase of wages, and through natural causes higher wages must follow a further reduction, is a sufficient answer to all objections."

The president also recommended that legislative interference of our law-making bodies be invoked for the purpose of prohibiting the employment of child-labor under fourteen years of age, and to prevent women from being employed more than eight hours.

On the important question of supporting the unemployed, the president made the following remarks in his biennial report: —

"The protective and benevolent features of the union should be enlarged by the adoption of an act of work-benefit. A member of the union, who is out of work for a long period, is in danger of soon being out of the union. If the number of the unemployed is large, demoralization steps in, and it becomes difficult to maintain the rate of wages. The fear that this benefit would encourage idleness among those who have but little ambition, has but little foundation, as the sum given would be so small and so guarded with conditions that the shiftless would soon be found out."

The president's decision in the New York trouble was indorsed, and the secession of the Progressives condemned by the convention. Mr. A. Strasser, of New York city, was re-elected, receiving 69 votes out of 87. The convention resolved to appoint a permanent organizer. In regard to the forms of labor, the following resolution was adopted: —

"WHEREAS we know that a reduction of the hours of labor furnishes employment to a larger number of men, we therefore recommend the consideration of this question to all members of the Cigar-makers' International Union, and urge them to use all their energy in effecting the reduction of the hours of labor to eight per day."

The convention increased the sick-benefit from $4.00 to $5.00 per week, and the death-benefit from $30.00 to $40.00 per member.

CALIFORNIA AND COLORADO.

The history of the movement in the Eastern, Middle and Western States is given in the fourth and fifth chapters of the book. At the present writing, the Knights of Labor have the greatest membership of any organization, and perhaps greater than all other organizations.

In the South, trades-unions have existed among the free white mechanics, tracing back to about 1850 or 1845, — the earliest days of the movement. The Knights of Labor are entitled to the credit of having accomplished more in the organization of the colored people than all other labor organizations. The history of the labor movement in the South would require a most exhaustive investigation, and might well fill a book.

The State of California, having specially to deal with the problem of Chinese labor, has demanded the sympathies as well as the attention of the labor organizations East. In another place, we devote considerable space to the Chinese question, and here give what little can be gathered of the organized effort in that State, furnished by E. Burdette Haskell, and supplement it by statements on the development of the question in Colorado, by J. R. Buchanan, member of the auxiliary Executive Board of the Knights of Labor.

THE LABOR MOVEMENT IN CALIFORNIA.

In California, of all places in the world, labor has probably had the hardest struggle to organize; and it will have in the future an equally hard task to accomplish its emancipation. The State was settled by a cosmopolitan population, and race jealousies and divisions consequently here flourish in excess. The main idea of the immigrants was to get money as soon as possible, and by any means. Thus the dollar is more of a god in California than in any other State. The early settlers were mainly of the reckless, criminal, improvident class of adventurers and a train of scheming camp-followers. This first class has nearly all died off. Their children, being deprived of proper schooling when young, are now deprived of proper labor by the presence of Chinese. They are, consequently, idle and discontented. The second class of immigrants grabbed all of the lands and city property, and now hold it and enjoy its fruits; they will not go into new enterprises, and they will not let go of the land, so that it may be made available for use by others. The result is stagnation in business. The want of moral training and education of any kind makes the population peculiarly corrupt and unscrupulous; and the labor organizations swarm with spies and jobbers.

The early history of labor movements on this coast is one of vicissitudes. The first recorded attempt at union in this city was made by the ship-carpenters, in 1856. This union was eminently successful, — in fact, too successful. Its dissolution was not less singular than its success; for its treasury became so plethoric that discussion among its members as to how the funds should be disposed of led to a disruption. In 1857, the journeymen tailors organized and elected officers. The union disbanded after three meetings. In 1863, the tailors again organized, their grievance being that they were not paid for extra work. The formation of the union was almost immediately followed by a strike against the amount of fancy-work put upon the coats of the period. The strike lasted several weeks, and was successful. The union died soon afterward. It was revived in 1873. Without a strike, the hours of labor were reduced from eleven to ten, and the organization was in a fair way to prosperity and longevity; but the action of its members precipitated several strikes, and the union at last dwindled away and died.

The first amalgamation of trades-unions took place about 1863, John M. Days leading the movement. A year later fourteen trades were represented in it, and the year following that it had six. It died during the struggle for an eight-hour law. In 1857, an eight-hour law went into effect in Australia, and was reported to be a success. The news, upon reaching this coast, caused a very general desire among workingmen for a decrease in the hours of labor. At this time, labor-saving machinery was making itself felt. A remedy for the resulting evil was seen in a reduction of hours, and it became a political war-cry. In 1865, it influenced the city election for members of the Legislature, and at the succeeding election eight hours for a day's labor became a law. In September, 1865, the ship-calkers adopted eight hours, and the ship-carpenters followed. The Trades-Council sent its president to Sacramento, in the interest of the movement, and he secured the appointment of a joint committee favorable to the eight-hour bill. It passed the Lower House by

64 ayes to 6 noes, and in the Senate was referred to a committee. It was attacked by the press. In January, 1867, the Senate defeated the bill by 15 ayes to 17 noes.

In 1866, a nine-hour movement was started; but the mechanics did not regard it favorably, and after a little agitation it fell through. Early in 1867, the eight-hour fight was renewed in earnest. An eight-hour league was organized, the unions formed the Mechanics' State Council. In it were represented the following unions: House-carpenters', lathers', brick-layers', stone-cutters', ship-joiners', gas-fitters', and laborers. The number of members is not known now. This organization advocated eight hours. Both parties adopted an eight-hour plank. On June 3d, the Mechanics' State Council paraded. On February 21, 1868, an eight-hour law was passed.

The passage of this bill was enthusiastically celebrated in San Francisco. Laws were passed to protect the wages of labor. The labor-men then relaxed their efforts, and these laws were soon evaded by having men work by the hour instead of by the day. Thus the eight-hour law never conferred a particle of benefit on the mechanic. The labor organizations soon dwindled away, and in three years only the brick-layers and plasterers remained organized. In 1874, the tailors made an attempt to federate the trades of San Francisco. Six unions met, but the federation soon fell to pieces. The brick-layers kept up their union, and observed the eight-hour law, until 1875, when a capitalist combination broke them up. The plasterers held out on eight hours until 1877, when their union succumbed in a strike for higher wages. When the labor agitations commenced, another attempt was made to amalgamate, and about fourteen unions were got together, having about 1,500 members. This federation died after the fall elections.

In 1877, the anti-Chinese agitation reached its culmination in the Kearney movement. Prior to appearing as a leader, Kearney had been on the side of capital and low wages. He attempted to gain admission to the Workingmen's party of the United States, was black-balled, and then started the "Workingmen's and Labor Union Party," making his headquarters on the Sand Lots. Much of his success was due to T. H. Bates and H. L. Knight, two of his lieutenants.

A convention was held in Humboldt Hall, January 24, 1878, which adopted the Workingmen's Party platform and constitution, the chief planks of which were anti-Chinese. Kearney was president, and Knight secretary of the party, which went actively to work through the city. Their outrages on the public peace called into being a "Safety Committee." Kearney was arrested several times for the violence of his language. Finally, his displays of physical cowardice utterly broke his hold, and he was hooted and jeered when he appeared on the Sand Lots. He was never in any respect a representative of labor, nor was his party.

In the early stages of the "Workingmen's Party," a federation of trades-unions was formed under the title of the "Trades-Assembly." The most notable of its performances was an ineffectual attempt to form a co-operative furniture factory. In April, 1882, the Trades-Assembly called a State Convention, in which were represented delegates from the trades-unions of Nevada and Oregon, and steps were taken against the Chinese. The means employed was the formation of a "League of Deliverance," which made considerable noise during its brief career, but accomplished nothing, and died out soon after its birth, side by side with the trades-assembly.

After the demise of the League of Deliverance, trades-unionism in San Francisco remained dormant until the early part of 1885. Early in that year, the International began to openly show itself as an encourager of trades organization and federation. On the 16th of March, a general convention of trades assembled at Irish-American Hall, and after three days' session launched "The Central Labor Union," which, however, succumbed to the vigorous attack of the politicians in the various unions. The Iron-moulders' Union was, however, more fortunate. They succeeded in perfecting a sub-federation of the iron trades, May 11, 1885, which still exists. The iron federation was but a preliminary step to a general federation of the trades and labor organizations of the Pacific coast. The coast seamen were the first after the iron-men to come to the front prominently. On the night of March 6, 1885, a party of coasting seamen gathered around a lumber-pile on Folsom-street wharf, and by the light of a friendly street-lamp formed a union. In the one year of its existence, it has gained ground until it now has a membership of over 3,000, with branches in Port Townsend, Eureka and San Pedro, covering the line of the entire coast. Its union has done much good in furnishing better board and rooms, by securing higher wages, and by acting as an agency where vessel-owners can get good men.

In the latter part of 1884, several cigar-makers, who were members of the Cigar-makers' Association of the Pacific Coast, withdrew from that organization, and formed themselves into a branch of the International Cigar-makers' Union of America. The reason for this action was that the constitution and by-laws of the association did not permit any of its members to work in a factory where Chinese were employed. The union has been very successful, has materially displaced Chinese control of the cigar-making business, and has eight hundred members. Several unions are now in operation through the State.

Last December, the Knights of Labor called a convention for the purpose of giving expression to the views of workingmen on the question of convict-labor and the Chinese; calling upon those renting property to Chinese to evict their tenants, and also demanded an enforcement of the laws as set down in the State Constitution. Several of the organizations which had sent delegates to the convention were displeased, and withdrew them. The iron trades, the Cigar-makers' Union, and other prominent organizations remained, however, and after passing a number of pertinent resolutions formed a plan for the federation of the trades and labor organizations of the Pacific coast. In the convention, the following were represented: Blacksmiths' Union, Boiler-makers' League, Sailing-Vessels' Cooks' and Waiters', Carpenters' and Joiners' Union No. 36, of Oakland; Local Assembly No. 855, of Sacramento; Lathers' Union, Local Assembly 1760, of San Francisco; Express Union, of San Francisco; Tinners' Union, of San Francisco; Local Assembly 1390, of San Francisco; Amalgamated Society of Engineers, of San Francisco; Steamship Protective Association, of California; United Order of Mechanics, of Vallejo; Boatmen's Protective Union, of San Francisco; Pavers' Union, of San Francisco; Iron-moulders' Union No. 164, of San Francisco; Independent Order of Associated Plasterers', Carpenters', and Joiners',

No. 22, of San Francisco; Furniture-makers' Union, Draymen and Teamsters' Union, Marine Engineers', Carpenters' and Joiners' Union, No. 58, of Los Angeles; Journeymen Boot and Shoemakers, of San Francisco; Local Assembly 1573, of San Francisco; Knights of Labor, 2999, of San Francisco; Knights of Labor, 3337, of San Francisco; Mechanics' Union, Storey County, Nevada; Typographical Union, of San Francisco, No. 21; Knights of Labor, 1580, of San Francisco; Saddle-treemakers, of San Francisco; Wood-carvers, of San Francisco; Knights of Labor, No. 2383; Musicians' Protective Union; Pacific Coast Association of Stationary Engineers; Penryn Stone-cutters; S. S. Firemen's Protective Association; Stone-cutters' Union, of San Francisco; Tailors' Protective and Benevolent Union, of San Francisco; White Cooks and Waiters, of San Francisco; Machinists' Union, of California; Federated Council of Iron Trades, Knights of Labor, 2861, of San Francisco; International Cigar-makers of America, No. 228, of San Francisco; Iron Laborers' Protective Association, of San Francisco; Carpenters and Joiners, of Alameda; Marine Carpenters, of San Francisco; Pacific Coast Seamen's Association; Clerks' Assembly, No. 3651, Knights of Labor; Bakers' Workmen Union; Boot and Shoemakers' "White-Labor" Union; Pacific Coast Division International Workingmen's Association; Under-wear Factory of M. J. Flavin, Stockton Branch of Pacific Coast Division International Workingmen's Association, Socialistic Labor Party, Coast Seamen's Union, Metal-roofers, Eureka Branch of the Coast Seamen's Union; of the Pacific Coast; International Workmen, Plumbers' Union, Coopers' Union, Pattern-makers' White Cigar-makers' Association; of the Pacific Coast; Wharf-builders' Protective Association, Los Angeles Trades-Council, Local Assembly 855, Knights of Labor, of Sacramento.

The Federation of Trades, when formed, included nearly all of the above. The following were elected officers: Frank Roney, president; Patrick McGreal, vice-president; T. W. Parkin, recording secretary; G. F. Wenzel, financial secretary; E. McKinley, corresponding secretary; W. C. Owen, statistical secretary; P. F. Murphy, treasurer; Committee on Organization, B. G. Haskell, P. Ross Martin, W. C. Owen, P. McGreal, L. N. Ahrens, H. W. Hutton; Edward Anderson, sergeant-at-arms; Finance Committee, M. Schneider, George Bayless, J. H. Ranons; Committee on Credentials, D. J. McCarthy, D. Chisholm, J. M. Clark; Committee on Reports, George Bayless, J. McDermott, E. McKinley.

After the adoption of a constitution, the Federation went ahead with its business. Since its organization, it has been very active in organizing local unions, and has taken an active and highly successful part in several movements.

THE LABOR QUESTION IN COLORADO.

Until within six or seven years, organized labor in Colorado and adjacent Territories has not amounted to much. The first organization in Colorado was Typographical Union No. 49, of Denver, chartered June 3, 1860. Now all the trades in Denver and in the principal towns of the State and Territories are organized. Denver has a trades-assembly, in which the unions are represented by delegates. In Leadville, Cheyenne, Ogden, Salt Lake, etc., the workers are principally organized in assemblies of the Knights of Labor. There was no important contest of labor and capital in that region until the great miners' strike in Leadville, 1880. This was caused by an attempt to reduce the wages of the miners from $4.00 and $6.00 per day to a uniform price of $3.00. The miners were organized into what was publicly known as the Miners' Union, but which were the Knights of Labor in their old, secret style. A majority of the 4,000 or 5,000 employees of the mines were in this organization. It decided to strike, after attempting to settle by arbitration. Some "scabs" were secured, but only a small force remained in the mines, and most of them were entirely shut down. The union, after getting most of those at work to leave, found the mines guarded by armed men, who, in some instances, fired on the union men. Excitement ran high. Both sides made public procession. A "Safety Committee of One Hundred," as it called itself, issued peremptory orders that certain leaders of the strike leave town. Only three obeyed. Influenced by misrepresentations, Governor Pitkin proclaimed martial law in Leadville, although he afterward said that the only disorderly element he could find there was that opposing the Miners' Union. The miners were beaten in the end; and it subsequently transpired that the whole affair was a stock-jobbing scheme, worked up by the owners of the property.

The next important event in labor circles in this region was the strike of the Union Pacific Railway employees, May 1, 1884, against a reduction of wages. The men organized, the shops were closed, and freight trains stopped. Assemblies of Knights of Labor were formed. Denver was made headquarters, and committees and organizers were sent all over the road. In three days, the company withdrew its order, and business was resumed. The men continued to organize. In August, a reduction was attempted by cutting a few at a time. Again work was suspended. A committee was sent to the company headquarters, and on the second day the reduction was withdrawn. A plan of concilation between the men and the company was then agreed upon, which is still in operation, and no serious trouble has since resulted.

In October, 1884, the coal-miners of Colorado, Wyoming and Utah organized at the various camps into assemblies of the Knights of Labor, formed a central organization, and with some of the operators created what they called a "Conciliation Board," for the purpose of settling differences as to wages, weights and screens, which had arisen at nearly all the mines. Failing to settle, a strike was ordered at most of the mines, and a bitter struggle began, — the hardest fight being with the Colorado Coal & Iron Co. "Scabs" were brought from the East and South, and worked under guards, families were turned out of company-houses, and a great deal of bad blood was shown. The trouble lasted through two months; but it finally died out. The strikers won in some places and lost in others, — the principal defeat being by the Colorado Coal & Iron Co. But the central organization of miners and the Conciliation Board were demolished; and now the miners look out for their interests locally, through their assemblies. Just at the close, on May 5, 1885, was inaugurated the celebrated Rio Grande strike. The Rio Grande Railroad Company, then in the hands of a receiver, began to discharge and otherwise discriminate against members of the Knights of Labor. Six men were unjustly discharged from the Denver shops, and the superintendent refused to reinstate or bring definite charges against them. It was decided to strike against this tyrannical action, although against the wish of a great many, who feared a contest with a road in the hands of the United States courts. The contest was one of the bitterest ever known in labor annals. Deputy United States marshals abounded, and the men were not allowed to go near the trainmen to persuade them not to work. Dynamite was placed on the track, and engines were blown up, but no lives were lost. Men were sent to jail for months for asking trainmen to leave the trains. The court decided that employees refusing to obey the order to keep off the company's ground, the company being in the hands of a receiver, were guilty of contempt of court, and men were imprisoned on this charge. Later developments go to show that the placing of dynamite on the tracks, and similar outrages, were done by deputies, who were drawing $5 per day, and who wanted the excitement continued. The strike was finally lost for lack of funds.

THE NATIONAL GRANGE OF THE PATRONS OF HUSBANDRY.

It is a remarkable coincidence, that the number of founders of the Grange was the same as of the Knights of Labor. From a union of ideas and efforts, by seven earnest men in each case, has sprung a great organization that covers the whole country. So far as known, also, six of the original founders are now living, — another coincidence with the founders of the Knights of Labor.

In January, 1866, Mr. O. H. Kelley, a clerk under the National Commissioner of Agriculture, was sent through the South, returning to Washington, April 21. He was impressed with the disorganization of the farmers of that section, and, after much thought, came to the conclusion that they should be organized into a secret league, devoted to their interests. He consulted Mr. J. R. Thompson, an officer in the Treasury Department, and Mr. William M. Ireland, chief clerk in the finance division of the Post-Office Department, to which Mr. Kelley had been transferred. Both of them were Masons, and they cordially indorsed the ideas of Mr. Kelley. Finding the need of the opinions of a practical agriculturist, they invited Mr. William Saunders, superintendent of the gardens and grounds of the Department of Agriculture, to join them. He consented. Wanting further advice, they invited Rev. John Trimble, of the Treasury Department, to criticise their labors. After a season, Rev. A. B. Grosh, then a clerk in the Agricultural Department, and Mr. F. M. McDowell, of Wayne, N. Y., were induced to labor with the other five; and these seven constituted the immortal founders of the Patrons of Husbandry. For nearly two years, they labored in preparing a scheme of organization, based on a ritual of four degrees each, for men and women. Having formed a constitution adapted to this ritual to govern them, they met, December 4,

1867, in the little brown building on the corner of Four-and-a-half street and Missouri avenue, and then and there constituted themselves as the National Grange of the Patrons of Husbandry, with Saunders as master, Thompson as lecturer, Ireland as treasurer and Kelley as secretary. The other offices were left vacant. For four years they labored zealously. Kelley resigned his clerkship and went, with neither scrip nor money, among the unknown farmers of the Northwest, to spread the Order. His only letter of credit was a sort of "To Whom it May Concern" epistle. He organized a grange at Harrisburg, Penn., one at Fredonia, N. Y., one at Columbus, O., and perhaps one or two others on his way to Northern Minnesota. His expenses were met by the $15 charter-fee of the granges he organized, and occasional pittances from his friends in Washington.

For four years this septuary brotherhood met frequently, and formally once a year as a National Grange. A quorum was not always present. At the Third Annual Session, Worthy Master Saunders delivered his inaugural, with Secretary Kelley as his sole auditory. When he finished, he asked leave to print in the next day's papers, which was granted.

The constitution required that every subordinate grange should be composed of not less than nine men and four women; and that fifteen such granges might ask for organization as a State grange. The first State grange was organized in Minnesota, February 23, 1869. By the Fifth Annual Session of the National Grange, January 3, 1872, about 200 granges had been organized; and during 1872, 1,074 were organized, about half of which were in Iowa and South Carolina. In 1873, 8,668 subordinate granges were organized, and 11,941 in 1874. Then came the attempt at co-operation and arbitration. The organization flourished marvelously. But lack of discipline, jealousy and envy soon wrought great injury. Politicians and other designing men began to get control of the granges. One grange was organized by forty-five bank-presidents, wholesale dealers, speculators, etc., in New York, and represented probably as many million dollars. In such ways was the foundation of the Order sapped. Reduced prices, secured for members of the granges from manufacturers under "confidential" pledges, were revealed, and damaged both sides. However, the prices remained reduced to a large extent. A perfect system of crop-reports was also adopted. Co-operative stores were established, which save large sums annually to their customers.

The Journal of Proceedings of the Nineteenth Annual Session, held at Boston, November 11–20, 1885, makes a pamphlet of 230 pages. It shows that the National Grange has about $50,000 in its treasury, and that since 1882 its receipts have more than met expenses. During 1885, 90 original charters were issued, divided among 23 States; and 150 dormant granges were reorganized between September 1, 1884, and September 1, 1885.

SOCIALISM IN AMERICA.

The industrial movement in this country is represented by the Trades-unions and Knights of Labor. In addition to this, there is a special movement, in which many labor organizations heartily sympathize, that makes finance the prominent issue. This, of course, assumes the political form. The movement grew out of the National Labor Congress immediately after the war.

In the early chapters of the history, we have given some account of the growth of Socialism. It was not until at the close of the war, that the present form of this movement became manifest. At present, we have the Socialistic Labor Party, the International Working-people's Association and the International Workingmen's Association. The Socialistic Labor Party at one time organized under the name of the Workingmen's Party of the United States. Its principles and measures are largely those now indorsed by the Knights of Labor This association had no affiliation with the anarchists. Anarchy means individualism, and it has gone to rot. Socialism means the introduction of democracy or republicanism in the economic as well as the political relations of men. Socialism makes no war upon capital; but its object is to demand the abolition of the control of the natural resources or natural wealth of the world by individuals or corporations. They believe in the national reservation of the land, control of the railroads, telephones, telegraphs, mines, and, finally, of all industries by the government.

The conservative leaders of the socialistic movement in America are largely the disciples of Carl Marx, and are at perfect harmony with the trades-unions. Some of them became refugees from Germany, immediately after the revolutions of 1848. One of the best representatives of this movement is Mr. F. A. Sorga, of Hoboken, New Jersey, — a man of education and deep discernment. He is of a retiring, modest disposition, and seldom associated publicly with the movement. He has accomplished a great deal in the distribution of the literature of the movement. One of the first societies to promulgate socialism was the Turnverein. Resolutions adopted by them show their hearty sympathy with the labor movement. They have proved their love for our country and its institutions, not only on the battle-field as soldiers, but in the civil walks of life as citizens. The International Working-peoples' Association favor the destruction of the existing class-rule, the establishment of the co-operative organizations of production, exchange of equivalent products without profit, regulation of all public affairs by free contracts. Members of this organization are divided in their opinions, — some of them inclining to the socialistic, and some of them to the anarchist opinion. The papers published in the interest of this organization are largely anarchist, and the anarchists themselves seem to be divided into two classes: those who believe in violent denunciation and agitation, and those who believe in violent action. As a rule, it is not safe to judge any organization by the papers conducted under individual control, like *Der Freheit*, Most's New York paper, or the *Alarm*, formerly edited by A. R. Parsons, which generally express the individual opinions of the writer.

The *Inquirer*, of Denver, Col., which is claimed as an advocate of this organization, is an ably conducted and moderately radical sheet. It favors the Knights of Labor, Trades-union organizations, and all legitimate means of the solution of the labor problem; and, while condemning violence, claims the advantage of the liberty of speech and of action, and utters manful protests against the evils of the wage-system.

The International Workingmen's Association is also largely socialistic.

They claim that the first duty is to educate the masses, prepare for the coming days of the revolution, and to so direct that there may be secured, as a result, a system of co-operation which will insure justice to all. In some of the larger cities, communistic societies exist, composed largely of French refugees and French citizens. Among the members of these societies, we find, as in the case of the Internationalists, both socialists and anarchists. The Socialistic party, as a rule, look to the establishment of a political party, and the control of the government, political and economical, by the wage-labor class. Their measures are similar to those advocated by other labor organizations. It can be said of the International and Socialistic propaganda that its speakers and writers are fluent in language, persistent in effort and determined in purpose.

BIOGRAPHY.

[In sketching the biographies of those who are or have been prominent leaders in the labor movement, only the barest outlines can be given. These outlines could well be filled in with interesting incident or instructive anecdote; but space forbids.]

Arthur, Peter M., was born in Scotland, about fifty-five years ago, and came to America when ten years of age, going to live on the farm of an uncle in New York; at the age of seventeen, he removed to Schenectady, N. Y., where, with money he had saved, he purchased a horse and wagon, and started a small jobbing business; when he was about eighteen years old, he got employment as wiper in an engine-house of the New York & Central Railroad, at Schenectady; he rose speedily to be fireman, and then engineer; he was early attracted to the organization of his craft, and in February, 1874, was chosen to its highest office; since that date, he has been annually re-elected to the office of Chief Engineer of the Brotherhood of Locomotive Engineers; his official headquarters, and consequently his residence, are at Cleveland, O.; his policy of using all conciliatory means in the settlement of difficulties, before resorting to strikes, has brought him into wide and favorable notice everywhere; under his administration, there have been but few serious strikes, and these occurred mostly in the early part of his incumbency; he possesses, in an unusual degree, the confidence of the order over which he presides; his public addresses have become noted for their vigor of language and plain-speaking.

Bailey, W. H.—Is a Canadian, and a native of Hamilton, Ontario; Mr. Bailey has done the cause good service, and is highly esteemed by his associates for the qualities that make up a straightforward and manly character.

Barry, James H., of San Francisco, is about 30 years old; is an eloquent and convincing orator and brilliant writer; editor and proprietor of *Weekly Star*, a Labor organ; was member of State Legislature a few years ago, and made an excellent record as an advocate of Labor and Reform.

Barry, Thomas B.—Born, July 17, 1852, at Cohoes, N. Y.; in 1860 went to work in knitting-mill, hours being from 5 A. M. to 6.30 P. M.; wages, $6.00 per month; first joined Carders' Union in 1867, which lived but a short time; in 1867 left knitting-mills to learn axe-polishing, but as company wanted six months' work for nothing, helped axe-makers instead; in 1869 effort was made to organize the trade, without success; for his share in strikes was black-listed by Manufacturers' Association, preventing him from getting work, and causing much distress to himself and family; directed the strike for ten hours in Saginaw Valley, from eleven and a half to twelve in saw-mills, and from fourteen to eighteen in lumber camps; was arrested five times for leading strikes; put under $30,000 bail, and sued by a lumber king for $10,000 damages; acquitted in one criminal suit, four still pending; in civil suit, judgment of $2.90 against him, but was appealed, and is now in supreme court. The strike was a success.

Buchanan, Joseph R.—Born in Hannibal, Marion County, Mo., December 6, 1851; educated in grammar pay-schools till 13; began earning his living; educated himself further, especially for business; at 19, kept books for large grain commission-house in Illinois; clerked until 1875; learned printing business; in 1876, edited and managed *The Republican*, daily, Louisiana, Pike county, Mo.; worked as printer and reporter on local papers in 1877 and

1878; went to Denver, November, 1878; compiled biographies of Colorado (1878) Legislature; managing editor of the *Democrat*, and business-manager six months of the *Daily Republican*, which succeeded the *Democrat*; joint-owner of a job office; in 1879 made honorary member of Typographical Union No. 49, and went to Leadville and worked at the case until the spring of 1880; was discharged for sympathizing with striking miners; returned to Denver in 1881, and worked at the case; in 1882, delegate to International Typographical Union, at St. Louis; started *Labor Enquirer*, December 16, 1882, with S. H. Laverty; soon bought him out; joined Knights of Labor as charter member of Labor Assembly 2327, December, 1882; organized the Union Pacific Railroad men in 1884, and settled strikes in May and August, on friendly terms, still continuing; delegate to General Assembly, at Philadelphia, 1884; then chosen member of General Executive Board; not a candidate for re-election; chosen assistant member at Cleveland.

CARLTON, ALBERT A., was born in Lynn, Mass., in 1847; at the age of ten years he began work in a shoe-shop, to add to the income of his father's family; he worked at his trade until July 16, 1865, when at the age of 17, he enlisted for the war; after meritorious services in the army, he returned to Lynn, and entered the shops as a shoe-cutter; he displayed an early interest in labor organizations, and was a member of the first cutters' unions, also of the Knights of St. Crispin; he was prominently identified with the Lynn Workingmen's Association, whose purposes were political; in 1877 he joined the Knights of Labor, as a member of Local Assembly 1715; he at once displayed ability as an organizer, and was chosen Master Workman of the district at its first session, — an office from which he retired at Lowell, January 19, 1886, having rendered brilliant services as an organizer of the Order; on his retirement he was presented with a gold watch and chain as a testimonial; he was elected delegate to the General Assembly at Detroit, 1879, but was unable to attend, owing to the lack of funds in the treasury; he served in General Assemblies at Cincinnati, Philadelphia, Hamilton, Cleveland and Richmond; January, 1886, his conspicuous ability as a public speaker, gained him an appointment at the hands of the Executive Board as general lecturer for the Order; in this latter position he has traveled far and wide, and delivered a large number of speeches.

CLINE, ISAAC.—Born at Winslow, N. J., January 12, 1835; when young, worked in window-glass factory; in early life, lived in Cincinnati, Millville, N. J., Winslow, Pittsburgh, and Croton, Penn.; in 1852, came again to Pittsburgh; apprenticed to learn blowing window-glass; went to Wheeling; again to Pittsburgh, where he joined first window-glass workers' organization, May, 1858; to Croton, in 1859, where he worked till May, 1861; formed a company of volunteers, joined 100th Pennsylvania, remained in service till July 27, 1865, serving with honorable distinction; became identified with Window-glass Blowers' Union in 1872; president of Artsman's Association; in 1881, chosen president of Local Assembly 300, and held place ever since; in 1884, helped organize window-glass workers of Europe, and form Universal Federation of Window-glass Workers, being its first president.

COOK, WILLIAM.—Born in Philadelphia, March 4, 1822; his grandfather on the maternal side was a Swede, and on the paternal side, English; attended the public schools until fifteen; apprenticed to the tailor's trade, serving six years; joined the Garment-cutters' Association in 1865; has been Worthy Foreman of his local for the past twelve years; his average attendance is the best in the local, being absent on an average from but four meetings a year.

CRAIN, WILLIAM H., of Cuero, Texas, was born at Galveston, Texas, November 25, 1848; graduated at Saint Francis Xavier's College, New York city, July 1, 1867, and received the degree of A. M several years afterwards; studied law in the office of Stockdale & Proctor, Indianola, and was admitted to practice in February, 1871; has practised law since that time; was elected a State Senator on the Democratic ticket in February, 1876; was elected as the Democratic candidate for district-attorney of the Twenty-third Judicial District of Texas in November, 1872; and was elected to the Forty-ninth Congress as a Democrat.

DALEY, EDWARD L.—Born in Danvers, Mass., October 6, 1855; educated in common schools until eleven; admitted to Holten high school in Danvers; graduated there at thirteen; apprenticed at shoemaker's trade, and worked at that, especially lasting, ever since; was member of Knights of St. Crispin in Danvers and Lynn; one of the sixteen who founded

Lasters' Protective Union in Lynn, in 1879, which was named by him; was its first secretary, and member of its Advisory Board its first two years; was chosen general secretary of Lasters' Protective Union of New England in April, 1885; unanimously re-elected in 1886; author of petition to Legislature of 1885 to abolish convict-labor; was among first to organize Lasters' Protective Unions in shoe-towns of Maine and New Hampshire; member of Local Assembly 715, Knights of Labor, since its organization.

DOUGLAS, WILLIAM L., shoe-manufacturer, of Brockton, Mass., was born in Plymouth, Mass., August 22, 1845, and was educated in his native place. He was a member of the Brockton Common Council in 1881 and 1882; and was a member of the House in 1882 and 1883, serving on the Committee on Towns the first year, and on the Finance Committee in 1883; member of Massachusetts Senate, 1886.

DYER, JOSIAH B., was born at Village of Cross, parish of Luxillian, county of Cornwall, England, January 5, 1843; joined Operative Stone-masons' Society, of England and Wales, when between seventeen and eighteen years old; learned stone-cutting on granite, freestone and limestone; before coming to this country worked for John Freeman & Sons, of Penryn, Cornwall, for about eight years; landed at Castle Garden, in March, 1871; worked at Fall River, Dix Island, East Cambridge, Boston, Graniteville, Mass., Ayer Junction, Lowell, etc.; he was elected Secretary of Granite-cutters' Union, November, 1878, to fill unexpired term of T. H. March; his brother, J. Edward Dyer, was General Secretary of the O. S. M. Society, of England and Wales, for about eleven years, and dying in office, the union erected a monument to his memory in Sheffield; he was born in a trades-union family, father and brothers being all union men; he was one of the charter members of the first Local Assembly of the Knights of Labor organized in Boston; as Secretary of the Granite-cutters' Union, he was removed, with headquarters of union, from Rockland to Boston, from Boston to Westerly, R. I., from Westerly, to Quincy, Mass., from Quincy to Philadelphia.

FARQUHAR, JOHN M., of Buffalo, was born near Ayr, Scotland, April 17, 1832; was educated at Ayr Academy; has been for thirty-three years a printer, editor, or publisher; is now a manufacturer of lubricants; was president of the National Typographical Union two terms, 1860–62; enlisted in the Union Army as a private in the Eighty-ninth Illinois Infantry, rose to the rank of major, and served as judge-advocate and as inspector on the staffs of Generals Willich, Beatty, and Wood in the Fourth Army Corps; participated in all the battles of the former Twentieth (McCook's) and Fourth Army Corps, excepting Missionary Ridge; never held civic office until elected to the Forty-ninth Congress as a Republican.

FORAN, MARTIN AMBROSE, of Cleveland, was born at Choconut, Susquehanna County, Penn., November 11, 1844; received a public-school and collegiate education; spent two terms in Saint Joseph's College, Susquehanna, Penn.; taught school three years; served in the Fourth Pennsylvania Cavalry from April, 1864, to July, 1865, as private; is a cooper by trade; was a member of the Constitutional Convention of Ohio, 1873; is a lawyer by profession, having been admitted, 1874, in the District Court of Cincinnati; was prosecuting attorney for the city of Cleveland, from April, 1875, to April, 1877; was elected to the Forty-eighth Congress, and was re-elected to the Forty-ninth Congress as a Democrat.

FOSTER, FRANK K., was born in Palmer (Thorndike), Mass., December 18, 1855; was educated in common schools and at Monson Academy; learned the printer's trade at the office of the *Churchman*, Hartford, Conn., afterwards working as compositor in various cities; his first connection with the labor movement was as a member of the Hartford Typographical Union, of which he was secretary; he came to Boston in 1880, and was president of the Cambridge Typographical Union, from which body he went as a delegate to the International Union, at St. Louis; by the latter body he was chosen delegate to the Federation of Trades Convention, at Cleveland, O.; he was delegate to this same body, in 1883, representing the Boston Central Trades and Labor Union, and was chosen secretary; first joined the Knights of Labor as a member of Local Assemby 2006, and was elected delegate to Convention of District 30, June, 1882; elected Secretary of District 30, 1883; delegate to General Assembly, at Cincinnati, 1883; elected chairman of the Executive Board of the General Assembly at that session; he has served as delegate to General Assemblies at Philadelphia, Hamilton, Cleveland and Richmond; has been a member of Executive Board of District No. 30 ever since its existence; September 30, 1886, nominated for Lieutenant-Governor of Massachusetts, by the Democratic Convention, at Worcester; founder and present editor of *Haverhill* (Mass.) *Daily and Weekly Laborer.*

FOSTER, WILLIAM H., secretary of the Federation of Trades, was born in Liverpool, England, May 3, 1847; taught school when but fifteen; went to learn the printing business, July 1, 1862, at Porta Down, county Armagh, Ireland, serving four years; finished his trade in Berylyton Steam Printing Works, Liverpool; became a journeyman, July 1, 1869; joined Liverpool Typographical Society as apprentice member; soon as had finished apprenticeship secured situation in Buxton, Derbyshire; came to America early in October, 1873; stayed in Philadelphia four or five weeks; went to Cincinnati; worked on *Gazette* till the celebrated lockout on July 18, 1874; went to Philadelphia soon after; in June, 1877, went to Cincinnati *Enquirer;* in 1878, elected president of Typographical Union No. 3 and secretary of Trades-Assembly, in formation of which he was a moving spirit; here acquired the title of the "Original Boycotter"; was leader in the successful efforts to make the *Enquirer, Sun, Gazette* and *Commercial* union offices; February 14, 1880, with Patrick Caulfield, started the *Exponent,* one of the pioneer labor papers; about this time elected delegate to the Twenty-eighth Session of the International Typographical Union; was chairman on committee on amalgamated unions, etc., whose action finally culminated in the first Trades-union Convention, at Pittsburgh, in November, 1881, when he represented the Cincinnati Trades-assembly,. elected secretary of the convention, which selected for the title of the new organization, "Federation of Trades and Labor Unions of the United States and Canada"; was secretary two years; at convention in Washington, 1885, was again elected secretary; in 1883, went to Philadelphia *Evening Call,* began active warfare against the non-union papers of that city; elected president of Typographical Union No. 2, in April, 1884; was delegate from No. 2 to preliminary meeting of Central Labor Union, of which body he has been secretary ever since..

GEORGE, HENRY.—Born September 2, 1839, in Philadelphia, of an old Pennsylvania family; educated in public schools until thirteen; classmate of Rev. R. Heber Newton; office boy in commercial house two years; went to sea; visited every part of the globe; returned to Philadelphia after two years; was printer short time; went to sea again; went to California and British Columbia; became compositor in San Francisco; in 1867 became a reporter; in five months became manager of the paper; in 1868, visited New York; interested in social question; wrote "Our Land and Our Land Policy"; in 1870, became editor of Sacramento paper; removed for opposing Pacific Railroad Company; started San Francisco *Daily Post,* originally Republican; joined Democrats in 1872; represented California in convention that nominated Greeley; began writing "Progress and Poverty" in 1877; finished in 1879; in 1880, removed to New York; since then has visited England, Ireland and Scotland; spoke on land question all over the Kingdom; is author of several books on social problems, which have been translated in many languages, and given him wide reputation; has also written much of leading American and English magazines.

HAYES, JOHN W.—Born in Philadelphia, December 26, 1854; when nine, was taken to Europe by parents, and remained several years; upon return, through financial reverses of family, went to work as brakeman on Pennsylvania railroad; served for eight years; settled in New Brunswick, N, J.; still lives there; in 1878, while on duty, was thrown on track, and train passed over his right arm, necessitating amputation; compelled to seek other employment, became a telegraph operator; in 1883, was delegate to the Chicago Telegraphers' Convention, which ordered the great strike, in which he took a prominent part; upon failure of strike, went into grocery business; now owns two large stores in New Brunswick; is one of the most prominent Knights of Labor in New Jersey, and his connection with the Order dates back to 1874; in 1879, he, with the assistance of several others, called the first New Jersey Congress, and has since been its president twice.

HILSEE, JAMES MADISON.—Born in the old "Dock" ward, now fifth, Philadelphia, October 2, 1821; attended private schools until nearly sixteen; then worked for his father, a tailor; is of the sixth generation of American stock which came originally from England; was member of the volunteer (hose) fire company from twenty-one until the disbandment of the volunteer fire department; the annals of the fire department of Philadelphia contain accounts of his daring feats in saving life and property; Mr. Hilsee is a bachelor; was one of the founders of the Garment-cutters' Association, and an active member in it until its dissolution; is an active member of his Knights of Labor assembly, and devotes much time and attention to the progress of the Order in the Quaker City.

HOWARD, ROBERT.—Born in Northwich, Cheshire, Eng., of Irish parents, 1844 or 1845; at eight, set to learn piecing in a Macclesfield silk-mill; removed to Bollington, where he got work as a piecer; moved to Stockport, where he got work as a bobbin-boy, being then but ten years old; at fifteen he became a spinner; at twenty-five, president of the Spinners' Union; declined offer as overseer, because he could not do the domineering required; prominent in the agitation for nine hours in textile industries; by conciliatory advice averted many strikes; in 1873, he came to Fall River; worked three years as spinner in the Flint Mill; in 1878, chosen secretary of the Fall River Spinners' Association; in 1879, chosen its permanent secretary; in 1880, chosen to the State House of Representatives, receiving the nomination of both parties, where he was foremost among the supporters of labor legislation; declined a renomination; in 1882, his friends in England sent him a splendid testimonial, to show their appreciation of his services; began the agitation, in Rhode Island, in 1883, for ten hours for women and children; prevailed on Governor Bourne to recommend such legislation, which was enacted in 1885; also advocated ten hours before the Maine Legislative Labor Committee; has frequently advocated labor reform measures before Massachusetts legislative committees; in 1885, chosen to State Senate from Second Bristol District as a Democrat; also became associate editor of *Wade's Fibre and Fabric;* from 1881 to 1885, he was treasurer of the Federation of Trades and Labor Unions of the United States and Canada; was once secretary of the National Cotton-spinners' Association; in May, 1885, the Cotton-spinners' Union of Fall River formed an assembly of the Knights of Labor, unanimously adopted his name and chose him as secretary. Mr. Howard, although a leader in labor matters, has always commanded the respect of both sides to an unusual degree.

JARRETT, JOHN.—Born January 27, 1843, at Elbow Vale, Monmouthshire, Eng., of Welsh parentage; left an orphan at twelve; put to work in iron-mill; at eighteen, came to America; went to Duncanville, Blair County, Penn.; worked as puddler four years; in November, 1865, went to Lochiel Mill, near Harrisburg; joined Puddlers' Union; in 1867 went to England to settle property affairs; remained there four years; worked at his trade; became head of Workingmen's Union, and won strike against reduction of wages; such a victory remarkable against the odds; in 1872 returned to America; joined Sons of Vulcan; chosen a vice-president in 1873; was prominent in organizing Amalgamated Association; chosen a vice-president and trustee; in 1879, chosen president to fill vacancy; in 1881, chairman of Federation of Trades; re-elected president of Amalgamated Association for three terms, retiring in October, 1883; chosen secretary of American Tinned-Plate Association, which office he now holds.

JONES, FRANK W., of Lynn, Mass., is foreman in a shoe-factory; was born in Stoughton, Mass., August 20, 1855, and was educated in the public schools; a member of the House the past two years; he served on the Committee on Election-Laws the first year, and on the Committee on Public Charitable Institutions the second; member of Massachusetts Senate, 1866.

KEEN, ROBERT WILLIAMSON.—Born in the old district of Spring Garden, April 8, 1832; traces ancestry back to 1638, to old Swedish settlers, before Penn's time; name then spelt "Kyn"; served apprenticeship to his father, a tailor; worked as journeyman until the war; enlisted for three-months' service in the Twenty-second Pennsylvania; re-enlisted in the Ninety-ninth Pennsylvania for three years; was wounded severely at the battle of Fredericksburg, December 13, 1862, but soon recovering, again took the field; was mustered out at the expiration of his term of service; is a member of Curry Post, No. 18, G. A. R.; joined the Garment-cutters' Association in 1867; at formation of first local assembly Knights of Labor he was chosen Worthy Foreman.

KENNEDY, JOSEPH SMITH.—Born in Philadelphia, February 1, 1821, of American parents; his great-great-grandfather was Scotch; his grandmother was one of the numerous families of Smiths of Chester County; educated at private school until fifteen; at sixteen apprenticed to a tailor; served five years; joined the Garment-cutters' Association two or three months after its formation, and was treasurer for some years, and until its dissolution; held the office of treasurer at the formation of the Knights of Labor, and was also elected Unknown Knight, retaining his office as treasurer until 1879.

LAWLER, FRANK, of Chicago, was born at Rochester, N. Y., June 25, 1842; attended a public school until thirteen years of age, when, owing to a serious accident which befell his father, he was compelled to leave school and seek employment in a brick-yard, where he continued to labor for two years; was news-agent on railroads for three years; learned the trade of ship-builder, was elected president of the Ship-carpenters' and Ship-calkers' Association, and took an active part in organizing trade and labor unions; became agent for *The Workingman's Advocate*, a newspaper; was appointed, upon the request of the trade and labor organizations, to a position in the Chicago post-office, which he held from 1869 to 1877; was elected a member of the Chicago City Council from the eighth ward in April, 1876, and was re-elected in 1878, 1880, 1882 and 1884; engaged in business in 1878 at Chicago as a liquor merchant, and was elected to the Forty-ninth Congress as a Democrat.

LEFFINGWELL, SAMUEL LANGDALE.—Born at Chillicothe, Ohio, of English and Scotch descent; was early apprenticed to a printer, and has always followed that trade; in July, 1850, he became a member of the Cincinnati Typographical Union, and has held important offices in printers' unions; in February, 1852, formed such a union at Columbus, Ohio; in 1856, was made president of the Cincinnati Typographical Union; in July, president of the one at Columbus; in July, 1875, joined the Knights of Labor, at Indianapolis; was commissioned organizer, and has organized more than a score of assemblies; represented Indianapolis Trades-Assembly, at first session of Federal Congress of Trade and Labor Unions; in 1882, was president of the Congress at Cleveland; has been delegate to several important sessions of General Assembly Knights of Labor; in September, 1885, organized Indiana State Federation Trade and Labor Unions; chosen president twice; established several labor papers, including the former organ of the International Typographical Union; in August, 1847, enlisted for the Mexican War, and served to its close; in August, 1861, was commissioned major in the Thirty-first Ohio; at battle of Mills Springs, transferred to Forty-fifth; major in Eighty-seventh; made prisoner at Harper's Ferry, September 15, 1862; paroled; mustered out, 1863; commanded a regiment in Southern Ohio to repel John Morgan; February, 1864 enlisted as private in First Ohio Cavalry; at battles of Decatur, Rome, Kenesaw, Marietta, Atlanta; January, 1865, assigned to special duty at Sherman's headquarters; honorably discharged, June 11, 1865.

LOVERING, HENRY B., of Lynn, was born at Portsmouth, N. H., April 5, 1841; was educated in the common schools of Lynn, and has since been connected with Lynn's great industry, the manufacture of shoes; was representative to the State Legislature in 1872 and 1874; was assessor in 1879 and 1880; was Mayor of Lynn in 1881 and 1882; was elected to the Forty-ninth Congress as a Democrat, supported by the People's Party.

MACAULEY, ROBERT CALVIN.—Born in County Antrim, Ire., February 2, 1840; at age of nine removed to Philadelphia; had strong tastes for mathematics and wonderful memory; before leaving Ireland could repeat large portions of the Bible and Burns' poems; reached Philadelphia, September 2, 1849; was placed at Nixon-street School; at eleven was apprenticed to a tailor, whom he shortly left because of his drunkenness; worked with other tailors for three years; at twenty-one started in business; was soon after married; in 1865, joined the Brotherhood of the Union; in 1866, giving up business, became a foreman, and joined Garment-cutters' Association; was chosen its secretary in 1867, and held the office until its dissolution; about this time joined the Knights of Pythias; was first secretary of Knights of Labor; became partner with Mr. Stephens, as R. C. Macauley & Co., 1128 Market street, which in time became the headquarters of the Knights of Labor; was chosen Master Workman in 1871, succeeding Mr. Stephens; in his administration first Assembly outside of original one was formed,—Ship-carpenters and Calkers, No. 2; gave up business and became foreman in wholesale clothing-house.

MAGUIRE, JAMES G., native Californian, 35 years of age; commenced life as a farmer boy, soon forsook the furrow for the anvil; at early age secured a school, and commenced the double task of teaching others, while studying law for himself; removed to San Francisco on being admitted to practice at the bar, and in a short time secured a lucrative practice; chosen judge of the Superior Court, which place he now holds; his papers on the Land Reform Question, published in the *Weekly Star*, have been widely read, and pronounced an able exposition of the subject.

McBride, John.—Born of humble parentage, in Wayne County, O., July 25, 1854; moved to Massillon, 1859; at nine commenced work in a coal mine; at sixteen joined Miners' Union; in 1883, by unanimous vote, elected its president, and again in 1884, 1885 and 1886; in 1881, nominated by the Democrats of Stark County for representative, defeated by only sixty-three votes; in 1883, again a candidate, elected by nearly seven hundred majority; again elected in 1885; in legislature recognized as one of the leaders on the Democratic side; in legislation favored the farmers; author of bill which gave first appropriation to Gettysburg Memorial Fund; in 1886, Democratic candidate for secretary of State.

McGaw, Homer L.—Born at Bethlehem, O., April 8, 1845; in 1853, entered a country rinting office as "devil"; at this early age he joined in a strike, which was a success; after leaving the army, went through college on the money he had saved in the army and working in coal-mines, printing offices, etc., graduating second in his class; became an accountant in Pittsburgh; before twenty-one was made cashier of the East Liberty Savings Bank, of that city; in 1868, he organized the book-keepers and salesmen of the city into a union, but it failed; the lessons of the panic of 1873 caused him, with others of similar views, to open correspondence with Eastern labor leaders, among whom was Uriah S. Stephens, founder of the Knights of Labor; one of the first assemblies of Knights was soon after organized in Mr. McGaw's printing office; chosen Master Workman of District Assembly 3, in January, 1884, holding the office one year, during which time all troubles were settled satisfactorily to all concerned, without collecting or expending a cent for strikes; chosen General Insurance Secretary of the Order in 1883, and has been re-elected by acclamation at every succeeding session; he has built up within the Order an assessment insurance association, which has cost its members about a cent a day for an indemnity of $500, and nearly $35,000 has already been paid by it to widows and orphans; retained by the Trades-Assembly of Western Pennsylvania to secure the repeal of the obnoxious conspiracy laws of the State.

McGuire, Peter J.—Born in New York city, July 6, 1852, of Irish parents; educated in public schools; studied evenings in Cooper Institute and evening high school; took high rank in all; in 1867, apprenticed to wood-joiner; in 1872, joined Union of his trade; has been very active in labor interests all his life, and very influential, being delegate repeatedly to important conventions; in 1880, secured passage of important labor bills in Missouri Legislature; organized labor bureau of that State; became Greenbacker in 1876, and stumped Missouri with great success in 1880; in August, 1881, organized Brotherhood of Carpenters and Joiners; in spring of 1881, arrested for conspiracy in labor troubles, refused release on half million offered bail; finally acquitted after seven hours' trial; drafted call for convention that formed Federation of Trades; delegate to International Workingmen's Congress in Switzerland, 1881; studied labor movement in Europe; helped Central Labor Union of New York; secured adoption of "Labor's Holiday"; since August, 1881, General Secretary of Brotherhood of Carpenters; re-elected for next two years; extricated it from debt, and put it on sound financial basis; has lectured in every State in Union, Canada, Nova Scotia and New Brunswick; addressed over 2,100 meetings; worked at his trade in nearly a score of cities, and always busy in cause of labor; in May, 1886, chosen secretary of National and International Trades-unions, and secretary of its standing committee; these are some of the principal points in his very active connection with labor interests.

McNeill, George E., was born in Amesbury, Mass., August 4, 1836; his father, John McNeill, was one of the first to unite with his neighbor, John G. Whittier, in the anti-slavery movement; he worked as a boy in the woolen-mills of his native town at the time of the great strike in 1851; about this time he learned the shoemaker's trade; settled in Boston in 1856; joined the Sons of Temperance, and filled the highest offices; he was a member of the grand Eight-hour League, and founded the Workingmen's Institute; he was appointed first Deputy of the Massachusetts Bureau of Statistics of Labor, under General H. K.

Oliver, serving until May, 1873; for eight years he was President of the Eight-hour League, also State Secretary of the Sovereigns of Industry, and President of the International Labor Union, of America, in which latter capacity he addressed public meetings in many States of the Union; in Chicago he addressed over 13,000 people, the labor societies having challenged Joseph Cook to meet him in debate; he was connected as editor and associate editor with the *New York Labor Standard*, *Fall River Labor Standard*, *Paterson Labor Standard* and *Paterson Home Journal;* he has attended many labor congresses and conventions in various parts of the country; as a member of the School Committee of Cambridge, Mass., succeeded in establishing free evening drawing-schools; he was appointed Treasurer of District 30, Knights of Labor, May, 1884; was elected to that position in January, 1885, and was subsequently made District Secretary-Treasurer; re-elected unanimously in January, 1886; resigned at the July session, 1886, receiving the thanks of the District Convention, appropriately engrossed on parchment, in consideration of his valuable services; he has been successful as an arbitrator of differences between employers and employees, notably in the great horse-car strike in Boston; in 1886, represented the Knights of Labor before committees of Congress in the winter and early spring of 1886.

MORROW, WILLIAM W., of San Francisco, was born near Milton, Wayne County, Ind., July 15, 1843; removed with his parents to Illinois in 1845, and settled in Adams County; went to California in 1859; received a common-school education, supplemented by private tuition in special branches; in the spring of 1862, joined a party which discovered gold-placers on the headwaters of the John Day River, in Oregon; engaged in mining for a season; returned East in January, 1863, intending to pursue a course of studies in some Eastern college; but the active operations of the government in the war of the Rebellion drew him to Washington, where he was appointed to a position in the office of the Secretary of the Treasury; served in the National Rifles, a military organization raised in the District of Columbia; appointed Special Agent of the Treasury Department in January, 1865, and placed in charge of a large shipment of treasure to California; employed during the next four years in confidential positions under the Secretary of the Treasury; studied law, was admitted to the bar in 1869, and has since been engaged in the practice of his profession; Assistant United States Attorney for California from 1870 to 1874; Chairman of the Republican State Central Committee of California from 1879 to 1882; Attorney for the State Board of Harbor Commissioners from 1880 to 1883; Chairman of the California Delegation to the National Republican Convention at Chicago in 1884, and was elected to the Forty-ninth Congress as a Republican.

O'NEILL, JOHN J., of St. Louis, was born June 25, 1846, of Irish parents; received a common-school education; was in the Government civil service during the war, and was afterwards engaged in manufacturing pursuits; was elected to the State Legislature from St. Louis in 1872, and re-elected in 1874 and 1876; was nominated for Congress in 1878 by the Workingmen's Party, but withdrew; was elected to the Municipal Assembly of St. Louis in 1879, and re-elected in 1881; was elected to the Forty-eighth Congress, and was re-elected to the Forty-ninth Congress as a Democrat.

PASCOE, DAVID M., born in Philadelphia, October 26, 1859; educated in public schools; at fifteen apprenticed to J. B. Lippincott & Company, publishers; served five years; remained journeyman until November, 1884, when he assumed control of the *Tocsin*, the labor paper of the Quaker City, which he still retains; at twenty-one, joined Typographical Union No. 2; in 1881, trouble being imminent over an increase in prices, it was deemed expedient to select a conservative committee to meet the employers, Mr. Pascoe was chosen, and the result was an amicable adjustment of the threatened rupture; at the Pittsburgh session of the International Typographical Union, the delegates from No. 2 reported five newspapers unionized within a year,—a creditable showing, brought about more through the conservative manner in which Mr. Pascoe and his co-laborers had acted towards the proprietors than any other reason; in April, 1884, elected secretary of local union; re-elected in 1885; in 1886, declined a third term; delegate to convention of International Union at Pittsburgh, and chairman of his delegation; youngest man ever selected by the Philadelphia Union as its delegate to the central body; elected secretary-treasurer; is an active member of the Central Labor Union, also of Local Assembly 3879 (printers), Knights of Labor, which he organized; during the strike in the carpet trade, in the winter of 1884–5, he stood in the shadow of the penitentiary for his fearless advocacy of the cause of the carpet-weavers.

POWDERLY, TERENCE VINCENT. — Born at Carbondale, Penn., January 24, 1849, of Irish parentage; had seven brothers and four sisters, being the eleventh child; attended school six years; at thirteen became a switch tender for D. & H. C. Co.; at seventeen entered its machine-shop; in 1869 went to Scranton shops of D. L. & W. R. R. Co.; in 1870 joined Machinists' and Blacksmiths' National Union; soon became its president; began studying the labor problem; in 1872 was married; trades-unions too narrow for him; in November, 1874, joined Local Assembly No. 88, Knights of Labor; soon induced all his union to join the Knights, and they organized Local Assembly No. 222, November, 1876; in 1876 a district assembly was organized, and he chosen secretary; in January, 1879, chosen General Worthy Foreman; in September, 1879, chosen Master Workman, which office he has held ever since; in 1878 was chosen Mayor of Scranton, also in 1880 and 1882, declining a nomination in 1884; has practically reorganized the Knights of Labor; has given his whole time and talents to their cause for several years, having spoken for the Order all over the United States and Canada; has been prominent in the Irish Land-League movement here, being chosen second vice-president in 1883.

SKEFFINGTON, HENRY J. — Born March 5, 1858, at Marysville, Yuba County, Cal., of Irish parents; soon after removed to Philadelphia, where has lived nearly ever since; educated in Catholic schools; at thirteen was sent to Portage City, Wis., to study for priest's orders; after one year returned to Philadelphia; after being apprenticed to several trades, learned trade of shoemaking, and has followed it ever since; reduction of wages caused hands to join Knights of Labor; he was too young to join, although desiring to, being only fifteen; joined Shoemakers' Local Assembly, No. 64, in winter of 1878; was soon advanced from subordinate offices to be Master Workman by unanimous vote; while in that office, successfully resisted reduction of wages, and helped women employees to regain a large reduction; these women subsequently founded first local assembly of women in the Order, being Garfield Assembly, No. 1684; largely by his efforts, shoemakers got charters as "locals" of their own; in spring of 1884, organized the body Brussels carpet-weavers, the first local of that trade in Philadelphia; November 15, 1884, two thousand ingrain carpet-weavers voted a strike against reduction of wages; in three weeks, Mr. Skeffington had them all members of Knights of Labor; in January, 1885, was sent to New York to organize shoemakers, which was done by six weeks of hard work; for over three years worked hard and successfully toward national organization of his craft, finally securely founding, June, 1884, National Executive Council of Shoe and Leather-workers of America, Knights of Labor; has been delegate repeatedly to important conventions.

STEPHENS, URIAH SMITH. — Born, August 3, 1821, near Cape May, N. J. Paternal grandfather killed in the Revolution; maternal ancestry, Quakers; educated for Baptist ministry; compelled to learn a trade; became a tailor; of studious and methodical habits; after serving apprenticeship as tailor, taught school in New Jersey; in 1845 removed to Philadelphia; in 1853 went to West Indies, Central America and California; in 1858 returned to Philadelphia; was cordial supporter of Fremont, in 1856, and of Lincoln, in 1860; about 1863 joined Garment-cutters' Association; when it dissolved, December 9, 1869, with six others, he founded the Knights of Labor; January 6, 1870, was chosen first Master Workman of General Assembly No. 1; December 28, 1871, was chosen statistician; in 1873 was chosen first District Master Workman of District Assembly No. 1; was instrumental in forming nearly every local assembly up to 1876, when health began to fail; January 1, 1878, was chosen first Grand Master Workman of the General Assembly; was recording secretary of his local assembly at his decease; was member of Masonic, Odd Fellows' and Knights of Pythias lodges, also; they were invited, through the press, to attend his funeral, but no labor organizations were so remembered; was buried in Mount Peace Cemetery, Philadelphia.

SWINTON, JOHN. — Born in Illinois, December, 1830; early learned printer's trade; moved to New York about 1850; studied medicine and law; chief of editorial staff of *Times* from 1860 through the war, and till Raymond's death in 1869; then with Horace Greeley on the *Tribune*, until about 1874; then chief of staff of the *Sun*, until 1883, when he resigned to start "John Swinton's Paper." In the Spring of 1874 became active champion of workingmen; that fall nominated with great enthusiasm by them for mayor, but polled only two hundred votes; has taken active part as public speaker, writer and worker, in all the movements of labor in New York since 1874, speaking at hundreds of meetings there, and all over the country; was very active in the railroad strike year of 1877, and presided at the great Tompkins Square demonstration; for the last few years has given up everything and sacrificed everything for the cause of labor.

TARSNEY, TIMOTHY E., of East Saginaw, was born at Ransom, Hillsdale County, Mich., February 4, 1849; was educated at the common schools; served seven years as a marine engineer, meantime reading law; entered the Law Department of Michigan University, in 1870, and graduated in the class of 1872; was justice of the peace, 1873 and 1874; was City Attorney in 1875-78, when he resigned, serving as *ex-officio* member of the board of supervisors at the same time, and was elected to the Forty-ninth Congress as a Democrat.

TREVELLICK, RICHARD F. — Born, May 2, 1830, at Saint Mary's, one of the Scilly Islands, England; early went to sea; from fifteen to twenty apprentice in a ship-yard; at twenty again went to sea, visiting Africa, India and China; in 1852 helped organize Eight-hour League, at Auckland, New Zealand; in 1857 joined eight-hour movement at Melbourne; in 1855 entered service of Pacific Mail Steamship Company at Panama; again went to sea; employed by United States in building docks and steamboats in Gulf of Mexico; elected president of Ship-carpenters' and Calkers' Union; successfully agitated for nine hours; again at sea; in 1862 foreman of Marine Railway, New York; went to Detroit; president of Ship-carpenters' and Calkers' Union, No. 4; in 1865, president of Ship-carpenters' and Calkers' International Union; discharged and blacklisted for connection with labor reform; organized trades-assembly; chosen president; chosen delegate to International Labor Congress in Europe; chosen president of National Labor Union, 1871-73.· in 1874-5 helped form Greenback party; in 1876 delegate to National Greenback convention and president of State Greenback convention; in 1880, presided over National Greenback convention also at Michigan State convention; was one of twelve founders, at Louisville, of National Labor Union and Industrial Brotherhood; is honorary member of seven trades-unions.

TURNER, FREDERICK. — Born in England in 1846; came to this country at 10; educated in schools of Philadelphia; graduated from its high school; learned the trade of gold-beating, which he worked before his duties as Secretary-Treasurer of the Knights of Labor became too burdensome; in 1873 he organized forty of his fellow gold-beaters as Local Assembly 20, and afterwards organized Local Assembly 28, the first in New York; chosen secretary-treasurer of the organization; twice re-elected one of the general Executive Board.

WEAVER, J. B., of Bloomfield, was born in Dayton, O., June 12, 1833; had a common-school education in his boyhood; graduated at the Law School of the Ohio University, at Cincinnati, in 1854; is a lawyer by profession, and one of the editors of the *Iowa Tribune*, published at Desmoines, Ia.; was elected District Attorney of the Second Judicia District of Iowa, in 1866, and served four years; was appointed by President Johnson assessor of internal revenue for the first district of Iowa, in 1867, and served six years; was elected to the Forty-sixth Congress; was nominated in 1880, at Chicago, by the National Party, as their candidate for President of the United States, and received about 350,000 votes; was elected to the Forty-ninth Congress by the Nationals and Democrats, having been nominated and supported by both, receiving 16,684 votes, against 16,617 votes for Campbell, Republican.

WEIHE, WILLIAM. — Born January 21, 1845, in Baldwin, Penn.; when a boy moved to Pittsburgh; about 1860 began working in bar-iron mill; afterward became a boiler worker; remained at that business until 1880; joined Sons of Vulcan; filled several local offices; in 1878 chosen member of Permanent Executive Committee; in 1879 chosen Trustee of Amalgamated Association, and succeeded President Jarrett, when he resigned; was re-elected in 1884; has served several terms on school board; in 1882 chosen as member of State Assembly by Workingmen and Democrats.

WILKINSON, JOSEPH, — Secretary of the Journeymen Tailors' National Union, was born in Ireland, March 23, 1856; he left school at the age of twelve to learn the tailor's trade in his native place; he arrived in the United States in 1872, and since then has been actively engaged in the labor movement in New York city; with J. P. McDonnell, of the Paterson

Labor Standard, Adolph Strasser and others, he founded the Amalgamated Trade and Labor Union, of New York city, and actively agitated for the enactment of beneficial labor legislation in New York State, such as the establishment of a Bureau of Labor Statistics, the abolition of prison convict-contract labor, reduction of the hours of labor, and the abolition of the manufacture of cigars in tenement-houses; the latter measure after being passed was decided unconstitutional by the Court of Appeals. When the call was issued in 1884 for a Convention of the Journeymen Tailors of the United States, in Chicago, he was elected by an almost unanimous vote to represent the New York union; in the convention he was prevailed upon to accept the secretaryship of the National Union, and was unanimously re-elected at the convention held in Baltimore, in August, 1885; though busily engaged in the labor movement, he still found time to improve his mind by study; he attended the evening high school in New York for three successive winters, and also belonged to the literary class attached to the Cooper Union, where he acquired a readiness in debate and eloquence of speech; he still works at his trade.

WRIGHT, JAMES LENDREW.—Born in County Tyrone, Ire., April 6, 1816, of Scotch-Irish ancestry; family soon removed to St. John, N. B., and to Philadelphia, when he was in his eleventh year; early education in Mt. Vernon grammar school and in private academy of Charles Mead; was early apprenticed to George W. Farr, tailor; served over six years; at his majority became member of Tailors' Benevolent Society; in 1847 begun in business in Frankfort, near Philadelphia, whither he removed in 1848; in 1854 became manager of large clothing-house; in 1862 helped organize Garment-cutters' Association; was its president many years, and when it dissolved; was very active in labor matters at this period, traveling much and forming many lodges, and paying most of his expenses; in 1878 had 54,000 votes as Greenback-Labor candidate for State treasurer, and 82,000 votes for Secretary of Internal affairs, by same parties; was chosen first Venerable Sage of Local Assembly No. 1, Knights of Labor; afterwards Master Workman; always an earnest and ready advocate of the Order.

O'DONOGHUE, DANIEL J.—Born in County Kerry, Ire., August 1, 1844; removed with parents in 1852 to Bytown, Can., which subsequently became Ottawa; at thirteen apprenticed himself to printer; remained there for following nine years; also was active member of St. Patrick's Literary Association, and of a volunteer fire company; joined volunteer militia rifle company and studied military tactics; refused to take oath of allegiance to Queen Victoria when Fenian movement arose, holding the order so to do an unjustifiable insult to Irish loyalty; removed to Buffalo, N. Y., soon after, and obtained situation on *Commercial Advertiser;* joined Typographical Union; spent a few weeks in Ottawa in May and June, and set on foot measures culminating in formation of a Typographical Union; worked in Chicago and Memphis for balance of year; then in New Orleans and Mobile, returning to Ottawa in following August; for next ten years worked at trade; helped form many local trades-unions; was several times president or secretary of local trades-councils; was first vice-president of Canada Labor Union, formed at Toronto, 1868-9; many times president of Ottawa Typographical Union; in 1874, chosen by workingmen of Ottawa to the Provincial Legislature to fill vacancy; in 1875, re-elected for the term of four years; was originator and advocate of many important labor measures, which became law; in 1879, removed to Guelph, unable to get work at trade in Ottawa on account of his trades-union sentiments; after eighteen months removed to Toronto, where now resides; in 1883, joined Knights of Labor; represented them at the Hamilton and Cleveland Conventions; in 1882, represented Toronto Typographical Union No. 91; since then Labor Assembly No. 2305, of which he was financial secretary for two years; is now Secretary of Legislative Committee of Trades and Labor Council; also employed in Ontario Bureau of Industries and Statistics; has been newspaper reporter, editor and publisher, and contributor to labor journals and various widely circulating newspapers of England.

STATISTICAL DIAGRAMS

SHOWING

THE GROWTH OF TRADES-UNIONISM IN THE UNITED STATES, DISPLACEMENT OF MANUAL LABOR BY MACHINERY, COST OF LIVING AND RATES OF WAGES, AND OTHER PHASES OF THE LABOR PROBLEM.

Prepared expressly for "The Labor Movement."

BY CHAS. F. PIDGIN,

CHIEF CLERK MASSACHUSETTS BUREAU OF STATISTICS OF LABOR.

EVERY science or art needs a definition — a short, easily remembered one. No more graphic or comprehensive one can be supplied for statistics than *history written in figures.* Since 1869, when the first bureau of statistics of labor was established, the history of the labor movement has certainly been written in figures, collected by the National and the various State bureaus, by city, State and National committees of investigation, by labor organizations, and by the individual efforts of persons interested in social and economic advancement.

The historian who uses figures has an advantage over the one who relies upon words alone; his readers can grasp in a one-page statistical table what ten pages of words would fail to express as plainly. Now, the artist has come to the aid of the statistical historian with colored maps, charts, and diagrams. Language, of course, will never lose its power to convey thought from mind to minds, but in statistical presentations the statistical table or diagram supplies the statement and argument, while words are used but for description or explanation.

The aim has been, in the following diagrams, to present some salient labor statistics in the most crystallized form. These tables have been prepared with the greatest care from the latest official statistics. They are closely in line with the subject of the Labor Movement, and are intended to illustrate both the history and the problem of which the book treats. Many of the subjects are such as have never before been the object of the engraver's art, such as those dealing with the causes and results of Strikes and Lockouts, the growth of Trades Unionism, and kindred topics. And yet these are of vital interest in connection with the present movement. The tables showing comparative wages, cost of living, the displacement of muscular labor by machinery, and the profits of employers and employees, teem with living interest, and are closely related to the general labor problem. The diagrams have all been prepared with scientific accuracy from official statistics, and the artist has been mathematically correct in reducing the original pen-and-ink sketches to the size of the printed page.

TRADES-UNIONISM IN THE UNITED STATES.

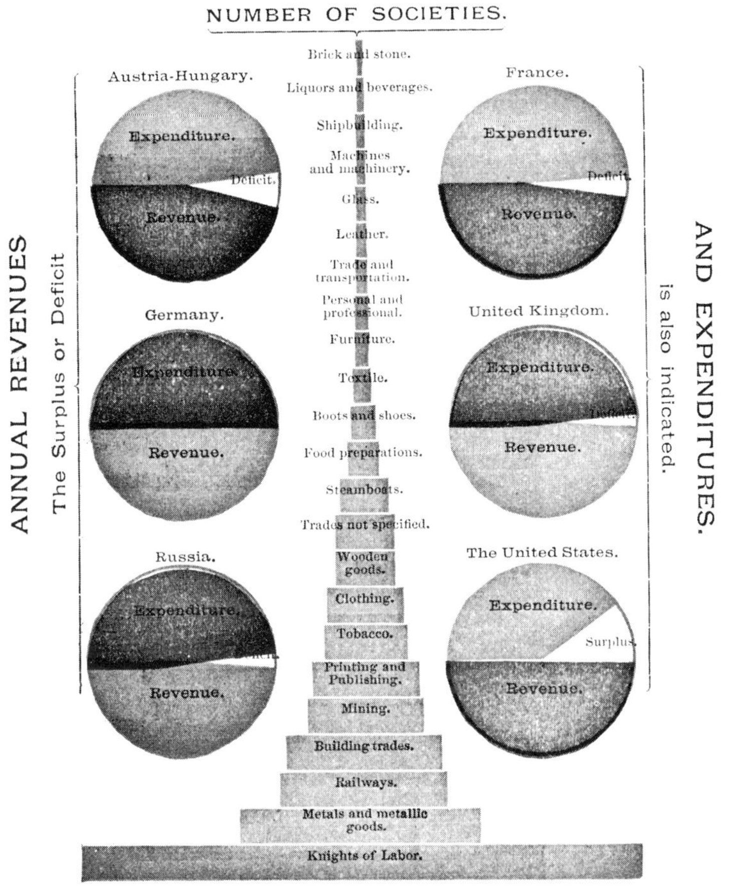

THE TARIFF QUESTION.—1885.

TOTAL IMPORTS.

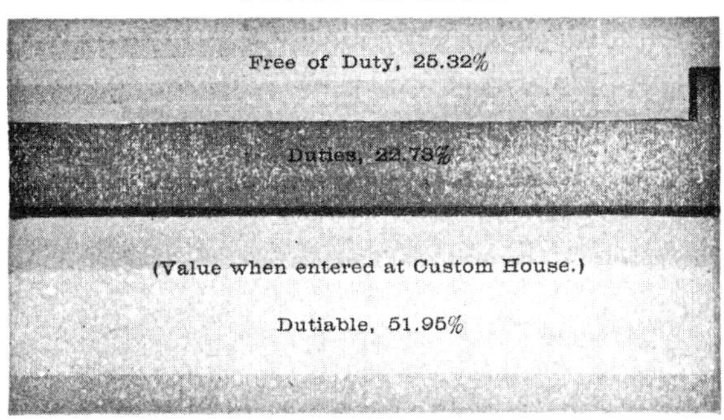

DISPLACEMENT OF MUSCULAR LABOR BY MACHINERY.

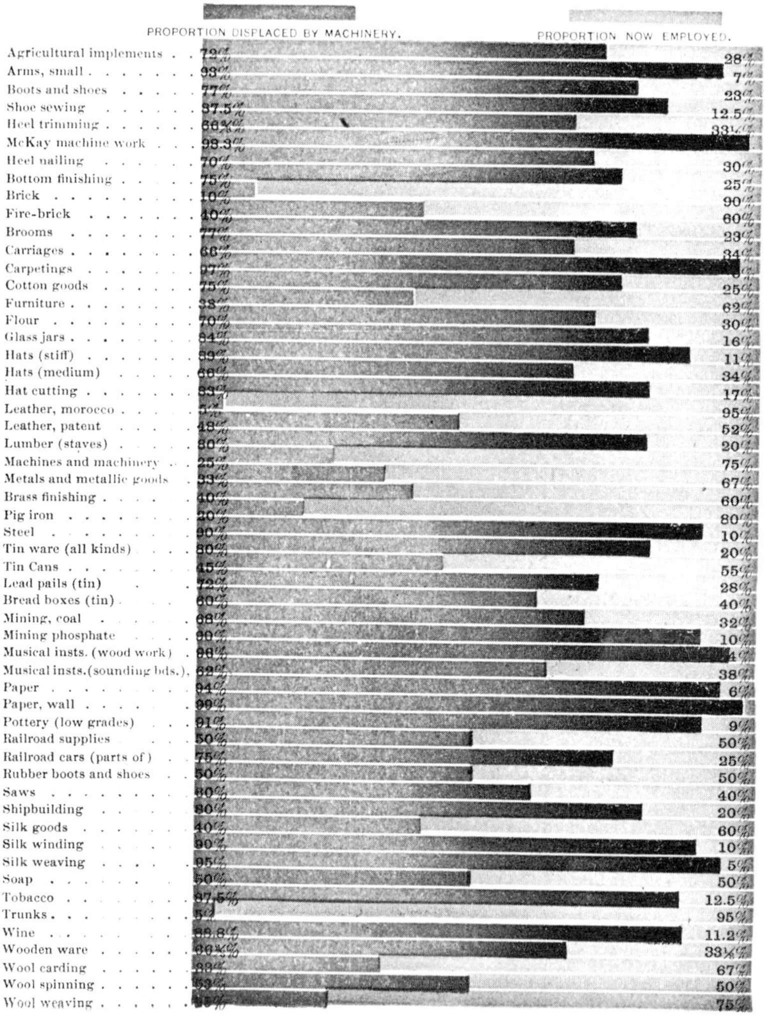

COMPARATIVE PRICES

IN THE UNITED STATES AND GREAT BRITAIN.

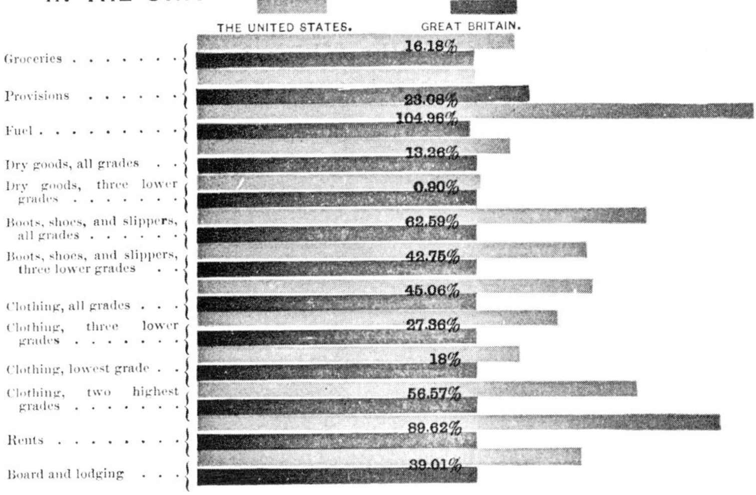

COMPARISON OF DAILY WAGES IN THE UNITED STATES: 1830 AND 1860.

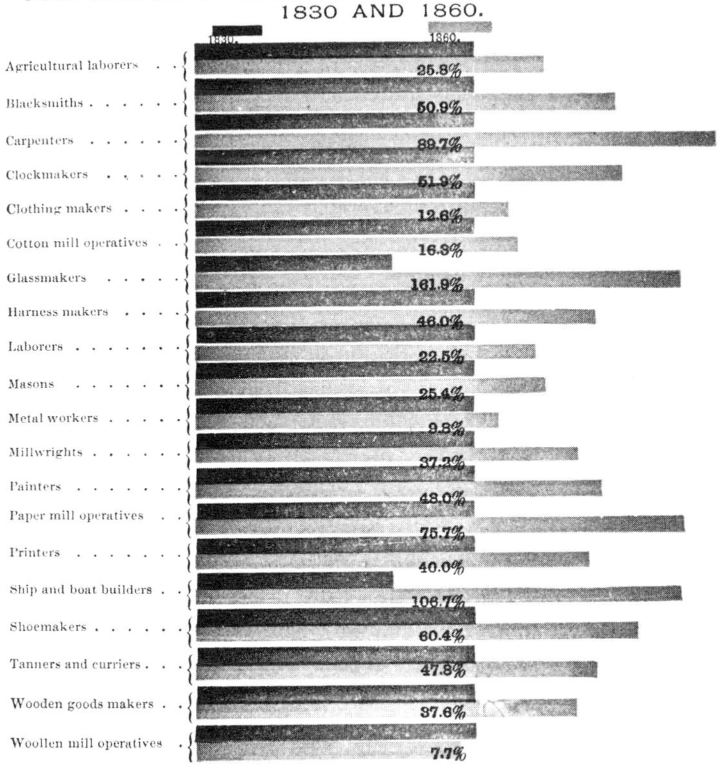

COST OF LIVING

IN THE UNITED STATES AND GREAT BRITAIN.

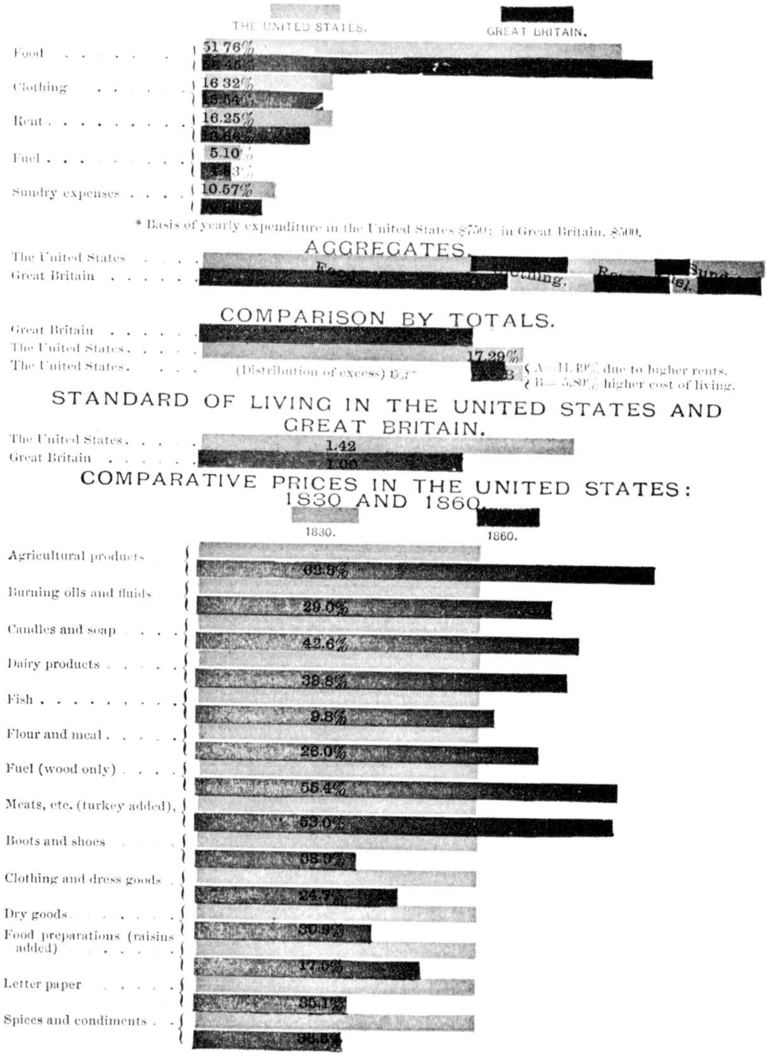

PROFITS: BY INDUSTRIES.

Relations of Stock Used, Wages Paid, Interest and Expenses, and Net Profit.

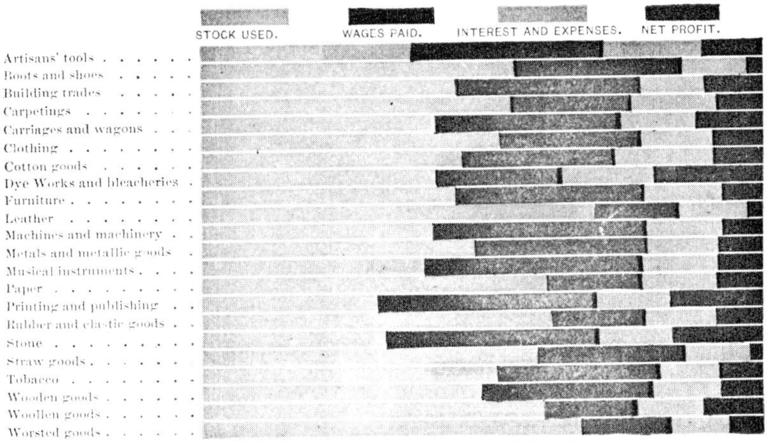

PROFITS: BY INDIVIDUALS.

Relation of the Yearly Earnings of Employé, and the Yearly Net Profit per Employé.

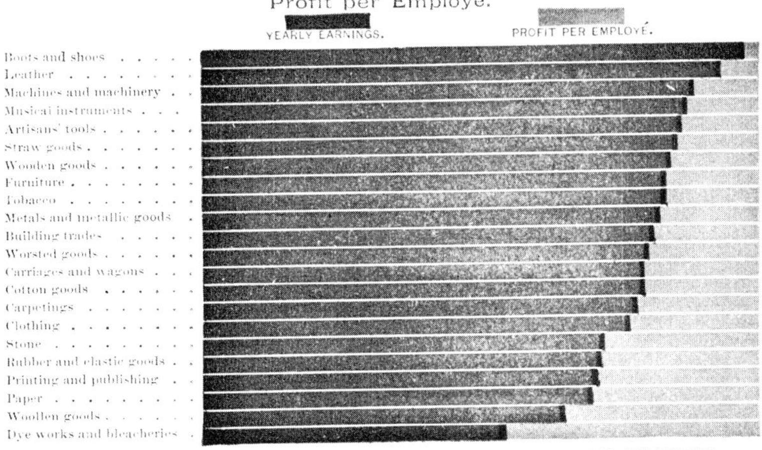

CAUSES OF STRIKES AND LOCKOUTS IN THE UNITED STATES.

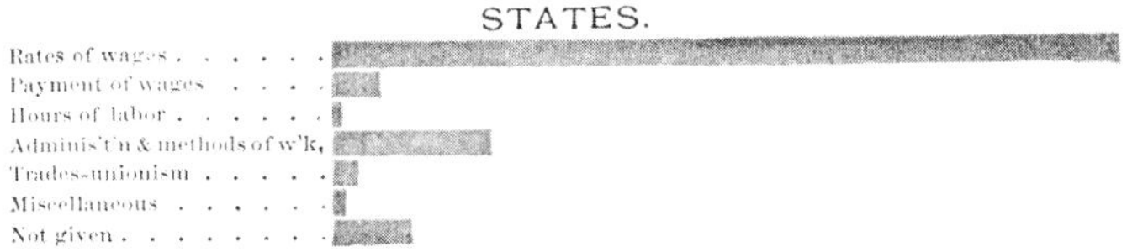

RESULTS OF STRIKES AND LOCKOUTS IN THE UNITED STATES.

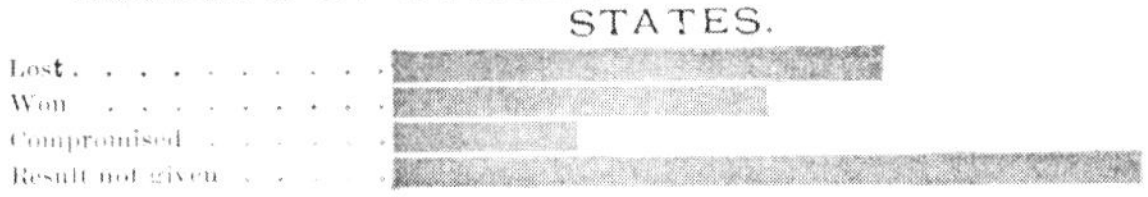

COMPARATIVE WAGES:
THE UNITED STATES AND GREAT BRITAIN.

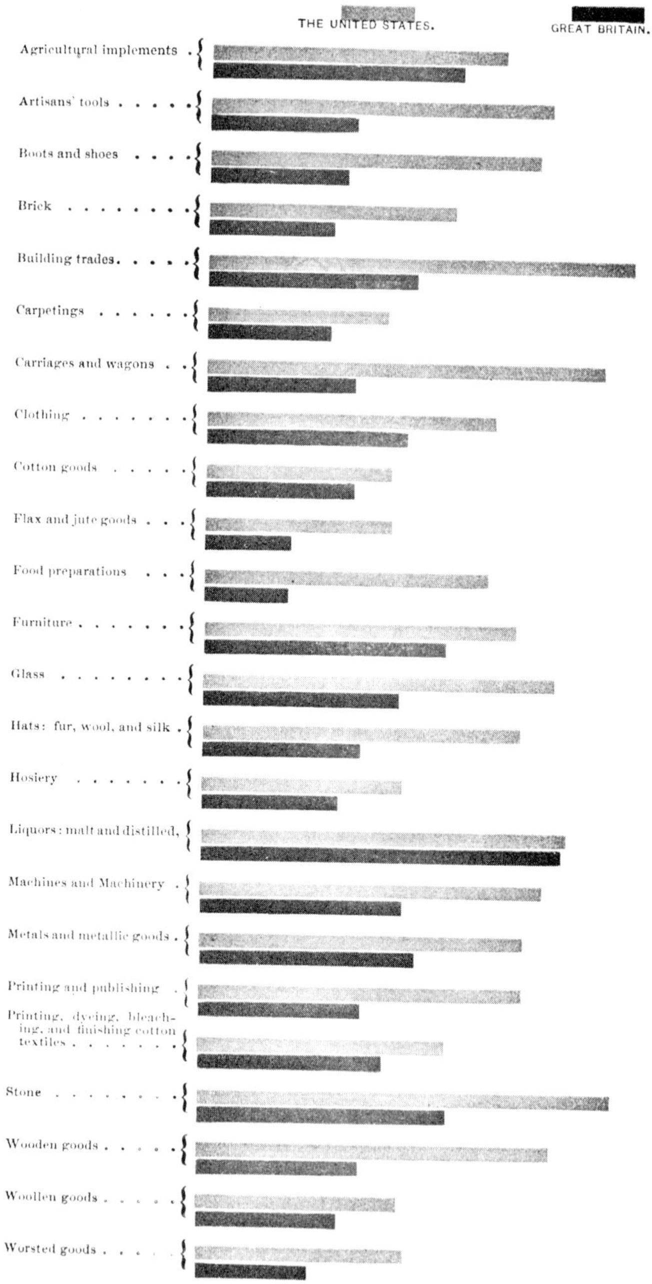

COMPARATIVE TABLE OF THE EARNINGS OF LABOR AND CAPITAL INVESTED IN MANUFACTURES, 1880, 1870.

STATE.	1880.		Per Cent. for Capital.	1870.		Per Cent. for Capital.
	Persons Employed.	Average Wages.		Persons Employed.	Average Wages.	
Alabama	10,017	$249.67	.26	8,248	$270.12	.56
Arizona	220	505.36	.46	84	542.65	.19
Arkansas	4,557	203.06	.48	3,206	210.21	.79
California	43,693	482.13	.36	25,392	517.35	.45
Colorado	5,074	456.11	.72	876	511.66	.25
Connecticut	112,915	386.14	.33	89,523	435.49	.37
Dakota	868	390.98	.66	91	231.93	.64
Delaware	12,638	337.66	.21	9,710	380.34	.26
District of Columbia	7,146	548.92	.46	4,685	426.80	.50
Florida	5,504	236.90	.38	2,749	359.98	.80
Georgia	24,865	211.78	.34	17,871	271.08	.55
Idaho	388	351.35	.57	265	424.04	.31
Illinois	144,727	396.80	.47	82,979	374.79	.48
Indiana	69,558	315.72	.39	58,852	312.08	.52
Iowa	28,372	342.80	.37	25,033	275.36	.53
Kansas	12,072	330.93	.48	6,754	352.01	.76
Kentucky	37,391	317.10	.36	30,636	308.28	.53
Louisiana	12,167	358.37	.47	30,071	152.75	.39
Maine	52,954	257.25	.30	49,180	290.40	.39
Maryland	74,945	252.25	.36	44,860	283.73	.52
Massachusetts	352,255	364.21	.38	279,380	422.54	.43
Michigan	77,601	326.17	.34	63,694	332.92	.40
Minnesota	21,247	405.37	.38	11,290	358.97	.43
Mississippi	5,827	204.67	.35	5,841	264.92	.49
Missouri	63,995	379.86	.41	65,354	475.18	.74
Montana	578	551.48	.56	701	529.02	.44
Nebraska	4,793	363.49	.54	2,665	536.55	.64
Nevada	577	800.35	.50	2,859	877.77	.59
New Hampshire	48,831	305.43	.30	40,783	338.94	.35
New Jersey	126,038	373.56	.40	75,552	432.13	.42
New Mexico	557	392.69	.42	427	391.29	.30
New York	527,533	357.55	.39	351,803	404.96	.51
North Carolina	18,109	151.34	.31	13,622	161.11	.49
Ohio	183,609	344.28	.37	137,102	357.66	.44
Oregon	3,373	494.23	.52	2,884	388.40	.53
Pennsylvania	387,072	372.16	.30	319,487	400.57	.39
Rhode Island	62,878	339.63	.32	49,417	391.65	.28
South Carolina	12,128	233.86	.35	8,141	189.62	.45
Tennessee	22,445	234.60	.39	19,412	278.21	.58
Texas	12,159	274.94	.47	7,927	225.53	.65
Utah	2,495	344.23	.34	1,534	257.73	.50
Vermont	17,540	300.14	.34	28,686	218.37	.24
Virginia	40,184	180.30	.43	26,974	190.66	.49
Washington	1,147	464.01	.23	1,026	560.36	.44
West Virginia	14,311	301.44	.33	11,772	367.15	.47
Wisconsin	57,109	329.45	.32	43,910	309.19	.42
Wyoming Territory	391	480.30	.30	505	692.38	.15
Totals	2,738,915	$346.10	.36	2,053,996	$377.59	.45

AGRICULTURE.

RELATIVE NUMBER OF CHILDREN AND OLD PERSONS ENGAGED.

STATE.	Total Number Engaged.	Males 10 to 15.	Females 10 to 15.	60 Years and Over.	Total of Non-Productive Age.	Total of Productive Age.
Alabama	380,630	53,854	20,608	26,929	101,491	279,139
Arizona	3,435	89	–	82	171	3,254
Arkansas	216,655	26,118	6,138	8,902	41,158	175,507
California	79,396	1,128	30	4,958	6,116	73,280
Colorado	13,539	335	6	563	904	12,635
Connecticut	44,026	1,214	3	8,115	9,332	34,684
Dakota	28,508	570	12	1,029	1,611	26,897
Delaware	17,849	1,634	36	1,711	3,380	13,469
Dist. of Columbia	1,464	11	–	126	137	1,327
Florida	58,731	5,649	2,680	4,173	12,502	46,229
Georgia	432,204	56,695	25,908	27,604	110,307	321,897
Idaho	3,858	50	–	132	182	3,676
Illinois	436,371	27,998	310	27,750	56,058	380,313
Indiana	331,240	25,413	253	24,063	49,729	281,511
Iowa	303,557	15,210	169	19,977	35,256	298,301
Kansas	206,080	11,781	83	9,274	21,138	184,942
Kentucky	320,571	30,141	885	22,132	53,158	267,413
Louisiana	205,306	20,045	16,416	18,572	55,023	150,283
Maine	82,130	1,968	10	15,499	17,467	64,663
Maryland	90,927	5,510	256	8,593	14,359	76,568
Massachusetts	64,973	1,229	10	13,403	14,642	50,331
Michigan	240,319	7,185	76	22,044	29,305	211,014
Minnesota	131,535	3,669	48	8,971	12,688	118,847
Mississippi	339,938	29,300	15,449	20,541	65,290	274,648
Missouri	355,297	24,043	255	22,672	46,970	308,327
Montana	4,515	51	2	97	150	4,365
Nebraska	90,507	3,233	81	4,050	7,365	83,142
Nevada	4,180	37	1	151	189	3,991
New Hampshire	44,490	1,012	4	9,139	10,155	34,335
New Jersey	59,214	1,878	6	7,481	9,365	49,849
New Mexico	14,139	926	9	986	1,921	12,218
New York	377,460	9,027	78	52,534	61,639	315,721
North Carolina	360,937	47,329	12,227	28,971	88,527	272,410
Ohio	397,495	17,729	90	40,287	58,106	339,389
Oregon	27,091	637	5	1,836	2,478	24,613
Pennsylvania	301,112	16,041	105	34,607	50,753	250,359
Rhode Island	10,945	192	1	1,941	2,134	8,811
South Carolina	294,602	27,453	16,602	21,683	55,738	238,864
Tennessee	294,153	36,338	5,728	21,819	63,875	230,278
Texas	359,317	31,592	7,485	17,763	56,840	302,477
Utah	14,550	1,351	17	507	1,875	12,675
Vermont	55,251	1,670	10	9,055	10,735	44,516
Virginia	254,099	22,601	3,370	25,132	51,103	202,996
Washington	12,781	225	5	555	785	11,996
West Virginia	107,578	7,944	195	8,767	16,906	90,662
Wisconsin	195,901	6,743	200	20,395	27,338	168,563
Wyoming Territory	1,639	19	–	40	59	1,580
Totals	7,670,493	584,867	135,862	625,711	1,246,440	6,424,053

PROFESSIONAL.

RELATIVE NUMBER OF CHILDREN AND OLD PERSONS ENGAGED.

STATE.	Total Number Engaged.	Males 10 to 15.	Females 10 to 15.	60 Years and Over.	Total of Non-Productive Age.	Total of Productive Age.
Alabama . . .	72,211	9,913	4,477	3,872	18,262	53,849
Arizona	8,210	102	17	70	189	8,021
Arkansas . . .	23,466	1,963	1,238	1,476	4,677	18,789
California . . .	121,435	1,252	793	3,521	5,866	115,569
Colorado . . .	24,813	240	155	384	679	24,134
Connecticut . .	51,296	443	854	3,197	4,294	47,002
Dakota	14,016	107	164	147	418	13,598
Delaware . . .	17,616	610	629	1,112	2,351	15,265
Dist. of Columbia	39,975	288	544	1,854	2,686	37,289
Florida	17,923	603	582	986	2,171	15,752
Georgia	104,269	7,298	5,123	4,974	17,395	86,874
Idaho	3,861	33	17	62	112	3,749
Illinois	229,467	4,310	5,050	7,951	17,311	212,156
Indiana	137,281	4,717	2,954	4,659	11,330	125,951
Iowa	103,932	1,667	2,197	3,175	7,039	96,893
Kansas	53,507	996	1,112	1,405	3,513	49,994
Kentucky . . .	104,239	4,649	4,069	3,715	12,433	91,806
Louisiana . . .	98,111	3,637	3,450	5,286	12,373	85,738
Maine	47,411	620	580	3,103	4,303	43,108
Maryland . . .	98,934	2,893	3,358	4,425	10,676	87,278
Massachusetts . .	170,160	1,293	1,605	10,866	13,364	156,796
Michigan . . .	143,249	2,160	2,914	4,487	9,561	133,688
Minnesota . . .	59,452	775	1,353	1,322	3,450	56,002
Mississippi . . .	49,448	2,688	1,990	2,770	7,448	42,000
Missouri	148,588	4,302	3,755	4,611	12,968	135,620
Montana . . .	6,954	40	22	56	118	6,836
Nebraska . . .	28,746	404	634	470	1,508	27,238
Nevada	10,373	53	38	159	250	10,123
New Hampshire .	28,206	253	345	1,804	2,402	25,804
New Jersey . . .	110,722	1,988	823	5,635	8,446	102,276
New Mexico . .	19,042	971	208	960	2,139	16,903
New York . . .	537,897	8,932	10,254	24,286	43,472	494,425
North Carolina .	69,321	6,757	5,962	3,760	16,479	52,842
Ohio	250,371	5,662	5,220	10,202	21,084	229,287
Oregon	16,645	182	93	427	702	15,943
Pennsylvania . .	446,713	15,110	11,569	21,376	48,055	398,658
Rhode Island . .	24,657	241	212	1,452	1,905	22,752
South Carolina .	64,246	3,704	3,220	3,353	10,277	53,969
Tennessee . . .	94,107	6,950	4,125	4,216	15,291	78,816
Texas	97,561	4,612	3,264	3,494	11,370	86,191
Utah	11,144	697	247	336	1,280	9,864
Vermont	28,174	406	875	1,752	3,033	25,141
Virginia	146,664	9,997	7,898	8,232	26,127	120,537
Washington . .	6,640	59	47	133	239	6,401
West Virginia . .	31,680	1,249	1,006	1,444	3,699	27,981
Wisconsin . . .	97,494	1,706	2,763	4,087	8,556	88,938
Wyoming Territory	4,011	33	25	30	88	3,923
Totals . . .	4,074,238	127,565	107,830	176,692	412,087	3,662,151

TRADE AND TRANSPORTATION.

RELATIVE NUMBER OF CHILDREN AND OLD PERSONS ENGAGED.

STATE.	TOTAL NUMBER ENGAGED.	MALES 10 TO 15.	FEMALES 10 TO 15.	60 YEARS AND OVER.	TOTAL OF NON-PRODUCTIVE AGE.	TOTAL OF PRODUCTIVE AGE.
Alabama	16,953	378	11	665	1,054	15,899
Arizona	3,252	5	–	21	26	3,226
Arkansas	9,233	81	1	203	285	8,948
California	57,392	429	27	1,379	1,835	55,457
Colorado	15,491	100	2	152	254	15,137
Connecticut	29,920	391	70	1,154	1,615	28,305
Dakota	6,219	30	2	39	71	6,148
Delaware	4,967	59	2	255	316	4,651
Dist. of Columbia	9,848	197	18	268	483	9,365
Florida	6,446	80	–	202	282	6,164
Georgia	25,222	41	14	675	730	24,492
Idaho	1,327	7	–	15	22	1,325
Illinois	128,372	1,564	179	2,677	4,420	123,952
Indiana	56,432	648	19	1,639	2,296	53,136
Iowa	50,872	330	16	1,119	1,465	49,407
Kansas	26,379	176	8	346	530	25,749
Kentucky	33,563	499	18	988	1,505	32,058
Louisiana	29,130	522	21	1,315	1,858	27,272
Maine	29,790	179	12	1,412	1,613	28,177
Maryland	49,234	797	75	1,578	2,450	46,784
Massachusetts	115,376	1,193	175	1,487	2,855	112,521
Michigan	54,723	500	56	1,466	2,022	52,701
Minnesota	24,349	208	6	355	569	23,780
Mississippi	12,975	154	2	366	522	12,453
Missouri	79,300	1,137	59	1,343	2,539	76,761
Montana	2,766	3	–	15	18	2,758
Nebraska	15,106	87	2	146	235	14,871
Nevada	4,449	11	–	50	61	4,388
New Hampshire	11,735	71	7	521	599	11,136
New Jersey	66,382	978	132	2,181	3,291	63,091
New Mexico	3,264	30	1	50	81	3,183
New York	339,419	6,856	931	10,295	18,082	321,337
North Carolina	15,966	306	11	603	920	15,046
Ohio	104,315	1,785	146	4,346	6,277	98,038
Oregon	6,149	52	1	126	179	5,970
Pennsylvania	179,965	3,418	386	6,643	10,447	169,518
Rhode Island	15,217	214	15	633	862	14,255
South Carolina	13,556	183	8	441	632	12,924
Tennessee	23,228	361	7	687	1,055	22,173
Texas	34,909	465	7	661	1,133	32,776
Utah	4,149	86	15	101	202	3,947
Vermont	8,945	80	3	410	493	8,462
Virginia	30,418	374	13	1,065	1,442	28,976
Washington	3,405	15	–	36	51	3,354
West Virginia	10,653	122	9	329	460	10,593
Wisconsin	37,550	463	60	1,145	1,668	35,882
Wyoming Territory	1,545	13	–	10	23	1,522
Totals	1,810,256	26,078	2,547	54,611	83,236	1,727,020

MANUFACTURES, MECHANICAL AND MINING.

RELATIVE NUMBER OF CHILDREN AND OLD PERSONS ENGAGED.

STATE.	TOTAL NUMBER ENGAGED.	MALES 10 TO 15.	FEMALES 10 TO 15.	60 YEARS AND OVER.	TOTAL OF NON-PRODUCTIVE AGE.	TOTAL OF PRODUCTIVE AGE.
Alabama	22,996	773	394	1,536	2,703	20,293
Arizona	7,374	9	3	75	87	7,287
Arkansas . . .	11,338	138	39	529	706	10,632
California . . .	118,282	621	193	3,781	4,495	113,787
Colorado . . .	47,408	140	8	523	671	46,737
Connecticut . .	116,091	3,755	3,083	4,479	11,237	104,854
Dakota	9,101	7	1	103	111	8,990
Delaware . . .	14,148	401	173	665	1,239	12,909
Dist. of Columbia	15,337	121	32	563	716	14,621
Florida	8,436	200	50	450	700	7,736
Georgia	36,167	895	659	1,793	3,347	32,820
Idaho	6,532	11	–	106	117	6,415
Illinois	205,570	3,228	1,557	6,394	11,179	194,391
Indiana	110,127	1,850	324	4,514	6,688	103,439
Iowa	69,941	625	80	2,928	3,633	66,308
Kansas	36,819	272	19	1,091	1,382	34,937
Kentucky . . .	61,481	1,354	415	2,647	4,416	67,065
Louisiana . . .	30,681	478	154	2,109	2,741	27,940
Maine	72,662	1,320	1,045	3,658	6,023	66,639
Maryland . . .	85,337	1,921	1,017	3,888	6,826	78,511
Massachusetts . .	370,265	8,591	7,272	13,973	29,836	341,429
Michigan . . .	130,913	1,765	433	4,490	6,688	124,225
Minnesota . . .	39,789	309	97	1,033	1,439	38,350
Mississippi . . .	13,145	188	121	785	1,094	13,051
Missouri	109,774	2,180	694	3,301	6,175	103,599
Montana	8,022	6	1	110	117	7,905
Nebraska . . .	18,255	92	13	409	514	17,741
Nevada	13,231	8	3	162	173	13,058
New Hampshire .	58,038	1,257	1,353	2,397	5,007	53,030
New Jersey . . .	160,561	5,113	3,377	5,639	14,129	146,432
New Mexico . .	4,377	18	34	97	149	4,228
New York . . .	629,869	13,719	10,899	22,856	47,474	582,395
North Carolina .	33,963	1,231	779	2,492	4,502	29,461
Ohio	242,294	6,106	1,795	11,011	17,912	224,382
Oregon	17,458	95	4	395	494	16,964
Pennsylvania . .	528,277	19,326	6,486	19,105	44,917	483,360
Rhode Island . .	66,160	2,957	2,576	1,977	7,510	58,650
South Carolina .	19,698	425	283	1,391	2,099	17,599
Tennessee . . .	36,082	643	196	2,015	2,854	33,228
Texas	30,346	265	34	1,079	1,378	28,968
Utah	10,212	158	32	538	728	9,484
Vermont	26,214	442	166	1,680	2,288	23,926
Virginia	63,059	1,769	577	3,943	6,289	56,770
Washington . .	7,296	38	2	142	182	7,114
West Virginia . .	26,288	527	32	1,231	1,790	24,498
Wisconsin . . .	86,510	1,328	425	3,504	5,357	80,953
Wyoming Territory	1,689	2	–	16	18	1,671
Totals . . .	3,837,112	86,677	46,930	147,503	281,110	3,556,002

GRAND TOTALS FOR UNITED STATES.

	Total Number Engaged.	Males 10 to 15.	Females 10 to 15.	60 Years and Over.	Total of Non-Productive Age.	Total of Productive Age.
Agriculture . . .	7,670,493	584,867	135,862	625,711	1,246,440	6,424,053
Professional . .	4,074,238	127,565	107,830	176,692	412,087	3,662,151
Trades and Transportation . .	1,810,256	26,078	2,547	54,611	83,236	1,727,020
Manufactures, Mechanical and Mining . . .	3,837,112	86,677	46,930	147,503	281,110	3,556,002
Grand Totals . .	17,392,099	825,187	293,169	1,004,517	2,022,873	15,369,226

INDEX.